The Songs of Genesis

ALSO BY STEVE ALDOUS

The World of Shaft: *A Complete Guide to the Novels, Comic Strip, Films and Television Series* (McFarland, 2015)

The Songs of Genesis

A Complete Guide to the Studio Recordings

Steve Aldous

McFarland & Company, Inc., Publishers
Jefferson, North Carolina

LIBRARY OF CONGRESS CATALOGUING-IN-PUBLICATION DATA

Names: Aldous, Steve, author.
Title: The songs of Genesis : a complete guide to the studio recordings / Steve Aldous.
Description: Jefferson, North Carolina : McFarland & Company, Inc., Publishers, 2020 | Includes bibliographical references and index.
Identifiers: LCCN 2020012329 | ISBN 9781476681382 (paperback : acid free paper) ∞
ISBN 9781476639840 (ebook)
Subjects: LCSH: Genesis (Musical group)—Discography. | Genesis (Musical group)—History—Chronology. | Rock music—Discography. | Progressive rock music—Discography. | Rock music—England—History and criticism. | Progressive rock music—England—History and criticism.
Classification: LCC ML156.7.G46 A43 2020 | DDC 782.42166092/2—dc23
LC record available at https://lccn.loc.gov/2020012329

BRITISH LIBRARY CATALOGUING DATA ARE AVAILABLE

ISBN (print) 978-1-4766-8138-2
ISBN (ebook) 978-1-4766-3984-0

© 2020 Steve Aldous. All rights reserved

No part of this book may be reproduced or transmitted in any form or by any means, electronic or mechanical, including photocopying or recording, or by any information storage and retrieval system, without permission in writing from the publisher.

Front cover: Members of Genesis in the recording studio (left to right) Phil Collins, Mike Rutherford and Tony Banks (Atlantic Records/Photofest)

Printed in the United States of America

*McFarland & Company, Inc., Publishers
Box 611, Jefferson, North Carolina 28640
www.mcfarlandpub.com*

To my wife Kathleen and my lovely family
who over the years have been indoctrinated
into the music of Genesis and have transformed
from reluctant listeners into genuine fans.

Acknowledgments

Over the years I have accumulated an extensive collection of Genesis related material including, books, magazines, music papers, radio interviews, TV interviews and much more. However, this material would only get me so far. In the last twenty years the Internet has become a universal library for new and archived material. It has helped me enormously in compiling this book.

I would particularly like to call out the following websites as having been invaluable in my research:

Mark Kenyon's *The Genesis Archive* is a superb noncommercial site hosting a massive collection of material about the band, including music press and magazine articles, press kits, video and audio material and fan submitted memorabilia. It is *the* "go to" resource for any serious Genesis fan. Mark has been very generous in donating his time and sharing some of his collection for use in this book.

Alan Hewitt's *The Waiting Room*, set up in 1987, is a dedicated fan's long-standing project and includes personal interviews with band members alongside articles, reviews and opinion. Phil Collins is an avid follower.

Dave Negrin's *The World of Genesis* contains an archive of excellent interviews that Dave has conducted with band members and technical crew over the years.

Michael Poloukhine's *A Genesis Discography* is a comprehensive catalogue of the band's worldwide releases.

There are many others. Where I have quoted from web or archive material to highlight specific points in the text, I have annotated the source in the chapter notes. I have also listed the key published works on the band as well as a selection of web resources in the section.

I'd also like to thank David Alff, editor at McFarland, for his advice and support as well as sharing his personal photographs of the band and allowing their use in this book.

Finally, my biggest thanks go to the band themselves—Tony Banks, Mike Rutherford, Phil Collins, Peter Gabriel, Steve Hackett, Anthony Phillips, Ray Wilson, John Mayhew, John Silver and Chris Stewart—for their inspiration, wonderful music and for being a huge part of my life.

Table of Contents

Acknowledgments — vi
Preface — 1
Introduction: From Charterhouse to Chart Toppers — 3
Notes on Cataloguing — 11

PART 1—THE FORMATIVE YEARS: SEPTEMBER 1963–SEPTEMBER 1970

1. The Genesis of Genesis — 14
2. Studio Album #1: *From Genesis to Revelation* — 27
3. The Road to Trespass — 40
4. Studio Album #2: *Trespass* — 47

PART 2—THE FIVE-MAN YEARS: OCTOBER 1970–MAY 1975

5. Studio Album #3: *Nursery Cryme* — 58
6. Studio Album #4: *Foxtrot* — 72
7. Studio Album #5: *Selling England by the Pound* — 87
8. Studio Album #6: *The Lamb Lies Down on Broadway* — 101

PART 3—THE FOUR-MAN YEARS: JUNE 1975–JULY 1977

9. Studio Album #7: *A Trick of the Tail* — 132
10. Studio Album #8: *Wind & Wuthering* — 146

PART 4—THE TRIO YEARS: AUGUST 1977–MARCH 1996

11. Studio Album #9: *…And Then There Were Three…* — 164
12. Studio Album #10: *Duke* — 181
13. Studio Album #11: *Abacab* — 200

14. Studio Album #12: *Genesis*	220
15. Studio Album #13: *Invisible Touch*	233
16. Studio Album #14: *We Can't Dance*	251

Part 5—Their Final Bow: June 1996–July 2000

17. Studio Album #15: *…Calling All Stations…*	274

Part 6—Looking Back and Reunions

18. Since 1998	294
Discography	303
Chapter Notes	310
Bibliography	327
Song Title Index	329
General Index	333

"I would probably describe myself as primarily a studio man. That's always going to be a special place for us; it's where we create our music."[1]

—Mike Rutherford

"We've always liked something to be distinctive about a song, even a simple song. There is usually an element of quirkiness about a Genesis song and that's important to us."[2]

—Tony Banks

"A lot of our older fans think that Genesis should be a brand name for progressive rock or whatever. But actually, Genesis is the name for a group of songwriters who have always done whatever we've felt like doing under that banner"[3]

—Phil Collins

"Nobody knew for certain, least of all us writers, where a song, once started, would end up—the democratic writing process open to a five-sided team was able to combine influences from science fiction to Greek mythology."[4]

—Steve Hackett

"I think when we got it right, we had something that none of us could do on our own. And there were different musical histories merging together in a powerful way."[5]

—Peter Gabriel

Preface

The songs of Genesis have been a huge part of my life, and this book is designed to tell the story behind each and every one of them. The book catalogues chronologically all the band's songs from their earliest demos in 1967 through to their last studio recording in 1997—a period of thirty years which saw Genesis progress from its schoolboy band origins into one of the biggest rock acts in the world. As well as offering opinions on each of the band's songs I provide background information on the recordings based on extensive research of archive material. Along the way I contrast my views with those of the band members themselves and of the music press, who in the post-punk days would often snub their noses at the mere mention of Genesis.

I first took notice of Genesis in the summer of 1980 when I heard the song [106] DUCHESS on the radio. I loved the melodic chorus and the drama of the music. I bought the single and played it to death on my dad's B&O turntable. Before this I had been familiar with the band but had not paid their music any close attention. I had liked the single [102] FOLLOW YOU, FOLLOW ME, but at the time I was into the disco strains of Earth, Wind & Fire, Michael Jackson and the soul of Stevie Wonder. I had grown up listening to and loving The Beatles and then the glam rock of the early 1970s. My dad had liked some of the fusion of jazz and rock evident in prog bands like Focus and Camel and he had mentioned Genesis as a band that I might like. By 1980, Genesis had adopted a more commercial approach to their music, while retaining the signature elements that made the band unique. Now was the time to explore their music further. I bought the album, *Duke*, and loved it. I worked my way backward through their catalogue and was amazed by the progressive nature of the band's musical development. I very quickly became a fan.

From then on Genesis became a big part of my life. My favorite band. As well as their albums, singles and videos I began collecting magazine and music press articles, reviews and books. I also videotaped their TV appearances and documentaries. I joined the fan club, Genesis Information. In the late 1990s, the arrival of the internet enabled me to obtain more and more information and I absorbed it to such an extent that I needed an outlet to get it all back out. This book is that outlet.

To use a cliché, the book is "a labor of love." It is something I started writing way back in 1998. I originally finished it two or three years later. Over the years I added to and honed the material and then…. I parked it. I went on to other things. Now, more than twenty years later I have finally fulfilled my vision of providing a complete guide to the songs of Genesis.

A major inspiration was Ian MacDonald's *Revolution in the Head: The Beatles Records and the Sixties*, originally written in 1994 and now in its third edition, published by Vintage. I found MacDonald's observations of the Fab Four's song output to be fascinating. I didn't always agree with his assessments, but his views were clearly and knowledgeably presented.

The book is still my go-to reference for the music of The Beatles. MacDonald catalogued the songs in the order they were recorded, and I have adapted a similar cataloguing system for this book. While I have musical experience, having played in a rock band for seventeen years, I am not a music scholar and could never emulate MacDonald's studied approach to his subject. However, I hope my enthusiasm for the music and my honest personal assessments will encourage readers to listen to the songs of Genesis with fresh ears. I am also hoping the book will introduce an extraordinary catalogue of songs to a new generation.

My aim is to provide a balanced critique of the band's music as well as the stories behind the songs. It is unashamedly my point of view, for I have no other. It is not just the view of a Genesis fan, but also that of a music fan. My tastes are quite diverse, but for me Genesis sit at the top of the tree. That doesn't mean to say that I think everything the band wrote and recorded was wonderful and that this book is a eulogy. In such a large and experimental body of music there are inevitably songs which do not work, whether that be musically, lyrically or conceptually. For example, many see [44] THE BATTLE OF EPPING FOREST as a great marriage of Peter Gabriel's whimsical storytelling and the band's intricate musical arrangement. I find it a bit of an ill-matched mess. However, one view that is almost unanimous among commentators on the band's output is that you'll have to go a mighty long way to find a better piece of music in the history of rock music than their epic [38] SUPPER'S READY.

My main challenge in writing this book was scope. Genesis have a huge output of material both as a band and individually, meaning that to cover it all would be a mammoth task. After all it has taken me twenty years to get to this point! I therefore decided to just focus on the band and leave the solo output for another day. I also decided to catalogue the songs based on their studio recordings. That is all the albums and singles, as well as archival demos. Many of Genesis' songs would benefit further from the live environment—songs like [46] THE CINEMA SHOW, [42] FIRTH OF FIFTH and [148] DOMINO really came alive on stage. These live versions are not separately catalogued; instead, I have made a reference to them in the text covering each studio entry.

While I provide a history of the band alongside the song entries for context, this book is not designed to be a definitive biography. I wanted to concentrate on the music. For those seeking a detailed history of the band I would refer you to Armando Gallo's excellent *I Know What I Like* and the band's own *Chapter & Verse*, both of which are detailed among others in the Bibliography.

Genesis tell us the well has run dry on their archive of material. Having released two *Archive* box sets and their full studio output in a further three career-spanning box sets, the band has certainly made the effort to give their fans everything they have. We probably now have access to a recording of every song that is available. It is also highly unlikely Genesis will produce any new music in the future. The last batch of new songs written and recorded by the band is now more than 20 years old. Phil Collins can no longer play drums and due to health issues is confined to a seat for most of his current live show. The official statement from the band is "never say never," but as the band members age the likelihood that they will ever record together again becomes increasingly remote.

The time is therefore right to celebrate the music of one of the most original bands in rock music history.

Introduction:
From Charterhouse
to Chart Toppers

Genesis have always sat outside of music fashions. Even when they were conquering the world with their *Invisible Touch* album in 1986, they did so while retaining an uncool image. The band let their music do the talking. Genesis was not about egos, pretty images, fashionable clothes and haircuts. The music is what mattered. Even in the heady heyday of progressive rock they remained songwriters first and foremost. While Yes, ELP and the like would be about the playing and technique, Genesis concentrated on song structure, dynamics and arrangement. They had set themselves up initially as a songwriting collective, looking for others to cover their material. When they could find no takers, they became a band intent on promoting their own songs. From 1969, freed of Jonathan King's desire to shape them into a pop band, they experimented with the song format. Their material moved away from the three-minute traditional verse-chorus-bridge structure to something much more experimental. Songs would link musical themes and passages into a whole that would move between changing moods and time signatures. This approach culminated in their 23-minute masterpiece [38] SUPPER'S READY.

By the time they got to 1976's album *Wind & Wuthering* the music scene was changing with the advent of punk followed by new wave. Genesis astutely realized they would not survive in an environment that took music back to its raw roots and said anyone can stand up and play. Genesis resolved to simplify their songwriting. As they shed members, the band's music became less complex and increasingly more structured around traditional form, while their lyrics moved from storytelling and fantasy to affairs of the heart and mind. As Genesis evolved, they lost some fans and gained many more new ones. By 1986, they had reached a peak of popularity that took them to being one of the top concert draws in the world. They remained at the top until Phil Collins' departure in 1996. A failed attempt to re-launch the band with new lead singer Ray Wilson spelled the end of Genesis as a recording unit. However, their 2007 reunion tour demonstrated that the band's music has outlasted them and has a timeless quality about it that has led to a reassessment of their contribution to popular music.

Evolution

The roots of Genesis were laid down by the evolving music scene of the mid to late 1960s. The decade saw an explosion in popular music unlike any witnessed before. The rock 'n' roll bands that had emerged during the 1950s had caused excitement by fusing elements of blues and jazz with melody and structure. The early 1960s saw further evolution and in Britain bands like The Beatles, The Rolling Stones and The Who led the way. In the United States, the soul hits of Motown and the slick pop harmonies of The Beach Boys dominated the airwaves. The music produced was fresh and original, expanding on the melody-driven song format to produce something fresh and innovative. The new music lit a fire in the baby boomers that would burn eternal and these ground-breaking bands and artists would inspire a new generation of musicians. Social culture was evolving too with the constraints of postwar Britain being replaced by a new period of optimism. The new generation suddenly had freedom to express themselves creatively and hope that they died before they got old.

The music scene continued to evolve and develop with artists exploring new territories of sound and composition. The Beach Boys' innovative use of recording techniques on their *Pet Sounds* album of May 1966 was a major influence on The Beatles, who took the approach to the next level with *Sergeant Pepper's Lonely Hearts Club Band*, released in June 1967. These experiments inspired others to explore new musical ideas and formats. Fueled by the drugs of the day, LSD being the most notable newcomer, the psychedelic music of the early Pink Floyd, The Doors, The Zombies, et al. pushed at the boundaries of song structure and instrumentation. Out of the psychedelic scene emerged bands willing to stretch musicianship, arrangement and song structures. The Nice, The Moody Blues, Family, Fairport Convention and Procol Harum introduced increasingly elaborate orchestration and folk elements into their music. The instrumentalist rather than the song would become the center of attention—the passion-fueled guitar work of Jimi Hendrix and the dynamic keyboard playing of The Nice's Keith Emerson being prime examples. Other bands began to emerge, with ELP (led by Emerson with bassist Greg Lake and drummer Carl Palmer), Jethro Tull, Yes, Van Der Graaf Generator and King Crimson all forming during this time. It was King Crimson's album *In the Court of the Crimson King* that became the template for what was to be termed "progressive rock" with its use of the Mellotron expanding the musical landscape with its orchestral simulation.

While in the early 1970s, Genesis was to become synonymous with the progressive rock genre, the band had started out in the mid–1960s as two pairs of songwriters nurturing their talent in the restrictive culture of a public school—Charterhouse, an all-male boarding school at that. This was not an environment associated with rock 'n' roll. The first pair was Anthony Phillips and Mike Rutherford, two guitarists with a liking for The Rolling Stones. The second pair was Tony Banks and Peter Gabriel, who were more inspired by the soul of Otis Redding and Nina Simone. Their early songwriting was aimed at creating a pop sound that captured the spirit of these inspirations as well as the emerging folk scene. The songs were derivative and lacking in hooks, but there was enough in them to impress Charterhouse old boy turned pop star and producer Jonathan King. He recorded two singles and an album with the band while they were still at school. Neither the singles nor the album were successful.

The members of Genesis are renowned for their bloody-mindedness and they resolved to go their own way and explore new musical territories to find a niche for themselves. All the band members were fans of The Beatles and had been impressed by the Fab Four's increasingly elaborate exploration of musical boundaries. The young men were also keen followers of the music scene in London and were particularly impressed by The Nice. Tony Banks was a huge fan of Keith Emerson and the band were amazed by The Nice's live energy.

Initially the quartet of writers had been looking to set up a publishing deal for their songs to be performed by other artists—something that was inspired by the team of writers in Tin Pan Alley who churned out hits for major artists. But in the late 1960s, by following in the footsteps of their heroes, more and more bands began to write and perform their own material. So, Genesis became a fully fledged band and started to write and hone their songs on the road. The result was a more experimental approach to composition, with ideas being pooled and pieced together to create more complex and longer songs. Genesis were signed up by Tony Stratton-Smith for Charisma and in 1970 recorded what they regard as their first "real" album, *Trespass*. From here on they would be categorized as part of the progressive rock movement, if in a lesser light than many of their peers. The growth of Genesis as a band would be a slow and steady one—one that would see them gain increased popularity with each album, all the way through to their commercial peak in the mid–1980s.

The River of Constant Change

Genesis' growth in popularity was coupled with a musical development that ensured the band retained its following through various changes in the musical climate. This level of resilience and adaptability is the secret of their longevity. Had Genesis continued to record music in the style of their early albums they would have disappeared in the punk revolution of the mid–1970s along with most of their contemporaries. Instead, the band adapted through contracting lineups and the evolving musical environment. This has had the result of polarizing fan opinion into two camps—those who love the early progressive approach with Peter Gabriel as lead singer and those who love the later, more pop orientated band, with Phil Collins as lead singer. Positions were largely established by the point at which fans came on board. Banks, Collins and Rutherford are consistent in explaining their evolution was a result of their changing tastes. It's a statement that makes sense when we look back at our own lives. For any band to survive for the length of time Genesis did, they had to remain interested and challenged by what they were creating. If the listener was to play the band's catalogue in sequence, then they would see a gradual and natural evolution from 1970's *Trespass* to 1991's *We Can't Dance*. If the listener was to play these two albums back to back, then they would be hard-pressed to conceive it was the same band. In reality, this wasn't physically the same band. Only two of the five Genesis members that recorded *Trespass* were involved with *We Can't Dance*, but all three who recorded *We Can't Dance* were involved in *Trespass*'s 1971 follow-up *Nursery Cryme*. The loss of lead singer Peter Gabriel in 1975 and guitarist Steve Hackett in 1977 reduced the lineup to its core elements of Tony Banks' keyboards, Mike Rutherford's bass and guitar and Phil Collins' drums and vocals. Banks' skill with harmony, Rutherford's craft with a tune and Collins' innovative rhythms and melodic sensibilities were perfectly matched to create a blend that none of them could create on their own.

What Genesis lost with Peter Gabriel's departure was the singer's surreal approach to lyrics, his mysterious persona and his musical experimentation, while in guitarist Steve Hackett they lost an innovator in sound and technique. That Genesis' music would become more structured as a result again seems natural. *A Trick of the Tail*, the album that followed Gabriel's departure, was the most song-orientated they had produced to date. *…And Then There Were Three…*, the album that followed Hackett's departure, eschewed the longer song format and simplified the sound.

On reflection, there are probably only three points in their career where Genesis made a conscious decision to shift their musical path. The first of these was their recording in 1974 of *The Lamb Lies Down on Broadway*. This album is musically very different from those that preceded it: *Trespass*, *Nursery Cryme*, *Foxtrot* and *Selling England by the Pound*. Those four albums had mixed expansive epics with the acoustic and the electric through changing moods and little musical repetition. [22] STAGNATION, [25] THE MUSICAL BOX, [31] THE FOUNTAIN OF SALMACIS, [40] DANCING WITH THE MOONLIT KNIGHT, [42] FIRTH OF FIFTH and [46] THE CINEMA SHOW are all considered classics of the band's catalogue. The 23-minute [38] SUPPER'S READY, which appeared on *Foxtrot*, is probably the pinnacle of the band's career. It is a suite of seven separate songs linked thematically and musically. The pieces were literally stitched together in the studio to produce an astonishingly dynamic whole, climaxing via the twisting instrumental "Apocalypse in 9/8" with the celebration of "As Sure as Eggs Is Eggs." These songs would be mixed with more whimsical content such as their first pop hit, [41] I KNOW WHAT I LIKE (IN YOUR WARDROBE). While the approach was far from formulaic, the band did not want to rest on their laurels. With *The Lamb Lies Down on Broadway* they explored the concept of a double album with a single story running through twenty-two shorter and contrasting pieces.

While the concept was dense and the story almost impenetrable, the individual songs were largely concise. [48] THE LAMB LIES DOWN ON BROADWAY, [54] BACK IN N.Y.C., [57] CARPET CRAWLERS and [56] COUNTING OUT TIME all had a more straight-ahead rock approach, while retaining the band's personality. Songs such as [52] IN THE CAGE and [65] THE COLONY OF SLIPPERMEN still allowed Genesis to stretch out more in terms of structure and complexity, but the band had undoubtedly made a big statement. Having reached this point, Gabriel could see no future for himself in the band—regarding the album as the limit to which he could exert his influence on its output. He had written all the lyrics and felt suffocated by the band's rigidity around ownership of instrumentation. Family problems and the desire to artistically spread his wings led to him leaving the band in 1975, at the end of the tour to support the album. With license to fully explore his own ideas, he would go on to establish a successful career both artistically and commercially.

Genesis' search for a replacement was deemed redundant when they realized the logical choice was already within their ranks. Phil Collins had always sung harmony vocal to Gabriel and the pair had often doubled-up on lead. While the music press was keen to write the band off under the misconception that Gabriel had been their creative core, the band was writing and recording what was to prove to be an assured first album as a quartet—*A Trick of the Tail*. As on *The Lamb* the songs were more straightforward and demonstrated a band full of confidence and ideas. Collins' influence on the composition and arrangement was evident on the jazzy and Latin-infused instrumental [78] LOS ENDOS, while Banks and Rutherford demonstrated how their unique chemistry fused their musical ideas with [73] SQUONK and the gorgeous [76] RIPPLES.... Hackett by now had released his first solo album, *Voyage of the Acolyte*, and was hungry for more. He, too, was developing a desire to stretch out on his own. After one more album with the band, 1976's *Wind & Wuthering*, he left during the mixing of the subsequent live album, 1977's *Seconds Out*.

This brings us to the second conscious change in musical direction, with the remaining trio's first album, *...And Then There Were Three...*, in 1978. Here the band resolved to write a collection of shorter songs, dispensing with any long instrumental passages. At this stage they hadn't refined their craft sufficiently and many of these shorter songs felt either overstuffed or inconsequential. The songs also missed Steve Hackett's sonic creativity, with Rutherford's lead guitar parts being rather simplistic and lacking any distinction. This was overcompensated by Banks' keyboards taking on a much greater lead role than ever before. The result was an album lacking in the variety they had striven in creating room for more songs. However, they did have one gem up their sleeve.

[102] FOLLOW YOU, FOLLOW ME was nearly left off the album—disliked by producer David Hentschel, with the band also feeling the song was too simplistic. The record company, however, liked it and saw the potential in its love song lyrics, simple melody and relaxing rhythms. The song was released as a single and became a top ten hit in the UK. Suddenly, Genesis began attracting females to their shows and their audience was now growing beyond their core fan base. The band redressed the inconsistencies seen on ...*And Then There Were Three*... with 1980s confident and energetic *Duke*. Here, they achieved the perfect marriage between the fusion side of the band and their increased desire for simplicity. Their first use of a drum machine, on [106] DUCHESS, would help them keep their writing more concise—something they would go on to explore further.

The third conscious change in direction came with the 1981 album *Abacab*. Punk had evolved into new wave. Bands such as The Police, Blondie and Talking Heads emerged out of the punk scene and added back the artistry punk had stripped from popular music, without reintroducing the pomposity punk had eradicated. The result was a cornucopia of styles incorporating the aggressive attitude of punk with the rhythms of reggae and the melodicity of pop. Bands began to integrate an electronic sound based around keyboard-led hooks, evident in pioneering artists such as Kraftwerk, Gary Numan and Orchestral Manoeuvres in the Dark. Also, during this period, Phil Collins had a huge hit with his debut solo album, *Face Value*. Its diverse content of soul, jazz and pop was a huge surprise to the music press, who had taken against bands like Genesis as the antithesis of the new era of popular music. Collins' debut single, "In the Air Tonight," was fresh and innovative in its sparse instrumentation with its huge drum sound. Collins had ironically initially developed this new sound with engineer Hugh Padgham while working with former band mate Peter Gabriel on the song "Intruder" for Gabriel's third album. Genesis wisely saw that producing another album in the style they had become identified with would see them lose momentum. The band could simply not survive without changing.

The trio resolved to make the music on *Abacab* different from anything they had recorded before. They would throw out any song in which they felt they were repeating themselves. There would be no extensive keyboard solos. The drums would be brought up in the mix. They would simplify the song format and keep the arrangements sparse. By this time, they had also bought their own studio and were able to record as they wrote, removing the need to book studio time and be restricted by cost. They employed Hugh Padgham as their engineer, replacing David Hentschel, who had worked with the band as co-producer/engineer since *A Trick of the Tail*.

The result was a fresh sounding album that would polarize their fans more than any before. The older fans, who wanted the band to carry on producing 10-minute epics with changing moods and long instrumental sections, were shocked by the new wave sensibilities the band had adopted for their new material. The pulsing rhythm of [119] ABACAB, the repetitive guitar riff of [122] KEEP IT DARK, the tuneless throwaway [125] WHO DUNNIT? all demonstrated a band unwilling to compromise. Genesis brought in the Earth, Wind & Fire horn section (who had played on Collins' *Face Value*) to play on two tracks in the sessions—the first time the band had used outside musicians since their 1969 debut. They wrote almost all the songs together, with only three individually written tracks recorded—all their future albums would see all tracks co-written by the trio from scratch. Tony Banks restricted his keyboard orchestration and use of harmonies. Mike Rutherford used his guitar more creatively, looping the lead guitar riff for KEEP IT DARK and broadening his sonic tableau on [128] ANOTHER RECORD.

From here it was apparent Genesis was not the band of 1972, 1975 or even 1978. The band had evolved and changed with the times to remain relevant but still retained a distinctiveness that set them apart from their contemporaries. Many older fans blamed Phil Collins and his solo success, claiming he had changed the band. This view is both incorrect and missing the point. The band's change of direction is something all three members pushed for to challenge themselves musically. *Abacab* certainly took this approach to the extreme and proved to be largely experimental, with the trio exploring how far they could comfortably go. Subsequent albums would see a slight redress in balance between simple song structures and more complex pieces. Genesis attracted new fans as a result, building up their audience with *Abacab*'s follow-up, *Genesis*, with its mix of short pop songs ([135] THAT'S ALL, [138] ILLEGAL ALIEN), longer pieces ([136/137] HOME BY THE SEA/SECOND HOME BY THE SEA) and innovation ([134] MAMA).

Genesis undoubtedly reached their commercial peak with 1986's *Invisible Touch*. By now, Phil Collins had established himself as a major solo star and was alternating his solo and band career—as were Banks and Rutherford, the latter having set-up his own side project band in Mike + The Mechanics. *Invisible Touch* would see the band at their most confident and assured. The album was a monster hit and it was not unreasonable to consider Genesis the biggest concert draw in the world at that time—with four sold-out nights at Wembley Stadium in 1987 evidence of their popularity. The band had incorporated the synth sounds of the day with electronic drums to create an album that was their closest ever to the current musical fashions. As such, in some ways, it is now probably their most dated sounding album production-wise. However, Genesis still managed to retain their musical identity with more challenging songs such as [148] DOMINO and [150] THE BRAZILIAN mixing with the hits.

Phil Collins' solo work was now beginning to take increasing precedence with a film career also under way. Banks and Rutherford even managed to record two albums each during the hiatus between *Invisible Touch* and *We Can't Dance*. The synth pop of the 1980s had given way to the more AOR rock-oriented sounds of the early 1990s. The trio would release what was to be their final album as a unit in competition with U2's *Achtung Baby* and Michael Jackson's *Dangerous*. *We Can't Dance* confirmed that Genesis' popularity remained just as strong while returning the band to a more organic sound—the synthetic productions of the mid–1980s now seeming somewhat passé. The CD format meant *We Can't Dance* included over 70 minutes of material and while the songs were well-crafted there were fewer moments that would surprise the listener. There was also a feeling of finality about the album. The closing ten-minute [165] FADING LIGHTS seemed to be the perfect song with which to say goodbye, with Banks deliberately closing his lyric with the word *remember*.

That said, there was nothing being said within the band that suggested they would not regroup for another album in a few years' time. Their tour was hugely successful and stretched into late 1992 and two live albums followed. Behind the scenes, however, things began to change in Phil Collins' life. A bitter divorce played out in the media in 1994 and lost the singer some of the popular support he had enjoyed over the previous thirteen years. He established a new relationship which took him to Switzerland. Finally deciding that juggling solo and band careers was no longer conducive with a domestic family life in Switzerland, in June 1996 it was announced Collins would leave Genesis.

Banks and Rutherford regrouped to write new songs together and see how things progressed. They produced a vast amount of material and agreed to carry on the Genesis name with a new singer, Scotsman Ray Wilson, who had been lead singer with grunge band Stiltskin—famous for the hit "Inside." The result was *...Calling All Stations...*, released in 1997. By now the musical landscape had changed dramatically. Grunge had taken hold in the U.S. with bands such as Nirvana, Pearl Jam and Soundgarden taking rock back to its exciting guitar driven roots, In the UK, indie bands such as Blur and Oasis looked backward to the vibe of the 1960s and mingled it with the sounds of the 1990s to produce what would be termed Britpop. Genesis' latest release seemed to suggest the band were stuck in a musical vacuum. Missing Collins' ear for simplicity and melody and his soulful vocal delivery, the music was dense and lacked heart. The songs were caught between a desire for a darker, more complex approach and the need to maintain the hits. The resulting album left fans of both the Gabriel and Collins eras largely cold and failed to bring in any new supporters. This was most startling in the United States, where the album disappeared without a trace and a planned tour was cancelled. The album was better received in the UK and Europe, but Banks and Rutherford's heart had gone out of the project. That is a shame as there were moments on the album that pointed toward a new direction—notably driving songs such as [174] THE DIVIDING LINE and the title track [168]. But there was no disguising that to many this was no longer Genesis.

Legacy

The modern-day music critic cites 1971–1975 as the classic Genesis period. A young band of five highly creative individuals pushing musical boundaries into new directions. It is hard to argue against a view that the band was at its creative peak during this period. *Selling England by the Pound* and *The Lamb Lies Down on Broadway* are the albums most music journalists signal as their best—both are listed in Robert Dimery's annual collection of *1001 Albums You Must Hear Before You Die* (Cassell). Even today's music fans in general hold this era in more reverence. The *All-Music Guide* only rates these two albums and *Foxtrot* with 5 stars—the highest rated post–Gabriel albums being *A Trick of the Tail* and *Abacab* with 4½ stars (the latter being the only 1980s album rated above 4 stars). The website *Rate-Your-Music* also shows *Selling England by the Pound*, *The Lamb Lies Down on Broadway* and *Foxtrot* as the band's highest rated.

The musical chemistry between Tony Banks, Phil Collins, Peter Gabriel, Steve Hackett and Mike Rutherford helped create a unique sound and style that was distinguishable from peers such as Yes, Pink Floyd and ELP. Genesis were always about the songs and while they employed musical technique, it would always be to the benefit of the composition and not to show off their musical technique as players. Outside of The Beatles, there is no other band that has ever had the breadth of songwriting capabilities Genesis had during this period. Even the Fab Four were largely reliant on Lennon and McCartney, with Harrison only increasing his output in the latter days. The fact that there have been successful solo careers for at least four of the five members of the band is testament to their individual talents. Ironically, only Tony Banks—who most consider to be the heart of Genesis—has failed to have any large-scale success outside of it.

It seems hard to believe that the band were only 21 years old when they wrote their masterpiece SUPPER'S READY. In today's immediacy driven society with its manufactured approach to popular music it is hard to imagine a band so young ever producing a piece of work so innovative again. What the band had during this period was a group of individuals with a shared vision and the drive to achieve it. On their first album together, 1971's *Nursery Cryme*, the five-piece unit sowed the seeds with the album's opening track [25] THE MUSICAL BOX. Its blend of acoustic guitar; changing moods and tempo; a driving electric guitar led midsection; and its climactic resolution as Tony Banks' organ chords heighten the drama played out by Gabriel's surreal lyrics. The song signaled the way forward for the band. [38] SUPPER'S READY on *Foxtrot* was the culmination of this thinking. The band's sound was further refined on *Selling England by the Pound* with John Burns a more sympathetic producer/engineer and a further expansion of their sound through keyboard synthesizers.

Many fans and critics would argue Genesis' musical creativity reached its peak on *The Lamb Lies Down on Broadway*. It was an album of such depth and range that it was hard to take in on its initial release. It baffled contemporary critics—even ardent supporters in the music press such as Chris Welch were bemused. Gabriel's story was full of imagery but left most listeners scratching their heads. So, why is it now regarded as a classic? It was certainly ahead of its time. There is a pre-punk energy to the central character of Rael, and it is very different from any other album they recorded. The band selected [57] CARPET CRAWLERS as the encore for their 2007 reunion, citing it as the song that best encapsulated their history. Like most of their albums, *The Lamb Lies Down on Broadway* has its moments of padding, but it remains perhaps the best distillation of their combined talent.

Once Gabriel had gone and Phil Collins had replaced him (again how many bands can claim to have matched Genesis for the level of success they achieved with two lead singers?), the band maximized the skills from the remaining members. Hackett's contributions to both *A Trick of the Tail* and *Wind & Wuthering* were among his best. Down to the core trio of Banks, Collins and Rutherford from 1978 the members honed their songwriting skills and went on to produce a string of hits, their staggering commercial success peaking with the three albums over the period 1983–1991: *Genesis, Invisible Touch* and *We Can't Dance*. The critics had pretty much abandoned the band with the advent of punk and, despite (or maybe because of) their growing popularity and Phil Collins' ascending star, their albums failed to garner the critical approval they had in their earlier years.

Genesis were never fashionable, with a snobbish music press sharpening their knives with greater intent as the band grew in popularity. Genesis were branded as ageing dinosaurs or charged as safe corporate rockers only in it for the money—their middle-class upbringing at odds with the working-class roots of most of the current bands. These criticisms were grossly unfair and did not reflect the band's willingness to take risks through experimentation, whether it be in composition, recording techniques or stage and lighting design. Genesis *never* played it safe. No two albums in their catalogue sound alike.

The band's last recorded album, *...Calling All Stations...*, was released in 1997—more than twenty years ago. Genesis' influence on modern music goes largely unrecognized by the critics, but not so by artists such as Radiohead, Rush, Phish and Elbow, who cite them as a key influence. The band has sold between 100 million and 150 million albums around the world and in March 2010 was finally inducted into The Rock and Roll Hall of Fame. The breadth of the band's career and output will always give rise to debate and argument, but no one can deny that Genesis and its individual members have left an indelible mark on popular music.

Notes on Cataloguing

The following is an account of the official studio recordings of Genesis catalogued by song. When I use the word "official" I am referring to those recordings sanctioned by the band. These include Genesis' early singles and debut album, *From Genesis to Revelation*, which were recorded for Decca with the rights still held by Jonjo Music. In the UK, the remainder of the band's output is now licensed by Virgin/EMI and published through Hit & Run Music. My core guiding principle for the cataloguing is the band's UK discography, but I have also referenced U.S. releases of each studio album and single, which are licensed through Atlantic/Rhino Records. I have not catalogued the band's live recordings, as this would overcomplicate things. Instead, I have referenced these recordings in the individual studio entry for the song, with notes around venue, song length and the live album or archive release the live version of the song is available on. The band's live albums and archive material are also listed in the Discography section.

For ease of reference I have used a numerical system to catalogue all officially released songs that appear on the band's studio albums, EPs and/or singles as well as later archive releases. The numbering starts at [1] for the band's first single, THE SILENT SUN, and ends at [186] for the band's last single, THE CARPET CRAWLERS 1999. The sequencing is based on the dates recorded from the earliest to latest. Where numerous songs were recorded for an album during dedicated sessions, the track sequencing or subsequent release date as a B-side single has been used as the ordering determinant.

As the band has released a vast amount of archive material in recent years, many demo or session recordings have become officially available. These songs have been prefixed with [D] and slotted into the sequence based on when they were recorded. So, the band's very first demo, PATRICIA, is coded as [D0a]. The [0] denotes that the demo of the song was recorded before [1] THE SILENT SUN. The [a] denotes that it was recorded before [D0b] SHE IS BEAUTIFUL. Unreleased material has been prefixed with [U]. There is only one track this applies to and that is [U186] NOWHERE ELSE TO TURN. The [186] denotes it would have been numbered such had it been released officially.

Each song entry includes the following detail:

[CAT REF] TITLE

Band Credit: Up until *The Lamb Lies Down on Broadway*, all songs were credited to Genesis, regardless of who wrote them. From *A Trick of the Tail* songs were credited to the specific writer(s).

Music: Where known I have identified the band member(s) responsible for writing the music. In most cases this will be a shared credit as the band's tendency was to work either from jam sessions, in partnership or by piecing separately written pieces together.

Lyrics: Here, again where known, I have identified the writer of the lyrics. The band tended to apportion this activity to a specific member who had an energy for the song or a specific lyrical concept.

Length: Song lengths are stated in their currently available version. Other lengths (e.g., edited versions for single releases) are noted in the text.

Musicians: This is a list of who played what on the track. For some of the band's earlier recordings this can be difficult to ascertain, notably on the acoustic numbers where any of up to three band members may be contributing guitar parts.

Recorded at: The studio where the song was recorded along with the date of the recording or the start to end dates of the album recording sessions, of which the song was a part.

Mixed at: The studio at which the song was mixed for its original release.

Producer: The name of the producer of the song.

Engineer: The name of the recording engineer who supported the producer.

Assistants: The name of any technical assistant on the recording.

Remix/Remaster release: Details of the technical crew involved in the remixing and remastering of the original recording.

UK/U.S. Release: Dates the song was released in each country. A date is provided for both the album release and when applicable, the single release. It should be noted there is much confusion over actual release dates which, until 1989, were loose. From 1989, albums and singles were generally released on Monday in the UK and Tuesday in the U.S. From 10 July 2015 this moved to Friday internationally. Here I have used what I believe to be the most accurate release dates based on my research. For single releases the catalogue number is also noted. Album catalogue details can be obtained in the main album listing. Single releases will also note whether the song was an A-side or B-side.

A description and review of the song including notes on its recording and, where relevant, comments from the band or production staff as well as music journalists.

Additional sections are added as appropriate including:

Alternative versions: Notes on other recorded versions such as demos or different mixes.

Single Release: Information about the single release of a song, which includes chart activity and other worldwide releases, although the primary focus is on the UK and U.S. markets.

Music Video: Description and detail relating to any promotional videos filmed for the song.

BBC Sessions: The band recorded songs over five sessions between 1970 and 1972 for the BBC. Notes are made about those sessions including venue, dates, technical credits and so on.

Live Performances: Details of the tours on which the song was performed and associated notes.

Live Recordings: Notes on any subsequent live recordings of the song, including venue and which album/single/archive release the live version of the song was included.

Archive Release: Demo recordings also include a note of which archive release the song is included on.

Most songs after are grouped in the sections of the album for which the sessions were recorded. This includes songs that did not make the album cut and were later released as B-sides to singles or as EPs. While in the early days the band attended studios for specific recording sessions of demos and their early single releases, between *Trespass* and *Selling England by the Pound* the band only recorded [32] Happy the Man as a dedicated isolated session. The only other "session" the band undertook separately after this was for their final release [186] The Carpet Crawlers 1999.

It is difficult when looking back in history, where documentation is sparse, to be 100 percent accurate about the details. The band themselves are sketchier about their own history than their fans. Therefore, for each album and song listing where information is unsubstantiated or where I have had to make an assumption, for example whether a band member played a specific instrument or had contributed backing vocals, I have included a (?) notation alongside.

Part 1

The Formative Years: September 1963–September 1970

Tony Banks (Keyboards)
Peter Gabriel (Vocals, Flute, Percussion)
Anthony Phillips (Guitars)
Mike Rutherford (Bass, Guitars)
Chris Stewart, John Silver, John Mayhew (Drums)

The original 1968 line-up of Genesis. From left, Anthony Phillips, Mike Rutherford, Tony Banks, Peter Gabriel and Chris Stewart. Decca promotional photograph.

1

The Genesis of Genesis

The seeds of Genesis were sown at an English public school, Charterhouse, situated on a hill overlooking Godalming in Surrey.[1] It was at this boarding school that **ANTHONY GEORGE "TONY" BANKS** (born in East Hoathly, Sussex, England, 27 March 1950) and **PETER BRIAN GABRIEL** (born in Chobham, Surrey, England, 13 February 1950) commenced their senior education aged 13 in September 1963.

Tony Banks was the fifth child of John and Nora Banks—he had an older brother, John (who also went to Charterhouse School) and three older sisters, Mary, Margaret and Pauline. Both his mother and grandmother were musical with his mother being a keen pianist. The young Tony Banks used to listen intently to her playing Chopin on the family grand piano and fell in love with the sound of the instrument. Noting her son's interest, Nora Banks arranged for him to have piano lessons. Schooled on popular classical pieces, the shy and introverted Banks quickly became technically proficient, although he did not enjoy the discipline of the grading process approach to learning. From the age of 7, Banks attended Boarzell, a boarding prep school in Hurst Green before moving on to Charterhouse as a matter of course six years later. As he progressed through Charterhouse, he concentrated his studies on the sciences. However, he continued to pursue his love of music and found a sympathetic teacher of classical piano in Leonard Halcrow, who helped him develop as a player by teaching him pieces by Rachmaninov. Banks also made great use of the house piano in his free time, playing pieces from sheet music or by ear. While he was schooled on classical musicians, he became increasingly interested in popular music—notably the songs of The Beatles and The Animals.

Peter Gabriel was the son of electrical engineer, Ralph Parton Gabriel. It was his mother, Edith Irene, who encouraged his interest in music and taught him to play the piano. After attending Cable House prep school in Woking, Gabriel entered Charterhouse—continuing a family tradition. He hated the school and felt, like many of his peers, both trapped and alone. He was conscious of his weight and the fact he had pimples and therefore resolved to attract attention to himself through the writing of songs. Musically, he was also fascinated by the drums and his first musical instrument was a bass tom-tom from which he went on to assemble his first kit. He would also go on to play in a school traditional jazz band called Milords. Gabriel himself admits that he was a more enthusiastic than talented drummer.

Having met on their first day at Charterhouse, Banks and Gabriel soon got to know each other through their shared interest in music and the pair used to battle it out over access to the house piano, on which they would play their favorite songs. Gabriel recalled the scramble to get to the instrument, "Sometimes this would mean clambering through the food hatch to beat the person running through the door. It was that critical."[2] The pair would also visit Record Corner, a store in Godalming town center, and use the booths provided to listen to the soul records of Otis Redding and James Brown.

Banks was introduced to The Beatles by a friend, Mark Weekes, and learned by ear to play much of their back catalogue, starting with "Eight Days a Week." Gabriel soon realized Banks was the better piano player and Banks that Gabriel was the better singer. The pair started to write music together, using original chord sequences and melodies to come up with songs that were challenging and different. As they wrote together, Banks and Gabriel soon became aware of two younger pupils who had also taken to writing songs and had formed a band. **MICHAEL JOHN CLEOTE CRAWFORD "MIKE" RUTHERFORD** (born in Portsmouth, Hampshire, England, 2 October 1950) had enrolled at Charterhouse in September 1964, while **ANTHONY EDWIN "ANT" PHILLIPS** (born in London, England, 23 December 1951) followed in April 1965.

Mike Rutherford's father, William Francis Henry Crawford Rutherford, was a Royal navy captain[3] and his mother, Anne, was a widow—her previous husband having died of cancer. The family moved around the country a lot due to the requirements of his father's navy service. Aged 7, young Michael attended boarding school at the Leas Hoylake on the Wirral in Cheshire. His mother was keen on the arts and the following year Rutherford was drawn to the guitar, initially by its shape. His parents bought him a Spanish guitar and paid for him to have lessons. His sister, Nicolette, was a fan of Elvis Presley and The Everly Brothers and Rutherford idolized Hank Marvin from The Shadows—being a big follower of their recordings with Cliff Richard. Anne later bought her son his first electric guitar, a Hofner, when he was 12. With his friend Dimitri Griliopoulos, a guitarist and drummer, he would play the hits of the day. The family later moved to Farnham, also in Cheshire, but Rutherford was placed for the next level of his schooling at Charterhouse, which put a physical distance of a couple of hundred miles between them.

Anthony Phillips started playing guitar at the age of 11 while he was at St. Edmund's boarding school, in Hindhead. It was here he joined the school band known as The Spiders. The only other competent musician in the band was his friend Rivers Job[4] (pronounced Jobe). Phillips' father was a wealthy banker and president of an insurance company and Phillips was brought up in the Putney and Roehampton areas of southwest London. Although they were music lovers, neither of his parents were players. He advanced his interest through school concerts and took his guitar with him to Charterhouse. Here, he reconnected with Rivers Job, who had moved to the school the previous year, thereby making Phillips' own entry to the school that much easier.

None of the quartet of Banks, Gabriel, Rutherford and Phillips enjoyed their schooldays. Charterhouse had a strict regime which was at odds with the increasingly liberated social attitudes of the time. It bred shy young men who were very insular, having been sheltered from the outside world and the opposite sex. Gabriel would endure many sleepless nights, while Rutherford became the victim of a housemaster who banned him from playing the guitar for much of his time there. "Unfortunately, I caught the place at a pretty weird time," Rutherford later commented, "as many traditions from the old English empire were becoming obsolete. I caught the brunt of those changes. A lot of kids ran away."[5]

As a release from the traumas of boarding school life the four boys reveled in their music. As Rutherford wasn't allowed to play guitar, he spent some of his time in the school choir—more to give him a musical outlet rather than from any religious standpoint. Later, with Phillips, he formed a school band called Anon.[6] Other members included Rob Tyrell on drums, Rivers Job on bass and Richard Macphail[7] on vocals. The budding musicians were highly influenced by The Beatles, The Who and The Rolling Stones and extensively covered The Stones' album *Out of Our Heads*. On 16 December 1965, Anon performed at a School Entertainment Day and included a set of three Rolling Stones songs ("We've Got a Good Thing Going," "Talkin' 'bout You" and "That's How Strong My Love Is"). Due to his ban, Rutherford was only loosely involved from thereon and eventually went on to form a band called Climax. Anon therefore employed another friend, Mick Colman, to bridge the gap. Rutherford would eventually realize Anon had the stronger musicians and returned on bass once Rivers Job had been excluded from the school for his insubordination.[8]

Meanwhile, Gabriel and Banks joined with trumpet player Johnny Trapman and drummer **CHRISTOPHER "CHRIS" STEWART** (born 1950 in Horsham, Surrey, England) to form The Garden Wall. While Stewart had a reputation as a bit of a rebel, The Garden Wall's music was not as rock 'n' roll as that of Anon. Stewart had been taught drums by Gabriel, who wanted to be freed up to sing and play flute. In terms of cover material, The Garden Wall were more interested in the soul songs of the day from artists such as Otis Redding and Percy Sledge.

In July 1966, the end of term concert featured both Anon and The Garden Wall. Phillips and Rutherford played in both bands, adding guitars and bass to The Garden Wall's sound. Banks played grand piano from below stage level (the piano was too heavy to get on stage), while Gabriel wore a very tall hat—maybe the first indication of his ultimate move into theatrical costume during his Genesis days.

During the summer vacation, Anon made a demo tape at Tony Pike Sound in Putney with the Anthony Phillips written and Rolling Stones-influenced song "Pennsylvania Flickhouse."[9] Nothing came of this and gradually the band began to disintegrate. Phillips and Rutherford eventually drifted towards Banks and Gabriel. Phillips had tuned into Banks' love of The Beatles, having heard him play their songs on the piano, while Gabriel stood singing using the dining room table as his stage. When Richard Macphail left Charterhouse to go to Millfield School, the two songwriting pairs linked up to work as a collective.

In December 1966, Phillips, Rutherford, Banks and Gabriel recorded six songs at the studio of their friend Brian Roberts.[10] The demos were intended to promote the quartet as a writing team but not as a band unit given their relatively limited capabilities with their respective instruments. The quartet aimed to sell their songs to music publishers. Initially, Phillips was to handle the singing until Banks persuaded him that Gabriel had the stronger voice, pointing to the character and excitement Gabriel brought to his vocal work. While Rutherford and Phillips were inspired by the British rock and blues scene, Gabriel and Banks were still primarily listening to the American soul of Stax and Motown and that influence came through in Gabriel's soulful approach to singing. As a result, the writing output of the two teams varied, being largely tied to their specific influences.

The tape the quartet recorded consisted of early versions of [D0c] TRY A LITTLE SADNESS, [2] THAT'S ME, "Listen on Five," "Don't Want You Back," [D0a] PATRICIA and [D0b] SHE IS BEAUTIFUL. Rutherford and Phillips had written all the songs, except for [D0b] SHE IS BEAUTIFUL, which was written by Banks and Gabriel. Phillips and Rutherford both later admitted [D0b] SHE IS BEAUTIFUL was the strongest song of the set.

[D0a] PATRICIA

Band Credit: Tony Banks/Peter Gabriel/Anthony Phillips/Mike Rutherford
Music: Anthony Phillips
Length: 3:05

Tony Banks—Acoustic Guitar; **Peter Gabriel**—Drums; **Anthony Phillips**—Lead Acoustic Guitar; **Mike Rutherford**—Bass; **Mick Colman**—Acoustic Guitar
Demo recorded at Brian Roberts' Home studio, 26 March 1967.
UK/U.S. Release: 22 June 1998 (4-CD: *Genesis Archive 1967–75*)

PATRICIA was one of the six pieces included on the original demo tape handed to Jonathan King. This version is the earliest demo Genesis has made available and was recorded during Easter 1967 at the home studio of their friend Brian Roberts. The surviving recording is rough but gives a fascinating insight into the band during its infancy, here joined by Mick Colman. The piece was written by Phillips about a girl he coveted when he was just 13 years old. It is an instrumental track written in D major and in 3/4 time which is based around a simple strummed acoustic guitar arrangement. Phillips provides the lead melody over Rutherford's uncomplicated bass line and Banks' accompanying acoustic guitar. The demo is also notable for the appearance of Gabriel on drums, who fails to acquit himself with any real distinction as he sticks rigidly to the waltz-like rhythm. Gabriel would later admit that what limited drumming abilities he had could be attributed to sheer enthusiasm rather than any level of technical expertise. While the song is pleasantly folky, it is being played by a group of inexperienced musicians finding their feet as both players and writers. It did, however, have a sufficiently strong enough hook to be developed later, with the addition of a vocal part, for *From Genesis to Revelation* as [12] IN HIDING.

Archive Release: This demo version was included on the 4-CD box set *Genesis Archive 1967–75*. A remastered version (3:05) appeared on the Edsel Records 2005 2-CD rerelease of *From Genesis to Revelation*.

* * *

In early 1967, an old boy already involved in the music business as a pop singer and music publisher visited Charterhouse. His name was Jonathan King.[11] King had achieved fame through his hit single "Everyone's Gone to the Moon" and therefore was perceived to have some clout in the music industry. He had set up his own music publishing company—Jonjo Music—with Joe Ronocoroni and Ken Jones, former manager of The Zombies. Being too shy themselves, the band persuaded one of their friends, John Alexander, to hand King their demo tape. King didn't play their tape until he was driving home in his MGB GT. He immediately latched onto Gabriel's voice and wanted to hear more.

During the summer of 1967, two of the original demo songs were rerecorded at Regent Sound Studios ([D0b] SHE IS BEAUTIFUL and [D0c] TRY A LITTLE SADNESS) as well as demos of two further songs, [5] WHERE THE SOUR TURNS TO SWEET and [18] IMAGE BLOWN OUT.

[D0b] SHE IS BEAUTIFUL[12]

Band Credit: Tony Banks/Peter Gabriel/Anthony Phillips/Mike Rutherford
Music & Lyrics: Tony Banks/Peter Gabriel
Length: 3:47
Tony Banks—Piano, Backing Vocals; **Peter Gabriel**—Lead Vocals; **Anthony Phillips**—Acoustic Guitar, Backing Vocals; **Mike Rutherford**—Acoustic Guitar, Backing Vocals
Demo recorded at Regent Sounds Studio, London, summer 1967.
UK/U.S. Release: 22 June 1998 (4-CD: *Genesis Archive 1967–75*)

This was the first song Banks and Gabriel wrote together. Banks came up with the chord sequence and bass part on piano, while Gabriel improvised the vocal melody line and wrote the lyrics. This was typical of how the pair worked as a writing team at the time, sometimes alternating roles. The song went through many changes from this original demo to the revised version, with new lyrics, that was included on *From Genesis to Revelation* as [8] THE SERPENT. This version of the song tells the story of a beautiful woman trapped by her fame after she has become a famous model. Banks' cheeky, snaking piano rhythm in D major accompanies Gabriel as he delivers a distinctive vocal interpretation of a set of awkward lyrics. Phillips and Rutherford strum along a little hesitantly on acoustic guitar. The song demonstrated, even at this early stage, Banks' desire to change standard harmonies and chord progressions as he switches key to A minor during the chorus and to D minor on the playout. The choral-styled backing vocals are typical of the late '60s (the band would dub themselves The Wild Boars) and now feel very dated. However, this was the best song from the original demo tape handed to Jonathan King and the one that piqued his interest, leading to it being rerecorded as this specific version recorded at Regent Studios.

Archive Release: This demo was included on the 4-CD box set *Genesis Archive 1967–75* released in 1998. A remastered version (3:45) appeared on the Edsel Records 2005 2-CD rerelease of *From Genesis to Revelation*.

[D0c] TRY A LITTLE SADNESS

Band Credit: Tony Banks/Peter Gabriel/Anthony Phillips/Mike Rutherford
Music & Lyrics: Tony Banks/Peter Gabriel
Length: 3:21
Tony Banks—Piano, Backing Vocals; **Peter Gabriel**—Lead Vocals; **Anthony Phillips**—Lead Acoustic Guitar, Backing Vocals; **Mike Rutherford**—Acoustic Guitar, Backing Vocals
Demo recorded at Regent Sounds Studio, London, summer 1967.
UK/U.S. Release: 22 June 1998 (4-CD: *Genesis Archive 1967–75*)

This was another of the songs included on the original demo tape handed to King. Like [D0b] SHE IS BEAUTIFUL, this version was a later recording made at Regent Studios during the summer of 1967. The band have been very honest about these early efforts, emphasizing they were songwriters looking to have their material performed by others. Their playing on these demos is reflective of their limited ability as musicians at this stage. TRY A LITTLE SADNESS adopts the standard pop song structure of three core musical sections comprising verse, chorus and bridge. Banks again plays a funky piano introduction to the song before settling into a straightforward rhythmic approach to accompany Phillips and Rutherford's heavily strummed acoustic guitars. Phillips provides a short and very tentative acoustic solo through the song's bridge. The track has a pleasant, but not especially memorable, melody. The lyrics are obscure but urge the young listener in a hip refrain around its title, rather untidily delivered in chorus by the band. Gabriel and Banks were huge Otis Redding fans and it is likely the title was a contrary spin on the soul singer's "Try a Little Tenderness."

Archive Release: This demo was included on the 4-CD box set *Genesis Archive 1967–75* released in 1998. A remastered version (3:18) appeared on the Edsel Records 2005 2-CD rerelease of *From Genesis to Revelation*.

* * *

Jonathan King was impressed enough by the band's latest demos to sign them to Jonjo Music on 30 August 1967, subject to yearly options.[13] "We were excited just by the fact that anyone was interested in our songs. We would have signed for life at that stage,"[14] commented Banks. King was initially interested in the band primarily as a writing team, something Phillips acknowledged, "We were signed as songwriters and I think he wanted to make us more of a group like Hedgehoppers Anonymous."[15]

Further song demos were recorded through 1967 and into 1968 at both Regent Sound Studios and Central Sound in London. These included [D0d] HIDDEN IN THE WORLD OF DAWN, [D4b] HEY!, [D0e] SEA BEE, [D0f] THE MYSTERY OF THE FLANNAN ISLE LIGHTHOUSE, [D0g] HAIR ON THE ARMS AND LEGS, [D4a] THE MAGIC OF TIME and [6] IN THE BEGINNING. Other songs that were recorded but have never been subsequently released included: "Barnaby's Adventure," "Fourteen Years Too Long," "Lost in a Drawer," "I'm Here," "2:30 Parktime (a.m. p.m.)," "There was a Movement," "Everywhere Is Here," "F#1" (which evolved into [25] THE MUSICAL BOX), "Humanity," "Sitting on Top of the World," "From the Bottom of a Well" and "You Got to Be Perfect."

[D0d] HIDDEN IN THE WORLD OF DAWN

Band Credit: Tony Banks/Peter Gabriel/Anthony Phillips/Mike Rutherford
Length: 3:10
Tony Banks—Piano, Backing Vocals; **Peter Gabriel**—Lead Vocals; **Anthony Phillips**—Acoustic Guitar, Backing Vocals; **Mike Rutherford**—Acoustic Guitar, Backing Vocals
Demo recorded at Regent Sounds Studio, London, October 1967.
UK/U.S. Release: 22 June 1998 (4-CD: *Genesis Archive 1967–75*)

A two-chord piano figure by Banks is backed by Phillips' picked acoustic guitar in the opening of this demo. Gabriel's delicate vocal, augmented by the band's ragged harmonizing, echoes the piano melody and lyrically describes the beauty and quiet of the dawn before the chaos of the day commences. It is a lyric that tries too hard to be poetic and merely comes across as fey, thereby weakening further what isn't musically a particularly strong song. It feels like there is a constant tussle between Banks' piano and Gabriel's vocal for the most part, as if Gabriel were singing over the top of an intended instrumental. That may be partly due to the lack of production with this recording being a demo with little attempt to get a balanced mix. Like all the demos from this period, the absence of a drummer means the songs lack rhythmic thrust beyond Banks' piano. The result is a very cluttered arrangement. Jonathan King was not keen on the song, wanting a simpler approach and more hook orientated approach to the band's music.

Archive Release: This demo was included on the 4-CD box set *Genesis Archive 1967–75* released in 1998.

[D0e] SEA BEE

Band Credit: Tony Banks/Peter Gabriel/Anthony Phillips/Mike Rutherford
Length: 3:04
Tony Banks—Piano, Backing Vocals; **Peter Gabriel**—Lead Vocals; **Anthony Phillips**—Acoustic Guitar, Backing Vocals; **Mike Rutherford**—Acoustic Guitar, Backing Vocals
Demo recorded at Regent Sounds Studio or Central Sound Studio, October 1967.
UK/U.S. Release: 22 June 1998 (4-CD: *Genesis Archive 1967–75*)

Another demo recorded in autumn 1967, SEA BEE sounds uncannily like [D0d] HIDDEN IN THE WORLD OF DAWN in both arrangement and approach, highlighting one of the band's problems at the time of getting variety into their song writing. Here again Banks' piano provides the basis for a delicate verse. There is a bit more attack in the chorus as Banks pushes for an aggressive major key chord progression from G to C via A sharp. Philips and Rutherford add an uncomplicated gently strummed acoustic guitar accompaniment. The song ends abruptly and feels unfinished both in conception and arrangement. As a demo of the band's writing talents it is one of their lesser tunes. The "Sea Bee" referred to in the lyrics is not a construction worker in the navy, but some mythical insect in flight over the sea. If there is any meaning to the lyrics it is not easily identifiable.

Archive Release: This demo was included on the 4-CD box set *Genesis Archive 1967–75* released in 1998.

[D0f] THE MYSTERY OF THE FLANNAN ISLE LIGHTHOUSE

Band Credit: Tony Banks/Peter Gabriel/Anthony Phillips/Mike Rutherford
Length: 2:35
Tony Banks—Piano, Backing Vocals; **Peter Gabriel**—Lead Vocals; **Anthony Phillips**—Acoustic Guitar, Backing Vocals; **Mike Rutherford**—Acoustic Guitar, Backing Vocals
Demo recorded at Regent Sounds Studio, London, October 1967.
UK/U.S. Release: 22 June 1998 (4-CD: *Genesis Archive 1967–75*)

This is a further demo recorded at the Regent Studio sessions in autumn 1967. The song opens with a repeated, grooving piano riff from Banks over descending chords, while Phillips and Rutherford again strum quietly away in the background. While this provides a promising start, the song soon settles into a familiar arrangement with the band's overly emphasized "Wild Boars" choral backing. The verse revolves around E flat, B flat and A flat, with Banks almost overlapping himself as he uneasily plays the galloping major key piano chords. The lyrics focus on the mystery of boats being attracted to a shrouded lighthouse and crashing against the rocks.[16] The song fades out with Banks playing a repeated riff over descending chords—it is the strongest musical section of the piece but is quickly gone.

Archive Release: This demo was included on the 4-CD box set *Genesis Archive 1967–75* released in 1998.

[D0g] HAIR ON THE ARMS AND LEGS

Band Credit: Tony Banks/Peter Gabriel/Anthony Phillips/Mike Rutherford
Length: 2:41
Tony Banks—Piano, Backing Vocals; **Peter Gabriel**—Lead Vocals; **Anthony Phillips**—Acoustic Guitar, Backing Vocals; **Mike Rutherford**—Acoustic Guitar, Backing Vocals
Demo recorded at Regent Sounds Studio, London, October 1967.
UK/U.S. Release: 22 June 1998 (4-CD: *Genesis Archive 1967–75*)

Banks' piano is again very dominant on this demo recording with Gabriel doing well to produce complementary vocal lines and melody. However, the song lacks the hook that Jonathan King was looking for and is bereft of rhythmic punch. Musically the piece ambles along aimlessly to its conclusion. Phillips and Rutherford's acoustic guitars are barely audible in the rough mix. The thoughtful lyrics tell the story of an old man trapped by his inability to solve the problems of the world. Gabriel's vocal textures attempt to capture the frustration and hopelessness outlined in the lyrics and provides a hint of the potential within. Fragments of this song were later used in the BBC recording of [D18c] FRUSTRATION in January 1970—part of the so-called *Jackson Tapes* collection.

Archive Release: This demo was included on the 4-CD box set *Genesis Archive 1967–75* released in 1998.

[1] THE SILENT SUN

Band Credit: Tony Banks/Peter Gabriel/
  Anthony Phillips/Mike Rutherford
Music & Lyrics: Tony Banks/Peter Gabriel
Length: 2:14
Tony Banks—Piano, Backing Vocals; **Peter Gabriel**—Lead Vocals; **Anthony Phillips**—Acoustic Guitar, Backing Vocals; **Mike Rutherford**—Bass, Backing Vocals; **Chris Stewart**—Drums and Percussion; **Unknown**—Strings
Recorded at Regent Sounds A Studio, London, December 1967.
Producer: Jonathan King. Engineer: Tom Allom.
Orchestral Arrangement: Arthur Greenslade.
UK Release: 22 February 1968[17] (A-side single b/w [2] THAT'S ME. Decca. F 12735)
U.S. Release: February 1968 (A-side single b/w [2] THAT'S ME. Parrot. 45-PAR-3018)
UK Album Release: 7 March 1969. (LP. *From Genesis to Revelation*)
U.S. Album Release: August 1974. (LP. *From Genesis to Revelation*)

Advertisement for the single release of [1] THE SILENT SUN placed in *Record Mirror* on 10 February 1968 (courtesy Mark Kenyon/The Genesis Archive).

Peter Gabriel received a letter from Joe Ronocoroni on behalf of Jonjo Music dated 29 November 1967 rejecting the band's latest batch of demos. Banks and Gabriel were frustrated with King's perceived lack of enthusiasm for the songs, which were veering into more lyrically and musically complex territory. King, however, was looking for hits. The band regrouped and discussed how they could rekindle King's interest. Knowing of King's love of the Bee Gees, Gabriel and Banks wrote THE SILENT SUN as a pastiche of the Gibbs Brothers' "To Love Somebody." Gabriel even delivered his best Robin Gibb impersonation on the second verse. The strategy worked as King was predictably impressed and took the band into the studio for sessions between December 1967 and April 1968 to record songs for their first two singles and he also finally gave the band its name—Genesis.[18]

At these sessions, the band recorded four songs for two separate single releases on the Decca label—[1] THE SILENT SUN backed with [2] THAT'S ME and [3] A WINTER'S TALE backed with [4] ONE-EYED HOUND. A further recording of ONE-EYED HOUND (referenced as "On the Trail of the One-Eyed Hound"), alongside another track "I'm Here," was made at Regent Studio on 17 April 1968.

THE SILENT SUN is a lightly romantic, midtempo piece with fanciful lyrics. The song is based around a simple repeated verse-chorus structure—utilizing just four regular chords (G major, C major, D major and A minor). Stylistically, it is a fusion of folk and pop styles and boasts a pleasing melody over an unimaginative acoustic arrangement that is made overly complex by the introduction of some intrusive strings. While Banks and Gabriel's cynical attempt to capture King's attention had worked, Phillips had major reservations about the approach, later noting, "It was a song I hated. As a young idealist I thought it was a sell-out."[19]

The mono recording was released as a single on the Decca label in the UK (and on London's Parrot label in the U.S.) on 22 February 1968. The single was first played on BBC Radio One by DJ Kenny Everett. It was also placed on the rotation list for Radio Caroline, until the pirate station was forced off the air only a month after the single's release. The band was hopeful of a hit and bought themselves outfits in the event they would be asked to appear on *Top of the Pops*.[20] Phillips later commented, "Mercifully it wasn't successful. I think if it had been successful it would have been the end of the band. The band would have got stuck, would never have developed a really original sound."[21] Banks echoed Phillips' views, although he felt the song could have been a hit given the right circumstances. It was possibly indicative of King's hesitancy about the band that he chose not to promote the single on his own TV show of the time, *Good Evening—I'm Jonathan King*.

The song did receive strong reviews from Chris Welch in *Melody Maker* and Derek Johnson in the *New Musical Express*. Johnson said the single was "a disc of many facets and great depth."[22] Both writers enjoyed the arrangement and the poetic nature of the lyrics. Their recommendations, however, had little impact on the single's sales.

The song would later be included in a slightly remixed form as "Silent Sun" on the band's debut album, *From Genesis to Revelation*, released just over a year later, with the single version also included on many of the subsequent rereleases.

Alternative Versions: THE SILENT SUN was remixed and reissued under the title "The Silent Sun 2006" as a CD single by Revvolution Records (REVVCDS002) under the band name of "Peter Gabriel and Genesis" on 8 January 2007, having previously been made available as an online download. A newly recorded drum track (player unknown) is more prominent in the mix here. The song was accompanied by a similar remix of [5] WHERE THE SOUR TURNS TO SWEET. Another remastered mono mix of THE SILENT SUN (2:14) along with an alternative mono mix (2:13), minus the strings, appeared on the *50 Years Ago* album of remixes and outtakes released in 2017.

[2] THAT'S ME

Band Credit: Tony Banks/Peter Gabriel/Anthony Phillips/Mike Rutherford
Music & Lyrics: Anthony Phillips/Mike Rutherford
Length: 2:39
Tony Banks—Piano, Backing Vocals; **Peter Gabriel**—Lead Vocals; **Anthony Phillips**—Guitar, Acoustic Guitar, Backing Vocals; **Mike Rutherford**—Bass, Backing Vocals; **Chris Stewart**—Drums and Percussion
Recorded at Regent Sounds A Studio, London, December 1967.
Producer: Jonathan King. Engineer: Tom Allom.
UK Release: 22 February 1968 (B-side single b/w [1] THE SILENT SUN. Decca. F 12735)
U.S. Release: 22 February 1968 (B-side single b/w [1] THE SILENT SUN. Parrot. 45-PAR-3018)

THAT'S ME was the B-side to [1] THE SILENT SUN and is an uptempo song about isolation and inner turmoil with the protagonist complaining about how everybody misunderstands him. The song was written by Phillips and Rutherford with Phillips' use of electric guitar the most interesting aspect as he provides a hesitant, but brief, solo early (0:59–1:14). "There's a glitch in the solo," recalled Phillips, "where it became known that I am supposed to have said 'oh fuck' when I missed the bend."[23] Crashing power chords in the closing section—obviously inspired by The Who guitarist Pete Townshend—make this the heaviest recording Genesis had produced in their initial batch. The band was still going for a feel they hoped would impress King and that desire to please is apparent here in a forced performance that sounds rushed in parts. Stewart's drumming is also weak, lacking the power and drive the piece needed.

The song was later included on several rerelease versions of the band's debut *From Genesis to Revelation*.

Alternative Versions: A remastered mono mix version of the song (2:37) appeared on the *50 Years Ago* album of remixes and outtakes in 2017.

[3] A WINTER'S TALE

Band Credit: Tony Banks/Peter Gabriel/Anthony Phillips/Mike Rutherford
Music & Lyrics: Tony Banks/Peter Gabriel
Length: 3:28
Tony Banks—Piano, Organ, Backing Vocals; **Peter Gabriel**—Lead Vocals; **Anthony Phillips**—Acoustic Guitar, Backing Vocals; **Mike Rutherford**—Bass, Backing Vocals; **Chris Stewart**—Drums and Percussion; **Unknown**—Brass
Recorded at Regent Sounds A Studio, London, between December 1967 and March 1968.
Producer: Jonathan King. Engineer: Tom Allom.
Orchestral Arrangement: Arthur Greenslade.
UK Release: 10 May 1968.[24] (A-side single b/w [4] ONE-EYED HOUND. Decca. F 12775)

Genesis' second single was released nearly three months after [1] THE SILENT SUN. A WINTER'S TALE is a simple song with a typical late-1960s folk/pop feel. The poetic lyrics draw on images of winter as a metaphor for the cooling of a relationship. Musically, the gentle verses lack distinction. However, the crescendo into the chorus is built around an agreeable melody, but the song is hampered by unsubtle backing vocal harmonies. Banks does, however, add some musical excitement with his lifting sustained organ chords using inversions to shift between A major, D major, B minor and F sharp major. The drama created by Banks' harmonies gave Gabriel the opportunity to inject some urgency and drive into his vocal performance. Again, a largely brass orchestral backing, arranged by Arthur Greenslade, was added to the track but here it is less intrusive than were the strings on THE SILENT SUN.

Banks was given the job of trying to persuade DJ Tony Blackburn to play the song on his BBC Radio One show, but the single ultimately failed to produce the resonance the band were looking for with the record buying public, despite another positive critical response. Derek Johnson was again impressed as he remarked in his review of the single for the *New Musical Express*, "The soul-searching lyric is impressive and gripping—and, while the melody could have done with a little more substance, it's a platter I can thoroughly recommend."[25]

A demo pressing by London records, sharing the same catalogue reference as the Decca disc, was produced but the single is not believed to have received an official release in the U.S. The song was, however, released as a single in Australia (again b/w [4] ONE-EYED HOUND) and was included as a bonus track on several rerelease versions of *From Genesis to Revelation*.

Interestingly this is the only song the band managed to sell to another artist under their original concept of a songwriter collective. An Italian singer, Carlo Pavone, recorded the song with new lyrics as "Chi Ti Ha Dato La Sua Vita," which was released by Arc Records in 1968. This version was swamped with strings, but otherwise remained faithful to the band's composition.

Alternative Versions: An in-studio work-in-progress sample (7:38) with studio conversations between the band and producer King as the song is started and stopped, appeared on the *50 Years Ago* album of remixes and outtakes in 2017. The final take from the recordings, included toward the end of this extended "in studio" version, is the one that was released as the single.

[4] ONE EYED HOUND

Band Credit: Tony Banks/Peter Gabriel/Anthony Phillips/Mike Rutherford
Music & Lyrics: Tony Banks/Peter Gabriel
Length: 2:30
Tony Banks—Piano, Organ, Backing Vocals; **Peter Gabriel**—Lead Vocals; **Anthony Phillips**—Guitar, Acoustic Guitar, Backing Vocals; **Mike Rutherford**—Bass, Backing Vocals; **Chris Stewart**—Drums and Percussion
Recorded at Regent Sounds A Studio, London, between December 1967 and March 1968.
Producer: Jonathan King. Engineer: Tom Allom.
UK Release: 10 May 1968. (B-side single b/w [3] A WINTER'S TALE. Decca. F 12775)

This seemingly Beatles influenced tune (note Phillips' harmonized electric guitar sound during the song's opening) finds the band sounding much more confident. There is still an occasional hesitancy to the playing, notably Phillips' acoustic lead lines, but the song has presence. The acoustic guitar takes the lead in the arrangement, while Phillips' electric underpins the chorus alongside Banks' piano. The song also hints at the feel Genesis would explore further on *Trespass*, with its faster passages contrasting with the surrounding gentler verses and featuring Stewart's best drumming for the band. The lyrics are obscure—basically representing the mutterings of a man committing a sin while in search of the one-eyed hound, suggesting this is the story of a man on the run. Gabriel contributes a strong and confident vocal and Banks' voice is dominant in the backing.

The song was later included as a bonus track on several rerelease versions of *From Genesis to Revelation*.

Alternative Versions: An alternative stereo mix using the original working title "On the Trail of the One-Eyed Hound" (2:39) appeared on the *50 Years Ago* album of remixes and outtakes in 2017. The cleaner mix and slightly longer edit includes a count-in by Gabriel while his vocal is more dominant in the mix. Banks' organ is also mixed slightly higher on the outro.

* * *

Despite Jonathan King's enthusiasm, the lack of success for both singles meant the band's preparation for stardom had to be postponed. King and the band remained undeterred and discussions commenced about the recording of an album. King had expressed concerns about the band's rhythm section, which would need to be addressed ahead of entering the studio. The band agreed and Chris Stewart, who was still attending school, was paid £300 to leave the band and sign away the rights to future royalties. Both the band and Stewart have since cited the drummer's lack of empathy with the music and an inability to add definition to the rhythm section as the reason behind the split.[26] Rutherford, supported by the band's friend John Alexander, was tasked with breaking the news.

Genesis quickly recruited a replacement drummer. Jazz fan **JONATHAN "JOHN" SILVER** was born in 1950 and educated at St. Edward's School, Oxford.[27] Gabriel had met Silver at Davis, Laing & Dick, a crammer (an institution to prepare students for exams) in London where they were both studying. They had struck up a rapport when Silver introduced the singer to new musical influences, including Randy Newman and The Beach Boys. Gabriel suggested Silver as a replacement for Stewart and the rest of the band agreed. Silver worked on further demos with the band through 1968 with further session recordings made at Central Sound Studio on Denmark Street in London as well as Regent Sounds.

[D4a] THE MAGIC OF TIME

Band Credit: Tony Banks/Peter Gabriel/Anthony Phillips/Mike Rutherford
Length: 2:01
Tony Banks—Piano; **Peter Gabriel**—Lead Vocals; **Anthony Phillips**—Acoustic Guitar; **Mike Rutherford**—Bass; **John Silver**—Percussion; **David Thomas**—Backing Vocals
Demo recorded at Regent Sounds Studio, early 1968.
UK/U.S. Release: 22 June 1998 (4-CD: *Genesis Archive 1967–75*).

A jazzy piano is played by Banks, in the manner of Dave Brubeck's "Take Five," over an uptempo skittering percussive rhythm from Silver using brushes on a Huntley & Palmers' biscuit tin. The drummer had been unable to get his kit into the studio and was forced to use the best alternative instrument available. Rutherford's walking bass line adds to the jazzy feel. This short song may have worked better as an instrumental, with Gabriel's vocals a little swamped in the rough mix and competing for attention with the skittering rhythm and Banks' dominant piano chords. The lyrics describe the fashioning of the land, rivers and seas over the passing of time as if guided by some ancient scripture. Banks grooves pleasantly on piano during the playout. The band's long-time friend David Thomas provided the harmony backing vocals to Gabriel.[28]

Archive Release: This demo was included on the 4-CD box set *Genesis Archive 1967–75* released in 1998.

[D4b] HEY!

Band Credit: Tony Banks/Peter Gabriel/Anthony Phillips/Mike Rutherford
Length: 2:28
Tony Banks—Piano, Backing Vocals; **Peter Gabriel**—Lead Vocals; **Anthony Phillips**—Acoustic Guitar, Backing Vocals; **Mike Rutherford**—Bass; **John Silver**—Drums, Percussion
Demo recorded at Central Sound Studio, London, 13 March 1968.
UK/U.S. Release: 22 June 1998 (4-CD: *Genesis Archive 1967–75*).

This demo was one of four tracks recorded at Central Sound Studio on 13 March 1968.[29] A bossa-nova rhythm opens the song, which again has a simple piano/acoustic guitar arrangement. Gabriel sings soulfully of a lost love over a simplistic chorus. There's a nice two-bar guitar/bass feature from Phillips and Rutherford, which repeats the song's core melody and Silver's galloping drums add a sense of urgent pace to the rhythm. Again, the mix is rough and the song feels underrehearsed, but it has promise in its hook before losing its way in another overly familiar arrangement that lacks any real musical spark.

Archive Release: This demo was included on the 4-CD box set *Genesis Archive 1967–75* released in 1998.

2

Studio Album #1: *From Genesis to Revelation*

UK Release: 7 March 1969. LP. Decca. SKL 4990 (stereo) LK 4990 (mono).
U.S. Release: August 1974. LP. London. PS 643.
Deluxe Edition Remaster:
UK Release: 2005. CD. Edsel Records. MEDCD 721.

Album Tracks
[5] WHERE THE SOUR TURNS TO SWEET
[6] IN THE BEGINNING
[7] FIRESIDE SONG
[8] THE SERPENT
[9] AM I VERY WRONG?
[10] IN THE WILDERNESS
[11] THE CONQUEROR
[12] IN HIDING
[13] ONE DAY
[14] WINDOW
[15] IN LIMBO
[1] SILENT SUN
[16] A PLACE TO CALL MY OWN

Other Songs Recorded
[17] BUILD ME A MOUNTAIN
[18] IMAGE BLOWN OUT

Genesis had prepared for their debut album with rehearsals at a series of country houses in the south of England and in the Midlands. These included Silver's parents' house in Oxford and David Thomas' in Hampshire. Genesis finally returned to Regent Sounds B Studio in the summer holidays of 1968 to record *From Genesis to Revelation*[1] with King as producer. The recording of the album was scheduled over ten days but was reportedly completed in three. The songs were captured on a four-track machine that left little room for overdubbing with the band concentrating on playing the songs live and using the best take. The downside of this method of working was that it put a strain on Gabriel's vocals as his voice tired through the recordings.

The band finalized a collection of their best songs, some of which were adapted from earlier demos. Together with King, they selected those that would ultimately ap-

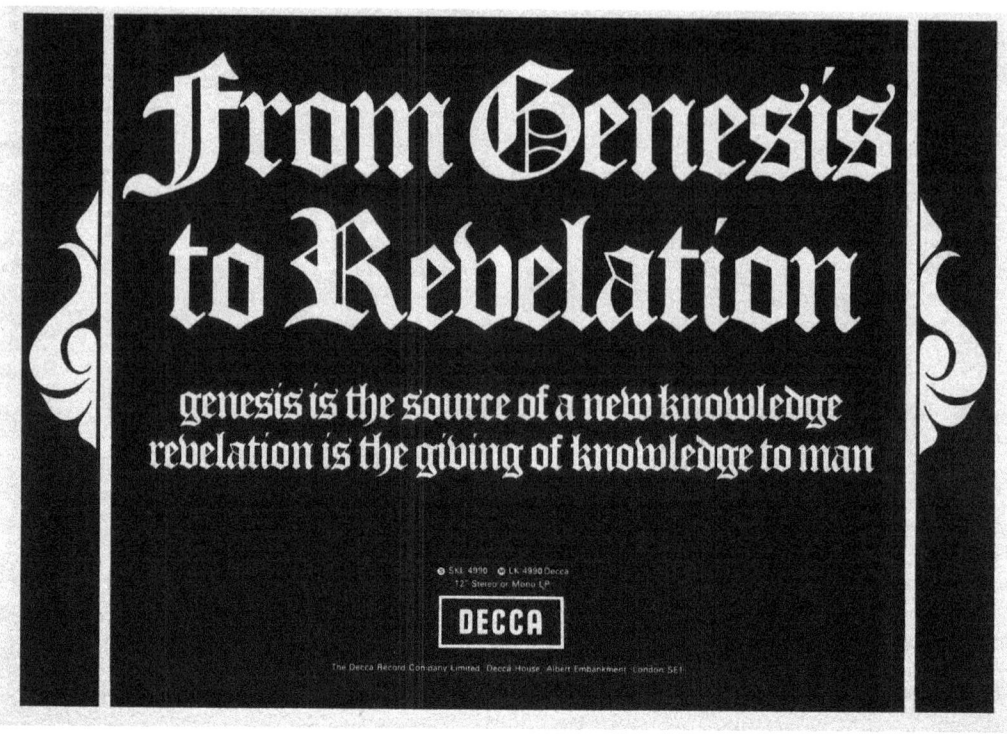

Advertisement for the release of Genesis' debut album, *From Genesis to Revelation* **placed in** *Record Mirror* **on 12 April 1969 (courtesy Mark Kenyon/The Genesis Archive).**

pear on the album. By this stage the band was utilizing more of the songs written by Banks and Gabriel.[2] While Phillips also contributed a few pieces, Rutherford was less involved in the writing at this stage. The band was keen to explore a crossover sound between folk and rock, but lyrically the album centered its theme on the story of the Bible—in this instance, the creation of the world. The theme came at King's suggestion and was aimed at giving the album a concept to hang the songs around. While this may seem more than a little pretentious, it did give the band a lyrical hook, leading them to rewrite lyrics to some of the songs in order to fit the concept. In retrospect, this decision could be judged a mistake as it led to many record shops dumping the album in their "Religious" sections.

King was not present for all the sessions, leaving the technical recording process to engineers Brian Roberts and Tom Allom, but he remained the project's guiding light. It was only later the orchestral parts, arranged by Arthur Greenslade and conducted by Lou Warburton,[3] were added to flesh out and commercialize the sound in a way The Moody Blues had done successfully. The band was unaware of King's plan and Phillips was particularly annoyed by the additions, feeling the new arrangements robbed the songs of some of their power. The rest of the band were more philosophical about the move. King later justified it by saying, "I like it with all the strings and links between the tracks. It was at a time when 'concept' albums had not really been invented, so it was one of the first. I think the added sweetness, and professionalism, makes it truly unusual and covers up any amateurism."[4]

[5] WHERE THE SOUR TURNS TO SWEET

Band Credit: Tony Banks/Peter Gabriel/Anthony Phillips/Mike Rutherford
Music & Lyrics: Tony Banks/Peter Gabriel
Length: 3:15
Tony Banks—Piano, Backing Vocals; **Peter Gabriel**—Lead Vocals; **Anthony Phillips**—Guitar, Backing Vocals; **Mike Rutherford**—Bass; **John Silver**—Drums, Percussion; **Unknown**–Strings & Horns
Recorded at Regent Sounds B Studio, London, August 1968 and 17–19 November 1968 (Orchestra). Producer: Jonathan King. Engineer: Brian Roberts & Tom Allom.
Orchestral Arrangement: Arthur Greenslade. Conductor: Lou Warburton.
UK Release: 7 March 1969. (LP: *From Genesis to Revelation*)
U.S. Release: August 1974. (LP: *From Genesis to Revelation*)
UK Single Release: 27 June 1969.[5] (A-side b/w [12] IN HIDING. Decca. F 12949. XDR 44553)

WHERE THE SOUR TURNS TO SWEET was originally recorded at Advision Studios in 1967 under the shorter title of "Sour Turns Sweet" as a potential single release with "From the Bottom of a Well" as its intended B-side. The band was unhappy with the recording and the single idea was dropped. While "From the Bottom of the Well" disappeared into obscurity, "Sour Turns Sweet" was included in the batch of songs to be recorded for *From Genesis to Revelation*.

Finger clicks over a climbing piano and bass riff present an uplifting gospel feel that signals the "religious" theme of the album. The verse switches to Phillips' gently strummed acoustic guitar and Banks' heavy piano major chords rotating from C to F to G and colored by Arthur Greenslade's string arrangement. It rather plods toward the chorus which returns to the opening riff, with Greenslade adding brass to the arrangement. Here the orchestration works reasonably well with the brass section giving the song depth to the arrangement allowing the backing vocal harmonies to be mixed down. Gabriel's vocals are assured throughout as he pleads the listener to join his throng. Originally, the song was to have a different chorus, but Banks and Gabriel felt it was weak and rewrote the chorus to repeat the theme of the intro. The song also fades with an outro reprising the piano/bass and finger-clicks figure of the intro. It makes for a fresh-sounding and appealing opener to the album.

Single Release: The song was released by Decca as an A-side single on 27 June 1969 in the UK (b/w [12] IN HIDING) without any chart success. Arthur Greenslade was credited on the label as Music Director. The song was also released as a single by Decca in New Zealand.

Alternative Versions: A 1968 demo of the song (3:06), minus the strings, was included on the 1998 box set *Genesis Archive 1967–1975*. A remixed version (3:18) with a newly added drum track (player unknown) was included as the "B-side" to the remixed single rerelease of [1] THE SILENT SUN (as THE SILENT SUN 2006) on CD in January 2007, having previously been available as an online download. A slightly longer remastered mono version (3:25) and new and cleaner mono mix without the strings (3:29) appeared on the *50 Years Ago* album of remixes and outtakes in 2017.

[6] IN THE BEGINNING

Band Credit: Tony Banks/Peter Gabriel/Anthony Phillips/Mike Rutherford
Music & Lyrics: Anthony Phillips/Peter Gabriel
Length: 3:45
Tony Banks—Piano; **Peter Gabriel**—Lead Vocals; **Anthony Phillips**—Guitar, Acoustic Guitar; **Mike Rutherford**—Bass; **John Silver**—Drums

Recorded at Regent Sounds B Studio, London, August 1968.
Producer: Jonathan King. Engineer: Brian Roberts & Tom Allom.
UK Release: 7 March 1969. (LP: *From Genesis to Revelation*)
U.S. Release: August 1974. (LP: *From Genesis to Revelation*)

A rumbling and distorted oscillating guitar effect provides an atmospheric opening to the second track on the album. It then fades into Rutherford's bouncing bass line, which is repeated throughout the verse. Banks' piano takes more of a back seat as Phillips' guitar work comes to the fore. The result is one of the strongest cuts on the album, with its grandiose story of the world's formation marrying well with the more urgent rhythms on show. Another Pete Townshend-inspired riff from Phillips' electric guitar gives the song its drive and Gabriel delivers a strong vocal performance that captures the drama of the natural event. Unfortunately, the impact is lessened by Gabriel's vocal being too far back in the mix and his voice being drenched with reverb.

Alternative Versions: A 1968 demo version (3:27) can be found on the box set *Genesis Archive 1967–75*. A new mono mix of the song (4:23), minus the drone intro and instead including the piano bridge to [7] FIRESIDE SONG, appeared on the *50 Years Ago* album of remixes and outtakes in 2017. Gabriel's vocals are much more up front here.

Single Release: A press testing had been completed for a potential UK single release but went no further. The song was much later released as a single by Decca (b/w [8] THE SERPENT) in Italy in 1974.

Live Performances: 1969/70. The song was performed on some of the band's early gigs.

Live Recordings: No officially released live recordings of the song exist.

[7] FIRESIDE SONG

Band Credit: Tony Banks/Peter Gabriel/Anthony Phillips/Mike Rutherford
Music & Lyrics: Tony Banks/Anthony Phillips/Mike Rutherford
Length: 4:18
Tony Banks—Piano, Acoustic Guitar, Backing Vocals; **Peter Gabriel**—Lead Vocals; **Anthony Phillips**—Acoustic Guitar, Backing Vocals; **Mike Rutherford**—Bass; **John Silver**—Percussion; **Unknown**—Strings
Recorded at Regent Sounds B Studio, London, August 1968 and 17–19 November 1968 (Orchestra).
Producer: Jonathan King. Engineer: Brian Roberts & Tom Allom.
Orchestral Arrangement: Arthur Greenslade. Conductor: Lou Warburton.
UK Release: 7 March 1969. (LP: *From Genesis to Revelation*)
U.S. Release: August 1974. (LP: *From Genesis to Revelation*)

Banks provides a harmonic piano introduction, using some smooth chord progressions, that acts as a linking passage between this and the previous track. The section showcases Banks' ear for harmony, but it has no direct link to the melodies employed in the song that follows. The listener can easily visualize the band sitting around a campfire with their acoustic guitars strumming away as they musically imagine the calm after the storm of the Earth's creation. The verse was written by Banks and originally had a much more complicated chord structure, some of which is echoed in his solo intro. He later decided to use a more basic structure and the song benefited from this. However, the thin orchestral strings are so intrusive they threaten to drown out the delicately strummed acoustic guitars, which may have been King's intention with a view to masking the more amateurish nature of the playing. Gabriel's lead vocals, along with the choral vocals from Banks and Phillips, may be too reverent in delivery but the chorus does carry a strong melody, which almost makes up for the strings ... but not quite.

Alternative Versions: A new mono mix of the song (3:38), without the strings, appeared on the *50 Years Ago* album of remixes and outtakes in 2017. The piano intro was moved to front the remix of [6] IN THE BEGINNING.

[8] THE SERPENT

Band Credit: Tony Banks/Peter Gabriel/Anthony Phillips/Mike Rutherford
Music & Lyrics: Tony Banks/Peter Gabriel
Length: 4:38
Tony Banks—Organ, Backing Vocals; **Peter Gabriel**—Lead Vocals; **Anthony Phillips**—Guitar, Acoustic Guitar, Backing Vocals; **Mike Rutherford**—Bass, Backing Vocals; **John Silver**—Drums, Percussion; **Unknown**—Strings
Recorded at Regent Sounds B Studio, London, August 1968 and 17–19 November 1968 (Orchestra).
Producer: Jonathan King. Engineer: Brian Roberts & Tom Allom.
Orchestral Arrangement: Arthur Greenslade. Conductor: Lou Warburton.
UK Release: 7 March 1969. (LP: *From Genesis to Revelation*)
U.S. Release: August 1974. (LP: *From Genesis to Revelation*)

THE SERPENT was initially recorded a year earlier as the demo [D0b] SHE IS BEAUTIFUL and was the song that originally encouraged Jonathan King to take the band on board. Here, the lyrics are reworked to conform with the theme of the album. Silver's galloping percussion, backed by a slightly detuned minor-key acoustic guitar, provides an interlude leading into the opening bass/guitar riff, which alternates between D minor and F major and is played in unison by Phillips and Rutherford. Banks' accompanying organ chords give the song a density of sound that is missing from most of the other songs on the album. The choral backing vocals, however, again prove to be musically distracting. Phillips' electric guitar work, however, weaves nicely into the musical passages and adds variety to the arrangement. The instrumental section surges with its changing tempos providing an early indication of the band's future direction. Overall, the song perhaps still feels a little cluttered—as if the band were trying to cram too many ideas into the four-minute space. Banks remains fond of it noting there was "an excitement about it we liked."[6]

Alternative Versions: A remastered version of the song (4:02), minus the interlude, appeared on the *50 Years Ago* album of remixes and outtakes in 2017. It is otherwise slightly longer due to a slightly extended fade out. A vocal only track (3:57), including Gabriel's lead and the band's backing, was also included.

Single Release: The song was released as a B-side single (b/w [8] IN THE BEGINNING) in Italy in 1974.

Live Performances: 1969/70. The song was performed on some of the band's early gigs.
Live Recordings: No officially released live recordings of the song exist.

[9] AM I VERY WRONG?

Band Credit: Tony Banks/Peter Gabriel/Anthony Phillips/Mike Rutherford
Music & Lyrics: Peter Gabriel/Tony Banks
Length: 3:31
Tony Banks—Piano; **Peter Gabriel**—Lead Vocals; **Anthony Phillips**—Acoustic Guitar, Backing Vocals; **Mike Rutherford**—Acoustic Guitar; **John Silver**—Percussion; **Unknown**—Horn

Recorded at Regent Sounds B Studio, London, August 1968 and 17–19 November 1968 (Orchestra).
Producer: Jonathan King. Engineer: Brian Roberts & Tom Allom.
Orchestral Arrangement: Arthur Greenslade. Conductor: Lou Warburton.
UK Release: 7 March 1969. (LP: *From Genesis to Revelation*)
U.S. Release: August 1974. (LP: *From Genesis to Revelation*)

Some wistful piano chords from Banks are heightened by a plucked acoustic guitar from Phillips to provide another interlude ahead of this track. What follows is an acoustic song with the lyrical theme of self-assessment. Banks' piano and the guitar work of Phillips and Rutherford are the basis for the verse. The song moves from minor key to major key for the more upbeat chorus with Silver adding some brief percussion. The understated horn backing behind both the verse and chorus is more effective than the orchestration on other tracks. Phillips adds his pure vocal harmony to the urgent chorus. The piano then returns with a strong passage and the backing harmonizing vocals remain gentle and melodic and work better than elsewhere on the album. But overall the track does not really take off musically and feels more like filler.

Alternative Versions: A cleaner remixed and remastered mono mix of the song (3:02) appeared on the *50 Years Ago* album of remixes and outtakes in 2017. It is slightly longer due to the extended fade out.

[10] IN THE WILDERNESS

Band Credit: Tony Banks/Peter Gabriel/Anthony Phillips/Mike Rutherford
Music & Lyrics: Anthony Phillips/Peter Gabriel/Tony Banks/Mike Rutherford
Length: 3:28
Tony Banks—Piano; **Peter Gabriel**—Lead Vocals; **Anthony Phillips**—Guitar, Acoustic Guitar; **Mike Rutherford**—Bass; **John Silver**—Drums, Percussion; **David Thomas**—Backing Vocals; **Unknown**—Strings
Recorded at Regent Sounds B Studio, London, August 1968 and 17–19 November 1968 (Orchestra).
Producer: Jonathan King. Engineer: Brian Roberts & Tom Allom.
Orchestral Arrangement: Arthur Greenslade. Conductor: Lou Warburton.
UK Release: 7 March 1969. (LP: *From Genesis to Revelation*)
U.S. Release: August 1974. (LP: *From Genesis to Revelation*)

An undulating piano figure from Banks leads off IN THE WILDERNESS before it builds to a chorus that seems a little forced. The strings are thankfully held in check and provide more appropriate coloring. The song plays like something that might have fit well in the Andrew Lloyd Webber musical *Jesus Christ Superstar* but lacks a distinctive hook. Banks' piano repeats the chorus on the play-out and acts as another bridge between songs. Gabriel was struggling with his vocals by the time the band came to record this song and his strained performance is most notable on the chorus where song transitions from F major to D major. Gabriel felt the music was pitched incorrectly for him, "You could hear this desperate sort of retching noise as I struggled for the high notes."[7] As he did on [D4a] THE MAGIC OF TIME, the band's friend David Thomas added lower harmony backing vocals. Thomas noted, "The vocal on [IN THE] WILDERNESS was done in about thirty takes. Peter had to go and take showers between each chorus! He found it was a good way of relaxing his voice."[8] Banks singled this track out as one of the strongest cuts on the album, feeling it had a more aggressive approach. He also felt that without the strings the song even had single potential.

Alternative Versions: A rough mix (3:00) of the track, minus the strings, was included on *Genesis Archive 1967–75*. It works better than the original album version. A cleaned up and remastered mono mix in a longer edit (3:23) appeared on the *50 Years Ago* album of remixes and outtakes in 2017.

Live Performances: 1969/70. The song was performed on some of the band's early gigs including their first professional gig at Brunel University in Acton on 1 November 1969.

Live Recordings: No officially released live recordings of the song exist.

[11] THE CONQUEROR

Band Credit: Tony Banks/Peter Gabriel/Anthony Phillips/Mike Rutherford
Music & Lyrics: Tony Banks/Peter Gabriel
Length: 3:40
Tony Banks—Piano, Organ, Backing Vocals; **Peter Gabriel**—Lead Vocals, Tambourine; **Anthony Phillips**—Guitar, Acoustic Guitar, Backing Vocals; **Mike Rutherford**—Bass, Backing Vocals; **John Silver**—Drums
Recorded at Regent Sounds B Studio, London, August 1968.
Producer: Jonathan King. Engineer: Brian Roberts & Tom Allom.
UK Release: 7 March 1969. (LP: *From Genesis to Revelation*)
U.S. Release: August 1974. (LP: *From Genesis to Revelation*)

After a brief low-key prelude reprise of [10] IN THE WILDERNESS on electric guitar by Phillips, the simply structured THE CONQUEROR kicks off in energetic style. Banks' driving piano riff in A major is repeated throughout the song and lifts only for the chorus. Gabriel confidently delivers a melodic vocal, which sadly is too far down in the mix, in this lyrical tale of a conqueror who points to all the things he hates and would like to destroy. The added organ backing from Banks lifts the song through its midsection in a more subtle way than the orchestration elsewhere on the album. Some electric guitar seeps in toward the end but again the part is positioned too far down in the mix and the overall the arrangement begins to feel cluttered in its tight mono mix. King had asked Silver to give the drums a Charlie Watts feel, which he duly complied with by mimicking Watts' playing on "Get Off My Cloud" over the chorus and outro. The result is one of the stronger songs on the album, which even renowned Genesis-basher Noel Gallagher would acknowledge as an influence in his writing the song "If Love Is the Law" for his High Flying Birds album *Who Built the Moon*.

Alternative Versions: A cleaner mono mix and remastered version of the song (3:27), minus the prelude and removing the fade out, appeared on the *50 Years Ago* album of remixes and outtakes in 2017. Gabriel's vocals are much further up in the mix.

[12] IN HIDING

Band Credit: Tony Banks/Peter Gabriel/Anthony Phillips/Mike Rutherford
Music: Anthony Phillips
Lyrics: Peter Gabriel
Length: 2:38
Tony Banks—Acoustic Guitar, Organ, Backing Vocals; **Peter Gabriel**—Lead Vocals; **Anthony Phillips**—Acoustic Guitar, Backing Vocals; **Mike Rutherford**—Bass; **John Silver**—Percussion; **Unknown**—Strings
Recorded at Regent Sounds B Studio, London, August 1968 and 17–19 November 1968 (Orchestra).
Producer: Jonathan King. Engineer: Brian Roberts & Tom Allom.
Orchestral Arrangement: Arthur Greenslade. Conductor: Lou Warburton.
UK Release: 7 March 1969. (LP: *From Genesis to Revelation*)

U.S. Release: August 1974. (LP: *From Genesis to Revelation*)
UK Single Release: 27 June 1969. (B-side b/w [5] Where the Sour Turns to Sweet. Decca/Jonjo Music. F 12949. XDR 44560)

In Hiding is a reworking of Anthony Phillips' instrumental [D0a] Patricia, with Gabriel adding lyrics to Phillips' original folky demo. The waltzing 3/4 rhythm is gently strummed on acoustic guitar and forms the basis for this easy-flowing song. Rutherford's bass, an addition for this version, is lacking in ideas and monotonously prods out the root note. The song does have a charming melody and Gabriel delivers his vocal effortlessly as he describes a man happy in his solitude. The strings are yet again surplus to requirements but fortunately they only appear briefly and do not spoil an otherwise modest, but affecting, song.

Single Release: The song was later included as the B-side to the UK single release of [5] Where the Sour Turns to Sweet on 27 June 1969.

Alternative Versions: The lead and backing vocals only track (2:35) and a new and longer stereo mix minus the strings (2:38), appeared on the *50 Years Ago* album of remixes and outtakes released as a download on 1 May 2017. As the latter is a true stereo mix it is believed the source must have been taken from the two sets of 4-track recordings, including the first tape before the band performance was pushed to one-track of the second tape to incorporate orchestration.[9]

[13] One Day

Band Credit: Tony Banks/Peter Gabriel/Anthony Phillips/Mike Rutherford
Music & Lyrics: Tony Banks/Peter Gabriel
Length: 3:20
Tony Banks—Piano, Backing Vocals; **Peter Gabriel**—Lead Vocals; **Anthony Phillips**—Acoustic Guitar, Backing Vocals; **Mike Rutherford**—Acoustic Guitar, Bass, Backing Vocals; **John Silver**—Drums, Percussion; **Unknown**—Strings & Horns
Recorded at Regent Sounds B Studio, London, August 1968 and 17–19 November 1968 (Orchestra).
Produced by Jonathan King. Engineered by Brian Roberts & Tom Allom.
Orchestral Arrangement: Arthur Greenslade. Conductor: Lou Warburton.
UK Release: 7 March 1969. (LP: *From Genesis to Revelation*)
U.S. Release: August 1974. (LP: *From Genesis to Revelation*)

A very twee acoustic guitar figure by Phillips is backed by orchestral strings and leads into a verse lifted by Banks' classically inspired piano arpeggios. While the marriage of music and vocals on the verse sound clumsy delivering the awkward lyrics, the chorus is much better and is prompted by the Beatles-like horn lines added to punctuate Gabriel's lyrics tell the story of a longing for love. Harmonizing backing vocals from the rest of the band help by adding a crescendo effect to the chorus. Banks later commented that One Day was "another song that was really nice when we used to play it but didn't sound good on the album."[10] Here Silver's drums and Rutherford's bass are buried in the mix, nullifying the dynamics of what in essence is a really promising song.

Alternative Versions: A rough mix (3:08), minus strings and brass is included on *Genesis Archive 1967–75*. A new and improved stereo mix (3:29), again minus the strings and brass, along with a remastered version (3:22) of the song appeared on the *50 Years Ago* album of remixes and outtakes in 2017. The stereo mix ends on a sustained piano chord which seemingly attempts to create an effect like that on The Beatles' "A Day in the Life."

[14] WINDOW

Band Credit: Tony Banks/Peter Gabriel/Anthony Phillips/Mike Rutherford
Music & Lyrics: Anthony Phillips/Mike Rutherford
Length: 3:33
Tony Banks—Piano, Acoustic Guitar, Backing Vocals; **Peter Gabriel**—Lead Vocals; **Anthony Phillips**—Acoustic Guitar, Backing Vocals; **Mike Rutherford**—Acoustic Guitar, Bass, Backing Vocals; **John Silver**—Drums; **Unknown**—Strings & Brass
Recorded at Regent Sounds B Studio, London, August 1968 and 17–19 November 1968 (Orchestra).
Producer: Jonathan King. Engineer: Brian Roberts & Tom Allom.
Orchestral Arrangement: Arthur Greenslade. Conductor: Lou Warburton.
UK Release: 7 March 1969. (LP: *From Genesis to Revelation*)
U.S. Release: August 1974. (LP: *From Genesis to Revelation*)

This is one of the few Phillips/Rutherford compositions on the album. It is also one of the weakest tracks. It starts with an oriental tinged piano rhythm, which is at odds with the lilting verse delivered quietly by Gabriel, who struggles with the dreamlike lyrics he is obviously uncomfortable singing. The French horns and strings are kept in the background of this meandering and forgettable song. Silver's drums enter the song at a late stage and are totally redundant. Rutherford and Phillips wrote the lyrics while sitting on top of the roof at their friend David Thomas' parents' house in Hampshire, having been inspired by the countryside that surrounded them. The lyrics take us on a fanciful flight of imagery and fantasy across the countryside.

Alternative Versions: A remastered mono mix of the song (3:34) (retitled "The Window") appeared on the *50 Years Ago* album of remixes and outtakes in 2017. Here the piano intro has been omitted and the fade out is longer by twenty seconds.

[15] IN LIMBO

Band Credit: Tony Banks/Peter Gabriel/Anthony Phillips/Mike Rutherford
Music & Lyrics: Tony Banks/Peter Gabriel/Anthony Phillips/Mike Rutherford
Length: 3:30
Tony Banks—Piano, Backing Vocals; **Peter Gabriel**—Lead Vocals; **Anthony Phillips**—Guitar, Acoustic Guitar, Backing Vocals; **Mike Rutherford**—Bass, Backing Vocals; **John Silver**—Drums; **Unknown**—Brass
Recorded at Regent Sounds B Studio, London, August 1968 and 17–19 November 1968 (Orchestra).
Producer: Jonathan King. Engineer: Brian Roberts & Tom Allom.
Orchestral Arrangement: Arthur Greenslade. Conductor: Lou Warburton.
UK Release: 7 March 1969. (LP: *From Genesis to Revelation*)
U.S. Release: August 1974. (LP: *From Genesis to Revelation*)

A brief and uncoordinated linking piano and acoustic guitar segment leads into a promising song with some interesting melodies and changes of pace, marred only by a lack of musical cohesion between the players. Banks' impressive grooving piano and Phillips' acoustic guitar continue to blend awkwardly and only serve to bring in the more effective horns over a very ordinary verse. Gabriel's vocals carry a little more soul here than on most of the other songs on the album, but again are almost drowned by the cloying harmonizing backing vocals. Just as the song is descending into blandness the band slows the tempo and goes for an epic and anthemic close, lifted by Gabriel's emotionally intense vocal delivery as he pleads for his god to set him free. This was a trait the band would use to much greater success on future albums, but here the whole arrangement and mix, with Phillips' screaming electric guitar buried, is so messy that it loses much of its intended impact. The song cried out for a stereo mix to give the arrangement room to breathe.

Alternative Versions: A remastered mono mix of the song (3:27) appeared on the *50 Years Ago* album of remixes and outtakes in 2017. This version omits the piano intro and has a twenty-second longer coda, which does not fade out.

Live Performances: 1969/70. The song was performed on some of the band's early gigs including their first professional gig at Brunel University in Acton on 1 November 1969.

Live Recordings: No officially released live recordings of the song exist.

Silent Sun

See [1] The Silent Sun.

[16] A Place to Call My Own

Band Credit: Tony Banks/Peter Gabriel/Anthony Phillips/Mike Rutherford
Music & Lyrics: Tony Banks/Peter Gabriel/Anthony Phillips
Length: 2:00
Tony Banks—Piano, Backing Vocals; **Peter Gabriel**—Lead Vocals; **Anthony Phillips**—Backing Vocals; **Mike Rutherford**—Bass, Backing Vocals; **Unknown**—Strings & Brass
Recorded at Regent Sounds B Studio, London, August 1968 and 17–19 November 1968 (Orchestra).
Producer: Jonathan King. Engineer: Brian Roberts & Tom Allom.
Orchestral Arrangement: Arthur Greenslade. Conductor: Lou Warburton.
UK Release: 7 March 1969. (LP: *From Genesis to Revelation*)
U.S. Release: August 1974. (LP: *From Genesis to Revelation*)

The album's closing song was developed from a much longer piece, which originally ran to around eight minutes in length. The band decided to eject the first two sections (largely written by Phillips), which they felt were not as strong musically, and retained just the final section which was a piano/vocal piece developed by Banks and Gabriel. Banks' seductive piano chords guide Gabriel through one of his strongest, if more restrained, vocal performances. The chorus again is a little clumsily placed but the play-out, which should have been further extended, is very strong. There is excellent use of the orchestral horn phrases, which add to the sound but fight to be heard above the overpowering string and vocal harmonies. The whole thing comes to a rather abrupt end with a quick fade just as the musicians seem to be warming up.

Alternative Versions: A Gabriel vocal a capella version (1:03) and a longer remixed mono version (2:22) of the song appeared on the *50 Years Ago* album of remixes and outtakes in 2017. The remix includes a count-in and excludes the strings and brass. It also has a longer play out.

[17] Build Me a Mountain

Band Credit: Tony Banks/Peter Gabriel/Anthony Phillips/Mike Rutherford
Length: 4:12
Tony Banks—Piano, Backing Vocals; **Peter Gabriel**—Lead Vocals; **Anthony Phillips**—Guitar, Backing Vocals; **Mike Rutherford**—Acoustic Guitar, Bass, Backing Vocals; **John Silver**—Drums

Recorded at Regent Sounds B Studio, London, 4 August 1968.
Produced by Jonathan King. Engineered by Brian Roberts & Tom Allom.
UK/U.S. Release: 22 June 1998. (4-CD: *Genesis Archive 1967–75*)

This is a rough mix recorded during the sessions with Jonathan King for *From Genesis to Revelation*. Phillips' electric guitar riff is unusual for this period in the band's development and opens the tune above some ascending acoustic guitar chords. Rutherford's clean running bass line drives the song, while Silver's drumming is adequate at best and perhaps not surprisingly is drowned in the mix. The playing isn't very good all round—Phillips hated his part and he was obviously still getting to grips with the electric guitar—and the chorus is weak, but there is a certain spirit in some of the instrumental phrasing that shines through the weakness of the playing. The compositional potential was there to be seen. Banks felt the song was better than some of those that ended up on the album. With a stronger chorus it would perhaps even have been one of the standout tracks.

Archive Release: This version was included on the 4-CD box set *Genesis Archive 1967–75* released in 1998.

Live Performances: 1969/70. The song was performed on some of the band's early gigs including their first professional gig at Brunel University in Acton on 1 November 1969.

Live Recordings: No officially released live recordings exist.

[18] IMAGE BLOWN OUT

Band Credit: Tony Banks/Peter Gabriel/Anthony Phillips/Mike Rutherford
Length: 2:12 (2005 Remaster Length: 2:46)
Tony Banks—Piano, Backing Vocals; **Peter Gabriel**—Lead Vocals; **Anthony Phillips**—Acoustic Guitar, Backing Vocals; **Mike Rutherford**—Bass; **John Silver**—Drums
Recorded at Regent Sounds B Studio, London, 4 August 1968.
Produced by Jonathan King. Engineered by Brian Roberts & Tom Allom.
UK/U.S. Release: 22 June 1998. (4-CD: *Genesis Archive 1967–75*)

A song originally included on the second demo tape made for King. This version was again recorded during the session for *From Genesis to Revelation*. It is based around a straight 4/4 piano rhythm that is close to the one Banks would later use on the song [77] A TRICK OF THE TAIL. The melody and rhythm have a Beatles-like quality that is accentuated by the sometime psychedelic lyrics referencing people digging holes in their minds. The cloying choral backing vocals, a feature of many of their early songs, date IMAGE BLOWN OUT badly. However, overall it is a promising short piece that pushed the band into exploring a bouncier more pop-orientated presentation.

Archive Release: This version was included on the 4-CD box set *Genesis Archive 1967–75* released in 1998.

Alternate Versions: A remastered longer version (2:46) appeared on the Edsel Records 2005 CD rerelease of *From Genesis to Revelation*. A demo version of the song (2:48), from the second tape for King recorded during the summer of 1967, appeared on the *50 Years Ago* album of remixes and outtakes in 2017.

* * *

From Genesis to Revelation was released on the Decca label on 7 March 1969. The band excitedly got their hands on the final product, presented in an all-black sleeve, which was King's response to The Beatles' "White Album" sleeve. Gabriel had wanted to have no text at all on the cover, but the gold text of the album title was added to at least give the record-buying public a reference point.

The promotional advertising for *From Genesis to Revelation* stated: "Genesis is the source of a new knowledge / Revelation is the giving of knowledge to man." It led to many retailers thinking the album was a religious recording and filing it accordingly. As a result, the album sold very few copies, reputedly only 649, and died an almost instant commercial death. It finally managed to grace the U.S. chart six years later, once the band had started to build a following in the territory, reaching #170. A single, [5] WHERE THE SOUR TURNS TO SWEET, was released to further promote the album on 27 June 1969, but that too flopped.

Genesis' first album is much better than it is often given credit for. A few of the songs displayed some of the strengths the band would go on to develop further with some effective, albeit short, instrumental passages on songs such as [6] IN THE BEGINNING, [8] THE SERPENT and [15] IN LIMBO. Where the album fell short was not so much in its writing but in its execution. The quality of the mix left a lot to be desired with many of the tracks overcrowded in their mono state and the limitations of 4-track recording equipment constraining a stereo mix, which also looked to add orchestration. The string arrangements had a thin sound and tended to swamp the band's instruments. Phillips was particularly perplexed and felt the orchestra's inclusion robbed the album of any power it may have had. The use of horns was a little more sparing and much more effective as a result.

Playing wise, the band was still in its infancy as was evidenced through moments of hesitancy and a distinct lack of confidence. Banks was perhaps the most musically competent and his work on piano and Farfisa organ already displayed a gifted sense of harmony. The guitar playing of Phillips and Rutherford remained simplistic and was restricted to largely strummed acoustic guitar work, although there was a brief and cautious snatch of electric guitar. Gabriel showed glimpses of the excellent vocalist he would become, with a textured and soulful quality to his voice. John Silver's drumming, on the other hand, was almost anonymous and was generally mixed way back.

The band's writing betrayed a lack of variation in song structure and arrangement. There was an overreliance on the creation of a folk/pop feel, which made for a very soft collection demonstrated by songs like [7] FIRESIDE SONG and [14] WINDOW. That said there was a higher level of quality to one or two of the choruses, which contained some charming melodies. Gabriel often cites Phillips as the band's strongest writer at this point and his ear for melody is apparent in many of these choruses, however Banks and Gabriel provided the strongest tunes overall.

While the album is largely forgotten today—even the band disregards it as part of their legacy due to the lack of artistic control and the rights still being held by Jonathan King—it at least provided a foundation for Genesis to build on in the years to come. Phillips summed the experience up when he described it as "an album embarked on in a very naïve way, but with a huge amount of fun."[11]

While the album had little exposure on release, there was one notably strong review in *International Times*, which said: "The album sets out to recall the memories of adolescence in all their fleeting naivety and it succeeds quite excellently. At times, however, the words border on the pretentious but then one's teens are often pretentious anyway, if it needles you though, involve yourself in Art Greenslade's intricate arrangements which are even better than those off the *Earth Opera* LP."[12]

Jonathan King has rereleased and repackaged the album in various formats and under various release titles over the years. In 2005 and 2011 remastered versions (by Peter Rynston and Jon Astley respectively) were released on CD in the UK, adding a second disc of demos, rough mixes and singles. On 1 May 2017, Jonathan King released *50 Years Ago* as a digital download, an album of new mixes and outtakes from recently rediscovered lost master tapes of the album sessions. King explained, "Some time ago we got a call from someone working for the Kassner Estate that an old warehouse was being emptied and had been found to contain hundreds of multi-track tapes from the Regent Sound Studios in the Sixties—including the Genesis sessions. So, we've done several remixes including strip downs and out takes and we're releasing it this month to celebrate 50 years of Genesis, the reason *50 Years Ago* includes some including strings and brass is because, on listening, they sounded great—so we've included some with as well as some without and some vocals only."[13] The tapes were originally believed to have been lost in a fire at the Iron Mountain warehouse in London. King was assisted in remixing and remastering the tapes by Steve Levine in his Liverpool studio. These remastered tracks give a greater clarity and added freshness to the recordings.

3

The Road to Trespass

In September 1968, having finished recording *From Genesis to Revelation*, the band returned to their education. Banks entered Sussex University to study Physics, Mathematics and Philosophy; Gabriel and Phillips continued studying for their A-levels, while Rutherford entered Farnborough Technical College. The members did, however, keep in touch with each other, notably during the Christmas holidays. Disheartened by the low sales of *From Genesis to Revelation* the band took to self-promotion—often visiting the BBC to canvass for interest in the record.

Banks had bought a Hammond L122 organ, which was delivered to his digs. Here he started to write more new music, including pieces that were later to be used in [38] SUPPER'S READY. Banks would also frequently stay with Gabriel at the singer's parents' house where the pair would work on musical ideas. Phillips and Rutherford had also invested in 12-string guitars and were beginning to write more original pieces. They found a way of complementing each other through their use of chords—with one playing a straight chord and the other an inversion thereby creating a fuller sound. During this period, they started to develop parts of songs such as [23] DUSK, [20] WHITE MOUNTAIN and [22] STAGNATION.

During the summer of 1969, the band moved from family home to family home to rehearse new songs. Gabriel had bought a decommissioned taxi as a method of transporting the band's equipment from location to location. All the band members' parents were very supportive and helped them out financially. In July, they stayed with Brian Roberts at his grandmother's home at Maher Lodge in Dormans Park, Chiswick. Roberts had technical interests in audio and used his equipment to record demos of the band using a Ferrograph tape recorder in a room above some stables that had been converted into a music studio.

Genesis turned professional at the end of that summer, once both Gabriel and Banks had committed themselves to the group. They bought more equipment including amplifiers and a Gibson bass for Rutherford and continued to demo songs of an increasingly complex and experimental nature. Most of these songs were written at Christmas Cottage, just outside Dorking, which was owned by the parents of Richard Macphail. In November 1969, the band moved in and remained there until April 1970. Rutherford noted, "The cottage period was incredibly formative. This is the time when we wrote totally as a band, and it was a period when we nearly killed each other too, in some respects."[1]

Genesis went about writing with increased intensity, shutting out the rest of the world. Macphail stayed on as housekeeper, road manager and chief supporter. Phillips and Rutherford were creating strong acoustic sounds with their 12-string guitars, their influences taken from Fairport Convention and Family. The writing process caused tensions within the band and there were regular standoffs between the three major writers—Banks, Gabriel and Phillips. These tensions also served to spark their creativity and while the earlier demos were mainly acoustic, later ones would become more adventurous in sound and structure. The band had been listening to King Crimson's *In the Court of the Crimson King* album and where impressed by its dynamics and the band's orchestral use of the Mellotron.[2] This encouraged Genesis to become more adventurous with their compositions. However, Jonathan King did not like the direction the new songs were taking and decided against renewing his option.

Their confidence hit by King's loss of interest, Banks and Gabriel became indecisive about whether they should continue with the band and considered further education and alternative career options—Gabriel looked at the possibilities of attending the London School of Film Technique. Eventually, encouraged by Phillips, who at this stage acted as the glue that held the band together, they committed themselves to Genesis.

John Silver, however, had decided to further his education in the U.S.,[3] so in September 1969 the band recruited a new drummer, **JOHN MAYHEW** (born 27 March 1947 in Ipswich, England, died 26 March 2009). Mayhew was a carpenter by trade and a jobbing musician who had played in bands both in his hometown of Ipswich and in London, notably the group Steamhammer. Mayhew circulated his telephone number among agents and his details were picked up at some point by Genesis. The band were impressed by his professional credentials and he was contacted by Rutherford.[4] After a quick audition at Christmas Cottage Mayhew was brought into the band.

Some of the demos and sessions recorded during this period have been subsequently made available via archive releases:

[D18a] GOING OUT TO GET YOU

Band Credit: Tony Banks/Peter Gabriel/Anthony Phillips/Mike Rutherford
Length: 4:54
Tony Banks—Piano; **Peter Gabriel**—Lead Vocals; **Anthony Phillips**—Guitar; **Mike Rutherford**—Bass; **John Mayhew**—Drums; **Tony Hill-Smith**—Backing Vocals; **Barry Johnston**—Backing Vocals, Tambourine
Demo recorded at Regent Sounds B Studio, London, 20 August 1969.
Engineer: Brian Roberts.
UK/U.S. Release: 22 June 1998. (4-CD: *Genesis Archive 1967–75*)

Phillips was the principal writer of this fast-paced Rolling Stones influenced song about an evil sorceress, describing it as "a hotchpotch of some of our slightly blues riffs."[5] It was a song that evolved considerably over the months as the band continued to hone it through rehearsals and liver performances. This version was captured when the song was in its early stages of development. The band received help from two friends—Tony Hill-Smith[6] and Barry Johnston on backing vocals—while Brian Roberts, again acted as recording engineer. Roberts was now working at Regent Sounds Studios and had managed to sneak the band into the studio to record this demo. At the same session the band also recorded versions of [23] DUSK (then titled "Family"), [20] WHITE MOUNTAIN and [D18f] PACIDY.

The feel of GOING OUT TO GET YOU is quite different for the band, with the funky groove of Banks' piano powered by Rutherford and Mayhew's pressing rhythm section. It acted as a precursor to songs such as [24] THE KNIFE and [27] RETURN OF THE GIANT HOGWEED, with its more aggressive approach. Phillips' lead guitar is mixed right down and Gabriel struggles a little with the upper register elements of the vocals in the verse. Also, Banks' piano playing sometimes runs away with him. The song does, however, demonstrate how the band's playing had by this stage already grown significantly in confidence since their debut album. Gabriel offers a brief flute line at 3:56 and Phillips sees the song out on lead guitar, which struggles to be heard in the mix. While the chorus isn't particularly strong and the song fades abruptly at the end, it is still a lively number and one that would be a popular inclusion in the band's live set. The song was also initially considered for inclusion on the second Genesis album, *Trespass*, but lost out to [24] THE KNIFE.

Archive Release: This demo version was first released on the retrospective 4-CD box set *Genesis Archive 1967–75* and later it appeared on the 6-CD box set collection *Genesis 1970–1975*.

Alternative Versions: The song was rerecorded and considered for single release in 1971, backed with a new song, "Wooden Mask," but unfortunately this never came to fruition and the recording of both songs from this session is now missing.[7]

Live Performances: 1969/70, 1970/1, 1971/2. The song remained a standard feature of the band's set for three years being played live between 1969 and 1972, during which time the song would go through its many changes. Banks later replaced the piano parts with organ, and the song would be lengthened and sped up.[8]

Live Recordings: No officially released live recordings exist.

[D18b] PROVOCATION

Band Credit: Tony Banks/Peter Gabriel/Anthony Phillips/Mike Rutherford
Music & Lyrics: Tony Banks/Peter Gabriel/Anthony Phillips/Mike Rutherford
Length: 4:10
Tony Banks—Organ, Mellotron; **Peter Gabriel**—Lead Vocals, Tambourine; **Anthony Phillips**—Guitar; **Mike Rutherford**—Bass; **John Mayhew**—Drums
Recorded at BBC Studios, Shepherd's Bush, London 9 January 1970.
Producer: Paul Samwell-Smith.
UK Release: 10 November 2008. (6-CD: *Genesis 1970–1975—Extra Tracks*)
U.S. Release: 11 November 2008. (6-CD: *Genesis 1970–1975—Extra Tracks*)

While Genesis were rehearsing at Richard Macphail's family Cottage in Dorking, a BBC producer approached them to write some music for a documentary he was filming about cult painter Mick Jackson.[9] Gabriel had been recording his flute in a session for Cat Stevens and was impressed with Stevens' producer, Paul Samwell-Smith.[10] So, when the band were asked to provide music to the BBC documentary, Gabriel suggested they use Samwell-Smith as producer.[11] The sessions were recorded on 9 January 1970 at the BBC's studios in Shepherd's Bush, but ultimately the documentary never aired. When, 30 years later, the band learned the master tapes were being sold at auction they managed to buy them back and released them as part of their *Genesis 1970–1975* box set under the title "Genesis Plays Jackson."[12]

Genesis had recorded four pieces of music—each themed around a human behavior or emotion. These pieces are interesting in that they demonstrate how Genesis would develop songs by joining together separately written pieces of music. PROVOCATION is the opening piece of the suite and like the other tracks, is largely a collection of musical ideas. The first half of the piece would be later developed as the intro and verse to [31] THE FOUNTAIN OF SALMACIS on *Nursery Cryme*, while the second half evolved into the instrumental section of [19] LOOKING FOR SOMEONE on *Trespass*. It is also interesting to contrast Phillips' guitar work, he is much more inventive and melodic here, with the stronger parts ultimately recorded by Hackett on *Nursery Cryme*. Gabriel added some vocals that delivered largely underdeveloped lyrical ideas and were not intended for the final version of the recording.[13]

Archive Release: This recording was first released on the *Extra Tracks* disc of the 6-CD box set collection *Genesis 1970–1975*.

[D18c] FRUSTRATION

Band Credit: Tony Banks/Peter Gabriel/Anthony Phillips/Mike Rutherford
Length: 3:42
Tony Banks—Piano, Organ; **Peter Gabriel**—Lead Vocals; Flute; **Anthony Phillips**—Acoustic Guitar; **Mike Rutherford**—Bass; **John Mayhew**—Drums
Recorded at BBC Studios, Shepherd's Bush, London 9 January 1970.
Producer: Paul Samwell-Smith.
UK Release: 10 November 2008. (6-CD: *Genesis 1970-1975—Extra Tracks*)
U.S. Release: 11 November 2008. (6-CD: *Genesis 1970-1975—Extra Tracks*)

The filmmaker's notes guided Genesis to write a piece based on unresolved music with contrasting tempos to emphasize the teasing nature of Jackson's work. What the band came up with was a piece that would be split into two distinct sections. The first has Banks' undulating piano theme as its focus. It was the same theme Banks would later use for [61] ANYWAY on *The Lamb Lies Down on Broadway*. While this early version has a different set of lyrics, which are largely underdeveloped and attempt to mirror the nature of Jackson's work, they do thematically signal the route to ANYWAY through their sensual nature. The song is very close to that final version until, at 2:02, Banks' piano signals an abrupt change to a less structured instrumental section. This is led by Gabriel on flute over acoustic guitar work from Phillips with Banks accompanying on organ. This latter section meanders through varying tempos over a jazzy groove. Rutherford's bass is a little uncertain in finding a groove as is Mayhew's drum work, resulting in a rhythmically messy section. The ideas on display here feel as if they are in their infancy and there is no real resolution to the progression of the music. The piece is therefore interesting primarily as a record of the band's approach to composition and the early development of ideas fulfilled much later.

Archive Release: This recording was first released on the *Extra Tracks* disc of the 6-CD box set collection *Genesis 1970–1975*.

[D18d] MANIPULATION

Band Credit: Tony Banks/Peter Gabriel/Anthony Phillips/Mike Rutherford
Length: 3:49
Tony Banks—Organ; **Peter Gabriel**—Lead Vocals; Tambourine; **Anthony Phillips**—Acoustic Guitar, Backing Vocals; **Mike Rutherford**—Acoustic Guitar, Bass; **John Mayhew**—Drums
Recorded at BBC Studios, Shepherd's Bush, London 9 January 1970.
Producer: Paul Samwell-Smith.
UK Release: 10 November 2008. (6-CD: *Genesis 1970-1975—Extra Tracks*)
U.S. Release: 11 November 2008. (6-CD: *Genesis 1970-1975—Extra Tracks*)

The brief for this piece was to depict a man manipulating a girl into lovemaking and to musically represent technology in the female form. The section begins with a 12-string acoustic guitar led piece, written by Phillips in F sharp,[14] which alternates between major and minor chords. Both Phillips and Rutherford play on this acoustic section over Banks' arpeggiating organ, which ultimately became the opening section of [25] THE MUSICAL BOX.[15] At 1:15 the piece evolves into a passage that was the basis for THE MUSICAL BOX's midsong instrumental section. The arrangement here is very close to the final version recorded for *Nursery Cryme*, although it does not include the electric guitar solo on the second instrumental section. This section then changes at 2:00 into an initially more reflective passage that gradually builds around a climbing organ figure from Banks, before fading over quieter and more ethereal chords.

The song is a fascinating look at the framework of what would become one of the band's signature moments. Whether Gabriel honed into Jackson's theme of sexual repression when he finalized his lyrics for THE MUSICAL BOX is an interesting point of debate.

Archive Release: This recording was first released on the *Extra Tracks* disc of the 6-CD box set collection *Genesis 1970–1975*.

[D18e] RESIGNATION

Band Credit: Tony Banks/Peter Gabriel/Anthony Phillips/Mike Rutherford
Length: 3:01
Tony Banks—Organ, Acoustic Guitar; **Peter Gabriel**—Flute; **Anthony Phillips**—Guitar, Acoustic Guitar; **Mike Rutherford**—Acoustic Guitar, Bass; **John Mayhew**—Drums
Recorded at BBC Studios, Shepherd's Bush, London 9 January 1970.
Producer: Paul Samwell-Smith.
UK Release: 10 November 2008. (6-CD: *Genesis 1970–1975—Extra Tracks*)
U.S. Release: 11 November 2008. (6-CD: *Genesis 1970–1975—Extra Tracks*)

The theme for the final piece was one of acceptance, whether it be acceptance of the manipulation outlined in the previous piece or merely a wider acceptance of the darker side of one's fantasies. The aim was for the music to have a more romantic feel while portraying the inner conflict created by base memories and a level of unresolved turmoil, but the gentle arrangement of the acoustic guitar opening is almost destroyed by Mayhew's heavy-handed drumming. Banks' chord structuring skills are evident in his organ work here and he would explore this further in various songs in the future. There are echoes of the opening to [31] THE FOUNTAIN OF SALMACIS between 1:08 and 1:20. What follows is a piece with constantly changing moods by contrasting brief heavy and light patches of music. A short series of heavy staccato chords played by all instruments ends the piece in abrupt fashion.

These four pieces, known collectively as "Genesis Plays Jackson," give great insight into the band's working methods and demonstrate Genesis' ambitious and challenging approach to writing. By gluing often wildly varying pieces of music, mood and tempo the band found they were able to create a much more dynamic whole. These embryonic pieces capture the raw performances of a creative band not afraid to experiment on tape and gives a glimpse of the drama Genesis would bring to their later work.

Archive Release: This version was first released on the *Extra Tracks* disc of the 6-CD box set collection *Genesis 1970–1975*.

[D18f] PACIDY

Band Credit: Tony Banks/Peter Gabriel/Anthony Phillips/Mike Rutherford
Music & Lyrics: Anthony Phillips/Mike Rutherford
Length: 5:42
Tony Banks—Organ, Backing Vocals; **Peter Gabriel**—Lead Vocals, Flute; **Anthony Phillips**—Acoustic Guitar, Backing Vocals; **Mike Rutherford**—Bass, Cello, Backing Vocals (?); **John Mayhew**—Drums

Recorded at BBC *Nightride* session, Maida Vale Studios Studio 4, London. 22 February 1970.
Producer: Alec Reid. Engineer: Mick Gomm.
UK Radio Broadcast: 1 April 1970 (BBC Radio One)
UK/U.S. Release: 22 June 1998. (4-CD: *Genesis Archive 1967–75*)

On 22 February 1970, Genesis recorded a session for the BBC's *Nightride* radio program at Maida Vale Studios. The session included six songs—[D18f] PACIDY, [D18g] SHEPHERD, [D18h] LET US NOW MAKE LOVE, [19] LOOKING FOR SOMEONE, [22] STAGNATION and [23] DUSK. The latter three songs would all be rerecorded a few months later for the band's *Trespass* album.[16]

PACIDY did not make the album, despite the band's fondness for the song. Phillips' 12-string guitar arpeggios open the piece as the guitarist plays straight chords rotating from A minor through E minor to F major and then to G major. The lyrics are pretentious and naïve—the kind of pseudo-romantic poetry only teenagers could write. Gabriel's vocals have too much reverb applied to them and are not very convincing. The whole track plods on with Gabriel introducing his flute to the musical landscape, which adds little to the arrangement. The piece does pick up when Banks contributes some undulating organ phrases from 3:00, which repeat the main theme. Mayhew's drum fills add urgency to the rhythm from 3:52 leading into a more propulsive playout. Overall, though, while the song demonstrates the band's increasingly effective use of 12-string guitars it is otherwise musically largely unmemorable.

Anthony Phillips would later use elements of this song on his own recording of "Field of Eternity" for his 1978 LP, *Private Parts and Pieces*.

Archive Release: The track was first released on the retrospective 4-CD box set *Genesis Archive 1967–75* and was later included on the *Extra Tracks* CD of the 6-CD collection *Genesis 1970–1975*.

Live Performances: 1969/70. The song was performed live at some of the band's earliest gigs and was the closing number on their first official live performance at Brunel University in Acton, London on 1 November 1969.

Live Recordings: No officially released live recordings exist.

[D18g] SHEPHERD

Band Credit: Tony Banks/Peter Gabriel/Anthony Phillips/Mike Rutherford
Music/Lyrics: Tony Banks/Anthony Phillips
Length: 4:00
Tony Banks—Lead Vocals (chorus), Backing Vocals, Piano; **Peter Gabriel**—Lead Vocals (verses) & Backing Vocals, Flute, Bass Drum, Tambourine; **Anthony Phillips**—Acoustic Guitar, Backing Vocals; **Mike Rutherford**—Acoustic Guitar; **John Mayhew**—Percussion
Recorded at BBC *Nightride* session, Maida Vale Studios Studio 4, London. 22 February 1970.
Producer: Alec Reid. Engineer: Mick Gomm.
UK Radio Broadcast: 1 April 1970 (BBC Radio One)
UK/U.S. Release: 22 June 1998. (4-CD: *Genesis Archive 1967–75*)

Also recorded at the *Nightride* sessions for the BBC in February 1970, SHEPHERD is notable as the only Genesis song to feature Banks contributing lead vocals—if only on the chorus. The song features a spiraling piano introduction, after which crashing acoustic guitar chords signal Gabriel's urging the people to listen and rejoice at the news he brings. What follows is a gentle verse with Gabriel's vocal melodies matching those of Banks' delicate piano figure. Banks' vocal on the chorus is polite rather than memorable and he comes across like a choirboy keen to impress, contrasting with Gabriel's more assured performance. The simple verse-chorus structure allows the band to tell a rather twee tale of a maiden waiting for her prince. From 3:04, the final section of the song sees Banks work his way up and down the piano keyboard prompted by a brief appearance from Gabriel on flute and bass drum. Aside from the opening, Phillips and Rutherford's acoustic guitar backing is relatively muted throughout.

Archive Release: The song was first released on the retrospective 4-CD box set *Genesis Archive 1967–75* and the later 6-CD collection *Genesis 1970–1975*.

Live Performances: 1970. The song was performed live at some of the band's earliest pre–*Trespass* gigs.

Live Recordings: No officially released live recordings exist.

[D18h] LET US NOW MAKE LOVE

Band Credit: Tony Banks/ Peter Gabriel/Anthony Phillips/Mike Rutherford
Music & Lyrics: Anthony Phillips
Length: 6:14
Tony Banks—Organ, Backing Vocals; **Peter Gabriel**—Lead Vocals, Flute, Tambourine; **Anthony Phillips**—Acoustic Guitar, Lead & Backing Vocals; **Mike Rutherford**—Acoustic Guitar, Bass, Backing Vocals; **John Mayhew**—Drums
Recorded at BBC *Nightride* session, Maida Vale Studios Studio 4, London. 22 February 1970.
Producer: Alec Reid. Engineer: Mick Gomm.
UK Radio Broadcast: 1 April 1970 (BBC Radio One)
UK/U.S. Release: 22 June 1998. (4-CD: *Genesis Archive 1967–75*)

Another song from the band's BBC *Nightride* session in February 1970. LET US NOW MAKE LOVE is a gently strummed acoustic number written by Phillips and as such it is indistinguishable from much of the other material Genesis recorded at this time. It had, however, been a popular live track and Phillips recalled, "I remember Nick Drake coming up to us and saying; 'who wrote that?' and then something like 'dangerous' because he thought it was so good."[17]

Gabriel's flute provides a 24-second introduction to this pastoral song with ornate and overly poetic lyrics that scans poorly (note 0:42). There is a lift into the chorus where Banks' sustained organ chords and Mayhew's mixed down drums fill out the sound. The song outstays its welcome by rotating verse-chorus repeatedly before a final section briefly threatens to add some variety until it somewhat disappointingly returns to its core melody. Phillips contributes the occasional snatch of lead vocals as well as harmony vocals to complement Gabriel.

The song was considered for inclusion on *Trespass* but was held back due to its perceived single potential. However, as Phillips left the band shortly after the album was recorded, plans for a dedicated release were shelved. Phillips later recorded a piano instrumental version of the song for the 1991 CD rerelease of his 1986 solo album, *Private Parts and Pieces VI: Ivory Moon*.

Archive Release: The song was first released on the retrospective 4-CD box set *Genesis Archive 1967–75* and the later 6-CD collection *Genesis 1970–1975*.

Live Performances: 1970. The song was performed live at the band's early gigs before being dropped from the set.

Live Recordings: No officially released live recordings exist.

4

Studio Album #2: *Trespass*

UK Release: 23 October 1970. LP. Charisma. CAS 1020.
U.S. Release: February 1971. LP. ABC Records/Impulse! AS-9205.
Remix/Remaster Release:
UK Release: 10 November 2008. CD/SACD/DVD. Virgin/Charisma. CASCDR 1020.
U.S. Release: 11 November 2008. CD/DVD. Atlantic/Rhino. R2 513942.

Album Tracks
[19] LOOKING FOR SOMEONE
[20] WHITE MOUNTAIN
[21] VISIONS OF ANGELS
[22] STAGNATION
[23] DUSK
[24] THE KNIFE

Peter Gabriel, supported by Richard Macphail, began hustling venues for gigs and Genesis started to actively promote the songs they had developed through live performance, despite still being poorly equipped to do so. When John Martin of the Marquee Martin agency tried to persuade the band to give it up, this only served to set their resolve even more firmly. Genesis toured their music relentlessly, often to disinterested audiences, but they slowly started to build a dedicated following. Their first major success was getting onto the bill at the Marquee Club in February 1970, where they supported Rare Bird.[1] John Anthony, Rare Bird's producer, was present at the gig and was impressed by what he heard from Genesis. On 3 March 1970, on Anthony's recommendation, Tony Stratton-Smith,[2] the boss of record label Charisma, caught Genesis at Ronnie Scott's club, where the band had

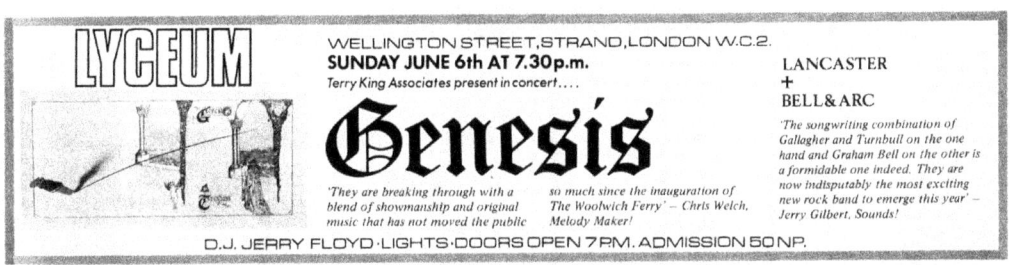

An advertisement promoting Genesis' show at The Lyceum Theatre in London on 6 June 1971 along with their album, *Trespass* (courtesy Mark Kenyon/The Genesis Archive).

a residency. The Charisma boss liked what he saw and signed the band to record an album that summer.[3] He noted, "They were so incredibly good. They were different. They had a language and feel of their own."[4]

Genesis' second album, *Trespass*, would be made compiled from pre-written songs the band had been testing and honing on the road.[5] These live performances enabled the band to refine the songs' arrangements and structures. The band's largely acoustic set would be sequenced to build in intensity from quiet beginnings toward an electric and energetic climax with the aggressive [24] THE KNIFE—then titled "Nice"—closing out the set. Banks recalled, "We had played live quite a bit and every song on the album had been performed on stage. We had a selection of at least twice as many songs as appeared on the album, and the versions changed rapidly."[6]

Genesis moved from the cottage they had rented in Dorking to the Gin Mill Club in Surrey to refine their material for the new album. The band upgraded some of their equipment and set about recording six songs at Trident Recording Studios in London during June and July 1970.[7] Phillips felt some of the better acoustic songs were overlooked for the album because they had not survived the road, where the harder songs had made more of a connection with the audience. But songs such as [23] DUSK and [19] LOOKING FOR SOMEONE were always strong contenders, while the signature tracks of the album were the ambitious [22] STAGNATION and the hard rocking [24] THE KNIFE.

Charisma assigned John Anthony to produce the album and he was assisted by Robin Cable. Anthony was Charisma's in-house producer (having worked with Van der Graaf Generator and Lindisfarne as well as Rare Bird) and immediately he struck up a rapport with the band. Being a former singer, Anthony would help Gabriel work on the vocal parts. Some critics suggested Anthony, having introduced the band to Stratton-Smith, was the

Genesis were signed by Charisma boss Tony Stratton-Smith after he saw them performing at Ronnie Scott's club in London in March 1970 (author's collection).

4. Studio Album #2: Trespass

main driving force behind the album, but this was strenuously denied by Gabriel in an interview at the time: "We look on him as another member of the band, rather than the one with all the power, the one who dictates what we want and what we don't want. The group did all the arrangements and we considered the type of sound we wanted before we went into the studio."[8] The tape operator on the album was future Genesis producer David Hentschel.

Phillips, who was tiring rapidly due to health issues,[9] had some disagreements with sound engineer Robin Cable about how the 12-string guitars should be miked. Although Phillips' challenging mood could be partly attributed to his ill health, it also served to demonstrate how the band had grown in confidence and had very clear ideas about how they wanted to sound. The band did feel Phillips was sympathetic to what they were trying to achieve, and the producer looked to get the best performance he could from them. John Anthony was proud of the album but felt the studio they had chosen did not do justice to the sound of the band. He also noted the limited skills of Mayhew as drummer and Rutherford as bass player—the latter was still learning his skills on the instrument, being primarily an acoustic and rhythm guitarist.

The recording sessions were completed within two months on an 8-track recorder. While an advancement on the 4-track equipment used for *From Genesis to Revelation*, it did restrict options for overdubs to the band's live interpretations. The band had completed an album they had felt they had more control over and better represented their qualities.

[19] LOOKING FOR SOMEONE

Band Credit: Tony Banks/ Peter Gabriel/Anthony Phillips/Mike Rutherford
Music: Tony Banks/ Peter Gabriel/Anthony Phillips/Mike Rutherford
Lyrics: Peter Gabriel
Length: 7:04
Tony Banks—Organ, Piano, Backing Vocals; **Peter Gabriel**—Lead Vocals, Flute, Bass Drum, Percussion; **Mike Rutherford**—Bass, Acoustic Guitar, Cello, Backing Vocals; **Anthony Phillips**—Guitar, Acoustic Guitar, Backing Vocals **John Mayhew**—Drums, Percussion, Backing Vocals
Recorded at Trident Studios, London, June/July 1970.
Producer: John Anthony. Engineer: Robin Geoffrey Cable.
2008 Remix/Remaster Release:
Mixed at The Farm, Surrey 2005/2006.
5.1 Surround sound and stereo mixes by Nick Davis. Assisted by Tom Mitchell.
UK Release: 23 October 1970. (LP: *Trespass*)
U.S. Release: February 1971 (LP: *Trespass*)

LOOKING FOR SOMEONE evolved from music written ahead of and used for the "Genesis Plays Jackson" sessions for the BBC under the title [D18b] PROVOCATION. While the piece developed from an idea from Gabriel, it is also an example of how the band would evolve songs on the road. Initially running at around thirteen minutes, the song was reduced to half that length before the album recording. It showcases a more confident Genesis. Gabriel calls out the title right from the outset and delivers a soulful vocal performance of his intense lyrics, which describe a journey of self-discovery. The lead singer is accompanied only by Banks' organ during this intro, before leading the band into a meandering song that blends elements of soul and folk. The song is a prime example of how the band had started to work by joining various incomplete pieces they had written to make a longer and more varied whole. The result is an arrangement and structure that includes various shifts in tempo and mood. Mayhew remembered, "we got stuck with LOOKING FOR SOMEONE and could not decide which direction to go in, and so one evening we said: 'That's it, enough. We'll go upstairs, just listen to some music and have a rest.' A couple of hours later we came downstairs, the blockage was past and we went on and finished the song."[10]

The initial section was developed from a short piece Gabriel had written with just piano and vocal. The song then works through a series of changes, including some fast jazz-rock passages mixed with slower folk-inspired acoustic stretches, which give a platform to different sides to the band's writing and playing. At 4:30, some dramatic chords and intensifying vocals leads to a section where Banks stabs out organ riffs and Phillips provides some interesting electric guitar runs, but Mayhew's drums tend to race away during these faster sections. The approach may have a "cut and paste" feel, but the band were determined to stretch themselves and be experimental. It prompted *Rolling Stone* to describe the song as "a creative rebirth in seven seamless minutes."[11]

Promo Single Release: While there was no official retail single release of the song, a promo UK Single backed with [21] VISIONS OF ANGELS (Charisma. GS1/GS2) was circulated to help promote the release of *Trespass*. In the U.S., a single-sided acetate pressing of the song was circulated to radio stations.

BBC Session: Another version of the song (7:18) was recorded a few months earlier, on 22 February 1970, at Studio 4, Maida Vale, London. The session was broadcast on BBC Radio One on 1 April 1970 and the song was later included on a BBC promotional CD. The studio recording was produced by Alec Reid and engineered by Mike Gomm. It is a good, professional recording with a muscular performance from the band (although Gabriel's vocals are a little too far down in the mix). The session recording was not included on the *Genesis Archive 1967–75* box set but can be easily found on the internet. The arrangement and lyrics were unchanged for the song's later inclusion on *Trespass*.

Live Performances: 1969/70, 1970/1. The song was performed regularly by the band through to the end of the *Trespass* tour before it disappeared from the live set. It was not performed on any subsequent tour.

Live Recordings: No officially released live recordings exist.

[20] WHITE MOUNTAIN

Band Credit: Tony Banks/ Peter Gabriel/Anthony Phillips/Mike Rutherford
Music & Lyrics: Anthony Phillips/Mike Rutherford
Length: 6:44
Tony Banks—Organ, Mellotron, Backing Vocals; **Peter Gabriel**—Lead Vocals, Flute; **Mike Rutherford**—Bass, Acoustic Guitar, Backing Vocals; **Anthony Phillips**—Guitar, Acoustic Guitar, Dulcimer, Backing Vocals; **John Mayhew**—Drums, Backing Vocals
Recorded at Trident Studios, London, June/July 1970.
Producer: John Anthony. Engineer: Robin Geoffrey Cable.
2008 Remix/Remaster Release:
Mixed at The Farm, Surrey 2005/2006.
5.1 Surround sound and stereo mixes by Nick Davis. Assisted by Tom Mitchell.
UK Release: 23 October 1970. (LP: *Trespass*)
U.S. Release: February 1971 (LP: *Trespass*)

Phillips and Rutherford were the principal writers of this atmospheric song, inspired by Jack London's novel *White Fang*.[12] It is the original tale of Fang, a wolf residing near the mythical White Mountain who is looking to take over as the pack leader. Despite the song's rather lame lyrics, the music demonstrated yet more development from the band as both players and writers. Banks' shimmering Mellotron, backed by Phillips and Rutherford's acoustic 12-string guitars, opens the song before the energy picks up through Banks' organ arpeggios and Rutherford's racing bass rhythms. Gabriel provides some light interludes with his flute, before the song moves into its finale prodded along by Rutherford's pounding bass notes and a thudding bass drum from Mayhew, creating a musical depiction of the fight between wolves. As the track fades, Gabriel whistles us out over some wistful chords from Banks, while an undulating choral melody fades in over flickering Mellotron and gentle guitar.

Already we can see a significant advance on anything Genesis recorded for their debut album. The playing is much more assured, with the band members having gradually honed their skills on the road. The more fantastical elements of the lyrics also pointed to the band's future direction with the dramatic story elements being well-served by the music.

Live Performances: 1970/1, 1976. The song was performed live at early gigs in 1970–1 before being dropped from the set. It was later resurrected in shortened form on the *A Trick of the Tail* tour in 1976, where it would be sung by Phil Collins with Gabriel having left the band.

Live Recordings: No officially released live recordings exist.

[21] VISIONS OF ANGELS

Band Credit: Tony Banks/Peter Gabriel/Anthony Phillips/Mike Rutherford
Music & Lyrics: Anthony Phillips
Length: 6:50
Tony Banks—Organ, Piano, Mellotron, Backing Vocals; **Peter Gabriel**—Lead Vocals, Flute; **Mike Rutherford**—Acoustic Guitar, Bass, Backing Vocals; **Anthony Phillips**—Guitar, Acoustic Guitar, Backing Vocals; **John Mayhew**—Drums
Recorded at Trident Studios, London, June/July 1970.
Producer: John Anthony. Engineer: Robin Geoffrey Cable.
2008 Remix/Remaster Release:
Mixed at The Farm, Surrey 2005/2006.
5.1 Surround sound and stereo mixes by Nick Davis. Assisted by Tom Mitchell.
UK Release: 23 October 1970. (LP: *Trespass*)
U.S. Release: February 1971 (LP: *Trespass*)

VISIONS OF ANGELS was originally written on piano by Anthony Phillips using a plodding rhythm and was recorded and considered for inclusion on *From Genesis to Revelation*. However, the song was shelved from that project with Phillips disappointed with the version developed at that time. The band continued to refine the song on the road and once they were satisfied recorded the revised version to be included on *Trespass*. The piece has a lovely melodic opening piano refrain leading into what is essentially a torch song that plays like a modern hymn. Phillips' lyrics were written about Gabriel's girlfriend (and later wife), Jill, whom the guitarist had developed a fascination with—something he kept secret from the band at the time.[13] The song also boasts a gorgeous spiraling chorus and Gabriel's vocal delivery is excellent, if a little muted in the mix—engineer Nick Davis would rectify in his 2008 remix. The band contributes some typically polite harmonizing backing vocals, which add further to the hymn-like qualities of the song. Rutherford provides fine urgent bass work under Banks' sizeable Mellotron and organ chords as the song picks up pace in a muscular midsection that would have made for a strong finale. Instead, we get another go-around of verses and chorus. The final chorus is repeated with increased intensity and leads into a rhythmic playout, over which Banks' Mellotron strings glide.[14] The song was perhaps Mayhew's strongest drumming performance on the album as he moves around the kit with more confidence during the instrumental sections and again during the climax.

Promo Single Release: The song was the B-side to a promotional UK Single of [19] LOOKING FOR SOMEONE (Charisma. GS1/GS2), which was circulated to radio stations to promote the release of *Trespass.*

Live Performances: 1969/70. The song was performed live at early pre–*Trespass* gigs before being dropped from the set.

Live Recordings: No officially released live recordings exist.

[22] STAGNATION

Band Credit: Tony Banks/Peter Gabriel/Anthony Phillips/Mike Rutherford
Music: Tony Banks/Peter Gabriel/Anthony Phillips/Mike Rutherford
Lyrics: Peter Gabriel
Length: 8:46
Tony Banks—Organ, Piano, Mellotron, Backing Vocals; **Peter Gabriel**—Lead Vocals, Flute, Accordion, Tambourine, Bass Drum, Percussion; **Mike Rutherford**—Bass, Acoustic Guitar, Cello, Backing Vocals; **Anthony Phillips**—Guitar, Acoustic Guitar, Backing Vocals; **John Mayhew**—Drums, Percussion
Recorded at Trident Studios, London, June/July 1970.
Producer: John Anthony. Engineer: Robin Geoffrey Cable.
2008 Remix/Remaster Release:
Mixed at The Farm, Surrey 2005/2006.
5.1 Surround sound and stereo mixes by Nick Davis. Assisted by Tom Mitchell.
UK Release: 23 October 1970. (LP: *Trespass*)
U.S. Release: February 1971 (LP: *Trespass*)

Gabriel's lyrics recount the aftereffects of a nuclear war in what was Genesis' most complex song recorded to date. STAGNATION originated from a long section of music the band had called "The Movement."[15] It goes through various changes of mood and themes throughout its near nine-minute length. During the recording Rutherford and Phillips laid down numerous folk-influenced guitar parts—the idea being to choose the most appropriate for the song. In the end, all the parts were mixed down onto one track, effectively cancelling each other out and creating a very dense sound which was further thickened by the addition of Banks' organ and Gabriel's flute. Banks later admitted, "We got very caught up; we used to have six or seven guitar tracks at once. STAGNATION had all these acoustic guitars playing the same thing and the final sound is very muddy."[16]

The song ultimately became a vehicle for the keyboardist to demonstrate his skills with sound and harmony. He contributes a haunting high-pitched whistling-organ solo over Phillips and Rutherford's complementary acoustic 12-string guitar figures very early in the song. Banks was initially a little reluctant to add what would become his first keyboard solo, a whistling pipe-like solo was therefore composed rather than improvised: "I had to be really cajoled into doing a solo the first time.... I got this first phrase which worked, then pretty much played scales and arpeggios for the rest of it!"[17] Following Banks' showpiece, the acoustic guitars strum vigorously as the song builds up to a faster organ-led section. At 5:05, Gabriel delivers an engaging vocal over a delicately undulating passage of music with beautiful harmonies before it evolves into a more rhythmic piece at 5:55. The song closes on a repeated spiraling phrase that runs from 6:55 and begins with Gabriel's flute before Banks'

4. Studio Album #2: Trespass

organ and Rutherford's bass take over.[18] Banks considers STAGNATION the best track on the album and one that helped shape the band's future direction.

BBC Sessions: (1) The song was earlier recorded (8:02) for BBC's *Nightride* radio program on 22 February 1970 at Studio 4, Maida Vale, London, which was broadcast on 1 April. The session was produced by Alec Reid and engineered by Mick Gomm. This version has different lyrics to its final section but is otherwise as would appear on *Trespass* later in the year.

(2) A second BBC recording (8:59) was made at a session on 10 May 1971 for *Sounds of the Seventies* at Studio T1, Kensington House, Shepherd's Bush, London and was subsequently broadcast on 31 May. This session was produced by Pete Dauncey and engineered by Adrian Revill. Phillips and Mayhew had left the band by this point and the recording features Phil Collins on drums and Steve Hackett on guitar. This version was included on *Genesis Archive 1967–75*.

Live Performances: 1969/70, 1970/1, 1972/3. The song was a regular feature in the band's set until 1973. The repeated motif from the final section would be used as part of the extended instrumental section of [41] I KNOW WHAT I LIKE (IN YOUR WARDROBE) from the 1977 tour onward.

Live Recordings: No officially released live recordings exist, excepting the segment used in I KNOW WHAT I LIKE (IN YOUR WARDROBE).

[23] DUSK

Band Credit: Tony Banks/Peter Gabriel/Anthony Phillips/Mike Rutherford
Music: Anthony Phillips/Mike Rutherford
Lyrics: Anthony Phillips
Length: 4:10
Tony Banks—Organ, Piano, Mellotron, Acoustic Guitar, Backing Vocals; **Peter Gabriel**—Lead Vocals, Flute; **Mike Rutherford**—Acoustic Guitar, Backing Vocals (?); **Anthony Phillips**—Acoustic Guitars, Backing Vocals; **John Mayhew**—Percussion, Backing Vocals (?)
Recorded at Trident Studios, London, June/July 1970.
Producer: John Anthony. Engineer: Robin Geoffrey Cable.
2008 Remix/Remaster Release:
Mixed at The Farm, Surrey 2005/2006.
5.1 Surround sound and stereo mixes by Nick Davis. Assisted by Tom Mitchell.
UK Release: 23 October 1970. (LP: *Trespass*)
U.S. Release: February 1971 (LP: *Trespass*)

The lilting melody written by Phillips and Rutherford, with a beautiful acoustic 12-string accompaniment, makes for a gently persuasive if insubstantial song. It can perhaps be viewed as a throwback to *From Genesis to Revelation* in its arrangement, but it contains stronger harmonizing vocals and a more confident all-round performance. Gabriel's lead vocals are delicately evocative of the music's reflective mood showing a maturity beyond his years. Phillips' lyrics reflect the helplessness we have in controlling the events that shape our lives. The song shifts sublimely from B major to B minor and ups its tempo for the instrumental bridge, which allows Gabriel to add simple lead flute lines and Banks a brief shimmer from the Mellotron. The bass piano notes responding to the acoustic guitar that close the song add a poignant note of finality.

Archive Release: A demo version, performed under the title "Family" (6:14), was recorded at Regent Studios on 20 August 1969 and is included on the 4-disc set *Genesis Archive 1967–75*. Friends Tony Hill-Smith and Barry Johnston contributed backing vocals and

Brian Roberts was the recording engineer. It is a strongly melodic acoustic piece, complete with metronome timekeeper and an earthier interpretation of the song. This recording includes a longer instrumental section, but the lyrics were the same.

BBC Session: The song was also recorded at the band's *Nightride* session for the BBC on Sunday 22 February 1970 at Studio 4, Maida Vale, London and broadcast on Radio One on 1 April. However, this specific recording is missing from the BBC archives.

Live Performances: 1970, 1970/1.

Live Recordings: No officially released live recordings exist.

[24] THE KNIFE

Band Credit: Tony Banks/Peter Gabriel/Anthony Phillips/Mike Rutherford
Music: Tony Banks/Peter Gabriel
Lyrics: Peter Gabriel
Length: 8:56
Tony Banks—Organ, Backing Vocals; **Peter Gabriel**—Lead Vocals, Flute, Bass Drum, Percussion; **Mike Rutherford**—Bass, Backing Vocals; **Anthony Phillips**—Guitar, Backing Vocals; **John Mayhew**—Drums, Backing Vocals (?); **John Anthony**—Backing Vocals
Recorded at Trident Studios, London, June/July 1970.
Producer: John Anthony. Engineer: Robin Geoffrey Cable.
2008 Remix/Remaster Release:
Mixed at The Farm, Surrey 2005/2006.
5.1 Surround sound and stereo mixes by Nick Davis. Assisted by Tom Mitchell.
UK Release: 23 October 1970. (LP: *Trespass*)
U.S. Release: February 1971 (LP: *Trespass*)
UK Single release: 21 May 1971. (A-side single b/w THE KNIFE [PART 2]. Charisma. CB 152)

THE KNIFE was the heavy and exciting closing song of the band's live set and along with STAGNATION was one of the two signature tracks on the album. The song was extended from a piece originally written by Banks and Gabriel on piano, before being transferred to organ as the band progressed the arrangement. Banks' galloping organ riff was inspired by the song "Rondo" by The Nice. Genesis even used a working title of "Nice" in the early stages of the song's development. The slashing guitar chords from Phillips during the intro are a musical interpretation of the wielded knife. The result is a memorable opening to an aggressive, almost violent, rocker with its racing organ phrases, dynamic electric guitar, distorted bass and propulsive drums. In the live environment, the song would set audiences alight following the quiet acoustic opening to the band's set.

The recorded version may lack some of the fire Genesis injected into their live performances, but nevertheless it captured the band's harder edge—something only hinted at until this point. THE KNIFE stands alongside [21] VISIONS OF ANGELS as Mayhew's best drumming performance on the album, further demonstrating the benefits of having road tested the material before recording. Gabriel really finds his feet as a vocalist here, with an intense and sinister performance as he lets himself loose with some psychotic lyrics that mirror his rebellious nature, in part inspired by Gandhi's attitude to violence. His lyrics painted the picture of the path that violent actions would inevitably lead us down and the fact that bloody revolutions tended to be followed by dictatorships. There is even time for Gabriel to deliver a flute solo during a quietly pulsing and introspective section before all carnage breaks loose and the band chant for their freedom while John Anthony calls on the armed forces to fire over the heads of the mob. This leads to a fast-paced instrumental section before the song's doom-laden climax over a punchy straight rhythm to emphasis each of Gabriel's words. THE KNIFE was Genesis' biggest and boldest statement to date.

Single Release: A single, which split the song over it's A- and B-sides, was released in May 1971 in the UK and Germany but did not chart. Banks recalled, "I don't think we looked on the single being anything more than a promotional tool for the album. We didn't think it was going to be a hit."[19] The single edit (side A) (3:17) of the song can be found on the expanded version of *Turn It On Again: The Hits*, subtitled *The Tour Edition,* released in 2007.

Live Performances: 1969/70, 1970/1, 1971/2, 1972/3, 1973/4, 1974/5 (occasionally), 1980 (occasionally), 1981 (rarely), 1982 ("Six of the Best" show). The song was a staple of the band's live set throughout Gabriel's tenure and became the most often played song from *Trespass.* It was later resurrected infrequently with Collins delivering a strained vocal on Genesis' early 1980s tours. It also became the encore at the "Six of the Best" one-off reunion concert in 1982 with Gabriel back at the microphone.

Live Recordings: A dynamic performance (9:47) was recorded at De Montford Hall, Leicester, 25 February 1973. This version was included on the 1973 album *Genesis Live.* The recording was produced by John Burns in conjunction with the band. It is perhaps the definitive recording of the song, with the added benefit of Phil Collins' more expressive drums and Steve Hackett's inventive use of lead guitar.

* * *

Trespass was released in the UK on 23 October 1970 but failed to chart until its release in 1984 when it reached #98 in the UK Album chart. The U.S. release followed in February 1971. The pastoral cover design was by Paul Whitehead. His album cover painting is of a couple looking out through a huge window onto the mountain scenery. The images matched the pastoral feel of most of the songs. The painting is slashed from right to left with a serrated knife to represent the jarring impact of the album's final track at the request of the band.

The album represented a major leap forward for Genesis. The band, having been freed from the creative shackles that Jonathan King had placed on them, enabling them to channel their energies into recording a more challenging and varied collection of songs. The arrangements were more complex, as were the structures with greater variation of mood and tempo. Genesis were now looking to express themselves over extended pieces, which would allow them to stretch and explore different musical themes and move away from the traditional verse-chorus-bridge template. As a result, there were many strong melodic moments captured, alongside some dramatic moments. These were often singular moments which would be linked to other sections rather than repeated.

Banks was becoming a major musical driving force, with his prompting organ, melodic piano and adventurous use of Mellotron, most effectively on [22] STAGNATION. Gabriel's vocals were more confident and mature, if a little back in the original mix—something that was rectified in Nick Davis' 2008 remix. The singer really enjoyed stretching his voice on the harder passages during [19] LOOKING FOR SOMEONE and [24] THE KNIFE. Phillips also made a major contribution the band's sound teaming up with Rutherford on some sensitive 12-string acoustic structures as well as his choral approach to vocal harmonies. Rutherford himself was starting to get to grips with the bass and produced some driving rhythms during [24] THE KNIFE. However, Mayhew's drumming lacked variety, although his contribution to [24] THE KNIFE was much more impressive. The drummer struggled to get to grips with the material and add anything creative to the more acoustic pieces. His time with the band would soon be up.

Despite the relaxed working relationship that producer John Anthony established with the band, he did not seem to be especially sensitive to their music with many of the tracks sounding a little muddy through overarrangement and excessive overdubbing due to limitations of the recording equipment. In particular, the drum sound was flat and lacked the required rhythmic thrust. On 11 November 2008, the vastly improved remixed and remastered version of the album was included in the *Genesis 1970–1975* box set release of the band's first five Charisma studio albums. This release significantly improves the dynamics and creates a much better stereo definition, finally giving the arrangements the necessary room to breathe.

The album was well-received by the music press on release. Michael Watts in his review for *Melody Maker* described the album as "tasteful, subtle and refined, but with enough spunk in the music to prevent the album from becoming a self-indulgent wallow in insipidity."[20] Jerry Gilbert in *Sounds* noted, "Genesis are still sadly underrated, but this should help rectify matters. Compelling rhythm and careful use of a variety of instruments predominantly keyboard and guitar. The group paint some nice original pictures and the material is strong and infectious, particularly the acoustic passages."[21]

Trespass feels like the first real Genesis album and the band would go on to build on the foundation it laid over the next four years, but this would be with a changed lineup.

Part 2

The Five-Man Years: October 1970–May 1975

Tony Banks (Keyboards)
Phil Collins (Drums, Vocals)
Peter Gabriel (Vocals, Flute, Percussion)
Steve Hackett (Guitars)
Mike Rutherford (Bass, Guitars)

The "classic" five-man Genesis line-up, seen in Central Park, Manhattan, New York, 1972. From left, seated—Phil Collins, Mike Rutherford, Tony Banks; standing, Peter Gabriel and Steve Hackett. Charisma promotional photograph (courtesy Mark Kenyon/The Genesis Archive).

5

Studio Album #3: *Nursery Cryme*

UK Release: 12 November 1971. LP. Charisma. CAS 1052.
U.S. Release: Early 1972. LP. Buddah/Charisma. CAS 1052.
Remix/Remaster Release:
UK Release: 10 November 2008. CD/SACD/DVD. Virgin/Charisma. CASCDR 1052
U.S. Release: 11 November 2008. CD/DVD. Atlantic/Rhino. R2 513944.

Album Tracks
[25] THE MUSICAL BOX
[26] FOR ABSENT FRIENDS
[27] THE RETURN OF THE GIANT HOGWEED
[28] SEVEN STONES
[29] HAROLD THE BARREL
[30] HARLEQUIN
[31] THE FOUNTAIN OF SALMACIS

Other Songs Recorded (separate dedicated session)
[32] HAPPY THE MAN

Soon after *Trespass* was completed Anthony Phillips stunned the band by quitting. His illness had triggered a chronic stage fright that was not helped by the stresses of the band's hectic touring schedule. This was compounded by the pressures created by promoters turning up to watch the band perform. Phillips' health deteriorated further through a bout of bronchial pneumonia, which hastened his decision to leave the band. Rutherford was Phillips' closest friend and he unsuccessfully tried to persuade him to carry on.[1]

Phillips had been a driving force for the band, which now had to seriously consider whether to carry on without one of their major writers and prime mover. After a long period of consideration, Genesis decided to continue and having done so also decided the rhythm section needed improving, so Mayhew was released as drummer. The band felt Mayhew had been slow to learn his trade and had found their songs difficult to play. Additionally, he was older than the rest of the band members and there had been a certain lack of chemistry.[2]

Following an ad in *Melody Maker* in July 1970, auditions for a "12-string guitarist who can also play lead; plus drummer sensitive to acoustic music" were held at Gabriel's parents' house in Chobham, Surrey. One of the drumming candidates was **PHILIP DAVID CHARLES "PHIL" COLLINS** (born 30 January 1951), who at that time was in a band called

5. Studio Album #3: Nursery Cryme

Flaming Youth. Collins attended the audition with his band mate Ronnie Caryl who was auditioning for the guitarist role.[3] Having arrived early and hearing his competitors perform while he went for a swim in the pool, Collins coasted through the audition playing bits of [39] TWILIGHT ALEHOUSE, [25] THE MUSICAL BOX, [24] THE KNIFE and [22] STAGNATION. Collins received the call telling him he had got the job on 8 August 1970.

Collins' upbringing had been very different from that of his new band mates. Born and raised in Chiswick, West London, his father, Greville, was an insurance salesman from the city, while his mother, June, was a theatrical agent. He had an older brother, Clive (who became a famous cartoonist) and a sister, Carole. Collins became interested in drumming when he was just 5 years old after two of his uncles had bought him a toy drum set. At the age of 14 he looked to pursue an acting career and entered Barbara Speake Stage School, where his mother was working. This culminated in a spell as the Artful Dodger in *Oliver!* on the West End stage. His acting ambitions took a dive when he had a disagreement with the director of the 1967 children's film *Calamity the Cow*. He gravitated back to drumming and was soon playing with the band Hickory, which later became Flaming Youth. The band's only album release was the concept album *Ark 2*. But having felt Flaming Youth had run its course, Collins started looking for other opportunities. Seeing the name of Tony Stratton-Smith, who Collins knew from the London music scene, heading the *Melody Maker* ad made up his mind.

Collins joined Banks, Gabriel and Rutherford for rehearsals at an old barn complex called the Maltings, in Farnham during September 1970 and performed his first gig at Medway College, Chatham in Kent on 2 October. All this took place before *Trespass* had even been released, so when the album came out later that month the band had to tour as a four-piece as the search for a guitarist continued. Genesis were temporarily augmented for eight shows in late October and early November by Caryl despite his playing style having been considered too bluesy for the band. Mick Barnard, who had been in the bands Farm and Smoky Rice, then took over on guitar for a short time after that. Barnard was recommended to the band by David Stopps, part-owner of the Friars Club in Aylesbury, where the band performed regularly. Barnard, however, did not seem to have the confidence required to hold the position on a permanent basis, lacking the required empathy for 12-string guitar work, and the band resolved to continue with their search.

Eventually Gabriel responded to an ad placed in the 12 December 1970 edition of *Melody Maker* by guitarist **STEPHEN RICHARD "STEVE" HACKETT** (born 12 February 1950). The ad read: "Imaginative Guitarist/Writer seeks involvement with receptive musicians, determined to strive beyond existing stagnant music forms." Hackett's challenging words struck a chord with the band. Gabriel and Banks made the trip to Hackett's flat on Ebury Bridge Road to meet the guitarist. Banks and Gabriel were impressed by a tape of music Hackett had recorded with his brother, John, which had obvious King Crimson influences employed in the composition and playing. They also felt Hackett's classical Spanish-style of playing would add an extra dimension to the overall sound. Hackett was invited to watch Genesis at the Lyceum in London on 28 December 1970 and he later met Rutherford, who was also impressed by Hackett's fondness of 12-string guitars.

Hackett was born in Pimlico, south central London to Peter and June Hackett. He and his younger brother John became interested in music from an early age. Steve, aged 12, chose guitar after flirting with both harmonica and recorder, while John pursued his interest on the flute. Hackett had a wide range of influences ranging from classical, to blues to pop, which helped shape his distinctive playing style. Having been schooled at Sloane Grammar School in Chelsea, Hackett pursued his musical interests through various bands before joining Quiet World with his brother John in 1970, playing on the album *The Road* recorded that year. Remaining unfulfilled, Hackett placed his ad in *Melody Maker* and Genesis came calling.

With the full band approval now secured, Hackett performed his first gig with Genesis on 14 January 1971 at the University College in London. The show was dogged by technical issues, and the guitarist wrongly assumed the band's bad mood was down to his performance. The band continued to promote *Trespass* around the UK as part of Charisma's "Six-Bob" tour package.[4] Between March and May 1971, the new five-piece Genesis began to write and rehearse new material for what was to become their third album, *Nursery Cryme*.

During the summer, manager Tony Stratton-Smith rented a cottage at Luxford House in Crowborough, East Sussex, which the band christened "Toad Hall." Here the band pooled ideas for their new songs.[5] The move enabled new members Collins and Hackett to get to know the other band members. Banks noted, "We moved to Strat's house in order to learn to play together. We needed to really rehearse together and work out a repertoire and everything."[6] To help get the sound he wanted, the band bought Hackett a new Les Paul guitar and a Hiwatt stack amplifier. The band members were also maturing as writers; challenging themselves to write darker material and expand their musical horizons. The sessions were protracted as Rutherford later commented, "It was not an easy writing session and we were at Tony Stratton-Smith's house and we battled away and it didn't come and it was a fight."[7] Banks and Gabriel would often disagree on the direction of songs, with Gabriel citing Banks' unwillingness to bend from his viewpoint when it came to keyboard parts. Hackett, being new to the band however, found the process more satisfying: "It was an album that I was very, very happy with at the time I'd done it…. I'd dome some session work beforehand but nothing really that I felt was 'me' and made a decent contribution to, so I was very happy with the album. I was ecstatic in fact."[8]

It was during this period the band got their first taste of success as *Trespass* became an unexpected hit in Belgium, prompting the band to play a gig there in March 1971 as well as take part in TV recording sessions. Genesis also continued to play venues in the UK during this period while fitting in a further TV recording in Brussels in June 1971. There was a famous incident at the band's show at Friars Club in Aylesbury, Buckinghamshire on 19 June 1971. Gabriel threw himself into a stage dive, only to see the startled audience move out of the way. The result was a broken ankle. He struggled back on stage to perform the encore only to be left sitting there in pain as the house lights went up and the rest of the band made their way to the dressing room. He would use a wheelchair for a few shows after this, only to roll off stage during one of those shows. This was pre–Spinal Tap.

Genesis left August free to record their new material at Trident Studios, again using John Anthony as producer. David Hentschel was promoted to engineer from his role as tape operator on *Trespass* and this led to an association with the band that would last until 1980, once he had taken on the role of producer for 1976's *A Trick of the Tail*. The band entered the studio in a less confident frame of mind than they had for *Trespass*. For that album they had honed the songs on the road. For this new batch of songs, most of which were freshly written, there were still uncertainties around arrangement. This resulted in multiple takes for each of the songs, which Collins felt robbed them of their edge. As a drummer he felt his best performance would be in the first two or three takes. The more takes the band put down the safer his performance became to ensure an error free take, being unable to overdub in the same way a guitarist or keyboard player could.

With the recording sessions and mixing concluded the band had a new album from its new lineup ready for release.

5. *Studio Album #3:* Nursery Cryme

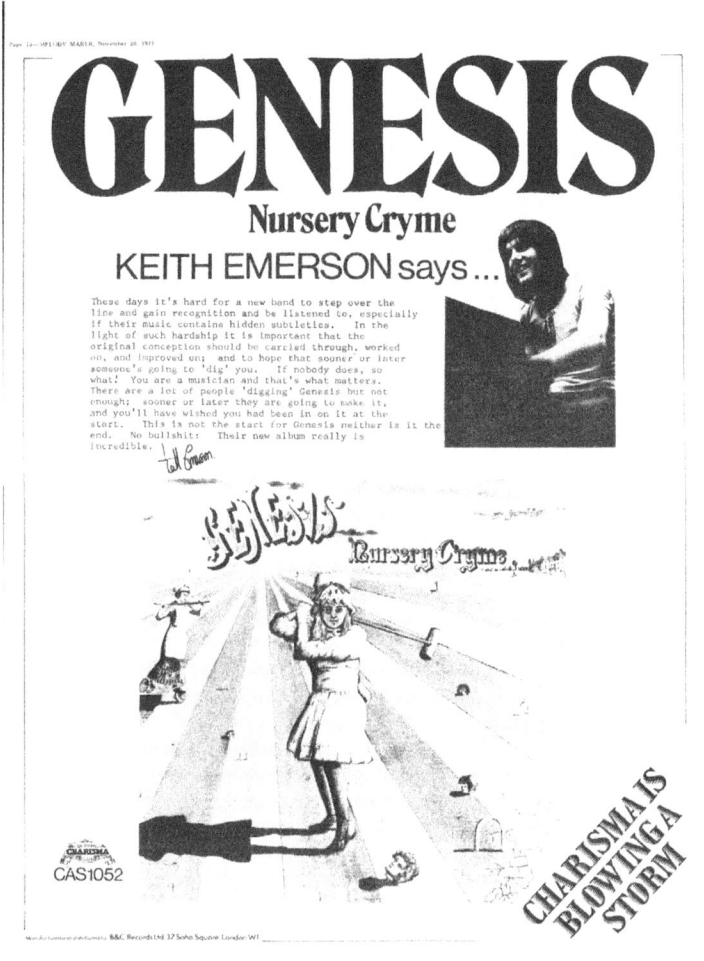

Advertisement promoting *Nursery Cryme*, including a glowing recommendation by Keith Emerson, placed in *Melody Maker* on 20 November 1971 (courtesy Mark Kenyon/The Genesis Archive).

[25] THE MUSICAL BOX

Band Credit: Tony Banks/Phil Collins/Peter Gabriel/Steve Hackett/Mike Rutherford
Music: Tony Banks/Mick Barnard/Phil Collins/Peter Gabriel/Steve Hackett/Anthony Phillips/Mike Rutherford
Lyrics: Peter Gabriel
Length: 10:30
Tony Banks—Organ, Electric Piano, Acoustic Guitar, Backing Vocals; **Phil Collins**—Drums, Backing Vocals; **Peter Gabriel**—Lead Vocals, Flute, Percussion, Oboe; **Steve Hackett**—Guitar, Acoustic Guitar; **Mike Rutherford**—Acoustic Guitar, Bass Pedals
Recorded at Trident Studios, London, August 1971.
Produced by John Anthony. Assistant Engineer: David Hentschel. Tape Jockey: Mike Stone.
2008 Remix/Remaster Release:
Mixed at The Farm, Surrey 2005/2006.
5.1 Surround sound and stereo mixes by Nick Davis. Assisted by Tom Mitchell.
UK Release: 12 November 1971. (LP: *Nursery Cryme*)
U.S. Release: Early 1972. (LP: *Nursery Cryme*)

THE MUSICAL BOX was the strongest example to date of the band's musical vision. It expanded on the musical complexity of [22] STAGNATION by linking together different thematic sections to make a dynamic whole. The song was rehearsed at the Maltings in Farnham during Collins' first session with the band. The basis for the song was the 12-string instrumental section "F#" written by Anthony Phillips and Rutherford in 1969, which itself was fleshed-out in [D18d] MANIPULATION on the "Genesis Plays Jackson" BBC session.[9]

The song was molded into its final shape while Genesis were touring as a four-piece with Banks playing guitar lead lines on keyboards and Rutherford on rhythm guitar while using pedals to cover the bass lines. It is a typical example of how Genesis liked to develop songs over time, both in rehearsals and live on the road. Temporary guitarist Mick Barnard was involved in stages of its development—notably the guitar parts toward the song's conclusion. By the time Hackett had replaced Barnard, the song was largely complete. Banks noted, "Steve was in the band a very short time when we recorded *Nursery Cryme*. All the guitar parts on THE MUSICAL BOX were written by Mick [Barnard]. Steve tended to play pretty much of what Mick had played 'cause there wasn't much time to learn new parts. Most of the guitar on it is Mike anyhow—all the rhythm guitar. There wasn't that much lead guitar on it."[10] The composition of the song was completed in the spring with Hackett's main creative contribution to the arrangement being to add the simulated sound of the titular musical box.

The opening gently coaxes the listener into the album with the acoustic guitar led passage in F sharp containing some pleasant flute from Gabriel. Collins provides backing vocals to Gabriel for the first time on record, immediately improving the vocal harmonies. At 3:38, the song moves into a dramatic uptempo section, as the story takes a dark and macabre turn. Gabriel's lyrics, which also take inspiration from his grandfather's house on Cox Hill,[11] examine repressive Victorian values from a bizarre perspective. The album liner notes detail the story for the song in which two young children playing croquet—a boy (Henry) and girl (Cynthia). Cynthia decapitates Henry with her croquet mallet. Later she finds a musical box in among Henry's belongings. When she opens the box, it plays "Old King Cole" and the spirit of Henry is summoned from within. His body ages rapidly while his mind remains unaltered. A lifetime of suppressed sexual desire comes to the surface and Henry looks for Cynthia to satisfy him, but they are disturbed by their nanny who hurls the music box at Henry and both are destroyed. Gabriel explained: "One of the influences on *Nursery Cryme* was the dark childhood of *The Turn of The Screw* (by Henry James). Also, *Great Expectations* (by Charles Dickens). These are very English and evocative. One of the reasons, I think, that films and programs about school are of interest to people is because that is when so much of your interface with the world gets formed."[12]

The band's desire to expand its musical soundscape was exemplified by Gabriel playing oboe on the "Old King Cole" section and Collins using mallets on his drums during Gabriel's flute solo. Banks' organ and Rutherford's rhythm guitar drives the instrumental midsection and almost immediately the strong impact of the two new members can be felt.[13] Hackett provides a blistering harmonic guitar solo using his influential tapping technique for the first time, which producer Anthony pans across the channels to create a swirling effect.[14] Collins' rolling drums give the song its rhythmic urgency.[15] The song's climax, from 7:38, was developed by Banks and Rutherford around the latter's chord sequence on rhythm guitar which was underpinned by his bass pedals. Banks complemented this by playing straight major chords on the organ. The keyboardist was pleased with how this sounded instrumentally, but Gabriel felt there needed to be a vocal on top. What he delivered was an increasingly intense performance of the release of the heightened sexual frustrations of

Old Henry as he implores young Cynthia to touch him. It proved enough to convince Banks to hand over the focus to Gabriel's vocals and lyrics. Hackett's guitar part for the closing section musically describes the hurried climax of their consummation and helps to shape a dramatic end to a Genesis classic.

Single Release: The song was included as the A-side on a three-track promo EP (Charisma. CG-EP) distributed by Buddah Records in June 1972 to further promote *Nursery Cryme* in the U.S. The tracks on the B-side were [26] FOR ABSENT FRIENDS and [31] THE FOUNTAIN OF SALMACIS.

BBC Sessions: (1) The song was recorded (11:54) for a BBC session for *Sounds of the Seventies* at Studio T1, Kensington House, Shepherd's Bush, London on 10 May 1971, which was subsequently broadcast on 31 May. The session was produced by Pete Dauncey and engineered by Adrian Revill.

(2) A second session, including Gabriel's story of "Old Henry" (12:26), was recorded in front of a live studio audience for the BBC's *In Concert* at BBC Paris Studios, London on 2 March 1972 and broadcast on 11 March.

Live Performances: 1971/2, 1972/3, 1973/4, 1974/5, 1977 (closing section), 1982 ("Six of the Best" show), 1992 (closing section). THE MUSICAL BOX would become a live favorite for many years being performed in full on each tour from 1971 to 1975, with Gabriel acting out the role of Old Henry with gusto. Rutherford acknowledged, "The studio version doesn't have the bite on the powerful sections that the song did live."[16] On later tours the song was excerpted down to its closing section and included as part of a medley.

Live Recordings: (1) An energetic performance of the whole song (10:56) at De Montfort Hall, Leicester, 25 February 1973 was included on the album *Genesis Live*, produced by John Burns and the band.

(2) A recording of the song's closing section (3:18) from one of the band's concerts at Palais des Sports, Paris between 11–14 June 1977, having segued from [48] THE LAMB LIES DOWN ON BROADWAY, appeared on the album *Seconds Out*. This was produced by David Hentschel and was played by the lineup of Banks, Collins (who handles the vocals), Hackett and Rutherford, augmented by Chester Thompson on drums.

(3) Another recording of the closing section as part of the "Old Medley" (19:32) from Niedersachsenstadion, Hanover, Lower Saxony, Germany on 10 July 1992 appeared on 1993's *The Way We Walk, Volume Two: The Longs* as part of the "Old Medley." This recording was produced by Nick Davis, Robert Colby and the band. The lineup here was Banks, Collins and Rutherford with Daryl Stuermer on guitar and Thompson on drums.

[26] FOR ABSENT FRIENDS

Band Credit: Tony Banks/Phil Collins/Peter Gabriel/Steve Hackett/Mike Rutherford
Music: Steve Hackett
Lyrics: Phil Collins/Steve Hackett
Length: 1:48
Tony Banks—Acoustic Guitar (?); **Phil Collins**—Lead & Backing Vocals; **Steve Hackett**—Acoustic Guitar; **Mike Rutherford**—Acoustic Guitar, Bass
Recorded at Trident Studios, London, August 1971.
Produced by John Anthony. Assistant Engineer: David Hentschel. Tape Jockey: Mike Stone.
2008 Remix/Remaster Release:
Mixed at The Farm, Surrey 2005/2006.
5.1 Surround sound and stereo mixes by Nick Davis. Assisted by Tom Mitchell.
UK Release: 12 November 1971. (LP: *Nursery Cryme*)
U.S. Release: Early 1972. (LP: *Nursery Cryme*)

A gentle acoustic song performed on acoustic guitar by Hackett on which Collins delivers his first ever lead vocal for the band. It is a short and wistful, if unmemorable, observation of two old ladies lamenting the passing of their husbands on a Sunday morning trip to church and is nicely sung by the drummer. Hackett likened the depiction of the ladies to two "Eleanor Rigbys." The music for the song was written by Hackett with Collins assisting with the lyrics. Rutherford recalled in his memoir the main reason for including the song on the album was because it had been written by the two new members. At the time, Collins regarded it as his "Ringo moment"—"more of an 'interlude' than a 'song.'"[17] Collins had initially intended for his vocal to be just a guide, to demonstrate the melody. The rest of the band liked the softness of his voice, which contrasted with Gabriel's harder and more textured sound and so was cemented Collins' first major vocal contribution to the band.

Single Release: The song was included as a B-side on a three-track EP (Charisma. CG-EP) distributed by Buddah Records to promote *Nursery Cryme* in the U.S. The other tracks were on the A-side [25] THE MUSICAL BOX and the other B-side [31] THE FOUNTAIN OF SALMACIS.

[27] THE RETURN OF THE GIANT HOGWEED

Band Credit: Tony Banks/Phil Collins/Peter Gabriel/Steve Hackett/Mike Rutherford
Music: Tony Banks/Phil Collins/Peter Gabriel/Steve Hackett/Mike Rutherford
Lyrics: Peter Gabriel
Length: 8:09
Tony Banks—Organ, Mellotron, Electric Piano, Backing Vocals; **Phil Collins**—Drums, Backing Vocals, Percussion; **Peter Gabriel**—Lead Vocals, Flute, Bass Drum, Percussion; **Steve Hackett**—Guitar; **Mike Rutherford**—Bass, Backing Vocals
Recorded at Trident Studios, London, August 1971.
Produced by John Anthony. Assistant Engineer: David Hentschel. Tape Jockey: Mike Stone.
2008 Remix/Remaster Release:
Mixed at The Farm, Surrey 2005/2006.
5.1 Surround sound and stereo mixes by Nick Davis. Assisted by Tom Mitchell.
UK Release: 12 November 1971. (LP: *Nursery Cryme*)
U.S. Release: Early 1972. (LP: *Nursery Cryme*)

THE RETURN OF THE GIANT HOGWEED is the heaviest song included on the album. It is similar in feel to [24] THE KNIFE, but without quite reaching the levels of excitement, paranoia and violence set by that song. Hackett provided the introduction, again using his pioneering tapping technique on electric guitar to play harmonic triplets during the song's opening. Banks doubled up with Hackett on the Hohner pianet Electric Piano. Gabriel, who also provided the blackly comic lyrics, sings aggressively of the invasion of the Giant Hogweed, a plant which proceeds to wipe out the country in true *Day of the Triffids* style.[18] His vocal urges the listener to flee from the Hogweed's overwhelming power as well as the need to find a way to destroy it.

While Banks' organ and Hackett's guitar dominate the arrangement, Collins and Rutherford add tight rhythmic power to drive the song along. Banks also provides a piano version of the riff during a long instrumental section before Hackett takes over again on guitar. At 6:55, the band crashes into a fast-paced musical climax with Banks' ascending organ chords depicting the savage attack of the plants as they wipe out all that stands in their way. A lively rocker this would become a popular feature of the band's live set.

BBC Sessions: (1) The song (7.50) was recorded for a BBC *Sounds of the Seventies* session at Studio T1, Transcription Service, Kensington House, Shepherd's Bush on 9 January 1972 and broadcast on 28 January. The session was engineered by John Walters and produced by John Muir.

(2) The song was also included in a second session (7:58) for BBC's *In Concert* series was recorded in front of a live studio audience at BBC Paris Studios, London on 2 March 1972. The performance engineered by Chris Lycett and produced by Jeff Griffin. It was broadcast nine days later.

Live Performances: 1970/1, 1971/2, 1972/3, 1973/4. THE RETURN OF THE GIANT HOGWEED would sound better live with the band's energy driven by the dynamic rhythm section of Rutherford and Collins. The song held a regular slot in the set until 1973 and occasionally took the place of [24] THE KNIFE as the closing number.

Live Recordings: A kinetic performance (8:14) at the Free Trade Hall, Manchester, 24 February 1973 was included on *Genesis Live*. This recording was produced by John Burns and the band.

[28] SEVEN STONES

Band Credit: Tony Banks/Phil Collins/Peter Gabriel/Steve Hackett/Mike Rutherford
Music: Tony Banks/Peter Gabriel/Steve Hackett
Lyrics: Tony Banks
Length: 5:08
Tony Banks—Organ, Mellotron, Piano, Backing Vocals; **Phil Collins**—Drums, Backing Vocals, Percussion; **Peter Gabriel**—Lead Vocals, Flute, Bass Drum, Percussion; **Steve Hackett**—Guitar; **Mike Rutherford**—Acoustic Guitar, Bass, Bass Pedals, Backing Vocals
Recorded at Trident Studios, London, August 1971.
Produced by John Anthony. Assistant Engineer: David Hentschel. Tape Jockey: Mike Stone.
2008 Remix/Remaster Release:
Mixed at The Farm, Surrey 2005/2006.
5.1 Surround sound and stereo mixes by Nick Davis. Assisted by Tom Mitchell.
UK Release: 12 November 1971. (LP: *Nursery Cryme*)
U.S. Release: Early 1972. (LP: *Nursery Cryme*)
UK Single Release: 29 May 1972. (B-side single b/w [32] HAPPY THE MAN. Charisma. CB 181)

This organ-led song is the most melodic track on the album. It also contains some typical Mellotron chord progressions in the key of G minor from Banks during the chorus and a choral backing similar in tone to those used on *Trespass*. Hackett wrote the instrumental bridge, while the bulk of the song was written by Banks and Gabriel. Banks was also responsible for the wordy lyrics, which tell the tale of an old man taking his chances in life. The strength of the new lineup is evident during the song's instrumental passages, particularly Rutherford's use of bass pedals behind Banks' expansive Mellotron chords. From 2:09 to 2:35, Gabriel is given the opportunity to contribute a delicate and extended flute refrain, which acts as a bridging interlude. Taken as a whole, the song is inconsequential but notable mainly for its moments of harmonic brilliance and Collins' inventive drumming. There's a neat playout reminiscent of the keyboard refrain from The Beatles' "Strawberry Fields Forever."

Single Release: SEVEN STONES would be used as the B-side to the UK single release of [32] HAPPY THE MAN on 29 May 1972.

Live Performances: 1971/2. The song was performed live occasionally on the tour that followed the album's release before disappearing from the set.

Live Recordings: No officially released live recordings of the song exist.

[29] Harold the Barrel

Band Credit: Tony Banks/Phil Collins/Peter Gabriel/Steve Hackett/Mike Rutherford
Music & Lyrics: Peter Gabriel
Length: 3:01
Tony Banks—Piano, Backing Vocals; **Phil Collins**—Secondary Lead Vocals, Drums, Backing Vocals, Percussion; **Peter Gabriel**—Primary Lead Vocals, Flute, Percussion; **Steve Hackett**—Guitar; **Mike Rutherford**—Bass, Backing Vocals
Recorded at Trident Studios, London, August 1971.
Produced by John Anthony. Assistant Engineer: David Hentschel. Tape Jockey: Mike Stone.
2008 Remix/Remaster Release:
Mixed at The Farm, Surrey 2005/2006.
5.1 Surround sound and stereo mixes by Nick Davis. Assisted by Tom Mitchell.
UK Release: 12 November 1971. (LP: *Nursery Cryme*)
U.S. Release: Early 1972. (LP: *Nursery Cryme*)

Largely written by Gabriel on piano and through his improvising harmonies with Collins, HAROLD THE BARREL has a music hall-feel and is an often hilarious and blackly comic tale of a restaurant owner at the end of his tether. Gabriel's lyrics describe how Harold, who after serving his own toes for tea, wants to commit suicide by jumping from the ledge of a tall building. Harold, his mother and the police are all portrayed in character to comic effect. Harold's mother being worried about how presentable Harold is with the media in attendance. Elements of *Monty Python*-esque humor are evident throughout in both the lyrics and the vocal delivery—notably the policemen imploring that they can help. Gabriel, often doubling with Collins, excels in breathing life into his characters.[19] Although the song is light relief, it is nevertheless enjoyable because of its execution and difference to the rest of the material on the album. The song ends effectively with Harold's dive from his ledge simulated by soft minor-key piano chords from Banks and Gabriel's fading vocal. It can best be judged as a precursor of better songs to come, such as [35] GET 'EM OUT BY FRIDAY and the "Willow Farm" section of [38] SUPPER'S READY, both on *Foxtrot*, as well as the less successful [44] THE BATTLE OF EPPING FOREST on *Selling England by the Pound*.

BBC Sessions: The song was also recorded in two versions, the first mix at (2:57) and the second mix at (2:52), at a *Sounds of the Seventies* BBC session at Studio T1, Transcription Service, Kensington House, Shepherd's Bush on 9 January 1972. The session, produced by John Muir and engineered by John Walters, was subsequently broadcast on 28 January and again on 17 March.

Live Performances: 1971/2, 1973/4. The song was performed live occasionally but was not a mainstay of the band's set.

Live Recordings: No officially released live recordings exist.

[30] Harlequin

Band Credit: Tony Banks/Phil Collins/Peter Gabriel/Steve Hackett/Mike Rutherford
Music: Mike Rutherford/Tony Banks
Lyrics: Mike Rutherford
Length: 2:56
Tony Banks—Harmony Vocals, Organ; Acoustic Guitar (?); **Phil Collins**—Harmony Vocals, Percussion; **Peter Gabriel**—Lead Vocals; **Steve Hackett**—Guitar, Acoustic Guitar (?); **Mike Rutherford**—Acoustic Guitar, Bass
Recorded at Trident Studios, London, August 1971.
Produced by John Anthony. Assistant Engineer: David Hentschel. Tape Jockey: Mike Stone.
2008 Remix/Remaster Release:

Mixed at The Farm, Surrey 2005/2006.
5.1 Surround sound and stereo mixes by Nick Davis. Assisted by Tom Mitchell.
UK Release: 12 November 1971. (LP: *Nursery Cryme*)
U.S. Release: Early 1972. (LP: *Nursery Cryme*)

This track, largely written by Banks and Rutherford, was based on Rutherford's twelve-string guitar melody. It marks a return to the folk-influenced acoustic writing and playing of their first two albums. Rutherford used a dual harmonic tuning to try and create the impression of two guitarists playing. The song carries some strong vocal harmonies between Gabriel and Collins, interpreting Rutherford's rather weak, wistful and reflective lyrics. The song's light fireside sing-along approach, however, feels a little out of place on an album of more progressive material and instrumentally the piece lacks any spark. Banks was disappointed with the playing on this song and Rutherford remembers it as being "pretty dodgy."[20]

BBC Session: HARLEQUIN was later recorded for a BBC session (2:39) at Studio T1, Transcription Service, Kensington House, Shepherd's Bush on 9 January 1972, and this song was broadcast on 17 March. The session was produced by John Muir and engineered by John Walters.

Live Performances: 1971/2. The song was performed live occasionally.

Live Recordings: No officially released live recordings exist.

[31] THE FOUNTAIN OF SALMACIS

Band Credit: Tony Banks/Phil Collins/Peter Gabriel/Steve Hackett/Mike Rutherford
Music: Tony Banks/Phil Collins/Peter Gabriel/Steve Hackett/Anthony Phillips/Mike Rutherford
Lyrics: Mike Rutherford
Length: 8:02
Tony Banks—Organ, Mellotron; **Phil Collins**—Drums, Backing Vocals, Percussion; **Peter Gabriel**—
    Lead Vocals, Percussion; **Steve Hackett**—Guitar; **Mike Rutherford**—Bass, Backing Vocals
Recorded at Trident Studios, London, August 1971.
Produced by John Anthony. Assistant Engineer: David Hentschel. Tape Jockey: Mike Stone.
2008 Remix/Remaster Release:
Mixed at The Farm, Surrey 2005/2006.
5.1 Surround sound and stereo mixes by Nick Davis. Assisted by Tom Mitchell.
UK Release: 12 November 1971. (LP: *Nursery Cryme*)
U.S. Release: Early 1972. (LP: *Nursery Cryme*)

The dramatic sweep of THE FOUNTAIN OF SALMACIS was largely conceived during the band's writing sessions at Tony Stratton-Smith's cottage in Crowborough. The epic nature of the track is evident from its opening spiraling organ lines and Mellotron crescendos bolstered by Rutherford's sumptuous descending sliding bass line. The song forged a new direction for the band toward orchestral inspired arrangements with Banks' increasingly inventive use of the Mellotron's sound library. During the writing sessions Banks adapted some earlier written material (a song called "Ketch," which formed part of the instrumental piece [D18b] PROVOCATION for the Jackson project with the BBC). This section had been written while the keyboardist was at Sussex University. He later added the Mellotron part and spiraling organ phrases with Hackett contributing some harp-like effects with his guitar. Banks also developed a chord sequence he liked running from E minor to C major and D major, while keeping the bass rooted to E. Banks acknowledged the part Hackett played in the song's sound, "We gained a certain quality on THE FOUNTAIN OF SALMACIS from having a fluent guitarist, Steve."[21] Hackett recalled, "I've always liked songs that were a heavy mellotron feature, because I felt it was the band exploring harmony and a certain kind of mysticism and … the whole kind of magic of mythology, narrative, stories."[22]

Rutherford and Collins tightly drive the song through its changing rhythms, moods and tempos, while Gabriel struggles manfully to be heard delivering Rutherford's mythological lyrics about the first hermaphrodite.[23] This is vintage Genesis marred only by some poor production and mixing, particularly on the vocals, which would later be vastly improved by Nick Davis' remix in 2008. Hackett's splendid gliding electric guitar solo over Banks' orchestral Mellotron chords during the finale gives the song an epic climax. The solo was written at midnight one night while the band were rehearsing at Luxford House. Hackett later explained its effect, "The guitar solo at the end was, I think, a breakthrough at the time. Previously we'd had both chords that sounded very orchestral, which I loved; but suddenly there was a solo over the top of that."[24]

The song demonstrated Genesis' increasing interest in the part that musical drama and contrasting moods played in adding to their lyrical story telling. The music's emphasis on orchestral inspired arrangements allowed Banks a variety of sounds that had not been available to him previously. The keyboard interplay with Hackett's exciting electric guitar, created an irresistible cocktail the band would expand on in the future. Francois Couture perfectly summed up the song in his review for *All Music Guide*: "Both highly cerebral and strongly emotional, THE FOUNTAIN OF SALMACIS played a role in the establishment of some progressive rock clichés, including the use of mythological themes and the perception that this style was directed toward the intellectual elite."[25]

Single Release: The song was included as the B-side on a three-track EP (Charisma. CG-EP) distributed by Buddah Records to promote *Nursery Cryme* in the U.S. The other tracks were on the A-side [25] THE MUSICAL BOX and the other B-side [26] FOR ABSENT FRIENDS.

BBC Sessions: (1) A recording of the song (7:41) was included as part of a *Sounds of the Seventies* BBC session at Studio T1, Transcription Service, Kensington House, Shepherd's Bush on 9 January 1972. The session, produced by John Muir and engineered by John Walters, was broadcast on 28 January and again on 17 March 1972.

(2) A second BBC recording (8:32) for their *In Concert* series was made in front of a live studio audience at BBC Paris Studios, London on 2 March 1972. The broadcast, produced by Jeff Griffin and engineered by Chris Lycett, was aired on 11 March.

Live Performances: 1970/1, 1971/2, 1972/3, 1978. The song, which is a favorite of both Banks and Hackett from the album, was regularly performed live between 1971 and 1973 and then later restored to the set in 1978, with vocals handled by Phil Collins.

Live Recordings: A performance of the song from the band's 1978 tour (8:37) was included on the European version of *Three Sides Live*, which later became the international version when remixed and remastered in 2008. The lineup was Banks, Collins and Rutherford, augmented by Daryl Stuermer (guitar) and Chester Thompson (drums). The recording was produced by Genesis and engineered by David Hentschel.

* * *

Nursery Cryme was released in the UK on 12 November 1971 and in the U.S. early the following year, but like *Trespass* it failed to chart.[26] While the playing was enhanced by the addition of Collins and Hackett, the writing on *Nursery Cryme* did not significantly advance on *Trespass*, something the band later acknowledged. The lesser songs fell slightly short as a set—despite the slick production in parts. Hints of the band's future success were abundant, however—Gabriel's theatrical vocals and macabre lyrics; Banks' increasingly symphonic approach to keyboards through the Mellotron; the angular guitar patterns of Hackett; Rutherford's more assured bass and his 12-string prowess; and Collins' dynamic drumming and vocal harmonies. These skills would advance over the next three albums in which the band would produce some of their finest music.

The material having been rehearsed through the spring and honed on the road, helped the band reduce the required studio recording time. However, this approach led to a tendency to overarrange some of the songs. The collection was a varied and perhaps, inevitably, inconsistent set. The dramatic approach to both [25] THE MUSICAL BOX and [31] THE FOUNTAIN OF SALMACIS proved to be instantly successful and demonstrated the band's willingness to broaden their method by writing structurally complex songs. Expansive in style with many changes of tempo and direction they would become live favorites for many years to come. The hard rocking [27] THE RETURN OF THE GIANT HOGWEED was a less successful attempt to recall the heavier feel of [24] THE KNIFE but became a popular live number. The other songs came across more as filler, being lighter and more reflective or comedic in mood: from the music hall approach to [29] HAROLD THE BARREL, the wistful [26] FOR ABSENT FRIENDS, the harmonic strains of [30] HARLEQUIN to the melodic simplicity of [28] SEVEN STONES.

Retrospectively the band have come to regard the album as transitional and one that was difficult to make. Banks noted he was still becoming familiar with both organ and Mellotron. Rutherford pointed to the fact that the new band were getting to know each other as writers—the loss of Phillips had been a big wrench for the band and for Rutherford personally—the pair having been a writing partnership in the early days. Collins also noted a strange vibe during the writing stage at Stratton-Smith's house, "I'm sure the house was haunted."[27]

The album's cover was again based on a painting by Paul Whitehead. This time the artist used the lyrics to THE MUSICAL BOX as his inspiration, depicting Cynthia playing croquet with Henry's decapitated head on the lawns outside a manor house. It was Whitehead's own personal favorite of his covers for the band.

Promotion of the album included a full-page ad in *Melody Maker* on 20 November 1971, with a ringing endorsement from keyboardist Keith Emerson: "This is not the start for Genesis, nor is it the end. No bullshit: Their new album really is incredible." In the U.S., a press release was issued by Buddah Records, who were Charisma's North American distributor, which included ringing endorsements from the UK music press. Jerry Gilbert commented in his review for *Sounds*, "The lineup's changed since the last album ... giving the group a far more positive sound. An extremely fine and absorbing album."[28]

Critical reaction to *Nursery Cryme* in the U.S., however, was mixed. Richard Cromelin, writing for *Rolling Stone*, gave a typical summation outlining that his problems with the album lay not with, "Genesis' concepts, which are, if nothing else, outrageously imaginative and lovably eccentric, nor with their musical structures—long, involved, multi-movement frameworks on which they hang their narratives—nor even with their playing, which does get pretty lethargic at points. It's the godawful production, a murky, distant stew that at best bubbles quietly when what is desperately needed are the explosions of drums and guitars, the screaming of the organ, the abrasive rasp of vocal cords."[29]

The band continued to attract a cult following through their live performances, revisiting such in-vogue places as The Friars Club in Aylesbury, where the owner, Dave Stopps, was a good friend who believed the venue to be Genesis' spiritual home. The Marquee Club in London was another venue where the band had built a following and they all felt a sense of achievement when they finally made it onto the bill.

Part 2—The Five-Man Years: October 1970–May 1975

In January 1972, the band began to capitalize on its growing reputation in Europe by returning to play foreign dates in Brussels, Belgium, where *Trespass* had been so popular. In February news reached the surprised band that *Nursery Cryme* had reached #4 in the Italian charts, further enhancing their reputation in mainland Europe and prompting a short tour of Italy in April, with many venues seeing two performances a day. Rutherford noted, "Italy really saved us, because they reacted to that album. England gave us a really hard time on it."[30] There was a short detour via Frankfurt, Germany, before returning to the UK to record a single and appear at the Lincoln Festival.

[32] HAPPY THE MAN

Band Credit: Tony Banks/Phil Collins/Peter Gabriel/Steve Hackett/Mike Rutherford
Music: Tony Banks/Phil Collins/Peter Gabriel/Steve Hackett/Mike Rutherford
Lyrics: Peter Gabriel
Length: 3:11
Tony Banks—Acoustic Guitar, Backing Vocals; **Phil Collins**—Drums, Backing Vocals, Percussion; **Peter Gabriel**—Lead Vocals, Flute, Percussion; **Steve Hackett**—Guitar; **Mike Rutherford**—Acoustic Guitar, Bass
Recorded at The Manor, London, 10 May 1972.
Produced by John Anthony.
2008 Remix/Remaster Release:
Mixed at The Farm, Surrey 2005/2006.
5.1 Surround sound and stereo mixes by Nick Davis. Assisted by Tom Mitchell.
UK Release: 12 May 1972. (A-side single b/w [28] SEVEN STONES. Charisma. CB 181)
U.S. Release: 22 June 1998. (4-CD: *Genesis Archive 1967–75*)

In May 1972, the band recorded this stand-alone single before enjoying a wonderful reception at the Lincoln Festival, helped by Gabriel's otherworldly appearance following his shaving the central part of his forehead. HAPPY THE MAN is a folk song about a wandering free-spirit and was written before Hackett joined the band. It was recorded at The Manor, which was Richard Branson's new studio, to which the band had been given access for a day. The song, which had been performed on the road for more than a year, was released as a single and demonstrated just how wrong the band was at the time for the singles market.[31] Rutherford, Hackett and Banks all played 12-string guitar on the opening section—a bright and jaunty piece based around an acoustic riff by Rutherford using one of his experimental tunings. Gabriel provided the lyrics

Advertisement promoting the standalone single [32] HAPPY THE MAN placed in *Melody Maker* on 3 June 1972 (courtesy Mark Kenyon/The Genesis Archive).

and Banks remarked, "I didn't have much to do with it really.... I quite liked it actually. That was quite good fun to do. Mike had another tuning on the guitar where everything was tuned to a chord and he played a riff on that that sounded good. I played guitar along with him and we built it from there."[32] However, as Collins would acknowledge in an interview with Chris Welch: "It was hard to get across in three minutes what the band is all about."[33] Hackett also felt the song to be inconsequential, "HAPPY THE MAN I think of as more of a throwaway song. There is not a lot to endear itself to me."[34] Welch in his review of the single for *Melody Maker* described the song as "a folksy tune rich in guitar chords, and emotional lead vocals."[35]

A disagreement between Charisma and producer John Anthony over the financial cost of the recording sessions led to a break in their relationship and the band would have to look elsewhere for a producer for their next album.

Alternative Versions: The song is available in its slightly edited single form, with a fade-in opening, on the *Genesis Archive 1967–75* (2.54) as well as *Turn It On Again: The Hits—Tour Edition* (3.08), including the full introduction. A remixed and remastered version (3:11) was included on the *Extra Tracks* CD of the *Genesis 1970–1975* box set.

Live Performances: 1970/1, 1971/2. The song was performed live irregularly over a two-year period.

Live Recordings: No official live recording of the track has been released.

6

Studio Album #4: *Foxtrot*

UK Release: 6 October 1972. LP. Charisma. CAS 1058.
U.S. Release: November 1972. LP. Buddah Records/Charisma. CAS 1058.
Remix/Remaster Release:
UK Release: 10 November 2008. CD/SACD/DVD. Virgin/Charisma. CASCDR 1058.
U.S. Release: 11 November 2008. CD/DVD. Atlantic/Rhino. R2 513946.

Album Tracks
[33] WATCHER OF THE SKIES
[34] TIME TABLE
[35] GET 'EM OUT BY FRIDAY
[36] CAN-UTILITY AND THE COASTLINERS
[37] HORIZONS
[38] SUPPER'S READY

Other Songs Recorded
[39] TWILIGHT ALEHOUSE

Genesis' cult status was beginning to gather momentum and the band was gaining confidence as they entered Island Studios in August 1972 to record their next album. The band had written and rehearsed new material initially in Blackheath, London before, via various venues, obtaining a room at Una Billings School of Dancing in Shepherd's Bush during the spring and summer of 1972.[1] The band also road-tested early versions of [33] WATCHER OF THE SKIES and [36] CAN-UTILITY AND THE COASTLINERS through their increasingly heavy touring schedule. Hackett described the process: "Whereas with its predecessor, *Nursery Cryme*, we'd taken the summer off and written and recorded together as a unit, bonding the team, this time we were on the run, in and out of the studio. I remember flying back from Italy to be in there a day or two ahead of the others, who were travelling by road, just to finish off my guitar parts on the end of [38] SUPPER'S READY."[2] Success in Europe had given the band the confidence to further explore their unique approach to song-writing, which would involve pooling musical ideas that the band would terms as "bits." The resultant album, *Foxtrot*, would give Genesis their biggest seller to date on home territory.

Being largely made up of ex-public-school boys, who were not the most forthcoming with praise, the environment within the band was very reserved. There was little effort made to complement other members on their contribution and there was a competitive edge to discussions on composition and arrangement. As a result, both Collins and Hackett

6. Studio Album #4: Foxtrot

felt very much like outsiders looking in and had been considering whether the band environment was right for them. While Collins' easygoing personality allowed him to relieve the tension through his humor, Hackett had a crisis of confidence going into the recording. The guitarist felt he was unable to bring any material to bear on the writing other than his short instrumental [37] HORIZONS. In a move that was out of character but summed up the feelings of the three ex-Charterhouse members, Banks, Rutherford and Gabriel allayed Hackett's fears by praising his unique guitar sound and playing style as well as confirming his importance to the band. Reassured, Hackett put aside any thoughts of leaving and entered the recording sessions with renewed enthusiasm.

Genesis had enjoyed working with Paul Samwell-Smith of the Yardbirds on their BBC recording for the Mick Jackson documentary and were keen to find a similarly sympathetic producer. Charisma, meanwhile, were keen for the band to have a hit single and suggested Bob Potter, who had worked with Simon and Garfunkel and Bob Dylan in the U.S. (with producer Bob Johnson) as well as Charisma's own Lindisfarne. Potter was brought on board, but his musical tastes were not matched with those of the band. His only real contribution to the album was working with Hackett on [37] HORIZONS. A disagreement with Banks over his intro to [33] WATCHER OF THE SKIES led to Potter leaving the project along with his engineer Tony Platt, who had also been working on the first half of [38] SUPPER'S READY.[3]

The band took a break from recording, while a new producer was found, and used the time to undertake a short eight-day tour of Italy. Upon returning to the UK they were still not happy with Potter's replacement, David Hitchcock, who had previously worked with the band Caravan, but they had finally found a sympathetic engineer in John Burns. Banks recalled, "We had just done the first bit of [38] SUPPER'S READY, with the original engineer and then we did the last half with John Burns as engineer. Suddenly there was power and excitement and I came out of the studio for the first time wanting to listen to something over and over again."[4] The album was completed with both Hitchcock and Burns on board.

The band worked in an increasingly creative and productive way on *Foxtrot* resulting in some of the material being jettisoned.[5] Out of a number of the bands "bits" the five members developed and compiled a suite of seven segments that when pieced together formed the epic [38] SUPPER'S READY, which would become widely acknowledged as the band's masterpiece.

[33] WATCHER OF THE SKIES

Band Credit: Tony Banks/Phil Collins/Peter Gabriel/Steve Hackett/Mike Rutherford
Music & Lyrics: Tony Banks/Mike Rutherford
Length: 7:22
Tony Banks—Organ, Mellotron, Backing Vocals; **Phil Collins**—Drums, Backing Vocals; **Peter Gabriel**—Lead Vocals, Tambourine, Bass Drum; **Steve Hackett**—Guitar; **Mike Rutherford**—Bass, Bass Pedals, Backing Vocals
Recorded at Island Studios, London, England, August–September 1972.
Producer: David Hitchcock and Genesis. Engineer: John Burns.
2008 Remix/Remaster Release:
Mixed at The Farm, Surrey 2005/2006.
5.1 Surround sound and stereo mixes by Nick Davis. Assisted by Tom Mitchell.
UK Release: 6 October 1972. (LP: *Foxtrot*)
U.S. Release: November 1972. (LP: *Foxtrot*)
U.S. Single Release: March 1973. (A-side Single b/w 'Willow Farm' from [38] SUPPER'S READY. Buddah Records/Charisma. CAR 103)

The huge opening Mellotron chords give Watcher of the Skies its otherworldly feel and set up a great atmosphere. Banks had been experimenting with the Mellotron sounds while trying to find an interesting chord sequence. He settled on two chords based around a solitary root bass note—B major 7th/F sharp and C sharp/F sharp. The resultant harmonic gave the effect of the instrument being slightly out of tune, thereby creating the introduction's eerie tension. Banks tried out the chords during a soundcheck at the Palasport in Reggio. The huge echo this venue created gave the sound added size and atmosphere encouraging Banks to develop it into a longer intro for the song. To achieve the sound he wanted Banks used as mix of brass, string, organ and piano accordion settings on an old Mellotron Mark 2, which the band had purchased from King Crimson. Banks was not initially keen on using a Mellotron but had been persuaded of its virtues by Crimson's Robert Fripp. Banks later commented the sound he created on the Mark 2 could not be replicated on the later versions of the Mellotron. Hackett recalled his personal contribution to the purchase of the instrument, "I remember pushing the band to acquire a Mellotron back in the '70s and, luckily, King Crimson had one to spare at the time—the 'Black Bitch' I think they called it on account of it always breaking down.... This song alone was a strong reason for re-approaching the early material—from Phil's inventive Morse code rhythm to Tony's momentous introduction which always sounded best in Italy's Palasports—an aircraft hangar type of rumble ideally suited to spacecraft impersonation."[6] The huge sound Banks created produced one of Genesis' most identifiable musical moments.

As the introduction reaches its conclusion at 1:30, the drums and bass launch into the main part of the song with an urgent staccato rhythm,[7] over which Gabriel sings the story of the Watcher—an alien arriving to find the Earth bereft of all human life. Following the vocal section, the song plays out a rhythmic struggle by alternating between 6/4 and 8/4 time-signatures before reaching its conclusion with a call and response between Hackett's guitar and Banks' organ. This leads into the closing section during which Banks returns to the Mellotron and heightens the tension through an ascending chord sequence.

Banks and Rutherford wrote the other-worldly lyrics while staring out at a deserted landscape from a Naples hotel window on a hot and sunny day during their Italian tour. The barren vista conjured up images of the desolate landscape the aliens would encounter. Rutherford liked the lyrics as written but felt they did not scan well, being hurried and clumsy in places and proving difficult for Gabriel to scan. Hackett, however, blamed the pace at which the band recorded, "To my ears now it sounds like a young band desperate to get the notes right in a race to the finish. Once we'd been playing it live for a while, we relaxed into it and it sounded bigger. The version that ended up on *Genesis Live* is more in-the-pocket. That rhythm is almost impossible for any band to play perfectly! It's full of pitfalls. Yet there's lots of weird and wonderful stuff; it's a band at its most creatively eccentric."[8]

Watcher of the Skies is an exciting and daring track. The song became a classic set opener for the next couple of tours and was a prime target for Gabriel's costumes and make-up.[9] The title was lifted from a line in John Keats' 1817 poem "On First Looking into Chapman's Homer."[10] Further influences for the song's subject included Arthur C. Clarke's *Childhood's End* as well as the Marvel comic strip hero The Watcher.

Watcher of the Skies was chosen to be performed live by Phish at Genesis' induction into the Rock & Roll Hall of Fame on 15 March 2010, which took place at the Waldorf-Astoria hotel in New York City.

6. Studio Album #4: Foxtrot

Single Release: A truncated version of the song (3:44) was prepared for release as a single, b/w the "Willow Farm" section (2:57) of [38] SUPPER'S READY, in the U.S. in March 1973. It would also be released in Italy, Germany and New Zealand. This version removed Banks' organ intro and included a different take of Gabriel's vocals as well as a different ending. The single edit was included on the *Genesis Archive 1967–75* box set.

BBC Session: A strong performance of the song (7:41) was also included as part of a BBC *Top Gear* session produced by John Peel and recorded at Studio T1, Transcription Service, Kensington House, Shepherd's Bush on 25 September 1972. The session was first broadcast on BBC Radio One on 9 November 1972.

Live Performances: 1971/2, 1972/3, 1973/4, 1974/5 (occasionally), 1976 (excerpt), 1982 (excerpt). Banks felt the song failed to follow-up on its atmospheric introduction but knew that Mellotron sequence would give the band a very strong and atmospheric concert opener. Adding to the music were the effects created by smoke machines and the lighting, which emphasized Gabriel's extravagant UV make-up and bat wings costume. The song would become the regular set opener from 1971 to 1974 and was also performed occasionally as an encore on the band's *Lamb* tour in 1974/5. Collins has stated it was much stronger live than on record. The opening Mellotron piece was blended with [70] IT for their later 1976 and 1982 tours.

Peter Gabriel in batwings performing [33] WATCHER OF THE SKIES, 1972. Charisma promotional photograph (courtesy Mark Kenyon/The Genesis Archive).

Live Recordings: (1) A live performance (8:34) recorded at De Montfort Hall, Leicester, on 25 February 1973 is included on *Genesis Live*. This recording is produced by John Burns and the band and is a great example of the power of the band's live performances at the time.

(2) The performance (8:01) at the Rainbow Theatre on 20 October 1973 was captured on the DVD audio version of *Live at the Rainbow*, which was issued with the box set *Genesis 1973–2007 Live*. The recording was by John Burns using the Rolling Stone mobile studio and produced by the band.

(3) The IT medley version (7:03), recorded on 8 July 1976 at the Apollo Theatre, Glasgow, Scotland, was included on 1982's European release of *Three Sides Live*. The band's lineup for this performance was Banks, Collins, Hackett and Rutherford, aug-

mented by Bill Bruford on drums. The recording was engineered by David Hentschel and produced by the band.

[34] Time Table

Band Credit: Tony Banks/Phil Collins/Peter Gabriel/Steve Hackett/Mike Rutherford
Music & Lyrics: Tony Banks
Length: 4:47
Tony Banks—Piano, Electric Piano; **Phil Collins**—Drums, Backing Vocals, Percussion; **Peter Gabriel**—Lead Vocals, Flute; **Steve Hackett**—Guitar; **Mike Rutherford**—Bass
Recorded at Island Studios, London, England, August–September 1972.
Producer: David Hitchcock and Genesis. Engineer: John Burns.
2008 Remix/Remaster Release:
Mixed at The Farm, Surrey 2005/2006.
5.1 Surround sound and stereo mixes by Nick Davis. Assisted by Tom Mitchell.
UK Release: 6 October 1972. (LP: *Foxtrot*)
U.S. Release: November 1972. (LP: *Foxtrot*)

An ornate piano opening is followed by a plodding rhythm in straight 4/4, a style that had been made popular by being employed on several compositions by The Beatles. This inconsequential but pleasantly melodic piece is typical of Banks. The approach to the song is akin to his later composition [74] Mad Man Moon, with his expansive use of harmonics. Hackett added complementary guitar arpeggios, which were fed through his Leslie cabinets. Hackett recalled, "I felt it was very much more a keyboard thing where the melody modulates and is almost a sort of Henry Mancini melody and I felt that all I needed to do was play underneath it. There was a little bit in there of mine, where I go into the area of distortion, and try to give the music some angst that it doesn't have at one point. I think my contribution to that track is fairly minimal, but if you play the track back without me, you would notice the difference."[11] The song represents an attempt at a more straightforward approach for the band, but it lacks a distinctive hook and therefore comes across as little more than filler, despite some effective passages. Banks also contributed the reflective folk-inspired lyrics, which tell the tale of an old oak table and the characters that have used it throughout its history.

[35] Get 'Em Out by Friday

Band Credit: Tony Banks/Phil Collins/Peter Gabriel/Steve Hackett/Mike Rutherford
Music: Tony Banks/Phil Collins/Peter Gabriel/Steve Hackett/Mike Rutherford
Lyrics: Peter Gabriel
Length: 8:36
Tony Banks—Organ, Electric Piano, Mellotron, Acoustic Guitar; **Phil Collins**—Drums; **Peter Gabriel**—Lead Vocals, Flute, Oboe, Percussion, Bass Drum; **Steve Hackett**—Guitar, Acoustic Guitar; **Mike Rutherford**—Bass, Bass Pedals
Recorded at Island Studios, London, England, August–September 1972.
Producer: David Hitchcock and Genesis. Engineer: John Burns.
2008 Remix/Remaster Release:
Mixed at The Farm, Surrey 2005/2006.
5.1 Surround sound and stereo mixes by Nick Davis. Assisted by Tom Mitchell.
UK Release: 6 October 1972. (LP: *Foxtrot*)
U.S. Release: November 1972. (LP: *Foxtrot*)

6. Studio Album #4: *Foxtrot*

The musical origins of this social satire can be traced back to the long piece of music called "The Movement" that the band had developed in the early days. It was a piece that provided a rich source for the band to take bits from and develop into new songs. Lyrically, GET 'EM OUT BY FRIDAY is a hilarious look at the unscrupulous property developers who housed families into high rise flats while their old houses where demolished in the name of progress. Its satire was prompted by a TV documentary exposing aggressive landlords and their rented housing in Islington. Reportedly Gabriel had been experiencing similar issues with the landlord to his flat on Camden Hill Road. This inspired him to create the song's prophetic theme and lyrics, which were written in the form of a miniplay. The plot features three characters: John Pebble, who is a business man attached to Styx Enterprises; Mark Hall (better known as "The Winkler"), who is tasked by Pebble to evict the council house tenants; Mrs. Barrow, one of the Harlow house tenants pursued by "The Winkler." When she refuses Pebble raises her rent. The second theme of the song concerns the idea of the human race controlling its own evolution. Gabriel invented the satirical idea of Genetic Control, where experiments would result in humans being restricted to four feet in height, so they take up less space, thereby enabling architects to design buildings that would house twice as many people for the same cost.

Musically the song meanders between soft passages and driving rhythms. Collins' skills as an arranger came to the fore when he suggested Banks make changes to the rhythm behind the riff he had been developing, which Banks stated, "made it to me twenty times better than I had thought it was."[12] The song is also more than a little cluttered instrumentally. That said, Rutherford's intricate running bass lines are among his best contributions to the band. This was as a by-product of the band's policy of laying down the music tracks before any vocals were developed. Lyrically the song is brilliant with Gabriel's biting satire still resonant today. His strengths in creating blackly comic characters and using witty wordplay are very much in evidence culminating in the ludicrous announcement from Genetic Control at the song's conclusion. The closing keyboard chords, over which the listener is urged by a memo from Saint Peter to invest, are beautifully sublime.

The song was later adapted as a comic strip by French cartoonists Jean Solé and Gotlib for the comic magazine *Fluide Glacial*. Alain Distler translated the lyrics—rather badly.

BBC Session: A version (8:46) was also recorded for a BBC *Top Gear* session recorded at Studio T1, Transcription Service, Kensington House, Shepherd's Bush on 25 September 1972. The recording was broadcast on Radio One on 9 November 1972. The session was produced by John Peel.

Live Performances: 1972/3. The song was performed live on the *Foxtrot* tour before disappearing from the set.

Live Recordings: A recording (9:14) from the De Montfort Hall, Leicester, on 25 February 1973, produced by John Burns and the band, was included on the 1973 album *Genesis Live*.

[36] CAN-UTILITY AND THE COASTLINERS

Band Credit: Tony Banks/Phil Collins/Peter Gabriel/Steve Hackett/Mike Rutherford
Music: Tony Banks/Steve Hackett
Lyrics: Steve Hackett
Length: 5:46
Tony Banks—Organ, Mellotron; **Phil Collins**—Drums, Backing Vocals; **Peter Gabriel**—Lead Vocals, Flute, Oboe, Percussion, Tambourine, Bass Drum; **Steve Hackett**—Guitar, Acoustic Guitar; **Mike Rutherford**—Acoustic Guitar, Bass, Bass Pedals

Recorded at Island Studios, London, England, August–September 1972.
Producer: David Hitchcock and Genesis. Engineer: John Burns.
2008 Remix/Remaster Release:
Mixed at The Farm, Surrey 2005/2006.
5.1 Surround sound and stereo mixes by Nick Davis. Assisted by Tom Mitchell.
UK Release: 6 October 1972. (LP: *Foxtrot*)
U.S. Release: November 1972. (LP: *Foxtrot*)

The working title for this song was the less inspired "Bye-Bye Johnny" and it was originally conceived as a piano led piece by Banks. Hackett later added the verse via an acoustic guitar arrangement and Banks swapped to Mellotron as the pair further refined the song, creating a much stronger overall sound. The song was honed on the road and later joined with another section which emerged from one of the band's jam sessions. The opening is built around Hackett and Rutherford's acoustic 12-string guitars alongside Gabriel's flute, before the main section kicks in. The epic feel to the song is enhanced during the midsection by Banks' big lush Mellotron chords, with the rising harmonies and symphonic sound prodded along by Rutherford's resonant bass pedals.

Hackett's lyrics tell the tale of old King Canute and his inability to hold back the tide as he orders the sea to retreat. He recalled, "I was looking for poetical lyrics and the idea of not being deceived by flattery, along with waves of the sea being described with huge waves of sound and bass pedal like a tolling bell."[13] The song's dramatic moments are accentuated by its dynamic instrumental surges underpinned by Rutherford's tasteful use of bass pedals freeing him up to play guitar. Collins' inventive drumming also adds to the drama, managing to punctuate the dramatic twists in the music. Banks would later cite the strong opening and closing sections, but pointed to the overall song being, "a bit fragmented."[14] It certainly crams a lot of ideas into a relatively short running time. As such it is less well remembered than other songs from this period, which is a shame as there is much to enjoy here.

Live Performances: 1971/2, 1972/3. The song was performed live in its early form (as "Bye Bye Johnny" and then later as "Rock My Baby") ahead of its eventual recording. It was then performed in its finished state on the early dates of the band's *Foxtrot* tour.

Live Recordings: No officially released live recording of the song exists.

[37] HORIZONS

Band Credit: Tony Banks/Phil Collins/Peter Gabriel/Steve Hackett/Mike Rutherford
Music: Steve Hackett
Length: 1:43
Steve Hackett—Acoustic Guitar
Recorded at Island Studios, London, England, August–September 1972.
Producer: David Hitchcock (credited), Bob Potter (uncredited) and Genesis. Engineer: John Burns.
2008 Remix/Remaster Release:
Mixed at The Farm, Surrey 2005/2006.
5.1 Surround sound and stereo mixes by Nick Davis. Assisted by Tom Mitchell.
UK Release: 6 October 1972. (LP: *Foxtrot*)
U.S. Release: November 1972. (LP: *Foxtrot*)

Hackett played this classically inspired solo piece on a 6-string Yamaha acoustic guitar in the early part of the recording sessions, while Bob Potter was still on board as producer. The recording was captured in full on the fourth take and was Potter's only real contribution to the finished album. It is a delightful acoustic interlude that is immaculately played. While it may be considered as filler, HORIZONS beautifully serves its purpose as a warm-up for the epic [38] SUPPER'S READY. It has since become regarded as something of a signature piece for the guitarist. The basis for the song was a Bach piece, "Prelude of Suite No. 1 in G major" for cello, played by Julian Bream as well as the renaissance composer William Byrd. Hackett adapted the theme and transposed the key to create the distinctive sound. He wrote the tune on a steel acoustic guitar and originally played it to the band on his electric guitar before reverting to its more natural nylon setting.

Live Performances: 1973/4 (occasionally). Hackett performed the instrumental as a solo spot on the *Selling England by the Pound* tour.

Live Recordings: No officially released live recording of the piece exists.

[38] SUPPER'S READY

I. Lover's Leap; II. The Guaranteed Eternal Sanctuary Man; III. Ikhnaton and Itsacon and Their Band of Merry Men; IV. How Dare I Be So Beautiful?; V. Willow Farm; VI. Apocalypse in 9/8 (co-starring the delicious talents of Gabble Ratchet); VII. As Sure as Eggs Is Eggs (Aching Men's Feet)

Band Credit: Tony Banks/Phil Collins/Peter Gabriel/Steve Hackett/Mike Rutherford
Music: Tony Banks/Phil Collins/Peter Gabriel/Steve Hackett/Mike Rutherford
Lyrics: Peter Gabriel
Length: 23:05
Tony Banks—Organ, Piano, Electric Piano, Mellotron, Acoustic Guitar, Backing Vocals; **Phil Collins**—Drums, Backing Vocals, Percussion, Tubular Bells, Whistle; **Peter Gabriel**—Lead & Backing Vocals, Flute, Oboe, Percussion, Tambourine, Bass Drum; **Steve Hackett**—Lead Guitar, Acoustic Guitar; **Mike Rutherford**—Rhythm Guitar, Acoustic Guitar, Bass, Bass Pedals, Cello, Backing Vocals
Recorded at Island Studios, London, England, August–September 1972.
Producer: David Hitchcock, Bob Potter (uncredited) and Genesis. Engineer: John Burns.
2008 Remix/Remaster Release:
Mixed at The Farm, Surrey 2005/2006.
5.1 Surround sound and stereo mixes by Nick Davis. Assisted by Tom Mitchell.
UK Release: 6 October 1972. (LP: *Foxtrot*)
U.S. Release: November 1972. (LP: *Foxtrot*)

In most fans' eyes SUPPER'S READY is the band's masterpiece and at 23 minutes it is the longest song they ever recorded and at the time was considered something of a gamble. Gabriel recalled, "There was some resistance in the band over the length of it, people were very nervous about it. We were taking risks with stuff that we knew was likely to be uncommercial, which wasn't guaranteed to get radio play and which was probably going to get knocked in reviews."[15] The band's long-standing friend and technical assistant Richard Macphail convinced them of its worthiness with his enthusiastic reaction when they played the song to him in its entirety. The fans lapped up the musical ebbs and flows through seven short pieces linked to form an epic suite and the piece has stood the test of time remarkably well.

The piece was largely written in the space of two weeks, mostly in the basement at Una Billings School of Dance, but not linked together until late in the recording process and it was only then that the band realized that they were onto a winner. The opening acoustic parts were recorded while Bob Potter was still on board as producer. The remainder of the first half of the song utilized David Hitchcock as producer and the second was overseen by engineer John Burns. Hackett recalled, "We edited it together like a film, although it was written as a whole."[16] When it got to writing the lyrics the band came up against time pressures, with Gabriel rushing to complete them as the backing tracks were being recorded.[17]

I. "Lover's Leap" (0:00–3:47)

The song's opening section is a gentle acoustic guitar piece written by Banks. He had come up with the music while the band were waiting in a gym in Cleethorpes to play a gig. The location created an atmospheric echo, which inspired Banks to get the sound he did. Hackett and Rutherford joined Banks to provide the arpeggiated 12-string guitar parts, while Banks also added a delicate electric piano sequence played on the Hohner pianet.

Gabriel's lyrical theme of bodily possession was inspired by an experience in the room at the top of his wife Jill's parents' house (which Gabriel had always found creepy). Jill had the feeling of being possessed and Gabriel thought he saw another face within her face. The couple had been spending time with producer John Anthony. Anthony had had a falling out with a girlfriend who was into magic. The feeling was Anthony's girlfriend's spirit had manifested itself in Jill, who began speaking in a strange voice and had to be restrained by Gabriel and Anthony. Jill was also receiving strange notes and messages at the time. Gabriel interprets the lyrics wonderfully with the three-part accompanying vocal harmonies being notable for missing the third note of the chord.

II. "The Guaranteed Eternal Sanctuary Man" (3:48–5:43)

Strong anthemic chords break the tranquility with Collins' drums kicking in and we realize that the band means business. This powerful and driving section had largely been composed by Banks a couple of years earlier, while he was still at Sussex University. Hackett contributes a soaring lead guitar lines over Banks' climbing organ chords and Rutherford's simple bass lines. Its strident theme would be repeated at a slower tempo with different lyrics for the song's "As Sure as Eggs Is Eggs" finale.

III. "Ikhnaton and Itsacon and Their Band of Merry Men" (5:44–9:42)

Children chant and a brief flute refrain from Gabriel follows before the song takes off with a stirring battle cry urged on by the unison of Banks' spiraling organ, Hackett's fluent tapping guitar lines on his new Gibson Les Paul, Rutherford's rhythmic guitar and Collins' propulsive drums. It makes for a musically exciting segment that showcased how far the band had progressed as musicians.

IV. "How Dare I Be So Beautiful?" (9:43–11:04)

A quiet reflective moment as we study the results of the battle and witness a solitary figure sitting by a pool. This was based on a guitar figure written by Banks, which echoed the feel of [25] THE MUSICAL BOX. The section was played in studio by Banks on piano, with the engineer removing the instruments attack creating a fading-in effect for each chord.[18] The title comes from a catchphrase used by their early champion and producer, Jonathan King, who according to Gabriel "used to look in the mirror and exclaim 'How dare I be so beautiful,' and I thought that was a great line to describe Narcissus in SUPPER'S READY."[19] Gabriel's line describing Narcissus' metamorphosis into a flower has entered into fan folklore.

V. "Willow Farm" (11:05–15:35)

Introduced by a heavy, jarring descending chord progression the song was developed in music hall-style by Gabriel on piano and was originally intended as a standalone song. Banks suggested the song be placed in the center of the suite to provide a deliberately stark contrast to the previous quiet and reflective section. Banks converted Gabriel's piano arrangement into a Mellotron/organ mix to produce the opening run-down. Gabriel excels with strong and absurdist *Monty Python*-inspired wordplay over a bouncy musical section, which stops abruptly as effects are used on Gabriel's voice to simulate a railway station change announcement. His vocals are then sped up as he delivers the madcap descriptive lyrics as bodies melt and rapidly change form. A tape speed problem, which caused the change in sections to drop down by part of a tone was rectified on the 2008 remix/remaster. The transition is a soft, moody musical interlude with Rutherford's bass pedal topped by Hackett's electric guitar and Banks' organ and Mellotron drone sounds. This leads into a delicate flute solo accompanied by acoustic guitars which then climbs into the dramatic "Guards of Magog" section that opens "Apocalypse in 9/8."

VI. "Apocalypse in 9/8" (co-starring the delicious talents of Gabble Ratchet)[20] (15:36–20:50)

The last two sections of the song form the epic finale which taken as a whole is among the best rock music ever written. The "Apocalypse in 9/8" segment was initially developed around Rutherford's rhythmic bass riff (a pattern using nine prodding beats to the bar played as 3+2+4). Banks, Rutherford and Collins improvised across the rhythm and Collins recalled shortly afterward, "It's the best thing we've done. It started off as a jam. Steve and Peter were away for some reason and Mike started playing this movement on bass pedals— totally abstract with no time signature at all. Then we tied it down and worked it out to a two-bar riff. I just knocked a beat out and it became a bar of nine."[21] Banks' blistering organ solo, initially a whimsical parody of Keith Emerson's playing style, increases in drama and intensity as the piece builds and rides over Collins and Rutherford's pounding 9/8 rhythmic phrases. The section was improvised over three bass notes (E, F sharp and B) enabling Banks to glide a solo across his lifting chord changes as the section progressed. Collins' skittering drum pattern is highly inventive as it plays around Rutherford's guitar and bass pedal rhythm and he later reflected, "I'm still immensely proud of the final recorded performance on the piece."[22] The final rise into the huge Mellotron chords, using the instrument's "three violins" tape setting, was originally intended to be accompanied by vocal harmonies, but Gabriel added the dramatic vocal entry to Banks' initial annoyance. However, the keyboard player very quickly realized how powerful the vocal was, "You get this massive dramatic C chord then Peter starts singing over the top. Initially I didn't want him spoiling my chords but then I realized how good it was. That's how you work as a group sometimes—you're fighting against each other, but the combination of those impulses produces something special."[23] Banks later noted, "The drums were in there playing heavily and it became such a big thing. And, I think particularly, the climax which occurs with the 'Apocalypse in 9/8,' which is a sort of extended keyboard solo that ends in massive chords with fantastic vocal performance from Peter, it still really works."[24] The piece then slows down again as the tension subsides and SUPPER'S READY enters its final phase…

VII. "As Sure as Eggs Is Eggs (Aching Men's Feet)"[25] (20:51–23:06)

The start of the final section reprises lyrics from "Lover's Leap" with Gabriel singing with increased intensity and a raw emotion. It is a beautifully anthemic melody that was thematically a slowed down reprise of the chord sequence for the earlier "The Guaranteed Eternal Sanctuary Man" section. The music is beautifully buttressed by Rutherford's deep bass pedals and Banks' staccato Mellotron brass simulation. Religious overtones are present with the depiction of the triumph of good over evil and are also cast throughout Gabriel's lyrics. They contain a direct reference to the biblical *Revelation 19:17* as Gabriel offers up his own reworking of these words from the Bible (*There's an angel standing in the sun. He cried with a loud voice, saying to all the birds that fly in the sky, Come! Be gathered together to the great supper of Go*) for the closing segment. Gabriel literally screams out the last line of the song from the bottom of his very soul, wringing every last drop of joyous elation, as he leads his children to the "New Jerusalem." As the song fades out its grand musical gestures it brings this masterpiece to a fittingly uplifting conclusion.

There is no doubt among most Genesis fans that SUPPER'S READY represents the band's creative high point. The band themselves knew they had taken a risk and succeeded beyond their expectations. Hackett likened the piece to "Elgar on acid"[26] believing at the time that none of their audience would like it. He was wrong, the band's audience lapped it up. Banks noted five years after the song had been recorded, "It's a number of contrasts. It's the loud against the soft and the very romantic against the incredibly stupid. And by doing that you make the romantic more romantic and the stupid more stupid."[27] It is these contrasts that give the song its epic feel and unpredictable quality. The pieces are perfectly placed to maximize the drama, which reaches its peak with "Apocalypse in 9/8" and "As Sure as Eggs Is Eggs."

Commenting on the song over 45 years later, Banks said, "I think if you've got the patience—unfortunately, not many people have the patience anymore—but if you've got the patience I think it's still rewarding now."[28] Collins too noted, "A lot of Genesis 'heads' regard it as our magnum opus, and I'd go along with that. It's greater than the sum of its parts, though some of those parts are brilliant, notably 'Apocalypse in 9/8 (co-starring the delicious talents of Gabble Ratchet)' and 'As Sure as Eggs Is Eggs (Aching Men's Feet).'"[29] Gabriel remains proud of the song placing it alongside the later double-album *The Lamb Lies Down on Broadway* as "one of the things I like best looking backwards."[30]

From a technical viewpoint, the band had been worried that SUPPER'S READY would not fit onto one side of the album due to its length—the longer the run time the shallower the grooves employed on the vinyl. The original rather abrupt fade at the end of "As Sure as Eggs Is Eggs" is evidence of their attempt to keep the running time as tight as possible. A more gradual fade was employed for the 2008 remix for CD.

Single Release: The "Willow Farm" section (2:57) was used as the B-side to the [33] WATCHER OF THE SKIES single released in the U.S. in March 1973 as well as Italy, Germany and New Zealand.

Live Performances: 1972/3, 1973/4, 1976, 1977, 1978 (closing section, once), 1982, 1986/7

6. Studio Album #4: Foxtrot

(closing section, occasionally), 1998 ("Lover's Leap"). Despite their initial nervousness, Genesis knew they had a song that would form the centerpiece of their live set for years to come. The song was condensed to its final two sections for the 1978 tour and these sections were later incorporated into a medley including [52] IN THE CAGE and [87] ...IN THAT QUIET EARTH in 1986/7 for the U.S. leg. The song was performed in its entirety for the last time on the 1982 "Encore" tour and again at the "Six of the Best" concert in which they reunited with Gabriel to raise funds for his WOMAD charity. The "Lover's Leap" opening was performed on the band's 1998 tour during the acoustic section of the show.

Live Recordings: (1) A performance (26:31), including Gabriel's introduction, from the Rainbow Theatre, London, on 20 October 1973 can be found on the *Genesis Archives 1967–1975* box set as well as the *Live at the Rainbow* disc (23:42) on the *Genesis 1973–2007 Live* box set. For these versions Gabriel recorded some of his vocals in the late 1990s, satisfying himself but annoying the purists. It was explained that this was due to technical difficulties with capturing Gabriel's voice due to his costumes causing problems for his microphone. But the number of edits made suggest this was also an artistic decision. The recording was engineered by John Burns and produced by the band with Nick Davis handling the remix.

(2) A further live recording (24:41) from Palais des Sports, Paris, taken from performances between 11–14 June 1977, with Collins providing splendid lead vocals, appeared on *Seconds Out*. This version used different sections from different evenings to get the best overall performance. The lineup here is Banks, Collins, Hackett and Rutherford, augmented by Chester Thompson (drums). The recording was produced and engineered by David Hentschel, with the band also credited as producers. Fans are split on whether they prefer Collins' vocal performance or Gabriel's original. Both are superb interpretations stamped with the character of the singer.

(3) A 1997 live acoustic recording of "Lover's Leap" (2:20) from the album launch event for ...*Calling All Stations*... at Cape Canaveral, Florida, on 28 August 1997 was included on the December 1997 CD single release of [170] SHIPWRECKED. The lineup for this recording was the final lineup of Banks, Rutherford and Ray Wilson. Nick Davis was engineer and co-produced with Banks and Rutherford.

* * *

Released on 6 October 1972, *Foxtrot* finally earned Genesis the recognition they had sought at home, by entering the UK Album chart at #12. The album saw the band finally fulfill their potential, both as writers and musicians. Producing songs as intelligent and diverse as this set in their early twenties demonstrated the group's rapidly growing writing skills and early maturity. They had also developed enormously as musicians through incessant touring and much of that energy was captured here, although again the main drawback was the production. Nick Davis' 2008 remix is therefore recommended as the best version of this album as it cleans up the sound and provides a stronger mix.

Foxtrot was also a huge success in Italy, where it topped the charts and earned the band a strong following that has survived throughout their career. Upon hearing the album Tony Stratton-Smith was moved to tears. [38] SUPPER'S READY convinced Stratton-Smith that the album was the one that would make Genesis' career and helped remove any lingering doubts he had about the band. Peter Gabriel' lyrics were becoming increasingly inventive and surreal, with satirical stories such as [35] GET 'EM OUT BY FRIDAY and "Willow Farm" from [38] SUPPER'S READY contrasting nicely with Banks and Rutherford's more fantastical and romantic lyrics for [33] WATCHER OF THE SKIES and

[36] Can-Utility and the Coastliners. Collins provided some exceptional creative drumming, particularly during the "Apocalypse in 9/8" section of [38] Supper's Ready. Steve Hackett was also advancing his skills as lead guitarist and contributed some assured electric and acoustic guitar work, overcoming the crisis of confidence he had going into the recording. His [37] Horizons was also an affecting little instrumental piece, which contrasted beautifully with the songs surrounding it. Collins and Hackett had given the band the added dimension it had needed on *Nursery Cryme* and with *Foxtrot* the five-piece unit had truly clicked into place.

The triumph, of course, was [38] Supper's Ready. This suite of linked short songs proved to be the perfect summation of the band's writing style with its meandering structure, swinging dynamics, moments of tension and drama and its brilliant instrumental passages. Banks, Collins and Rutherford had begun to write more closely as a unit, developing rhythmic and harmonic ideas—most notably on the "Apocalypse in 9/8" section. Gabriel's apocalyptic vision was well served by the band, particularly during the song's closing sections where the epic scope really comes through and Gabriel delivers his vocals with conviction and panache. The only relatively weak tune on the album was [34] Time Table, which seemed like a return to earlier, gentler days. The song did contain some nice piano melodies from Banks, but it remains largely forgettable in this otherwise very strong set of songs.

The cover for the album was again painted by Paul Whitehead. In his painting Whitehead depicted interspersed literal interpretations of songs from the album, depicting the Four Horsemen of the Apocalypse as well as the six saintly shrouded men and the seventh in front holding a cross high in his hands. There was also a group of hunters sat on their horses with hounds held back by the sea as a woman in a red dress and a fox's head stands on top of some broken ice.[31] In the distance amidst the hills is a tower block of flats ready for demolition. Whitehead later remembered the other references on the cover, "The band and I also felt it important to include images that reflected the state of the world and the planet at the time. In the water in the upper right-hand corner, you'll see a U.S. nuclear submarine, which represents the presence of the U.S. Naval Fleet off the coast of Scotland. Many people in Britain, including members of Parliament, were unhappy with the fact that the U.S. maintained a fleet of nuclear subs 'only 30 minutes by missile' away from the Soviet Union. The 2 dolphins and fish rising up from the ocean were representing the marked increases in water pollution (caused by the nuclear subs?) and its effects on all living things, while the man with his head buried in the sand (to the left of the Saints) represented 'the music business' who had yet to treat the band and its music with much respect."[32] The lack of proper perspective adds to the surreal feel, but it all comes across as a little heavy-handed by the artist. None of the band were entirely happy with the cover and it proved to be Whitehead's last for the band.

The band members were much more positive about *Foxtrot* than they had been about *Nursery Cryme*. Each felt that [38] Supper's Ready was by far the best thing they had recorded to date. Banks noted, "*Foxtrot* is just a really exciting album, full of melodrama, with great ups and downs and contrasts."[33]

Critics were also seeing the strength of the material. Jerry Gilbert in his review for *Sounds* noted, "Lyrically and musically *Foxtrot* comes across as a total mind trip, with imagination and musical ideas being allowed to run wild and in turn stretch the imagination of the listener."[34] *Billboard* believed, "Genesis should begin to make US headway with this interesting set."[35] With this in mind, Genesis indeed embarked on their first U.S. tour just before Christmas 1972, determined to crack the market.

The band further cemented its European success with another tour, which included a gig in front of 18,000 fans at the Rome Palasport. Their UK dates were the first in which they topped the bill on their home territory. The show at the Rainbow Theatre in London, on 9 February 1973, is regarded by many, including the band, as a highlight. During the tour Peter began to experiment with costumes. Initially his idea was to have someone walk around the theater dressed in a red dress and foxes head, like the character in Paul Whitehead's painting. He began to plan this with Genesis' booking manager, Paul Conroy. In the end Gabriel decided to take matters into his own hands. The sight of Gabriel himself wearing the fox's head and a red dress as he wandered back on stage for the closing sections of [25] THE MUSICAL BOX managed to provoke a stunned reaction from the Irish audience at a boxing ring in Dublin on 28 September 1972.[36] To avoid any confrontation with the rest of the band, he had kept his plans secret and his bandmates were as surprised as the audience. When Gabriel was pictured in costume on the front page of *Melody Maker* the following week, the band realized they were onto something good and it helped significantly increase their income for subsequent gigs. Gabriel's costumes would become more and more elaborate over the next couple of years and ultimately become a bone of contention within the band.

* * *

Genesis followed their UK tour with dates in France, Italy and Germany before a second visit to the U.S. in the middle of 1973. They also took in dates in Canada for the first time. With a heavy touring schedule and a lack of new material, the band followed *Foxtrot* with their first live album, simply titled *Genesis Live*. It was released on 20 July 1973 as a holding operation due to the slow writing process that would cause delays with their follow-up, *Selling England by the Pound*, and as an offering to fans following the cancellation of a concert at the Empire Pool, Wembley on 25 May.[37] It was suggested to the band that the album be drawn from tapes recorded by King Biscuit for their American radio show. The recordings were taken from two concerts—The Free Trade Hall, Manchester, from 24 February 1973 and De Montfort Hall, Leicester, two days later. However, the band had never intended for the tapes to be used for a commercial release and they had to be persuaded by Charisma that the move would help build the band's reputation due to their strong live following and powerful performances.

An initial test pressing is reputed to have been carried out as a three-sided album including [38] SUPPER'S READY and Gabriel's in-between song banter and stories but no actual copies of this pressing have ever surfaced. As Charisma was keen to market the album as a low-cost single LP, and the band were also unhappy with the live version of SUPPER'S READY from those shows, the epic track was omitted from the final pressing.

The album proved to be a good representation of the band's live show.[38] Genesis had gained a growing reputation as a strong live act and the album confirms that. Although it omitted other staple numbers such as [31] FOUNTAIN OF SALMACIS, the songs that were selected were among their strongest live items. [25] THE MUSICAL BOX and [27] RETURN OF THE GIANT HOGWEED seemed to find an extra dimension in the live arena. [24] THE KNIFE provided a powerful climax. Collins later remarked that the band had always felt they sounded better on record until the tapes of this album convinced them otherwise. Genesis was knitting together well as a unit with a driving rhythm section, a gifted lead guitarist, one of the best keyboardists in rock and an enigmatic vocalist in Gabriel. Unfortunately, the disc cannot convey the costumes and staging, which added to the live experience, but it still serves as an excellent representation of their stage show at the time.

[39] Twilight Alehouse

Band Credit: Tony Banks/Phil Collins/Peter Gabriel/Steve Hackett/Mike Rutherford
Music: Tony Banks/Peter Gabriel/Anthony Phillips/Mike Rutherford
Lyrics: Steve Hackett
Length: 7:48
Tony Banks—Organ, Mellotron; **Phil Collins**—Drums, Backing Vocals, Percussion; **Peter Gabriel**—Lead & Backing Vocals, Flute, Bass Drum, Percussion; **Steve Hackett**—Guitar; **Mike Rutherford**—Acoustic Guitar
Recorded at Island Studios, London, England, August–September 1972.
Produced by Genesis. Engineered by John Burns.
2008 Remix/Remaster Release:
Mixed at The Farm, Surrey 2005/2006.
5.1 Surround sound and stereo mixes by Nick Davis. Assisted by Tom Mitchell.
UK Release: October 1973. (Flexi-disc single: *ZigZag* Magazine #35. Charisma). 22 February 1974. (B-side single b/w [41] I Know What I Like [In Your Wardrobe]. Charisma. CB 224)
U.S. Release: March 1974. (B-side single b/w [41] I Know What I Like [In Your Wardrobe]. Atlantic/Charisma. FC-26002)

Peter Gabriel pleads the case for alcoholic beverage on the chorus of this fragmented song. The song's origin dates to early 1969 and it was fully developed while Anthony Phillips was still in the band. A gentle acoustic section with distant organ over a pounding bass drum provides the introduction to this song about an alcoholic. The band then launches into a chorus focused around the organ/guitar dynamic, which attempts to capture a bluesy feel. Hackett referenced this in a later interview saying, "It had an interesting verse and a chorus that really aspired to be a Blues but I don't think the band were sufficiently prepared at that point to let their hair down … and so I didn't come up with any Blues licks for them! (Laughter). I could have played all over it. I could have played the harmonica on it and done it justice and I don't even have a copy of that song."[39] The song rotates around these sections in a slow and repetitive way. Gabriel gets to contribute a midsong flute solo over a long meandering instrumental section. The arrangement feels a little cluttered through its many undulating instrumental passages and its urgent chorus. Collins provides some excellent drumming and his use of bass drum disguises the lack of a bass guitar, while his fills accentuate Banks' keyboard lines and the stabbing guitar rhythm through the long playout—the latter being less structured than most of the band's instrumental offerings. Ultimately, Twilight Alehouse comes across as a failed experiment.

This recording was later included on the *Genesis Archive 1967–75* box set and again in remixed form on the *Extra Tracks* CD in the *Genesis 1970–1975* box set.

Single Release: Twilight Alehouse was released as a free flexi-disc with *Zig Zag* magazine (Issue #35, Vol. 3, Number 11) in October 1973 as well as with souvenir programs during the band's tour the same month. It was later released as the B-side to the [41] I Know What I Like single in February 1974. Remaining copies were gifted to the first thousand members of the fan club Genesis Information in 1976.

BBC Session: A recording (7:58) was made for a BBC *Top Gear* session produced by John Peel and recorded at Studio T1, Transcription Service, Kensington House, Shepherd's Bush on 25 September 1972. It was first broadcast on 9 November 1972.

Live Performances: 1969/70, 1970/1, 1971/2, 1972/3. The song was featured in the band's live set for their first official gig at Brunel University in Acton, London on 1 November 1969 and was a regular feature in their live set during their early dates.

Live Recordings: No official live recording of the song has been released.

7

Studio Album #5:
Selling England by the Pound

UK Release: 13 October 1973. LP. Charisma. CAS 1074.
U.S. Release: 12 November 1973. LP. Atlantic. SD 19277.
Remix/Remaster Release:
UK Release: 10 November 2008. CD/SACD/DVD. Virgin/Charisma. CASCDR 1074.
U.S. Release: 11 November 2008. CD/DVD. Atlantic/Rhino. R2 513943.

Album Tracks

[40] DANCING WITH THE MOONLIT KNIGHT
[41] I KNOW WHAT I LIKE (IN YOUR WARDROBE)
[42] FIRTH OF FIFTH
[43] MORE FOOL ME
[44] THE BATTLE OF EPPING FOREST
[45] AFTER THE ORDEAL
[46] THE CINEMA SHOW
[47] AISLE OF PLENTY

Genesis struggled with the writing sessions for their next album, which took place at a doctor's big old house near Chessington Zoo in Surrey. Being in a residential area, the band did not endear themselves to their neighbors as Hackett recalls, "we used to get these irate neighbors who used to come over and say 'you're playing too loud! What do you think you are doing; you are disturbing the livestock!' It was one of those sort of things basically full of interruptions really."[1] As a result the sessions became very edgy as tensions developed within the band. Banks remembered, "We all thought about leaving the band, almost every week, in different ways. That was one of the worst times."[2]

The sessions were the first for which Genesis had set specific time aside to write an album from scratch. They were looking to compose via jams and improvisation rather than developing pre-existing ideas and joining pieces together. The brief was for the band to focus on their Englishness as a response to the increasing popularity of American music. After a promising start, inspiration seemed to desert them and they struggled to get their improvisations to produce enough material to develop into finished songs. Collins recalled, "We seemed to be spreading ourselves all over the place and it wasn't really coming together that well."[3] Banks also acknowledged the problems, "we hit a period when nothing seemed to happen; we just went over the same bits again."[4] Rutherford pointed out that the band had written much of the material they ultimately used in the first two weeks, stating the three month window they had allowed themselves meant they used the time to keep tinkering with it.

Steve Hackett   Mike Rutherford   Peter Gabriel   Phil Collins   Tony Banks

Genesis in 1973. From left, Steve Hackett, Mike Rutherford, Peter Gabriel, Phil Collins and Tony Banks. Atlantic promotional photograph used for *Genesis Archive 1967–1975* (courtesy Mark Kenyon/The Genesis Archive).

Collins had become increasingly frustrated with the writing difficulties and lack of focus. For a time, it was feared he might leave the band as he had been dabbling with a bunch of session musicians under the name of Zox and the Radar Boys playing pub gigs. Collins had been listening to the jazz fusion band Mahavishnu Orchestra a lot during this period, which encouraged him to find like-minded players. Some of these musicians joined Collins in eventually forming Brand X. During the summer of 1973, Collins also teamed up with Rutherford and Anthony Phillips to help the band's former lead guitarist with a demo recording of his song "Take this Heart." Collins sang the lead vocal. The three musicians then looked at the possibility of recording a further demo of "Silver Song," a song Phillips had written in 1969 for the band's then drummer John Silver as he left the band. Charisma liked the demo and Phillips, Rutherford and Collins later recorded the song at Island Studios in October 1973 as a prospective single, with "Only Your Love" as its intended B-side. It was intended to market it as a Phil Collins single. In an interview with Peter Harvey of *Record Mirror*, Collins remarked, "I don't see any great success for it, but if it gets some nice reviews I might do an album of my own."[5] Ultimately, the single was never released (allegedly due to pressures exerted by Charisma) but both songs were later included on the 2015 deluxe release of Anthony Phillips' *The Geese and the Ghost* album.

Hackett was also having personal problems following a split with his first wife. This reduced him to largely offer guitar parts rather than any partly or completed pieces. Banks, meanwhile, had obtained the smaller Mellotron M400 and for the first time would work with a synthesizer using the ARP pro-soloist. This helped to broaden the band's sound and was particularly effective on his solo for [46] THE CINEMA SHOW. The band finally managed to hone down the material into a collection of songs to record. Not all material written during the sessions was used. Some of it was taken away by band members and used in later solo material. For example, a Mike Rutherford guitar piece would later become the end section of a song called "Compression" he recorded during his *Smallcreep's Day* sessions in 1979. Steve Hackett finished a song he had started writing with Peter Gabriel and used it on his *Genesis Revisited* album under the title "Déjà vu," with vocals provided by Paul Carrack. Hackett later commented, "There's something particularly stirring about the melody that we originally came up with on that."[6]

After months of writing, arranging and arranging their new songs Genesis finally entered Island Studios to record their new album in August 1973. They had quickly settled on John Burns as producer following his excellent engineering work on *Foxtrot*. Burns was also sympathetic to the band's music and was therefore a good choice. There were arguments in the band about what material should be included on the album. None of the band was willing to compromise and it ultimately led to a very long album at just shy of fifty-four minutes.

[40] DANCING WITH THE MOONLIT KNIGHT

Band Credit: Tony Banks/Phil Collins/Peter Gabriel/Steve Hackett/Mike Rutherford
Music: Tony Banks/Phil Collins/Peter Gabriel/Steve Hackett/Mike Rutherford
Lyrics: Peter Gabriel
Length: 8:03
Tony Banks—Organ, Mellotron, Acoustic Guitar; **Phil Collins**—Drums, Backing Vocals, Percussion; **Peter Gabriel**—Lead Vocals, Oboe, Percussion; **Steve Hackett**—Lead Guitar, Acoustic Guitar; **Mike Rutherford**—Rhythm Guitar, Acoustic Guitar, Bass
Recorded at Island Studios, London, England, August 1973.
Producer: John Burns and Genesis. Engineer: John Burns. Assistant Engineer: Rhett Davis.
2008 Remix/Remaster Release:
Mixed at The Farm, Surrey 2005/2006.
5.1 Surround sound and stereo mixes by Nick Davis. Assisted by Tom Mitchell.
UK Release: 13 October 1973. (LP: *Selling England by the Pound*)
U.S. Release: 12 November 1973. (LP: *Selling England by the Pound*)

"DANCING WITH THE MOONLIT KNIGHT opens with something that alludes to Scottish plainsong and ends up with fusion, crazy time signatures.... English hymns and the occasional big band rhythm—you've got what Genesis was all about."[7] These words from Steve Hackett sum up the opening track of *Selling England by the Pound*. Gabriel's a capella vocal, which leads into a song about Britannia and her values, is certainly an unusual and memorable way to open a rock album. The initial delicate acoustic textures are a throwback to the band's earlier albums. The song builds toward a propulsive and largely instrumental midsection where Hackett, who would later acknowledge this as his favorite Genesis song, provides some creative lead guitar incorporating both his tapping and sweep-picking techniques over a racing rhythm from Collins and Rutherford. Banks utilizes the choral sounds of his new Mellotron M400 to good effect and adds low rumbling synth noises followed by some deft organ chords. The solo exits via a powerful riff over which Gabriel contributes strong vocals where he is pushing at times for an R&B approach. His lyrics—a commentary on contemporary England—are laced with domestic brand references. The band had worked on this section of the song for some considerable time, constantly refining it. This frustrated Banks and Collins in particular. The song plays out through a floating and almost hypnotic 12-string guitar arpeggio from Rutherford, which is complemented by Banks' Mellotron and Gabriel's understated duck noises using an Oboe reed.[8] The melody is reprised at the end of [46] THE CINEMA SHOW as it leads into [47] AISLE OF PLENTY.

The words "Paper late" were sung repeatedly by Collins during the band's soundchecks on the 1980 *Duke* tour. The band would later develop the phrasing into a song—titled [131] PAPERLATE—to be recorded during the *Abacab* sessions.

Live Performances: 1973/4, 1978 (rarely), 1980 (opening section), 1982 (excerpt, "Six of the Best" show), 1998 (opening section). The song was played live by the band throughout the tour that followed. It was also performed occasionally on their 1978 tour, segueing into the closing section of [25] THE MUSICAL BOX, with Collins providing lead vocals. The opening section was used on the 1980 tour where it segued into [57] CARPET CRAWLERS. Gabriel would perform the song again with the band at the "Six of the Best" show at Milton Keynes in 1982. Ray Wilson added his vocal interpretation to this section as part of the band's acoustic break during their 1998 tour.

Live Recordings: (1) A performance (7:05) from the Rainbow Theatre in London on 20 October 1973 can be found on *Genesis Archives 1967–1975* and with Gabriel's introduction to the audience on the *Live at the Rainbow* bonus disc in the *Genesis 1973–2007 Live* box sets (9:05). Gabriel controversially recorded some of his vocals in the mid- to late 1990s for these releases. The recording was engineered by John Burns using the Rolling Stone mobile studio and produced by the band, with Nick Davis handling the remix.

(2) An acoustic recording of the song's opening section (2:06) from their 13 December 1997 performance at RTL Studios, Paris, can be found on the [172] NOT ABOUT US CD single. The lineup was Banks, Rutherford and Wilson, augmented by Anthony Drennan (guitar). The song was recorded by Christopher Hedge and mixed by Nick Davis.

[41] I KNOW WHAT I LIKE (IN YOUR WARDROBE)

Band Credit: Tony Banks/Phil Collins/Peter Gabriel/Steve Hackett/Mike Rutherford
Music: Tony Banks/Phil Collins/Peter Gabriel/Steve Hackett/Mike Rutherford
Lyrics: Peter Gabriel
Length: 4:10
Tony Banks—Organ, Synthesizer, Mellotron; **Phil Collins**—Drums, Percussion, Harmony Vocals; **Peter Gabriel**—Lead Vocals, Flute, Percussion; **Steve Hackett**—Guitar; **Mike Rutherford**—Bass, Electric Sitar
Recorded at Island Studios, London, England, August 1973.
Producer: John Burns and Genesis. Engineer: John Burns. Assistant Engineer: Rhett Davis.
2008 Remix/Remaster Release:
Mixed at The Farm, Surrey 2005/2006.
5.1 Surround sound and stereo mixes by Nick Davis. Assisted by Tom Mitchell.
UK Release: 13 October 1973. (LP: *Selling England by the Pound*)
U.S. Release: 12 November 1973. (LP: *Selling England by the Pound*)
UK Single Release: 22 February 1974.[9] (A-side single b/w [39] TWILIGHT ALEHOUSE. Charisma. CB 224)
U.S. Single Release: March 1974. (A-side single b/w [39] TWILIGHT ALEHOUSE. Atlantic/Charisma. FC-26002)

A low rumbling Mellotron drone from Banks gives this song its avant-garde opening and close. Gabriel's addition of a talking drum over the introduction proved to be the first evidence of his interest in African music. Co-producer/engineer John Burns describes how the opening section was created: "They just all made noises and weird things and we put it all together with that 'R-A-A-O-A-R!' opening. Then I took a talking drum in that I brought back from Nigeria, because I had just come from Nigeria after working with Ginger Baker, and Peter played that on the song. That's the 'D-O-O-N! D-O-O-N!' sound you hear in the beginning of I Know What I Like, but Peter played it completely differently than the Africans. He played it between his knees and squeezed his legs together. It really gave it some character."[10]

The surreal feel is carried over into Gabriel's witty lyrics, which came late in the writing process. The theme was influenced by discussions with Betty Swanwick about her painting *The Dream*, which was later adapted for the cover of the album (with added lawn mower). The scene Gabriel paints with his lyrics is populated by strange characters feeding off the British self-consciousness, focusing on a young groundsman who is more than happy to just mow the grass. Structurally simple, the song is very melodic—notably in its sing-along chorus. It had developed from a guitar riff by Hackett, which he and Collins had worked on during the *Foxtrot* rehearsals at Una Billings, with the guitarist using a sitar-guitar played through his Leslie cabinet. At that time, the rest of the band were not keen to use it, believing the simple melody to be too close to the sound of The Beatles. As Hackett and Collins persisted through to the latest writing sessions, Banks added his fuzz electric piano and organ which gave the song new lease of life. He also added the basis for the chorus. While Gabriel was never comfortable with the song, due to its relative simplicity, he knew the audience would like it. Gabriel and Collins worked on the vocal melody basing it on the part Hackett had developed on guitar and the pair sang the chorus as a duet. Banks' proprietorial nature was in evidence when, while he was away from the studio, the rest of the band had an idea for an outro and Gabriel recorded the part on the Mellotron. On his return Banks took the band to task over them using his keyboard set-up.

The resultant song was the most commercial the band had recorded to date and became an obvious choice for single release. Its sing-along chorus hook was infectious enough to give the band their first minor hit.

Single Release: A UK promo single of the song was released on 25 January 1974 alongside a press ad that stated this was the intended single release date, but the retail release was delayed due to a vinyl shortage in the industry caused by the oil crisis. The song (edited to 3:35, removing the droned intro) was finally released as a single in late February 1974. The single eventually reached #21 in the UK charts over a month later spending seven weeks in the Top 50. The band were on tour in America when they heard of its success. The song was played on *Top of the Pops* with the all-female in-house dancers Pan's People performing a routine after the band refused to authorize use of footage from a live performance filmed at Shepperton Studios—much to the annoyance of Tony Stratton-Smith, who saw it as a great promotional opportunity. Hackett too had been frustrated that the song wasn't released as a single earlier, feeling its chance to make a significant impression had gone with it already being available on the album. When the song hit the charts, Gabriel was quick to point out, "I don't think this single is the best track for people who haven't heard us before, but it's served its purpose. It's just not representative of the kind of things people like the most."[11] The single was also released in several European countries as well as the U.S. (where it was further edited to 2:51 and distributed by Atlantic Records), Japan and New Zealand.

Live Performances: 1973/4, 1976, 1977, 1978, 1980, 1981, 1982, 1992, 2007. I Know What I Like became a live favorite and was performed on most of the band tours that followed—the exceptions being their 1984, 1986/7 and 1998 tours. On the *Selling England* tour Gabriel wore a military helmet and clamped some straw between his lips as he mimed the pushing along of a heavy lawnmower by the groundsman. Gabriel and Collins later sang the song as a duet during the encore at the 1982 Milton Keynes reunion concert, under the banner "Six of the Best," with Hackett joining the band on stage at this point in the show. During Collins' tenure as singer, the band would add elements of other songs to flesh out an instrumental section to allow Collins to add his own unique tambourine dance and audience interplay.

Live Recordings: (1) A performance of the song (5:36) from the Rainbow Theatre in London on 20 October 1973 can be found on both *Genesis Archive 1967–75* and *Genesis 1973–2007 Live* box sets (5:23). This is the only officially released live recording with Gabriel on lead vocals. John Burns engineered and the band produced with Nick Davis handling the remix.

(2) Collins' vocal rendition can first be heard on a recording (8:45) from Pavillon de Paris, Paris, between 11–14 June 1977 on *Seconds Out*. This version includes added interaction between Collins and the audience along with a brief melody reprise from [22] STAGNATION. The lineup here was Banks, Collins, Hackett and Rutherford, augmented by Chester Thompson (drums). The recording was engineered and produced by David Hentschel with the band sharing production credit.

(3) In 1992 the song was incorporated into the "Old Medley." A recording (19:32) of the medley from the Niedersachsenstadion, Hanover, Germany, show on 10 July appeared on *The Way We Walk—Volume Two: The Longs*. It would later be remixed and appear on the sequenced double *The Way We Walk* (19:43) as part of the *Genesis Live 1973–2007* box set. The lineup was Banks, Collins and Rutherford, augmented by Daryl Stuermer (guitar) and Thompson (drums). The recording was produced by Nick Davis, Robert Colby and the band.

(4) A recording (6:45) from the 2007 reunion tour concert at Old Trafford, Manchester, on 7 July was included on *Live Over Europe 2007*, which was released later the same year. The lineup was again Banks, Collins and Rutherford, augmented by Stuermer and Thompson. The recording was made by Bernard Natier and produced by Nick Davis.

[42] FIRTH OF FIFTH

Band Credit: Tony Banks/Phil Collins/Peter Gabriel/Steve Hackett/Mike Rutherford
Music: Tony Banks
Lyrics: Tony Banks/Mike Rutherford
Length: 9:35
Tony Banks—Organ, Piano, Synthesizer, Mellotron, Acoustic Guitar; **Phil Collins**—Drums, Backing Vocals, Percussion; **Peter Gabriel**—Lead Vocals, Flute; **Steve Hackett**—Lead Guitar; **Mike Rutherford**—Rhythm Guitar, Bass, Bass Pedals
Producer: John Burns and Genesis. Engineer: John Burns. Assistant Engineer: Rhett Davis.
2008 Remix/Remaster Release:
Mixed at The Farm, Surrey 2005/2006.
5.1 Surround sound and stereo mixes by Nick Davis. Assisted by Tom Mitchell.
UK Release: 13 October 1973. (LP: *Selling England by the Pound*)
U.S. Release: 12 November 1973. (LP: *Selling England by the Pound*)

FIRTH OF FIFTH was developed from a section of another earlier piece the band had been working on titled "The Block." It was built from three segments written by Banks before the *Foxtrot* sessions. The pieces had originally been dropped as Collins found them difficult to play along to. When Banks introduced them for the new album's writing and rehearsal sessions, he had the idea of developing them into three separate songs. Rutherford suggested linking them together and the group arranged the pieces into a whole song.

The song opens with a classical-styled grand piano solo from Banks, which moves in and out of complex time signatures and leads into a sequence of powerful descending chords as the rest of the band join in. Over this, Gabriel sings Banks and Rutherford's romantic lyrics about a Scottish river,[12] which are designed to be a metaphor for life as Banks explained, "Mike and I wrote the lyrics together. We were a bit stuck for an idea for a lyric. We started off writing very simply about a river, then the river became a bit more ... a river of life.... You know, it's quite allegorical and I don't think it's our most successful lyric."[13]

FIRTH OF FIFTH really comes to life during its elongated instrumental midsection (3:08 to 8:34). Banks used a gently undulating melody for Gabriel's flute and his piano before transferring it to Hackett's guitar. This helped to heighten the drama by building momentum in the melody through the stepped move from acoustic to electric sound. Banks had originally planned this section as a piano piece, but this changed once Hackett had played the section with treatment to his guitar as he explained: "There was the Echoplex, so suddenly I'm working with an echo unit. And it happened to work particularly well with the pedal I had and the fuzz box I had back in the day. Fortunately, most of the time it would feed back on a high F sharp when I hit that, so it sounded as if the notes went on forever. And it was a particularly good melody played on guitar. Played on piano, it sounds like a French Impressionistic thing. But when played on guitar, it's got something Egyptian or Middle Eastern. Once I started playing it on guitar, Tony was like, 'Oh, let's do it as a band. Let's do it with big keyboards.'"[14] The result is one of the strongest instrumental segments the band ever recorded. Hackett's solo is the most expressive he produced for the band and Banks' symphonic Mellotron chords glide gloriously over the guitarist's fluid wailing lead. Banks achieved the thick string sound by applying split echoes to the Mellotron and the result produced an extremely effective swell. Collins and Rutherford provide a driving rhythm section, further prompted by Rutherford's ground shaking bass pedals.

Inspiration for the song came from an unexpected source as Banks explained years later: "James Brown, Otis Redding and Ben E. King were all really influential on us. I put this particular track [James Brown's 'It's a Man's Man's Man's World'] in as I almost, kind of but not quite, used the chord sequence when I wrote what became the guitar solo for FIRTH OF FIFTH. I slightly inverted it as I loved the way it went to the major chord when you were expecting it to go to the minor; it just gives it such an incredible lift that it sends shivers down your spine every time you hear it! I'm not a huge James Brown fan apart from that track, but it's just such a wonderful song."[15]

The song became a firm favorite with fans of the band. Its sandwich structure: vocal section—long instrumental—reprise vocal section, would be successfully repeated by the band many times during their career.

Live Performances: 1973/4, 1976, 1977, 1981, 1982 ("Six of the Best" show only), 1983/4 (instrumental section), 1992 (instrumental section), 1998 (instrumental section), 2007 (instrumental section). FIRTH OF FIFTH would also become a tour favorite benefiting hugely from the dynamics of the live arena. It was played on each subsequent tour through to 1981 (minus the piano intro) and then the instrumental section only on each tour from 1984 (excluding 1986/7). Collins believed the song benefited greatly from the addition of a second drummer from the 1976 tour onward, with first Bill Bruford and then Chester Thompson helping to add greater rhythmic drive to the instrumental section.

Live Recordings: (1) A live version of the song (8:29) recorded at the Rainbow Theatre, London, on 20 October 1973 can be heard on both *Genesis Archive 1967–75* and the *Live at the Rainbow* disc *Genesis 1973–2007 Live* box set (8:33). Hackett reworked some of his guitar parts in the mid- to late 1990s for these releases. The recording was engineered by John Burns and produced by the band.

(2) Collins' vocal performance of the song (8:56) from Palais des Sports, Paris, between 11–14 June 1977 can first be heard on *Seconds Out*. The lineup was Banks, Collins, Hackett and Rutherford, augmented by Chester Thompson (drums). The recording was produced by David Hentschel and the band.

(3) A live recording (9:29) from the Nassau Coliseum, Long Island, New York, on 29 November 1981 was issued as a flexi-disc with *Genesis Magazine* from Genesis Information Society in May 1983. This version was also included as the B-side on the 12-inch single release of THAT'S ALL on 7 November 1983. The lineup is Banks, Collins and Rutherford, augmented by Daryl Stuermer (guitar) and Chester Thompson (drums). This is the first live release to feature Stuermer's fluid interpretation of Hackett's signature solo. The engineer on the recording was Geoff Callingham with the band taking production credit.

(4) Later performances and recordings featured only the instrumental section. The performance at Niedersachsenstadion, Hanover, Germany, on 10 July 1992 and 7 July 2007 is available on *The Way We Walk: The Longs* as part of the "Old Medley" (19:32). The lineup is Banks, Collins and Rutherford, again augmented by Stuermer and Thompson. Production is by Nick Davis, Robert Colby and the band.

(5) The instrumental section (4:39) appeared again on *Live Over Europe 2007* respectively. This was a recording from Old Trafford, Manchester, on 7 July 2007. The lineup is Banks, Collins and Rutherford, once more augmented by Stuermer and Thompson. The recording was made by Bernard Natier and produced by Nick Davis.

[43] MORE FOOL ME

Band Credit: Tony Banks/Phil Collins/Peter Gabriel/Steve Hackett/Mike Rutherford
Music & Lyrics: Mike Rutherford/Phil Collins
Length: 3:11
Phil Collins—Lead & Backing Vocals; **Mike Rutherford**—Acoustic Guitar
Recorded at Island Studios, London, England, August 1973.
Producer: John Burns and Genesis. Engineer: John Burns. Assistant Engineer: Rhett Davis.
2008 Remix/Remaster Release:
Mixed at The Farm, Surrey 2005/2006.
5.1 Surround sound and stereo mixes by Nick Davis. Assisted by Tom Mitchell.
UK Release: 13 October 1973. (LP: *Selling England by the Pound*)
U.S. Release: 12 November 1973. (LP: *Selling England by the Pound*)

Phil Collins contributes a delicate lead vocal (his second for the band after [26] FOR ABSENT FRIENDS on *Nursery Cryme*) and adds his own harmonies to this gentle acoustic number, which has a lilting melody. It is a contrast to the rest of the album due to its simplicity of arrangement, lack of pretension and in its subject matter concerning personal relationships. While regarded as little more than filler, it is well played and provides a brief diversion from some of the more bizarre tracks on the album. Collins and Rutherford wrote the song sitting on the steps to the studio and producer John Burns championed it to the rest of the band, "I said, 'That would be great on the album!' Because it was so different that it was Phil singing, and I thought it was a nice little ditty to include on the thing. I just said to the rest of the band that this is going on, and they all said fine. It was two against two on the song's inclusion initially. Obviously, Mike and Phil liked it. I threw in my vote, and said 'It's only a very short song, and it's a bit different.' In the end, it made the album."[16]

Single Release: The track was included as a B-side to the [41] I Know What I Like single releases in Portugal and Brazil.

Live Performances: 1973/4. The song was performed live on the subsequent *Selling England* tour, allowing Collins to step forward from the drum kit to join Rutherford, before being dropped from the set for subsequent tours.

Live Recordings: The version recorded at the Rainbow Theatre, London, on 20 October 1973 can be heard on both *Genesis Archive 1967–75* (4:01), with a short intro by Gabriel, and the *Live at the Rainbow* disc of the *Genesis 1973–2007 Live* box set (3:24). The recording was produced by John Burns and the band.

[44] The Battle of Epping Forest

Band Credit: Tony Banks/Phil Collins/Peter Gabriel/Steve Hackett/Mike Rutherford
Music: Tony Banks/Phil Collins/Peter Gabriel/Steve Hackett/Mike Rutherford
Lyrics: Peter Gabriel
Length: 11:43
Tony Banks—Organ, Mellotron; **Phil Collins**—Drums, Backing Vocals, Percussion; **Peter Gabriel**—
 Lead & Backing Vocals, Flute, Percussion; **Steve Hackett**—Guitar; **Mike Rutherford**—Bass
Recorded at Island Studios, London, England, August 1973.
Producer: John Burns and Genesis. Engineer: John Burns. Assistant Engineer: Rhett Davis.
2008 Remix/Remaster Release:
Mixed at The Farm, Surrey 2005/2006.
5.1 Surround sound and stereo mixes by Nick Davis. Assisted by Tom Mitchell.
UK Release: 13 October 1973. (LP: *Selling England by the Pound*)
U.S. Release: 12 November 1973. (LP: *Selling England by the Pound*)

The Battle of Epping Forest plays like a mini-opera and attempts to unfold its lyrically dense character-driven narrative over meandering and overarranged music. Like [42] Firth of Fifth, this song was derived from an older piece titled "The Block"—but here the battle for space between the busy musical arrangement and the word-heavy lyrics strangles it.

A traditional marching band rhythm and fanfare open the song. Hackett created the simulation of the gang's marching feet on guitar by playing through a fuzz box and using an octave divider and echoplex. He then suggested fading the resultant sound in to create the image of an approaching army. The impact is striking and gives the song a promising start. Lyrically, it is a tale of riots on the streets of London sparked by two rival gangs. The subject matter was inspired by a real-life incident that had been reported in the news a year earlier. Gabriel explained: "I keep cuttings that interest me. Battle of Epping Forest was taken from a genuine news story in *The Times*.[17] When I went back to find the story I'd misplaced it, so I fabricated the whole thing around the story of two gangs fighting over protection rights in London's East End."[18] His final lyrics read more like a miniplay than words to a song, with the use of multiple characters to enact the story. Gabriel pondered over whether his imagined conclusion, in which he left the matter to be decided on the toss of a coin, was strong enough, but he loved the irony of it and kept it in the final lyric.

In his vocal performance, Gabriel experimented with voices and vocal textures in amusingly portraying an array of characters including Mick the Prick, Bob the Nob and Harold Demure to name a few. However, the whole thing is far too long and lacks any musical focus. The song's overarrangement is symptomatic of the band's writing methods at the time, where musical pieces would be rehearsed and arranged to a point where they were almost self-contained instrumentals before Gabriel would fight for space to add his vocals over the top. Here, both instrumental and vocals run at such a pace there is no room for the song to breathe and the whole thing feels like a haphazard aural assault. Gabriel realized his lyrics didn't really fit with the music, but the band had committed too far to enable them to make any last-minute changes to the musical structure or arrangement.

While in its entirety THE BATTLE OF EPPING FOREST fails to satisfy, the instrumental work is generally well played with some complex passages, but there are also moments where rhythmically the song is too awkward. Looking back Banks commented, "The trouble is there is so much going on in that song, I find it a very uncomfortable song actually. I find the rhythm of the middle section very uncomfortable. Steve at the time said we should not have done it that way and I'm absolutely with him on that."[19] The result was a song that did not fully satisfy anyone in the band. Collins pointed to its overcrowded nature and Gabriel's wordy lyrics, "It's like, three-hundred words per line. There was no space. All the air had been sucked out of it."[20] Retrospectively Gabriel agreed, "I spent a lot of time building up the characters. I was quite reluctant to edit as severely as I should have done. It did end up too wordy."[21]

The song can therefore be viewed as a failed marriage of music and vocals. The music is often rambling and until the finale lacks any sequences of note. The lyrics are creative but betray the separate origin despite Gabriel's imaginative interpretation. It is therefore one of the few long songs by the band lacking in dramatic tension or any satisfying musical progression.

Live Performances: 1973/4. The song was performed on the following tour only. It was so closely linked to Gabriel's lyrical and vocal work that Genesis would not attempt to play the song once he had left the band.

Live Recordings: The performance (12:23) from the Rainbow Theatre, London, on 20 October 1973 is available on the box set *Genesis 1973–2007 Live* on the *Live at the Rainbow* disc. The recording was engineered by John Burns and produced by the band.

[45] AFTER THE ORDEAL

Band Credit: Tony Banks/Phil Collins/Peter Gabriel/Steve Hackett/Mike Rutherford
Music: Steve Hackett/Mike Rutherford
Length: 4:15
Tony Banks—Piano, Organ, Mellotron; **Phil Collins**—Drums, Backing Vocals, Percussion; **Peter Gabriel**—Flute; **Steve Hackett**—Guitar, Acoustic Guitar; **Mike Rutherford**—Acoustic Guitar, Bass
Recorded at Island Studios, London, England, August 1973.
Producer: John Burns and Genesis. Engineer: John Burns. Assistant Engineer: Rhett Davis.
2008 Remix/Remaster Release:
Mixed at The Farm, Surrey 2005/2006.
5.1 Surround sound and stereo mixes by Nick Davis. Assisted by Tom Mitchell.
UK Release: 13 October 1973. (LP: *Selling England by the Pound*)
U.S. Release: 12 November 1973. (LP: *Selling England by the Pound*)

An inoffensive and melodic instrumental written in G major by Hackett with a piece from Rutherford added at the conclusion. The song has something of a medieval feel in its acoustic instrumentation and musical phrasing. Banks' piano and Hackett's nylon guitar seem to compete against each other for the same space, making the arrangement feel cluttered. This opening section would have worked better as a solo acoustic guitar piece from Hackett, with Banks' piano accompaniment superfluous to the mix. The second section slows and stretches into a more successful melodic segment led by Hackett's precise electric guitar solo, which glides over Banks' sedate chord progressions on piano, although again the instrumentation underneath feels overcrowded. The piece can be regarded as filler on an album with perhaps more than its fair share. It was Banks' least favorite Genesis tune, which he described as "pseudo-classical without any real spirit."[22] He also, with perhaps an overdose of self-criticism, described his own playing as "atrocious."[23] He and Gabriel did not want the song on the album, while Hackett did. None of the band were prepared to compromise on the track sequencing of *Selling England by the Pound*, hence all the songs the band had recorded ended up on the album.

Single Release: The song was used as the B-side to the [41] I KNOW WHAT I LIKE single in France.

[46] THE CINEMA SHOW

Band Credit: Tony Banks/Phil Collins/Peter Gabriel/Steve Hackett/Mike Rutherford
Music: Tony Banks/Phil Collins/Mike Rutherford
Lyrics: Tony Banks/Mike Rutherford
Length: 10:41
Tony Banks—Synthesizer, Acoustic Guitar; **Phil Collins**—Drums, Harmony Vocals, Percussion; **Peter Gabriel**—Lead Vocals, Flute, Oboe; **Steve Hackett**—Lead Guitar, Acoustic Guitar; **Mike Rutherford**—Rhythm Guitar, Acoustic Guitar, Bass, Bass Pedals
Recorded at Island Studios, London, England, August 1973.
Producer: John Burns and Genesis. Engineer: John Burns. Assistant Engineer: Rhett Davis.
2008 Remix/Remaster Release:
Mixed at The Farm, Surrey 2005/2006.
5.1 Surround sound and stereo mixes by Nick Davis. Assisted by Tom Mitchell.
UK Release: 13 October 1973. (LP: *Selling England by the Pound*)
U.S. Release: 12 November 1973. (LP: *Selling England by the Pound*)

Along with [42] FIRTH OF FIFTH, THE CINEMA SHOW was to become a fan favorite mainstay of their live set for many years to come. A beautiful 12-string acoustic opening, written by Rutherford, sees Gabriel tell the tale of two young lovers, wittily named Romeo and Juliet. The first half of the song is all acoustic and contains some strong melodic moments despite a slightly dragging length and a needless fluttering flute solo from Gabriel. Collins' backing vocals harmonize superbly with Gabriel's lead throughout and most notably during the chorus. Banks and Rutherford's lyrics were inspired by T.S. Eliot's long poem *The Wasteland*, which contained vignettes of contemporary society using alternating narrations. In the song we get the viewpoint of both Romeo and Juliet and their respective aspirations for their evening assignation. Gabriel has since commented he was not overly fond of the lyrics, although he did prompt his band mates to use the names of the characters from Shakespeare's play.

At 5:50, the song moves into a jazzy instrumental section in a 7/8 rhythm, which is pounded out by Collins' drums and Rutherford's rhythm guitar and bass. This section was largely written through improvisation at Chessington by Banks, Collins and Rutherford and they stitched together the best pieces from their jam sessions, mirroring the method they would later use as a trio. Banks recalled, "Mike came out with a riff in 7/8, which had a great feel, and by restricting his playing a little he allowed me to make the chord changes ... so with Mike just hitting the bottom three or four strings of the guitar I managed to write endless bits on the rhythm. Just before we came to do the album, we put them in order and the final section of CINEMA SHOW developed."[24] Rutherford also remembered, "I'm moving around chords, Tony's reacting and improvising over them, and between the two of us we're coming up with something that would go on to be the essence of the Genesis sound for the next twenty years. And the drumming's great too."[25] The section also contains some of Banks' best instrumental solo work on the ARP Pro-Soloist and Rutherford's use of thunderous bass pedals. Charisma boss Tony Stratton-Smith wasn't convinced by the longer instrumental approach, fearing the band were veering into Emerson, Lake and Palmer territory, but the band felt they were exploring new ground. While it ends a little unconvincingly it does avoid what was to become a Genesis trait by not reprising the vocal section. Instead, it segues via a fade into an acoustic passage that leads into [47] AISLE OF PLENTY. The segue accounts for the time differential between the original release and Nick Davis' remaster, with the latter moving this connecting piece to the start of the following track.

Live Performances: 1973/4, 1976, 1977, 1978, 1981 (instrumental section), 1982 (instrumental section), 1983/4 (instrumental section), 2007 (instrumental section). The song would become an exciting addition to their stage set with the instrumental section really coming alive through more muscular playing of its dynamic rhythm by Collins and Rutherford. It would also be sung later by Collins on his first three tours as lead vocalist. The instrumental section was resurrected to form part of the "In the Cage Medley" from 1981 to 1984 and again in 2007.

Live Recordings: (1) The 20 October 1973 performance (11:05) at the Rainbow Theatre was captured on the *Live at the Rainbow* disc of the box set *Genesis 1973–2007 Live*. The recording was engineered by John Burns and produced by the band. Banks took the opportunity to fix an error on the synth solo for this release.

(2) A recording (10:58) from Pavillon de Paris on 23 June 1976 with Collins taking on the lead vocals featured on *Seconds Out*. The band lineup was Banks, Collins, Hackett and Rutherford, augmented by Bill Bruford (drums). The recording was produced by David Hentschel and the band.

(3) A large segment of the instrumental section was used as part of the "In the Cage Medley" and a recording (11:53) from the National Exhibition Centre in Birmingham, England, on 23 December 1981 can be heard on *Three Sides Live*. The band lineup was Banks, Collins and Rutherford, augmented by Daryl Stuermer (guitar) and Chester Thompson (drums). This recording was engineered by Geoff Callingham and produced by the band.

(4) A segment of the instrumental section was later again used as part of the "In the Cage" medley (13:30) on the 2007 reunion tour. A recording made by Bernard Natier and produced by Nick Davis, from Old Trafford, Manchester, on 7 July was included on *Live Over Europe 2007*. The band lineup was again Banks, Collins and Rutherford, again augmented by Stuermer and Thompson.

[47] AISLE OF PLENTY

Band Credit: Tony Banks/Phil Collins/Peter Gabriel/Steve Hackett/Mike Rutherford
Music: Steve Hackett
Lyrics: Peter Gabriel
Length: 1:58
Tony Banks—Organ, Mellotron; **Phil Collins**—Drums, Percussion; **Peter Gabriel**—Lead & Backing Vocals; **Steve Hackett**—Guitar, Acoustic Guitar; **Mike Rutherford**—Acoustic Guitar, Bass
Recorded at Island Studios, London, England, August 1973.
Producer: John Burns and Genesis. Engineer: John Burns. Assistant Engineer: Rhett Davis.
2008 Remix/Remaster Release:
Mixed at The Farm, Surrey 2005/2006.

7. Studio Album #5: Selling England by the Pound

5.1 Surround sound and stereo mixes by Nick Davis. Assisted by Tom Mitchell.
UK Release: 13 October 1973. (LP: *Selling England by the Pound*)
U.S. Release: 12 November 1973. (LP: *Selling England by the Pound*)

[46] THE CINEMA SHOW segues into this short acoustic piece, which comes across as an afterthought being presented as a coda to both the previous song and the album. It can also be seen as a prelude to some of the atmospheric instrumentals that appeared on *The Lamb Lies Down on Broadway*. The lyrics contain plenty of clever wordplay from Gabriel as he references well-known British shopping brands. Musically the song reprises themes from the album's opening song [40] DANCING WITH THE MOONLIT KNIGHT—creating a bookend feel the band would repeat on future albums. A light and strangely hypnotic looping play-out, with Gabriel calling out supermarket pricing structures in the backing, closes the album.

* * *

Selling England by the Pound was released on 13 October 1973 and performed well in the UK charts, becoming Genesis' first top 10 hit by reaching #3 as well as charting in the U.S. at #70 following its release there a month later. The album was also noteworthy for providing the band with their first hit single, [41] I KNOW WHAT I LIKE (IN YOUR WARDROBE), which reached #21 in the UK charts.

Having parted company with Paul Whitehead, Genesis were looking for a fresh approach to the album cover. Peter Gabriel had become fascinated with the artwork of British painter Betty Swanwick. Her painting *The Dream* had become the inspiration for Gabriel's lyrics to I KNOW WHAT I LIKE (IN YOUR WARDROBE). When it came to the selection of the cover for the album, the band asked Swanwick to add a lawnmower to her original painting. This she did happily, and the final cover remains one of the band's most iconic.

Genesis had enjoyed working with John Burns as producer and were pleased with the improved recording quality that emerged from the sessions. Despite the superior sound, the record company was not overly enthusiastic about the album and neither were certain members of the band—notably Banks and Rutherford who felt it wasn't as consistent as *Foxtrot*. Banks told Armando Gallo, "I don't think the album succeeds on every level but there were attempts to just try and do things a little more imaginatively."[26] Conversely, *Selling England by the Pound* is regarded by fans and critics as possibly Genesis' strongest and most representative album. Steve Hackett concurs, pointing to the experimental nature of the instrumentation and the surreal lyrics.

The music press was largely impressed. In its review *Sounds* noted, "The compositions are melodic and naturally intuitive in their construction, the playing is sweet and extremely precise, and the composition of the album as a whole is such that it remains fluid and carefully wrought for the best possible impact."[27] In her review for *New Musical Express*, Barbara Charone noted it was "the band's best, most adventurous album to date."[28] In the U.S., however, *Rolling Stone* writer Paul Gambaccini was less convinced but nevertheless remained mildly supportive: "Musically their artiness is, in small doses, engaging. And a band that is trying to do something different in a stagnant pop scene deserves encouragement."[29]

Contemporary reviewers often cite this as Genesis' strongest work. In their "Buyer's Guide," *Planet Rock* described the album as being, "Full of romantic longing and unrequited love—it's all so brilliantly, *terribly* English."[30] In his review for *All Music Guide*, Stephen Thomas Erlewine noted, "It plays as a collection of short stories, fables, and fairy tales, and it is also a rock record, which naturally makes it quite extraordinary as a collection, but also as a set of individual songs."[31] Despite these glowing tributes it is hard to argue against the view of Banks and Rutherford that the album is a mixed bag. It has some very strong creative musical moments on its standout tracks, but there is a large gap in quality between the best tracks and the rest. The album is also more heavily instrumental than before, as demonstrated by the long passages on [42] FIRTH OF FIFTH and [46] THE CINEMA SHOW as well as the wholly instrumental [45] AFTER THE ORDEAL. Gabriel did, however, contribute increasingly whimsical and surreal lyrics, particularly for the single [41] I KNOW WHAT I LIKE (IN YOUR WARDROBE) and the long rambling opus [44] THE BATTLE OF EPPING FOREST. The former worked beautifully with its simple catchy melodies masking a more complex arrangement, but the latter sank in its own self-indulgence and lack of cohesion with the real battle being between the band's densely arranged music and Gabriel's wordy and demanding lyrics and vocals. Collins enjoyed another lead vocal spot on the delicate and short [43] MORE FOOL ME, which provided contrast, but [45] AFTER THE ORDEAL, an inconsequential instrumental, was little more than filler.

Technically, the band's playing was very assured and certainly their strongest performance to date—something they acknowledged at the time. Banks was beginning to delve into the world of synthesizers with interesting results. Rutherford was showing great rhythmic prowess on bass, while Collins' drumming was inventive and highlighted perfectly the drama in the music—notably during the instrumental stretches. Hackett contributed possibly his best work for the band with some fluent guitar pieces—his solo on [42] FIRTH OF FIFTH being his best with the band and it became something of a signature piece. Gabriel's vocals also benefited from the clearer production and at last managed to cut through the sometime dense soundscape. Despite the album's compositional inconsistencies, *Selling England by the Pound* confirmed Genesis' commercial breakthrough and produced four songs that are among the strongest in the band's catalogue.

Genesis filmed the highlights of their live set for an Italian TV special at arranged audience sessions at Shepperton Studios on 30 and 31 October 1973.[32] The band was unhappy with the result as Collins commented, "When we saw the film, we couldn't say anything to each other. It wasn't right."[33] The band continued to promote their music in the U.S. with a tour spanning November and December 1973. To help with their live promotion Genesis recruited Tony Smith, who had worked in partnership with British promoters Mike Alfandary and Harvey Goldsmith, as their new manager. The band had discovered that poor book-keeping had left them significantly in debt.[34] Smith had a reputation for being very organized and having lots of contacts in the business. By managing to persuade Smith to take on the challenge, the band had removed any conflict Tony Stratton-Smith might have had being both manager of the band as well as the band's record label. The U.S. tour was well received critically and their growing reputation as a live act was further enhanced during a 1974 tour of the UK. Gabriel continued to expand his use of costumes to help act out the songs on stage, which naturally focused the attention of the music press on the lead singer. This was an increasing source of frustration to the rest of the band, who felt they were now being perceived as Gabriel's backing musicians. There were several attempts to put the press right on the matter. Collins noted in an interview with *Record Mirror* at the time, "We're all aware of each other's importance and out of the limelight Peter just blends in with the rest of us. Anyway, luckily it's got better and people don't see it like that anymore."[35]

In the UK, the band was voted top stage act by the *New Musical Express* readers, but despite their newfound success, the band remained heavily in debt and was determined to crack the U.S. market. This led to a think of approach for their next album. Having explored in detail the very essence of Englishness they would now look across the water for their inspiration.

8

Studio Album #6:
The Lamb Lies Down on Broadway

UK Release: 22 November 1974. 2LP. Charisma. CGS 101.
U.S. Release: 25 November 1974. 2LP. Atlantic/ATCO Records. SD 2–401.
Remix/Remaster Release:
UK Release: 10 November 2008. 2-CD/2SACD/DVD. Virgin/Charisma. CGCDSR-1.
U.S. Release: 11 November 2008. 2-CD/DVD. Atlantic/Rhino. R2 513945.

Album Tracks

[48] THE LAMB LIES DOWN ON BROADWAY
[49] FLY ON A WINDSHIELD
[50] BROADWAY MELODY OF 1974
[51] CUCKOO COCOON
[52] IN THE CAGE
[53] THE GRAND PARADE OF LIFELESS PACKAGING
[54] BACK IN N.Y.C.
[55] HAIRLESS HEART
[56] COUNTING OUT TIME
[57] CARPET CRAWLERS
[58] THE CHAMBER OF 32 DOORS
[59] LILYWHITE LILITH
[60] THE WAITING ROOM
[61] ANYWAY
[62] HERE COMES THE SUPERNATURAL ANAESTHETIST
[63] THE LAMIA
[64] SILENT SORROW IN EMPTY BOATS
[65] THE COLONY OF SLIPPERMEN
[66] RAVINE
[67] THE LIGHT DIES DOWN ON BROADWAY
[68] RIDING THE SCREE
[69] IN THE RAPIDS
[70] IT.

Work began on writing *The Lamb Lies Down on Broadway* during May 1974 following the completion of the *Selling England by the Pound* tour. The band had made the conscious decision to write a concept album with songs linking to form an overall story. This would advance the approach explored in [38] SUPPER'S READY to its natural conclusion. Various

Genesis take a break from writing *The Lamb Lies Down on Broadway* in 1974. From left, Phil Collins, Mike Rutherford, Tony Banks, Peter Gabriel and Steve Hackett. Atlantic promotional photograph (courtesy Mark Kenyon/The Genesis Archive).

ideas were shared before the band finally settled on Gabriel's allegorical and surreal story of self-discovery set in New York City based around a Puerto Rican kid named Rael.[1] Gabriel had fought his corner, believing his proposal to be the strongest—particularly when compared to Rutherford's suggestion of adapting Antoine de Saint Exupéry's kids' story *The Little Prince*.[2] Gabriel was keen to set the story around a contemporary, street-wise, figure rather than a character from fables. He took his influences from a variety of sources including Swiss psychologist Carl Jung, the musical *West Side Story*, the 1678 novel *Pilgrim's Progress* and the 1970 symbolic western *El Topo*. Gabriel explained: "The first idea came from when I was in New York and it was just a dream. It sounds interesting when you go back over the day and you start dreaming through some of the events, but your mind starts pulling in other things that you didn't see the first time around. And there were other sort of bits of dream images and sounds. It sounded just like an abstracted story, which I sort of put together."[3]

The story is so dense that no one, including Gabriel himself, can adequately convey its meaning. It comes across more as a collection of dreamlike lyrical images than a cohesive narrative. Over the years, many in-depth books and essays have been written analyzing Gabriel's concept. Its willful obscurity has been its pull. Despite its baffling story, Rutherford later acknowledged the wisdom of going with Gabriel's proposal,[4] although Banks still feels it is the weakest thing about the album in has often stated that it doesn't engage him personally. Collins simply stated when asked, "I don't know what it's about. I'm just the drummer. Ask Peter."[5]

Having submitted his story proposal and obtained the group's consent, Gabriel insisted on writing all the lyrics himself. The band had previously split the writing of lyrics between each of them, so the singer's demand for a monopoly led to some initial reluctance before finally being agreed. While Gabriel developed the story framework for his lyrics in a separate room with a piano to help write melodies, the rest of the band wrote the music in another. In this very moment Genesis had physically divided themselves and the seeds of discontent that would lead to Gabriel's eventual departure had been sown.

The bulk of the writing for the album was completed at Headley Grange, a large but rather rundown poorhouse built in 1795 situated in East Hampshire. It had previously been used by Led Zeppelin as a base from which they would live, write and record songs and the band had worked on their *Physical Graffiti* album there. Zeppelin also sublet the property to other bands. The last tenants before Genesis were The Pretty Things, who had just vacated the property. Genesis moved in with their families in mid–May 1974, with a lease on the property until the end of July. On arrival, they found it overrun with rats that would scratch at the walls at night, and the band members were surprised at the almost derelict nature of the building. Zeppelin had warned Genesis that they believed the building to be haunted—no doubt providing inspiration for the eerie [60] THE WAITING ROOM. With rats in the rafters the noises at nighttime would have been disconcerting. The initial writing sessions went very well as Rutherford remembered, "We started writing and it just came out very easily. After the previous album, it was a big relief. We realized quite quickly that we had three good sides—not just two good sides and another side, but three good sides. So, we had to go for a double."[6]

It was during the writing that Gabriel was approached by film director William Friedkin, who had recently made the acclaimed horror film *The Exorcist*, to work on some ideas for a future movie.[7] Friedkin had been impressed by the surreal nature of Gabriel's story from the cover of *Genesis Live*, which fitted with his vision for revolutionizing the film industry. The band were adamant that Gabriel was committed to them and to the album and that he should not take up the offer as it would effectively leave them in limbo. Gabriel, however, decided he could not pass on Friedkin's offer and left the band to spend some time developing the project. After a couple of weeks away, Friedkin seemingly lost interest in the project and had become wary of the effect it would have on the band. Tony Stratton-Smith intervened and helped smooth the waters for Gabriel's return to the fold. Rutherford managed to convince Gabriel a compromise could be struck for future ventures and the singer committed to finishing the album before embarking on any other side projects.

Banks, Collins, Rutherford and Hackett had written most of the music through jam sessions,[8] often based around a theme or lyrical idea, while Gabriel was further developing Rael's story. Gabriel was struggling to keep pace with his writing of the lyrics and vocal melodies. He requested new linking pieces of music to be written to bridge elements of the story and initially refused the band's offer of help with finishing the lyrics, rejecting suggestions from Banks and Hackett for [63] THE LAMIA and [62] HERE COMES THE SUPERNATURAL ANAESTHETIST. However, he would later relent, allowing Banks and Rutherford to work on [67] THE LIGHT DIES DOWN ON BROADWAY.

As the band's lease at Headley Grange had run its course, Genesis moved to Glaspant Manor in South Wales in late July to record the album in a converted barn, later known as Swift Cottage. The band had hired The Island Mobile Studio,[9] using John Burns as producer and David Hutchins as engineer. "It was basically a cowshed with a pitched roof," Burns remembered. "I had to send out hardboard to nail up around the drums."[10] The move away from using a dedicated recording studio freed the band up and they worked creatively with Burns. The location also allowed Gabriel to experiment with vocal sounds, using the natural acoustics of the outbuildings and rooms around the property. Collins also felt the location improved the sound of his drums, giving them more of a live feel.

Another event that alienated Gabriel from his colleagues was the birth of his first child, Anna-Marie, on 26 July 1974. Gabriel's wife, Jill, had experienced a traumatic delivery and their daughter spent the first month of her life on an incubator. Gabriel spent long hours travelling to and from St. Mary's Hospital at Paddington, which further slowed down the process of writing the lyrics for the album. Gabriel felt increasingly distant as the band showed little sympathy for his plight—none of them had children of their own at the time. He had also become increasingly frustrated with Banks not allowing him to develop musical ideas on the keyboards. Banks now readily admits he adopted a parochial attitude to the instrument, but at the time his lack of flexibility fueled Gabriel's discontent and frustration.

The final recording of the vocals and overdubs, followed by the mixing of the album, took place a month later at Island Studios on Basing Street in London.[11] This allowed Gabriel further time to complete his lyrics. Burns and the band worked around the clock to get the album finished. For the mixing, Gabriel and Collins took the evening/night shift and Banks, Hackett and Rutherford the day shift. The sessions remained tense with the band running up against time pressures created by the volume of music they had recorded and a forthcoming tour with a heavy production load.

During the mixing, the band learned that Brian Eno was in the upstairs studio recording his second solo album, *Taking Tiger Mountain (By Strategy)*. Gabriel approached Eno and asked if he could treat some of his vocals through Eno's computerized effects unit (he would also add some treatment to Hackett's guitar). Eno agreed and in exchange Collins played drums on Eno's track "Mother Whale Eyeless." Eno and Collins get on so well that Collins would drum on two of Eno's later albums—*Another Green World* and *Music for Films*. Eno received a credit on *The Lamb Lies Down on Broadway* for his "Enossification," something that irks Banks to this day as it suggests he took a larger role in the creative process than was the case.

With the mixing finally complete, albeit hurriedly,[12] in mid–October the band were ready to unveil their new concept double-album.

[48] THE LAMB LIES DOWN ON BROADWAY

Band Credit: Tony Banks/Phil Collins/Peter Gabriel/Steve Hackett/Mike Rutherford
Music: Tony Banks/Peter Gabriel
Lyrics: Peter Gabriel
Length: 4:52
Tony Banks—Piano, Electric Piano; **Phil Collins**—Drums, Backing Vocals, Percussion; **Peter Gabriel**—Lead Vocals; **Steve Hackett**—Guitar; **Mike Rutherford**—Bass
Recorded at Glaspant Manor, Carmarthenshire, Wales, with the Island Mobile Studio, and Mixed at Island Studios, August–October 1974.
Producer: John Burns and Genesis. Engineer: David Hutchins.
2008 Remix/Remaster Release:
Mixed at The Farm, Surrey 2005/2006.
5.1 Surround sound and stereo mixes by Nick Davis. Assisted by Tom Mitchell.
UK Release: 22 November 1974. (2LP: *The Lamb Lies Down on Broadway*)
U.S. Release: 25 November 1974. (2LP: *The Lamb Lies Down on Broadway*)

8. Studio Album #6: The Lamb Lies Down on Broadway

U.S. Single Release: December 1974. (A-side single b/w [56] COUNTING OUT TIME. Atlantic/ATCO. 45–7013)

Rael's long and complex story begins with this insistent song largely written by Banks and Gabriel. Banks' cross-handed spiraling piano figure, a technique requiring great synchronization and giving the impression of a speedier delivery, opens the song. A fly buzzes its way across Banks' piano—an effect Hackett achieved by hammering notes on his Gibson Les Paul guitar and routing through two fuzz boxes. The band crash in at 0:30 with two big major chords moving from E flat to G flat before settling on B flat and then switching to E for the opening verse. Gabriel declares the title and the defining theme of the album—and we're off. The singer lyrically paints a picture of Manhattan as he introduces us to his street kid protagonist. Immediately, as the riffing electric guitar and classical piano punch out the sound, we know this is a harder-edged Genesis. The sound is earthy, with a heavier rock arrangement.

When challenged around the conceptual nature of their album, the band likened it to The Who's 1969 double-album *Tommy* rather than Yes' 1973 double opus *Tales from Topographic Oceans*, being keen to distance themselves from the latter's excesses. The title track validates that comparison. The rhythm is urgent and driven by Rutherford's propulsive six-string Micro-Frets Signature Baritone bass work, which he played through a Marshall fuzz treatment and an acoustic amp giving the instrument its distinctive sound. Banks added his RMI 368x Electra Piano to the track as an overdub at Island Studios. The softer midsection features Banks' electric piano and Hackett's lead guitar coloring Gabriel's vocal lines. The lyric switches to the first person in the final verse as we enter Rael's head as he tries to get a grip on his actions. Gabriel delivers an aggressive angst-ridden vocal while he lyrically steals the Drifters' lyrical hook from their 1963 song "On Broadway" as he closes out the song.

Single Release: THE LAMB LIES DOWN ON BROADWAY was released as an edited single (3:15) in the U.S. b/w [56] COUNTING OUT TIME in December 1974 but failed to chart. It was also released as an EP in Brazil, with [56] COUNTING OUT TIME and [53] THE GRAND PARADE OF LIFELESS PACKAGING, and as a B-side to [57] CARPET CRAWLERS in Italy. The song was later included on a 4-track EP released in Brazil in 1975 with [56] COUNTING OUT TIME, [53] THE GRAND PARADE OF LIFELESS PACKAGING and [54] BACK IN N.Y.C.

Live Performances: 1974/5, 1976, 1977, 1978 (rarely), 1981, 1982, 1983/4 (excerpt), 1992 (excerpt), 1998. The band performed the whole album on the 1974/5 tour to support its release. Following Gabriel's departure, the song was retained in the set for both the 1976 and 1977 tours with Phil Collins delivering his vocal interpretation. It was performed rarely on the 1978 tour and was later incorporated into medleys in 1983/4 and 1992. In 1998, when Ray Wilson replaced Collins, the song returned to the set in its entirety, but it would not be performed on Collins' return in 2007.

Live Recordings: (1) A live recording (6:29) at the LA Shrine Auditorium on 24 January 1975 can be heard on *Genesis Archive 1967–75* as part of that box set's presentation of the entire concert. The recording was mixed by Nick Davis and Geoff Callingham and produced by the band. Gabriel recorded parts of his vocal for the new mix of this song and others. Other mistakes across the show were also corrected by band members with the help of Nick Davis to ensure the best possible performance was captured. To some this may be judged as dishonest—by presenting a performance that did not exist at the time. There are certainly moments when the Gabriel of 1975 contrasts quite jarringly with the Gabriel of the 1990s, his voice having thickened and deepened over the intervening years. The other band corrections are less obvious and will only be spotted by those familiar with the untampered source material. The result is a patchwork presentation that may have best been left alone, with the mistakes intact, as a raw but genuine representation of the band's live performance.

(2) A recording (4:59) of a performance from one of the shows at Palais des Sports, Paris, between 11–14 June 1977 appeared on *Seconds Out*. This is the first live recording of the song to feature Collins' vocal. This version lacks the rhythmic punch of the album recording. The band lineup was Banks, Collins, Hackett and Rutherford, augmented by Chester Thomson (drums). David Hentschel co-produced with the band.

(3) A segment of the song was included in the "Old Medley" that the band performed on their 1992 tour. A recording (19:32) at Niedersachsenstadion, Hanover, Germany, on 10 July appeared on *The Way We Walk—Volume Two: The Longs* and the remixed double-CD *The Way We Walk* as part of the *Genesis Live 1973–2007* box set. The lineup was Banks, Collins and Rutherford, augmented by Daryl Stuermer (guitar) and Thompson. The recording was produced by Nick Davis, Robert Colby and the band.

[49] FLY ON A WINDSHIELD

Band Credit: Tony Banks/Phil Collins/Peter Gabriel/Steve Hackett/Mike Rutherford
Music: Tony Banks/Phil Collins/Peter Gabriel/Steve Hackett/Mike Rutherford
Lyrics: Peter Gabriel
Length: 2:45
Tony Banks—Synthesizers, Organ, Mellotron; **Phil Collins**—Drums, Percussion; **Peter Gabriel**—Lead Vocals; **Steve Hackett**—Guitar, Acoustic Guitar; **Mike Rutherford**—Acoustic Guitar, Bass, Bass Pedals
Recorded at Glaspant Manor, Carmarthenshire, Wales, with the Island Mobile Studio, and Mixed at Island Studios, August–October 1974.
Producer: John Burns and Genesis. Engineer: David Hutchins.
2008 Remix/Remaster Release:
Mixed at The Farm, Surrey 2005/2006.
5.1 Surround sound and stereo mixes by Nick Davis. Assisted by Tom Mitchell.
UK Release: 22 November 1974. (2LP: *The Lamb Lies Down on Broadway*)
U.S. Release: 25 November 1974. (2LP: *The Lamb Lies Down on Broadway*)

[48] THE LAMB LIES DOWN ON BROADWAY fades away via a gently strummed 12-string guitar piece which alternates between E minor and G major. Banks offers the Mellotron's choral sound to add width to the arrangement. Gabriel sings quietly setting the scene of some form solidifying over Times Square. It is in fact a descriptive lyric telling how Rael is entombed in dust blown into Manhattan on high winds. The wind leaves him hovering in the air waiting for the inevitable collision with oncoming traffic. The song then literally blasts into life as the metaphoric "fly" hits the windshield at 1:18 and the band explode in unison. It's an astonishingly dramatic moment, the musical equivalent of a jump-scare in a horror movie. Banks would later describe this as the band's finest recorded moment. The song then moves into an elegantly drifting instrumental section, again played around the two chords of E minor and G major, where Banks' lush keyboards establish the mood. Rutherford described the evocative music as imagining Egyptian boats floating down the Nile river and this led to the working title "Pharaohs down the Nile." Collins' John Bonham–like heavy backbeat and Rutherford's pounding bass power the music along beneath Banks' symphonic keyboard chords. Hackett's soaring and weeping guitar solo paints an aural picture of Rael's sub-conscious descent through a black cloud into an alternate reality. Hackett, who cites the song as one of his personal favorites from the album, has since commented on

8. *Studio Album #6: The Lamb Lies Down on Broadway*

his inspiration for the solo, "I went for Egyptian phrases as we made the same modulation from E to F sharp that roughly parallels the modulation on Ravel's 'Bolero' at the end; a tone up in other words. It gave the piece that tonic lift and I suppose what would be trite in song, you know, when the chorus goes up like that, in an instrumental piece works really well."[13]

Live Performances/Recordings: See [50] BROADWAY MELODY OF 1974.

---

[50] BROADWAY MELODY OF 1974

Band Credit: Tony Banks/Phil Collins/Peter Gabriel/Steve Hackett/Mike Rutherford
Music: Tony Banks/Phil Collins/Peter Gabriel/Steve Hackett/Mike Rutherford
Lyrics: Peter Gabriel
Length: 2:11
Tony Banks—Synthesizers, Mellotron; **Phil Collins**—Drums, Percussion; **Peter Gabriel**—Lead Vocals; **Steve Hackett**—Guitar; **Mike Rutherford**—Bass
Recorded at Glaspant Manor, Carmarthenshire, Wales, with the Island Mobile Studio, and Mixed at Island Studios, August–October 1974.
Producer: John Burns and Genesis. Engineer: David Hutchins.
2008 Remix/Remaster Release:
Mixed at The Farm, Surrey 2005/2006.
5.1 Surround sound and stereo mixes by Nick Davis. Assisted by Tom Mitchell.
UK Release: 22 November 1974. (2LP: *The Lamb Lies Down on Broadway*)
U.S. Release: 25 November 1974. (2LP: *The Lamb Lies Down on Broadway*)

[49] FLY ON A WINDSHIELD segues into BROADWAY MELODY OF 1974 with a tight rhythm section in which Rutherford pushes out a solitary prodding E bass note mirrored by Hackett's guitar. Collins keeps his drumming simple and Banks provides some lush Mellotron chords behind the rhythm. Gabriel delivers the splendidly allegorical and surreal lyrics, describing an absurd parade along Broadway, with panache. He name-checks a cast of popular culture icons and makes them synonymous with the social decline in New York City at that time.[14] By now the listener will have realized that this album is going to be a challenging listen, with Gabriel's dark fantasy being brought to life by the band's inventive music. The song's title was inspired by a series of MGM musicals that ran from 1936 to 1940.

Live Performances: 1974/5, 1976, 1982 ('six of the Best' show, FLY ON A WINDSHIELD only). Both FLY ON A WINDSHIELD and BROADWAY MELODY OF 1974 were performed live on the 1974/5 tour as part of the band's presentation of the whole album. The songs were also performed after Gabriel's departure as an instrumental on the 1976 tour,[15] then again in full, with Gabriel back on vocals, at the "Six of the Best" reunion benefit concert at the National Bowl in Milton Keynes on 2 October 1982.

Live Recordings: The performance from the LA Shrine Auditorium on 24 January 1975 (2:54/2:19) is available on *Genesis Archive 1967–75* with vocals recorded by Gabriel in the late 1990s (on [49] FLY ON A WINDSHIELD only) along with the guitar solo by Hackett. The same recording of both tracks (2:54 / 2:18) also appeared as a bonus on the remixed and remastered *Genesis Live*, which was issued as part of the box set *Genesis 1970–1975*. The recording was mixed by Nick Davis and Geoff Callingham and produced by the band.

---

[51] CUCKOO COCOON

Band Credit: Tony Banks/Phil Collins/Peter Gabriel/Steve Hackett/Mike Rutherford
Music: Tony Banks/Phil Collins/Peter Gabriel/Steve Hackett/

Lyrics: Peter Gabriel
Length: 2:13
Tony Banks—Piano; **Phil Collins**—Backing Vocals, Percussion; **Peter Gabriel**—Lead & Backing Vocals, Flute; **Steve Hackett**—Guitar; **Mike Rutherford**—Acoustic Guitar, Bass
Recorded at Glaspant Manor, Carmarthenshire, Wales, with the Island Mobile Studio, and Mixed at Island Studios, August–October 1974.
Producer: John Burns and Genesis. Engineer: David Hutchins.
2008 Remix/Remaster Release:
Mixed at The Farm, Surrey 2005/2006.
5.1 Surround sound and stereo mixes by Nick Davis. Assisted by Tom Mitchell.
UK Release: 22 November 1974. (2LP: *The Lamb Lies Down on Broadway*)
U.S. Release: 25 November 1974. (2LP: *The Lamb Lies Down on Broadway*)

At this point in the story Rael regains consciousness and finds himself wrapped in a cocoon. He starts to explore his surrounding and concludes that he is secured in some form of cave. CUCKOO COCOON is a short but beautifully harmonic and gently meandering guitar-led track, with Hackett playing ninths and sevenths between the major chords of D and C in the verses before moving up to F and G. Gabriel delivers a pleasantly melodic vocal, with his own tight backing harmony and Collins adding a second more understated vocal beneath. Gabriel also provides a couple of simple solo flute refrains with Banks inserting some tinkling piano, which adds to the dreamy feel of the piece. Hackett's watery guitar sound effect was created via his Leslie amp and gives the track its warmth. The effect was achieved accidentally due to a malfunction in the tape Echoplex unit, which resulted in a double tracking effect.

Live Performances: 1974/5. The song was included as part of the band's presentation of the whole album.

Live Recordings: A recording (2:17) from the LA Shrine Auditorium on 24 January 1975 is available on *Genesis Archive 1967–75* on which Gabriel recorded his vocals and flute in 1998. The recording was mixed by Nick Davis and Geoff Callingham and produced by the band.

[52] IN THE CAGE

Band Credit: Tony Banks/Phil Collins/Peter Gabriel/Steve Hackett/Mike Rutherford
Music: Tony Banks/Phil Collins/Peter Gabriel/Steve Hackett/Mike Rutherford
Lyrics: Peter Gabriel
Length: 8:12
Tony Banks—Organ, Synthesizers; **Phil Collins**—Drums, Backing Vocals, Percussion; **Peter Gabriel**—Lead Vocals; **Steve Hackett**—Lead Guitar; **Mike Rutherford**—Rhythm Guitar, Bass, Bass Pedals; **Brian Eno**—Voice/Guitar Synthesizer
Recorded at Glaspant Manor, Carmarthenshire, Wales, with the Island Mobile Studio, and Mixed at Island Studios, August–October 1974.
Producer: John Burns and Genesis. Engineer: David Hutchins.
2008 Remix/Remaster Release:
Mixed at The Farm, Surrey 2005/2006.
5.1 Surround sound and stereo mixes by Nick Davis. Assisted by Tom Mitchell.
UK Release: 22 November 1974. (2LP: *The Lamb Lies Down on Broadway*)
U.S. Release: 25 November 1974. (2LP: *The Lamb Lies Down on Broadway*)

Rael wakes up in a cold sweat and finds he is no longer inside the cocoon. The cave morphs around him and the stalactites and stalagmites form themselves into a cage. From inside his prison Rael spots his brother, John, who turns and walks away leaving the cage to dissolve and Rael to spin uncontrollably. IN THE CAGE energetically fuses urgent rhythms with soulful vocals into one of the best pieces on the album. A throbbing heartbeat bass pattern brings us slowly into the song as Gabriel's descriptive lyrics set the scene, depicting Rael waking from his sleep. Collins and Rutherford then propel the song forward, beating a fast and pressing rhythm beneath Banks' stabbed organ phrases, which alternate between E flat minor and B flat minor. Here, the band evocatively creates an aural representation of the claustrophobic environment Rael finds himself in.[16] Banks explained the song's development, "Well, apart from the solo, the rest of IN THE CAGE I wrote at home and I came in with it and it developed a certain sort of way. So, a lot of things were sections we brought in, but as you develop them with the group you change them."[17] Banks had originally envisioned it as a dramatic piece in 3/4, but Collins brought his own rhythmic ideas to the song and altered it 7/8 as two sets of two and a three, helping to add an element of excitement that hadn't been there before.

The song switches from minor to major key as it moves into the chorus section. After the second chorus a fast and fluid synth solo from Banks leads to the song's dramatic peak at 4:10 as a repeated guitar riff is played by Rutherford over his sustained E flat bass pedal note and Banks' changing chords. The section demonstrates the keyboard player's mastery of harmonics as a tool in heightening musical tension and drama as Gabriel sings of Rael seeing his Brother John outside of the cage and imploring him for help. There is another cultural reference as Gabriel recites Burt Bacharach's "Raindrops Keep Falling on My Head" from 1969's *Butch Cassidy and the Sundance Kid* as the songs spirals into its play out.

This was also one of two tracks on which Brian Eno helped with vocal and guitar effects. Banks felt the song was overlooked on the album and points to the fact that it only really took off in the live environment. IN THE CAGE became a stage favorite from 1978 onward and it would lead off the feature medley section on numerous follow-up tours.

Live Performances: 1974/5, 1978, 1980, 1981, 1982, 1983/4, 1986/7, 2007. IN THE CAGE was performed on the subsequent tour as part of the full presentation of the album. Following Gabriel's departure, the song was not performed again until the 1978 tour from when it became a main stay of the set, with additional old songs added onto the end to make a medley on subsequent tours. The energy the band brought to the song in the live arena took it to another plane. While it was dropped for Collins' last tour in 1992 it was resurrected on his return to the band in 2007.

Live Recordings: (1) The performance at the LA Shrine Auditorium on 24 January 1975 was recorded (7:56) and included on *Genesis Archive 1967–75*, with recorded vocals from Gabriel added in the mid- to late 1990s. The recording was mixed by Nick Davis and Geoff Callingham and produced by the band.

(2) A recording of the medley (11:53) from National Exhibition Centre, Birmingham, on 23 December 1981 was included on *Three Sides Live*. The lineup was Banks, Collins and Rutherford, augmented by Daryl Stuermer (guitar) and Chester Thompson (drums). The recording was engineered by Geoff Callingham and produced by the band.

(3) Another medley (13:30) was recorded from the European leg of the band's reunion tour at the show at Old Trafford, Manchester, on 7 July 2007 and appeared on *Live Over Europe 2007*. The lineup was again Banks, Collins, Rutherford, Stuermer and Thompson. The recording was made by Bernard Natier and produced by Nick Davis.

[53] THE GRAND PARADE OF LIFELESS PACKAGING

Band Credit: Tony Banks/Phil Collins/Peter Gabriel/Steve Hackett/Mike Rutherford
Music: Tony Banks/Phil Collins/Peter Gabriel/Steve Hackett/Mike Rutherford

Lyrics: Peter Gabriel
Length: 2:46
Tony Banks—Synthesizers, Piano; **Phil Collins**—Drums, Backing Vocals, Percussion; **Peter Gabriel**—Lead Vocals; **Steve Hackett**—Guitar; **Mike Rutherford**—Bass; **Brian Eno**—Voice Synthesizer
Recorded at Glaspant Manor, Carmarthenshire, Wales, with the Island Mobile Studio, and Mixed at Island Studios, August–October 1974.
Producer: John Burns and Genesis. Engineer: David Hutchins.
2008 Remix/Remaster Release:
Mixed at The Farm, Surrey 2005/2006.
5.1 Surround sound and stereo mixes by Nick Davis. Assisted by Tom Mitchell.
UK Release: 22 November 1974. (2LP: *The Lamb Lies Down on Broadway*)
U.S. Release: 25 November 1974. (2LP: *The Lamb Lies Down on Broadway*)

THE GRAND PARADE OF LIFELESS PACKAGING was written late in the process to fill a gap in Gabriel's story. The music was written during an improvisation session where for once the band was working with Gabriel's completed lyrics. Gabriel was partly inspired by Aldous Huxley's 1932 novel *Brave New World*, notably the opening hatchery sequence where the citizens are factory engineered through artificial wombs. At this point in the story Rael stops spinning and sits on a polished floor. In front of him a saleslady demonstrates a production line of packages. On closer inspection Rael discovers the packages are lifeless bodies—some of which are members of his street gang. Rael flees in fear of his safety. As he runs along the factory floor, he spots his brother John in the line with the number 9 stamped on his forehead and Rael is transported into a reconstruction of his life.

Musically, the piece is based on a two-chord sequence from Banks played in twos, which the band worked across three keys. It features an incredibly strong vocal performance from Gabriel and is thematically an allegorical swipe at the growth of consumerism. The atmospheric opening involves the whistle of a steam engine followed by a rhythmic build as the marching parade of packages passes by Rael. Structurally the song stays in this one area, but the tension is heightened as Gabriel's vocals build in intensity with added synthesized vocal effects by Brian Eno at the song's conclusion. Collins' drumming is highly percussive throughout making maximum use of his expansive kit as he adds considerable rhythmic propulsion to the track.

Single Release: The song was included on a 4-track EP released in Brazil to promote the album in 1975.

Live Performances: 1974/5. The band also rehearsed the song for their 1978 tour but found it did not work as well when taken out of context within the album.

Live Recordings: The performance (4:25) from the LA Shrine Auditorium on 24 January 1975 was captured and included on *Genesis Archive 1967–75*, with recorded vocals from Gabriel added sometime between 1995 and 1998. The recording was mixed by Nick Davis and Geoff Callingham and produced by the band.

[54] BACK IN N.Y.C.

Band Credit: Tony Banks/Phil Collins/Peter Gabriel/Steve Hackett/Mike Rutherford
Music: Tony Banks/Phil Collins/Peter Gabriel/Steve Hackett/Mike Rutherford
Lyrics: Peter Gabriel
Length: 5:45
Tony Banks—Synthesizers; **Phil Collins**—Drums, Backing Vocals, Percussion; **Peter Gabriel**—Lead Vocals; **Steve Hackett**—Guitar; **Mike Rutherford**—Bass; **Brian Eno**—Voice Synthesizer

8. Studio Album #6: The Lamb Lies Down on Broadway

Recorded at Glaspant Manor, Carmarthenshire, Wales, with the Island Mobile Studio, and Mixed at Island Studios, August–October 1974.
Producer: John Burns and Genesis. Engineer: David Hutchins.
2008 Remix/Remaster Release:
Mixed at The Farm, Surrey 2005/2006.
5.1 Surround sound and stereo mixes by Nick Davis. Assisted by Tom Mitchell.
UK Release: 22 November 1974. (2LP: *The Lamb Lies Down on Broadway*)
U.S. Release: 25 November 1974. (2LP: *The Lamb Lies Down on Broadway*)

BACK IN N.Y.C. is often described as punk-prog and the song certainly carries an attitude of rebellion and aggression that pdates the punk explosion of 1976. During the reconstruction of his life, Rael observes himself as an angry young man with destructive tendencies who is coming to terms with the onset of puberty. Rael's angst is brilliantly conveyed via an electrifying vocal performance from Gabriel. The song is the heaviest on the album and is based around Banks' harsh synth arpeggios and some powerful rhythm work from Rutherford and Collins. It opens, like [52] IN THE CAGE, with Rutherford's bass creating a heartbeat effect. The main repeated riff was written by Rutherford on a six-string bass guitar, with Banks adapting it into a phrase for his ARP synth. It feels like a template for the techno rock that Gary Numan would champion only a few years later. The verses are largely in 7/4. The meter then alternates with the 3/4 timing in the chorus before moving to 9/4 in the bridge at 3:31. This shifting of time signatures gives the song a stop/start feel that musically mirrors Rael's level of agitation. Gabriel is really straining at points to convey the passion and aggression of the protagonist in his vocal performance as Rael's actions descend into destruction. Daryl Easlea, for *Prog*, described the song as "one of the hardest things the group ever recorded with Gabriel moving frequently from a scream to a whisper."[18] The singer's delivery certainly equals the emotion he poured into the closing section of [38] SUPPER'S READY. Banks felt the band, probably led by himself, had nearly overcomplicated the song by adding in too many elements, but this is a minor quibble. All the band members acknowledge it is one of the strongest songs on the album. It is certainly one of the band's most distinctive and impressive recordings.

Single Release: The song was included on a 4-track EP released in Brazil to promote the album in 1975.

Live Performances: 1974/5, 1980 (occasionally), 1982 ('six of the Best' show). The song was performed on the subsequent tour as part of the band's presentation of the whole album. Following Gabriel's departure, it was not included in the set again until 1980, when Phil Collins gave a strained interpretation, as he struggled to maintain the aggressive vocal delivery—notably at the Madison Square Gardens' gig in New York City that June. This accounted for its infrequent use on the tour and the song was subsequently dropped. When Gabriel returned for the one-off reunion at the Milton Keynes Bowl in 1982, the song was used as the concert opener with the singer being carried on stage in a coffin.

Live Recordings: The performance (6:19) from the LA Shrine Auditorium on 24 January 1975 was captured and included on *Genesis Archive 1967–75*. Due to his dissatisfaction with aspects of his original vocal performance, Gabriel rerecorded vocal parts sometime between 1995 and 1998. Another version of this performance (6:11) is available on the remastered and remixed *Genesis Live*, released as part of the *Genesis 1970–1975* box set in 2009. Here the vocal is largely Gabriel's original. Neither version really captures the full aggression of the studio recording. The recordings were mixed by Nick Davis and Geoff Callingham and produced by the band.

[55] Hairless Heart

Band Credit: Tony Banks/Phil Collins/Peter Gabriel/Steve Hackett/Mike Rutherford
Music: Tony Banks/Phil Collins/Steve Hackett/Mike Rutherford
Length: 2:10
Tony Banks—Synthesizers, Organ, Piano; **Phil Collins**—Drums, Percussion, Vibraphone; **Steve Hackett**—Guitar; **Mike Rutherford**—Acoustic Guitar, Bass Pedals
Recorded at Glaspant Manor, Carmarthenshire, Wales, with the Island Mobile Studio, and Mixed at Island Studios, August–October 1974.
Producer: John Burns and Genesis. Engineer: David Hutchins.
2008 Remix/Remaster Release:
Mixed at The Farm, Surrey 2005/2006.
5.1 Surround sound and stereo mixes by Nick Davis. Assisted by Tom Mitchell.
UK Release: 22 November 1974. (2LP: *The Lamb Lies Down on Broadway*)
U.S. Release: 25 November 1974. (2LP: *The Lamb Lies Down on Broadway*)

HAIRLESS HEART is an instrumental piece that acts as an antidote to the power and aggression of [54] BACK IN N.Y.C. as Rael watches himself being shaved of all his hair. Hackett provided the main musical ideas around this piece. The track opens with a classical acoustic motif double-tracked with a gentle electric guitar backing by Hackett over some undulating synth lines and organ arpeggios from Banks. This leads into a short, pleasant and charming instrumental piece in D minor, which adds more than a hint of melancholy via its minor-key setting. Banks provides a warm, relaxing and flowing melody over a simple chord structure. Collins adds a tasteful drum pattern and Rutherford contributes single bass pedal notes emphasizing each change in the harmonic structure and adding emphasis to the gliding feel of the chord changes.

Live Performances: 1974/5. The song was played as part of the band's presentation of the whole album but was dropped from the set following this tour.

Live Recordings: The performance (2:22) from the LA Shrine Auditorium on 24 January 1975 was captured and included on *Genesis Archive 1967–75*. The recording was mixed by Nick Davis and Geoff Callingham and produced by the band.

[56] Counting Out Time

Band Credit: Tony Banks/Phil Collins/Peter Gabriel/Steve Hackett/Mike Rutherford
Music: Peter Gabriel
Lyrics: Peter Gabriel
Length: 3:41
Tony Banks—Synthesizers, Piano; **Phil Collins**—Drums, Backing Vocals, Percussion; **Peter Gabriel**—Lead Vocals; **Steve Hackett**—Guitar; **Mike Rutherford**—Bass
Recorded at Glaspant Manor, Carmarthenshire, Wales, with the Island Mobile Studio, and Mixed at Island Studios, August–October 1974.
Producer: John Burns and Genesis. Engineer: David Hutchins.
2008 Remix/Remaster Release:
Mixed at The Farm, Surrey 2005/2006.
5.1 Surround sound and stereo mixes by Nick Davis. Assisted by Tom Mitchell.
UK Release: 15 November 1974.[19] (A-side single b/w [68] RIDING THE SCREE. Charisma. CB 238)
UK Album Release: 22 November 1974. (2LP: *The Lamb Lies Down on Broadway*)
U.S. Release: 25 November 1974. (2LP: *The Lamb Lies Down on Broadway*)
U.S. Single Release: December 1974. (B-side single b/w [48] THE LAMB LIES DOWN ON BROADWAY. Atlantic/ATCO. 45-7013)

A hilarious account of Rael's first sexual encounter and his need to buy a book to instruct him in the finer art of lovemaking. It was referred to by the band as "Sex Song" during

8. Studio Album #6: The Lamb Lies Down on Broadway

Advertisement promoting *The Lamb Lies Down on Broadway* **and the lead-off single** [56] **COUNTING OUT TIME placed in** *Melody Maker* **on 30 November 1974 (courtesy Mark Kenyon/ The Genesis Archive).**

the recording. Of course, the whole thing ends prematurely with Rael displeasing his mistress and earning a slap in the face before returning to the bookstore for a refund. It is a typical piece of Gabriel whimsy and it blends music hall humor with straight rock guitar riffs as the song rhythmically bounces from verse to chorus. Gabriel delivers his risqué lyrics, about the female erogenous zones and how to manipulate them, with obvious relish and Collins adds witty harmonics. The song's main hook is Hackett's simple guitar riff on the chorus. Hackett also contributes a jolly treated guitar solo, ahead of the final verse-chorus combo. Here he uses an EMS Synthi Hi-Fli guitar synthesizer to enable the guitar to simulate the sound of a brass wind instrument. The song's closing moments have Gabriel and Collins wailing out vocal noises and bringing a conclusion to this bright and breezy interlude.

Single Release: The song is possibly the most straightforward in approach on the album and was therefore was an obvious selection for a single. It was released in the UK in November 1974 ahead of the album in slightly edited form (3:39, with a modified intro) but failed to chart. The single was also released across Europe and followed in the U.S. a month later, where it was the B-side to [48] THE LAMB LIES DOWN ON BROADWAY. Its chart progress won't have been helped by the scathing review in *Melody Maker* which stated: "This really is a woeful, dreary three-and-a-half minutes' worth, chugging along like the runaway train going uphill, with only a few whoops and strange noises at the end to brighten it."[20] The song was also included on a 4-track EP released in Brazil in 1975.

Live Performances: 1974/5. Like many songs from the album, COUNTING OUT TIME was only performed as part of the band's tour of *The Lamb Lies Down on Broadway.*

Live Recordings: The performance (4:00) from the LA Shrine Auditorium on 24 January 1975 was included on the box set *Genesis Archive 1967–75*. The recording was mixed by Nick Davis and Geoff Callingham and produced by the band.

[57] CARPET CRAWLERS

Band Credit: Tony Banks/Phil Collins/Peter Gabriel/Steve Hackett/Mike Rutherford
Music: Tony Banks/Phil Collins/Peter Gabriel/Steve Hackett/Mike Rutherford
Lyrics: Peter Gabriel
Length: 5:15
Tony Banks—Synthesizers, Electric Piano; **Phil Collins**—Drums, Backing Vocals, Percussion; **Peter Gabriel**—Lead Vocals, Flute; **Steve Hackett**—Guitar; **Mike Rutherford**—Acoustic Guitar, Bass, Bass Pedals
Recorded at Glaspant Manor, Carmarthenshire, Wales, with the Island Mobile Studio, and Mixed at Island Studios, August–October 1974.
Producer: John Burns and Genesis. Engineer: David Hutchins.
2008 Remix/Remaster Release:
Mixed at The Farm, Surrey 2005/2006.
5.1 Surround sound and stereo mixes by Nick Davis. Assisted by Tom Mitchell.
UK Release: 22 November 1974. (2LP: *The Lamb Lies Down on Broadway*)
U.S. Release: 25 November 1974. (2LP: *The Lamb Lies Down on Broadway*)
UK Single Release: 18 April 1975. (A-side Single b/w [60] THE WAITING ROOM [here referred to as 'Evil Jam' (Live)]. Charisma. CB 251)

Late in the writing process Gabriel still had sections of his story that he required music for. CARPET CRAWLERS (also referred to as "The Carpet Crawlers" or "Carpet Crawl") was one such example.[21] At this juncture in the story, Rael continues his journey and finds himself in a carpeted corridor where he encounters people slowly crawling along the floor toward a wooden door at the end. Through the door, Rael sees a candle-lit table containing a feast. Beyond the table is a spiral staircase, which twists upward until it disappears out of site.

Musically, the song is based on a doodle worked on quickly by Banks and Rutherford. The urgent need for its completion meant the pair kept the song structure and chords simple—Gabriel already had the lyrics prepared and the band created the music around the chord sequence of D major, E minor and F sharp minor. This allowed the singer to write a seductive vocal melody using the piano at his wife's parent's house in Kensington. The opening to the song was based on a piece of improvisation the band found while listening back through a batch of cassettes that Collins had compiled during the recording sessions. Rutherford recalled, "I was sitting in the kitchen one night drinking beer, playing back one of the jam tapes of the day, and there it was—one of those bits that at the time we hadn't really rated but, with renewed perspective, was potentially quite interesting."[22]

A gentle spiraling keyboard refrain provides a gentle introduction, before the rest of the band join for the verse. The catchy chorus hook is sung by both Gabriel and Collins—their vocal harmonies complementing each other with Collins' falsetto riding over Gabriel's low timbre. The song continues to gradually build adding subtle layers with each verse as Gabriel's vocals grow in intensity, before finally fading away as the chorus is repeated in overlapping fashion. The result is perhaps the strongest song on the album and one that stands out even when isolated from the story concept, despite the descriptive nature of Gabriel's lyrics.

Single Release: The song was released as a single as "The Carpet Crawlers" in a slightly edited version (4:33) in the UK in April 1975,[23] backed with a live recording of [60] THE WAITING ROOM (EVIL JAM) from the LA Shrine Auditorium on 24 January 1975. The single failed to chart but was also released in Italy (b/w [48] THE LAMB LIES DOWN ON BROADWAY) and Brazil (b/w [56] COUNTING OUT TIME). In his review of the single release for *Melody Maker*, Colin Irwin bizarrely described the song as "doomy and ghostlike, rather like Rasputin prowling round Alderley Edge in search of voluptuous virgins to devour."[24] Other reviewers, such as *Zig Zag*'s Andy Childs, could see the quality of the song: "It's tuneful, devoid of any clever instrumental pyrotechnics, and has the most ear-grabbing sing-along chorus I've heard in a fair old time."[25] Gabriel regards his melody as one of the strongest he wrote for the band and described it as a pop song. Banks believes the lyric stopped the song from becoming a hit as it is effectively a linking piece between [56] COUNTING OUT TIME and [58] THE CHAMBER OF 32 DOORS, suggesting a need to be familiar with the story, although he acknowledged that the chorus had a more universal appeal.

Rerecording: Between 1994 and 1999 *The Lamb* lineup of the band rerecorded the song in shortened form as [186] THE CARPET CRAWLERS 1999 (see separate entry) for digital download and single release. However, this version was recorded via a series of overdubs utilizing the production expertise of Trevor Horn rather than as a band performance. Collins provided lead vocals for the final verse. This version was also included on the 1999 compilation album *Turn It On Again: The Hits*, while the original version appeared on *The Platinum Collection* released in 2004.

Live Performances: 1974/5, 1976, 1977, 1980, 1981, 1982 ('Six of the Best' show), 1992 (occasionally), 1998, 2007. The song became one of the most popular in the band's live set and was also a favorite among the band members. The song was performed on the subsequent tour of *The Lamb*. Later performances would omit the opening introductory verse. The song was also performed at the one-off "Six of the Best" reunion at the Milton Keynes Bowl in 1982. Indeed, the band's fondness for the song led to it being chosen as the encore on their 2007 reunion tour and therefore the last song they ever performed.

Live Recordings: (1) The performance (5:45) from the LA Shrine Auditorium on 24 January 1975 was captured and included on the box set *Genesis Archive 1967–75*. The recording was mixed by Nick Davis and Geoff Callingham and produced by the band.

(2) A version sung by Collins (5:27) from Palais des Sports and recorded between 11–14 June 1977 was included on *Seconds Out*. This version feels a little light and lacks the harmonic interplay of the original. The lineup was Banks, Collins, Hackett and Rutherford, augmented by Chester Thompson (drums). David Hentschel and the band co-produced.

(3) A further live recording (6:00) from Old Trafford, Manchester, on 7 July 2007 appeared on *Live Over Europe 2007*. This is a much stronger performance with Collins delivering an emotive vocal and the band even interjected a sequence from their 1999 rerecorded

Advertisement promoting the [57] CARPET CRAWLERS single release placed in *New Musical Express* on 26 April 1975 (courtesy Mark Kenyon/The Genesis Archive).

version. The lineup was Banks, Collins and Rutherford, augmented by Daryl Stuermer (guitar) and Thompson. The recording was made by Bernard Natier and produced by Nick Davis.

[58] THE CHAMBER OF 32 DOORS

Band Credit: Tony Banks/Phil Collins/Peter Gabriel/Steve Hackett/Mike Rutherford
Music: Tony Banks/Phil Collins/Peter Gabriel/Steve Hackett/Mike Rutherford

8. Studio Album #6: The Lamb Lies Down on Broadway

Lyrics: Peter Gabriel
Length: 5:45
Tony Banks—Mellotron, Organ, Piano; **Phil Collins**—Drums, Backing Vocals; **Peter Gabriel**—Lead Vocals; **Steve Hackett**—Guitar; **Mike Rutherford**—Bass
Recorded at Glaspant Manor, Carmarthenshire, Wales, with the Island Mobile Studio, and Mixed at Island Studios, August–October 1974.
Producer: John Burns and Genesis. Engineer: David Hutchins.
2008 Remix/Remaster Release:
Mixed at The Farm, Surrey 2005/2006.
5.1 Surround sound and stereo mixes by Nick Davis. Assisted by Tom Mitchell.
UK Release: 22 November 1974. (2LP: *The Lamb Lies Down on Broadway*)
U.S. Release: 25 November 1974. (2LP: *The Lamb Lies Down on Broadway*)

There is a religious/country feel that pervades the final song from the first side of the CD and second side of the LP.[26] Rael ascends the spiral staircase that he came across at the close of [57] CARPET CRAWLERS and finds a circular chamber with thirty-two doors and only one way out. There is a lively crowd of people in the chamber and Rael finally silences them before finding himself huddling in a corner.

While the song was largely developed by Gabriel, the dramatic midtempo introduction is one of the rare showcases for Hackett's guitar and here he provides the lead lines over some chunky bass pedals from Rutherford and a rhythm from Collins' drums that heightens the drama. The song then rolls over into a more urgent rhythm as Gabriel introduces his vocal to advance the story. The verse then slows again over a sparse moody accompaniment prompted by Rutherford's bass and colored by Hackett's lead guitar. Hackett liked the cinematic quality of the music and commented on how he weaved his guitar parts through the questioning song attempting to mirror the theme of the lyrics. On the chorus the song rhythmically and stylistically takes on the referenced country feel, with Banks adding piano to the mix, before it returns to its two-part verse. Banks contributes a mix of Mellotron strings and Hammond organ to fill out the sound as the two styles then interchange before the song returns to the chorus and ends on a desolate refrain by Gabriel over Banks' singular piano chords. The song was a stylistic departure for the band demonstrating that their desire to experiment enabled them to create challenging music.

Live Performances: 1974/5. The song was only performed as part of the band's tour of *The Lamb Lies Down on Broadway*.

Live Recordings: The performance (5:52) from the LA Shrine Auditorium on 24 January 1975 was captured and included on *Genesis Archive 1967–75*. A remixed version (5:58) was included on the 2009 release of *Genesis Live* as part of the *Genesis Live 1973–2007* box set. The recording was mixed by Nick Davis and Geoff Callingham and produced by the band.

[59] LILYWHITE LILITH

Band Credit: Tony Banks/Phil Collins/Peter Gabriel/Steve Hackett/Mike Rutherford
Music: Tony Banks/Phil Collins/Peter Gabriel/Steve Hackett/Mike Rutherford
Lyrics: Peter Gabriel
Length: 2:49
Tony Banks—Synthesizers; **Phil Collins**—Drums, Backing Vocals, Percussion; **Peter Gabriel**—Lead Vocals; **Steve Hackett**—Guitar; **Mike Rutherford**—Bass
Recorded at Glaspant Manor, Carmarthenshire, Wales, with the Island Mobile Studio, and Mixed at Island Studios, August–October 1974.
Producer: John Burns and Genesis. Engineer: David Hutchins.
2008 Remix/Remaster Release:
Mixed at The Farm, Surrey 2005/2006.

5.1 Surround sound and stereo mixes by Nick Davis. Assisted by Tom Mitchell.
UK Release: 22 November 1974. (2LP: *The Lamb Lies Down on Broadway*)
U.S. Release: 25 November 1974. (2LP: *The Lamb Lies Down on Broadway*)

LILYWHITE LILITH is one of the most melodic tracks on the album and proves to be a brief but lively opener for the second disc on the CD and LP. Gabriel lyrically describes how Rael is led by a blind woman through the crowded chamber and into a cave where they are dazzled by a blazing light. Gabriel was inspired for the song's title by some nature books he had been studying about animals that live beneath the earth's surface and never see daylight and are therefore very pale in color. He used this idea for the character of Lilith and to imagine her wax-like pale skin.

Musically, the song evolved from sections of a longer piece the band had written and performed in 1971 under the working title "The Light." Collins brought the bones of that song into the band forming the basis for both the guitar riff and the verse melody. Collins' strong drumming alongside the driving bass and rhythm guitar riffs of Rutherford and Hackett steer the piece. Hackett also contributes some effective lead work and Collins' close harmonizing to Gabriel's lead vocals adds further character. The song plays out over a repeated staccato rhythm and floating keyboards as it evolves into [60] THE WAITING ROOM.

Live Performances: 1974/5, 1977 (once). LILYWHITE LILITH was performed on the subsequent tour as part of the band's presentation of the whole album. It was later performed just once on their 1977 tour, during the first show at the Rainbow Theatre in London on 1 January, with Collins handling the lead vocals.

Live Recordings: The performance (3:04) from the LA Shrine Auditorium on 24 January 1975 was captured and included on *Genesis Archive 1967–75*. The recording was mixed by Nick Davis and Geoff Callingham and produced by the band.

[60] THE WAITING ROOM

Band Credit: Tony Banks/Phil Collins/Peter Gabriel/Steve Hackett/Mike Rutherford
Music: Tony Banks/Phil Collins/Peter Gabriel/Steve Hackett/Mike Rutherford
Length: 5:17
Tony Banks—Synthesizers; **Phil Collins**—Drums, Percussion; **Peter Gabriel**—Flute, Oboe, Percussion, Sonic Effects; **Steve Hackett**—Guitar; **Mike Rutherford**—Bass
Recorded at Glaspant Manor, Carmarthenshire, Wales, with the Island Mobile Studio, and Mixed at Island Studios, August–October 1974.
Producer: John Burns and Genesis. Engineer: David Hutchins.
2008 Remix/Remaster Release:
Mixed at The Farm, Surrey 2005/2006.
5.1 Surround sound and stereo mixes by Nick Davis. Assisted by Tom Mitchell.
UK Release: 22 November 1974. (2LP: *The Lamb Lies Down on Broadway*)
U.S. Release: 25 November 1974. (2LP: *The Lamb Lies Down on Broadway*)

At this juncture in the story Rael is left to face his fears as the light envelopes him and a group of strange and disconcerting sounds fill the air around him. THE WAITING ROOM is no traditional Genesis instrumental. Instead it is the edited sonic product of a near twenty-minute unstructured improvisation with the only brief to somehow work from evil to good. Hackett and Banks were in their element creating as many eerie sounds from their instruments as was possible during the "evil" first half as Banks recalled, "We switched off all the lights and just made noises. And the first time it was really frightening."[27] Gabriel created additional effects from his Oboe by blowing the reeds into a microphone and from his flute by running the instrument through an echoplex effect using tape delay. A loud thunderclap breaks the atmosphere and takes the band into a more structured second part, which represented the transition from evil to good. This is a highly inventive change of mood without the band missing a beat. Collins recalled in his interview for the remasters DVD that while the band were improvising inside it was pouring with rain outside, but at the precise moment the switch of mood in the music takes place the sun came out forming a rainbow.

Ultimately, THE WAITING ROOM may fall into the category of "more fun to play than to listen to," but Collins loved the freedom it gave the band to express themselves describing it as one of the album's "stand-out moments."[28] Whatever you may think of the piece as "music," it is certainly unlike anything the band had written before or since. It pitches perfectly into the story of Rael and illustrates the character's phobias and anxieties. To that extent it fulfills its role perfectly and should always be played and judged in the context of its position in the story.

Live Performances: 1974/5, 1977 (excerpt, once). THE WAITING ROOM was performed on the subsequent tour and rechristened "Evil Jam" as the band would improvise the sounds and atmosphere on stage, sometimes for up to ten minutes, as Banks explained at the time, "Some nights it's great, some nights it's awful, which is really nice because it means there's a challenge to it. And when it goes well it lifts you up for the rest of the set. When things go badly you concentrate on thinking of tomorrow."[29] A brief excerpt was also used on the first date of the band's 1977 tour as a link between [59] LILYWHITE LILITH and [83] WOT GORILLA?

Live Recordings: The performance (6:15) at the LA Shrine Auditorium on 24 January 1975 was captured and included on *Genesis Archive 1967–75*. The recording was remixed by Nick Davis and Geoff Callingham. The same live performance (edited to 4:04) was also used as the B-side to the [57] CARPET CRAWLERS single release in April 1975 under the title of "The Waiting Room (Evil Jam)" and was produced by John Burns and the band.

[61] ANYWAY

Band Credit: Tony Banks/Phil Collins/Peter Gabriel/Steve Hackett/Mike Rutherford
Music: Tony Banks/Phil Collins/Peter Gabriel/Steve Hackett/ Anthony Phillips/Mike Rutherford
Lyrics: Peter Gabriel
Length: 3:17
Tony Banks—Piano, Synthesizers; **Phil Collins**—Drums, Backing Vocals, Percussion; **Peter Gabriel**—Lead Vocals; **Steve Hackett**—Guitar; **Mike Rutherford**—Bass
Recorded at Glaspant Manor, Carmarthenshire, Wales, with the Island Mobile Studio, and Mixed at Island Studios, August–October 1974.
Producer: John Burns and Genesis. Engineer: David Hutchins.
2008 Remix/Remaster Release:
Mixed at The Farm, Surrey 2005/2006.
5.1 Surround sound and stereo mixes by Nick Davis. Assisted by Tom Mitchell.
UK Release: 22 November 1974. (2LP: *The Lamb Lies Down on Broadway*)
U.S. Release: 25 November 1974. (2LP: *The Lamb Lies Down on Broadway*)

Gabriel sings of Rael's journey through a dark cave he finds himself in and explores how the protagonist starts to contemplate his own death. Banks' undulating piano melody was originally written as part of the [D18c] FRUSTRATION section of the music recorded in 1970 for the BBC TV documentary on painter Mick Jackson. Banks' semi-classical approach to the piano figure played through spiraling arpeggios is backed by an understated bass from Rutherford and tasteful drumming from Collins. There is a dramatic midsection break, which ends in a brief guitar solo from Hackett that adds some life to an otherwise surprisingly dull song, which has too many stops and starts meaning that while it is just over three minutes in length it feels much longer. Banks also adds some color along the way via his synth melody lines. Gabriel delivers his vocal straight with few flourishes, but the song serves little more purpose than to advance the story.

Live Performances: 1974/5. The song was only performed as part of the band's tour of *The Lamb Lies Down on Broadway*.

Live Recordings: The performance (3:28) at the LA Shrine Auditorium on 24 January 1975 was captured and included on *Genesis Archive 1967–75*, with Gabriel updating some vocals. This performance was later added to the *Genesis Live* remix/remaster release (3:33) in 2009 with further additional vocals from Gabriel. The recording was mixed by Nick Davis and Geoff Callingham.

[62] HERE COMES THE SUPERNATURAL ANAESTHETIST

Band Credit: Tony Banks/Phil Collins/Peter Gabriel/Steve Hackett/Mike Rutherford
Music: Tony Banks/Phil Collins/Peter Gabriel/Steve Hackett/Mike Rutherford
Lyrics: Peter Gabriel
Length: 2:49
Tony Banks—Synthesizers, Mellotron; **Phil Collins**—Drums, Harmony Vocals, Percussion; **Peter Gabriel**—Lead Vocals, Flute; **Steve Hackett**—Guitar; **Mike Rutherford**—Acoustic Guitar, Bass
Recorded at Glaspant Manor, Carmarthenshire, Wales, with the Island Mobile Studio, and Mixed at Island Studios, August–October 1974.
Producer: John Burns and Genesis. Engineer: David Hutchins.
2008 Remix/Remaster Release:
Mixed at The Farm, Surrey 2005/2006.
5.1 Surround sound and stereo mixes by Nick Davis. Assisted by Tom Mitchell.
UK Release: 22 November 1974. (2LP: *The Lamb Lies Down on Broadway*)
U.S. Release: 25 November 1974. (2LP: *The Lamb Lies Down on Broadway*)

Gabriel's brief introductory lyric serves as a link in the story and song is split into two distinct sections as Rael sees a figure that he believes to be Death, but Death merely sprays an anesthetic into his face. Hackett was the main writer of this track, which gave him one of his few solo spots on the album. In the first twenty-five seconds Gabriel, backed strongly by Collins, sings a gentle and whimsical melody over a strummed acoustic rhythm guitar from Rutherford. The song then breaks out with the full band joining into an electric instrumental section. This features a lovely melodic guitar solo from Hackett, working short staccato lead lines over Rutherford's continued strummed rhythm. Banks adds harmonic textures though his synthesizer and Mellotron. The section ends on a brief crescendo and then the band suddenly stops playing while Hackett and Banks create the ambient link into the next track. It is another short, but evocative piece that advances the story.

Live Performances: 1974/5. The song was only performed as part of the band's tour of *The Lamb Lies Down on Broadway*.

Live Recordings: the performance (3:57) at the LA Shrine Auditorium on 24 January 1975 was captured and included on *Genesis Archive 1967–75*. The recording was mixed by Nick Davis and Geoff Callingham.

[63] THE LAMIA

Band Credit: Tony Banks/Phil Collins/Peter Gabriel/Steve Hackett/Mike Rutherford
Music: Tony Banks/Phil Collins/Peter Gabriel/Steve Hackett/Mike Rutherford
Lyrics: Peter Gabriel
Length: 6:58
Tony Banks—Synthesizers, Organ, Piano; **Phil Collins**—Drums, Backing Vocals, Percussion; **Peter Gabriel**—Lead Vocals, Flute; **Steve Hackett**—Guitar; **Mike Rutherford**—Acoustic Guitar, Bass
Recorded at Glaspant Manor, Carmarthenshire, Wales, with the Island Mobile Studio, and Mixed at Island Studios, August–October 1974.
Producer: John Burns and Genesis. Engineer: David Hutchins.
2008 Remix/Remaster Release:
Mixed at The Farm, Surrey 2005/2006.
5.1 Surround sound and stereo mixes by Nick Davis. Assisted by Tom Mitchell.
UK Release: 22 November 1974. (2LP: *The Lamb Lies Down on Broadway*)
U.S. Release: 25 November 1974. (2LP: *The Lamb Lies Down on Broadway*)

THE LAMIA depicts Rael's encounter with the seductive and erotic snake-like Lamia in their pool. Here Rael is drained of his energy by the creatures. The Lamia die and Rael eats their flesh before exiting the cavern. As he turns and looks back, he sees the stage has been reset for the next visitor. Gabriel's inspiration for the lyrics came from the poem *Lamia*, written in 1819 by John Keats, which describes the god Hermes discovering a woman's spirit prisoned within the body of a serpent.

It is during the early sections of this long, theatrical and rippling song that the listener may start to drift. The melody is like that used on [61] ANYWAY, with Banks' immaculately played piano figure again providing the lead over which Gabriel vocally describes Rael's encounter through his highly descriptive lyrics of the Lamia's lair and its serpentine sensuality. Again, the music has stop/start moments that fragment the song. Hackett, however, counts this as one of his favorite pieces from the album and enlivens the track with some splendid lead guitar work, "I aimed to make the guitar sound both bluesy and classical and as sensual as the lyric."[30] As the song progresses Banks adds synth lines which are both atmospheric and melodic and Gabriel contributes an intervening flute motif. Collins' drumming is tasteful throughout helping to lift moments where the music swells. The tune finally takes off with Hackett's searing solo that concludes the song—his playing is both inventive and spine-chilling and his performance adds some late drama to rescue what is otherwise a track that feels overstretched.

Live Performances: 1974/5. On stage this was a strong costume moment for Gabriel as he becomes enveloped in a tube of fabric symbolizing the Lamia's snaking dance. It proved to be another point in the set where the singer would often struggle to get the microphone in position to deliver his vocal.

Live Recordings: The performance (7:12) at the LA Shrine Auditorium on 24 January 1975 was captured and included on *Genesis Archive 1967–75*. The recording was mixed by Nick Davis and Geoff Callingham.

[64] SILENT SORROW IN EMPTY BOATS

Band Credit: Tony Banks/Phil Collins/Peter Gabriel/Steve Hackett/Mike Rutherford
Music: Tony Banks/Phil Collins/Steve Hackett/Mike Rutherford
Length: 3:01
Tony Banks—Synthesizers, Mellotron; **Phil Collins**—Percussion; **Steve Hackett**—Guitar; **Mike Rutherford**—Bass; **Brian Eno**—Sonic Effects

Recorded at Glaspant Manor, Carmarthenshire, Wales, with the Island Mobile Studio, and Mixed at Island Studios, August–October 1974.
Producer: John Burns and Genesis. Engineer: David Hutchins.
2008 Remix/Remaster Release:
Mixed at The Farm, Surrey 2005/2006.
5.1 Surround sound and stereo mixes by Nick Davis. Assisted by Tom Mitchell.
UK Release: 22 November 1974. (2LP: *The Lamb Lies Down on Broadway*)
U.S. Release: 25 November 1974. (2LP: *The Lamb Lies Down on Broadway*)

This instrumental track was based on a piece the band had written called "Victory at Sea" and was used here as an ambient link. It is intended to musically describe Rael's frame of mind following his encounter with the Lamia. The piece is based around a repeated six-note guitar pedal motif by Hackett backed by the swells of the choral section from Banks' Mellotron. The overall visual image conjured by the music is of slow boats gliding down a river blanketed in mist—as the instruments slowly fade in and then away it is easy to imagine the boat emerging from the mist and disappearing again. The title is lifted from a line of Gabriel's lyric for [63] THE LAMIA and is representative of Rael's sad refrain. Collins adds elegant percussion and the track is one of his personal favorite musical moments from the album, for which he cites the improvisational nature of its composition as the group at its strongest. This is also one of the tracks to which Brian Eno contributes his "Enossification," here helping to create the shimmering sound effects.

Live Performances: 1974/5. The piece was only performed as part of the band's tour of *The Lamb Lies Down on Broadway*.

Live Recordings: The performance (3:15) at the LA Shrine Auditorium on 24 January 1975 was captured and included on *Genesis Archive 1967–75*. The recording was mixed by Nick Davis and Geoff Callingham.

[65] THE COLONY OF SLIPPERMEN

I. Arrival; II. A Visit to the Doktor; III. The Raven

Band Credit: Tony Banks/Phil Collins/Peter Gabriel/Steve Hackett/Mike Rutherford
Music: Tony Banks/Phil Collins/Peter Gabriel/Steve Hackett/Mike Rutherford
Lyrics: Peter Gabriel
Length: 8:12
Tony Banks—Synthesizers, Organ; **Phil Collins**—Drums, Lead Vocals (as 'John'), Backing Vocals, Percussion; **Peter Gabriel**—Lead Vocals, Flute; **Steve Hackett**—Guitar; **Mike Rutherford**—Acoustic Guitar, Bass; **Brian Eno**—Voice Synthesizer (?)
Recorded at Glaspant Manor, Carmarthenshire, Wales, with the Island Mobile Studio, and Mixed at Island Studios, August–October 1974.
Producer: John Burns and Genesis. Engineer: David Hutchins.
2008 Remix/Remaster Release:
Mixed at The Farm, Surrey 2005/2006.
5.1 Surround sound and stereo mixes by Nick Davis. Assisted by Tom Mitchell.
UK Release: 22 November 1974. (2LP: *The Lamb Lies Down on Broadway*)
U.S. Release: 25 November 1974. (2LP: *The Lamb Lies Down on Broadway*)

THE COLONY OF SLIPPERMEN is a three-part suite and is the longest piece on the album at just over eight minutes in length:

I. "Arrival" (0:00–3:26)

Written under the working title of "Chinese Jam," the segment opens with an echoing mandarin-like sound created by unrelated phrases played by Hackett and Banks. These are delicately interwoven with blocky percussion from Collins. The fast-paced musical section is based around Banks' rotating organ riff, while Gabriel's lyrics describe Rael's arrival at a colony of hideously disfigured freaks. Rael has contracted a sexually transmitted disease from the Lamia and Gabriel delivers his lyrics in character as the Slipperman tries to reassure the diseased Rael that he is not alone in his suffering. The song then splits into more operatic dialogue between Rael and the Slipperman backed by some more eerie synth sounds.

II. "A Visit to the Doktor" (3:27–4:17)

As the song enters its second phase Rael finds his brother, John, among the Slippermen. John explains the only cure for them is to visit Doktor Dyper for a castration to be performed. Banks' riffing organ leads this section with Rutherford's prodding bass line while Collins' drums urge the song along with gusto. Gabriel delivers more surreal and witty wordplay with his lyrics describing Rael's disease of the genitalia and the likely castration that will follow. He also delivers some strange treated voices, likely courtesy of Brian Eno, in character for the Slippermen who prepare to assist Doktor Dyper perform the operation to remove Rael's manhood.

III. "The Raven" (4:18–8:12)

In the final segment, Gabriel provides a sung narration over an urgent rhythm. Having survived the operation Rael and John are presented with their genitalia secured in yellow plastic tubes, which they wear around their necks as trophies. A raven then swoops down to steal Rael's trophy and John again deserts him. The song evolves into a splendid gliding synth solo from Banks, which leads into the final section where the raven flies off with the tube containing Rael's castrated phallus. We're now back into a dialogue exchange between Rael, the Slipperman and briefly John (whose one-line is sung by Collins). The song then fades out as the raven drops the tube into the river below.

Co-producer/engineer John Burns was not initially happy with the sound of the song on which he had intended to create the aural equivalent of a vast lair, "I put it through an echoplex, which is like a delay echo. So, I mixed the echoplex in mono into the middle of the stereo. I put the whole track through it with the stereo out the side but the echoplex signal coming out of the middle."[31] The song does have some interesting moments and the shifts in action lead to shifts in the tone and pace of the music. Out of the context of the story, however, it would be difficult to listen to this piece in isolation.

Live Performances: 1974/5, 1980 ("Raven" excerpt), 1981 ("Raven" excerpt), 1982 ("Raven" excerpt), 1983/4 ("Raven" excerpt). THE COLONY OF SLIPPERMEN was only performed in its entirety on the subsequent tour. It caused some friction in the band over Gabriel's cumbersome costume, covered in lumps with inflated genitalia being revealed after having crawled through an inflatable phallus. While the appearance was theatrically impressive, it was musically impractical with the singer again struggling to get the microphone anywhere near his mouth. The resonant "Raven" keyboard solo proved very popular and was added to the band's medley led by [52] IN THE CAGE during their tours from 1980 to 1984.

Live Recordings: (1) The performance (8:47) at the LA Shrine Auditorium on 24 January 1975 was captured and included on *Genesis Archive 1967–75*. The recording was mixed by Nick Davis and Geoff Callingham.

(2) The snipped "Raven" keyboard solo appears as part of the "In the Cage Medley" (11:53) recorded at National Exhibition Centre in Birmingham, England on 23 December 1981 appears on *Three Sides Live*. The lineup here was Banks, Collins and Rutherford, augmented by Daryl Stuermer (guitar) and Chester Thompson (drums).

[66] RAVINE

Band Credit: Tony Banks/Phil Collins/Peter Gabriel/Steve Hackett/Mike Rutherford
Music: Tony Banks/Steve Hackett
Length: 2:06
Tony Banks—Synthesizers; **Steve Hackett**—Acoustic Guitar
Recorded at Glaspant Manor, Carmarthenshire, Wales, with the Island Mobile Studio, and Mixed at Island Studios, August–October 1974.
Producer: John Burns and Genesis. Engineer: David Hutchins.
2008 Remix/Remaster Release:
Mixed at The Farm, Surrey 2005/2006.
5.1 Surround sound and stereo mixes by Nick Davis. Assisted by Tom Mitchell.
UK Release: 22 November 1974. (2LP: *The Lamb Lies Down on Broadway*)
U.S. Release: 25 November 1974. (2LP: *The Lamb Lies Down on Broadway*)

This is another ambient instrumental bridge describing musically how Rael helplessly watches the tube drift away down the river. It is a gentle and poignant piece of music, which utilizes the eerie whistling wind-like sounds of Banks' synth alongside Hackett's acoustic guitar chord tremolos to conjure up a sense of place as Rael traverses the ravine. This shimmering musical idea would also later be reworked on 1976's *Wind & Wuthering* as [86] UNQUIET SLUMBERS FOR THE SLEEPERS…

RAVINE, like [64] SILENT SORROW IN EMPTY BOATS, was added to the recording late in the day to provide a story bridge between two songs. It also served to create stage time for Gabriel to switch costumes. Anyone who has seen the stage performance will understand why this was necessary.

Live Performances: 1974/5. The piece was only performed as part of the band's tour of *The Lamb Lies Down on Broadway*.

Live Recordings: A recording (1:39) at the LA Shrine Auditorium on 24 January 1975 was captured and included on *Genesis Archive 1967–75*. The recording was mixed by Nick Davis and Geoff Callingham.

[67] THE LIGHT DIES DOWN ON BROADWAY

Band Credit: Tony Banks/Phil Collins/Peter Gabriel/Steve Hackett/Mike Rutherford
Music: Tony Banks/Phil Collins/Peter Gabriel/Steve Hackett/Mike Rutherford
Lyrics: Tony Banks/Mike Rutherford
Length: 3:32
Tony Banks—Synthesizers; **Phil Collins**—Drums, Backing Vocals, Percussion; **Peter Gabriel**—Lead Vocals, Flute; **Steve Hackett**—Guitar; **Mike Rutherford**—Bass

8. Studio Album #6: *The Lamb Lies Down on Broadway*

Recorded at Glaspant Manor, Carmarthenshire, Wales, with the Island Mobile Studio, and Mixed at Island Studios, August–October 1974.
Producer: John Burns and Genesis. Engineer: David Hutchins.
2008 Remix/Remaster Release:
Mixed at The Farm, Surrey 2005/2006.
5.1 Surround sound and stereo mixes by Nick Davis. Assisted by Tom Mitchell.
UK Release: 22 November 1974. (2LP: *The Lamb Lies Down on Broadway*)
U.S. Release: 25 November 1974. (2LP: *The Lamb Lies Down on Broadway*)

Rael follows the tube as it is carried along the river by the rapids. Above he sees a skylight that leads back to Broadway, but as he contemplates his way out, he spies his brother John struggling in the rapids below.

THE LIGHT DIES DOWN ON BROADWAY is a slowed down musical reprise of the title theme and a repeated section of [63] THE LAMIA. By returning to earlier themes, it is designed to signal that we are now entering the final act of the story. Gabriel had been struggling to finish his lyrics in time for the deadline and reluctantly had to accept outside help. Banks and Rutherford stepped in to complete the lyrics to this song, Gabriel having given the pair his brief as to where the song fitted into the plot. The finished lyrics fitted well into the body of the story, describing the action in the third person. By this stage of the album all but a few listeners will have likely given up on trying to make sense of Gabriel's vision and just sit back to enjoy the music. The song fades out via Banks' oscillating synthesizer and Gabriel's flute before there is time to dwell too long.

Live Performances: 1974/5. The song was only performed as part of the band's tour of *The Lamb Lies Down on Broadway*.

Live Recordings: A recording [3:37] at the LA Shrine Auditorium on 24 January 1975 was captured and included on *Genesis Archive 1967–75*. The recording was mixed by Nick Davis and Geoff Callingham.

[68] RIDING THE SCREE

Band Credit: Tony Banks/Phil Collins/Peter Gabriel/Steve Hackett/Mike Rutherford
Music: Tony Banks/Phil Collins/Peter Gabriel/Steve Hackett/Mike Rutherford
Lyrics: Peter Gabriel
Length: 4:07
Tony Banks—Synthesizers; **Phil Collins**—Drums, Backing Vocals, Percussion; **Peter Gabriel**—Lead Vocals; **Steve Hackett**—Guitar; **Mike Rutherford**—Bass
Recorded at Glaspant Manor, Carmarthenshire, Wales, with the Island Mobile Studio, and Mixed at Island Studios, August–October 1974.
Producer: John Burns and Genesis. Engineer: David Hutchins.
2008 Remix/Remaster Release:
Mixed at The Farm, Surrey 2005/2006.
5.1 Surround sound and stereo mixes by Nick Davis. Assisted by Tom Mitchell.
UK Release: 15 November 1974. (B-side single b/w [56] COUNTING OUT TIME. Charisma. CB2 238)
UK Album Release: 22 November 1974. (2LP: *The Lamb Lies Down on Broadway*)
U.S. Release: 25 November 1974. (2LP: *The Lamb Lies Down on Broadway*)

This is the strongest track on the second disc, working well in the context of the story and as an individual piece of music. Rael struggles down the cliff to the water's edge and dives into the cold rapids. He is swept along and past John but manages to hold himself steady on a rock enabling him to grab John's arm.

The song is led by Banks' pacey and melodic synth lead with weeping punctuation that is pushed along by Collins' odd-metered rhythm mirrored by Rutherford's bass. Gabriel delivers a soulful vocal capturing Rael's desperation as he tries to save his brother from drowning. A spiraling keyboard line from Banks over the band's dynamic backing depicts Rael's dive into the water before the song fades via Gabriel's humorous vocal reference to Evel Knievel, which was inspired by the stunt-rider's ill-fated leap across Snake River Canyon on 8 September 1974.

Single Release: The song was included as the B-side to [56] COUNTING OUT TIME, which was released in November 1974 ahead of the album.

Live Performances: 1974/5, 1981 (excerpt), 1982 (excerpt), 2007 (excerpt). The song was performed live on the subsequent tour only as part of the band's presentation of the whole album. The keyboard led "dive" section was later used as an excerpt in the band's medley led by [52] IN THE CAGE on their 1981, 1982 and 2007 tours.

Live Recordings: (1) A recording (4:30) at the LA Shrine Auditorium on 24 January 1975 was captured and included on *Genesis Archive 1967–75*. The recording was mixed by Nick Davis and Geoff Callingham.

(2) The short keyboard led "dive" segment is part of the "In the Cage Medley" that appeared on *Three Sides Live*. See [52] IN THE CAGE.

(3) Another version of the medley appeared on *Live Over Europe 2007*. See [52] IN THE CAGE.

[69] IN THE RAPIDS

Band Credit: Tony Banks/Phil Collins/Peter Gabriel/Steve Hackett/Mike Rutherford
Music: Tony Banks/Phil Collins/Peter Gabriel/Steve Hackett/Mike Rutherford
Lyrics: Peter Gabriel
Length: 2:22
Tony Banks—Synthesizers, Piano; **Phil Collins**—Drums, Backing Vocals, Percussion; **Peter Gabriel**—Lead Vocals; **Steve Hackett**—Guitar; **Mike Rutherford**—Acoustic Guitar, Bass
Recorded at Glaspant Manor, Carmarthenshire, Wales, with the Island Mobile Studio, and Mixed at Island Studios, August–October 1974.
Producer: John Burns and Genesis. Engineer: David Hutchins.
2008 Remix/Remaster Release:
Mixed at The Farm, Surrey 2005/2006.
5.1 Surround sound and stereo mixes by Nick Davis. Assisted by Tom Mitchell.
UK Release: 22 November 1974. (2LP: *The Lamb Lies Down on Broadway*)
U.S. Release: 25 November 1974. (2LP: *The Lamb Lies Down on Broadway*)

We're now well into the final act of the story as Rael knocks his brother unconscious in the water and together they ride the rapids until they finally slow down and Rael manages to drag John to safety. As he turns his brother's limp body to face him, he is staggered to see not his brother's face, but his own.

A short, gently strummed 12-string acoustic guitar rhythm from Rutherford opens the song as Gabriel initially sings softly to convey Rael's exhaustion from his efforts to save his brother. The rest of the band join in at 0:54 with Banks' piano building in intensity alongside Hackett's guitar. Hackett's wailing lead lines and Gabriel's tortured vocals capture Rael's anguish, and guide the song toward its final twist as he turns his brother to see he is looking down at his own face. The moment of shock for Rael is captured by the siren that leads off directly into [70] IT.

Live Performances: 1974/5. The song was only performed as part of the band's tour of *The Lamb Lies Down on Broadway*.

Live Recordings: A recording (2:25) at the LA Shrine Auditorium on 24 January 1975

8. Studio Album #6: The Lamb Lies Down on Broadway

was captured and included on *Genesis Archive 1967–75*. The recording was mixed by Nick Davis and Geoff Callingham.

[70] IT.

Band Credit: Tony Banks/Phil Collins/Peter Gabriel/Steve Hackett/Mike Rutherford
Music: Tony Banks/Phil Collins/Peter Gabriel/Steve Hackett/Mike Rutherford
Lyrics: Peter Gabriel
Length: 4:19
Tony Banks—Synthesizers; **Phil Collins**—Drums, Backing Vocals, Percussion; **Peter Gabriel**—Lead Vocals; **Steve Hackett**—Guitar; **Mike Rutherford**—Acoustic Guitar, Bass
Recorded at Glaspant Manor, Carmarthenshire, Wales, with the Island Mobile Studio, and Mixed at Island Studios, August–October 1974.
Producer: John Burns and Genesis. Engineer: David Hutchins.
2008 Remix/Remaster Release:
Mixed at The Farm, Surrey 2005/2006.
5.1 Surround sound and stereo mixes by Nick Davis. Assisted by Tom Mitchell.
UK Release: 22 November 1974. (2LP: *The Lamb Lies Down on Broadway*)
U.S. Release: 25 November 1974. (2LP: *The Lamb Lies Down on Broadway*)

The final track of this monumental album is more ironic than epic. Banks' revving synth siren guides us into a fast and seemingly rushed play-out. A mesmerized Rael finds his presence being absorbed and in a state of transition as he watches both bodies melt into a haze and finally dissolve leaving the listener to puzzle the meaning of this twist in the tale. Using clever wordplay, the open question posed by the story's finale demonstrated Gabriel's intent to leave the listener to decide the nature of Rael's story. It is a tale that is undoubtedly challenging and adventurous, with some listeners likely switched off by its surreal and off-beat nature and others turned on by the same attributes. Lyrically, Gabriel, perhaps sensing a backlash, is already on the defensive suggesting in his lyrics that listeners who judge the story as pretentious have only fooled themselves.

Musically, Hackett's guitar lead lines glide over Rutherford's fast-paced acoustic rhythm and the whole thing is propelled along by Collins' urgent drumming. Gabriel loved his cultural references and uses them freely on the album. Here, the song fades Gabriel riffs lyrically on the Rolling Stones' number "It's Only Rock and Roll." Banks had his doubts about the song as an album closer and its use as such will no doubt have further cemented his mixed feelings about the album's story as a whole: "I never felt that it really concluded very well. I thought the song IT. was not very strong ender and so I have a slightly funny feeling about it all."[32]

Live Performances: 1974/5, 1976. The song was performed in its entirety only on the subsequent tour as part of the band's performance of the whole album. A cut-down version, with Collins on vocals and Bill Bruford on drums, was performed on the band's 1976 tour and linked with the opening/closing instrumental sequences from [33] WATCHER OF THE SKIES.

Live Recordings: (1) A recording (4:20) at the LA Shrine Auditorium on 24 January 1975 was captured and included on *Genesis Archive 1967–75*. The recording was mixed by Nick Davis and Geoff Callingham. Due to technical issues the live recording of IT. was not available, so the band created a "live" version using the studio recording along with new vocals from Gabriel.

(2) A recording of the medley version noted above was made at the Apollo Theatre in Glasgow, Scotland, 8 July 1976 (7:03) and was included on *Three Sides Live*. The band lineup

was Banks, Collins, Hackett and Rutherford, augmented by Bruford. Collins took on vocal duties. The recording was engineered by Geoff Callingham and produced by the band.

* * *

Genesis had briefly considered issuing their new album in two parts over a period of six months, Gabriel feeling it would have given them more time to hone the lyrics on the album's latter half. Common sense prevailed and *The Lamb Lies Down on Broadway* was finally released as a double album on 22 November 1974. Its gatefold sleeve, a photographic design by Hipgnosis which gives it the look of a graphic novel, was a move away from the painted covers of their earlier albums. It featured male model Omar as Rael with panels shot in black and white depicting scenes from Gabriel's story—three on the front cover and three on the back. The story itself was printed in full on the inside gatefold with further shaped photographs depicting more of the story. The disc sleeves contained the lyrics. A new logo for the band was designed by George Hardie, using Greek lettering in an Art Deco style.

The album received mixed reviews on release in the music press. Barbara Charone in *Sounds* was one of the few offering a positive perspective stating, "*The Lamb Lies Down on Broadway* sticks out of the present vinyl rubble like a polished diamond."[33] But many critics were bemused by the obscure and demanding storyline and density of musical ideas. Chris Welch, a big supporter of the band, commented in *Melody Maker*, "There is a vast amount of music to wade through, with some 24 titles and only a few themes worthy of such interminable development."[34] Pete Erskins of *New Musical Express* noted, "the listener finds himself wading knee-deep in symbolism…. In the process the burden borne by the music causes it certain arthritic problems."[35]

Gabriel had anticipated such a reaction, observing that critics had started to take a dislike to what they saw as the pretensions behind concept albums. As a result, the album was perhaps the most controversial of the band's career, splitting opinion between those who thought it a masterpiece of inventiveness and those who dismissed it as an overblown, overindulgent, sprawling mess. Gabriel's story was so obscure that it could not be absorbed in just one sitting and it required a commitment from the listener. It was therefore not surprising that the album was a relative disappointment, sales-wise, in the UK.

Over the years *The Lamb Lies Down on Broadway* has grown significantly in reputation and appreciation. Stephen Thomas Erlewine noting for *All Music Guide*, "it's a considerable, lasting achievement."[36] Jon Michaud, in an article on the album for *The New Yorker* magazine commented, "While no one would ever mistake it for the first Clash album, there is far more grit to be found in *The Lamb* than in *Tales from Topographic Oceans*."[37] *Classic Rock Review* observed, "Serendipitously, it all came together with some truly brilliant moments both musically and lyrically."[38]

As with any argument there are truths on both sides. There are many moments where the band's creativity really shines through. The main problem is that most of these are on the first disc. The music on the second disc is less exciting taken as a whole, although again there are moments of brilliance. It was difficult for the band to consistently keep the quality levels at the absolute pinnacle during what amounted to just over ninety-four minutes of music. Additionally, the band's occasional need to turn to pieces written earlier in their career was further evidence of the rushed approach to completing the album.

The songs had a generally more electric and heavier slant than on previous work and their arrangements were brave and bold, showing Genesis were determined not to stand still. Gone were the twee acoustics and dynamically swinging epics. In their place came a collection of largely concise songs and musical moods that relied more on atmosphere and character to convey the surreal nature of the story. Tracks such as [48] the title cut, [57] Carpet Crawlers, [54] Back in N.Y.C., [56] Counting Out Time and [52] In the Cage stand up very well on their own. This is largely due to the strength of the music and the individual nature of the musical approach to these pieces.

The album's main weakness lies is in its pacing. As noted, the first disc is excellent and taken on its own would stand as a tremendous piece of work. The second disc is almost universally inferior to the first. As such, the flow of the album does not work in its entirety as the story loses momentum and the listener starts to drift during some long, dull sections. The album also lacks a satisfying climax, with [70] It. coming across as a rushed conclusion. That said there is no doubt this album is one of the most important of the band's career. It marks a sharp change in direction and a willingness to experiment with their compositional methods and sound. There are moments of inventiveness that produce some of the best music the band ever recorded, and it was a fitting last album for Gabriel. His vocal performance here was undoubtedly his strongest. Lyrically his single-mindedness had led him to becoming insular and a little too self-indulgent and obscure and it is of note that the band lightened up considerably after his departure. But Gabriel's contribution to the growth of Genesis was enormous and here he made his most significant contribution.

Naturally, of the five band members, Gabriel feels closest to the album: "It's a much wider album than past efforts. In the past our records haven't come off as strong as I would have liked; it's been down to live performances. But this has the best the band has to offer. On the right wing there are conventional pop songs and on the left wing more sound pictures drawn by the music which we'd only done before in rehearsal never on plastic."[39] Rutherford is more neutral in his assessment, "It was interesting, but I preferred *Foxtrot*."[40] Collins enjoyed the writing process and the creativity it sparked remarking in his autobiography, "It's one of the few Genesis albums I can put on and be surprised by."[41] Hackett, however, looks back on the period less fondly. He was having marriage problems at the time and he saw himself as a creative bystander for the most part and felt the album was overly indulgent saying, "As a piece of music I think *The Lamb Lies Down on Broadway* tends to come unglued in a number of places."[42] He did feel it was possibly Banks' strongest contribution to the band to date. The keyboardist had increasingly experimented with synthesized sound on the album creating some strong ambient instrumental pieces. Banks' own views of the album, however, were mixed: "Looking back I think the songs were great, individually at least. It was the overall concept that was flawed. It was willfully obscure, even by our standards!"[43]

After an initial and costly hiccup in October 1974 due to Hackett injuring his hand,[44] which resulted in the initial UK leg being postponed until the following spring, Genesis embarked on a long and ambitious tour. The album would be played in its entirety over 102 dates. The set was hampered somewhat by some of the songs not being suited to the live environment and a slide show, which provided visuals to help interpret the story to audiences, prone to technical problems. Rutherford also later reflected on the limitations this presented to the band by not being able to perform other songs from their catalogue, with only [25] The Musical Box, [33] Watcher of the Skies and [24] The Knife being performed as encores.

Stage effects were elaborate, as was Gabriel's stage costume design—notably his Slipperman costume. Collins became frustrated at the impact this theatricality had on the performance of the music, as Gabriel often struggled to get the microphone anywhere near his mouth. Then, in December 1974, came the news that the rest of the band had both been expecting and dreading. Gabriel had initially informed the band's manager, Tony

Smith, of his decision to quit in late November in Cleveland. Smith had asked him to take a couple of days to think it through, but Gabriel had his mind made up. Among the considerations was the band's financial position. Genesis had been in significant debt and was still over £100,000 in the red, despite Smith having taken over the management of their affairs. Gabriel reflected, "I think there was the thought that a lot of years of work had gone in on the musical side and in terms of people's livelihoods in terms of buying houses for families and all this practical stuff and we were just getting to the point where that might become a reality, and I wanted to get out so that was another sort of layer of guilt."[45]

After some extensive discussions, the band managed to persuade Gabriel to see the tour out and the last gig the five played together was at St. Etienne in France during May 1975 where in recognition of the event Gabriel played "The Last Post" in the dressing room on his oboe. At this point, only Gabriel, the rest of the band and their management knew of his decision. Gabriel agreed to delay any announcement to the press while the band considered its future. However, rumors of his departure began to leak out and on 12 July 1975 *NME* published a short piece under the headline "Gabriel to Leave Genesis Is Denied." Charisma's spokesperson, Peter Thompson, was trotted out to play a straight bat to the press. A month later, *Melody Maker* too speculated "Gabriel Out of Genesis?" in its lead headline on 16 August—again despite initial denials from both Tony Stratton-Smith and Charisma. Finally, realizing the rumors were proving far too strong, Gabriel released a detailed press statement, which was published on 23 August, confirming his departure and the reasons behind his decision.[46] The remaining members of Genesis were back together by this point writing their next album and looking for a new lead vocalist, while the music press were writing their obituary. Collins agreed to an interview with *NME* the following week and responded positively to questions from Tony Tyler about the band's future: "Peter's leaving isn't the blow that some people seem to think it is."[47]

Gabriel would not speak to the music press again for another three months. He finally agreed to an interview with Chris Welch of *Melody Maker* stating, "I wanted to make sure my heart felt good. It was time for a change for me and the band. Things weren't right. And it was tying me down to one role."[48] The comments highlighted Gabriel's creative frustration at having to compromise in a band environment. He wanted more control and the room to explore his musical ideas to the full—he was particularly frustrated by Banks' territorial attitude to the keyboards. Despite this there was no personal animosity in the split and Gabriel was positive about Genesis' future without him, "From what I've heard there's some good stuff going on, far better recorded than before. I never felt we captured our live energy on record. I think they're over-compensating for me by doing fewer instrumental passages which isn't the best idea—though I'll probably be slammed for saying so. As long as Phil does the singing it'll be all right, he sings a lot like me."[49]

The Lamb Lies Down on Broadway was not to be Gabriel's swansong with the band as we'll come to later. Additionally, plans to make a film version of the album were later discussed, in 1979, when Collins reported that Gabriel was working on a screenplay. However, these plans never came to fruition, although talk around the five-man lineup performing the whole album resurfaced on occasions over the years, notably in 2005, until Collins' health issues finally laid any hopes of that to rest.

Part 3

The Four-Man Years: June 1975–July 1977

Tony Banks (Keyboards)
Phil Collins (Vocals, Drums)
Steve Hackett (Guitars)
Mike Rutherford (Bass, Guitars)

The four-man Genesis line-up, without Peter Gabriel, in 1976. From left, Mike Rutherford, Phil Collins, Tony Banks and Steve Hackett. Atco promotional photograph (courtesy Mark Kenyon/The Genesis Archive).

9

Studio Album #7: *A Trick of the Tail*

UK Release: 13 February 1976. LP. Charisma. CDS 4001.
U.S. Release: 13 February 1976. LP. Atlantic/ATCO. SD 36–129.
Remix/Remaster Release:
UK Release: 2 April 2007. CD/SACD/DVD. Virgin/Charisma. CDSCDR4001.
U.S. Release: 15 May 2007. CD/DVD. Atlantic/Rhino. R2 128700.

Album Tracks

[71] Dance on a Volcano
[72] Entangled
[73] Squonk
[74] Mad Man Moon
[75] Robbery, Assault and Battery
[76] Ripples…
[77] A Trick of the Tail
[78] Los Endos

Other Songs Recorded

[79] It's Yourself

Following the departure of Peter Gabriel, the band decided to take some time out to reflect on their future. During this period Steve Hackett recorded his first solo album, *Voyage of the Acolyte*. He recruited Mike Rutherford to assist on bass as well as to co-write the track "Shadow of Hierophant," which was developed from a piece they had worked on in the band. Phil Collins contributed drums and percussion throughout as well as adding lead vocals to "Star of Sirius." Rutherford also continued to work with Anthony Phillips, writing and recording new songs for what was to become Phillips' debut solo album, *The Geese and the Ghost*. Collins would add his vocals to two tracks on that album—"Which Way the Wind Blows" and a duet with Vivienne McAuliffe "God If I Saw Her Now." Collins also continued to work as a session drummer in his downtime, with artists as diverse as Argent, Brian Eno, Eddie Howell, John Cale and Tommy Bolin. The busy drummer also joined a loose jazz fusion band that was to become Brand X—an outfit he would work with intermittently over the next five years.[1]

Tony Banks, meanwhile, had been approached by Tony Stratton-Smith to oversee an orchestrated album of Genesis songs, something that did not progress beyond the initial planning stage. He therefore spent his time writing new material in preparation for the band's next album. Stung by the music press' assumption that Gabriel had written most of the songs, the band made the decision to credit songs directly to the writer(s) rather than to the band unit as had been policy on previous albums. Banks laughingly recalls, "I came in with the most complete songs. Mike came in with sections as did Steve. As it happened the bits we used to finish them off were my bits. So, I ended up being credited on every track on this album, which was sort of quite funny."[2]

The news of Gabriel's departure, having been leaked to the press in August 1975 while the band were writing their new album, led to music journalists assuming the band was finished. Hackett's solo album being released shortly after and Collins having already begun working with the future Brand X only helped fan the flames. The band soldiered on regardless and began rehearsals for their new album in Maurice Plaquet's basement on Churchfield Road, East Acton.[3] Hackett, who was still putting the finishing touches to *Voyage of the Acolyte*, would join them three days later. It quickly became clear that Genesis could function without Gabriel and indeed his departure had left more creative room for the other writers. The trio of Banks, Collins and Rutherford took confidence from their previous contributions to the group—such as the instrumental sections of [46] THE CINEMA SHOW and the "Apocalypse in 9/8" section of [38] SUPPER'S READY. Rutherford remembers, "we had a great time. We wrote [73] SQUONK and [71] DANCE ON A VOLCANO. It just sort of happened and sounded great. But we could have gone in and it could have been crap and then we would have been in trouble. That was an important week, I think."[4]

Recording of the album took place at Trident Studios in London in October and November 1975. It was the band's first album to be produced by David Hentschel, who also managed to get a much cleaner sound to the recording. The band had known Hentschel for a few years and the producer was a good friend of Collins, who respected his skills in attaining a more natural drum sound. Having met Collins while working as a tape operator on *Nursery Cryme*, the pair had linked up again at Trident Studios on one of Collins' many sessions outside the band.[5] It was here Collins asked Hentschel if he would be interested in producing the band. Hentschel was also an accomplished keyboard player and had a strong knowledge of synthesizers. Banks had been branching out into the world of synths since *Selling England By the Pound*, and his sound would blossom on this album.

Once Genesis had put down all the backing tracks to the songs, they decided to start the auditioning process for Peter Gabriel's replacement. An ad was placed in *Melody Maker*, "Singer wanted for Genesis-type group," and many potential replacement singers sent in tapes.[6] The band reduced these to a dozen or so real contenders. The auditions were held each Monday over five or six weeks during the autumn using the band's back catalogue (including [42] FIRTH OF FIFTH and [24] THE KNIFE) as well as the new material, which Collins would guide them on. The band ultimately went into the studio with Mick Strickland, formerly of the band Witches Brew, to test him on the new songs but he struggled with the key to [73] SQUONK, the backing track for which, like all the songs, had already been committed to tape.

In retrospect, it should have been obvious to Banks, Hackett and Rutherford that their new singer had been under their noses all along. Collins had sung lead vocals on two previous Genesis songs—the acoustic duo [26] FOR ABSENT FRIENDS on *Nursery Cryme* and [43] MORE FOOL ME on *Selling England by the Pound*. In addition, he had regularly backed up Gabriel and the pair had also contributed dual vocals on songs such as [29] HAROLD THE BARREL, [46] THE CINEMA SHOW and [57] CARPET CRAWLERS. Collins had been penciled in to sing two of the softer songs on the new album—[72] ENTANGLED and [76] RIPPLES…. The rest of the band had not considered him for the heavier songs, believing his voice to be too pure. Following the failed attempt to bring Strickland on board, Collins' frustration finally boiled over and he put himself forward.

Collins had already been touted as a potential lead vocalist to Steve Hackett by Yes front man Jon Anderson at the drummer's wedding. Hackett had referenced Collins' vocal work on his solo album and Anderson knew of Collins' ability and said he would be a good choice. He took on [73] SQUONK and immediately impressed the others with his ability to handle the difficult melody and attack the song. Rutherford recalled, "Phil did the vocal on [73] SQUONK which was a big step for him as it has quite an aggressive vocal, and he sounded great, so we went with that."[7] He worked his way through the rest of the songs and ultimately completed the album.

The band were pleased with the results and had found the environment liberating without the tensions that had blighted their previous album. Rutherford recalled in 2007, "The whole concept of *The Lamb* was darker, longer, and it was a real uphill battle to finish. That's why *A Trick of the Tail* was easier to make. It was lighter, Phil was singing, and we had a whole new scenario with a breath of fresh air."[8]

[71] DANCE ON A VOLCANO

Music: Mike Rutherford/Tony Banks/Steve Hackett/Phil Collins
Lyrics: Mike Rutherford
Length: 5:57
Tony Banks—Synthesizers, Mellotron; **Phil Collins**—Lead & Backing Vocals, Drums, Percussion; **Steve Hackett**—Lead Guitar; **Mike Rutherford**—Rhythm Guitar, Bass, Bass Pedals,
Recorded at Trident Studios, London, October–November 1975.
Producer: David Hentschel and Genesis. Engineer: David Hentschel and Nick 'Haddock' Bradford.
2007 Remix/Remaster Release:
Mixed at The Farm, Surrey 2005/2006.
5.1 Surround sound and stereo mixes by Nick Davis. Assisted by Tom Mitchell, Tom Webster and Tom Tunney.
UK/U.S. Release: 13 February 1976. (LP: *A Trick of the Tail*)

Written very early on in the sessions, DANCE ON A VOLCANO sounds liberating. The track opened a new era for the band with the first chance to hear Collins as lead vocalist performing a heavy number. The confident opening showed that Genesis was as strong as ever, with Rutherford's chiming twelve-string guitar figure underlined by his thunderous bass pedals. Collins' rhythmic punctuation is synchronized with Hackett's lead guitar melody and Banks' textured keyboards. The sound is wide and dynamic and in his review for *All Music Guide* Donald Guarisco noted "the band's skill at creating a cinematic mood."[9] The song is indeed one of the band's strongest with the dramatic intro leading into an urgent rhythm in 7/8 creating the tension over which Collins immediately demonstrates his vocal ability to handle the material through his confident delivery of the opening lines, which vividly describe the dangerous path of ascent of the metaphorical volcano.

Rutherford felt the song "kind of embodied all that Genesis did well, which was quite majestic powerful stuff, interesting rhythms, good melodies… the intro had a drama and excitement…. I'm not sure the rest of it was always up to scratch but the intro and the sort of first bit I thought was very strong."[10] The steam effects are created by Collins' inspired use of symbols removing the delay to create a short sharp sound. Collins' inventive drumming as he negotiates the song's changing rhythmic patterns demonstrates why he is regarded as one of rock music's all-time greats. The song is one of the band's most musically complex and impressive as it weaves its way through different time signatures and rhythms before playing out with a fast and jazzy instrumental dance led by Hackett's lead guitar. Banks wasn't keen on the outro feeling it wasn't played as well as it could have been.

The opening of the song would be briefly reprised in the closing section of the instrumental [78] Los Endos, creating a bookend effect to the album. The two pieces would later be linked together in the live environment, allowing for a drum duet between Collins and future tour drummer Chester Thompson to act as the bridge.

Live Performances: 1976, 1977, 1978, 1980, 1981, 1982, 1992 (excerpt). The song became a key component of the band's live set for several years, being included on each tour from 1976 to 1982. And then, in cut down form, as part of the "Old Medley" on their 1992 tour. Its exciting dynamic sound made Dance on a Volcano perfect for the live environment.

Live Recordings: (1) A live recording of the song (5:09) from Palais des Sports, Paris, between 11–14 June 1977 was included on the album *Seconds Out*. This version removes the outro and replaces it with a drum duet between Collins and Thompson that would lead into [78] Los Endos. The recording was produced by David Hentschel and the band.

(2) An excerpt section of the song opened the "Old Medley" [19:32] recorded on 10 July 1992 at Niedersachsenstadion, Hanover, Germany, and was included on the live album *The Way We Walk: Volume 2: The Longs*. The lineup was Banks, Collins and Rutherford, augmented by Daryl Stuermer (guitar) and Thompson. The recording was produced by Nick Davis, Robert Colby and the band.

[72] Entangled

Music: Steve Hackett/Tony Banks
Lyrics: Steve Hackett
Length: 6:27
Tony Banks—Synthesizers, Mellotron, Acoustic Guitar, Backing Vocals; **Phil Collins**—Lead & Backing Vocals, Percussion; **Steve Hackett**—Guitar, Acoustic Guitar; **Mike Rutherford**—Acoustic Guitar, Bass, Bass Pedals
Recorded at Trident Studios, London, October–November 1975.
Producer: David Hentschel and Genesis. Engineer: David Hentschel and Nick 'Haddock' Bradford.
2007 Remix/Remaster Release:
Mixed at The Farm, Surrey 2005/2006.
5.1 Surround sound and stereo mixes by Nick Davis. Assisted by Tom Mitchell, Tom Webster and Tom Tunney.
UK/U.S. Release: 13 February 1976. (LP: *A Trick of the Tail*)
U.S. Single Release: May 1976. (A-side single b/w [76] Ripples.... Atlantic/ATCO. 45–7050)

Beautiful vocal harmonies glide over the dreamlike counter-harmony of a 12-string acoustic guitars, played by Hackett, Rutherford and Banks, that encapsulates the song's lyrical subject of hypnosis. The lyrics are delivered via a sensitive vocal from Collins. *Classic Rock Review* noted the song's "ethereal musical soundscape, like an old English folk song."[11] The music for the verses was written by Hackett, following the guitarist's experimentation with a light acoustic 12-string sound, and this was the strongest of the pieces he had written. His lyrics were based on a painting by his then girlfriend, Kim Poor. The guitarist recalled, "I remember when I first had the lyric ready and I showed it to Phil who was going to sing it and he said this has got a *Mary Poppins* feel to it ... 'Over the Rooftops and Houses.' Indeed, the whole world of Disney cartoons and the attendant music was a huge influence on Genesis."[12] Collins double-tracks his own lead vocals through the verses with a harmonizing countermelody. Banks added the chorus section, which had originally been written on piano in 6/8 thus matching the time signature of Hackett's verse to create the perfect match. The piano melody from the chorus became the vocal melody delivered by Collins with Banks adding further backing harmonies.

The second section of the song, from 4:23, is instrumental and features Banks' ARP Pro Solo Synthesizer I choral sound, with added vibrato, which he played expressively using the synthesizer's touch sensitive keyboard, to emulate a female soprano. Banks adds further harmonics through the choral sounds from the Mellotron. Banks' haunting melody floats over Hackett and Rutherford's gentle guitars and is given depth by the bass pedal notes added by Rutherford. Banks noted, "It produced what is probably my favorite track on that album, ending with a great cathedral-type feeling."[13]

It's a beautiful piece of music that demonstrates the versatility of the band and the individual members' ability to complement each other's playing.

Single Release: The song was released as a shortened promo single (3:24) in the U.S. and Canada, backed with a similarly shortened version of [76] RIPPLES.... For the retail single release, in May 1976, both songs were restored to their full length. For the French promo single release, the following month, it was backed with [77] A TRICK OF THE TAIL.

Live Performances: 1976. Hackett recalls, "We had lots of twelve-strings that were all prone to go out of tune live, I recall. So much of the early, well, the good stuff of the band was dogged by the fact that doing it live was very difficult because we had so many guitarists and so many guitars."[14]

Live Recordings: A somewhat hesitant performance (6:57) was recorded at Bingley Hall, Staffordshire, on 10 July 1976, mixed for its by Nick Davis, was included in the *Genesis Archive #2 1976–1992* box set released on 6 November 2000. The band was augmented by Bill Bruford (drums).

[73] SQUONK

Music: Mike Rutherford/Tony Banks
Lyrics: Mike Rutherford
Length: 6:30
Tony Banks—Organ, Synthesizers; **Phil Collins**—Lead & Backing Vocals, Drums, Percussion; **Steve Hackett**—Lead Guitar; **Mike Rutherford**—Rhythm Guitar, Bass, Bass Pedals
Recorded at Trident Studios, London, October–November 1975.
Producer: David Hentschel and Genesis. Engineer: David Hentschel and Nick 'Haddock' Bradford.
2007 Remix/Remaster Release:
Mixed at The Farm, Surrey 2005/2006.
5.1 Surround sound and stereo mixes by Nick Davis. Assisted by Tom Mitchell, Tom Webster and Tom Tunney.
UK/U.S. Release: 13 February 1976. (LP: *A Trick of the Tail*)

One of Rutherford's strongest guitar riffs forms the core of this straight-ahead rocker and is prodded along by his pulsing bass pedal notes, which he later supplements with his bass guitar. Initially Rutherford wasn't too keen on the riff: "I didn't really think much of it," he told *NME* a year later. "I hadn't seen it as they had. I really didn't think it would come out like that. Everybody said, 'Let's try it.' And we did one run through and it had that sound it's got on the album straight away."[15] The song also benefits from a tight, heavy and crisp backbeat from Collins, inspired by his admiration of Led Zeppelin drummer John Bonham. Banks and Rutherford had heard Zeppelin's "Kashmir" on the radio and loved the huge drum sound Bonham had created. Genesis did not have a strong reputation for heavy songs, despite moments on *The Lamb Lies Down on Broadway*, and Rutherford was keen to explore this side of the band. He and Banks resolved to write a song, under a working title of "Indians," initially with a similar feel to the Zeppelin tune and Collins was only too pleased to oblige in creating a like-minded drum pattern. While the band may have been aiming to mirror Zeppelin's approach and sound, what they ended up with was a hybrid between the two bands with Banks writing the song's softer midsection to create a bridge between the flanking driving sections.

Lyrically the song tells the story of a mythical creature called a "squonk' that when captured by its hunter dissolves in a pool of its own tears.[16] Collins delivers a soulful, at times bluesy, vocal rendition straight from the opening lines describing the creature. This was the song which, when Collins delivered his vocal in rehearsal, persuaded his bandmates that he could handle the heavier material. In fact, it was his first vocal recording for the album. Rutherford recalls, "We got a lot of confidence from doing that song; we proved to ourselves that we could keep going after Peter left."[17] Collins has also since commented that he felt the song was a musical standout on the album.

Live Performances: 1976, 1977, 1978, 1980, 1983/4 (excerpt). SQUONK was to become a popular inclusion in Genesis' live set, being played on each of the band's next four tours between 1976 and 1980 (opening the set in 1977), then again as part of a long medley on their 1983/4 tour.

Live Recordings: A rather flat live version of the song (6:39) recorded at Palais des Sports, Paris, between 11–14 June 1977, appeared on *Seconds Out*, released the following year. The band was augmented by Chester Thompson on drums. The recording was produced by David Hentschel and the band.

[74] MAD MAN MOON

Music & Lyrics: Tony Banks
Length: 7:35
Tony Banks—Piano, Synthesizers; **Phil Collins**—Lead & Backing Vocals, Drums, Percussion; **Steve Hackett**—Guitar; **Mike Rutherford**—Bass
Recorded at Trident Studios, London, October–November 1975.
Producer: David Hentschel and Genesis. Engineer: David Hentschel and Nick 'Haddock' Bradford.
2007 Remix/Remaster Release:
Mixed at The Farm, Surrey 2005/2006.
5.1 Surround sound and stereo mixes by Nick Davis. Assisted by Tom Mitchell, Tom Webster and Tom Tunney.
UK/U.S. Release: 13 February 1976. (LP: *A Trick of the Tail*)

This is a typical reflective Banks composition piecing together various piano themes he had written into an overall song without a central hook. The song also contains a central instrumental section of spiraling piano and synth motifs, which allows Banks space to express himself harmonically with unusual chord changes and progressions. "It's more, dare I say, a feminine track. Melancholy. I was very pleased when I wrote it, especially the verses. The noodling in the middle is quite fun, but if you listen carefully, it's beyond my playing ability."[18]

In his lyric Banks lays down his philosophy on the need for balancing contrasts in the world in presenting a philosophy of what is good to some can be the opposite to others. His lyric referencing unwanted snow in June is likely a reference to the shock felt in the UK on 2 June 1975 when large parts of the country saw heavy snowfall. Collins delivers an earnest, almost melancholic, vocal over a lyric that reads better than it scans. Collins readily admits he often struggles with Banks' lyrics as well as his written vocal melodies, which were "out of my usual comfort zone, especially having to learn them in the studio."[19]

Reflecting on the song, Banks noted he was pleased with the outcome citing this as one of his favorite pieces of music on the album: "One of my favorite chord changes of all time comes at the end of MAD MAN MOON, coming out of the middle section and into the last verse. It goes from E flat minor 7th to G minor 7th with a D in the bass. It's an uplifting sort of change."[20] Chris Welch summed up MAD MAN MOON in his review for *Melody Maker* noting, "Here is a classical grandeur that sounds contrived and self-conscious in the hands of some recently successful super-groups. By Genesis it is done with musical good taste and intelligence."[21]

[75] ROBBERY, ASSAULT AND BATTERY

Music: Tony Banks
Lyrics: Phil Collins
Length: 6:18
Tony Banks—Organ, Synthesizers; **Phil Collins**—Lead & Backing Vocals, Drums, Percussion; **Steve Hackett**—Guitar; **Mike Rutherford**—Bass
Recorded at Trident Studios, London, October–November 1975.
Producer: David Hentschel and Genesis. Engineer: David Hentschel and Nick 'Haddock' Bradford.
2007 Remix/Remaster Release:
Mixed at The Farm, Surrey 2005/2006.
5.1 Surround sound and stereo mixes by Nick Davis. Assisted by Tom Mitchell, Tom Webster and Tom Tunney.
UK/U.S. Release: 13 February 1976. (LP: *A Trick of the Tail*)

With doubt over the future of the band following Peter Gabriel's departure, the remaining members had begun to work on their own projects. During this period Banks had started to write extensively for what may have become a solo album if Genesis decided not to carry on. He had accumulated two complete songs—[74] MAD MAN MOON and [77] A TRICK OF THE TAIL and various bits that became parts of [71] DANCE ON A VOLCANO, [76] RIPPLES… and [72] ENTANGLED. He had also written the bulk of what was to become ROBBERY, ASSAULT AND BATTERY.

Lyrically, this is a darkly humorous piece and another story-based song. The subject concerns a thief who is caught in the act of burglary and shoots his discoverer, only to end up being chased and arrested by the police. It is a continuation of the style of song Peter Gabriel used to thrive on—see [29], [35] and [44]. Collins proved he could bring his own personality to his interpretation of the lyrics using his Artful Dodger–like vocal delivery to inhabit the main character. Banks provides an extended driving instrumental midsection chase sequence in 13/8 that enlivens a song that otherwise plods a little, seeming much longer than its six-minutes as it winds its way through varying rhythms and time signatures. The patchwork quilt feel is likely evidence of Banks pasting together several individually written pieces in the hope of creating a satisfying whole. In the end ROBBERY, ASSAULT AND BATTERY feels cluttered and unfocused and as such it is the weakest song on the album.

Music Video: A promotional video, directed by Bruce Gowers, who also shot the video for Queen's "Bohemian Rhapsody," included scenes of the band acting out the story intercut with a performance of the song in their traditional stage set-up.

Live Performances: 1976, 1977. The song enabled Collins to demonstrate his acting chops by slipping easily into character and hamming it up for the audience.

Live Recordings: A recording (6:02) from the performances at Palais des Sports, Paris, between 11–14 June 1977 was included on the album *Seconds Out*, released later the same year. The band was augmented by Chester Thompson on drums. The recording was produced by David Hentschel and the band.

[76] RIPPLES…

Music: Mike Rutherford/Tony Banks
Lyrics: Mike Rutherford
Length: 8:05
Tony Banks—Piano, Synthesizers; **Phil Collins**—Lead & Backing Vocals, Drums, Percussion; **Steve Hackett**—Guitar, Acoustic Guitar; **Mike Rutherford**—Acoustic Guitar, Bass
Recorded at Trident Studios, London, October–November 1975.
Producer: David Hentschel and Genesis. Engineer: David Hentschel and Nick 'Haddock' Bradford.
2007 Remix/Remaster Release:
Mixed at The Farm, Surrey 2005/2006.
5.1 Surround sound and stereo mixes by Nick Davis. Assisted by Tom Mitchell, Tom Webster and Tom Tunney.
UK/U.S. Release: 13 February 1976. (LP: *A Trick of the Tail*)
UK Single Release: 12 March 1976. (B-side single b/w [77] A TRICK OF THE TAIL. Charisma. CB 277)
U.S. Single Release: May 1976. (B-side single b/w [72] ENTANGLED. Atlantic/ATCO. 45–7050)

RIPPLES… is quite simply one of the most beautiful songs the band has ever recorded. Hackett and Rutherford's delicate 12-string guitars set the atmosphere for Collins to sing the fragile opening lines describing the "Bluegirls." The song's theme of the uncontrollable aging process and the ravages of time replaced an initially much raunchier direction for Rutherford's lyrics as he recalled, "All I had was this one lyric about 'Bluegirls come in every size.' Bluegirls is a term for schoolgirls in England, referring to the blue uniforms many of them wear. So, I wound up writing this really obscene set of lyrics for RIPPLES… and I sang those words until I wrote the final version of the song. I never showed them to anyone, they were too kinky."[22]

The traditional verse-chorus approach is lifted by the introduction of Collins' drums on the second chorus and was described by Barbara Charone in *Sounds* as "a hypnotic melody that you'll find yourself humming."[23] It is delivered with heart by Collins and soars over some pleasant acoustic 12-string guitar playing from Hackett and Rutherford, Banks' climbing piano and Rutherford's tasteful understated bass. The song then moves into a brooding instrumental midsection, written by Banks and featuring a restrained solo from Hackett on electric guitar. "I thought it had something interesting about it," recalled Hackett. "Mainly, for the guitar combinations to be honest. The 12-string work, from Mike and myself, and the thing that sounds like a backwards guitar solo which was played forwards but was a sign of things to come."[24] The song finally returns to its rousing repeated chorus for the playout. The mix of gorgeous melodies, wonderful harmonies and the band's mastery of the 12-string guitar sound make this one of Genesis' most accomplished recordings.

Single Release: A shortened version (4:15) of the song was included as the B-side to the U.S. and Canada radio promo single releases of [72] ENTANGLED, while the full version was included on the official U.S. release in May 1976. In Italy, RIPPLES… was an A-side promo single release (4:25) in March 1976 backed with [79] IT'S YOURSELF. In the UK the song was used as the B-side to the [77] A TRICK OF THE TAIL single release in March 1976.

Music Video: A promotional video for the full-length version of the song was shot by Bruce Gowers with the band performing to the backing track. The video was one of three promos shot for the album.

Live Performances: 1978, 1980, 1983/4 (excerpt), 2007. The song wasn't performed live by the band until their 1978 tour. It was also very briefly included as part of a longer medley on their 1983/4 tour. When Banks, Collins and Rutherford reunited for a final Genesis tour in 2007 the song was reintroduced to the set and was one of the show's highlights.

Live Recordings: (1) A performance (9:54) recorded at the Lyceum Theatre, London, on 6 May 1980 was included on the *Genesis Archive #2 1976–1992* box set. The lineup was Banks, Collins and Rutherford, augmented by Daryl Stuermer (guitar) and Chester Thompson (drums). The recording was mixed by Nick Davis and captures the intimacy of the venue.

(2) A recording [7:57] from Republic Strahov Football Stadium in Prague, Czech Republic, on 20 June 2007 was included on the *Live Over Europe 2007* album. The lineup was again Banks, Collins and Rutherford, augmented by Stuermer and Thompson. The recording was made by Bernard Natier and produced by Nick Davis. This latter-day version shortens the midsection solo and contains Collins' most heartfelt vocal rendition of the song. It's a wonderful performance.

[77] A Trick of the Tail

Music & Lyrics: Tony Banks
Length: 4:35
Tony Banks—Piano, Synthesizers, Mellotron, Backing Vocals; **Phil Collins**—Lead & Backing Vocals, Drums, Percussion; **Steve Hackett**—Guitar; **Mike Rutherford**—Bass
Recorded at Trident Studios, London, October–November 1975.
Producer: David Hentschel and Genesis. Engineer: David Hentschel and Nick 'Haddock' Bradford.
2007 Remix/Remaster Release:
Mixed at The Farm, Surrey 2005/2006.
5.1 Surround sound and stereo mixes by Nick Davis. Assisted by Tom Mitchell, Tom Webster and Tom Tunney.
UK/U.S. Release: 13 February 1976. (LP: *A Trick of the Tail*)
UK Single Release: 12 March 1976. (A-side single b/w [76] Ripples…. Charisma. CB 277)

A Beatle-esque bouncy piano rhythm and melody in F sharp minor, inspired by the Fab Four's "Getting Better" but possibly more closely resembling their later "Your Mother Should Know," underpins another fantasy tale. This time Banks tells the story of a mythical beast with horns that appears in a modern city far away from its homeland and how it is captured and put on show where it would be mistreated. A group of people release the beast and encourage it to lead them to its homeland, where they see a golden spire before the beast disappears along with their dreams of treasure.

The song can, perhaps, be viewed as a thinly disguised social comment on racism and exploitation. Banks got the story idea after reading William Holding's book *The Inheritors*.[25] Musically, the lively piano melody for the song pre-dates the *Foxtrot* era of the band. Banks resurrected it feeling the song would add a quirky feel to the album and replicate the approach of some of Gabriel's earlier more off-the-wall lyrics, such as [29] Harold the Barrel. The resultant song is both the lightest and most straightforward piece on the album, being pleasantly short and concise. Collins is vocally much more at home interpreting Banks' quirky lyrics and melody here. It is the closest thing the band had written to date to a straight-ahead pop song since their debut album.

Single Release: The song was released as a single in the UK and other regions of Europe in March 1976, but perhaps surprisingly had little success. In the UK it was backed with [76] RIPPLES…. The song was also included as the B-side for the single release of [72] ENTANGLED in France.

Music Video: A promotional video was shot by Bruce Gowers to help the single. It included some special effects fun, with a miniaturized Collins wearing furry boots, long scarf, braces, red linen hat and smoking a thin pipe while exploring Banks' piano and Hackett's guitar. In a later interview with VH1 in 1994, Collins admitted to being embarrassed by the video, which can perhaps now best be viewed as a quirky period piece.

[78] LOS ENDOS

Music: Phil Collins/Steve Hackett/Mike Rutherford/Tony Banks
Length: 5:52
Tony Banks—Synthesizers, Mellotron; **Phil Collins**—Drums, Percussion, Background Vocals; **Steve Hackett**—Lead Guitar, Acoustic Guitar; **Mike Rutherford**—Rhythm Guitar, Acoustic Guitar, Bass, Bass Pedals
Recorded at Trident Studios, London, October–November 1975.
Producer: David Hentschel and Genesis. Engineer: David Hentschel and Nick 'Haddock' Bradford.
2007 Remix/Remaster Release:
Mixed at The Farm, Surrey 2005/2006.
5.1 Surround sound and stereo mixes by Nick Davis. Assisted by Tom Mitchell, Tom Webster and Tom Tunney.
UK/U.S. Release: 13 February 1976. (LP: *A Trick of the Tail*)

Advertisement promoting the release of the [77] A TRICK OF THE TAIL single placed in *New Musical Express* on 27 March 1976 (courtesy Mark Kenyon/The Genesis Archive).

LOS ENDOS,[26] the closing track of *A Trick of the Tail*, is one of the band's strongest instrumentals and repeats themes from [71] DANCE ON A VOLCANO and [73] SQUONK in its closing section. Collins had been keen to loosen up the Genesis sound. He had been listening to a lot of jazz-rock fusion music and was looking to get an element of it into the band's playing to provide a contrast to its traditional compositional and structured approach. The drummer recalled, "It was the first time I thought Genesis played the type of music they'd never played before—American music vaguely in the mold of Weather Report."[27]

The slow shimmering Mellotron opening is based around three chords and was lifted from a song that didn't make the album—[79] It's Yourself. It was Collins' suggestion to dissolve this sequence into a fast Latin jazz-rock rhythm which repeated the same chord sequence and involved Hackett's guitar synchronizing with Banks' keyboards. "You can hear in the introduction the guitar is sailing in," recalled Hackett. "That's how I wrote it. I was thinking orchestral string melody, film music—not that I've ever arranged it that way. But Phil said, 'Yes, we can do it that way, or we could do it with this fast baión rhythm.' The attack is fast from the word go, and accents, of course, are all important in that school of thought."[28]

The track contains some energetic drumming from Collins, who is clearly enjoying the freedom the piece gives him, and a propulsive bass line from Rutherford. It was the piece Collins had most involvement with on the album and he had used Santana's "Promise of a Fisherman" from their *Borboletta* album, notably the drumming of Airto Moreira, as the template for his rhythmic ideas. Collins would hum improvised melodies over the rhythm, which Banks and Hackett would later translate for their keyboard and guitar parts. Collins told *NME* a year later: "It wasn't a blowing tune, but it was the first time we'd tried anything in that vein. To me, it was great to do that kind of thing with Genesis rather than playing it with Brand X."[29] Banks' melodic keyboard phrases are echoed by Hackett's guitar on the playout, riffing on the themes from [73] Squonk. It also includes a mixed-down vocal reference by Collins to Gabriel's departure by quoting a line from the lyrics to the closing section of [38] Supper's Ready.

The band enjoyed the change of approach, citing Los Endos as one of the most adventurous pieces on the album and the it would become a mainstay in their live set for years to come.

Live Performances: 1976, 1977, 1978, 1980, 1981, 1982, 1983/4, 1986/7, 2007. Los Endos was played on every tour from 1976 to 1986/7. From 1977, and on most subsequent tours, it was linked to [71] Dance on a Volcano with a drum duet by Collins and Chester Thompson bridging the two songs and acting as the set closer. Los Endos was brought back into the set for the band's 2007 reunion tour.

Live Recordings: (1) A recording (6:20) of an energetic performance of the song from Genesis' shows at Palais des Sports, Paris, between 11–14 June 1977 was included on the following year's live album, *Seconds Out*. The band was augmented by Thompson on drums. The recording was produced by David Hentschel and demonstrated the energy the band brought to this track in the live environment.

(2) A recording (6:24) from the reunion tour was made at Twickenham, London, on 8 July 2007 and included on the album *Live Over Europe 2007*. Like the *Seconds Out* version this is an excellent example of the power and rhythmic dynamics the instrumental brought to the set. The lineup of Banks, Collins and Rutherford was augmented by Daryl Stuermer (guitar) and Thompson. The recording was made by Bernard Natier and produced by Nick Davis.

[79] It's Yourself

Music: Mike Rutherford/Phil Collins/Steve Hackett/Tony Banks
Lyrics: Phil Collins

Length: 6:16
Tony Banks—Synthesizers, Mellotron; **Phil Collins**—Lead & Backing Vocals, Drums, Percussion; **Steve Hackett**—Guitar, Acoustic Guitar; **Mike Rutherford**—Acoustic Guitar, Bass Pedals
Recorded at Trident Studios, London, October–November 1975.
Producer: David Hentschel and Genesis. Engineer: David Hentschel and Nick 'Haddock' Bradford.
2007 Remix/Remaster Release:
Mixed at The Farm, Surrey 2005/2006.
5.1 Surround sound and stereo mixes by Nick Davis. Assisted by Tom Mitchell, Tom Webster and Tom Tunney.
UK Release: 18 February 1977. (B-side single [4:30] b/w [82] YOUR OWN SPECIAL WAY. Charisma. CB 300)
U.S. Release: 6 November 2000. (3-CD: *Genesis Archive #2: 1976–1992*)

This slow and delicate ballad about a young teenage girl who decides to run away from home was a theme Genesis would return to again on [104] VANCOUVER two years later. Here, acoustic guitars are beautifully played over some warm, deep bass pedal notes before the band moves into a long and aimless, almost acid-like, freeform instrumental section (at 4:15) that recalls the backward taping methods sometimes employed by The Beatles. Hackett commented, "We thought it was a bit 'Kensington Market.' That was one of the places that was the focus of the Hippie scene in the Sixties."[30]

Originally titled "Beloved Summer," the song went through various edits either losing a verse or part of the instrumental section. It is a throwaway song that lacks any real substance outside of its pleasant sonics. The band felt the song failed to match the quality of the rest of the material they wrote and left it off the album, but the three-chord bridge (2:55 to 4:15) as the song transitions into the spaced-out instrumental closing section was reused as the introduction to, and the chordal basis for, [78] LOS ENDOS.

Single Release: The song wasn't released in the UK until just over a year later when it was used in edited form as the B-side (4:30) to the band's single release of [82] YOUR OWN SPECIAL WAY. However, it had appeared in Italy in March 1976 as the B-side (5:45) to the [76] RIPPLES… single.

Alternative Versions: The song was later included on *Genesis Archive #2 1976–1992* at 5:26 minus a verse and in its fullest and remixed form (6:15) on the *Genesis 1976–1982* box set released in April 2007.

* * *

A Trick of the Tail was released on 13 February 1976 and reached #3 in the UK charts where it resided for 39 weeks becoming the band's biggest seller to date. Despite only peaking at #31 in the U.S., worldwide sales doubled those for *The Lamb Lies Down on Broadway* and helped alleviate the band's financial problems. The album cover was designed by Colin Elgie at Hipgnosis and featured a storybook texture with characters from the songs drawn on a parchment colored background with the album title in script. The cover was a great representation of the music the listener would find within.

Genesis had proved they were still a viable proposition without their former charismatic front man Peter Gabriel. Critics responded well to the album. In *Sounds*, Barbara Charone said, "Genesis have not sacrificed anything or cheated themselves to attain such successful results. Only the strong survive. And Genesis possess great strength. A triumph."[31] Writing for *Melody Maker*, Chris Welch was equally as enthusiastic: "Whether this album will have the lasting appeal and impact of earlier classics like *Foxtrot*, time will tell, but from first impressions this is certainly one of the best recorded and produced works to bear the Genesis seal of quality."[32]

With *A Trick of the Tail* Genesis had wanted to prove themselves as writers following Gabriel's departure. Many sections of the press had assumed that Gabriel was the main writer and therefore predicted the band's downfall now that he had left. The album proved that Genesis were alive and well and were more than capable of progressing without their former charismatic front man.

The opening cut, [71] DANCE ON A VOLCANO, really confirms this, with one of the best intros the band has produced, which immediately pulls the listener in. It also contains one of the stronger vocal performances from Collins, who at this stage was still at his best on the more delicate material, such as the gorgeous ballads [72] ENTANGLED and [76] RIPPLES.... The album had tremendous variety, seemingly drawing on each band member's strengths as writers and players. [73] SQUONK showcased the heavier side of the group with a strong repeated guitar riff from Rutherford, [78] LOS ENDOS Collins' jazz-rock influences and [76] RIPPLES... contained some inventively eerie lead guitar from Hackett. Banks came more to the fore with his increasingly impressive symphonic approach to keyboards, producing some stunning harmonies on tunes like [72] ENTANGLED and [74] MAD MAN MOON.

Banks was the main writing contributor and produced some of his best work here. The songs he co-wrote with Rutherford stand with the very best of the band's catalogue. Collins' drumming also reached new heights on this record, mixing the powerful and the simple [73] SQUONK with the technically brilliant [71] DANCE ON A VOLCANO and [78] LOS ENDOS. The drummer was certainly fired up by his new role in the band: "During *A Trick of the Tail* I felt like I was doing something constructive. Before I felt like I was marking time."[33] The album's success, both critically and commercially, would give Genesis the confidence to produce a follow-up very quickly.

For the first time, three promotional videos were shot for songs from the album including [77] A TRICK OF THE TAIL, [76] RIPPLES... and [75] ROBBERY ASSAULT AND BATTERY. Each of these is available on the DVD *Genesis—The Video Show* as well as the 2007 remix SACD/DVD included as part of the box set *Genesis 1976–1982* and as a standalone release on 2 April 2007.

To allow Collins to take the front man role on the subsequent tour, the band recruited former Yes and King Crimson drummer Bill Bruford. Bruford was a friend of Collins and had visited him as he was rehearsing for

In 1976, to promote *A Trick of the Tail*, their first post–Gabriel album, Genesis were joined on tour by former Yes drummer Bill Bruford, right, enabling Phil Collins, left, to take on front man duties. Charisma promotional photograph (courtesy Mark Kenyon/The Genesis Archive).

9. Studio Album #7: A Trick of the Tail

the Brand X album *Unorthodox Behaviour*. To Collins' surprise and delight, Bruford suggested he help Genesis out by taking the drummer's stool for the upcoming tour, which would also feature dual drumming from Collins and Bruford on most of the instrumental sections.

Genesis relocated themselves in Dallas, Texas, for rehearsals and the subsequent tour ran from March to July 1976 taking in Canada, the U.S., the UK and Europe. Collins' first show as lead singer was on 26 March at the London Arena in London, Ontario, Canada. He was an immediate hit with audiences, projecting a much more accessible image compared to Gabriel's mysterious persona. Collins grew in confidence as the tour progressed, but on this tour still shared on-stage song introductions with Rutherford and Hackett.

The Glasgow Apollo and Bingley Hall, Stafford, shows were filmed by Tony Maylam and released as the 45-minute *Genesis: In Concert* in cinemas on a double bill with *White Rock*, a documentary covering the 1976 Winter Olympics.

Genesis hit the UK cinemas in 1977 with *Genesis: In Concert* filmed by Tony Maylam during the band's 1976 tour. The film was shown on a double-bill with *White Rock*, a documentary covering the 1976 Winter Olympics with music by Yes' Rick Wakeman. This advertisement appeared in *Melody Maker* on 29 January 1977 (courtesy Mark Kenyon/The Genesis Archive).

10

Studio Album #8: *Wind & Wuthering*

UK Release: 17 December 1976. LP. Charisma. CDS 4005.
U.S. Release: 17 December 1976. LP. Atlantic/ATCO. SD 36–144.
Remix/Remaster Release:
UK Release: 2 April 2007. CD/SACD/DVD. Virgin/Charisma. CDSCDR4005.
U.S. Release: 15 May 2007. CD/DVD. Atlantic/Rhino. R2 128764.

Album Tracks

[80] Eleventh Earl of Mar
[81] One for the Vine
[82] Your Own Special Way
[83] Wot Gorilla?
[84] All in a Mouse's Night
[85] Blood on the Rooftops
[86] Unquiet Slumbers for the Sleepers…
[87] …In That Quiet Earth
[88] Afterglow

Other Songs Recorded

[89] Match of the Day
[90] Pigeons
[91] Inside and Out

Genesis decided on a quick follow-up to the successful *A Trick of the Tail*, but the recording of their new album sowed the seeds of another split. The bulk of the writing for the album was completed by Tony Banks and Mike Rutherford with contributions from Steve Hackett and the material was rehearsed during the hot summer of 1976. Hackett, buoyed by his solo success, felt under pressure from the band to concentrate on group activities rather than further explore outlets for his own material. He therefore felt that he should get his fair share of the writing space on the album. This led to disagreements with the rest of the group who felt the best material should be used, regardless of who wrote it. Hackett became frustrated with the committee approach to agreeing material and later commented, "My development as a writer created a difficult situation—within the group there were so many writers that we couldn't contain it. I was interested in instrumental music and the balance was shifting more to songs, to simplifying, and I felt that the wackiness was being toned down, maybe in search of a new audience, maybe less elitist and I was maybe more purist than that."[1]

10. Studio Album #8: Wind & Wuthering

While Hackett did offer ideas to the band during their six-week writing period, the other members did not find his material to be attractive. Collins noted: "A lot of his things–5/4, 7/8, 9/8 bits—were all over the place, it wasn't really happening."[2] Hackett was disappointed two of his songs in particular—"Please Don't Touch" and "Hoping Love Will Last," which would both appear on his second solo album, *Please Don't Touch*, were rejected by the rest of the band. But as he was a less forceful personality than Banks and Rutherford, he ultimately backed down.

Despite his frustrations, Hackett did enjoy working on the album but increasingly he was beginning to feel more of an outsider. In an online interview, he commented: "I was already working outside the group, I was already thinking of Randy Crawford and working with other gifted, gifted people. Tremendously gifted people, singers, people who are geniuses in their own right. I felt that I still had a lot to learn and the only way to do that was by immersion in separate cultures; black, American, white American and not be exclusively involved with European music."[3]

The band decamped to Relight Studios in Hilvarenbeek, Holland, to record the album in September 1976. Banks recalled, "We were advised we might make some money if we recorded in Holland. You're allowed to keep 25 percent more of your money if you record your album out of the country."[4] The location was rural and remote, situated next to a pig farm, and the band camped at the studio with producer David Hentschel and their technical crew. It was the first time Genesis had recorded outside the UK. The group enjoyed the isolation as it helped them to focus on recording their new music. Hentschel recalled, "We'd eat at the studio every night, have stuff sent in, it was totally cut off, but that enabled us to concentrate."[5]

The songs had been well rehearsed by the band and the recording process was quick with most songs being captured on the third or fourth take. The recording of the album was

Advertisement promoting the release of *Wind & Wuthering* placed in *Melody Maker* on 8 January 1977 (courtesy Mark Kenyon/The Genesis Archive).

therefore completed in just two weeks. The process was helped by the fact that Genesis and Hentschel had already established a working relationship on *A Trick of the Tail*. The band and their crew returned to London and Trident Studios in Earl's Court in October to add overdubs and complete the mix.

During this period, Phil Collins' son, Simon, was born. Collins could only spend a couple of days with his wife and new child before reimmersing himself in the album. "It was one of those moments where you now think 'What the fuck did I do that for? What the hell was I thinking about?' You miss so much because you don't think about it and my attitude at the time was that this is what I do for a living."[6] Collins was not heavily involved in the writing of the album—with his contribution restricted to ideas for the jazz-fusion tinged [83] WOT GORILLA? and the chorus to [85] BLOOD ON THE ROOFTOPS—instead his main role in the process was as an arranger.

The album's title was derived from two pieces: The "Wind" comes from John Buchan's novel *The House of the Four Winds*, the title (also inspired by a Chinese restaurant in New York) was also adapted by Hackett for a piece that later became the quiet bridge for [80] ELEVENTH EARL OF MAR. Another inspiration was the Victorian poet Christina Rossetti's poem "Who Has Seen the Wind?"—a line also used in [82] YOUR OWN SPECIAL WAY; the "Wuthering" alludes to the novel *Wuthering Heights* by Emily Brontë, the last nine words of the closing sentence of her novel being used as the split title for the instrumental section preceding [88] AFTERGLOW.

[80] ELEVENTH EARL OF MAR

Music: Tony Banks/Steve Hackett
Lyrics: Mike Rutherford/Steve Hackett
Length: 7:43
Tony Banks—Synthesizers, Organ, Mellotron; **Phil Collins**—Lead & Backing Vocals, Drums, Percussion; **Steve Hackett**—Lead Guitar, Acoustic Guitar, Kalimba; **Mike Rutherford**—Rhythm Guitar, Bass, Bass Pedals
Recorded: Relight Studios, Hilvarenbeek, Holland, September–October 1976.
Mixed: Trident Studios, London, October 1976.
Producer: David Hentschel and Genesis. Engineer: David Hentschel. Assistant: Pierre Geoffroy Chateau and Nick "Cod" Bradford.
2007 Remix/Remaster Release:
Mixed at The Farm, Surrey 2005/2006.
5.1 Surround sound and stereo mixes by Nick Davis. Assisted by Tom Mitchell.
UK/U.S. Release: 17 December 1976 (LP: *Wind & Wuthering*).

ELEVENTH EARL OF MAR was developed under the working title "Scottish" and opens with a foreboding Tony Banks Mellotron chord sequence written in E flat major, which ultimately transitions to D major. The sound had reminded Rutherford of the Scottish Highlands and triggered the subject matter for his lyrics. It is a beautifully textured introduction with its crescendos reminiscent of the intro to [31] THE FOUNTAIN OF SALMACIS. It leads into a complex and urgent organ led verse-chorus section accentuated by Collins' rot tom fills, which switches tempos around its basic 4/4 meter. The chorus section was written by Hackett and the song demonstrates how well Banks and Hackett's challenging approach to harmonies and sound benefited the band. The song propels its way through these changes before arriving at a beautiful and dynamic slowed-down midsection (3:55 to 6:08), also written by Hackett, in A minor. This section, played by the guitarist on a Kalimba and with added nylon guitar, had originally been intended as a separate song to have been titled "The

House of the Four Winds." This section reaches a dramatic climax with Collins' multilayered vocal harmonies riding over Hackett's neat repeated riff and Rutherford's thunderous bass pedals, before returning to the song's uptempo basis.

Rutherford's lyric tells the story of Scottish nobleman John Erskine, who led a Jacobite rebellion in 1715. The opening lines of the song were lifted from D.K. Broster's book *The Flight of the Heron*.[7] Rutherford felt the song "had a tremendous energy."[8] Banks noted the lack of immediacy that is normally needed to open an album—with the song requiring multiple hearings from the listener for it to sink in. He also noted, "Often we'd add the lyrics when we'd finished the music and there's no doubt some songs lost it at that point. The words did something the music didn't need, they attracted too much attention to themselves."[9] Banks' comments make sense to a point, as the song demonstrates the band's strengths in creating musical dynamics, but the lyrical tale here sits well with the music. ELEVENTH EARL OF MAR may have challenged listeners, but for those patient enough to absorb its subtleties it is a highly rewarding opener.

Live Performances: 1977, 1978, 1983/4 (excerpt). The song was used as the set opener on the 1978 tour. The intro would later be used as part of a medley performed on their 1983/4 tour.

Live Recordings: No official live recording of the song has been released.

[81] ONE FOR THE VINE

Music & Lyrics: Tony Banks
Length: 9:59
Tony Banks—Piano, Synthesizers, Mellotron; **Phil Collins**—Lead & Backing Vocals, Drums, Percussion; **Steve Hackett**–Guitar; **Mike Rutherford**—Acoustic Guitar, Bass
Recorded: Relight Studios, Hilvarenbeek, Holland, September–October 1976.
Mixed: Trident Studios, London, October 1976.
Producer: David Hentschel and Genesis. Engineer: David Hentschel. Assistant: Pierre Geoffroy Chateau and Nick "Cod" Bradford.
2007 Remix/Remaster Release:
Mixed at The Farm, Surrey 2005/2006.
5.1 Surround sound and stereo mixes by Nick Davis. Assisted by Tom Mitchell.
UK/U.S. Release: 17 December 1976 (LP: *Wind & Wuthering*).

Banks worked meticulously on honing ONE FOR THE VINE over a period of a few months between the release of *A Trick of the Tail* and the recording of *Wind & Wuthering*. In a similar approach to the one he took for [74] MAD MAN MOON on the previous album, Banks weaved together various musical segments, chordal structures and key changes into an overall package. He noted, "It's an idea I've wanted to do for a long time of using a lot of instrumental ideas, which flow one from the other without repeating themselves."[10] He demoed the song to the band in its entirety, singing the melody himself. His dogged persistence as much as the music persuaded the band to rehearse and record it. In the studio Banks and Collins laid down the basic backing track on a Steinway grand piano, and drums then the whole band added their additional parts as overdubs. Banks felt this approach left the song underrehearsed and noted it would improve once played live. However, the method allowed Banks the space to experiment with the Mellotron and his armory of synthesizers to create the orchestral textures that give the song its character. Hackett also adds some undertested guitar parts, which add to the song's character without distracting from Banks' core melodies.

Lyrically, ONE FOR THE VINE tells the story of an unwitting false prophet—a stranger in a strange land who is accepted as a Christ-like figure. It is told musically via its soothing piano-led melody. The story was inspired by Michael Moorcock's 1970 novel, *Phoenix in Obsidian*.[11] The faster instrumental midsection gives the song a contrasting change of pace, emphasizing Banks' tendency to indulge his love of harmonics. The keyboardist likened the end section to a triumphant march as it reveals the irony that the protagonist was indeed the Christ-like figure all along.

The song is typical of its composer and a great example of what the band would term a "journey" song—one that does not follow the traditional verse-chorus structure, instead weaving its way through different thematic sections with rhythm and tempo changes creating a more dramatic presentation. As such it may remain a connoisseur's piece, but those who have empathy with Banks' approach to composition will find much to enjoy.

Live Performances: 1977, 1978, 1980. The song became an even more effective live piece where theater acoustics helped to convey the dynamics created by its many mood changes. It was played live on the three tours that followed before disappearing from the band's set.

Live Recordings: A live version of the song (11:04), recorded at the Theatre Royal, Drury Lane, London, on 5 May 1980, appeared on the European release of *Three Sides Live* in 1982 as well as the later remastered international version in 1994 and remix in 2009. The band lineup was Banks, Collins and Rutherford, augmented by Daryl Stuermer (guitar) and Chester Thompson (drums). The recording was engineered by David Hentschel and produced by the band with Nick Davis handling the remix.

[82] YOUR OWN SPECIAL WAY

Music & Lyrics: Mike Rutherford
Length: 6:17
Tony Banks—Synthesizers, Organ, Electric Piano; **Phil Collins**—Lead & Backing Vocals, Drums, Percussion; **Steve Hackett**—Lead Guitar, Acoustic Guitar; **Mike Rutherford**—Rhythm Guitar, Acoustic Guitar, Bass
Recorded: Relight Studios, Hilvarenbeek, Holland, September–October 1976.
Mixed: Trident Studios, London, October 1976.
Producer: David Hentschel and Genesis. Engineer: David Hentschel. Assistant: Pierre Geoffroy Chateau and Nick "Cod" Bradford.
2007 Remix/Remaster Release:
Mixed at The Farm, Surrey 2005/2006.
5.1 Surround sound and stereo mixes by Nick Davis. Assisted by Tom Mitchell.
UK/U.S. Release: 17 December 1976 (LP: *Wind & Wuthering*)
UK Single Release: 18 February 1977. (A-side single b/w [79] IT'S YOURSELF. Charisma. CB 300)
U.S. Single Release: March 1977. (A-side single b/w [87] ...IN THAT QUIET EARTH. Atlantic/ATCO. 45–7076)

A seemingly straightforward love song written by Rutherford for his wife, Angie, while staying in a hotel overlooking the Copa Cobana in Brazil. It joins together three separate pieces of music he had written in three different time signatures. The song was reportedly inspired by the poem "Who Has Seen the Wind?" by Christina Georgina Rossetti. It has a lovely acoustic opening and verse, written in 3/4 and based around Rutherford's weirdly open-tuned 12-string guitar.[12] It gives way to a chorus that seems ill-fitting, exposing the song's stitched together nature, with more than a hint of country feel in Hackett's lead guitar lines. To cap it all the midsong keyboard led instrumental section, on which Banks employs a delicate sound akin to a musical box using his Fender Rhodes electric piano, meanders aimlessly and takes any momentum out of the song.

The love song lyric coupled with the gentle acoustic guitar was to become a Rutherford specialty. The bassist's strength was in his ear for a simple melody and chord structure and it would later stand him in good stead with his writing outside the band for his own Mike + The Mechanics project. This song is a tentative first step along that road. Collins recognized it as, "the most commercial track on the album."[13] Rutherford felt the song was underarranged, with its acoustic verse working against it. Banks agreed: "It was a song that fell together.... I think it could have been done better in a different way. The first bit's lovely, but I always felt the marriage between verse and chorus wasn't quite right."[14]

Flyer issued to record stores promoting the February 1977 single release of [82] YOUR OWN SPECIAL WAY. Note the typo for its B-side with [79] IT'S YOURSELF here billed incorrectly as "You Yourself" (courtesy Mark Kenyon/The Genesis Archive).

The song certainly highlighted the band's aim to explore simpler structures and more conventional personal relationship-based lyrics, while retaining the elements of composition and musicianship that set them apart from the more commercial bands of the period. The song's limited success upon its release as a single, suggests they had not yet achieved that goal and would lead to a decision to tighten their writing even further on their next album.

Single Release: Rutherford's first solo penned song became a minor hit on its edited single release (3:49) in the UK (reaching #43). The edit removed the ponderous midsong instrumental section. The song was further edited (3:03) for its single release in the U.S., where it peaked at #62 on the singles chart.

Live Performances: 1977 (occasionally), 1986/7 (Australian leg). The song was performed on occasion on the band's *Wind & Wuthering* tour before being dropped from the set. It reappeared during the Australian leg of the 1986/7 tour when the band used a string quartet to satisfy local union laws to back a purely acoustic version of the song. This version is more laid back and Collins delivers a heartfelt vocal rendition.

Live Recordings: A recording (6:51) from the Sydney Entertainment Centre in December 1986 featured on the band's [162] HOLD ON MY HEART CD-maxi single and later as part of the *Genesis Archive #2: 1976–1992* box set. The lineup was Banks, Collins and Rutherford, augmented by Daryl Stuermer (guitar) and Chester Thompson (drums) and joined by the Robert Ingram string section arranged by Peter Robinson. The recording was engineered by Geoff Callingham and mixed by Nick Davis.

[83] WOT GORILLA?

Music: Tony Banks/Phil Collins
Length: 3:20
Tony Banks—Synthesizers; **Phil Collins**—Drums, Tubular Bells, Percussion; **Steve Hackett**–Guitar; **Mike Rutherford**—Bass
Recorded: Relight Studios, Hilvarenbeek, Holland, September–October 1976.
Mixed: Trident Studios, London, October 1976.
Producer: David Hentschel and Genesis. Engineer: David Hentschel. Assistant: Pierre Geoffroy Chateau and Nick "Cod" Bradford.
2007 Remix/Remaster Release:
Mixed at The Farm, Surrey 2005/2006.
5.1 Surround sound and stereo mixes by Nick Davis. Assisted by Tom Mitchell.
UK/U.S. Release: 17 December 1976 (LP: *Wind & Wuthering*).

WOT GORILLA? is a percussive instrumental inspired by Collins' love of free-form jazz-rock fusion. It adapts one of Banks' keyboard themes from the earlier [81] ONE FOR THE VINE adding Collins' rhythmic flourishes. The piece opens with some shimmering tubular bells, played delicately by Collins to create the illusion that they are chiming in the wind. Collins' driving drum pattern fades in and gives the piece its rhythmic propulsion, Banks' keyboard phrases are punctuated by a soaring guitar part from Hackett and punchy bass work by Rutherford. The result is a pleasing diversion from the more earnest tracks on the album. The short instrumental rattles along at a decent lick before fading out on the same shimmering bells that introduced it. While it is agreeable, musically there is no real progression and the track stays in one mood and tempo throughout giving the impression of a brief interlude to the sweeping music that surrounds it. However, it was one of Collins' favorite tracks on the album, allowing him the freedom to express his percussive ideas:

"it was a bit more of my Los Endos thing coming in the door. It was my fusion, kind of Weather Report-ing side of me I was suddenly able to make Tony Banks plays this stuff and they seemed to like it."[15]

The song was originally to be linked to Hackett's "Please Don't Touch' before that song was dropped by the band. The guitarist was less keen on Wot Gorilla? and later commented, "to my mind, [Wot Gorilla?] was a very inferior instrumental—a real doodle of an idea."[16] Hackett acknowledged the strong rhythms but pointed to the lack of harmonic development, which he felt was more adequately displayed on his rejected song.

Live Performances: 1977 (once). The instrumental was only performed once only, at the band's opening gig of their 1977 tour at the Rainbow Theatre on New Year's Day—where it followed [59] Lilywhite Lilith and the intro to [60] The Waiting Room as part of a short medley.

Live Recordings: No official live recording is available.

[84] All in a Mouse's Night

Music & Lyrics: Tony Banks
Length: 6:38
Tony Banks—Synthesizers; **Phil Collins**—Lead & Backing Vocals, Drums, Percussion; **Steve Hackett**—Lead Guitar; **Mike Rutherford**—Rhythm Guitar, Bass
Recorded: Relight Studios, Hilvarenbeek, Holland, September–October 1976.
Mixed: Trident Studios, London, October 1976.
Producer: David Hentschel and Genesis. Engineer: David Hentschel. Assistant: Pierre Geoffroy Chateau and Nick "Cod" Bradford.
2007 Remix/Remaster Release:
Mixed at The Farm, Surrey 2005/2006.
5.1 Surround sound and stereo mixes by Nick Davis. Assisted by Tom Mitchell.
UK/U.S. Release: 17 December 1976 (LP: *Wind & Wuthering*).

Banks composed this "Tom and Jerry" cartoon tale put to music. It is one of the songs Collins highlights when he talks about the band's lyrics reading better than they are sung. "That's why I have a soft spot for the later years of Genesis," said Collins later, "when I could at least sing other people's words, by then a little more personal, with some kind of emotion."[17] You can understand how he would find it difficult to put energy and emotion as a vocalist into the twee story presented here. But the band were keen to present a contrast to some of their more cosmic ideas and produce a song with a more whimsical nature. The song is lyrically expressed as a mini play from the point of view of the loving couple, who discover the mouse, the mouse itself and the cat who tries to rid the household of the rodent. It is very much a comic song with the cat failing to defeat the mouse and fabricating a story in order to save face.

Musically, the song progresses nicely using Banks' vast array of synthesizers to create a wide sonic landscape and some lovely chord transitions with Rutherford's bass prodding at the melody. His keyboard lines convey the scurrying activity of the chase. Hackett's scratching and bubbling guitar effects are brought more to the fore in Nick Davis' remix and are like those he used in [65] The Colony of Slipperman on *The Lamb Lies Down on Broadway*. His guitar solo on the instrumental play-out is also a highlight, showing how skillful the Hackett was at working with Banks' shifting harmonies.

Ultimately, the song's subject matter means it all feels a little too lightweight, despite the occasional dramatic punch of the music. Banks later noted, "The riffs were good, but the lyric was a little self-conscious. I don't think it's bad, it's just not up there with my other two. It has that humorous element in it, in contrast to some of the heavyweight tracks elsewhere on the album. It's important in that sense."[18]

Live Performances: 1977 (UK leg). The song was regular part of the set during the UK leg of the *Wind & Wuthering* tour but was dropped once the band moved to North America and Europe.

Live Recordings: No official live version of the song is available.

[85] BLOOD ON THE ROOFTOPS

Music: Steve Hackett/Phil Collins
Lyrics: Steve Hackett
Length: 5:27
Tony Banks—Piano, Mellotron; **Phil Collins**—Lead & Backing Vocals, Drums, Percussion; **Steve Hackett**–Lead Guitar, Acoustic Guitar, Auto Harp; **Mike Rutherford**—Acoustic Guitar, Bass
Recorded: Relight Studios, Hilvarenbeek, Holland, September–October 1976.
Mixed: Trident Studios, London, October 1976.
Producer: David Hentschel and Genesis. Engineer: David Hentschel. Assistant: Pierre Geoffroy Chateau and Nick "Cod" Bradford.
2007 Remix/Remaster Release:
Mixed at The Farm, Surrey 2005/2006.
5.1 Surround sound and stereo mixes by Nick Davis. Assisted by Tom Mitchell.
UK/U.S. Release: 17 December 1976 (LP: *Wind & Wuthering*).

BLOOD ON THE ROOFTOPS is one of the Genesis' most underrated songs, likely due to it never having been performed live by the band. The song has built a strong following over the years and the band themselves have come to appreciate it more. It opens with an excellent nylon classical guitar piece by Hackett backed by Banks' lightly orchestral Mellotron work, which gives the song a brooding and melancholic atmosphere. Collins then enters with a delicate vocal conveying a lyric that sums up the feel of rainy days when there is little to do but watch TV. Inspired by the songwriting of Jimmy Webb,[19] this slow-tempo piece satirizes society's then obsession with television and is full of references to the programs and news events of the day. Musically simple in structure and lush in soundscape, the song is split into the verses written by Hackett and a lovely chorus written separately and sometime earlier by Collins, which he developed lyrically around the title phrase.

Whereas [82] YOUR OWN SPECIAL WAY unsuccessfully glued together unconnected musical sections, here the separate pieces weave seamlessly making this one of the strongest tracks on *Wind & Wuthering*. The symphonic feel to the arrangement is generated by Banks' imaginative use of the Mellotron and the Steinway grand piano, which lifted the song in the studio. Originally the lyrics were to have been a romantic love ballad, but Hackett ultimately decided to contrast this with the other romantic songs on the album by writing a more cynical piece with the occasional political reference. Banks and Rutherford both retrospectively felt it was one of the guitarist's strongest contributions to the band. Banks recalled, "It's a beautiful song and because I had nothing to do with the writing of it, I can be a little more detached; it still moves me when I hear it now."[20]

While the song was never performed live by the band it was briefly considered for inclusion in the set of their 2007 reunion tour.

10. Studio Album #8: Wind & Wuthering

[86] UNQUIET SLUMBERS FOR THE SLEEPERS...

Music: Steve Hackett/Mike Rutherford
Length: 2:19
Tony Banks—Synthesizers; **Phil Collins**—Percussion; **Steve Hackett**—Guitar, Acoustic Guitar; **Mike Rutherford**—Acoustic Guitar, Bass
Recorded: Relight Studios, Hilvarenbeek, Holland, September–October 1976.
Mixed: Trident Studios, London, October 1976.
Producer: David Hentschel and Genesis. Engineer: David Hentschel. Assistant: Pierre Geoffroy Chateau and Nick "Cod" Bradford.
2007 Remix/Remaster Release:
Mixed at The Farm, Surrey 2005/2006.
5.1 Surround sound and stereo mixes by Nick Davis. Assisted by Tom Mitchell.
UK/U.S. Release: 17 December 1976 (LP: *Wind & Wuthering*).

This is the first of three interlinked tracks to close the album, the first two of which are instrumental. It is another showcase for Hackett's skills on his nylon classical acoustic guitar, with some ghostly synth effects from Banks added on top. The piece had its origins in a version of [66] RAVINE, on which Hackett and Banks had experimented with sonic textures. It is a typically inspired piece of playing by Hackett, with both electric and acoustic guitar providing a haunting melody over Rutherford's strummed 12-string. Collins' echoed percussion conjures cold images into the musical landscape.

Originally the track was to have been joined with [87] ...IN THAT QUIET EARTH as a solitary band credited composition but the rest of the band had sensed Hackett's frustration with much of his compositional work being passed over, so a decision was taken to split the music into two distinct tracks and give the guitarist an additional credit on the album.

[87] ...IN THAT QUIET EARTH

Music: Steve Hackett/Mike Rutherford/Tony Banks/Phil Collins
Length: 4:54
Tony Banks—Synthesizers; **Phil Collins**—Drums, Percussion; **Steve Hackett**—Lead Guitar; **Mike Rutherford**—Rhythm Guitar, Bass, Bass Pedals
Recorded: Relight Studios, Hilvarenbeek, Holland, September–October 1976.
Mixed: Trident Studios, London, October 1976.
Producer: David Hentschel and Genesis. Engineer: David Hentschel. Assistant: Pierre Geoffroy Chateau and Nick "Cod" Bradford.
2007 Remix/Remaster Release:
Mixed at The Farm, Surrey 2005/2006.
5.1 Surround sound and stereo mixes by Nick Davis. Assisted by Tom Mitchell.
UK/U.S. Release: 17 December 1976 (LP: *Wind & Wuthering*).
U.S. Single Release: March 1977 (B-side single b/w [82] YOUR OWN SPECIAL WAY. Atlantic/ATCO. 45-7076)

Collins' elongated drum roll is followed by a gliding lead electric guitar figure from Hackett which alternates with Banks' harmonizing keyboards in a fast-paced 9/8 rhythm, taking the two-part instrumental section into an energetic new territory. Hackett's lead guitar soars over Collins' inspired drumming as he moves around the rhythm before the music changes tempo, reverting to a straight 4/4 meter with heavy backbeat as it shifts in key from A major to E major. This second section is rhythmically driven by Rutherford's heavy rhythm guitar riff, prodding bass and Collins' complementary drums. This lays the foundation for Banks to deliver one of his trademark solos and the instrumental showcases the band's musical strengths. Hackett remarked, "It was very good. You had the fast and the slow—the compelling slow rhythm, setting up all those marching band aspects. You have the implied army coming at you."[21] It is certainly an exciting piece and one the band's best instrumental compositions.

Single Release: The instrumental was released as the B-side (4:45) to the U.S. single release of [82] YOUR OWN SPECIAL WAY.

Live Performances: 1977, 1983/4, 1986/7. The piece was played live in link with [88] AFTERGLOW on the 1977 tour and was later played as part of a longer medley on the 1983/4 and 1986/7 tours, which were sandwiched by [52] IN THE CAGE and [88] AFTERGLOW or occasionally on the latter tour the finale of [38] SUPPER'S READY.

Live Recordings: No official live version of the song is available.

[88] AFTERGLOW

Music & Lyrics: Tony Banks
Length: 4:14
Tony Banks—Synthesizers, Organ, Mellotron; **Phil Collins**—Lead & Multitracked Backing Vocals, Drums, Percussion; **Steve Hackett**—Lead Guitar; **Mike Rutherford**—Rhythm Guitar, Bass, Bass Pedals
Recorded: Relight Studios, Hilvarenbeek, Holland, September–October 1976.
Mixed: Trident Studios, London, October 1976. Remixed: The Farm, Surrey, 2006.
Producer: David Hentschel and Genesis. Engineer: David Hentschel. Assistant: Pierre Geoffroy Chateau and Nick "Cod" Bradford.
2007 Remix/Remaster Release:
Mixed at The Farm, Surrey 2005/2006.
5.1 Surround sound and stereo mixes by Nick Davis. Assisted by Tom Mitchell.
UK/U.S. Release: 17 December 1976 (LP: *Wind & Wuthering*).

Wind & Wuthering closes with possibly its strongest, as well as its simplest, track. AFTERGLOW is structured around a rotating verse and chorus that builds in intensity as it progresses. Banks wrote this midtempo song very quickly, the music coming out spontaneously, but then he became worried that the melody he had written was too close to that for the seasonal standard "Have Yourself a Merry Little Christmas." He eventually realized there were enough differences in the songs to avoid accusations of plagiarism.

Hackett's guitar figure on the verse utilizes a descending pattern that resolves and repeats as Banks continuously loops the song. The anthemic approach adds drama and passion with its lifting key changes (switching from G major to E flat major for the chorus then to C major for the final chorus) heightening the drama. "There's a lot you can do with key changes to make a song more interesting."[22] Banks later noted. The final chorus lift ends the song on a note of optimism, contrasting with its first-person narrative of emotional despair resulting from some form of physical disaster, not a broken relationship as is often cited.

Collins delivers a strong vocal, his range coping well with the song's ascent and growing intensity. He also adds his own three-layered backing harmonies (inspired by 10cc's "I'm Not in Love"). It was Hackett who suggested the vocal harmony loops when a problem with the tape machine led to producer David Hentschel looking to the band for ideas to try out. The revolving instrumental play-out serves to add a note of finality to the emotional drama and demonstrates how Collins' musical ear helped him highlight Banks' harmonic phrases through his clever use of drum fills and cymbals.

Live Performances: 1977, 1978, 1980, 1981, 1982, 1983/4, 1986/7 (occasionally), 2007. The song would become a fan stage favorite, being performed on each tour over the next ten years. It was also performed on the band's reunion tour in 2007. Each time the song would close out an instrumental section or medley, which from 19810 was topped by [52] IN THE CAGE.

Live Recordings: (1) A live version of the song (4:29) recorded at Palais des Sports, Paris, 13 July 1977 appeared on *Seconds Out*. This was de-coupled from the instrumental [87] ...IN THAT QUIET EARTH and presented as a standalone piece. This performance lacks the power in Collins' vocal performance it would gain on later tours. The band was augmented by Chester Thompson on drums. The recording was produced by David Hentschel and the band.

(2) The recording (5:14) featured on *Three sides Live* was taken from the National Exhibition Centre, Birmingham, on 23 December 1981. At this point the song formed the conclusion to the [52] IN THE CAGE medley and this version was a dynamic performance by the band. The lineup of Banks, Collins and Rutherford was augmented by Daryl Stuermer (guitar) and Thompson. The recording was engineered by Geoff Callingham and produced by the band.

(3) A more restrained performance, protecting Collins' ageing voice, and again completing a medley begun with IN THE CAGE, was captured on *Live Over Europe 2007* (4:27) from Old Trafford, Manchester, on 7 July 2007. The lineup was again Banks, Collins and Rutherford, augmented by Stuermer and Thompson. The recording was made by Bernard Natier and produced by Nick Davis.

[89] MATCH OF THE DAY

Music: Tony Banks/Phil Collins/Mike Rutherford
Lyrics: Phil Collins
Length: 3:29
Tony Banks—Synthesizers; **Phil Collins**—Lead & Backing Vocals, Drums, Percussion; **Steve Hackett**—Guitar, Acoustic Guitar; **Mike Rutherford**—Rhythm Guitar, Acoustic Guitar, Bass
Recorded: Relight Studios, Hilvarenbeek, Holland, September–October 1976.
Mixed: Trident Studios, London, October 1976. Remixed: The Farm, Surrey, 2006.
Producer: David Hentschel and Genesis. Engineer: David Hentschel. Assistant: Pierre Geoffroy Chateau and Nick "Cod" Bradford.
2007 Remix/Remaster Release:
Mixed at The Farm, Surrey 2005/2006.
5.1 Surround sound and stereo mixes by Nick Davis. Assisted by Tom Mitchell.
UK Release: 20 May 1977 (EP: *Spot the Pigeon*. Charisma. GEN 001)
U.S. Release: 15 May 2007 (6-CD: *Genesis 1976–1982*)

Three further songs were recorded during the *Wind & Wuthering* studio sessions but were left off the album. The songs would later be released in the UK as an EP, *Spot the Pigeon*. The EP, released while the band was on tour, charted in the UK at #14. It was also released in many other territories around the world, but not in the U.S.—although Atlantic did release the EP in Canada.

MATCH OF THE DAY was the lead-off track and was joined by [90] PIGEONS and [91] INSIDE AND OUT. The title for the EP was a play on the "Spot the Ball" competitions prevalent in the UK at the time, where people were invited to put a cross on a photographic scene from a football match to indicate where they believed the ball should be, having been removed from the picture. It is a humorous song built around Rutherford's bouncy and melodic bass line and Hackett's jangly guitar, which looks at the world of soccer through the band's cynical eyes. Musically, Banks was the main writer and commented that he had basically reused the bass riff from [57] Carpet Crawlers in sped up form. Banks felt that musically the song was just about passable, notably during the riff in its middle section. Collins referenced that the band had tried to bring in some of the "hipper grooves of the day."[23] While the music does have elements which achieve that objective, the lyrics, written by Collins, are slightly cringe-worthy and Collins himself would later admit to being embarrassed by them. The spoken word outro, however, accurately and comically depicts the experiences of fans avoiding hooliganism on the terraces in the 1970s. Writer Daryl Easlea agreed, noting: "it's a fabulous time capsule of what Association Football used to be like in the UK."[24]

Overall, however, the keyboardist summed up his thoughts: "Match of the Day I think is one of the worst things we have ever done and I was mainly responsible for that and I can't stand it."[25] Accepted as a novelty song it has a certain comedic appeal, but none of the band were impressed enough to include it on their *Genesis Archive #2 1976–1992* collection, although it would later appear in remixed form in the *Genesis 1976–1982* box set.

[90] Pigeons

Music: Tony Banks/Phil Collins/Mike Rutherford
Lyrics: Tony Banks
Length: 3:12
Tony Banks—Synthesizers; **Phil Collins**—Lead & Backing Vocals, Drums, Percussion; **Steve Hackett**—Guitar; **Mike Rutherford**—Banjolele, Bass
Recorded: Relight Studios, Hilvarenbeek, Holland, September–October 1976.
Mixed: Trident Studios, London, October 1976. Remixed: The Farm, Surrey, 2006.
Producer: David Hentschel and Genesis. Engineer: David Hentschel. Assistant: Pierre Geoffroy Chateau and Nick "Cod" Bradford.
2007 Remix/Remaster Release:
Mixed at The Farm, Surrey 2005/2006.
5.1 Surround sound and stereo mixes by Nick Davis. Assisted by Tom Mitchell.
UK Release: 20 May 1977 (EP: *Spot the Pigeon*. Charisma. GEN 001)
U.S. Release: 6 November 2000 (3-CD: *Genesis Archive #2:1976–1992*)

Like [89] Match of the Day, Pigeons is another novelty song. The song was inspired by an article Rutherford had read about the nuisance value of the pigeons flying around the Foreign Office with its guano covered roof. Another rather jolly melody, this time based around a one-note guitar figure from Hackett with a heavily strummed banjolele from Rutherford. Rutherford's bass is also grounded in B flat with Banks adding chordal harmonies on top. The song would have been out of place among the more melancholic and expansive material used on *Wind & Wuthering*. While it is well recorded, it is an ultimately lightweight track that served its purpose better on the *Spot the Pigeon* EP. Banks remembered, "It was a lot of fun as it was so different. The idea of doing a whole song around one note was something that I had wanted to do for a long time, changing the chords underneath it."[26] Rutherford, however. is less fond of the song, particularly the lyrics, and sees it as representative of its time. Nick Davis' 2006 remix adds effects to Collins' vocals, creating the impression of a "speaker on a soapbox" on the verse.

[91] Inside And Out

Music: Tony Banks/Phil Collins/Steve Hackett/Mike Rutherford
Lyrics: Mike Rutherford

10. Studio Album #8: Wind & Wuthering

Length: 6:45
Tony Banks—Synthesizers; **Phil Collins**—Lead & Backing Vocals, Drums, Percussion; **Steve Hackett**—Lead Guitar, Acoustic Guitar; **Mike Rutherford**—Rhythm Guitar, Acoustic Guitar, Bass
Recorded: Relight Studios, Hilvarenbeek, Holland, September–October 1976.
Mixed: Trident Studios, London, October 1976. Remixed: The Farm, Surrey, 2006.
Producer: David Hentschel and Genesis. Engineer: David Hentschel. Assistant: Pierre Geoffroy Chateau and Nick "Cod" Bradford.
2007 Remix/Remaster Release:
Mixed at The Farm, Surrey 2005/2006.
5.1 Surround sound and stereo mixes by Nick Davis. Assisted by Tom Mitchell.
UK Release: 20 May 1977 (EP: *Spot the Pigeon*. Charisma. GEN 001)
U.S. Release: 3 March 1978. (B-side single b/w [102] FOLLOW YOU, FOLLOW ME. Atlantic. 3474)

Where the other two songs on *Spot the Pigeon* would have been out of place on *Wind & Wuthering*, INSIDE AND OUT would have been right at home. Maybe it was the rather downbeat and controversial subject matter of Rutherford's lyrics—dealing with the story of a man falsely accused of rape—which tipped the balance against it. Structurally, the song is split into two sections. The first section, "Inside," is a largely acoustic ballad played on 12-string guitar by Hackett and Rutherford with a beautiful, wistful melody. It deals with the basis for the man's imprisonment told from his point of view and that of his brother and the police. The playing on this section recalls the band's delicate acoustic work on [76] RIPPLES... with its intricate acoustic arrangement. The second section, "Out," is a high energy uptempo instrumental piece featuring some fine synth lines from Banks and lead guitar work from Hackett with Rutherford adding the crashing Pete Townshend–like rhythm guitar chords during the closing bars. Musically, this section is designed to represent the sense of relief the prisoner feels on being set free.

Hackett felt the song should have been included on *Wind & Wuthering* at the expense of [83] WOT GORILLA? as he believed it to be more representative of the music the band was producing, "lots of good noises; lots of good ideas; lovely twelve-string work, if I may say so. Interesting playing from everybody ... a good tune!"[27] Banks too felt the song was a strong contender, preferring it to [82] YOUR OWN SPECIAL WAY.

Live Performances: 1977 (occasionally). The song was performed live on during the May to July South American, UK and European legs of the band's 1977 tour to promote the release of the EP.

Live Recordings: No official live recordings of the song have been released.

* * *

Released on 17 December 1976, *Wind & Wuthering* finds Genesis consolidating on the triumphs of *A Trick of the Tail* without ever quite matching that record's variety and songwriting quality. That said, there are moments on the album where the band captures powerfully dramatic and emotional moods. Musically it is very sober and often classically orchestral in sound, with Banks further getting to grips with the possibilities of his synthesizers. Hackett's prowess on the acoustic guitar also came to the fore on this album, with some lovely playing. The guitarist pointed out, "The album has a broader spectrum of sound and a more varied composition. You have to listen to it a couple of times to really appreciate it. We experimented more with sound, we tried to avoid certain clichés of mellotron and synthesizers ... we wanted to try different arrangements."[28] Banks felt it was "a romantic album, which is probably why I like it as much as I do. Perhaps that area of music excites me more in a way. The chords are much more expansive, which I like and the changes more yearning."[29]

The liveliest instrumental moments, however, are built around the rhythmic backbone of Rutherford's bass and rhythm guitars alongside Collins' skillful drumming and percussion. This is particularly evident on [87] ...In That Quiet Earth. A couple of attempts to introduce simpler song structures have mixed results. Rutherford's [82] Your Own Special Way—a love song with ill-fitting sections—is eclipsed by Banks' wonderful [88] Afterglow, which makes for a superb anthemic album closer. Collins' singing is a little more assured here than on *Trick*, but lyrically he is given little with which to inject any soul or emotion—only on [88] Afterglow does he really get the chance to get some passion behind the lyrics.

The album required an investment from the listener and those who were prepared to absorb its many intricacies were rewarded with perhaps the band's most musical album to

STEVE HACKETT · TONY BANKS · CHESTER THOMPSON · MIKE RUTHERFORD · PHIL COLLINS

GENESIS

When Bill Bruford proved unavailable for the *Wind & Wuthering* tour, Genesis hired former Frank Zappa drummer Chester Thompson. He is pictured flanked by Steve Hackett and Tony Banks at the left and Mike Rutherford and Phil Collins at the right. Atco promotional photograph (courtesy Mark Kenyon/The Genesis Archive).

date. This is likely the reason it remains one of Banks' favorites, as it clearly represents his most personal musical statement. Rutherford, however, found the album less satisfying, believing the band was treading water.

Upon release the album charted at #7 in the UK and #26 in the U.S. The critical reception was largely positive with David Brown in *Record Mirror* noting, "it's an album to grow into, and a lot of people will take the time for their unmatched blend of music."[30] Barbara Charone of *Sounds*, echoed Brown's viewpoint by listening to the album eight times for her own review picking out different observations along the way before finally noting, "Genesis make Yes redundant. And The Pink Floyd too. Don't listen to me, here it for yourself. It's addictive stuff. Just smell the heather, Heathcliff."[31]

Wind & Wuthering also become a personal favorite with Hackett—the guitarist having been given a chance to express his classical playing on [85] BLOOD ON THE ROOFTOPS and [86] UNQUIET SLUMBERS FOR THE SLEEPERS…. Despite his appreciation of much of the album, Hackett felt the song selection left a couple of strong tracks that had been recorded on the side-lines—[90] PIGEONS and [91] INSIDE AND OUT, which he preferred to YOUR OWN SPECIAL WAY and WOT GORILLA?

No promotional videos were shot for songs from the album, although it is rumored a video was filmed for [89] MATCH OF THE DAY, with Collins singing on the terraces at Queens Park Rangers F.C. The band did however appear on the *Mike Douglas Show* in America and lip-synced to [88] AFTERGLOW and [82] YOUR OWN SPECIAL WAY.

Genesis went back on the road in January 1977 to promote the album. Bill Bruford was unable to return on drums having formed his own band UK, so the band turned to Chester Thompson as his replacement. Collins had seen Thompson perform with Weather Report and had also been impressed by his dual drumming with Ralph Humphrey on "More Trouble Every Day" from Frank Zappa's album *Roxy and Elsewhere (Live)*. Collins managed to track him down, via bassist friend Alphonso Johnson, while he was playing in the musical *The Wiz*. Collins offered him the job there and then, without the need for an audition. Thompson accepted and immediately flew over to the UK to rehearse with the band for the upcoming tour.

The *Wind & Wuthering* tour, ran through to July 1977, taking in the UK, U.S., Canada, Brazil and Europe. It included three nights at the start of the tour to promote the reopening of London's Rainbow Theatre. The dates were announced on 13 November 1976, before Genesis had even confirmed their new drummer. A live album, *Seconds Out*, was compiled from shows recorded during four nights at Paris' Palais des Sport between 11 and 14 June 1977. [46] THE CINEMA SHOW, a recording from the previous year at Pavillon de Paris, Paris, on 23 June 1976 with Bill Bruford on drums, was also included. The album was designed to be a representation of the current live set-up with Collins on vocals handling many of the tunes recorded during Gabriel's tenure as lead singer. It also provided the band with an opportunity to release a first live recording of their epic [38] SUPPER'S READY.

It was during the mixing of *Seconds Out* that Hackett's disillusionment came to a head. He had become increasingly frustrated by the lack of material he was getting through the band committee. Having recorded a solo album, *Voyage of the Acolyte*, which had given him a taste for greater creative control, he wanted to release more solo material. When the other band members were unwilling to compromise on band activities Hackett made his decision to leave. Collins explained, "Steve, unfortunately didn't write songs that appealed as much to everybody as Tony or Mike did but I thought his frustration at that time seemed unreasonable."[32]

Genesis completed the mixing of *Seconds Out* without Hackett and the album was released on 15 October 1977. A week before its release the announcement of Hackett's departure was made to the music press. Hackett noted in an exclusive interview for *Melody Maker*, "My decision to leave was not to do with Genesis specifically, but to do with the whole group ethic which I have grown to regard as a bit dubious… an individual's ideas get diluted, especially in a corporate group like Genesis with so many writers."[33]

Part 4

The Trio Years: August 1977–March 1996

Tony Banks (Keyboards)
Phil Collins (Vocals, Drums)
Mike Rutherford (Guitars, Bass)

From August 1977, Genesis were reduced to the trio of, from left, Mike Rutherford, Phil Collins and Tony Banks. Charisma promotional photograph (courtesy Mark Kenyon/The Genesis Archive).

11

Studio Album #9: ...And Then There Were Three...

UK Release: 31 March 1978. LP. Charisma. CDS 4010.
U.S. Release: 31 March 1978. LP. Atlantic. SD 19173.
Remix/Remaster Release:
UK Release: 2 April 2007. CD/SACD/DVD. Virgin/Charisma. CDSCDR4010.
U.S. Release: 15 May 2007. CD/DVD. Atlantic/Rhino. R2-128572.

Album Tracks
[92] DOWN AND OUT
[93] UNDERTOW
[94] BALLAD OF BIG
[95] SNOWBOUND
[96] BURNING ROPE
[97] DEEP IN THE MOTHERLODE
[98] MANY TOO MANY
[99] SCENES FROM A NIGHT'S DREAM
[100] SAY IT'S ALRIGHT JOE
[101] THE LADY LIES
[102] FOLLOW YOU, FOLLOW ME

Other Songs Recorded
[103] THE DAY THE LIGHT WENT OUT
[104] VANCOUVER

Following Steve Hackett's departure Genesis reconvened in August 1977 to write and record their first album as a trio. The album title ...And Then There Were Three... was the band's humorous take on their dwindling numbers. The title referenced a line taken from the Frank J. Green song adaptation of the children's poem "Ten Little Indians," which had been used in the first film adaptation of Agatha Christie's similarly title mystery, retitled And Then There Were None (1945). The only brief the band had going into the sessions was to write shorter, more concise, songs—the trio having felt that Wind & Wuthering had taken the band to one extreme with its musical complexity and romanticism. Rutherford commented later, "We missed not having some lightweight moments, like [89] MATCH OF THE DAY and [90] PIGEONS on Wind & Wuthering. So, we said to ourselves, 'Let's not make the songs quite so long. To get more variety on it.' I feel that set the mood of the album more than Steve's departure."[1] Banks confirmed the brief was to "Keep it shorter, more variety, get more quirky pieces in."[2]

Rutherford was tasked with handling lead guitar as well as rhythm and bass duties. He later recalled, "I remember discussing getting in another guitarist, what with Steve's fluidity and style, but I think we felt at that stage that we'd been together quite a long time as the three of us, and to bring a new person in, to make them understand the way we worked, to make them fit, was quite a big ask. So, we thought we'd just try without it and see."[3] The album would prove to be a steep learning curve for Rutherford, as he readily admitted: "The truth is I could barely play lead guitar. You don't suddenly become a lead guitarist. You have to work your way up to it. For the first couple of albums after Steve, I thought I was doing okay. I covered things fine as a songwriter, but as the albums moved along, my guitar playing started getting better. I felt more comfortable playing lead. I think I'm a songwriter who plays guitar, rather than a virtuoso guitarist, but I'm very comfortable with the lead parts I play."[4] Although Rutherford was not the most gifted lead player, he was able to create atmospheres through his playing. This in turn meant more of the lead work going to Banks' keyboards.

The bulk of the writing of the album fell to Banks and Rutherford as Collins was distracted by marriage problems and many of the tracks were individual compositions by the pair. The band used Shepperton Studios over a period of roughly six weeks to hone the material ahead of going into the studio. While Collins had not been a major writing contributor at this point, his skills as an arranger along with his rhythmic creativity were essential to the band's output. Also, having one band member fewer on the creative committee gave the remaining trio much needed space, as Banks later confirmed. "Making ...*And Then There Were Three...* was a very pleasurable experience. We weren't in each other's way because we had such definite roles—we felt very complete in the studio."[5]

The band returned to Relight Studios in Holland during September 1977 to record the album, with David Hentschel again on board as producer. Banks commented on the move, "One thing we find from going abroad is that when you record in a small town in Holland, there's nothing going on that will distract you from recording. We start about 11:00 in the morning and work right through until about 3:00 the next morning. On ...*And Then There Were Three...*, we did that for 12 days straight with no distractions. It's hardest on the engineer/producer. Obviously, he's got to stay there all the time, through every little overdub and everything. But the guys who aren't playing can have a rest."[6]

Although the songs were already written as the band went into the studio, the arrangements were still sparse as Rutherford remembered, "with only three of us it meant some of the songs weren't going to sound right until we put the overdubs on. The basic track was often quite sparse and then we put the important bits over the top. But we knew quite quickly whether the basic tracks were okay."[7]

Final mixing of the album was completed at Trident Studios the following month.

[92] DOWN AND OUT

Music: Tony Banks/Phil Collins/Mike Rutherford
Lyrics: Phil Collins
Length: 5:27
Tony Banks—Organ, Mellotron, Synthesizers; **Phil Collins**—Lead & Backing Vocals, Drums, Percussion; **Mike Rutherford**—Guitar, Bass, Bass Pedals
Recorded: Relight Studios, Hilvarenbeek, Holland, September–October 1977.
Mixed: Trident Studios, London.
Producer: David Hentschel and Genesis. Engineer: David Hentschel. Assistants: Pierre Geoffroy Chateau and Steve Short.

2007 Remix/Remaster Release:
Mixed at The Farm, Surrey 2005/2006.
5.1 Surround sound and stereo mixes by Nick Davis. Assisted by Tom Mitchell.
UK/U.S. Release: 31 March 1978. (LP: ...And Then There Were Three...).

The song, which opened ...And Then There Were Three..., was developed under the working title of "5/8" due to its odd-metered rhythm. Rutherford noted the song originated during the rehearsals for the album in August 1977. The band had been trying out ideas for openings to songs and Down and Out had its origins in one of Rutherford's guitar riffs. It also uses highly atmospheric high-octave chord transitions from Banks' synthesizers, which give the impression of dawn breaking. Rutherford's rhythmic riff in 5/8 then introduces a cautionary tale of the evils of corporate business, notably within record companies—emphasized by its working title "The Man with the Big Cigar." Collins explained, "The idea was to have song about an American record company, no names just companies, that are quite prepared to toss you out when you become passé. The chorus is spoken from the artist's point of view and the verses are from the company's point of view, basically cut and thrust."[8]

This song is probably most typical of the band on the album. Collins' expressive tom-filled drum patterns provide the drive over Rutherford's prodding bass pedals, gliding over which are Banks' stabbed staccato organ phrases and layered keyboard textures. With its urgent tempo, which Collins describes as "complex rhythmically, you can tap your foot through it, but it will come out somewhere else,"[9] it is one of the strongest cuts on the album and proved to be a winning opening track. However, Rutherford was unsure retrospectively noting, "The heavier tracks, like Down and Out, don't sound so good. That kind of song needs more room to stretch out."[10] Collins also struggled to convey the rhythm to drummer Chester Thompson during tour rehearsals. Daryl Stuermer, who joined the band as guitarist and bass player for the tour, also noted the band's confusion over the rhythm. Each member seemingly having a different perspective of where the first beat was in the 5/8 timing for the opening note.

Live Performances: 1978 (early dates). Down and Out was performed on some early dates of the subsequent tour but was later dropped as the band struggled to come to terms with the song's rhythmic complexity.

Live Recordings: No official live recordings of the song are available.

[93] Undertow

Music & Lyrics: Tony Banks
Length: 4:47
Tony Banks—Electric Grand Piano, Mellotron, Synthesizers; **Phil Collins**—Lead & Multitracked Backing Vocals, Drums, Percussion; **Mike Rutherford**—Guitar, Fretless Bass
Recorded: Relight Studios, Hilvarenbeek, Holland, September–October 1977.
Mixed: Trident Studios, London.
Producer: David Hentschel and Genesis. Engineer: David Hentschel. Assistants: Pierre Geoffroy Chateau and Steve Short.
2007 Remix/Remaster Release:
Mixed at The Farm, Surrey 2005/2006.
5.1 Surround sound and stereo mixes by Nick Davis. Assisted by Tom Mitchell.
UK/U.S. Release: 31 March 1978. (LP: ...And Then There Were Three...).

Undertow is a solo composition by Banks, which he noted, "was a slightly different way for me to write—slightly less chord dependent and a bit more dependent on the melody."[11] It was Banks' first use of the Yamaha CP70 electric grand piano, an instrument he would use expansively over the next few years and on which here he uses its distinctive chorus setting to great effect. Rutherford added a soft fretless bass part. Once the band had laid down the basic tracks—with guitar, piano and drums—it was decided the mix was already sounding full due to the input of the CP70. Collins recorded multitracked background vocal loops in a similar way to [88] AFTERGLOW, here they were held down in the mix so as not to be overly intrusive. Banks' gentle CP70 piano-led verse is married to a soaring chorus decorated with lush keyboard textures and Rutherford's big fretless bass notes. Reflective and yearning lyrics were becoming a Banks trademark and here they are nicely sung by Collins, whose crisp drumming also helps to lift the chorus. Rutherford has little to do other than offer some tasteful guitar lines on top of his bass.

The theme of the chorus was later reworked into an instrumental track, "From the Undertow" for Banks' first solo album *A Curious Feeling* (1979) and was also used as the main theme in Banks and Rutherford's score to the film *The Shout* (1978). Banks had originally intended to use the instrumental intro for a much longer version of UNDERTOW, but the group's determination to become more concise on this album meant it was discarded.

The song was originally planned to be sequenced as Track 8 on the album but was later swapped with [98] MANY TOO MANY and [99] SCENES FROM A NIGHT'S DREAM to move to Track 2. While UNDERTOW was among Banks and Rutherford's favorites songs from *...And Then There Were Three...* it was never performed live.

[94] BALLAD OF BIG

Music: Tony Banks/Phil Collins/Mike Rutherford
Lyrics: Phil Collins
Length: 4:50
Tony Banks—Electric Grand Piano, Organ, Synthesizers; **Phil Collins**—Lead & Backing Vocals, Drums, Percussion; **Mike Rutherford**—Guitar, Roland Guitar Synthesizer, Bass, Bass Pedals
Recorded: Relight Studios, Hilvarenbeek, Holland, September–October 1977.
Mixed: Trident Studios, London.
Producer: David Hentschel and Genesis. Engineer: David Hentschel. Assistants: Pierre Geoffroy Chateau and Steve Short.
2007 Remix/Remaster Release:
Mixed at The Farm, Surrey 2005/2006.
5.1 Surround sound and stereo mixes by Nick Davis. Assisted by Tom Mitchell.
UK Release: 3 March 1978. (B-side single b/w [102] FOLLOW YOU, FOLLOW ME)
UK/U.S. Album Release: 31 March 1978. (LP: *...And Then There Were Three...*).

The introduction to BALLAD OF BIG, which was developed under the working title "The Ballad of Big Jim," recalls a hazy desert scene as Collins' shimmering cymbals and Banks' sparse electric grand piano set the scene. The introduction also uses sonic effects created by Rutherford by rubbing the guitar strings with a bottleneck. This contributed the distinct wobble that gave the song an almost Eastern feel.

Collins' lyrics tell a tale of the old Wild West—one of two such songs on the album ([97] DEEP IN THE MOTHERLODE being the other). Big Jim Cooley is a U.S. marshal who takes a bet to take a herd of cattle on a long drive, but he ultimately meets a grizzly death at the hands of Indians. The song is one of only three written by all three band members on the album as Collins recalled, "This is one of the songs that was born out of one man's verse and another's chorus and someone else's intro."[12] It has a nagging chorus, heightened by Rutherford's pounding bass and Banks' repeated Hammond organ riff. The verse holds a different tempo and mood trying to conjure up a musical description of the cattle drive. Rutherford used a Roland Guitar Synthesizer, which he had purchased while the band was in the studio, on the outro which creates a neat phased effect.

Single Release: While the song is not one of the more memorable on the album, it was included as the B-side of the band's first single from the album, [102] FOLLOW YOU, FOLLOW ME.

Live Performances: 1978 (occasionally). The song was an irregular feature of the set for the subsequent tour but was not played on any subsequent tour.

Live Recordings: No official live recordings of the song are available.

[95] SNOWBOUND

Music & Lyrics: Mike Rutherford
Length: 4:31
Tony Banks—Electric Grand Piano, Mellotron, Synthesizers; **Phil Collins**—Lead & Backing Vocals, Drums, Percussion; **Mike Rutherford**—Guitar, Acoustic Guitar, Bass, Bass Pedals
Recorded: Relight Studios, Hilvarenbeek, Holland, September–October 1977.
Mixed: Trident Studios, London.
Producer: David Hentschel and Genesis. Engineer: David Hentschel. Assistants: Pierre Geoffroy Chateau and Steve Short.
2007 Remix/Remaster Release:
Mixed at The Farm, Surrey 2005/2006.
5.1 Surround sound and stereo mixes by Nick Davis. Assisted by Tom Mitchell.
UK/U.S. Release: 31 March 1978. (LP: *...And Then There Were Three...*).

Rutherford was consciously trying to encourage Banks and Collins to help develop a different approach with SNOWBOUND, to avoid falling into the trap of repeating old phrasings and arrangements. Originally the track had a faster tempo and it was decided to have Collins slow it down to a ballad. The result is a very pretty song, with Rutherford's delicate 12-string acoustic guitar guiding the verse, which evokes images of children playing in the snow. According to Rutherford, it is "a romantic song about a guy who gets inside a snowman outfit to hide from everybody, he was paranoid, and he gets stuck!"[13]

The band adds another big soaring chorus, which is played over a slow but heavily emphasized beat from Collins further helped by some tastefully placed bass notes from Rutherford. Banks used a pitch-bend pedal linked to his Polymoog string sound to get the rising effect to his keyboard that gives the chorus its sonic lift. Collins delivers one of his best vocal performances on the album by deftly marrying the breathy verse to the rising crescendo of its chorus. Rutherford noted, "[Phil's] singing is exceptionally good on this song, but then I think his singing has improved all round on this album."[14] The end result is a beautiful song which may be a little repetitive but remains effective due to its simplicity of structure and economy of execution.

[96] BURNING ROPE

Music & Lyrics: Tony Banks
Length: 7:10
Tony Banks—Electric Grand Piano, Mellotron, Synthesizers; **Phil Collins**—Lead & Backing Vocals, Drums, Percussion; **Mike Rutherford**—Guitar, Bass
Recorded: Relight Studios, Hilvarenbeek, Holland, September–October 1977.

Mixed: Trident Studios, London.
Producer: David Hentschel and Genesis. Engineer: David Hentschel. Assistants: Pierre Geoffroy Chateau and Steve Short.
2007 Remix/Remaster Release:
Mixed at The Farm, Surrey 2005/2006.
5.1 Surround sound and stereo mixes by Nick Davis. Assisted by Tom Mitchell.
UK/U.S. Release: 31 March 1978. (LP: ...And Then There Were Three...).

At just over seven minutes this Tony Banks composition is the longest cut on the album. Banks' multilayered introduction based around his piano chords features some scampering drum work from Collins, who works his way tirelessly around his kit. This leads into a verse featuring another of Banks' reflective lyrics on the theme of regret. While the vocal is delivered competently by Collins, it lacks the fire of some of his later work, perhaps again reflecting his lack of empathy with Banks' rather literate lyrics. The song is notable for featuring a tuneful guitar solo from Rutherford (from 4:03 to 5:10) over some big chords from Banks, who utilizes the Mellotron and Polymoog choral and string settings. The solo soars elegantly over Banks' backing and Collins dynamic drums. His part was written for him by Banks, who deliberately kept it simpler than would have been the case had Hackett still been on board. Rutherford was happy with his interpretation, noting it was his best solo on the album.

While Banks was writing the song, he envisaged it being much longer and similar in approach to [81] ONE FOR THE VINE. It was initially planned to feature various sections of music over a series of tempo changes. Ultimately, Banks decided to fall in line with the band's brief to produce shorter songs for the album. The basic track was again built around drums, piano and bass and the band members were not initially excited by the song. Once in the studio, Banks was able to add layers of keyboards that gave it more texture and Rutherford warmed to it. Collins, however, has never been keen on the track, saying shortly after his departure from the band had been announced, "It's a cruel thing to say, but it's a song like this that made me leave Genesis. Tony Banks will never talk to me again after this is published—this is one of his songs—but to me this song is a period piece. It doesn't make it in the twentieth century. I know there are people who like this music, but I just couldn't get up on stage and play or sing this material anymore."[15] Collins also noted his powerful drum fills during the song's opening was an attempt by him to make the track more interesting.

Live Performances: 1978. The song was a regular feature of the band's set for the ...And Then There Were Three... tour but did not feature on subsequent tours.

Live Recordings: A recording (7:29) from the Houston Hofheinz Pavilion on 22 October 1978 was included on CD2 of the *Genesis Archive #2: 1976–1992* box set. The band was augmented by Daryl Stuermer (bass) and Chester Thompson (drums). The recording was mixed by Nick Davis.

[97] DEEP IN THE MOTHERLODE

Music & Lyrics: Mike Rutherford
Length: 5:15
Tony Banks—Organ, Mellotron, Synthesizers; **Phil Collins**—Lead & Backing Vocals, Drums, Percussion; **Mike Rutherford**—Guitar, Guitar Synthesizer, Bass, Bass Pedals
Recorded: Relight Studios, Hilvarenbeek, Holland, September–October 1977.
Mixed: Trident Studios, London.

Producer: David Hentschel and Genesis. Engineer: David Hentschel. Assistants: Pierre Geoffroy Chateau and Steve Short.
2007 Remix/Remaster Release:
Mixed at The Farm, Surrey 2005/2006
5.1 Surround sound and stereo mixes by Nick Davis. Assisted by Tom Mitchell.
UK/U.S. Release: 31 March 1978. (LP: ...And Then There Were Three...)
U.S. Single Release: September 1978. (A-side single as 'Go West Young Man [In the Motherlode]' b/w [99] SCENES FROM A NIGHT'S DREAM. Atlantic. 3511)

DEEP IN THE MOTHERLODE, like [94] BALLAD OF BIG, is set in the American West. The song's story centered on a miner urged by his family to seek out their fortune during the American Gold Rush. The song was developed under the working title "Heavy." A later working title, "Go West Young Man," was used for the U.S. single release and the phrase remains the hook of the chorus. It is a reference to a quote from Horace Greeley, who, on July 13, 1865, famously advised in an editorial he wrote: "Go west, young man, go west and grow up with the country."

The song was penned by Rutherford and is a straight-ahead rock song with a pounding, bouncy, pulsing bass track typical of him. Rutherford's repeated treated guitar riff is augmented by some floating keyboards from Banks. Collins lays down a heavy backbeat and further colors the music with his well-place drum fills. The song seamlessly changes time signatures through its various sections and while it is similar in feel to its companion piece [94] BALLAD OF BIG, it is much more accessible and successful. Of note is a quiet midsong segment from 2:03 that gives way to a dramatic reintroduction to the main riff at 3:22. Rutherford was very happy with the mix of the final track, which required little overdubbing. He did, however, have reservations about his lack of technique in his use of a bottleneck on his guitar at the end of the song.

Single Release: The song was released as a single in September 1978 in the U.S. and Canada, in edited form (3:35, rather clumsily omitting the quiet midsection) but failed to chart in either territory. The 12-inch single release in the U.S. is the album version. The song also received a Japanese single release.

Live Performances: 1978, 1980. DEEP IN THE MOTHERLODE worked effectively in the live environment and was performed over the next two tours, being promoted to set opener in 1980.

Live Recordings: A strong performance was recorded at Drury Lane, London, on 5 May 1980 (5:54) and was included on CD2 of the *Genesis Archive #2 1976–1992* box set. The band was augmented by Daryl Stuermer (bass) and Chester Thompson (drums). The recording was mixed by Nick Davis.

[98] MANY TOO MANY

Music & Lyrics: Tony Banks
Length: 3:31
Tony Banks—Electric Grand Piano, Mellotron, Synthesizers; **Phil Collins**—Lead & Backing Vocals, Drums, Percussion; **Mike Rutherford**—Guitar, Bass
Recorded: Relight Studios, Hilvarenbeek, Holland, September–October 1977.
Mixed: Trident Studios, London.
Producer: David Hentschel and Genesis. Engineer: David Hentschel. Assistants: Pierre Geoffroy Chateau and Steve Short.
2007 Remix/Remaster Release:
Mixed at The Farm, Surrey 2005/2006.
5.1 Surround sound and stereo mixes by Nick Davis. Assisted by Tom Mitchell.

11. Studio Album #9: ...And Then There Were Three...

UK/U.S. Release: 31 March 1978. (LP: *...And Then There Were Three...*)
UK Single Release: 23 June 1978. (A-side single b/w [103] THE DAY THE LIGHT WENT OUT and [104] VANCOUVER. Charisma. CB 315)

With MANY TOO MANY Banks attempted to write a simple love song for the first time. The keyboardist noted, "It wasn't until confidence came and we were feeling more at home with life that I wrote a genuine 'love gone wrong' song, which was MANY TOO MANY. At the same time Mike wrote [102] FOLLOW YOU, FOLLOW ME. There was less hiding behind myths and legends; we could move in a straight-forward direction."[16] The slow CP-70 electric grand piano based ballad builds elegantly through its verses toward an anguished chorus delivered with vocal gusto by Collins. Lyrically the theme is of lost love, one that the band would return to even more successfully during the 1980s. Banks was a little self-conscious with the subject matter, which was a departure for him as a writer. There is certainly a lack of raw emotion in the lyrics, with Banks making a more literate attempt to describe the anguish of lost love. Collins redresses this through his strong vocal interpretation, pointing the way to the more mature vocal performance he would deliver on *Duke*. Banks had fun pointing out that this song included the band's first to use the word "mama"—during the chorus. He noted that Collins initially had reservations with the use of the word, but Banks managed to persuade him that Stevie Wonder used it all the time in his songs. The term would be used more overtly in their 1983 classic [134] MAMA.

The basic track was once again built from piano, bass and drums. The band had briefly considered using an orchestra before Banks managed to produce a string sound that he was happy with. He used a mix of Roland RS-202 String Synthesizer and Mellotron with a rough edge to create the lush string sound, the keyboardist feeling the Polymoog came up short in that department.[17] He then added the Roland's brass settings to the mix in order to create a fat orchestral sound. Rutherford's lead guitar during the chorus is lifted higher in Nick Davis' remix and this improves its effect. Rutherford also contributed a shorter solo than he had done for [96] BURNING ROPE. Here, Rutherford and Banks worked on various options in terms of sound and melody for the solo before settling on a rather simple, but effective coda (from 2:53) to the song.

Along with [102] FOLLOW YOU, FOLLOW ME this is the simplest song on the album and is also one of the best. The song was originally sequenced as Track 2 for the album but was later moved down in the order, having been swapped with [93] UNDERTOW.

MANY TOO MANY was never performed live, though it was rehearsed ahead of their 1978 tour. By 2007, Rutherford had reappraised the piece which, like [85] BLOOD ON THE ROOFTOPS, he considered a forgotten song. He noted its great sound and how it successfully adopted a simpler style for the band. "The verse especially is really good," he noted. "We were finding once again slightly simpler styles of playing and writing and once again Tony lyrically was a little simpler here."[18] Additionally, during the preparation for the 2007 reunion tour, Banks suggested playing the song, but ultimately the band decided against this.

Single Release: MANY TOO MANY was released as a single in the UK on 23 June 1978 peaking at #43 and spending five weeks in the UK singles chart. The single was also released in Germany, Italy, Norway, Holland, Australia and Japan.

Music Video: A promotional video was filmed in the U.S. for the song to support its worldwide release. The band also performed to a backing track at a sound check at Knebworth for the BBC's 1978 documentary *Three Dates with Genesis*. This version was used to promote the single in the UK.

[99] SCENES FROM A NIGHT'S DREAM

Music: Tony Banks
Lyrics: Phil Collins
Length: 3:29
Tony Banks—Organ, Synthesizers; **Phil Collins**—Lead & Backing Vocals, Drums, Percussion; **Mike Rutherford**—Guitar, Bass
Recorded: Relight Studios, Hilvarenbeek, Holland, September–October 1977.
Mixed: Trident Studios, London.
Producer: David Hentschel and Genesis. Engineer: David Hentschel. Assistants: Pierre Geoffroy Chateau and Steve Short.
2007 Remix/Remaster Release:
Mixed at The Farm, Surrey 2005/2006.
5.1 Surround sound and stereo mixes by Nick Davis. Assisted by Tom Mitchell.
UK/U.S. Release: 31 March 1978. (LP: ...*And Then There Were Three*...)
U.S. Single Release: September 1978. (B-side single b /w [97] DEEP IN THE MOTHERLODE as 'Go West Young Man [In the Motherlode].' Atlantic. 3511)

SCENES FROM A NIGHT'S DREAM is probably the least effective song on ...*And Then There Were Three*.... Rutherford, who contributes one of the track's strongest elements in its slick bass line, noted, "This song is a slightly lighter element that might not have got onto the album in the normal course of events."[19] Collins wrote the lyrics to Banks' music, which he based on the dreams of the comic strip character Little Nemo.[20] The subject matter may be considered surprisingly twee considering Collins' later contributions to the band and the direction he took as a solo artist. His lyrics replaced an initial set prepared by Banks. The band had rehearsed the song with Banks' lyrics but once it had been recorded, they decided it was too wordy and considered leaving the song off the album. Later, at Trident Studios, during the mixing process, Collins suggested rearranging the melody with his new lyrics. Once recorded Collins also added answering vocal harmonies into the mix. The result is an uptempo song, which musically has perhaps too many changes for its relatively short length. The song is also very similar in arrangement to others on ...*And Then There Were Three*..., highlighting one of the album's key faults with Banks' keyboards taking most of the lead lines on as Rutherford was still finding his feet as a lead guitarist.

The song was originally sequenced as Track 3 on the album, to follow [98] MANY TOO MANY until both tracks were swapped with [93] UNDERTOW.

Single Release: The song was chosen as the B-side for the U.S. single release of [97] DEEP IN THE MOTHERLODE—which was released under the title of "Go West Young Man"—in September 1978.

[100] SAY IT'S ALRIGHT JOE

Music & Lyrics: Mike Rutherford
Length: 4:21
Tony Banks—Electric Grand Piano, Synthesizers; **Phil Collins**—Lead & Backing Vocals, Drums, Percussion; **Mike Rutherford**—Acoustic Guitar, Guitar, Bass
Recorded: Relight Studios, Hilvarenbeek, Holland, September–October 1977.
Mixed: Trident Studios, London.
Producer: David Hentschel and Genesis. Engineer: David Hentschel. Assistants: Pierre Geoffroy Chateau and Steve Short.
2007 Remix/Remaster Release:
Mixed at The Farm, Surrey 2005/2006.
5.1 Surround sound and stereo mixes by Nick Davis. Assisted by Tom Mitchell.
UK/U.S. Release: 31 March 1978. (LP: ...*And Then There Were Three*...)

SAY IT'S ALRIGHT JOE was the penultimate track recorded during the *...And Then There Were Three...* sessions and is a solo composition by Rutherford which pays tribute to the saloon torch songs made popular by many U.S. postwar crooners, such as Frank Sinatra's rendition of Doris Tauber and Johnny Mercer's "One for My Baby." As such the song represents another change of approach for the band. It also gave Collins a tremendous opportunity to ham it up on stage, by enthusiastically taking on the role of the drunk at the end of the bar.

Rutherford initially found the song to be uninspiring and didn't think it would work, but when Banks provided some synth overdubs it developed its distinctive feel. The quiet and reflective moments during the verses are given a dramatic contrast as the song bursts into life in true Genesis fashion as it enters the chorus. However, here these moments seem inappropriate in a song of such short length and maudlin subject matter. As a result, the piece feels contradictory and unsatisfying—as if the band did not have the courage of their convictions in keeping the song as a slow, moody and intense ballad. The verses are strong in this respect with Collins conveying the weariness of the down-on-his-luck protagonist who has turned to the bottle. The bombastic chorus only serves to break the mood and as a result the song is one of the least satisfying on the album.

When the band remixed *...And Then There Were Three...* in 2006, they discovered the original multitrack master was missing from their archive and therefore it did not get the full 5.1 remix, instead receiving a simulated mix.

Live Performances: 1978, 1980. Collins enjoyed delivering the vocal on the album but would bring the song more to life on stage as he adopted the persona of the drunk at the end of the bar complete with whisky and cigarette.

Live Recordings: No official live recording of the song has been released.

[101] THE LADY LIES

Music & Lyrics: Tony Banks
Length: 6:08
Tony Banks—Electric Grand Piano, Organ, Mellotron, Synthesizers; **Phil Collins**—Lead & Backing Vocals, Drums, Percussion; **Mike Rutherford**—Guitar, Acoustic Guitar, Bass
Recorded: Relight Studios, Hilvarenbeek, Holland, September–October 1977.
Mixed: Trident Studios, London.
Producer: David Hentschel and Genesis. Engineer: David Hentschel. Assistants: Pierre Geoffroy Chateau and Steve Short.
2007 Remix/Remaster Release:
Mixed at The Farm, Surrey 2005/2006.
5.1 Surround sound and stereo mixes by Nick Davis. Assisted by Tom Mitchell.
UK/U.S. Release: 31 March 1978. (LP: *...And Then There Were Three...*)

Banks' THE LADY LIES is another song that Collins describes as "a great instrumental period piece."[21] It certainly has a storybook element to the lyrics that harks back to their earlier albums—a situation the band members were slowly beginning to distance themselves from. Here, the fantasy parable tells the tale of an evil and mysterious lady in a medieval forest who seduces travelers who fail to battle against their own basic desires. Musically, the song provided one of the few opportunities on the album for the band to stretch out during its protracted instrumental play-out. Rutherford noted, "The ending was meant to be cacophonous with the sort of jazz style that happens when the musicians get that really happy look. It sounded very strong even after we'd put down the basic track."[22]

The basic track had a slinky feel that the trio got on the second or third take, emphasizing their comfort with working with each other in the studio. Banks picked a synth patch that would emphasize the sensuality of the song and its villain. It is an instrumentally muscular song driven by Collins' lightning percussion in 12/8 over Banks' stabbed piano chords and Rutherford's thrusting bass—and for once the mood changes seem appropriate in a song given more room to stretch. Banks also adds a pleasant synth solo through the middle section (2:40 to 3:48). As Rutherford noted, the end section has a freeform blow-out as the band just pile on the energy. It would have been a great close to the album, but Genesis had a surprise up its sleeve.

Live Performances: 1978, 1980. Collins would bring the song further to life on stage by acting out the parts of good and evil with music hall glee, deliciously playing up the evil elements to the tale as he stroked an imagined villainous moustache.

Live Recordings: A rather theatrical performance recorded at the Lyceum Ballroom, London, on 6 May 1980 (6:07) was released on CD3 of the *Genesis Archive #2: 1976–1992* box set. Here, the band was augmented by Daryl Stuermer (bass) and Chester Thompson (drums). Collins later admitted his vocal strayed a little too much into Anthony Newley territory as he hammed up his performance. The recording was engineered by Craig Schertz and later remixed by Nick Davis. A performance, drawn from the Lyceum show the following night, had previously been released in August 1982 as a gifted flexi-disc in *Flexipop* magazine.

[102] FOLLOW YOU, FOLLOW ME

Music: Tony Banks/Phil Collins/Mike Rutherford
Lyrics: Mike Rutherford
Length: 4:03
Tony Banks—Organ, Synthesizers; **Phil Collins**—Lead & Backing Vocals, Drums, Percussion; **Mike Rutherford**—Guitar, Bass, Bass Pedals
Recorded: Relight Studios, Hilvarenbeek, Holland, September–October 1977.
Mixed: Trident Studios, London.
Producer: David Hentschel and Genesis. Engineer: David Hentschel. Assistants: Pierre Geoffroy Chateau and Steve Short.
2007 Remix/Remaster Release:
Mixed at The Farm, Surrey 2005/2006.
5.1 Surround sound and stereo mixes by Nick Davis. Assisted by Tom Mitchell.
UK Release: 3 March 1978. (A-side single b/w [94] BALLAD OF BIG. Charisma. CB 309)
U.S. Release: 3 March 1978 (A-side single b/w [91] INSIDE AND OUT. Atlantic. 3474)
UK/U.S. Album Release: 31 March 1978. (LP: *...And Then There Were Three...*)

Genesis had their first major hit with this relaxed and rhythmic love song, which became the lead-off single release from *...And Then There Were Three....* The band had planned to end the album on a lighter note by using FOLLOW YOU, FOLLOW ME as a postscript following the tour de force of the closing section to [101] THE LADY LIES. At the time Rutherford did not consider this the strongest cut from the album, despite it being chosen for single release. Years later, however, he reflected on the ease of the song's composition (developed under the working title of "Calypso") recalling that it came along almost by accident. Initially the band had a view of this being a longer song. Collins had made recordings of the band's jam sessions in a way that prefaced their approach from *Duke* onward. The idea was to use several elements from these sessions and piece them together into a song, but the band ultimately decided to base FOLLOW YOU, FOLLOW ME around the character

11. Studio Album #9: ...And Then There Were Three... 175

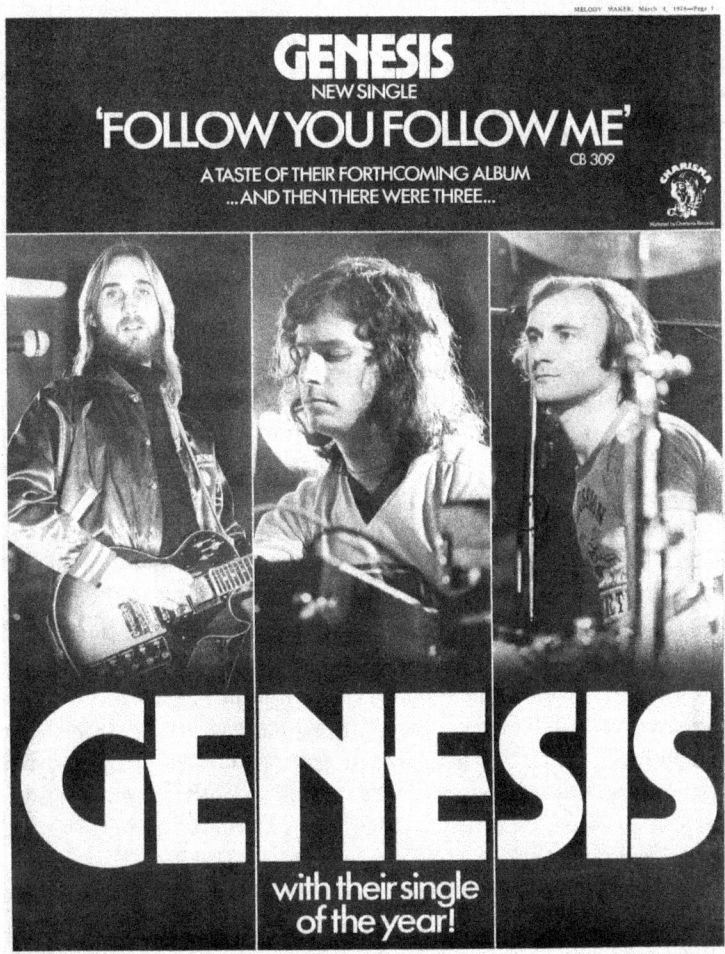

Advertisement for the single release of [102] FOLLOW YOU, FOLLOW ME placed in *Melody Maker* on 4 March 1978 (courtesy Mark Kenyon/The Genesis Archive).

of its South American rhythm and restrict the musical structure to a simple verse-chorus approach.

The song's memorable gentle intro was achieved by channeling Rutherford's guitar through an MXR Flanger effects pedal, which helped create the phasing sound on his plucked melody. The simple progression of Banks' organ chords beneath Rutherford's guitar lines gave Collins the basis from which to add a lovely undulating melodic vocal. Rutherford was encouraged by his wife, Angie, to express his emotions and he wrote the romantic lyrics very quickly. Banks had already contributed a similarly themed, but more literate lyric for [98] MANY TOO MANY and he too encouraged Rutherford to follow suit. Rutherford was almost embarrassed by the simplicity of his final lyrics—feeling the song was almost too banal. This was a sentiment shared by producer David Hentschel, who did not believe the song to be strong enough for the album. As a result, it was close to being shelved when the band decided to remix it. Collins had also been desperate to get the band to write material with more of a groove and noted, "We had been to Brazil by then, so the Latin flavor may have come from that, certainly the Guica I used was bought by me in Brazil."[23] However, the core basis for the song was Rutherford's memorable guitar figure and the easy progressions of Banks' chords. The band tried out the song with different tempos and levels of aggression, but it was only when they slowed down the rhythm and gave it a more relaxed feel that it all came together.

The final mix further highlighted Collins' South American influence on his percussive rhythm, which is backed by Rutherford's lovely flanged guitar part and steered by Banks' melodic synth lines. Even Banks' cheery midsong solo is brief, restrained and perfectly in keeping with the song's relaxed and happy feel. This was the band doing what it does best—writing as a unit and coming up with something totally fresh. Collins was later delighted to hear from tour drummer Chester Thompson that the song was a favorite with Weather Report—for whom Collins had a lot of respect.

FOLLOW YOU, FOLLOW ME is undoubtedly one of the most important songs of the band's career and proved Genesis could make an impact on the singles charts and get radio play. In his review for *All Music Guide*, Stephen Thomas Erlewine summed up the song as follows, "Its calm, insistent melody, layered with harmonies, is a perfect soft rock hook, although there's a glassy, almost eerie quality to the production that is also heard throughout the rest of the record."[24]

Single Release: The song opened the band up to a much wider audience through its single release ahead of the album on 3 March 1978. The single spent thirteen weeks on the UK singles chart peaking at #7 and became their biggest hit to date. The band later commented that more females started to attend their concerts from this point onward. As well as being a major single release in the UK, the song received similar promotion in the U.S., where it was strangely released with a different mix (3:19), which had less keyboards and percussion and a different rhythmic emphasis utilizing more pronounced sustained bass notes. The song became a hit across Europe, reaching the top ten in both Germany and Switzerland.

Music Video: A promotional music video was recorded for the song during the tour rehearsals and featured the band lip-synching a performance.

Live Performances: 1978, 1980, 1982, 1984, 1986/7 (U.S. and Australia legs), 1992 (excerpt), 1998 (acoustic version), 2007. The band felt obliged to play the song on stage due to its success, but they were never fully happy with it in the live environment. Rutherford commented, "FOLLOW YOU, FOLLOW ME is not a good live song. We did an okay version of it. Had it not been a hit single we probably would never have done it."[25] On the 2007 tour Collins also doubled up on drums, resulting in a more sympathetic interpretation.

Live Recordings: (1) A rather heavy-handed performance (4:58) recorded at the Lyceum Ballroom, London, on 6 May 1980 was released on *Three Sides Live*. The band was augmented by Daryl Stuermer (bass) and Chester Thompson (drums). The recording was engineered by David Hentschel and produced by the band.

(2) A brief snatch of the song was referenced in "The Old Medley" (19:32) recorded at Hannover, Germany, on 10 July 1992 was featured on *The Way We Walk, Volume Two: The Longs* and in the 2009 recompiled and remixed *The Way We Walk*. The lineup was again augmented by Stuermer and Thompson with production by Nick Davis, Robert Colby and the band.

(3) An acoustic version (2:56) from the 13 December 1997 warm-up performance at RTL Studios, Paris, can be found on the [172] NOT ABOUT US CD single. The lineup was Banks, Rutherford and Ray Wilson (vocals), augmented by Anthony Drennan (guitar) and Nir Zidkyahu (percussion). The recording was recorded by Christopher Hedge and mixed by Nick Davis.

(4) A much better and softer version (4:19) was captured for *Live Over Europe 2007*

at Parc des Princes, Paris, on 30 June 2007. The lineup was Banks, Collins and Rutherford once more augmented by Stuermer and Thompson (percussion) with Collins delivering his vocal from behind the drum kit. The recording was made by Bernard Natier and produced by Nick Davis.

[103] THE DAY THE LIGHT WENT OUT

Music & Lyrics: Tony Banks
Length: 3:12
Tony Banks—Organ, Synthesizers, Electric Grand Piano; **Phil Collins**—Lead & Backing Vocals, Drums, Percussion; **Mike Rutherford**—Guitar, Bass
Recorded: Relight Studios, Hilvarenbeek, Holland, September–October 1977.
Mixed: Trident Studios, London.
Producer: David Hentschel and Genesis. Engineer: David Hentschel. Assistants: Pierre Geoffroy Chateau and Steve Short.
2007 Remix/Remaster Release:
Mixed at The Farm, Surrey 2005/2006.
5.1 Surround sound and stereo mixes by Nick Davis. Assisted by Tom Mitchell.
UK Release: 23 June 1978. (B-side single c/w [104] VANCOUVER b/w [98] MANY TOO MANY. Charisma. CB 315)
U.S. Release: 6 November 2000. (3-CD: *Genesis Archive #2:1976–1992*)

THE DAY THE LIGHT WENT OUT did not make the cut for *...And Then There Were Three...*. It is not one of Banks' proudest moments as a lyricist as he himself readily acknowledged, "It's a toss-up between that [[89] MATCH OF THE DAY] and THE DAY THE LIGHT WENT OUT as to which is the worst lyric we ever wrote."[26] The lyric was likely inspired by a real incident in New York City on July 13–14, 1977, when the city was decimated by looting and disorder following a widespread power outage. Used in this short form setting the song just doesn't work and is possibly the worst song Banks wrote for the group. Collins must have really struggled to scan Banks' dense lyrics at the pace in which he had to deliver them. His vocal performance is therefore less of an interpretation and more of a test of endurance. Too much is crammed into its relatively short length with no musical build. It is like being thrown into a song that is already halfway through and then finishes before you've taken anything in. Nick Davis' remix does give the song some extra punch by mixing up Rutherford's power guitar chords, however it is not one of the band's better moments.

Single Release: THE DAY THE LIGHT WENT OUT was included as a B-side to the [98] MANY TOO MANY single, coupled with [104] VANCOUVER. It was also later included on CD3 of *Genesis Archive #2 1976–1992* and in remixed form on the *Extra Tracks* Disc of the *Genesis 1976–1982* box set.

[104] VANCOUVER

Music: Mike Rutherford
Lyrics: Phil Collins
Length: 3:03
Tony Banks—Electric Grand Piano, Organ, Synthesizers; **Phil Collins**—Lead & Backing Vocals, Percussion; **Mike Rutherford**—Acoustic Guitar, Bass
Recorded: Relight Studios, Hilvarenbeek, Holland, September–October 1977.
Mixed: Trident Studios, London.
Producer: David Hentschel and Genesis. Engineer: David Hentschel. Assistants: Pierre Geoffroy Chateau and Steve Short.

2007 Remix/Remaster Release:
Mixed at The Farm, Surrey 2005/2006.
5.1 Surround sound and stereo mixes by Nick Davis. Assisted by Tom Mitchell.
UK Release: 23 June 1978. (B-side single c/w [103] THE DAY THE LIGHT WENT OUT b/w [98] MANY TOO MANY. Charisma. CB 315)
U.S. Release: 6 November 2000 (3-CD: *Genesis Archive #2:1976–1992*)

VANCOUVER was the second song from the sessions that didn't make the cut for *...And Then There Were Three....* Rutherford wrote the gentle, reflective music and Collins contributed the lyrics. The title of the song may have been a reference to the singer/drummer's marital problems and thematically it covers a daughter's frustration with the lack of attention being given to her by her constantly arguing parents. The song's title references the home of Andrea Collins' mother—the Collins family had visited her during 1977. Whether this is a biographical song, or merely a point of reference is not clear. Collins' marriage would not recover from his almost constant absence through the band's relentless touring schedule and Andrea later moved to Vancouver with their children in 1979, following the couple's eventual split.

Where [103] THE DAY THE LIGHT WENT OUT failed to come to terms with its short length VANCOUVER is more successful. The song is built around a nice acoustic guitar figure from Rutherford and Hammond organ textures from Banks. The instrumentation conveys the sad feelings of the young girl who looks to run away from home, before realizing what she would be leaving behind. It's the band's take on The Beatles' "She's Leaving Home." Here, the parents also see that they are partly to blame—Collins' lyric cleverly creating a balancing viewpoint. While the song is slight it has a charm that showed the more human and emotional side of the band.

Single Release: The song was later included as a B-side to the [98] MANY TOO MANY UK single release on which it was coupled with [103] THE DAY THE LIGHT WENT OUT. It was also later included on CD3 of *Genesis Archive #2 1976–1992* and in remixed form on the *Extra Tracks* Disc of the *Genesis 1976–1982* box set.

* * *

...And Then There Were Three... was released on 31 March 1978. It was as a transitional album in more ways than one. The concise nature of the songs and the limitations of Rutherford's lead guitar playing were contributing factors that meant the band came to regard the album as one of their lesser efforts. Rutherford said of the songs, "By doing all short songs to get more variety, we ended up with a narrower framework." And of his playing, "I managed to scrape through the lead part, just. And when I hear it back it sounds slightly dodgy because I lacked—and consequently the album lacked—Steve's ability and his lovely way of playing, which I didn't possess. Of all our albums *...And Then There Were Three...* was the weakest without a doubt."[27] Banks agreed, "Looking back, most of this album was written by Mike and myself individually and we felt we were playing a bit as session guys on each other's songs.... It's a bit like *Nursery Cryme* this album, it's not one of my favorites. I can't work out why. I listened to it the other day because we had it on compact disc. The best tracks were [93] UNDERTOW, [102] FOLLOW YOU, FOLLOW ME and [100] SAY IT'S ALRIGHT JOE."[28] Collins acknowledged only a few months after the album's release that his lack of contribution to the writing had made the album less exciting for him, "I thought it was rather light on the jazzier, fusion end of our music. Things like [78] LOS ENDOS and [87] ... IN THAT QUIET EARTH weren't apparent because I hadn't come up with the rhythmic ideas that give those things the kiss of life."[29]

11. Studio Album #9: ...And Then There Were Three...   179

Despite Collins' concerns, songs such as the heavy [92] DOWN AND OUT, the racing [99] SCENES FROM A NIGHT'S DREAM and the reflective [100] SAY IT'S ALRIGHT JOE although shorter in length were still structurally more complex than most rock songs of the day. However, the brevity of the songs meant changes of mood and atmosphere sat less comfortably than when the band allowed themselves room to breathe. Only where the structures and arrangements were simplified did the songs stand up, such as on the sad [98] MANY TOO MANY and the uplifting and rhythmical [102] FOLLOW YOU, FOLLOW ME. It is not surprising that these two tracks were selected for single release. Throughout the album, Collins' expressive drums pinpoint the musical highlights well, but the increased reliance on Banks' layers of keyboards exposed a lack of variety in the arrangements. Rutherford is obviously feeling his way on lead guitar but delivers some undemanding passages, particularly his neat solo on the longest cut—[96] BURNING ROPE.

While the album marked a step away from their longer songs, it would take another couple of albums before the transition from prog-rock to pop-rock would see them dominate the 1980s. The music press reaction, however, was cool. In *NME*, Steve Clarke noted, "Genesis might well be advised to rethink drastically—perhaps even call it a day."[30] In *Rolling Stone*, Michael Bloom observed, "The melodies have never been less substantial, while the songs revel in pettiness and two-bit theatricality. In short, this contemptible opus is but the palest shadow of the group's earlier accomplishments."[31] Chris Welch, on the other hand, was more positive in his review for *Melody Maker* calling it a "strong, confident album."[32] Hugh Fielder of *Sounds* was also impressed stating, "no Genesis fan having given the album three spins is going to be disappointed."[33]

Commercially the album was a big hit in the UK, where it reached #3 on the UK Album chart, while in the U.S. it reached #14 and became their first Gold (and eventually Platinum) record. Promotional videos were shot for the [102] FOLLOW YOU, FOLLOW ME and [98] MANY TOO MANY singles, while the band made their debut appearance, albeit nit in person, on the UK weekly TV music show *Top of the Pops* where the promo video for the former was used.

The subsequent nine-month

Phil Collins on stage in July 1978 at the Merriweather Post Pavilion, Columbia, Maryland (photograph by David Alff).

tour saw talented guitarist Daryl Stuermer join the band as for live performances after Alphonso Johnson (Weather Report), who had also been auditioned on recommendation from Chester Thompson, suggested him as an ideal candidate.[34] Rutherford auditioned Stuermer in New York having sent the guitarist four songs to learn. The two played together on sections from each song before Rutherford reached a quick decision on behalf of the band to hire Stuermer.

The *...And Then There Were Three...* tour ran from March to December 1978, taking in three trips to the U.S. as well as tours of Europe, Canada and Japan. The band could only manage a solitary UK appearance, at the Knebworth Festival on 24 June. The tour proved to be a technical tour de force with an impressive light and laser show highlighted by six or eight huge hexagonal mirrors suspended above the stage.

Mike Rutherford on guitar and Chester Thompson on drums in July 1978 at the Merriweather Post Pavilion, Columbia, Maryland (photograph by David Alff).

12

Studio Album #10: *Duke*

UK Release: 28 March 1980. LP. Charisma. CBR 101.
U.S. Release: 24 March 1980. LP. Atlantic. SD 16014.
Remix/Remaster Release:
UK Release: 2 April 2007. CD/SACD/DVD. Virgin/Charisma. CBRCDR101.
U.S. Release: 15 May 2007. CD/DVD. Atlantic/Rhino. R2 128636.

Album Tracks
[105] BEHIND THE LINES
[106] DUCHESS
[107] GUIDE VOCAL
[108] MAN OF OUR TIMES
[109] MISUNDERSTANDING
[110] HEATHAZE
[111] TURN IT ON AGAIN
[112] ALONE TONIGHT
[113] CUL-DE-SAC
[114] PLEASE DON'T ASK
[115] DUKE'S TRAVELS
[116] DUKE'S END

Other Songs Recorded
[117] OPEN DOOR
[118] EVIDENCE OF AUTUMN

Genesis put activities on hold during 1979 to allow Phil Collins time to attempt to patch up his broken marriage. The band's heavy workload throughout 1978 had created a rift between Collins and his wife, Andrea. "The 1978 ...*And Then There Were Three*... tour lasted all year, and it finished my marriage," Collins recalled. "I was going to live in Canada because my wife's parents lived there. Mike and Tony both started work on solo albums, which gave me a lot of time to sort myself out."[1] After a couple of months, Collins realized the situation was irretrievable and moved back to the new home the couple had recently bought at Old Croft in Shalford, Surrey.

Meanwhile, Tony Banks and Mike Rutherford had taken the hiatus as an opportunity to record their first solo albums (*A Curious Feeling* and *Smallcreep's Day* respectively). Rutherford said, "We hadn't had much communication with Phil during this period, although

Tony Smith was obviously in touch with him. We hadn't set a timescale. It was up to Phil to say when he felt ready to start working with us again."[2] Collins, therefore, immersed himself into recording the Brand X album *Product* and playing a handful of live dates, as well as helping out on sessions with John Martyn and his old bandmate Peter Gabriel. Collins also began to write songs, as a form of therapy—pouring out his heart into his music. Like his fellow band members, Collins had set up a home studio with the help of Genesis technician, Geoff Callingham. Collins used a Roland CR-78 drum machine to lay down basic rhythm tracks.[3] His studio also contained a drum kit, an 1820 Collard & Collard piano gifted by his Great-Aunt Daisy, Fender Rhodes piano and a Prophet 5 synthesizer. Many of the songs he wrote were of an autobiographical nature, triggered by his marital problems. At this stage Collins had no immediate plans to release the songs, he was merely offloading his emotions in the only way he knew how.

When the three band members decided to reconvene at Collins' house for rehearsals for the new Genesis album, they tried to inject more of a collaborative feel into the writing than had been apparent on ...*And Then There Were Three*.... "We started writing as a group again," said Rutherford, "which used to bring all those magical moments. We hadn't really had those for a long time."[4] Rutherford also commented on how relaxed the atmosphere was for the writing sessions, "Phil was living on his own in his house in Guildford, we wrote it there. That was quite nice too—in one of the bedrooms actually. A nice environment. Phil was writing a lot more now and we started writing songs together again."[5]

Collins found he had a lot of time on his hands, so he immersed himself completely into the sessions. The band had slated some solo songs for inclusion on the album and for the first time a couple of Collins' own compositions were to be used. Collins explained to BBC Radio One DJ Kid Jensen in an interview coinciding with the release of *Duke*, "On this album, I put two of my songs for the first time. Up until last year I didn't write anything on my own and last year I wrote a lot of songs and so we decided to use two of mine and Mike and Tony. We started rehearsing three each of theirs and because of the amount of group stuff, there was only a limited amount of time and so we decided to have a couple from each and from day one down to the finished album it is down to what tracks excite everybody the most irrelevant of who wrote what, you know?"[6]

There has always been a playful dispute between Collins and Banks as to whether Collins played them "In the Air Tonight," the song that was to become the drummer's signature tune, in the batch of demos he shared. Collins later recalled via a post on his website, "Tony Banks, to this day, says that I didn't play 'In the Air Tonight,' but I did. I played it because (a) I was proud of it and (b) because I felt it only right to play them everything, I thought they'd like … remember I didn't know that I had a solo album in me yet. Though I knew the songs were going to be out in some shape or form…. Tony and Mike chose [109] Misunderstanding and [114] Please Don't Ask. Misunderstanding had a Beach Boys flavor (!) … mainly due to 'Sail on Sailor' from *Holland*, a great B.B. [Beach Boys] Album … and Please Don't Ask (one of my most personal songs ever) as it had an ELO feel that Tony liked!!! I did feel that the simplicity of some songs like 'If Leaving Me Is Easy' would be lost if I handed it over, but we'll never know now."[7] Collins' newfound confidence as a writer also translated into his performance as a singer where he managed to inject more of his personality into his interpretations of the songs. This more confident approach from Collins, was not lost on Banks and Rutherford as Banks later reflected, "After all those vocals he did on his demos, *Duke* was the first time Phil really sounded like a singer, a total singer."[8]

During the writing, Genesis had shaped together a suite of music from the material they had written together, which was ultimately split into three sections on the album.

12. Studio Album #10: Duke

Banks confirmed, "It would have gone [105] BEHIND THE LINES, [106] DUCHESS, [107] GUIDE VOCAL, [111] TURN IT ON AGAIN, [115] DUKE'S TRAVELS, [116] DUKE'S END, which is how we performed it live. One reason we didn't do it was because we didn't want the comparisons with [38] SUPPER'S READY and felt it wasn't the moment to do a combined thing like that. As it is there is quite a lot of linkage between those tracks anyhow. The first three are linked. At the time, we were talking about this the bit that became [111] TURN IT ON AGAIN was just a link. We just went once around the whole sequence (the two bits) and then went into [115] DUKE'S TRAVELS. We did it and recorded all the stuff and I thought that's much too strong just to do once. So, we did it twice."[9]

In November 1979, Genesis took their material to Abba's Polar Studios in Sweden to record with David Hentschel producing the band for what would become the last time. Both Rutherford and Banks had the used the studio for their solo albums, both also produced by Hentschel, and had been impressed with the facilities. Collins recalled the studio, "had a big live room. It's a fantastic studio…. That to me was the first time we started to sound good on record."[10]

The album was mixed at Maison Rouge, London, in January 1980 and mastered at Trident Studios.

[105] BEHIND THE LINES

Music: Tony Banks/Phil Collins/Mike Rutherford
Lyrics: Mike Rutherford

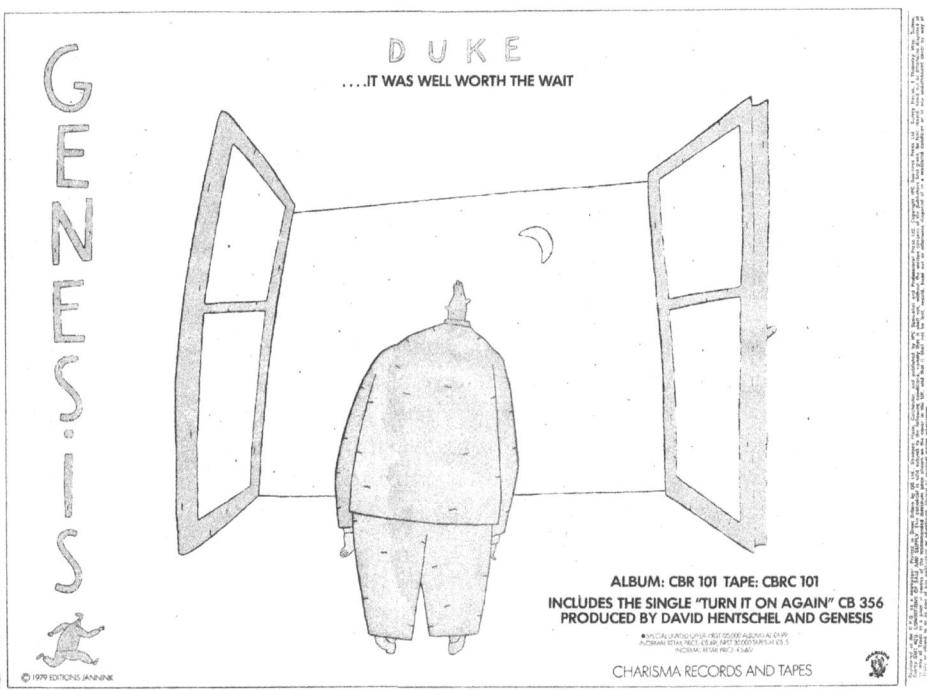

Advertisement for the release of *Duke* placed in *Melody Maker* on 29 March 1980 (courtesy Mark Kenyon/The Genesis Archive).

Length: 5:31
Tony Banks—Synthesizers, Electric Grand Piano, Duck; **Phil Collins**—Lead & Backing Vocals, Drums, Percussion, Duck; **Mike Rutherford**—Guitar, Bass
Recorded at Polar Studios, Sweden, November–December 1979.
Mixed at Maison Rouge, London, January 1980.
Producer: David Hentschel and Genesis. Engineer: David Hentschel. Assistant: Dave Bascombe.
2007 Remix/Remaster Release:
Mixed at The Farm, Surrey 2005/2006.
5.1 Surround sound and stereo mixes by Nick Davis. Assisted by Tom Mitchell.
UK Release: 3 March 1980 (B-side single edited as 'Behind the Lines—Part 2' b/w [111] TURN IT ON AGAIN. Charisma. CB 356)
UK Album Release: 28 March 1980 (LP: *Duke*)
U.S. Release: 24 March 1980 (LP: *Duke*)
U.S. Single Release: 10 May 1980 (B-side single b/w [109] MISUNDERSTANDING. Atlantic. 3662)

BEHIND THE LINES was the first song developed during the group writing sessions for the album at Collins' house. The band jammed for hours over a drum machine pattern on which they used funkier rhythms. The band's change in writing approach demonstrated how the use of the drum machine could open up their music. The result is a bright, optimistic statement to open the album and showed a confident desire to expand their musical palette from the material written for ...*And Then There Were Three*....

The song opens with a synth simulated brass fanfare rotating a two-chord phrase across four keys backed by some energetic drumming from Collins.[11] At 2:15, the song settles down into a vocal section over a bouncing piano rhythm on the Yamaha CP-70 electric grand based around the same chord sequence and punctuated by the synthesized brass section. Collins had been listening to the music of Earth, Wind & Fire and loved the brass sound they had. To replicate this on both BEHIND THE LINES and [111] TURN IT ON AGAIN he and Banks had to trigger the sound from Banks' Yamaha CS-80 synthesizer, using a duck call implement. They ended up giving the duck call an instrumental credit on the album in the hope it would raise some curiosity from the music press—but to their dismay not one reviewer mentioned it. Collins recalled, "Before I got to know Earth, Wind & Fire and we wanted to get the horn sound on BEHIND THE LINES and TURN IT ON AGAIN, the only way to do it was for me to trigger a vocoder and a synthesizer, and I was fooling around with a duck call, which I played into a microphone, that went through a synthesizer, from the synthesizer to the vocoder. It ended up sounding like a horn section when it wasn't, so we called it the duck."[12]

The song also immediately highlights Collins' leap forward as a vocalist. Here he injects a much more confident and passionate delivery than had been the case on the previous three studio albums. The more grounded nature of the band's lyrics also gave him something to feed off. Collins had originally been assigned lyric writing duty for the song, but his overly cynical ideas (he was looking to respond to criticism of the band in the music press) were vetoed and Rutherford provided an alternative concerning a fan's infatuation with a celebrity. This thematically links well with the next two songs—[106] DUCHESS and [107] GUIDE VOCAL.

BEHIND THE LINES is also noted for being covered by Collins on his 1981 debut solo album *Face Value*. The idea came to him during the mixing process for *Duke*, when to save time the band would fast-forward the tapes to get to certain editing points. As BEHIND THE LINES played at its sped-up rate over the speakers, they noted the potential for a more uptempo and funkier feel to the song. The idea stuck with Collins, which he then looked to create on his solo version. He also took the opportunity to employ the Earth Wind & Fire's horn section—the inspiration for the original brass simulation.

Single Release: The second half of the song, titled BEHIND THE LINES–Part Two (3:54), was released ahead of the album as the B-side to the [111] TURN IT ON AGAIN single on 7 March 1980 and the full-length version (5:39) to [109] MISUNDERSTANDING in May in the U.S..

Live Performances: 1980, 1981, 1982, 2007 (excerpt). The song became a live favorite for three successive tours, including its presentation as the lead-off tack of the linked "Duke Suite" in 1980. On the 2007 reunion tour, the fanfare opening instrumental section was coupled with [116] DUKE'S END and used to open the band's set.

Live Recordings: (1) A recording (5:26) from the Nassau Coliseum, Long Island, New York, on 29 November 1981 was included on their live album *Three Sides Live*. The band was augmented by Daryl Stuermer (guitar) and Chester Thompson (drums) for both official live recordings. This recording was engineered by Geoff Callingham and produced by the band.

(2) A performance of the 2007 reworked version, retitled "Duke's Intro" (3:48), was recorded at Old Trafford, Manchester, on 7 July 2007 and included on their subsequent album *Live Over Europe 2007*. The recording by Bernard Natier was produced by Nick Davis.

[106] DUCHESS

Music: Tony Banks/Phil Collins/Mike Rutherford
Lyrics: Tony Banks
Length: 6:37
Tony Banks—Electric Grand Piano, Synthesizers, Backing Vocals; **Phil Collins**—Lead & Backing Vocals, Drums, Percussion, Drum Machine; **Mike Rutherford**—Guitar, Bass, Bass Pedals, Backing Vocals; **David Hentschel**—Backing Vocals
Recorded at Polar Studios, Sweden, November–December 1979.
Mixed at Maison Rouge, London, January 1980.
Producer: David Hentschel and Genesis. Engineer: David Hentschel. Assistant: Dave Bascombe.
2007 Remix/Remaster Release:
Mixed at The Farm, Surrey 2005/2006.
5.1 Surround sound and stereo mixes by Nick Davis. Assisted by Tom Mitchell.
UK Release: 28 March 1980 (LP: *Duke*)
U.S. Release: 24 March 1980 (LP: *Duke*)
UK Single Release: 12 May 1980. (A-side single b/w [117] OPEN DOOR. Charisma. CB 363)

DUCHESS showcases the band at its very best in a concise melodic anthem. A slow undulating and pattering Roland CR-78 drum machine pattern, programmed by Collins, is accompanied by soothing synth string chords from Banks to guide a long introductory instrumental section—indeed the working title for the song was "Drum Machine." Some background percussion from Collins, using the manual panel on the Roland, is eventually stepped up by a real military marching snare drum, which serves to open the song up. Banks used his electric grand piano to try and mimic the drum machine and this rhythm would form the verse section of the song. The strong chorus contains Collins' best vocal performance for the band to date and is guided along by the rise and fall of Banks' piano harmonies, while being given a deep bottom end through huge bass pedal notes from Rutherford. Banks recalled, "It was an important song, it was very simple, but it has almost as much emotion as [38] SUPPER'S READY. We'd learned to abbreviate things by then."[13]

This was the first song on which Genesis used a drum machine. Banks recalled, "It would carry on without you having to do anything, whereas a drummer always wants to do something fiddly."[14] The band decided to keep the drum machine part on record as it created its own distinctive mood and atmosphere. This allowed the band creative room to experiment in the studio, where the song came alive. Banks also cites DUCHESS as one of his favorite tracks in all Genesis history and his simple lyric is the story of the rise and fall of a female rock star—the "Duchess" of the title. Banks recorded both the melody and lyrics while improvising and played a version as a guide for Collins to work from. It was at this point Banks really noted the extra dimension Collins brought to the song through his vocal interpretation, which lifted it to a new level. "All the elements are there, but when he sang it—it's not just that he's got a better voice than me—all the kind of embellishments and tales and things that happened on it just transformed it completely from being something like a session guy might do to something that a singer does and his own character is right across it for that reason. The resultant effect is very, very strong."[15]

Collins also marks the song as a personal favorite and was pleased with the drum sound he captured through various close and distant microphones with the drum sound clipped through a severe limiter. It was an effect he would later perfect on his solo album *Face Value* with "In the Air Tonight."

Stevie Chick in *The Guardian* summed up the song perfectly as "one of the finest tracks in the entire Genesis discography... with Collins' soulful vocal powered by Banks' driving piano chords and some truly colossal drums."[16]

Single Release: DUCHESS was released as the second UK single from *Duke* (edited to 4:21 to exclude the prolonged drum machine intro) on 12 May 1980. The single reached #46 in the UK charts and stayed on the chart for five weeks. Non-album track [117] OPEN DOOR was the B-side. The song was also released as a single in the Netherlands and Italy. In Germany and Australia, it appeared as the B-side to the preferred single release of [109] MISUNDERSTANDING.

Music Video: A low-key video for the song was shot by Stuart Orme in and around the Liverpool Empire Theatre during Genesis' 1980 UK theater tour. The band looked to be enjoying using the old theater as they donned caretaker coats and delivered their performance from various parts of the building, including hauling Banks' upright piano onto the steps of the theater's circle.

Live Performances: 1981, 1982. The song was performed as part of the "Duke Suite" on the *Duke* tour, while linked solely to [105] BEHIND THE LINES the following year.

Live Recordings: A live recording (6:43) from Nassau Coliseum, Long Island, New York, on 29 November 1981 was included on the live album *Three Sides Live*. The band was augmented by Daryl Stuermer (guitar) and Chester Thompson (drums). The recording was engineered by Geoff Callingham and produced by the band.

[107] GUIDE VOCAL

Music & Lyrics: Tony Banks
Length: 1:21
Tony Banks—Electric Grand Piano, Synthesizers; **Phil Collins**—Lead Vocals; **Mike Rutherford**—Bass
Recorded at Polar Studios, Sweden, November–December 1979.
Mixed at Maison Rouge, London, January 1980.
Producer: David Hentschel and Genesis. Engineer: David Hentschel. Assistant: Dave Bascombe.
2007 Remix/Remaster Release:
Mixed at The Farm, Surrey 2005/2006.
5.1 Surround sound and stereo mixes by Nick Davis. Assisted by Tom Mitchell.
UK Release: 28 March 1980 (LP: *Duke*)
U.S. Release: 24 March 1980 (LP: *Duke*)

Strangely developed under the working title "AC-DC," GUIDE VOCAL is Banks' short torch song. It tells of a bitter retort from a jilted mentor sung with passion by Collins over a sparse slow-tempo and moody arrangement of electric grand piano, synth strings and bass. It serves as the coda to the two opening songs [105] BEHIND THE LINES and [106] DUCHESS, from which it is segued. Collins really gets across the bitterness of the protagonist in his wonderfully nuanced delivery of the closing lines, which also provide a neat conclusion to this opening trio of songs. The strong core melody was later reprised very effectively in [115] DUKE'S TRAVELS.

Live Performances: 1980. The song was performed as part of the "Duke Suite."
Live Recordings: No official live recording of the song has been released.

[108] MAN OF OUR TIMES

Music & Lyrics: Mike Rutherford
Length: 5:35
Tony Banks—Synthesizers; **Phil Collins**—Lead & Backing Vocals, Drums, Percussion; **Mike Rutherford**—Guitar, Guitar Synthesizer, Bass
Recorded at Polar Studios, Sweden, November–December 1979.
Mixed at Maison Rouge, London, January 1980.
Producer: David Hentschel and Genesis. Engineer: David Hentschel. Assistant: Dave Bascombe.
2007 Remix/Remaster Release:
Mixed at The Farm, Surrey 2005/2006.
5.1 Surround sound and stereo mixes by Nick Davis. Assisted by Tom Mitchell.
UK Release: 28 March 1980 (LP: *Duke*)
U.S. Release: 24 March 1980 (LP: *Duke*)

MAN OF OUR TIMES was written by Rutherford under the working title "Dark Green." The guitarist took his inspiration for the repeated driving guitar synthesizer riff from Gary Numan's synth classic "Cars." In many ways, the song mirrors the approach taken with [54] BACK IN N.Y.C., another song built around one of Rutherford's stuttering and repeated riffs. Rutherford used the ARP Avatar guitar synthesizer to double-up with his lead guitar to create the part's final processed sound. The use of the guitar synthesizer freed the guitarist up to present his music across a wider tapestry. Later, in his personal memoir, Rutherford would play down MAN OF OUR TIMES, saying it was best forgotten as a failed experiment. He described his lyrics as "another way of looking at that frightened figure, defiantly representing his times but a bit empty behind the front."[17]

Despite Rutherford's personal reservations, this is one of the heaviest songs performed by the band with the guitarist's repeated riff driving the soaring chorus. Collins' staccato drum rhythm gouges its way through the arrangement emphasizing the off beat. Collins delivers a searing vocal performance, albeit mixed back by producer David Hentschel to give more size to the music. His repeated phrasing of the word "tonight" may have been a precursor to the later [144] TONIGHT, TONIGHT, TONIGHT.

MAN OF OUR TIMES is one of the standout individual written tracks on the album. It was never performed live, maybe due to Rutherford's misgivings about it, and is a largely forgotten gem from this fertile period for the band.

[109] MISUNDERSTANDING

Music & Lyrics: Phil Collins
Length: 3:15

188 Part 4—The Trio Years: August 1977–March 1996

Tony Banks—Electric Grand Piano, Synthesizers; **Phil Collins**—Lead & Backing Vocals, Drums, Percussion; **Mike Rutherford**—Guitar, Bass
Recorded at Polar Studios, Sweden, November–December 1979.
Mixed at Maison Rouge, London, January 1980.
Producer: David Hentschel and Genesis. Engineer: David Hentschel. Assistant: Dave Bascombe.
2007 Remix/Remaster Release:
Mixed at The Farm, Surrey 2005/2006.
5.1 Surround sound and stereo mixes by Nick Davis. Assisted by Tom Mitchell.
UK Release: 28 March 1980 (LP: *Duke*)
U.S. Release: 24 March 1980 (LP: *Duke*)
U.S. Single Release: 10 May 1980. (A-side single b/w [105] BEHIND THE LINES. Atlantic. 3662)
UK Single Release: 8 September 1980 (A-side single b/w [118] EVIDENCE OF AUTUMN. Charisma. CB 369)

Collins' first solo composition for Genesis is a "girl breaks boy's heart" story set to a bouncing, overlapping, soft-rock rhythm. The simplest and most direct song on the album, it caught the imagination of the American record-buying public having been released as the album's lead-off single in the U.S. on 10 May 1980. It became Genesis' first hit there by reaching #14 on the U.S. Hot 100. Collins recalled his rhythmic influences for the song as "Sail on Sailor" by the Beach Boys, "Rocky Mountain Way" by Joe Walsh and "Hold the Line" by

Advertisement for the single release of [109] MISUNDERSTANDING placed in *Sounds* on 6 September 1980 (courtesy Mark Kenyon/The Genesis Archive).

Toto, all of which had a similar loping beat popular in the States. Collins' working title for the song was "OT OT" or Toto spelled backward.

The song was one of two selected by Banks and Rutherford as standouts from the demos Collins had been working on prior to the band regrouping in late 1979. This version is faithful to Collins' original vision for the song, as comparisons to his demo (released as part of the remaster set for his album *Face Value*) would prove. Banks reinterpreted Collins' piano part and added some synth strings, while Rutherford contributed simple guitar phrasing as accompaniment. Banks later commented: "If it had never been brought out as a single, I'd probably like it better. But when you take it out of context and make it 'The Single,' in other words representing the whole album—which is what it was doing in the States—it just seemed rather insubstantial."[18] The keyboardist had a point in that the song was a distinct contrast to some of the more dramatic material on the album, but in showcasing Collins' writing talents and ear for a catchy melody, it signaled the way forward for the band in an era where progressive rock was being derided and the new wave/punk revolution demanded music in its simplest and sparsest form. The song's success in the U.S. also served to build Genesis' profile in that territory.

Alternative Versions: Collins' original demo version of the song (2:53) was included on the bonus CD for the remastered 2016 rerelease of Collins' *Face Value* album.

Single Release: The song was the band's lead single from the album in the U.S. (slightly sped-up at 3:04), being released on 10 May 1980. The single was backed with [105] BEHIND THE LINES—Part Two. In the UK the song was released as the third single from the album on 8 September 1980 backed with [118] EVIDENCE OF AUTUMN, reaching #42 in the UK Singles Chart.

Music Video: A music video was shot by Stuart Orme to support the single release on both sides of the Atlantic. The shoot took place in Los Angeles and featured Collins driving a 1950s model Ford convertible with Banks (on upright piano) and Rutherford (on guitar) following in the back of a pickup.

Live Performances: 1980 (U.S. leg), 1981, 1982, 1983/4. The song was performed live on the subsequent tour to support *Duke*, but only on the U.S. leg following its success there as a single release. It then featured in the full set on the next three tours.

Live Recordings: A sprightly performance (4:06) was captured at the Savoy Theatre in New York City, New York, on 28 November 1981 and included on *Three Sides Live*. The band was augmented by Daryl Stuermer (guitar) and Chester Thompson (drums). The recording was engineered by Geoff Callingham and produced by the band.

[110] HEATHAZE

Music & Lyrics: Tony Banks
Length: 4:59
Tony Banks—Electric Grand Piano, Synthesizers; **Phil Collins**—Lead & Backing Vocals, Drums, Percussion; **Mike Rutherford**—Guitar, Bass
Recorded at Polar Studios, Sweden, November–December 1979.
Mixed at Maison Rouge, London, January 1980.
Producer: David Hentschel and Genesis. Engineer: David Hentschel. Assistant: Dave Bascombe.
2007 Remix/Remaster Release:
Mixed at The Farm, Surrey 2005/2006.
5.1 Surround sound and stereo mixes by Nick Davis. Assisted by Tom Mitchell.
UK Release: 28 March 1980 (LP: *Duke*)
U.S. Release: 24 March 1980 (LP: *Duke*)

HEATHAZE is a lovely, reflective Tony Banks composition, one of his best for the band. His use of the Yamaha CP-70 electric grand piano is highly effective emphasizing the melancholic nature of the lyrics through the beautiful harmonies he plays. Mirroring [76] RIPPLES..., Banks tackles the subject of the passing of time, here played against a lazy backbeat from Collins—his use of snare just behind the beat demonstrates his skillful interpretation of the material. The effect of the marriage of Banks' harmonies, alternating between major and minor chords, with Collins and Rutherford's easygoing rhythm gives the song the feel of being played at the end of a weary hot summer's day. Collins delivers the sad, almost self-pitying, lyric with soulful passion in his vocal performance. The gentle verses crescendo into an emotive chorus, where the singer bemoans his feeling of alienation.

This is another song that was largely forgotten after the album's release. The indirect nature of Banks' lyrics may be one reason why the song did not receive more attention. It is something Collins has often reflected upon. The singer's more naturalistic approach to lyrics is often a stark contrast to Banks' more literate method. Collins would later connect with the record buying public through his honest and heartfelt writing. Banks' struggle for solo success can be partly attributed to his more distant approach and maybe to his penchant for, in his own words, going "A Chord Too Far."[19] That said his lyrics here are written in the first person and are an attempt to convey a more personalized approach and show some emotion, if on a more intellectual level. As such, HEATHAZE can be considered a classy thinking man's ballad. Francis Couture, in his review for *All Music Guide*, certainly agreed, "It could be considered one of the band's strongest achievements since Peter Gabriel's departure, at least composition-wise, if it weren't for the fact that the song was never played live and didn't get any farther than its album release."[20]

[111] TURN IT ON AGAIN

Music: Tony Banks/Phil Collins/Mike Rutherford
Lyrics: Mike Rutherford
Length: 3:52
Tony Banks—Electric Grand Piano, Synthesizers, Duck (?)[21]; **Phil Collins**—Lead & Backing Vocals, Drums, Percussion, Bass Pedals, Duck (?); **Mike Rutherford**—Guitar, Bass Pedals
Recorded at Polar Studios, Sweden, November–December 1979.
Mixed at Maison Rouge, London, January 1980.
Producer: David Hentschel and Genesis. Engineer: David Hentschel. Assistant: Dave Bascombe.
2007 Remix/Remaster Release:
Mixed at The Farm, Surrey 2005/2006.
5.1 Surround sound and stereo mixes by Nick Davis. Assisted by Tom Mitchell.
UK Release: 3 March 1980 (A-side single b/w [105] BEHIND THE LINES edited as 'Behind the Lines—Part 2.' Charisma. CB 356)
UK Album Release: 28 March 1980 (LP: *Duke*)
U.S. Release: 24 March 1980 (LP: *Duke*)
U.S. Single Release: August 1980 (A-side single b/w [118] EVIDENCE OF AUTUMN. Atlantic. 3751)

TURN IT ON AGAIN provided Genesis with their second UK Top 10 hit single and would become a live favorite. The basis for the song is Rutherford's repeated guitar riff played in 13/8, which is mirrored by Banks' bouncing piano. When Rutherford presented his riff to the band it was originally in a much slower tempo.[22] Collins again called on his Earth, Wind & Fire influence in envisioning a much more uptempo approach and suggested this to Rutherford. This gave the song the necessary lift with Rutherford's pulsing bass pedals and Collins' crisp backbeat injected further increasing the energy. In the days before sequencers, the pulse effect for the bass pedal part was originally achieved by Rutherford using an echo effect to trigger every alternate note. When the band went into the studio to record the song, Rutherford wanted to play the riff real-time by triggering the bass pedals with his fist. When he got tired Collins took over. The odd time signature established by Rutherford's signature riff would prove confusing to listeners as Collins recalled, "You can't dance to it. You see people trying to dance to it every now and again. They get on the off beat but they don't know why."[23]

The piece, developed under the working title "Tamia," had initially been intended as a linking section to join [107] GUIDE VOCAL to [115] DUKE'S TRAVELS in the envisioned "Duke Suite." As the band began to realize its potential, they expanded it by repeating the main riff section, adding Banks' part midsong and then craftily bringing in the main hook as the outro rather than as a repeated chorus. Banks explained, "We kind of put [Rutherford's riff]—the bit he didn't use on *Smallcreep's Day*, curiously enough—with the bit I didn't use on *A Curious Feeling* and put these two together. We made it much more rocky; both bits became much more rocky. My bit was a bit more epic, and Mike's bit was a bit slower and a bit more heavy metal. And then Phil gave it a much more straightforward drum part; perhaps neither of us would have thought that we would want that on that bit […] We put on one or two other bits, too."[24]

Rutherford's lyrics relate to a lonely man's infatuation with the characters he sees on TV as he becomes increasingly isolated from the outside world, thereby creating a thematic link with the earlier sections of the originally designed suite. Collins delivers a sprightly vocal performance making TURN IT ON AGAIN a benchmark song for the band. It pointed the way forward to a more direct pop/rock approach that would lead to them filling stadiums on subsequent tours. The song, however, still retained a musical complexity that made Genesis such an original band and rightly sits alongside their classics.

Single Release: The song was released as a slightly shortened (3:44) lead-off single in the UK on 3 March 1980. It reached #8 on the UK Singles chart and was backed with [105] BEHIND THE LINES—Part Two. In Europe the single reached #1 in Italy. It was released in August in the U.S., where [109] MISUNDERSTANDING had been chosen as the first single. For this release the track was more heavily edited (3:27) by shortening the intro and fading the song earlier. Here the single peaked at #58.

Music Video: A music video was shot to promote the single by Stuart Orme and featured the band miming to the song on a studio stage set.

Live Performances: 1980, 1981, 1982, 1983/4, 1986/7, 1992, 1998, 2007. The song was performed on every tour the band undertook from 1980. It quickly became a stage favorite and on the 1983/4 and 1986/7 tours became the encore with an added medley of the band's favorite pop and rock hits tagged on as a sing-along. This also gave Collins the opportunity to engage with the audience in true Blues Brothers fashion by donning shades and a black hat.

Live Recordings: (1) TURN IT ON AGAIN is the song with the most officially available live recordings from Genesis' catalogue. The performance (5:16) at Nassau Coliseum in Uniondale, New York, on 29 November 1981 was included on *Three Sides Live*. The band was augmented by Daryl Stuermer (bass) and Chester Thompson (drums). A neat instrumental play-out was added to the song on which Collins doubled up on drums with Thompson. The recording was engineered by Geoff Callingham and produced by the band.

(2) A performance from the Philadelphia Spectrum on 27 November 1983, including the add-on medley of "Everybody Needs Somebody to Love"; "(I Can't Get No) Satisfaction"; "The Last Time"; "All Day and All of the Night"; "In the Midnight Hour" (9:26), was used as the B-side to the band's 12-inch [138] ILLEGAL ALIEN single in late January 1984.

The medley was edited out for the 7-inch release (5:24). The band was again augmented by Stuermer and Thompson. The recording was mixed by Hugh Padgham.

(3) A live recording from the band's performance at Knebworth on 30 June 1990 as part of the Silver Clef Award Winners Show also including a medley: "Everybody Needs Somebody to Love"; "Reach Out (I'll Be There)"; "Pinball Wizard"; "In the Midnight Hour" (11:10), was released on that year's *Knebworth—The Album*. The lineup was Banks, Collins and Rutherford, augmented by Collins' touring band of Stuermer (guitar), Thompson (drums), Rahmlee Michael Davis (trumpet), Harry Kim (trumpet), Louis Satterfield (trombone), Don Myrick (saxophone), Brad Cole (keyboards), Leland Sklar (bass), Bridgette Bryant, Arnold McCullar and Fred White (backing vocals). The recording was mixed by Christopher Marc Potter and produced by Chris Kimsey and Steve Smith.

Flyer issued to record stores for the single release of [111] Turn It On Again and promoting an already sold-out UK tour (courtesy Mark Kenyon/The Genesis Archive).

(4) A further recording (7:11) from the band's 1992 tour appeared as a B-side to the [160] TELL ME WHY CD single in February 1993. It was later added to the remixed and repackaged version of the live album *The Way We Walk* in 2009 as part of the *Genesis 1973– 2007 Live* box set. Again, the band was augmented by Stuermer (bass) and Thompson. The recording was engineered and mixed by Nick Davis.

(5) A live acoustic performance (2:37) from the band's *…Calling All Stations…* album launch set at Cape Canaveral on 28 August 1997 appeared on the CD single release of [170] SHIPWRECKED. The lineup was Banks, Rutherford and Ray Wilson (vocals), augmented by Nir Zidkyahu (percussion). The recording was engineered by Nick Davis.

(6) The final live release of the song (4:26) was from the band's 2007 reunion tour, where a recording from the Amsterdam Arena on 1 July was used. The band lineup was Banks, Collins and Rutherford, augmented by Stuermer and Thompson.

[112] ALONE TONIGHT

Music & Lyrics: Mike Rutherford
Length: 3:57
Tony Banks—Synthesizers; **Phil Collins**—Lead & Backing Vocals, Drums, Percussion; **Mike Rutherford**—Acoustic Guitar, Bass
Recorded at Polar Studios, Sweden, November–December 1979.
Mixed at Maison Rouge, London, January 1980.
Producer: David Hentschel and Genesis. Engineer: David Hentschel. Assistant: Dave Bascombe.
2007 Remix/Remaster Release:
Mixed at The Farm, Surrey 2005/2006.
5.1 Surround sound and stereo mixes by Nick Davis. Assisted by Tom Mitchell.
UK Release: 28 March 1980 (LP: *Duke*)
U.S. Release: 24 March 1980 (LP: *Duke*)

This acoustic guitar led Mike Rutherford song was specifically written for *Duke*, rather than being a leftover from his solo work. Rutherford explained, "I think it is always a problem when you have a situation where you are writing material and you are saying; 'Is this for the solo? Or is this for the group?' and what we did last year was do the solo albums, write them, finish them and then start writing for the group album so there was no kind of overlap. I did this for the group one at the time."[25] The song was developed under the working title "South Coast" and presents a sad and confused first-person perspective on a broken relationship. Rutherford uses major chords to draw on the protagonist's positive thoughts of hope and then reverts to minor chords to convey his feelings of loss and loneliness. It is well sung by Collins, who gives a heartfelt rendition of the lyrics, no doubt drawing on his own personal experience. The verse is based around a melancholic and gentle acoustic guitar melody building to a big chorus, with the entrance of Collins' drums, which transitions from B minor 7th to A major. It perhaps suffers from overarrangement during this chorus crescendo, with Banks' armory of keyboards and Collins' strong drum fills adding emphasis to the melodramatic switch of mood.

Charisma wanted to release ALONE TONIGHT as the lead-off single—much to the chagrin of the band who were championing [111] TURN IT ON AGAIN. The band members won that contest. With the song never having been performed live, it is largely forgotten—Francis Couture noting dismissively in his review for *All Music Guide*, "the song is simply too easy to forget, which is exactly what happened to it."[26] That summary is perhaps a little unfair on a song, that while unassuming, demonstrates the more sensitive side of the band.

[113] CUL-DE-SAC

Music & Lyrics: Tony Banks
Length: 5:04
Tony Banks—Electric Grand Piano, Synthesizers; **Phil Collins**—Lead & Backing Vocals, Drums, Percussion; **Mike Rutherford**—Guitar, Bass
Recorded at Polar Studios, Sweden, November–December 1979.
Mixed at Maison Rouge, London, January 1980.
Producer: David Hentschel and Genesis. Engineer: David Hentschel. Assistant: Dave Bascombe.
2007 Remix/Remaster Release:
Mixed at The Farm, Surrey 2005/2006.
5.1 Surround sound and stereo mixes by Nick Davis. Assisted by Tom Mitchell.
UK Release: 28 March 1980 (LP: *Duke*)
U.S. Release: 24 March 1980 (LP: *Duke*)

CUL-DE-SAC harks back in style and arrangement to the material on *…And Then There Were…* in its attempt to cram a lot of musical ideas into a relatively short length. The soft piano led opening gives way to some huge synth chords which are given added drama by Collins' rolling drum fills. The verses and chorus merge in progressive fashion and the song could have happily sat in any of the band's previous three albums. The chorus keyboard riff is trademark Banks and is reminiscent of his solo work on *A Curious Feeling*. Collins offers dynamic drumming throughout and Rutherford contributes his best lead guitar solo to date to complement Banks' expansive chords. Banks noted, "That song is my most successful attempt at size. That and [38] SUPPER'S READY are the kinds of thing where the size comes totally from the keyboards."[27]

Lyrically CUL-DE-SAC tells the story of the demise of the dinosaur, using the subject as a warning metaphor of an evolutionary "cul-de-sac" for the human race. Banks' overly literate lyrics again proved a problem for Collins, as did the arrangement: "As soon as I have trouble playing something, he [Banks] knows he shouldn't have played it and he should have kept it."[28] Banks, on the other hand, felt the song, developed under the working title "P.F.J.," was more important for its music and its grandiose feel, thereby setting it apart from other material on the album. However, like most of the solo compositions from *Duke*, CUL-DE-SAC remains largely forgotten with Collins' lack of enthusiasm for it potentially offsetting Banks' keen ear for musical drama and elaborate chord structures.

[114] PLEASE DON'T ASK

Music & Lyrics: Phil Collins
Length: 4:02
Tony Banks—Electric Grand Piano, Synthesizers; **Phil Collins**—Lead & Backing Vocals, Drums, Percussion; **Mike Rutherford**—Guitar, Bass
Recorded at Polar Studios, Sweden, November–December 1979.
Mixed at Maison Rouge, London, January 1980.
Producer: David Hentschel and Genesis. Engineer: David Hentschel. Assistant: Dave Bascombe.
2007 Remix/Remaster Release:
Mixed at The Farm, Surrey 2005/2006.
5.1 Surround sound and stereo mixes by Nick Davis. Assisted by Tom Mitchell.
UK Release: 28 March 1980 (LP: *Duke*)
U.S. Release: 24 March 1980 (LP: *Duke*)

PLEASE DON'T ASK was another song Collins had written during the 1979 hiatus, that would have appeared on *Face Value* had Genesis not used it for *Duke*. The song is highly personal and is written in the form of an awkward meeting with his ex-wife. Collins explained, "It was about kids, it was about what was happening, it was about my problems—my situation. I've never really written anything like that since. It's that stuff 'Don't say it, I know why' and 'maybe we should try.' It is a conversation really."[29] His vocal performance conveys the pain of a man separated from his wife and kids and Banks' fluid interpretation of Collins' written piano figure adroitly captures the confused emotions. The mood here is emphasized by the extensive use of melancholic minor 7th chords and is close enough to Collins' original demo to maintain its authenticity. Like [112] ALONE TONIGHT, the chorus is again a little overblown in terms of arrangement and threatens to detract from the emotional impact of the lyrics to this heart-breaking song.

Collins noted at the time, "I'd have liked to have played piano on it but we have territorial rights within the band which is fair enough and so I'll do another version of it on my own album."[30] In the end he decided against this and would instead bring his own interpretation of the group-written [105] BEHIND THE LINES to that project. Collins would also retrospectively note that the song would have benefited through being slowed down in tempo and played more as a traditional ballad. That said, it remains a lovely low-key addition to the album adding to the melancholic feel of many of the tracks and demonstrating that Genesis could dispense with their intellectual tag and show they also had a heart.

Alternative Version: Collins' original demo (4:01) was included on the bonus disc for the 2017 rerelease of *Face Value*. This version, although very rough in form, is probably the most revealing version of the song. It also confirms the band altered very little from the original core arrangement.

[115] DUKE'S TRAVELS / [116] DUKE'S END

Music: Tony Banks/Phil Collins/Mike Rutherford
Lyrics: Tony Banks
Length: 10:49 (8:39 / 2:10)
Tony Banks—Electric Grand Piano, Synthesizers; **Phil Collins**—Lead & Backing Vocals, Drums, Percussion; **Mike Rutherford**—Guitar, Guitar Synthesizer, Bass
Recorded at Polar Studios, Sweden, November–December 1979.
Mixed at Maison Rouge, London, January 1980.
Producer: David Hentschel and Genesis. Engineer: David Hentschel. Assistant: Dave Bascombe.
2007 Remix/Remaster Release:
Mixed at The Farm, Surrey 2005/2006.
5.1 Surround sound and stereo mixes by Nick Davis. Assisted by Tom Mitchell.
UK Release: 28 March 1980 (LP: *Duke*)
U.S. Release: 24 March 1980 (LP: *Duke*)

The last two tracks on *Duke* complete what would have originally been the planned "Duke Suite." They are predominantly linked largely instrumental pieces with DUKE'S END reprising themes from the band compositions earlier in the album. There is an energy to the playing summed up by Rutherford's observation, "it sounds very live it doesn't sound studio; it sounds like three guys playing which is something to do with Polar Studios."[31]

A shimmering wash of synthesizers from Banks sees a gradual fade in of Collins' battery of drums at 1:30, in which he plays a repeated African-styled pattern. This leads into one of Banks' best instrumental performances as DUKE'S TRAVELS evolves into a galloping keyboard-led section (the working title for the piece was "Swish Jazz") that has a hint of Scottish Highland fling to it. Collins then doubles the beat for a midsection, which peaks with Rutherford's screaming lead guitar line, the sound for which he achieved through using the

ARP Avatar guitar synthesizer. The instrumental surges reach a peak at 6:10 and the piece moves into a powerful reprise of [107] GUIDE VOCAL. This forms the resolution of DUKE'S TRAVELS with Collins' searing vocals packing an emotional wallop to Banks' bitter lyric. As the reprise slows to a halt a bridging section led by Banks' Prophet 5 synth pipe organ/flute refrain, an alleged nod to King Crimson's *In the Court of the Crimson King*, takes us into a repeat of the opening synthesized brass fanfare from [105] BEHIND THE LINES. With DUKE'S END, the band really comes together to produce a bombastic and high energy climax to the album. It is a muscular piece of music with the three players creating a huge sound. It is undoubtedly the band's strongest instrumental work since [46] THE CINEMA SHOW on *Selling England by the Pound* and demonstrates how the Banks-Collins-Rutherford trio had always been the instrumental heart of the band. Collins' drumming throughout is among his very best for the band.

While the themes of DUKE'S END recalled both [105] BEHIND THE LINES and [111] TURN IT ON AGAIN, Banks refutes claims that "The Duke Suite" had any form of concept: "There wasn't supposed to be any particular thematic relationship between the songs in any way and on this album there isn't either there is no concept at all. We have only ever done that once and that was with *The Lamb Lies Down on Broadway*, all the other albums have been totally separate."[32] Regardless, DUKE'S TRAVELS and DUKE'S END provide a very satisfying end to one of the band's strongest albums.

Live Performances: 1980, 2007 (excerpt). The pieces were included as the band performed a live rendition of "The Duke Suite" on the subsequent tour. Parts of the piece were utilized during the 2007 reunion tour as explained below.

Live Recordings: (1) A recording of DUKE'S TRAVELS/DUKE'S END (9:32) from the Lyceum Theatre, London, on 7 May 1980 was included on *Genesis Archive #2 1976–1992*. The band was augmented by Daryl Stuermer (bass) and Chester Thompson (drums) on both officially released live versions. This version doesn't quite match up to the studio recording but remains an energetic performance. The recording was engineered by David Hentschel and later mixed by Nick Davis.

(2) On the 2007 tour DUKE'S END was incorporated with the opening to [105] BEHIND THE LINES to form "Duke's Intro" (3:48) as the concert opener. The midsection of DUKE'S TRAVELS formed part of the longer [52] IN THE CAGE/[46] THE CINEMA SHOW/DUKE'S TRAVELS/[88] AFTERGLOW medley (17:57). Both "Duke's Intro" and the "In the Cage Medley" recordings from Old Trafford, Manchester, on 7 July 2007 were included on *Live Over Europe 2007*. The recording was made by Bernard Natier and produced by Nick Davis.

[117] OPEN DOOR

Music & Lyrics: Mike Rutherford
Length: 4:06
Tony Banks—Electric Grand Piano, Synthesizers; **Phil Collins**—Lead & Backing Vocals; **Mike Rutherford**—Acoustic Guitar, Bass
Recorded at Polar Studios, Sweden, October 1979 to December 1979.
Mixed at Maison Rouge, London, January 1980.
Producer: David Hentschel and Genesis. Engineer: David Hentschel. Assistant: Dave Bascombe.
2007 Remix/Remaster Release:
Mixed at The Farm, Surrey 2005/2006.
5.1 Surround sound and stereo mixes by Nick Davis. Assisted by Tom Mitchell.
UK Release: 12 May 1980 (B-side single b/w [106] DUCHESS. Charisma. CB 363)
U.S. Release: 4 June 1982 (2LP: *Three Sides Live*)

12. Studio Album #10: Duke

OPEN DOOR is another sad, angst-ridden acoustic song, written by Rutherford—the first of two additional songs recorded during the *Duke* sessions that did not make the album. Lyrically we sit inside a man's thoughts about being separated from his lover, recalling the day he left with the image of her framed in the open doorway. The lyrics poignantly capture the pain of separation with the finality of its closing lines and Collins delivers a fragile vocal that accurately conveys the emptiness felt by the protagonist. Rutherford keeps the chords simple on the chorus moving from C to F to B flat and then to G minor, while Banks' piano tastefully accompanies his gentle acoustic guitar. Banks also adds some low-key orchestral string and reed instrument sounds behind his piano accompaniment in this otherwise sparsely arranged, there is no percussion, but beautifully haunting song.

Single Release: Originally released as the B-side to the band's [106] DUCHESS single in the UK. The song was later included on *Genesis Archive #2 1976–1992* and again on the *Extra Tracks* CD for the *Genesis 1976–1982* box set.

[118] EVIDENCE OF AUTUMN

Music & Lyrics: Tony Banks
Length: 4:57
Tony Banks—Electric Grand Piano, Synthesizers; **Phil Collins**—Lead & Backing Vocals, Drums, Percussion; **Mike Rutherford**—Guitar, Bass
Recorded at Polar Studios, Sweden, October 1979 to December 1979.
Mixed at Maison Rouge, London, January 1980.
Producer: David Hentschel and Genesis. Engineer: David Hentschel. Assistant: Dave Bascombe.
2007 Remix/Remaster Release:
Mixed at The Farm, Surrey 2005/2006.
5.1 Surround sound and stereo mixes by Nick Davis. Assisted by Tom Mitchell.
UK Release: 8 September 1980 (B-side single b/w [109] MISUNDERSTANDING. Charisma. CB 369)
U.S. Release: August 1980 (B-side single b/w [111] TURN IT ON AGAIN. Atlantic. 3751)
U.S. Album Release: 4 June 1982 (2LP: *Three Sides Live*)

The second track left off *Duke* is this Tony Banks penned song, which is typical of the keyboardist in that it goes through a series of themes and mood changes while still managing to retain a cohesive identity. A doom-laden opening with the simulated sound of a solitary tolling bell, no doubt contributing to the working title "Bring Out Your Dead," leads into a more traditional Genesis delivery. The song would not have felt out of place on *Wind & Wuthering*, with its short instrumental midsong interlude reminiscent of that used in [81] ONE FOR THE VINE. Collins' vocal performance lacks the bite and emotion he had on other tracks, again emphasizing the difficulty he frequently had in interpreting Banks' often overly literate lyrics. The song affords Banks the opportunity to indulge himself by experimenting with harmonics and changing rhythms. The basis for the song is the Yamaha CP70 electric grand piano, to which the keyboardist adds some lush string sounds. Rutherford's unobtrusive bass notes complement Banks' orchestration and Collins deftly adapts his drumming to the changing tempos.

Lyrically, the song is laid out in three acts with the boy meeting the girl of his dreams, then recalling the day she left him and finally reminiscing about his lost love. Banks' lyrics are descriptive but lack the soul that Collins would bring to his own songs on the album. As a result, the song is very pleasant and beautifully played but is not particularly affecting and Banks recalled, "EVIDENCE OF AUTUMN and CUL-DE-SAC it was a choice of which one went on the album and I think we went with the right one really."[33]

Single Release: Originally released in August in the U.S. as the B-side to the [111] TURN

It On Again single and in the UK as the B-side to the [109] Misunderstanding single, the song was later included on *Genesis Archive #2 1976–1992* and again on the *Extra Tracks* CD for the *Genesis 1976–1982* box set.

* * *

Duke was released in the UK on 28 March 1980 and was the first Genesis album to top the UK Album chart. It also reached the band's highest charting position in the U.S. at #11, where it was released four days earlier. The album eventually went platinum on both sides of the Atlantic and found Genesis back on top form. Where the songs on ...*And Then There Were Three...* had often sounded jaded, here there was the freshness of a rejuvenated band. This was likely to have been sparked by the return to group writing through jam sessions for half the album and Collins' growing confidence as a writer, having spent much of 1979 developing his first set of songs.

Collins' performance on this album reached a new peak, with not only some inventive drumming but also a stronger and more soulful vocal delivery, something he acknowledged, "I've put more power and guts into my vocals. I had to take a crash course in singing after Peter Gabriel left but now I'm moving into overdrive."[34] Most of the lyrics gave him something to get behind and he gave the songs strong identities with some expressive singing. Rutherford was also more confident on guitar, contributing fine work on [108] Man of Our Times and [113] Cul-de-sac. His bass work remained tasteful, particularly on [106] Duchess and [111] Turn It On Again. Banks used more piano here than of late and this approach gave the songs an energy and brightness that was missing on the last album. His writing was also more assured with songs more successfully fitting the shorter format.

The album's one downside was the original mastering. Although a certain live feel was captured with the use of Abba's Polar Studios, the album as originally released lacked in bottom end, producing a muddy bass sound. Banks attributes this to the mastering at Maison Rouge. This was remedied by Nick Davis when he remixed and remastered the album for its rerelease in 2006, where he managed to better capture the live spirit of the recordings.

The music critics' response remained mixed as the band had fallen out of favor with the press, who were keen to be seen keeping abreast of the rapidly changing musical fashions. Lynn Hanna of the *New Musical Express* was one such observer, "*Duke* is an innately conservative album. There's the snobbish connotations of the title; the group's strict adherence to their old musical form; and, inherent in the lyrics, the preaching of the cocooned commentator who has internalized his disappointments and made a virtue out of a pessimism that is the ultimate, escapist protection."[35] Hugh Fielder of *Sounds* on the other hand noted, "No Genesis fan could be disappointed with *Duke* which means the band have fulfilled their main commitment."[36] Many modern commentators see this album as marking the end of the progressive era of Genesis and the start of the pop era. The album certainly contains the best of both worlds. In his retrospective review for *All Music Guide*, Stephen Thomas Erlewine notes, "This is modernist art rock, quite dissimilar to the fragile, delicate *Selling England by the Pound*, and sometimes the precision of the attack can be a little bombastic. Nevertheless, this is a major leap forward in distinguishing the sound of Genesis, the band, and along with a new signature sound come pop songs, particularly in the guise of Misunderstanding and Turn It On Again."[37] The move away from extended songs had begun with ...*And Then There Were Three...* but here the band seemed more concerned with letting the album evolve naturally rather than forcing the direction. The return to group composition produced some exceptional material with these songs largely overshadowing the material written by individuals. That isn't to say the individually penned songs are lacking, in fact each has its own defined character and sits well on the album. The success of the group compositions meant the band had suddenly found a formula that could work for them going forward—building songs out of improvisation and being creative in the arrangement.

Promotional videos were shot for the single releases of [111] TURN IT ON AGAIN, [106] DUCHESS and [109] MISUNDERSTANDING and the band appeared for the first time in person on BBC's *Top of the Pops* to promote the former.

The memorable album cover utilized a drawing from a children's book by Lionel Koechlin. Collins recalled, "Originally it was part of an A-B-C book for children and it was Q for question and it had a picture of Albert looking out the window like on the cover, but with a Q above it and a question mark. We just god rid of the Q."[38] It is remarkable for its simplicity and therefore contrasts to previous covers. As such, it stands out as one of the band's best.

Genesis toured the album extensively through theater-based UK venues between 17 March and 30 June 1980, taking in the Canada and U.S. from late May. Granada TV filmed a documentary on the band's gigs at Liverpool and the BBC recorded the Lyceum Ballroom shows for TV and radio.

Genesis was now set up to embark on its most commercially successful decade.

13

Studio Album #11: *Abacab*

UK Release: 18 September 1981.[1] LP. Charisma. CBR 102.
U.S. Release: 24 September 1981. LP. Atlantic. SD 19313.
Remix/Remaster Release:
UK Release: 2 April 2007. CD/SACD/DVD. Virgin/Charisma. CBRCDR102.
U.S. Release: 15 May 2007. CD/DVD. Atlantic/Rhino. R2 128508.

Album Tracks
[119] ABACAB
[120] NO REPLY AT ALL
[121] ME AND SARAH JANE
[122] KEEP IT DARK
[123] DODO / [124] LURKER
[125] WHODUNNIT?
[126] MAN ON THE CORNER
[127] LIKE IT OR NOT
[128] ANOTHER RECORD

Other Songs Recorded
[129] NAMINANU
[130] SUBMARINE
[131] PAPERLATE
[132] YOU MIGHT RECALL
[133] ME AND VIRGIL

This was the first Genesis album to surface following Collins' major solo success with his album, *Face Value*. Genesis were already working on their new album when Collins' debut effort sailed to the top of the UK Album chart and into the U.S. Top 10. The confidence the album's success gave to Collins enabled him to exert more influence on the band's approach to writing and arranging. Evidence of this can be seen in songs like [120] NO REPLY AT ALL and [131] PAPERLATE, both of which included the Earth, Wind & Fire horn section, which he had used on his own album. He was likely the catalyst for the band's decision to avoid what they would term as their own clichés. *Duke* had been a turning point for the group, with a more direct approach to both the music and lyrics. As a result, the band resolved to make the transition away from their trademark musical statements and push themselves into new areas. Banks was happy to be more sparing with his keyboard arrangements and adopt a less expansive use of chords. Collins' drums would get more prominence in the mix, recreating the big drum sound he had perfected on *Face Value*.

To help them achieve their desired new stripped-down sound, the band decided to change their co-producer/engineer and David Hentschel gave way to Hugh Padgham. Hentschel confirmed, "Phil's solo success and the sound he was getting with Hugh were surely a big influence, not only on my position, but very obviously on the future of Genesis as well."[2] Padgham had worked with Collins on his debut album and previously on Peter Gabriel's third self-titled album. During the recording of Gabriel's album, in the spring and summer of 1979, Collins and Padgham had developed a huge live drum sound, which had been used to great effect on the album's opening track "Intruder." Padgham later explained how the sound was arrived at: "One day Phil was playing in the studio and I inadvertently pressed the talkback button. Out came this ginormous sound, which everyone in the control room said sounded incredible. They all said, 'Let's have a bit of that on something' but the problem was that because the talkback was built into the desk it couldn't be recorded. [Having found a way to loop back the sound through the desk] We started recording and almost for a laugh I switched in a noise gate. That's where the cut-off sound came from. So, we now had something that sounded enormous but with no die away."[3] When it came to Collins recording his solo album, he and Padgham recreated the drum sound for Collins' "In the Air Tonight," which became a hit single, largely based on the huge drum fill entrance at 3:41. The sound Collins and Padgham had created would be a major influence on 1980s pop, with drums coming more to the fore—Banks and Rutherford were no exception.

Another major factor in the making of the album was the band using their recording facilities, having bought Fisher Lane Farm in November 1980 and built a studio using the original cow shed. This meant Genesis were now able to record songs as and when they were written. Collins recalled, "*Abacab* was the first album we did here and it was a coincidence that it was the beginning of a new era for us because we were rehearsing it, writing it, coming in and recording it and the attitude was, it sounds like it is, let's not screw with it."[4] They would also use drum machines more extensively during the writing process, freeing up Collins to improvise vocal melodies over Banks and Rutherford's music. This also meant the songs would not suffer from being overrehearsed before being recorded, as had sometimes been the case in the past. The band was able to capture on tape the raw early feel of a track and resist the temptation to overembellish the arrangement. The trio were also able to experiment with musical ideas more and as a result they ended up with an abundance of material for the album.

As the studio was still being built, Genesis decided to rehearse their material in the main house of The Fisher Lane Farm complex. Once the band had started writing the album, they realized they were going over old ground. Much of the early material was jettisoned in favor of the pieces that had a more experimental and original approach. Collins recalled, "We had one track which had the working title 'Fast Bass,' which we went ahead and recorded. We started thundering along on this 'Fast Bass' tune when suddenly we all stopped. We said, 'This is what people expect to hear from Genesis.'"[5] Collins was also keen to disassociate the band from being tagged in one musical area, "Frankly the term 'art rock' has been a pain in the ass. People have to put you in certain areas. We had synthesizers, we played tunes that weren't three chords, we had different time signatures. Therefore, we were like Emerson, Lake and Palmer."[6]

The album was written and recorded over a period of fourteen weeks with the band working 12 to 14 hours per day. Banks, Collins and Rutherford produced the album them-

Advertisement for the single release of [119] ABACAB placed in *Melody Maker* on 15 August 1981 (courtesy Mark Kenyon/The Genesis Archive).

selves for the first time. They even had to take over the technical side for one week when Hugh Padgham was taken ill. Not having to keep to a studio schedule ensured the band could fully explore their new ideas and take their time in getting the right final mix for the song. Genesis were inspired by their new approach and wrote enough songs to fill a double album, which allowed them to be more selective. This ensured the songs which forged a new direction for the band were given prominence. The result was a bold new Genesis and the band's most experimental album since *The Lamb Lies Down on Broadway*.

[119] ABACAB

Music: Tony Banks/Phil Collins/Mike Rutherford
Lyrics: Mike Rutherford
Length: 6:57
Tony Banks—Synthesizers; **Phil Collins**—Lead & Backing Vocals, Drums, Percussion; **Mike Rutherford**—Guitar, Bass Pedals

13. Studio Album #11: Abacab

Recorded and Mixed at The Farm, Chiddingfold, Surrey, March to July 1981.
Producer: Genesis. Engineer: Hugh Padgham.
2007 Remix/Remaster Release:
Mixed at The Farm, Surrey 2005/2006.
5.1 Surround sound and stereo mixes by Nick Davis. Assisted by Tom Mitchell.
UK Release: 17 August 1981 (A-side single b/w ANOTHER RECORD. Charisma. CB 388)
UK Album Release: 18 September 1981 (LP: *Abacab*)
U.S. Release: 24 September 1981 (LP: *Abacab*)
U.S. Single Release: December 1981 (A-side single b/w [125] WHO DUNNIT? Atlantic. 3891)

ABACAB was the working title the band used as an aide memoire to the structure of the song—A-B-A-C-A-B being the musical segments for the verse-chorus-verse-bridge-verse-chorus sequence. Collins described the three sections as follows: "A is Booker T and the MGs, B is The Rolling Stones and C is 'Friday on My Mind' [the Easybeats hit]."[7] The final edit of the song followed a different structure, however, but the title had by then stuck. This brash, midtempo song exemplified the direction the band was taking by blending elements of their progressive background with newfound pop sensibilities and filtering them through a new wave lens to produce a fresh new sound. The sparse sound helps highlight the interplay between Banks' clean simulated organ played through his Prophet 10 synthesizer and Rutherford's riffing guitar. Collins positively spits out the vocal lines and his drumming, with emphasis on the back beat, is urged on by Rutherford's pulsing bass. The lyrics, written by Rutherford, are as abstract as the album's cover and make little sense but appear to thematically be a representation of paranoia. The sound is fresh and the arrangement simple.

The song moves into a prolonged instrumental jam from 3:31, with Banks, using the chunky sound of the ARP Quadra synthesizer, and Rutherford riffing off each other with call and response phrases. This section, which is totally improvised, seems to wander rather aimlessly with little build on the initial idea. Banks noted, "We just jammed until the tape ran out."[8] He recalls the jam originally lengthened the song to fifteen minutes. The band was keen to keep that version for the album, which with the weight of material they had written, was being touted as a potential double. Ultimately, they were talked out of it and as the album reduced to a single disc, so too ABACAB was cut down to its final seven-minute length. A sped-up tape sample of the Earth, Wind & Fire horn section was discreetly used during the instrumental section. The song was sequenced as the opening and title track of the album and boldly heralded the arrival of the new Genesis.

Single Release: The song was further edited (4:11 in the UK and 3:59 in the U.S.) for its release as a single. Instead of moving into the extended jam the intro is repeated as the outro, which then merely fades out. ABACAB was the lead single release, ahead of the album, in the UK with [120] NO REPLY AT ALL chosen in the U.S. ABACAB went on to reach #9 in the UK charts and #26 in the U.S. charts on its subsequent release there. The full-length version of the song would later be included as a B-side, along with [129] NAMINANU, on the UK 12-inch single release of [122] KEEP IT DARK.

Music Video: A video to promote the single release was shot by B. Ryner with the band miming a performance of the edited version of the song in a rehearsal studio setting.

Live Performances: 1981, 1982, 1983/4, 1986/7. The song was performed on each of the next four tours but was dropped from the set following the *Invisible Touch* tour. It was reportedly rehearsed ahead of the 2007 reunion but dropped as Collins felt he could not get behind the lyrics, claiming not to understand what the song was meant to be about.

Live Recordings: (1) A recording (8:47) from the National Exhibition Centre in Birmingham on 23 December 1981 included on *Three Sides Live*. The lineup was augmented by Daryl Stuermer (bass) and Chester Thompson (drums) on both official live recordings.

The recording of this workmanlike performance was engineered by Geoff Callingham and produced by the band.

(2) A stronger and more energetic performance (8:37) was recorded at Wembley Stadium, London, on 4 July 1987 and included as a B-side to the INVISIBLE TOUCH (LIVE) UK single release on 9 November 1992. The recording was engineered by Nick Davis and Geoff Callingham with Davis co-producing alongside the band.

[120] NO REPLY AT ALL

Music: Tony Banks/Phil Collins/Mike Rutherford
Lyrics: Phil Collins
Length: 4:33
Tony Banks—Electric Grand Piano, Synthesizers; **Phil Collins**—Lead & Backing Vocals, Drums, Percussion; **Mike Rutherford**—Guitar, Bass; **Don Myrick**—Saxophone; **Louis "Lui Lui" Satterfield**—Trombone; **Rahmlee Michael Davis**—Trumpet; **Michael Harris**—Trumpet
Recorded and Mixed at The Farm, Chiddingfold, Surrey, March to July 1981.
Producer: Genesis. Engineer: Hugh Padgham.
Horns Arranged by Thomas "Tom Tom 84" Washington.
2007 Remix/Remaster Release:
Mixed at The Farm, Surrey 2005/2006.
5.1 Surround sound and stereo mixes by Nick Davis. Assisted by Tom Mitchell.
UK Release: 18 September 1981 (LP: *Abacab*).
U.S. Release: 9 September 1981 (A-side single b/w DODO. Atlantic. 3858)
U.S. Album Release: 24 September 1981 (LP: *Abacab*).

NO REPLY AT ALL was the first of two collaborations with the Earth, Wind & Fire horn section during the sessions. It is the least effective of the pair, with [131] PAPERLATE flowing much better as a complete song. The song was written under the working title "Nationwide" with the band improvising over a drum machine pattern, which would be used more audibly on the live version of the song. The song opens with Banks playing a cross-handed keyboard figure on his Prophet 5, mirroring the technique he used on [48] THE LAMB LIES DOWN ON BROADWAY. Rutherford adds a funky, calypso-like bass line to give the piece its groove. There is a nicely played midsection bridge on which Banks adds a refrain using the Yamaha CP-70 electric grand piano, which helps give the song some variety. Collins delivers a passionate lead vocal performance, interpreting his own lyrics about a relationship growing stale, further demonstrating the band's grounding of its subjects in matters of the heart.

Once the band had the basic track down on tape, Collins felt the arrangement needed the addition of a brass section and suggested this to Banks and Rutherford. His colleagues were unsure not having used outside musicians in the studio since their debut album, excepting Brian Eno's sonic contribution to a couple of tracks on *The Lamb Lies Down on Broadway*. Rutherford agreed to fly out to Los Angeles with Collins and Hugh Padgham to work with the EWF horns and their arranger, Thomas Washington (credited as Tom Tom 84). The horns effectively add punctuation to the rhythm with stabbed notes and phrases also helping to add color to the arrangement. Rutherford was now convinced the horn parts had a positive impact on the track, and later he commented, "It actually saved the song because it wasn't really happening and it really brought the song to life but it didn't take away anything that was there already; it added to it which was very good."[9] When he heard the tapes, Banks too was finally convinced.

Single Release: NO REPLY AT ALL was used as the lead-off single (4:37) from the album in the U.S. It peaked at #29 but stayed on the U.S. Singles chart for 18 weeks. The song was not released as a single in the UK.

Music Video: A promotional video was shot by Stuart Orme, with the band enjoying themselves mimicking the horn section players in a staged rehearsal setting.

Live Performances: 1981, 1982 (four shows on the U.S. leg). The song would be played live on the subsequent tour. It would also be performed briefly on the band's 1982 tour. For the occasional performance the band were joined on stage by the EWF horn section.

Live Recordings: A recording (4:56) from the Savoy Theatre, New York City, on 28 November 1981, minus the horn section, which Daryl Stuermer replicated on guitar, is included on CD3 of the *Genesis Archive #2 1976–1992* box set. The lineup was also augmented by Chester Thompson (drums). The recording was engineered by Craig Schertz and mixed by Nick Davis.

[121] ME AND SARAH JANE

Music & Lyrics: Tony Banks
Length: 6:02
Tony Banks—Electric Piano, Synthesizers, Drum Machine (?); **Phil Collins**—Lead & Backing Vocals, Drums, Percussion, Drum Machine (?); **Mike Rutherford**—Guitar, Bass
Recorded and Mixed at The Farm, Chiddingfold, Surrey, March to July 1981.
Producer: Genesis. Engineer: Hugh Padgham.
2007 Remix/Remaster Release:
Mixed at The Farm, Surrey 2005/2006.
5.1 Surround sound and stereo mixes by Nick Davis. Assisted by Tom Mitchell.
UK Release: 18 September 1981 (LP: *Abacab*)
U.S. Release: 24 September 1981 (LP: *Abacab*)

The band started recording ME AND SARAH JANE, a Banks solo composition, as early as the second day in the studio. While this is a more traditional Genesis track and contrasts with much of the material on the album, there is a freshness in Banks' approach to opening himself up to broader influences. The first half of the song is set up by an undulating Roland CR78 drum machine pattern and is played to a reggae rhythm by Banks, which he explained "is just two notes and the chords working round it so it sounds like you are playing everything but you are not and then I change the two notes to another two notes and so right up to the 'standing on a corner' bit and up to there that is done pretty much the same way and I quite like doing that, it is quite fun to see how far you can go and get away with it really. I like the way the key changes in that, you know."[10]

Developed under the working title "Spike," lyrically Banks tells a tale of love gone cold. He initially developed some random lyrics and evolved them into the story. He recalled a year later, "It's sort of doomy stuff. I tend to write sad songs, or if they're happy they're happy/sad. But I'm not really as melancholy a person as people think."[11] Banks recorded a guide vocal for Collins to replace. This was something that encouraged Banks to perform his own vocals when he came to record his next solo album, *The Fugitive*. Collins had been advocating for some time that if Banks and Rutherford sung their own lyrics, they would understand the need for them to be less literate and more able to capture the emotion or sentiment of a song. Banks achieves a much better balance here and Collins has fun playing with the lyrics and the rhythm of his vocal delivery.

The beautifully played romantic bridge contains a spine-tingling swirling synth sound over Rutherford's sliding bass notes. This then leads into a rhythmically more straightforward final section, with Rutherford coming to the fore with some chopping guitar chords. The song plays out in more traditional grandiose and dramatic style as Collins vocally takes us through to its doom-laden climax. This section gives Banks the opportunity to stretch through his harmonic range to great effect.

The band would revisit the two-part song structure with a short bridging section on a handful of songs later in their career. Here it helps give ME AND SARAH JANE both a traditional Genesis feel, while adopting new musical ideas that demonstrated their willingness to challenge themselves as writers.

Live Performances: 1981. The live environment suited the dynamics of the song, but it would only be performed on the *Abacab* tour.

Live Recordings: An intimate recording (6:02) from the Savoy Theatre in New York City on 28 November 1981 was included on *Three Sides Live*. The lineup was augmented by Daryl Stuermer (bass) and Chester Thompson (drums). The recording was engineered by Craig Schertz, mixed by Geoff Callingham and produced by the band.

[122] KEEP IT DARK

Music: Tony Banks/Phil Collins/Mike Rutherford
Lyrics: Tony Banks
Length: 4:32
Tony Banks—Electric Grand Piano, Synthesizers; **Phil Collins**—Lead & Backing Vocals, Drums, Percussion; **Mike Rutherford**—Guitar, Bass
Recorded and Mixed at The Farm, Chiddingfold, Surrey, March to July 1981.
Producer: Genesis. Engineer: Hugh Padgham.
2007 Remix/Remaster Release:
Mixed at The Farm, Surrey 2005/2006.
5.1 Surround sound and stereo mixes by Nick Davis. Assisted by Tom Mitchell.
UK Release: 18 September 1981 (LP: *Abacab*)
U.S. Release: 24 September 1981 (LP: *Abacab*)
UK Single Release: 26 October 1981 (A-side single b/w [129] NAMINANU. Charisma. CB 391. 12" version adds [119] ABACAB)

Genesis describe KEEP IT DARK as their "punk song." Its repetitive riff and the sparseness of its arrangement all nod to the punk philosophy that anyone can write and play a song. There is undoubtedly a new wave spirit that permeates this standout track, in much the same way as it had done on [119] ABACAB. However, that statement hides a conceptually complex song that could not be easily played in a live environment, as the band would later find out. Rutherford recalled how difficult it was to even get the song right in the studio, "A song like KEEP IT DARK is so simple it's not a question of playing the right notes and you're halfway there. It's all down to feel.... KEEP IT DARK took months of recording until it gelled. Unless there was some magic there it didn't sound like anything special at all. It was all down to feel."[12] Indeed the song was developed under the working title "Odd" and came out of the same rehearsal session that produced ABACAB. The song's guitar riff is played over a pounding piano bass note with some sharp keyboard phrases in a 6/4 time-signature, giving the false impression that nothing is quite in time. Collins' drums were looped in the studio to create the same hypnotic effect for his drum pattern as if it were being played by a drum machine. The song also has something of a feel of The Beatles' "Magical Mystery Tour" in its almost psychedelic experimentation. Banks stays away from his usual penchant for big chords until the chorus, thereby creating an even stronger effect when he finally unleashes his harmonies.

13. Studio Album #11: Abacab

Advertisement for the single release of [122] KEEP IT DARK placed in *Sounds* on 24 October 1981 (courtesy Mark Kenyon/The Genesis Archive).

Banks' lyrics tell the story of a man who has returned to his home after having been abducted by aliens but being unable to tell anyone of his experience. He explained: "the idea was that this character had to pretend that he'd just been robbed by people and that's why he'd disappeared for a few weeks, and in fact what had happened [was] he'd been to the future and gone to this fantastic world where everything was wonderful and beautiful and everything… but he couldn't tell anybody that, because no one would believe him and the powers that be kept him silent."[13] The keyboardist would later cite KEEP IT DARK as his personal favorite track from the album. It is probably the strongest example of the band's willingness to challenge its own conventions. That is does so successfully is a testament to the trio's skills as writers and arrangers. Here, they achieve maximum impact with the minimum of fuss and in so doing created something very different from any other band, while remaining uniquely Genesis.

Single Release: KEEP IT DARK was released as a single in the UK on 26 October 1981 (b/w non-album track [129] NAMINANU) reaching #33 in the UK Singles chart and staying on the chart for 4 weeks. The 12-inch single also included the album version of [119] ABACAB.

Music Video: A video to promote the single was shot by Stuart Orme on the streets of Amsterdam, with the band dressed in trench coats and fedoras: Banks playing a miniature toy keyboard; Rutherford a guitar neck; Collins using his drumsticks to beat out the rhythm on fresh air and brick walls. For the chorus the band is transported to a field with Collins donning a white suit and sunglasses adding to the psychedelic feel.

Live Performances: 1983/4. The band struggled to capture the atmosphere of the song when rehearsing it for their 1981 tour and it wasn't until 1983/4 that they finally got around to playing it to a live audience. The live performances failed to fully capture the atmosphere of the studio version and the song was dropped from the set for subsequent tours.

Live Recordings: No official live recording of the song has been released.

[123] DODO / [124] LURKER

Music: Tony Banks/Phil Collins/Mike Rutherford
Lyrics: Banks
Length: 7:31
Tony Banks—Synthesizers, Synth Bass; **Phil Collins**—Lead & Backing Vocals, Drums, Percussion; **Mike Rutherford**—Guitar, Bass, Bass Pedals
Recorded and Mixed at The Farm, Chiddingfold, Surrey, March to July 1981.
Producer: Genesis. Engineer: Hugh Padgham.
2007 Remix/Remaster Release:
Mixed at The Farm, Surrey 2005/2006.
5.1 Surround sound and stereo mixes by Nick Davis. Assisted by Tom Mitchell.
UK Release: 18 September 1981 (LP: *Abacab*)
U.S. Single Release: 9 September 1981 (DODO B-side single b/w NO REPLY AT ALL Atlantic. 3858)
U.S. Release: 24 September 1981 (LP: *Abacab*).

DODO/LURKER evolved from two separate pieces the band had developed under the working titles "German I" and "German II." The tracks were split on the album but effectively formed one long song of over seven minutes and would become known as simply DODO once played live. The length and evolving musical structures led to this being considered the most progressive song on the album and the closest in spirit to traditional Genesis, but it is also very much grounded in the band's new sound.

DODO opens with big, bombastic synth chords from Banks and expansive drum fills from Collins before a strange off-beat rhythm heralds the vocal verse section. The verses are full of chopping rhythms and dramatic punctuation with Banks' snaking keyboard lines prodded by Collins' crisp drumming and a pulsing bass that Banks played from his Yamaha-CS80 fed through a fuzz box. The lyrics are largely abstract, referencing concern over the need to kill animals for our own purposes. Banks recalled, "the lyrics were ones which sounded good when a person sang them rather than worrying about what they actually meant and that is true of quite a few of the tracks in a way. That is why we haven't got the lyrics written on the album because we have wanted to steer things away from the emphasis on what they mean and put it on what they sound like. That's not to say that the lyrics don't mean anything and in the case of DODO it's more like the phrases that mean something; there is a prevailing theme in them and in the main it was designed thinking around the way Phil would sing it and how it would sound good."[14]

At 5:09, DODO breaks into LURKER, which begins with a spoken section from Collins to introduce the "Lurker." This gives way to a charming lead synth phrase by Banks, before returning to some more grandiose chords over which Collins sings an abstract riddle, which has no answer. The band then plays out over some climaxing chords like a huge orchestra. This is Genesis acknowledging its past but doing so in a new and dynamic way. Collins confirmed, "DODO is to a lot of people a very traditional Genesis song. But to me and Tony and Mike, the way it was written and performed wasn't quite the same as the way we used to do things. We came up with a slightly better way of doing it."[15] DODO/LURKER showed Genesis could hone its strengths through new arrangements and with a modern sensibility and is one of the standout songs on the album.

Fans of the band continue to discuss whether DODO/LURKER was intended to be part of a longer suite ending with [130] SUBMARINE and [129] NAMINANU. Banks even referenced this in interviews following the album's release, "Originally, we had four tracks which we joined together of which these are the first two and the other two we decided to shelve because they weren't very strong and so in a way we consider them as separate songs in fact there is a definite break point and then you are into a different kind of feel."[16] Many fans claim the answer to the riddle posed during LURKER was SUBMARINE, despite Banks' denial: "I'm afraid to say really that there is no real solution. You can search for your own one if you like. It was a bit of a joke. When I was writing it, I honestly didn't really have a specific idea in mind. If you can find out what the answer is, perhaps you can tell me!"[17] Collins had provided early tapes of the recordings to an Italian music journalist for *Ciao 2001* magazine. The journalist describes the longer suite containing two codas based around a soft melodic organ section by Banks (potentially SUBMARINE) and a rhythmic chant from various sounds (potentially NAMINANU). Collins confirmed that these codas were removed as they were too close in feel to earlier material that the band were looking to move away from.

Single Release: DODO (5:08) was included as the B-side to the [120] NO REPLY AT ALL single released in the U.S. in September 1981.

Live Performances: 1981, 1982, 1983/4. The song would thrive in the stage environment on their next three tours and opened the set on their 1983/4 tour.

Live Recordings: A recording (7:19) from the National Exhibition Centre in Birmingham on 23 December 1981 was included on *Three Sides Live*. The lineup was augmented by Daryl Stuermer (bass) and Chester Thompson (drums). The recording was engineered by Geoff Callingham and produced by the band.

[125] WHO DUNNIT?

Music: Tony Banks/Phil Collins/Mike Rutherford
Lyrics: Phil Collins
Length: 3:24
Tony Banks—Synthesizers; **Phil Collins**—Lead & Backing Vocals, Drums, Percussion; **Mike Rutherford**—Guitar, Bass
Recorded and Mixed at The Farm, Chiddingfold, Surrey, March to July 1981.
Producer: Genesis. Engineer: Hugh Padgham.
2007 Remix/Remaster Release:
Mixed at The Farm, Surrey 2005/2006.
5.1 Surround sound and stereo mixes by Nick Davis. Assisted by Tom Mitchell.
UK Release: 18 September 1981 (LP: *Abacab*)
U.S. Release: 24 September 1981 (LP: *Abacab*)
U.S. Single Release: December 1981 (B-side single b/w [119] ABACAB. Atlantic. 3891)

Genesis had been determined to reinvent themselves on *Abacab* and their resolve is no more apparent than on WHO DUNNIT? which continues to polarize opinion. A song that most older fans, and even the band's studio crew loathe, but the band loves, it is a real one-off. It demonstrates a post-punk/new wave awareness that would surprise the band's critics. It's really a throwaway joke based on an annoyingly repetitive melody and lyric. It potentially should have been left in the studio or consigned to the B-side to one of the singles. It was therefore a brave decision to include this doodling, unstructured, discordant piece of music on the album. Even the band themselves were initially dubious about its inclusion at the expense of the elegant [132] YOU MIGHT RECALL but were persuaded by Atlantic president Ahmet Ertegun. It can therefore best be viewed as a statement of intent—Genesis breaking free from the shackles of their past.

Collins adopts a cockney wide boy accent to get into character, as he had done previously on [75] ROBBERY ASSAULT AND BATTERY. Here, he is a villain claiming false arrest by repeatedly chanting the he didn't do whatever it is he is being accused of. The song, which was developed under the working title "Weirdsynth," is a sonic experiment that doesn't really stand up to repeated listens. Banks distorts a variety of sounds on his keyboard by holding down notes while changing the tones, as he explains: "WHO DUNNIT? is based on a rather sort of abuse of the Prophet 5 and there are only three things on it in fact which are; drums, guitar and the Prophet 5. It sounds like there are a lot of other things going on because the synthesizer is going through a lot of peculiar sounds, but it was a fun thing to do. That demonstrates something, but I don't think any one track could demonstrate the variety of the album. I think the album does that itself really."[18] Collins and Rutherford had picked up on Banks' sounds and the trio improvised for thirty minutes, before honing the track down to its final version.

The song basically cycles in three sections before finishing on a blistering down-tuning tom-tom fill. Collins explained the band's process, "We did lots of different versions of WHO DUNNIT? And we did a really nasty version of it that everyone suddenly picked up on and we honed that into a song."[19] The band all loved the perverse nature of the song. Banks summed it up when he said: "It's a daft track, but it certainly characterizes the spontaneity of the sessions. I was abusing the synthesizer during a rehearsal, and Mike and Phil got so fed up with me doing it they said 'Okay, we'll put it down.' Then Phil wrote an idiotic lyric to it. I thought it was great."[20]

Single Release: WHO DUNNIT? was released as the B-side to the U.S. single release of [119] ABACAB.

Live Performances: 1981, 1982, 1983/4 (occasionally). The song was performed live on their next three tours with Rutherford playing drums alongside Chester Thompson, Banks wearing a snorkel and rest of the band, also including Daryl Stuermer on guitar, wearing assorted headgear. Fans in Europe let their feelings be known about the song, most notably in Leiden in the Netherlands on 3 October 1981, where the band were booed for playing it.

Live Recordings: No official live recording of the song has been released.

[126] MAN ON THE CORNER

Music & Lyrics: Phil Collins
Length: 4:27
Tony Banks—Synthesizers; **Phil Collins**—Lead & Backing Vocals, Drums, Drum Machine; **Mike Rutherford**—Guitar, Bass
Recorded and Mixed at The Farm, Chiddingfold, Surrey, March to July 1981.
Producer: Genesis. Engineer: Hugh Padgham.
2007 Remix/Remaster Release:

Mixed at The Farm, Surrey 2005/2006.
5.1 Surround sound and stereo mixes by Nick Davis. Assisted by Tom Mitchell.
UK Release: 18 September 1981 (LP: *Abacab*)
U.S. Release: 24 September 1981 (LP: *Abacab*)
UK Single Release: 8 March 1982 (A-side single b/w [130] SUBMARINE. Charisma. CB 393)
U.S. Single Release: 9 March 1982 (A-side single b/w [130] SUBMARINE. Atlantic. 4025)

For *Abacab*, Banks, Collins and Rutherford decided to write most of their material through band jam sessions. However, they also agreed to include one solo-written track each. This album would be the last on which they would do so. MAN ON THE CORNER is Collins' solo contribution and it is very similar in its sparse arrangement to some of his songs on *Face Value*. Developed under the working title "Lonely Man," it is built around a slow, skittering Roland TR-808 drum machine pattern with Banks playing a repeated sustained Prophet 5 chord sequence, thereby establishing the melancholic mood. The lyric tells the story of a lonely and solitary man who is a stranger in his own community. A sad figure, he stands on a street corner and shouts at the passers-by. Thematically it is Collins' first acknowledgment of the homeless issue, a theme he would return to later in his solo work with "Another Day in Paradise." The real drums make a big entrance at 2:17, adding percussive emphasis alongside Rutherford's succinct bass phrases. Rutherford's guitar is mixed down to add sketchy color along the way. While the song helps give the album a nice balance in its basic simplicity, it is a little inconsequential—almost a throwaway idea that has been extended.

Single Release: MAN ON THE CORNER was released as a single in the UK (b/w non-album track [130] SUBMARINE) on 8 March 1982, reaching #41 on the UK Singles chart, and would be edited to (3:40) for a U.S. single release where it peaked at #40 on the chart.

Music Video: A promotional video was shot by Stuart Orme with the band in their stage gear simulating a performance of the song.

Live Performances: 1981, 1982, 1983/4 (North American leg). MAN ON THE CORNER was performed on the subsequent *Abacab* tour and again occasionally on their 1983/4 tour. Banks and Rutherford always found the song difficult, despite its simple musical structure. Rutherford explained, "Every time we played it live, we had to pay absolute attention to keep the beat. When you know where 'one' is you are all right, but if you miss that moment it is a catastrophe. I remember many evil looks from Phil on stage when we played that song."[21]

Live Recordings: A recording (4:04) from the Savoy Theatre, New York City, on 28 November 1981 appeared on CD3 of *Genesis Archive #2 1976–1992*. The lineup was augmented by Daryl Stuermer (bass) and Chester Thompson (drums). The recording was engineered by Craig Schertz and mixed by Geoff Callingham.

[127] LIKE IT OR NOT

Music & Lyrics: Mike Rutherford
Length: 4:58
Tony Banks—Synthesizers; **Phil Collins**—Lead & Backing Vocals, Drums, Percussion; **Mike Rutherford**—Guitar, Bass
Recorded and Mixed at The Farm, Chiddingfold, Surrey, March to July 1981.
Producer: Genesis. Engineer: Hugh Padgham.
2007 Remix/Remaster Release:
Mixed at The Farm, Surrey 2005/2006.
5.1 Surround sound and stereo mixes by Nick Davis. Assisted by Tom Mitchell.
UK Release: 18 September 1981 (LP: *Abacab*)
U.S. Release: 24 September 1981 (LP: *Abacab*).

Mike Rutherford's solo-composition contribution to *Abacab* was developed under the working title "Don" from an old piece he had found on a cassette tape. Driven by a typical pounding Rutherford bass line, the song harks back to *Duke* by using a more expansive soundscape. Collins' opening drum fill leads to a short instrumental version of the chorus before a gentler verse section takes over in which Banks adds light arpeggios. The chorus has a swinging Rutherford bass rhythm and is a more traditional Genesis arrangement with the guitar more prominent in the mix and Banks contributing some lush synth chords. Collins sings with passion about a marital break-up and there are traces of bitterness and anger in the lyrics. The repetitive nature of the latter section of the song is broken by a guitar-led key change at 3:40, which helps to elevate it into the climax as Collins increases the intensity of his vocals. Ultimately, LIKE IT OR NOT is a pleasant, but undistinguished, addition to the album and its inclusion at the expense of other group-written tracks is likely to be the result of the band's democratic approach to the use of solo compositions.

Live Performances: 1981 (rarely on North America leg). The song was performed live on the subsequent tour over six shows in Canada and the U.S. Collins did not feel comfortable with the song on stage and attempts to shift the key down for its closing section seemed to jar and take the impetus out of the song. The band quickly decided to drop the song from the set.

Live Recordings: No official live recordings of the song have been released.

[128] ANOTHER RECORD

Music: Tony Banks/Phil Collins/Mike Rutherford
Lyrics: Phil Collins
Length: 4:38
Tony Banks—Electric Grand Piano, Synthesizers; **Phil Collins**—Lead & Backing Vocals, Drums, Percussion; **Mike Rutherford**—Guitar, Bass
Recorded and Mixed at The Farm, Chiddingfold, Surrey, March to July 1981.
Producer: Genesis. Engineer: Hugh Padgham.
2007 Remix/Remaster Release:
Mixed at The Farm, Surrey 2005/2006.
5.1 Surround sound and stereo mixes by Nick Davis. Assisted by Tom Mitchell.
UK Release: 17 August 1981 (B-side single b/w ABACAB. Charisma. CB 388)
UK Album Release: 18 September 1981 (LP: *Abacab*)
U.S. Release: 24 September 1981 (LP: *Abacab*).

The album's closing number was developed under the working title "Westside" using material originally written during the *Duke* sessions. ANOTHER RECORD opens with a slow, beautiful and simple arpeggiated piano refrain from Banks. Above this Rutherford adds an atmospheric weeping lead guitar refrain as Banks fades in and out his synth string chords. The bluesy feel of the intro makes for the most impressive song opening on the album and promises more than it ultimately delivers. At 0:42, The intro gives way to a more traditional pop/rock approach for the main song. Collins' lyrics tell the story of a veteran rock & roll star whose fame has long-since faded. Banks' repeated chopping piano chords of A major and G major are perfectly matched with Collins' drums, producing a syncopated rhythm. The song shifts to B minor for its repeated and catchy chorus. Banks also adds a moody synthesized harmonica sound in the playout which rhythmically returns to the looping piano riff from the verse as Collins humorously and repeatedly urges us to play something else.

The song's sad theme of a performer past his prime who has fallen upon hard times thematically repeats that of the last verse of [106] DUCHESS and can perhaps be viewed as a companion piece. Tonally, however, it plays against the rhythmically upbeat approach of the music and gives the song an oddly contradictory feel. The result has many nice moments but is found wanting as a cohesive whole.

Single Release: ANOTHER RECORD was included as the B-side to the UK single release of [119] ABACAB, which was released ahead of the album.

[129] NAMINANU

Music: Tony Banks/Phil Collins/Mike Rutherford
Lyrics: Phil Collins
Length: 3:54
Tony Banks—Synthesizers; **Phil Collins**—Lead & Backing Vocals, Drums, Percussion; **Mike Rutherford**—Guitar, Bass, Bass Pedals
Recorded and Mixed at The Farm, Chiddingfold, Surrey, March to July 1981.
Producer: Genesis. Engineer: Hugh Padgham.
2007 Remix/Remaster Release:
Mixed at The Farm, Surrey 2005/2006.
5.1 Surround sound and stereo mixes by Nick Davis. Assisted by Tom Mitchell.
UK Release: 26 October 1981 (B-side single b/w KEEP IT DARK. Charisma. CB 391)
U.S. Release: 6 November 2000 (3-CD: *Genesis Archive #2: 1976–1992*)

The first of the five additional group-written tracks developed and recorded during the sessions for *Abacab* was released as a B-side to [122] KEEP IT DARK a month later. NAMINANU is a lively jazz/rock instrumental with a repeated improvised chanted chorus melody by Collins, which became the song's title.[22] The chant melodically mirrors Banks' organ lines, which have a similar feel to those used on [24] THE KNIFE. The song has a fast-paced rhythm and contains some splendid lead guitar work by Rutherford. Collins is obviously enjoying the opportunity to stretch around his kit with some heavy drumming giving the piece its "live" sound. Banks adds some big punctuating synth chords to further flesh out the sound. The piece's fusion approach is typical of Collins penchant as a drummer for bringing life to Banks' intricate melodies. The drummer noted, "NAMINANU was, like WOT GORILLA? a rhythm-based piece. My Zawinul influence again."[23] *Rolling Stone* described the song as "The most naggingly catchy gibberish in the Genesis discography."[24] The track is repetitive but is given a lift when Collins moves his drums into double-time during the song's lively conclusion.

It is alleged the band originally looked to this song (along with [130] SUBMARINE) to form part of a double-coda to [123] DODO/[124] LURKER but decided against using it on the album due to it failing to meet their conditions of a challenging new sound.

Single Release: NAMINANU was later included as the B-side to their [122] KEEP IT DARK single in the UK, released on 26 October 1981. It would also be included on *Genesis Archive #2 1976–1992* and on the Extra Tracks CD from the *Genesis 1976–1982* box set.

[130] SUBMARINE

Music: Tony Banks/Phil Collins/Mike Rutherford
Length: 4:37
Tony Banks—Synthesizers; **Phil Collins**—Drums, Percussion; **Mike Rutherford**—Guitar, Bass
Recorded and Mixed at The Farm, Chiddingfold, Surrey, March to July 1981.

Producer: Genesis. Engineer: Hugh Padgham.
2007 Remix/Remaster Release:
Mixed at The Farm, Surrey 2005/2006.
5.1 Surround sound and stereo mixes by Nick Davis. Assisted by Tom Mitchell.
UK Release: 8 March 1982 (B-side single b/w Man on the Corner. Charisma. CB 393)
U.S. Release: 9 March 1982 (B-side single b/w Man on the Corner. Atlantic. 4025)

Submarine is an aptly titled instrumental piece, which gently builds from a quiet opening, creating the impression of an approaching vessel in the ocean's murky depths. Banks' piped keyboard melody gently undulates over layers of lush synths. Rutherford adds power chords and a gliding lead guitar melody to heighten the tension as the vessel passes over before fading away into the distance. Collins' drumming demonstrates his skill at picking out the nuances in Banks' melodies and his ability to build drama within an arrangement.

Like [129] Naminanu, the piece is rumored to have been one of two codas originally planned to follow [123] Dodo/[124] Lurker. Again, the more traditional approach to the arrangement and composition ultimately led to its exclusion from the album, once the band had decided against pursuing a double album. It wonderfully captures a mood and atmosphere totally in keeping with its title and is a pleasant diversion from the more challenging music the band had written during the sessions.

Single Release: Submarine was released as the B-side to the [126] Man on the Corner single in the UK, U.S. and across Europe.

Alternative Versions: It would later be included in an elongated (5:14) edit[25] on *Genesis Archive #2 1976–1992* and finally in a new mix on the *Extra Tracks* CD from the *Genesis 1976–1982* box set.

[131] Paperlate

Music: Tony Banks/Phil Collins/Mike Rutherford
Lyrics: Phil Collins
Length: 3:25
Tony Banks—Electric Grand Piano, Synthesizers; **Phil Collins**—Lead & Backing Vocals, Drums, Percussion; **Mike Rutherford**—Guitar, Bass; **Don Myrick**—Saxophone; **Louis "Lui Lui" Satterfield**—Trombone; **Rahmlee Michael Davis**—Trumpet; **Michael Harris**—Trumpet
Recorded and Mixed at The Farm, Chiddingfold, Surrey, March to July 1981.
Producer: Genesis. Engineer: Hugh Padgham.
Horns Arranged by Thomas "Tom Tom 84" Washington.
2007 Remix/Remaster Release:
Mixed at The Farm, Surrey 2005/2006.
5.1 Surround sound and stereo mixes by Nick Davis. Assisted by Tom Mitchell.
UK Release: 17 May 1982 (EP: *3x3*. Charisma. GEN 1)
U.S. Release: 18 May 1982. (A-side single b/w You Might Recall. Atlantic. 4053)
U.S. Album Release: 4 June 1982 (2LP: *Three Sides Live*)

During the writing of *Abacab*, Collins identified two songs that would benefit from the addition of the Earth, Wind & Fire horn section he had used on his solo album *Face Value*. The first, [120] No Reply at All, was included on the album and was a minor hit in the U.S. on its release as a single. Paperlate was the second and was held back for release as the lead track for the *3x3* EP the following year.[26] The seeds for the song were planted during soundchecks on the *Duke* tour, where Collins would repeatedly sing the words "Paper late" from the opening of [40] Dancing with the Moonlit Knight to help get microphone levels. He recalled in the EP's sleeve notes, "I started getting into a rhythmic thing. It devel-

Advertisement for the release of the *3x3* EP placed in *Sounds* on 15 May 1982 (courtesy Mark Kenyon/The Genesis Archive).

oped into a natural jam, everybody coming in, one by one. The sound guy taped what he was getting and I brought out the tape at the new album sessions. We agreed to hone it into a spin-off song, condensing the title to a single word."27

The result is arguably the stronger of the two tracks featuring the horns and one of the strongest songs written during the sessions. A skittering drum fill opens this bouncy and catchy song based around Banks' rhythmic piano riff which is punctuated by the horn section and solidly guided by Rutherford's funky bass lines. Collins' drumming accurately highlights the key components of the music—the drummer being one of the most gifted and inventive rhythmic interpreters in popular music at the time. Vocally, Collins delivers the uplifting lyrics with a relish that demonstrated his level of enthusiasm for the project. Dave Thompson's review of the song for *All Music Guide* summed up the song by describing, "a horn-honking romp with just the ghosts of '60s soul playing around its chorus and a buoyancy that fed readily into the mood of the U.K. charts of the day."28

The song would later be included on the U.S. version of *Three Sides Live*, with the fourth side being comprised of studio outtakes from *Duke* and *Abacab*. Later it would be included on the box sets *Genesis Archive #2 1976–1992* and in remixed form on *Genesis 1976–1982*.

Single Release: The song was included as the first track on the band's *3x3* EP, which also included [132] YOU MIGHT RECALL and [133] ME AND VIRGIL, released on 17 May 1982. The EP peaked at #10 on the UK Singles chart.[29] The song also hit the U.S. charts as a single release reaching #32. Five years later, the song would be included as a B-side on the 12-inch single release of [144] TONIGHT, TONIGHT, TONIGHT.

Music Video: While no promotional video was shot for the single, the band's appearance on *Top of the Pops* on 27 May 1982, miming (rather badly) to the track, is now widely used on music video channels.

Live Performances: 1982 (rarely on the North American leg). PAPERLATE was occasionally performed live over four shows on the band's 1982 tour where they were joined by the EWF horn section.

Live Recordings: No official live recording has been released.

[132] YOU MIGHT RECALL

Music: Tony Banks/Phil Collins/Mike Rutherford
Lyrics: Tony Banks
Length: 5:35
Tony Banks—Electric Grand Piano, Synthesizers; **Phil Collins**—Lead & Backing Vocals, Drums, Percussion; **Mike Rutherford**—Guitar, Bass
Recorded and Mixed at The Farm, Chiddingfold, Surrey, March to July 1981.
Producer: Genesis. Engineer: Hugh Padgham.
2007 Remix/Remaster Release:
Mixed at The Farm, Surrey 2005/2006.
5.1 Surround sound and stereo mixes by Nick Davis. Assisted by Tom Mitchell.
UK Release: 17 May 1982 (EP: *3x3*. Charisma. GEN 1)
U.S. Release: 18 May 1982. (B-side single b/w PAPERLATE. Atlantic. 4053)
U.S. Album Release: 4 June 1982 (2LP: *Three Sides Live*)

YOU MIGHT RECALL is a romantic love song and was originally slated for inclusion on the *Abacab* album, but ultimately lost out to the brash and quirky [125] WHO DUNNIT? when Atlantic president Ahmet Ertegun persuaded the band to go for the "ugly" ahead the "pretty." The song was developed under the working title "Jangly." Collins noted Rutherford's guitar sound, "represented a cross between Django Reinhardt and the jangly noise of our playing."[30] Rutherford's guitar is accompanied by a chittering drum pattern and catchy melodic keyboard riff. These elements set the tone for a light but decidedly catchy pop song. The glowing romance of the lyrics is typical of Banks and provides a neat contrast to the more abstract nature of most of the material written during the sessions. The song potentially suffers from a lack of progression by staying in one mood throughout, something the band had been keen to explore in order to avoid their historic tendencies toward more complex song structures. The band added a key change toward the end to give the song its anticipated lift. There are many who argue the band made the wrong decision to leave this song off the album at the expense of WHO DUNNIT? It is certainly strong enough and would not have been out of place on *Abacab*, but the band were resolute in their determination to show they were moving with the times.

Single Release: The song was included on the *3x3* EP in the UK and was used as the B-side to the [131] PAPERLATE single in the U.S. and other parts of the world. In the U.S., the song would be also be included on the fourth side of their *Three Sides Live* LP with other studio outtakes from *Duke* and *Abacab*. It would later appear on the box set *Genesis Archive #2 1976–1992* and the Extra Tracks CD in remixed form in the *Genesis 1976–1982* box set.

[133] ME AND VIRGIL

Music: Tony Banks/Phil Collins/Mike Rutherford
Lyrics: Phil Collins
Length: 6:19
Tony Banks—Electric Grand Piano, Synthesizers; **Phil Collins**—Lead & Backing Vocals, Drums, Percussion; **Mike Rutherford**—Acoustic Guitar, Guitar, Bass
Recorded and Mixed at The Farm, Chiddingfold, Surrey, March to July 1981.
Producer: Genesis. Engineer: Hugh Padgham.
2007 Remix/Remaster Release:
Mixed at The Farm, Surrey 2005/2006.
5.1 Surround sound and stereo mixes by Nick Davis. Assisted by Tom Mitchell.
UK Release: 17 May 1982 (EP: *3x3*. Charisma. GEN 1)
U.S. Release: 4 June 1982 (2LP: *Three Sides Live*)

ME AND VIRGIL is another Genesis tale of the Old West (see [94] and [97]), this time relating its story in the first person to give it a more personal perspective. Collins' lyrics recount the tale through the eyes of one of two young boys left alone with their mother on the prairie after their father dies. When later their mother dies, the boys decide to leave their homestead and spread their wings. The band worked on the song under the working title "Chunky" and developed it through jam sessions by linking musical passages in much the same way they had on earlier albums. Collins would later admit to finding his lyrics embarrassing: "I've said before that it's inevitable in a career as long as mine and Genesis' that there will be a few dogs, and this is one. I think I was trying to see if we could do something like The Band ... we couldn't."[31]

It's an evocative song, with a sparse arrangement enhanced by Banks' synthesized violins, utilizing the sampling keyboard the Synclavier. Padgham and Collins achieve a similar vocal effect (through clipping the reverb) to that achieved on "The Roof if Leaking" on Collins' *Face Value* album. The overall combined effect was to create the musical imagery of isolation in a broad flat landscape with a big sky. The short midsong instrumental section (5:00 to 5:25) features a psychedelic lead guitar solo from Rutherford, which seems ill-fitting, despite Collins' best efforts to improve it: "Mike recorded his guitar solo for it. I was candid and said 'really '67 acid stuff man, I don't think we should use it.' He replied, 'Do you know, I think you're right, yes you're right.' He did it again and it was much better. But if I hadn't spoken my mind, we'd have used the first version."[32]

For all its faults the song has a certain charm and is very different in its approach to sound and arrangement. Yes, the lyrics are a little clichéd and perhaps feel out of place on a Genesis record, but the willingness of the band to experiment and shake things up would inevitably lead to a few misfires. This just happens to be one of them.

While the song was included on the studio outtakes side of *Three Sides Live* in the U.S. Collins vetoed the track's inclusion on *Genesis Archive #2 1976–1992*. Banks remarked, "Phil objected to ME AND VIRGIL because he read the lyric to it and maybe felt a bit self-conscious about it and I think musically it is quite a good song."[33] However, it was later included on the *Genesis 1976–1982* box set on the *Extra Tracks* CD.

Single Release: The song was third track included on the *3x3* EP released in the UK on 17 May 1982.

Live Performances: 1981 (twice on European leg). The band performed the song live on the first two shows of the Spanish leg of their tour,\ before it was dropped and never performed again.

Live Recordings: No official live recording of the song has been released.

* * *

Abacab was released on 18 September 1981 reaching #1 on the UK Albums chart and #7 in the U.S. following its release there a few days later. Its bold, direct, experimental and challenging approach alienated some of the band's older fans—but it also brought in many more new fans at the same time. Collins had attracted a wide audience with his solo album *Face Value* and many admirers of that album were now willing to give Genesis a chance. The band were philosophical about the reaction of their older fan base. Banks commented, "I can understand it when some of our older fans feel disillusioned by our recent success. It's a psychological thing I think."[34]

Abacab proved to be a real turning point for Genesis in their calculated attempt to reinvent themselves. As such the album was a hit and miss affair. Even the album's cover, a painted abstract artwork of colors presented in four different versions, was a break with tradition. Other factors that helped the band establish a new identity included a further move toward group compositions; the building of their own studio; and the decision to produce themselves. Hugh Padgham, who was brought on board as engineer, helped capture a live sound in the studio, stripping away the production sheen that had been evident on their previous two albums as a trio and adding an earthier quality. Rutherford noted, "There's a lot of space on *Abacab*. People tend to think of Genesis as a wall of sound, but I think that's a thing of the past. This album is more the way we've been sounding when we've been rehearsing."[35]

The album ultimately proved to be a stepping-stone to greater things. It may have been a step back in terms of consistency of song quality, but it was a big step forward in rejuvenating Genesis for the 1980s and beyond. The band went to great lengths to ensure they did not fall into their old clichés. Banks was more sparing with the big keyboard sounds and played simpler chord progressions; Collins provided some lively and powerful drumming, capitalizing on the sound he had found with Padgham on his work outside the band; and Rutherford established a more atmospheric and characterful approach to lead guitar. The songs that worked best, like [123] Dodo/[124] Lurker, [119] Abacab and [122] Keep It Dark, were those which were identifiably Genesis but offered a new slant on sound or composition. This approach would be further refined over the next two albums.

The music press was quick to identify Collins as the catalyst of change following his newfound solo success. He was responsible for the hiring of Hugh Padgham as engineer and for suggesting the use of the Earth, Wind & Fire horn section. However, it was a band decision, with no dissenters, to simplify their arrangements and approach to songwriting. Banks, Collins and Rutherford were all equally involved in the writing process, which now saw an even split in contribution for the first time. A vast number of group-written songs were recorded during the sessions and the album could have been the first to be 100 percent co-written but for their early decision to include one solo composition each—a reduction from the two each included on *Duke*.

The music press was quick to pick up on the change. Paul Colbert in his review for *Melody Maker* called the album, "their least consistent, and therefore least predictable release of the last three years…. If Genesis are hunting for a new audience, then *Abacab* could be seen as an album of hooks all baited in a different way to see which one catches."[36] David Fricke noted in *Rolling Stone*, "Keep It Dark and the mischievous [125] Who Dunnit? ring out with a post-punk industrial clang."[37] Cathi Wheatley observed in *Sounds*, "Genesis prove with this album that they will not allow the grass to grow under their highly revered feet."[38] Retrospectively *All Music Guide* noted, "*Duke* showcased a new Genesis—a sleek, hard, stylish trio that truly sounded like a different band from its first incarnation—but *Abacab* was where this new incarnation of the band came into its own."[39]

What at the time seemed a remarkably bold move can now be seen as a test to see how far the band could stretch themselves away from people's pre-conceptions of the band. Banks noted, "*Abacab* I think was an experiment in many ways and it was quite successful from that point of view—much more streamlined, almost got a bit of abstract quality, which we tried to demonstrate with the cover as well, going away from the sort of pretty covers, to something which was just very blatant and straightforward. That was the sort of the aim, really, and I think maybe the albums that came after *Abacab* brought a little bit of the old stuff back in sometimes. But it was a necessary change for us to do, otherwise I don't think we would have survived."[40]

Collins agreed, "In retrospect *Abacab* was a transition period. At the time it was the best thing we were doing. As all these new albums are, though. In each new album we are going to try to do different things."[41] Perhaps the band was trying a little too hard to be different … but at least they were trying.

Genesis toured *Abacab* in 1981 and followed up with a live album, *Three Sides Live*, a year later. With the band having recorded a further three studio albums since their previous live album, *Seconds Out*, they wanted to document the period 1978–81, which had seen a great transition in the Genesis sound as they reduced to a trio. Genesis embarked on a small venue "Encore" tour in the U.S., Europe and the UK in 1982 to support *Three Sides Live*, which also included the "Six of the Best" WOMAD benefit concert. This show reunited Genesis (including Stuermer and Thompson) with Peter Gabriel in an effort to dig him out of financial trouble.[42] The one-off gig was played at Milton Keynes on 2 October 1982. Steve Hackett flew in from South America to join the band for the encore.

14

Studio Album #12: *Genesis*

UK Release: 3 October 1983. LP. Charisma/Virgin. GEN LP1.
U.S. Release: 7 October 1983. LP. Atlantic. A1-80116-1.
Remix/Remaster Release:
UK Release: 1 October 2007. CD/SACD/DVD. Virgin/Charisma. GENCDR1.
U.S. Release: 20 November 2007. CD/DVD. Atlantic/Rhino. R2 300924.

Album Tracks
[134] Mama
[135] That's All
[136] Home by the Sea / [137] Second Home by the Sea
[138] Illegal Alien
[139] Taking It All Too Hard
[140] Just a Job to Do
[141] Silver Rainbow
[142] It's Gonna Get Better

After a break of seven months following the completion of their "encore" tour, Genesis reconvened to record their next studio album. The eponymous *Genesis* was the result and it is the album that took the writing approach started on *Duke* then enhanced on *Abacab* to its natural conclusion. With their Fisher Lane Farm Studio now complete, the band was able to write and record its music simultaneously. There would be no solo compositions used for the band from hereon. Banks recalled, "As soon as we came up with an idea that was good, we could put it straight down onto tape and begin to develop it immediately. We've often found in the past that when you take two or three months to write before recording, you get some incredibly strong moments during the writing but which you can't recreate in the studio. It was important that we made sure that that didn't happen."[1]

The stripped-down approach demonstrated on *Abacab* had been taken into the trio's solo albums of 1982/3. These outlets removed any potential tension within the group setting by providing a vehicle for individually written material. Banks' *The Fugitive* and Rutherford's *Acting Very Strange* were very different from their debut albums, which had remained close to the Genesis sound. Both Banks and Rutherford had also decided to handle lead vocals themselves. Both had also taken the approach used for *Abacab* into their solo work. Banks adopted a more concise writing style with simpler lyrics. Rutherford too stripped down his sound with the songs having a more organic feel. Banks also found time to score the Michael Winner film *The Wicked Lady*. Collins, meanwhile, had completed his second solo album, *Hello, I Must Be Going!* and produced albums for both John Martyn (*Glorious Fool*) and Abba's Frida (*Something's Going On*). He had also worked as drummer with Robert Plant on his album *Pictures at Eleven* playing on six of the eight tracks and he subsequently joined Plant on a short tour.

In the writing of *Genesis* there was a partial return to the more traditional Genesis style of songs. *Abacab* had been a deliberate attempt by the band to shake things up, with the fans, the music press and themselves. The band had been keen to demonstrate that they were still valid in the post-punk music world. The songs they had written for *Abacab* were reflective of this. Now, more confident and relaxed, Genesis got back to what the band did best. However, the writing was not without its problems. The band would normally have some bits left over from previous ventures or that had been developed between albums—ideas to kick-start the writing process. For this album they had absolutely nothing. They would have to write and record the whole album from scratch. To do this the band recorded long jam sessions and went back to review them in order to extract parts they felt were worth developing further. Over the first couple of days, working under this new approach was difficult with the group finding ideas hard to come by as they were getting used to the new approach. On the third day, ideas started to flow and eventually the songs began to take shape.

Hugh Padgham was again on board as engineer for the album, having worked once more with Collins on his solo album. This time he would also act as co-producer with Geoff Callingham credited with providing technical assistance. Genesis recorded enough material to fill the album, but had no additional tracks, meaning there was no selection

Genesis in 1983. From left, Mike Rutherford, Tony Banks and Phil Collins. Charisma promotional photograph (courtesy Mark Kenyon/The Genesis Archive).

process as to what would appear on the album and what would be left off. Every finished song they wrote and recorded was included.

Phil Collins also video recorded the studio activity, fly on the wall style, on his newly purchased camera. The results can be seen on the DVD Video Extras disc of the 2007 remix and reissue included in the *Genesis 1983–1998* box set. The footage showed the band developing a mix of direct pop songs alongside experimental and progressive music.

[134] MAMA

Music: Tony Banks/Phil Collins/Mike Rutherford
Lyrics: Phil Collins
Length: 6:52
Tony Banks—Synthesizers; **Phil Collins**—Lead & Backing Vocals, Drums, Percussion; **Mike Rutherford**—Guitar, Bass, Drum Machine
Recorded and Mixed at The Farm, Chiddingfold, Surrey, May to August 1983.
Producer: Genesis with Hugh Padgham. Engineer: Hugh Padgham. Technical Assistance: Geoff Callingham.
2007 Remix/Remaster Release:
Mixed at The Farm, Surrey 2005/2006.
5.1 Surround sound and stereo mixes by Nick Davis. Assisted by Tom Mitchell.
UK Release: 29 August 1983 (A-side single b/w [142] IT's GONNA GET BETTER. Charisma. MAMA 1)
U.S. Release: 30 August 1983 (A-side single b/w [142] IT's GONNA GET BETTER. Atlantic. 7-89770)
UK Album Release: 3 October 1983. (LP. *Genesis*)
U.S. Album Release: 7 October 1983. (LP. *Genesis*)

Advertisement for the release of the self-titled album *Genesis* placed in *Sounds* on 15 October 1983 (courtesy Mark Kenyon/The Genesis Archive).

If any song demonstrated the band's new approach to writing and recording, it was MAMA. The song was developed from Rutherford's experimentation with a Linn LM-1 electronic drum machine pattern, which he fed through a gated reverb and his Mesa Boogie guitar amplifier. The resultant sound is rough and distorted, but highly distinctive. The band then improvised over the pattern for half-an-hour and most of the song emerged from that initial session. The finished song ferments a steamy, sweaty atmosphere with Banks playing some haunting synth voices over a droned E bass note on the Prophet 10. He also added a triggered chopping minor key keyboard rhythm MIDI'd from the cowbell sound of the drum machine. Alongside this he sampled a Japanese Koto using the Emulator for the plunking sound produced in the call and response with Rutherford's guitar that follows the chorus.

Collins wrote the lyrics, having improvised about half of them during the writing. This is the hottest song the band ever recorded, not least for its subject matter. Collins explained the song was "about a young teenager that's got a mother fixation with a prostitute that he's just happened to have met in passing and he has such a strong feeling for her and doesn't understand why she isn't interested in him. It's a bit like [British actor] David Niven in *The Moon's a Balloon*, I don't know if you've read that book, he's very young, just come out of cadet college or whatever, and he meets this quite, you know, 45-year-old prostitute who he has a fantastic time with. He's special to her but it definitely can't go any further than what it is and that's really what the song is about, with sinister overtones."[2]

Collins delivers a searing, passionate vocal performance that comes to a head with a manic, evil laugh at 2:42, inspired by Grandmaster Flash and the Furious Five's "The Message."[3] Collins' vocals are heavily treated with reverb enabling the singer to accentuate tonally harder aspects of the words, emulating one of his heroes—John Lennon. The song builds in tension through a bridging section featuring some of Banks' strongest sustained harmonics to which Rutherford adds guitar power chords to increase the drama and Collins introduces a level of anxiety to his vocal. The real drums, employing the gated reverb effect created by Collins and Padgham, enter at 4:10 and take the song to another plane as it intensifies both musically and vocally for its final two verses. Banks remarked, "The drum entry was a bit like 'In the Air [Tonight]' but it seemed so right for the song we wouldn't fight it.... I think MAMA is one of the strongest things we've ever been involved in."[4]

All three members of the band place the song among their best work. It is a tortured and brooding masterpiece unlike anything else on the music scene at the time. It showed that Genesis could still produce highly original music.

Single Release: MAMA was released as the lead-off single (b/w [142] IT'S GONNA GET BETTER) for the *Genesis* album on 29 August 1983 in edited form (6:07) removing the penultimate verse. It was further edited for radio play (5:18) shortening the intro and the brief interplay between Banks and Rutherford after the chorus. The 12-inch single release is the longest edit of the song (7:28) with an elongated playout. MAMA would become the band's highest charting single in the UK peaking at #4 and staying on the chart for ten weeks. In the U.S. it only reached #73.

Music Video: A promotional video was shot by Stuart Orme on a set designed to replicate a brothel in a hot and sweaty country somewhere in the Far East. Shot in black and white the video transitions to color during its build toward the climax.

Alternative Versions: A "work in progress" recording (10:43) from the session was included on CD3 of the *Genesis Archive #2 1976–1992* box set. This gives great insight into the band's writing process and shows how Genesis edited down longer jam sessions to hone a song into its final state.

Live Performances: 1983/4, 1986/7, 1992 (rarely on U.S. leg), 1998, 2007. MAMA would feature in the band's live set on each subsequent tour, although it was dropped from the set early in the 1992 tour due to the difficulties it caused for Collins' voice. The song was performed in full on the 1983/4 tour and early dates on the band's 1986/7 tour, before being edited down to include just the second of the last two verses after the drum entrance, again to protect Collins' voice. It also became the set opener on the 1986/7 tour. On the 1998 tour, Ray Wilson handled the vocals admirably on his brief stint with the band. For the 2007 reunion tour, the band dropped the key and Collins sang the song with a less aggressive attack, which enabled it to be played throughout the tour.

Live Recordings: (1) A live recording (6:50) from 4 July 1987 at Wembley Stadium, London, appeared on *The Way We Walk, Volume One: The Shorts*. It would be remixed and remastered (6:48) for the reissue of *The Way We Walk* on the *Genesis Live 1973–2007* box set in 2009. The lineup was augmented by Daryl Stuermer (bass) and Chester Thompson (drums) on all official live recordings. This recording was produced by Nick Davis, Robert Colby and the band.

(2) A further recording (6:57) from Commerzbank-Arena, Frankfurt, on 5 July 2007 was included on *Live Over Europe 2007*. This recording by Bernard Natier was produced by Nick Davis.

[135] THAT'S ALL

Music: Tony Banks/Phil Collins/Mike Rutherford
Lyrics: Phil Collins
Length: 4:26
Tony Banks—Electric Grand Piano, Synthesizers; **Phil Collins**—Lead & Backing Vocals, Drums, Percussion; **Mike Rutherford**—Guitar, Bass
Recorded and Mixed at The Farm, Chiddingfold, Surrey, May to August 1983.
Producer: Genesis with Hugh Padgham. Engineer: Hugh Padgham. Technical Assistance: Geoff Callingham.
2007 Remix/Remaster Release:
Mixed at The Farm, Surrey 2005/2006.
5.1 Surround sound and stereo mixes by Nick Davis. Assisted by Tom Mitchell.
UK Release: 3 October 1983. (LP. *Genesis*)
U.S. Release: 7 October 1983. (LP. *Genesis*)
UK Single Release: 7 November 1983 (A-side single b/w [139] TAKING IT ALL TOO HARD. Virgin/Charisma, TATA-1. 12-inch version adds FIRTH OF FIFTH [live])
U.S. Single Release: 8 November 1983 (A-side single b/w [137] SECOND HOME BY THE SEA. Atlantic. 7-89724)

Advertisement for the release of the single [134] MAMA placed in *Sounds* on 27 August 1983 (courtesy Mark Kenyon/The Genesis Archive).

If [134] MAMA has echoes of Lennon, then THAT'S ALL has more than a hint of McCartney. The song was a complete contrast to its predecessor's dark and brooding atmosphere. It is an infectious pop song driven by bouncy piano chords, with Banks using the Yamaha CP-70 electric grand, over a country and western styled bobbing bass line from Rutherford. Banks also provides a breezy organ solo during the bridge, using the Synclavier to imitate a Hammond B-3 organ, and Rutherford plays the song out with a most jolly lead guitar part, repeating the song's main riff. Collins adopted a Ringo-style approach to his drum part to complete the Fab Four feel.

Collins' lyrics tell the story of a couple who never seem to see eye to eye. It is a lyric he is comfortable writing and has a more naturalistic feel than either of his bandmates as he recalled, "Mike and Tony have always had problems saying 'I love you' in a word, in a lyric. *And* I've never had a problem doin' that. You know, it's part of me; I'm very honest and direct."⁵ The working title for the song was "George and Martha." This is likely a double reference: firstly, to the British TV comedy series *George & Mildred*, which featured a bickering married couple played by Yootha Joyce and Brian Murphy; secondly to The Beatles song "Martha My Dear," written by Paul McCartney, which featured a similarly jaunty piano rhythm. The song originally developed from a guitar riff that Rutherford had been working on, which Banks sampled on the Emulator and considerably slowed down. From there he translated it to a piano phrase resulting in the bouncing line that would run throughout the song. Banks was also keen to keep the song simple and not go for any extravagant chords, continuing the band's strategy begun on *Abacab*.

THAT'S ALL is a great example of Genesis' ear for melody and not being afraid to show their influences. The song proved very popular with radio stations, earning the band a wider audience and it continued the perfect start to the album.

Single Release: The song was released as the second single from *Genesis* in the UK (b/w [139] TAKING IT ALL TOO HARD) and reached #16 on the UK Singles chart. In the U.S. (b/w [137] SECOND HOME BY THE SEA) it was even more successful peaking at #6 and becoming their first single to hit the *Billboard* Hot 100 Top 10.

Music Video: A promotional video, the first shot by director Jim Yukich, featured the band as homeless men in an abandoned factory.

Live Performances: 1983/4, 1986/7. The song was performed on the following two tours before being dropped from the set. The song was always popular with audiences and the band obviously enjoyed playing it, as is evidenced on the video records of their concert performances. It was briefly rehearsed for, but not performed on, the band's 1998 tour featuring Ray Wilson on vocals.

Live Recordings: A recording (4:59) from Wembley Stadium, London, on 4 July 1987 was included on *The Way We Walk, Volume One: The Shorts*. A remixed and remastered version of this performance (4:58) appeared on the reissued *The Way We Walk* on the *Genesis Live 1973–2007* box set in 2009. The lineup was augmented by Daryl Stuermer (bass) and Chester Thompson (drums). The recording was engineered by Nick Davis and Geoff Callingham and produced by Davis, Robert Colby and the band.

Poster issued to record stores for the single release of [135] THAT'S ALL (courtesy Mark Kenyon/The Genesis Archive).

[136] Home by the Sea /
[137] Second Home by the Sea

Music: Tony Banks/Phil Collins/Mike Rutherford
Lyrics: Tony Banks
Length: 11:14 (5:07 / 6:07)
Tony Banks—Electric Grand Piano, Synthesizers; **Phil Collins**—Lead & Backing Vocals, Drums, Electronic Drums, Percussion; **Mike Rutherford**—Guitar, Bass, Bass Pedals
Recorded and Mixed at The Farm, Chiddingfold, Surrey, May to August 1983.
Producer: Genesis with Hugh Padgham. Engineer: Hugh Padgham. Technical Assistance: Geoff Callingham.
2007 Remix/Remaster Release:
Mixed at The Farm, Surrey 2005/2006.
5.1 Surround sound and stereo mixes by Nick Davis. Assisted by Tom Mitchell.
UK Release: 3 October 1983. (LP. *Genesis*)
U.S. Release: 7 October 1983. (LP. *Genesis*)
U.S. Single Release: 31 October 1983 (B-side single Second Home by the Sea b/w [135] That's All. Atlantic. 7-89724)

Developed under the working title "Heavy Simmons Vibe," in reference to the booming electronic drums played by Collins in what was to become the latter section, Second Home by the Sea, this is the longest song on the album at just over eleven minutes. As such, the song recaptures much of the magic of early Genesis and utilizes the sandwich structure the band had introduced on [42] Firth of Fifth.

The song tells the tale of a burglar breaking into a house situated by the sea only to discover it is haunted and the ghosts force him to stay and listen to their stories for the remainder of his life. The lyric was written by Banks using Collins' improvised vocal phrasing "Home by the Sea" and the eerie feel of the music to shape his story. Musically the song was honed from a one-hour jam session of improvisations around a Linn drum machine pattern laid down by Collins. Recording their improvisations, the band collated a rough structure and then rerecorded their parts once they had agreed on the final arrangement. The first part of the song was based around staccato guitar chords and spiraling synth phrases, with some nice prompting from Rutherford's bass and sharp drumming from Collins over an oriental sounding rhythm. An eerie and atmospheric midsection provides the bridge to one of the band's best instrumentals driven by a soaring melodic synth solo from Banks and propelled along by Collins' thunderous Simmons drum lick. Rutherford joins the party for a brief lead guitar solo before a reprise of the first part of the song closes it out. Banks explained how the instrumental section was developed, "we were just out there improvising and Phil was just playing in three and Mike and I were just playing over the top of that and all of the little moments coalesced and it sounded fantastic ... we had two thirty minute tapes of it. Mike and I just sat down and marked the best bits.... We learned exactly what we played and if we changed the chord on the third beat of the bar, we did it and I did exactly the notes I did on his things and then we just stuck it all together and one bit that sounded good we played twice."[6]

The result is one of the band's very best compositions that is among the band's most powerful and majestic pieces. It provides a perfect finish to a near-perfect Side One of the LP.

Single Release: The Home by the Sea section (4:46) of the song was released as a single in the Netherlands, Australia and New Zealand. Second Home by the Sea (6:00) was used as the B-side on the Australasia version as well as to [135] That's All in the U.S. It was later used in edited form (4:54) on the enhanced CD single release of [169] Congo released on 15 September 1997.

Music Video: A video was shot by Jim Yukich with the band in stage gear on their rehearsal stage as a simulated performance, but with no live audience. The promo film was shot at Reunion Arena, in Dallas, Texas, on 21 January 1984.

Live Performances: 1983/4, 1986/7, 1992, 1998, 2007. The song became known simply as HOME BY THE SEA once it entered the live environment. It would be performed on all the band's subsequent tours and become a stage highlight. In his introduction to the song Collins would whip up enthusiastic audience participation as he attempted to create the impression of the stadium being levitated, while the lights were lowered toward the stage.

Live Recordings: (1) A recording (12:18), believed to be from the 1983/4 tour,[7] was included on the CD single release of [162] HOLD ON MY HEART as part of the *Invisible Series* (Volume 3). The lineup was augmented by Daryl Stuermer (bass) and Chester Thompson (drums) on all three official live recordings. This recording was engineered by Geoff Callingham and mixed by Nick Davis.

(2) A further live recording (12:14) from Niedersachsenstadion, Hanover, on 10 July 1992 was included on *The Way We Walk, Volume Two: The Longs* and in remixed/remastered form on the 2009 combined version of *The Way We Walk*. The lineup was again augmented by Stuermer and Thompson. The recording was produced by Nick Davis, Robert Colby and the band.

(3) A third official live recording (11:58) was mixed from one of the shows at LTU Arena, Düsseldorf, on either 26 or 27 June 2007 and Circus Maximus, Rome, on 14 July 2007. This recording was included on *Live Over Europe 2007*. The lineup was once again augmented by Stuermer and Thompson. The recording by Bernard Natier was produced by Nick Davis.

[138] ILLEGAL ALIEN

Music: Tony Banks/Phil Collins/Mike Rutherford
Lyrics: Mike Rutherford
Length: 5:15
Tony Banks—Electric Grand Piano, Synthesizers, Backing Vocals; **Phil Collins**—Lead & Backing Vocals, Drums, Percussion, Trumpet; **Mike Rutherford**—Guitar, Bass, Backing Vocals
Recorded and Mixed at The Farm, Chiddingfold, Surrey, May to August 1983.
Producer: Genesis with Hugh Padgham. Engineer: Hugh Padgham. Technical Assistance: Geoff Callingham.
2007 Remix/Remaster Release:
Mixed at The Farm, Surrey 2005/2006.
5.1 Surround sound and stereo mixes by Nick Davis. Assisted by Tom Mitchell.
UK Release: 3 October 1983. (LP. *Genesis*)
U.S. Release: 7 October 1983. (LP. *Genesis*)
UK Single Release: 30 January 1984 (A-side single b/w [111] TURN IT ON AGAIN [live]. Virgin/Charisma. AL 1)
U.S. Single Release: 23 January 1984 (A-side single b/w [111] TURN IT ON AGAIN [live]. Atlantic. 7-89698)

Even in the days before political correctness, ILLEGAL ALIEN still managed to get the band into dodgy waters in America. It deals, in a light-hearted way, with the flood of illegal immigrants coming into the U.S. from Mexico. The song can perhaps be judged as offensive by its stereotypical approach to Mexicans, which was not helped by the cod-Mexican accent Collins adopted for his vocals. Further controversy emerged in Rutherford's lyrics resulting in the song being edited for its 7-inch single release, promotional video and radio play to exclude references to a young girl offering sexual favors to be allowed to cross the border. There is no doubt that Genesis did not set out to cause offense and meant this to be a humorous and satirical lyric, which would draw attention to the plight of the Mexicans. Banks noted, "In fact it's meant to be sympathetic towards illegal aliens."[8] The lyrics had been inspired by the band's own experience at trying to obtain visas to reenter the U.S. while on tour. While the song was indeed intended to be sympathetic to the population south of the U.S. border, in a modern context it can be considered a misjudgment. Whatever one's personal view about the questionable lyrics and performance it does have a memorable chorus hook.

The sound effects that open the song mingle traffic noises and synth sounds among other things. This leads into a light catchy tune that coasts along on a buoyant rhythm. As the song evolved so did Collins' drum part as he recalls, "We went through a few different drum parts on ILLEGAL ALIEN. I initially was trying for a more sophisticated drum part than the song actually required. Eventually I ended up with that basic rock-and-roll part-two and four on the snare, one and three on the bass. That's what made the tune work."[9] The song also contains a relaxed piano-led midsection with more heavy sound effects utilizing everyday samples, such as a telephone ringing, captured using Banks' Emulator. During this section Collins also adds a tuneless trumpet, while he is joined by Banks and Rutherford in singing the repeated chorus. The band brushed off the criticism of the song but would go on to find better satirical material on 1991's *We Can't Dance* with [155] JESUS HE KNOWS ME.

Single Release: ILLEGAL ALIEN was released as a single, in edited form (4:33), backed with a live version of [111] TURN IT ON AGAIN. It peaked in the UK Singles chart at #46 (staying on the chart for five weeks) and in the U.S. at #44. The song was also included as a B-side on the Australasia single release of [136] HOME BY THE SEA.

Music Video: A promotional video was shot by Stuart Orme at the same time as that for [134] MAMA, reusing some of the sets. The band were dressed as stereotypical Mexicans, with Collins wearing a black wig and handlebar moustache.

Live Performances: 1983/4. Collins gave a humorous introduction to the song, portraying the band as "fugitives from justice," backed with a snippet of the *Dragnet* theme. The band would often be joined on stage by the road crew for the final sing-along chorus.

Live Recordings: A recording (5:31) from the L.A. Forum, Los Angeles, on 14 January 1984 was included on CD2 of the *Genesis Archive #2 1976–1992* box set. The lineup was augmented by Daryl Stuermer (bass) and Chester Thompson (drums). The recording was mixed by Nick Davis.

[139] TAKING IT ALL TOO HARD

Music: Tony Banks/Phil Collins/Mike Rutherford
Lyrics: Phil Collins
Length: 3:58
Tony Banks—Electric Grand Piano, Synthesizers; **Phil Collins**—Lead & Backing Vocals, Drums, Percussion; **Mike Rutherford**—Acoustic Guitar, Bass
Recorded and Mixed at The Farm, Chiddingfold, Surrey, May to August 1983.
Producer: Genesis with Hugh Padgham. Engineer: Hugh Padgham. Technical Assistance: Geoff Callingham.
2007 Remix/Remaster Release:
Mixed at The Farm, Surrey 2005/2006.
5.1 Surround sound and stereo mixes by Nick Davis. Assisted by Tom Mitchell.
UK Release: 3 October 1983. (LP. *Genesis*)
U.S. Release: 7 October 1983. (LP. *Genesis*)
UK Single Release: 7 November 1983 (B-side single b/w [135] THAT'S ALL. Virgin/Charisma, TATA-1)
U.S. Single Release: June 1984 (A-side single b/w [141] SILVER RAINBOW. Atlantic. 7-89656)

TAKING IT ALL TOO HARD is a nicely judged acoustic ballad that flows effortlessly and is immaculately played. Rutherford's tuneful acoustic guitar work and Banks' Yamaha CP-70 electric grand piano complement each other perfectly. They are backed by Collins' tasteful drums and shuffling percussion along with Rutherford's unfussy bass. The song unusually opens with its chorus, which works around a rooted A bass note around which the band progress the major chord sequence through D, A and G before changing to B minor for the hook. The verse shifts to a D minor key and the bridge takes us to B flat major. The shift between the straight minor and major keys musically reflects the shifting tone in the song's lyrics, which contrast emotions of sadness and acceptance. Collins delivers a heartfelt vocal interpretation of his own lyrics on one of the album's simplest, yet most polished, tracks. It's the kind of song Collins made his trademark in the '80s with its honest from-the-heart perspective and is warmly affecting.

The well-crafted ballad would become a feature on each album from now on (see [146], [158] and [162]) and was seen by some of the band's older fans as Genesis losing its identity by being drawn into the mainstream. This view misses the point. Time does not stand still. We do not live in a bubble where everything remains unchanged. The band had rightly found it necessary to evolve in order to survive and Banks, Collins and Rutherford had identified a desire to write songs in a shorter format as well as retain some of their creative experimentation as a contrast. That the band became more popular was a result of their opening the music up to a wider audience. The process had begun more than five years earlier with [102] FOLLOW YOU, FOLLOW ME and [98] MANY TOO MANY on ...*And Then There Were Three*.... Now the band was refining its craft as well as continuing to produce challenging music. The Genesis of 1983 was producing different music to the Genesis of 1977, but it was still distinctively Genesis.

Single Release: The song was released as an A-side single in June 1984 in the U.S. and Canada (b/w [141] SILVER RAINBOW). It reached #50 on the *Billboard* Hot 100, staying on the chart for twelve weeks. No promotional video was shot to support the single. In the UK it was used as the B-side to [135] THAT'S ALL.

[140] JUST A JOB TO DO

Music: Tony Banks/Phil Collins/Mike Rutherford
Lyrics: Mike Rutherford
Length: 4:47
Tony Banks—Electric Grand Piano, Synthesizers; **Phil Collins**—Lead & Backing Vocals, Drums, Percussion; **Mike Rutherford**—Guitar, Bass
Recorded and Mixed at The Farm, Chiddingfold, Surrey, May to August 1983.
Producer: Genesis with Hugh Padgham. Engineer: Hugh Padgham. Technical Assistance: Geoff Callingham.
2007 Remix/Remaster Release:
Mixed at The Farm, Surrey 2005/2006.
5.1 Surround sound and stereo mixes by Nick Davis. Assisted by Tom Mitchell.
UK Release: 3 October 1983. (LP. *Genesis*)
U.S. Release: 7 October 1983. (LP. *Genesis*)

JUST A JOB TO DO was written under the working title "M.J." and tells the story of a hit man hunting down his target. It's an unusual subject matter for the band and one that sits a little uncomfortably with the busy and quirky melody and rhythms presented. The verses are light in arrangement with some flashy synth runs from Banks, who also provides a thick repeated synth lead riff, which is urged along by Rutherford's calypso-like guitar figure. The chorus slips into a more conventional rock feel with Rutherford's power guitar chords and prompting bass taking over. Here again, as on [138] Illegal Alien, the midsong bridge is the highlight of the song, with Banks reverting to piano and Collins delivering some emotive vocals. Musically too, this section proves to be much stronger than the rather awkward verse.

The song is largely forgotten in Genesis' vast catalogue and is the only song on the album not to be used as a B-side on a single release. It is certainly not among the band's strongest pieces. It feels a little out of character and musically contrived. The album sessions were restricted to only nine recorded tracks. There were no leftovers to give the band a selection process. Their new method of writing from scratch had proved challenging as well as exciting and the well of creativity was running a little dry after a succession of solo albums. Just a Job to Do feels like the result of the band grasping hard to be creative, but finding the juices were not flowing as freely. The band have always had mixed feelings about the song, with Banks even contradicting himself, on the one hand saying, "I heard Just a Job to Do recently on the radio and I thought 'Was that really us?' It was awful."[10] And on the other hand, "That's a pretty good song when you hear it now."[11]

[141] Silver Rainbow

Music: Tony Banks/Phil Collins/Mike Rutherford
Lyrics: Tony Banks
Length: 4:30
Tony Banks—Electric Grand Piano, Synthesizers; **Phil Collins**—Lead & Backing Vocals, Drums, Percussion; **Mike Rutherford**—Guitar, Bass
Recorded and Mixed at The Farm, Chiddingfold, Surrey, May to August 1983.
Producer: Genesis with Hugh Padgham. Engineer: Hugh Padgham. Technical Assistance: Geoff Callingham.
2007 Remix/Remaster Release:
Mixed at The Farm, Surrey 2005/2006.
5.1 Surround sound and stereo mixes by Nick Davis. Assisted by Tom Mitchell.
UK Release: 3 October 1983. (LP. *Genesis*)
U.S. Release: 7 October 1983. (LP. *Genesis*)
U.S. Single Release: June 1984 (B-side single b/w [139] Taking It All Too Hard. Atlantic. 7-89656)

Silver Rainbow has an atmospheric synth opening in D minor from Banks, over which Collins adds a breezy percussion and sings Banks' lyrical *Alice in Wonderland* absurdities. Collins' electronic drums then kick in with Banks' piano providing a pacey counter-rhythm—indeed the song had been worked on under the title "Adam Ant" due to Collins' galloping drum pattern. Banks' lyrics concern a young man's plan of conquest of the opposite sex and in its subject is reminiscent of [46] The Cinema Show. The song is another catchy piece with a standard verse-chorus structure. The "Silver Rainbow" referenced here is a metaphor for the zipper as Banks mixes his *Alice* imagery with the more basic needs of an adolescent male. The song's climb and fall through the chorus can be seen to symbolize the young male's hopes being raised and dashed. The absurd nature of the song has a winning charm.

While again the song does not sit with the band's best work, Silver Rainbow has some interesting ideas. Like [140] Just a Job to Do, it has been largely forgotten by Genesis and was never performed live. However, the band have grown fonder of the song over time with Collins later recalling, "Someone sent me a 6-CD set, a drummer fan, and they send me the stuff they like that I've done and one of these tracks was Silver Rainbow. Then you know when you play a song and you say 'What's that bit? That's a really great bit.' And this song kept on coming by me. I'd never even thought of it since we did it, but it sounded really, really great."[12]

Single Release: The song was used as the B-side to the June 1984 single release of [139] TAKING IT ALL TOO HARD in the U.S. and Canada.

[142] IT'S GONNA GET BETTER

Music: Tony Banks/Phil Collins/Mike Rutherford
Lyrics: Mike Rutherford
Length: 5:14
Tony Banks—Electric Grand Piano, Synthesizers; **Phil Collins**—Lead & Backing Vocals, Drums, Percussion; **Mike Rutherford**—Guitar, Guitar Synthesizer, Bass
Recorded and Mixed at The Farm, Chiddingfold, Surrey, May to August 1983.
Producer: Genesis with Hugh Padgham. Engineer: Hugh Padgham. Technical Assistance: Geoff Callingham.
2007 Remix/Remaster Release:
Mixed at The Farm, Surrey 2005/2006.
5.1 Surround sound and stereo mixes by Nick Davis. Assisted by Tom Mitchell.
UK Release: 29 August 1983 (B-side single b/w [134] MAMA. Charisma. MAMA 1)
U.S. Release: 30 August 1983 (B-side single b/w [134] MAMA. Atlantic. 7–89770)
UK Album Release: 3 October 1983. (LP. *Genesis*)
U.S. Album Release: 7 October 1983. (LP. *Genesis*)

The closing track of *Genesis* opens with one of those happy accidents. Banks had tried to get a string sound sample using the Emulator but failed. However, on playing back the sound as four simultaneous notes he created an overlapping phrase in B minor, which generated a mysterious sound he liked, and the band used it as the song's distinctive introduction. The verse section features a prominent midtempo weaving synth bass riff from Rutherford, using the ARP Guitar synthesizer, over which the guitarist strums a jangly pattern and Banks colors in using his tasteful synth patches. The verses feel a little labored, but the chorus has a melodic quality with its uplifting sing-along lyric demonstrating the optimistic reassurance offered in the title. The song's message of keeping hope and faith in times of struggle was unusually upbeat for Genesis and created a welcome contrast to some of their more cynical and surreal lyrics seen elsewhere on the album. The chord structure is kept simple and, like [139] TAKING IT ALL TOO HARD, the song commences with its uplifting chorus in B major before switching to B minor for the more downbeat verses. Banks' piano playout is nicely understated as his overlapping string sample reappears beneath to close out the song.

Single Release: IT'S GONNA GET BETTER was the B-side to the [134] MAMA single in the UK and U.S. For the 12-inch single release an extended edit [6:28] featuring an extra chorus and longer playout was used.[13]

Live Performances: 1983/4. The song would work better on stage with the two-chord outro section being extended to include a blissful guitar solo by touring guitarist Daryl Stuermer and vocal ad libs from Collins.

Live Recordings: A recording (7:31) from the L.A. Forum, Los Angeles, on 14 January 1984 was included on CD2 of the *Genesis Archive #2 1976–1992* box set. The lineup was augmented by Stuermer and Chester Thompson (drums). The recording was produced by Nick Davis.

* * *

Upon its release on 3 October 1983, *Genesis* would confirm the band's increasing popularity by charting well on both sides of the Atlantic—it would be the band's third consecutive #1 in the UK 9 in the U.S. It featured a photographic album cover by Bill Smith of a collection of toy shapes that lacked any real inspiration and the band have never been keen on it.

Being the first album entirely written from scratch and then recorded simultaneously in the studio, it is a hit-and-miss affair. It contains some truly inspired work in [134] MAMA and [136] HOME BY THE SEA/[137] SECOND HOME BY THE SEA, along with some quality pop material. The LP Side One is about as near perfect as the band would get, but the quirkier tracks on Side Two were less successful, making for an uneven sequence. The band would acknowledge this themselves in many subsequent interviews. Banks recalled, "When I listen to the *Genesis* album, I really love the first side. [134] MAMA, [135] THAT'S ALL and [136/137] HOME BY THE SEA are my favorite tracks. The second side is less exciting, but there are some nice moments."[14] Rutherford concurred adding, "Side 1 is great.... Side 2 hasn't really lasted. They've all fallen by the wayside."[15]

That said most of the other songs did contain some memorable moments. [140] JUST A JOB TO DO and [138] ILLEGAL ALIEN contained excellent bridge sections. [135] THAT'S ALL was a lovely Beatle-esque/country tune, which connected with the record buying public. [139] TAKING IT ALL TOO HARD was a finely crafted ballad suggesting things to come and mirroring Collins' solo work. [141] SILVER RAINBOW has grown in favor over the years and remains a charming song. [142] IT'S GONNA GET BETTER may lack enough distinction to be an album closer but has its uplifting moments despite being a little too ponderous in the verses.

The music press, as was becoming the custom, greeted the album with mixed reviews. Hugh Fielder in *Sounds* was largely positive and opened his review by saying, "Whatever else you want to accuse Genesis of, you certainly can't say they're stuck in a rut anymore. Their last three albums have wrung more changes than many younger and supposedly fresher groups have managed in half a dozen."[16] J.D. Considine, writing for *Rolling Stone* felt, "*Genesis* seems little more than an attempt to be all things to all fans."[17] In his retrospective review for *All Music Guide*, Stephen Thomas Erlewine noted, "It has a little bit too much of everything—too much pop, too much art, too much silliness—so it doesn't pull together, but if taken individually, most of these moments are very strong, testaments to the increasing confidence and pop power of the trio, even if it's not quite what long-time fans might care to hear."[18]

By this point, Phil Collins' increasing solo success, while raising the profile of the band, threatened to overshadow the contribution of Banks and Rutherford. But, as with *Abacab*, this was a truly group collaboration and the first to be wholly conceived in the studio by the trio as a writing team, an approach they would perfect with their next album. In retrospect, therefore, *Genesis* is a further move toward the crafted pop-rock approach they would perfect on *Invisible Touch* and is best remembered for one of the most blisteringly atmospheric rock songs ever recorded in [134] MAMA.

The band would tour the album extensively across the U.S. and Canada between 6 November 1983 and 20 February 1984, before returning to the UK for five dates at Birmingham's NEC Arena at the end of February.

15

STUDIO ALBUM #13:
Invisible Touch

UK Release: 9 June 1986. CD/LP. Virgin/Charisma. GEN CD2/GEN LP2.
U.S. Release: 6 June 1986. CD/LP. Atlantic. 7 81641–2/ Atl-81641-1-E.
Remix/Remaster Release:
UK Release: 1 October 2007. CD/SACD/DVD. Virgin/Charisma. GENCDR2.
U.S. Release: 20 November 2007. CD/DVD. Atlantic/Rhino. R2 301244.

Album Tracks

[143] INVISIBLE TOUCH
[144] TONIGHT, TONIGHT, TONIGHT
[145] LAND OF CONFUSION
[146] IN TOO DEEP
[147] ANYTHING SHE DOES
[148] DOMINO (PART ONE—IN THE GLOW OF THE NIGHT;
PART TWO—THE LAST DOMINO)
[149] THROWING IT ALL AWAY
[150] THE BRAZILIAN

Other Songs Recorded

[151] DO THE NEUROTIC
[152] FEEDING THE FIRE
[153] I'D RATHER BE YOU

Invisible Touch was recorded in the aftermath of Phil Collins' huge success with his *No Jacket Required* album, which had been a much more upbeat set including hits such as "Sussudio," "One More Night" and the sublime "Take Me Home." The album, and his much-vaunted appearance at both UK and U.S. *Live Aid* concerts, had sent Collins' star into the stratosphere. He was now also as much in demand as a producer, working with Earth, Wind & Fire's Philip Bailey on *Chinese Wall* and Eric Clapton on his album *Behind the Sun*. In press interviews, Collins was keen to stress that his own personal success was not getting in the way of Genesis, "Because we know each other so well, there's no room for three individual egos when we get into the same room. As long as I'm proud of the stuff Genesis does, that's good enough for me."[1]

Mike Rutherford had also had some success with his *Mike + The Mechanics* album, notably the key singles "Silent Running" and "All I Need Is a Miracle," which both reached the Top 10 (#6 and #5 respectively) in the U.S. Tony Banks, meanwhile, had been working

From left, Phil Collins, Mike Rutherford and Tony Banks released what was to become Genesis' biggest selling album, *Invisible Touch*, in June 1986. Virgin/Charisma promotional photograph (courtesy Mark Kenyon/The Genesis Archive).

on a couple of film soundtracks (*Quicksilver* and *Lorca and the Outlaws*), the best work from which would be compiled into the album *Soundtracks* released in March 1986.

The confidence within the band was therefore high going into the sessions for the album, as would become evident in the quality of the songs they wrote. The three members had absorbed a lot of influences outside of the band and the new music they would produce together would again move in a new direction.

Invisible Touch was written and recorded during the autumn and winter of 1985/6 at The Farm. The process the trio adopted was the same as for *Genesis*, continuing the approach of writing from scratch through improvisation. This would involve Banks and Rutherford playing over a drum machine pattern set by Collins. Collins would improvise vocal melodies over the top—often including nonsense phrases, but sometimes distinct enough to form part of the final lyric. This time the trio were more at home with the approach as Rutherford recalled: "We just play for a couple of hours on the first day, it's just long jam sessions—if someone came in at the wrong moment, it might sound horrible—but because we're completely unafraid of playing anything which is complete rubbish, or in the wrong key, that's how we find things. We don't mind branching off—very often we'll be playing and Tony will stab a chord or lead line that sounds fantastic and that'll lead whoever's following onto a new path. It's purely spontaneous improvisation when the three of us go in that produces the musical sound that is Genesis."[2]

While the music was written by the group together, the lyrics to the songs were again divided between the band individually. Each member would select the songs they felt most affinity with as Banks confirmed: "In the main, it's best to let the lyrics to a song be done by one person, who can carry through an idea."[3]

The band wrote eleven songs during the sessions for the album—including two elongated pieces that would let them explore different moods and stretch the music. The remaining songs were shorter and more pop orientated and there were a couple of instrumentals. The band would later report how pleased they were with their output, each of the trio feeling the songs improved on their last album.

Hugh Padgham returned for his third and final stint as engineer and would also act as co-producer. Padgham was assisted by Paul Gomersall, while Geoff Callingham offered technical support. The Fisher Lane Farm Studio had been upgraded during the previous year by Sam Toyishima. There was a debate regarding the studio window, which Toyishima had wanted removed, but this was ultimately retained at the insistence of the band. Happy with their new environment, Collins, Rutherford and Banks reached their creative peak in terms of writing output both individually and within the group environment. The completed album was mastered by Bob Ludwig at Masterdisc in New York City.

[143] INVISIBLE TOUCH

Music: Tony Banks/Phil Collins/Mike Rutherford
Lyrics: Phil Collins
Length: 3:30
Tony Banks—Synthesizers; **Phil Collins**—Lead & Backing Vocals, Electronic Drums, Drum Machine; **Mike Rutherford**—Guitar, Bass
Recorded and Mixed at The Farm, Chiddingfold, Surrey, October 1985 to February 1986.
Producer: Genesis and Hugh Padgham. Engineer: Hugh Padgham. Assistant: Paul Gomersall.
2007 Remix/Remaster Release:

Postcard promoting the limited-edition single release of [143] INVISIBLE TOUCH in June 1986 (author's collection).

Mixed at The Farm, Surrey 2005/2006.
5.1 Surround sound and stereo mixes by Nick Davis. Assisted by Tom Mitchell.
UK Release: 26 May 1986 (A-side single b/w [148] Domino 'The Last Domino.' Virgin/Charisma. GENS 1. 12" version adds Invisible Touch [extended remix]) and 16 November 1992 (A-side single/CD single Invisible Touch [live] b/w [119] Abacab [live]. Virgin. GENS 10/GENDX 10. CD single adds The Brazilian [live])
U.S. Release: 27 May 1986 (A-side single b/w [148] Domino 'The Last Domino.' Atlantic. 7-89407. 12" version adds Invisible Touch [extended remix])
UK Album Release: 9 June 1986 (CD/LP. *Invisible Touch*)
U.S. Album Release: 6 June 1986 (CD/LP. *Invisible Touch*)

Invisible Touch emerged from jam sessions for another piece that would become "The Last Domino" section of [148] Domino. Rutherford had been working on a guitar riff and Collins ad-libbed the eventual vocal chorus line over the top. The source of influence was evident from the off for this bouncy track, notably in its Linn-LM1 drum machine rhythm as Collins explained: "We didn't know the song would be a hit. It was just a case of thinking: 'Well, I like this, lots of other people might.' I can hear something of Prince and Sheila E in the drum machine—I was a fan of both."[4] Collins also cited Sheila E's song, "The Glamourous Life" as an influence on his lyrics. That song's subject matter of a woman manipulating the men in her life would be reworked by Collins from the male perspective. Rutherford's guitar riff is propelled along by Collins' electronic drums, while Banks fleshes out the verse with his tasteful synth backing. Collins sings confidently and infectiously on the chorus. Banks then contributes a speedy sequenced synthesized midsection over a fast beat before the song falls back into the chorus. Banks noted of the bridge: "I recorded eight different sequencer parts, quite arbitrarily, in step time. A couple of things I actually wrote ahead of time, and on the others I did it roughly—playing a chord and punching that in, and then another chord, and then a gap. The best one was the most random, which is the one that becomes the most prominent by the end of that section. I just faded them into the mix slowly and brought the whole thing up at the end. By building on this one chord, it's almost like you've changed key when you come back into the song, when in fact you're back in the original key."[5] There is a lifting key change as the song plays out over the repeated chorus.

Invisible Touch is pure pop and remains a firm personal favorite of Collins, "The melody, lyrics and title were mine, and it was a song that I championed during the writing of the *Touch* album."[6] It has a sing-along chorus and is played with obvious enjoyment by the band. The arrangement may now seem a little dated with its keyboard sequencing and electronic drums, but the song proved to be a crowd-pleaser for the band's newfound fan base.

Single Release: Invisible Touch was the worldwide lead-off single (b/w The Last Domino) and would be released a couple of weeks ahead of the album. The song would stall at #15 on the UK Singles chart but would stay on the chart of eight weeks. In the U.S., however, the song was a smash hit and the album's first ever #1 single hitting the top spot on 17 July 1986, staying at the top for three weeks and on the chart for seventeen weeks. It would be the first of five successive Top 5 singles from the album in the States. The song was ironically replaced at the top of the chart by Peter Gabriel's "Sledgehammer." A remix (5:58) by John "Tokes" Potoker was included on longer formats of the single. This version would appear on CD3 of the *Genesis Archive #2 1976–1992* box set. Aspects of the remix would be used by the band for the live version. The song would also later be released as a live single in the UK on 9 November 1992 to promote the live album *The Way We Walk, Volume One: The Shorts,* faring better in the UK by reaching #7.

Music Video: A video was shot by Jim Yukich with the band ad-libbing using props and swapping instruments with each other on a film set. This more naturalistic and charming approach allowed Collins to adopt his recognizable front-man persona.

Live Performances: 1986/7, 1992, 1998, 2007. The song was performed live on each subsequent tour. From 1992 it would be segued from a shortened version of [144] Tonight, Tonight, Tonight and was the set closer on the band's 2007 reunion tour.

Live Recordings: (1) A recording (5:03) from The Forum, Inglewood, Los Angeles, 13–17 October 1986 was included as a B-side to [149] Throwing It All Away released on 8 June 1987. The lineup for this and subsequent live recordings was augmented by Daryl Stuermer (bass) and Chester Thompson (drums). This recording was engineered and mixed by Craig Schertz and George Massemburg.

(2) Another live performance from the same tour (5:00), recorded at Wembley Stadium, London, on 4 July 1987, featured on the [154] No Son of Mine CD single. The track was engineered by Geoff Callingham and Steve Riddel and mixed and produced by Hugh Padgham.

(3) The live single version (5:41), released in November 1992, was recorded at Niedersachsenstadion, Hanover, Germany, on 13 July 1992 and this recording was also included on *The Way We Walk, Volume One: The Shorts.* The recording was produced by Nick Davis, Robert Colby and the band. This version was remixed and remastered by Nick Davis (5:28) for the 21 September 2009 reissue of the album as simply *The Way We Walk* as part of the *Genesis Live 1973–2007* box set.

(4) A recording (5:35) from the free Rome concert on 14 July 2007 was included on *Live Over Europe 2007.* The performance was recorded by Bernard Natier and Nick Davis produced.

[144] Tonight, Tonight, Tonight

Music: Tony Banks/Phil Collins/Mike Rutherford
Lyrics: Phil Collins
Length: 8:53
Tony Banks—Synthesizers; **Phil Collins**—Lead & Backing Vocals, Electronic Drums, Percussion, Drum Machine; **Mike Rutherford**—Guitar, Bass, Bass Pedals

Poster issued to UK record stores for the single release of [144] Tonight, Tonight, Tonight in March 1987 (courtesy Mark Kenyon/The Genesis Archive).

Recorded and Mixed at The Farm, Chiddingfold, Surrey, October 1985 to February 1986.
Producer: Genesis and Hugh Padgham. Engineer: Hugh Padgham. Assistant: Paul Gomersall.
2007 Remix/Remaster Release:
Mixed at The Farm, Surrey 2005/2006.
5.1 Surround sound and stereo mixes by Nick Davis. Assisted by Tom Mitchell.
UK Release: 9 June 1986 (CD/LP. *Invisible Touch*)
U.S. Release: 6 June 1986 (CD/LP. *Invisible Touch*)
UK Single Release: 9 March 1987 (A-side single/CD single b/w [148] Domino 'In the Glow of the Night.' Virgin/Charisma. GENS 4/CD EP 1. 12" version adds [131] Paperlate and an extended remix of Tonight, Tonight, Tonight. CD version adds extended remixes of Tonight, Tonight, Tonight and [143] Invisible Touch)
U.S. Single Release: 10 March 1987 (A-side single b/w [148] Domino "In the Glow of the Night." Atlantic. 7-89290. 12-inch version adds [131] Paperlate and an extended remix of Tonight, Tonight, Tonight)

One of two longer songs on the album, Tonight, Tonight, Tonight oozes atmosphere with its repeated sustained opening two-chord synth sequence punctuated by eerie lead guitar work from Rutherford. The opening section of the song was developed through a group jam. The drum machine pattern allowed Banks to hold a drone note on the Prophet 10 as he plays chords on top alternating between B flat major and D minor over A before stepping up to C major and D major on the lead into the chorus, which alternates between D minor seventh and G major. The song demonstrates Banks' ability to create evocative atmospheres through his use of harmonics, which has always been one of the signature elements of the band. While the chords used here are straight, his deft use of inversions to progress between sequences makes the transitions seamless.

The track had the working title "Monkey/Zulu" with the "Monkey" a reference to Collins' lyrics concerning a drug addict with withdrawal symptoms looking for his next fix. Collins recalled, "The 'Coming down like a monkey' line was improvised while we wrote the song and, like we do with a lot of songs where the lines are improvised, tried to include it in the lyric. So, I got stuck with trying to write a song about monkeys!"[7] The song's changing mood and build of tension to the chorus effectively convey the desperation of the protagonist. The "Zulu" reference is to the African feel of the popping Linn drum machine pattern Collins had set up.

The instrumental midsection features Collins tapping out experimental drum sounds over which Banks developed an undulating melody and chord progression. This leads into a more bombastic link, with Collins' anguished vocals betraying the protagonist's increasing frustration and desperation. The song plays out over repeats of the chorus in grand style as Collins goes all out vocally with Rutherford's guitar soaring in and out.

Tonight, Tonight, Tonight has an epic feel in the best Genesis tradition. Its basis being in the atmosphere set by the drum machine allowing for long-sustained keyboard textures repeating a similar effect to that achieved on [134] Mama. Its anthemic chorus made it a popular live number.

Single Release: The song was used on American TV to promote Michelob beer in their "The night belongs to Michelob" campaign. This encouraged the band to release it as a single on 2 March 1987, edited down to 4:32 by removing the instrumental midsection. As a result, the song reached #3 and spent fifteen weeks on the U.S. *Billboard* Hot 100 chart. In the UK it reached #18 and spent seven weeks on the chart. A 12-inch remix [11:47], by John "Tokes" Potoker, was also released and later included on the *Genesis Archive #2 1976–1992* box set. The song was edited to 4:28 for its inclusion on the 1999 compilation *Turn It On Again: The Hits.*

Music Video: A promotional video was shot by Jim Yukich depicting scenes from the song, with the band interjecting. Shot at night at the Bradbury Building in Los Angeles, a location used for the sci-fi classic *Blade Runner*, Yukich gave the video a cinematic feel and added visual references to the movie.

Live Performances: 1986/7, 1992 (excerpt), 2007 (excerpt). The song would be performed in its entirety on the subsequent 1986/7 tour. From the following tour in 1992 the band played the first part of the song, up to the midsection instrumental, and then segued into [143] INVISIBLE TOUCH.

Live Recordings: (1) A recording (9:33) from Wembley Stadium in London on 4 July 1987 was included as the B-side to the band's [160] TELL ME WHY single, released on 8 February 1993. The lineup was augmented for this and subsequent live recordings by Daryl Stuermer (bass) and Chester Thompson (drums). This recording was engineered by Geoff Callingham and produced by Nick Davis, Robert Colby and the band.

(2) An excerpt recording (3:36) from Niedersachsenstadion, Hanover, Germany, on 13 July 1992 was included on *The Way We Walk, Volume One: The Shorts*. This was later remixed (3:49) for the reissued version of the both volumes of the album as a single package in the *Genesis Live 1973–2007* box set. The recording was engineered by Nick Davis and Geoff Callingham and produced by Davis, Robert Colby and the band.

(3) Another excerpt recording (3:49) from Circus Maximus, Rome on 14 July 2007 was included on *Live Over Europe 2007*. The performance was recorded by Bernard Natier and produced by Nick Davis.

[145] LAND OF CONFUSION

Music: Tony Banks/Phil Collins/Mike Rutherford
Lyrics: Mike Rutherford
Length: 4:46
Tony Banks—Synthesizers, Synth Bass; **Phil Collins**—Lead & Backing Vocals, Drums, Electronic Drums, Percussion, Drum Machine; **Mike Rutherford**—Guitar, Bass
Recorded and Mixed at The Farm, Chiddingfold, Surrey, October 1985 to February 1986.
Producer: Genesis and Hugh Padgham. Engineer: Hugh Padgham. Assistant: Paul Gomersall.
2007 Remix/Remaster Release:
Mixed at The Farm, Surrey 2005/2006.
5.1 Surround sound and stereo mixes by Nick Davis. Assisted by Tom Mitchell.
UK Release: 9 June 1986 (CD/LP. *Invisible Touch*)
U.S. Release: 6 June 1986 (CD/LP. *Invisible Touch*)
UK Single Release: 17 November 1986 (A-side single/CD single b/w [152] FEEDING THE FIRE. Virgin/Charisma. GENS 3/ SNEG 3-12. 12-inch version adds LAND OF CONFUSION [extended remix]. CD version adds [151] DO THE NEUROTIC)
U.S. Single Release: 18 November 1986 (A-side single b/w [152] FEEDING THE FIRE. Atlantic. 7-89336. 12-inch version adds LAND OF CONFUSION [extended remix])

One of the most popular songs on the album, LAND OF CONFUSION features Rutherford's Keith Richards style guitar riffing over a stomping sequenced synth bass line from Banks, which the keyboardist recalled, "Originally it was an addition to the song, but it ended up being one of the major aspects of it."[8] The bass drum was also sequenced from a drum machine, with Collins adding drum fills. Rutherford noted that his rather simplistic lyrics were a protest about how we are making a mess of the world we live in. He dictated the words he had written to Collins while he had a heavy dose of flu and later recalled "I was in kind of a delirious state with a very high temperature and I dictated it to him and I remember thinking, 'I think I told him the right thing,' 'was it all rubbish or was it any good?'"[9]

Advertisement to promote the November 1986 single release of [145] LAND OF CONFUSION. The advertisement and promotional video utilized puppets created by the satirical TV series *Spitting Image*'s Fluck & Law (author's collection).

Collins delivers a confident and exciting vocal performance adding to the song's energy. This is also another song that contains a memorable contrasting bridge, here featuring some soft synth chords in the key of C sharp minor from Banks as Collins slows the tempo while moving to the Simmons electronic kit before the main riff kicks back in.

A powerful driving rocker given a modern sound, LAND OF CONFUSION provided a great contrast to the songs immediately surrounding it, demonstrating the band's sequencing expertise. The song would later be famously covered by Heavy Metal band Disturbed for their 2005 album *Ten Thousand Fists*. Genesis acknowledged this version by confirming it influenced the way they would play the song live with a slightly harder edge on their 2007 reunion tour.

Single Release: LAND OF CONFUSION was the third single from the album. Released on 17 November 1986 the song reached #16 in the UK and stayed in the Top 20 for seven weeks and on the chart for twelve weeks. It was released simultaneously in the U.S. and reached #4 staying on the chart for twenty-one weeks. In the UK, the single was backed with non-album tracks [152] FEEDING THE FIRE (on both 7-inch and 12-inch) and [151] DO THE NEUROTIC (on 12-inch only). The 12-inch single also included an extended remix (6:55) by John Potoker, which would later be included on the *Genesis Archive #2 1976–1992* box set. A live 1992 rehearsal version (5:00) mixed by Robert Colby would be included on the CD single release of JESUS HE KNOWS ME.

Music Video: A promotional video was shot to promote the single by John Lloyd and Jim Yukich and featured puppets created by Peter Fluck and Roger Law, who were responsible for the satirical TV show *Spitting Image*. The video, which is highly amusing, features a large cast of political and celebrity puppets and won the Grammy for Best Concept Music Video during its 30th Annual Awards.

Live Performances: 1986/7, 1992, 1998, 2007. The song would prove to be a strong live number and was played on each subsequent tour the band undertook, opening the set for their 1992 tour. Ray Wilson would handle the vocals on the 1998 tour.

Live Recordings: (1) A recording (5:16) from Niedersachsenstadion, Hanover, Germany, on 11 July 1992 was included on the live album *The Way We Walk, Volume One: The Shorts*. The lineup for both officially released live recordings was augmented by Daryl Stuermer (bass) and Chester Thompson (drums). This recording was engineered by Nick Davis and Geoff Callingham and produced by Davis, Robert Colby and the band. It would later be remixed (5:13) by Davis and included on the reissued album *The Way We Walk*, which was included in the *Genesis Live 1973–2007* box set.

(2) A recording (5:11) from Olympic Stadium, Helsinki, Finland, on 11 June 2007 from the reunion tour was included on *Live Over Europe 2007*. The performance was recorded by Bernard Natier and produced by Nick Davis.

[146] IN TOO DEEP

Music: Tony Banks/Phil Collins/Mike Rutherford
Lyrics: Phil Collins
Length: 5:02
Tony Banks—Electric Grand Piano, Synthesizers; **Phil Collins**—Lead & Backing Vocals, Drums, Percussion, Drum Machine; **Mike Rutherford**—Guitar, Acoustic Guitar, Bass
Recorded and Mixed at The Farm, Chiddingfold, Surrey, October 1985 to February 1986.
Producer: Genesis and Hugh Padgham. Engineer: Hugh Padgham. Assistant: Paul Gomersall.
2007 Remix/Remaster Release:
Mixed at The Farm, Surrey 2005/2006.
5.1 Surround sound and stereo mixes by Nick Davis. Assisted by Tom Mitchell.
UK Release: 9 June 1986 (CD/LP. *Invisible Touch*)
U.S. Release: 6 June 1986 (CD/LP. *Invisible Touch*)
UK Single Release: 25 August 1986 (A-side single b/w [151] DO THE NEUROTIC. Virgin/Charisma. GENS 2)
U.S. Single Release: April (?)1987 (A-side single b/w [153] I'D RATHER BE YOU. Atlantic. 7-89316)

During the writing of *Invisible Touch*, Genesis were approached by HandMade Films, the production company funding the Bob Hoskins gangster vehicle *Mona Lisa*, to provide a song for the movie.[10] HandMade had originally wanted to capitalize on Collins' solo success. However, the approach was made against the wishes of the film's producers, who had to hurriedly design a montage sequence which would have Hoskins touring the seedy porn stores of Soho in London to incorporate the song.[11] While the music for the song had already been written before the approach from HandMade, Collins wrote the lyrics to fit the film's theme of an ex-con who is besotted with the high-class call girl he is paid to drive to clients. The result is the perfect Genesis ballad. Tastefully performed and arranged, everything about this song feels right and almost effortless. The marriage of Rutherford's acoustic guitar with Banks' piano and synth string support is beautiful. The alternating minor and major chords perfectly capture the confused emotions of Hoskins' character in the film. This is capped by Collins' emotive vocal and tasteful drumming. The midsong bridge is also exquisitely played. The band had originally struggled to come up with a chorus as Collins later recalled, "In the end, I said 'Aah.... I think I've got a chorus,' very sheepishly. But that's probably the only time it's happened."[12] It would be the only piece of music brought in from outside of the writing sessions.

Critics of the band would cite IN TOO DEEP as another example of a lack of distinction between Genesis' songs and those of Collins as a solo performer. Collins certainly has a deft way of vocally interpreting a ballad, his vocal performance carrying the right amount of fragility. While there is no denying the song is less distinctively Genesis, it remains a quality composition that demonstrated the band's level of confidence in their writing.

Single Release: On 25 August 1986, the song became the second single released from the album in the UK. The single, which was backed with the non-album track [151] DO THE NEUROTIC, peaked at #19 and remained on the chart for nine weeks. The UK 7-inch release featured a slightly edited (4:39) version of the track, while the full album version was included on the 12-inch release. In the U.S., the song was released as a single in the spring of 1987 backed with another non-album track [153] I'D RATHER BE YOU. It peaked at #3 in June 1987, remaining on the chart for seventeen weeks.

Music Video: A promotional video was shot by Jim Yukich with band seen against the backdrop of a blank cinema screen, perhaps referencing *Mona Lisa*, however no shots from the film were included.

Live Performances: 1986/7 (U.S. and Australia legs). IN TOO DEEP was performed on the U.S. leg of their 1986/7 tour and again in Australia, where the band used a string orchestra (dubbed The Invisible Strings) to conform with local music union laws.

Live Recordings: A recording (5:28) from The Forum, Inglewood, Los Angeles, in October 1986 was included as a B-side to the [157] I CAN'T DANCE CD single (volume 2 of the *Invisible Series*). The lineup was augmented by Daryl Stuermer (guitar) and Chester Thompson (drums). This recording was engineered by Geoff Callingham and mixed by Nick Davis. It would later be included on the live album (5:36) *The Way We Walk, Volume One: The Shorts* and its remixed version on the reissue of *The Way We Walk* included in the *Genesis Live 1973–2007* box set.

[147] ANYTHING SHE DOES

Music: Tony Banks/Phil Collins/Mike Rutherford
Lyrics: Tony Banks
Length: 4:20
Tony Banks—Synthesizers; **Phil Collins**—Lead & Backing Vocals, Drums, Percussion; **Mike Rutherford**—Guitar, Bass
Recorded and Mixed at The Farm, Chiddingfold, Surrey, October 1985 to February 1986.
Producer: Genesis and Hugh Padgham. Engineer: Hugh Padgham. Assistant: Paul Gomersall.
2007 Remix/Remaster Release:
Mixed at The Farm, Surrey 2005/2006.
5.1 Surround sound and stereo mixes by Nick Davis. Assisted by Tom Mitchell.

UK Album Release: 9 June 1986 (CD/LP. *Invisible Touch*)
U.S. Album Release: 6 June 1986 (CD/LP. *Invisible Touch*)

ANYTHING SHE DOES is an uptempo pop song, which surprisingly was never released as a single. It is based around a squirming brassy lead synth line from Banks,[13] propelled by some crisp drumming from Collins and punchy guitar and bass work from Rutherford. Banks created a sampled horn sound on his E-mu Emulator II for the main instrumental hook. The sound is believed to have been taken from the band's own song [131] PAPERLATE, which used the Earth, Wind & Fire horn section. The subject of Banks' lyrics was the pin-up girls that decorate the walls of garages. The song centers around the fantasies the newspaper and magazine editors fabricated around the girls and the obsessions they created in their male readers. It is another example of a lyric that may be regarded as rather crass to a modern audience, its lightly satirical intent likely to be lost in a sea of political correctness. Banks noted with tongue-in-cheek, "I'm sure people think we light joss sticks, wear white shirts and pray all the time for inspiration, but we actually cut out pictures of scantily clad women and stick them on the wall. This song is about girls like that."[14]

The band have never performed the song live and it was the only song from the album not to feature in the set on the subsequent tour. Banks claims this is because the song proved too difficult to play.

Music Video: The humorous slant of the song was exploited in a promotional video shot by Jim Yukich. It featured the band preparing to go on stage while their security guard, played with zeal by distinctly politically incorrect British comic Benny Hill,[15] tried to prevent a host of female fans from getting backstage. The video would be used on the jumbotron screens to introduce the band during their 1986/7 tour, the final shot showing the band making their way to the stage.

[148] DOMINO

I. In the Glow of the Night; II. The Last Domino

Music: Tony Banks/Phil Collins/Mike Rutherford
Lyrics: Tony Banks
Length: 10:45
Tony Banks—Synthesizers, Synth Bass; **Phil Collins**—Lead & Backing Vocals, Drums, Electronic Drums, Percussion, Drum Machine; **Mike Rutherford**—Guitar, Bass
Recorded and Mixed at The Farm, Chiddingfold, Surrey, October 1985 to February 1986.
Producer: Genesis and Hugh Padgham. Engineer: Hugh Padgham. Assistant: Paul Gomersall.
2007 Remix/Remaster Release:
Mixed at The Farm, Surrey 2005/2006.
5.1 Surround sound and stereo mixes by Nick Davis. Assisted by Tom Mitchell.
UK Release: 26 May 1986 (B-side single "The Last Domino" b/w [143] INVISIBLE TOUCH. Virgin/Charisma. GENS 1) and 9 March 1987 (B-side single/CD single "In the Glow of the Night" b/w [144] TONIGHT, TONIGHT, TONIGHT. Virgin/Charisma. GENS 4/CD EP 1)
U.S. Release: 27 May 1986 (B-side single "The Last Domino" b/w [143] INVISIBLE TOUCH. Atlantic. 7–89407) and 10 March 1987 (B-side single "In the Glow of the Night" b/w [144] TONIGHT, TONIGHT, TONIGHT. Atlantic. 7–89290)
UK Album Release: 9 June 1986 (CD/LP. *Invisible Touch*)
U.S. Album Release: 6 June 1986 (CD/LP. *Invisible Touch*)

The two-part DOMINO emphasized the strengths of the new Genesis when it came to the longer songs. Here, the trio linked two separate pieces they had written to create a dynamic whole. Banks outlined the thinking: "In musical terms, it was like the two songs were fairly separate. But the idea of going one into the other then reprising a little bit of the idea of the first one at the end of the second one, came a bit later really. It felt right. The first part felt like it lent itself to going into something with a little bit more than just being a sort of one-off song."[16]

The first section, "In the Glow of the Night," is a soft-focused piece telling the tale of how one man's decision can have unintended consequences on others. Banks' lyrics were inspired by the 1982 Lebanon War with the setting a Beirut hotel room where a couple watch bombs fall on the city. The concept of cause and effect is completed in the song's second part, which has an uptempo beat to contrast with the first. "The Last Domino" developed from a standalone jam session, which was initially titled "Hawkwind" as Banks' chords were reminiscent of that band's driving rhythm to the song "Silver Machine." Here, Genesis goes into overdrive with another sequenced and almost overlapping bass line from Banks to some thrashing guitar chords from Rutherford and Collins' pounding electronic drums. Banks' bass notes are topped with haunting melodramatic chords and an urgent keyboard line, which are resolved with the arrival of Collins' vocals.

Banks explained the concept behind the song: "The first part is very personal, coming from an individual's point of view of how he might be affected by what one person set in motion without realizing what he was doing. It's a war situation I was thinking of where a guy has lost his woman, and his attitude of 'look what you've done' in speaking to the guy who pressed the button that made the whole thing happen. The second half is a different approach. It's a more surreal approach to the idea with a nightmarish quality to it. The domino itself is the idea that there's nothing you can do if you're next in line. It sounds good when it's sung and it's also a good image."[17]

In its structuring DOMINO is much more of a traditional Genesis composition with its two-part structure mirroring the approach taken with songs like [91] INSIDE AND OUT and [123] DODO/[124] LURKER. Rutherford reflected, "It's an area we've done before but when you make it work it's still very exciting. To me it's one of the best things we've done."[18] The two parts are totally distinctive, but the lyrical theme and a slow eerie section that serves as the bridge make it into a seamless progressive song. The playout builds in excitement as Rutherford's slashing guitar and Banks' gorgeous overarching synth lead lines guide Collins' passionate vocals to a natural conclusion.

As on some of his previous songs, Collins found Banks' lyrics a little difficult to interpret recalling, "I used to think, 'How do I sing this thing about double glazing? How do I sing this and convince an audience?' I found it awkward, because I was getting more personal in my song writing, and here I was singing things I didn't understand—just syllables."[19] Collins' reservations about the lyrics aside, this is a strong example of how Genesis could still produce moments of musical drama and substance alongside more pop friendly compositions. DOMINO hones the band's newfound pop sensibilities into a complex piece of music, successfully merging the old with the new.

Single Release: Both sections of the song were used individually as B-sides to singles from the album with "In the Glow of the Night" backing [144] TONIGHT, TONIGHT, TONIGHT and "The Last Domino" backing [143] INVISIBLE TOUCH on both sides of the Atlantic.

Live Performances: 1986/7, 1992, 1998, 2007. The song became a constant in the band's live set being performed on every subsequent tour. Collins would play along with the crowd demonstrating the domino effect by having the lighting crew spotlight different sections of the audience in turn. On the 1998 tour the vocals were provided by Ray Wilson with Nir Zidkyahu on drums and Tim Drennan on bass.

Live Recordings: (1) A recording (11:19) from Wembley Stadium, London, between 2–4 July 1987 was released as a gift standalone 3-inch CD single with the original VHS release of *Live at Wembley Stadium*. As on the other two official live releases, the lineup was augmented by Daryl Stuermer (bass) and Chester Thompson (drums). This recording was engineered by Geoff Callingham and Steve Riddel and produced and mixed by Hugh Padgham.

(2) A performance (11:21) from Niedersachsenstadion, Hanover, Germany, on 10 July 1992 was included on *The Way We Walk, Volume Two: The Longs* and in remixed form (11:25) on the reissued *The Way We Walk* as part of the *Genesis Live 1973–2007* box set. This recording was engineered by Nick Davis and Geoff Callingham and produced by Davis, Robert Colby and the band.

(3) The performance (11:34) from the free concert held at Circus Maximus, Rome, on 14 July 2007 was included on *Live Over Europe 2007*. The recording was made by Bernard Natier and produced by Nick Davis.

[149] THROWING IT ALL AWAY

Music: Tony Banks/Phil Collins/Mike Rutherford
Lyrics: Mike Rutherford
Length: 3:51
Tony Banks—Electric Grand Piano, Synthesizers; **Phil Collins**—Lead & Backing Vocals, Drums, Percussion; **Mike Rutherford**—Guitar, Bass
Recorded and Mixed at The Farm, Chiddingfold, Surrey, October 1985 to February 1986.
Producer: Genesis and Hugh Padgham. Engineer: Hugh Padgham. Assistant: Paul Gomersall.
2007 Remix/Remaster Release:
Mixed at The Farm, Surrey 2005/2006.
5.1 Surround sound and stereo mixes by Nick Davis. Assisted by Tom Mitchell.
UK Release: 9 June 1986 (CD/LP. *Invisible Touch*)
U.S. Release: 6 June 1986 (CD/LP. *Invisible Touch*)
U.S. Single Release: 5 August 1986 (A-side single b/w [151] DO THE NEUROTIC. Atlantic. 7-89372)
UK Single Release: 15 June 1987 (A-side single b/w [153] I'D RATHER BE YOU. Virgin/Charisma. GENS5.
  12-inch version adds THROWING IT ALL AWAY [live] replacing the studio version and [143] INVISIBLE TOUCH [live])

THROWING IT ALL AWAY is another near perfect pop ballad, this time played midtempo, further emphasizing the very strong overall quality of the album and the confidence of the band at the time. The song was developed under the working title "Zeppo."[20] As the chorus was being developed the song was transformed from the basis of a heavy Rutherford guitar riff with an aggressive backbeat from Collins, into a midtempo shuffling rhythm. Banks provides some lovely piano work behind Rutherford's repeated riff, while Collins' catchy improvised chorus vocal gives the song its hook. During the chorus Rutherford's bass tastefully counter-balances Banks' sublime chord changes, which work from C major seventh to B flat suspended second to F major with added ninth and G suspended fourth. This is a wonderful example of Banks' use of complex harmonies to add a unique feel to a simply structured song. Rutherford's lyrics are a philosophical reflection on how splitting couples don't appreciate each other until it is too late. Once the band had recorded the song, it was nearly shelved as Rutherford explained at the time, "we lost interest in it for a bit. In my mind it became a B-song. But then I heard it yesterday and it sounded great."[21]

Francis Couture perfectly summed up the song in his review for *All Music Guide* by saying, "This love song featured heartfelt vocals, a simple piano accompaniment, and Mike Rutherford's trademark rhythm guitar, plus a very catchy chorus. Nothing striking, but all the elements came together nicely and adult contemporary radio stations played it extensively."[22] THROWING IT ALL AWAY certainly got a lot of airplay and is affecting in a seemingly effortless simplicity.

Single Release: The song proved to be very popular when released as a single in the U.S. in August 1986, where, backed with the non-album instrumental [151] DO THE NEUROTIC, it reached #4 in October on the *Billboard* Hot 100 and spent sixteen weeks on the chart. It wasn't until 15 June 1987, a year after the album was released, that the song was put out as a single in the UK. It reached #22 on the UK Singles chart where backed with [153] I'D RATHER BE YOU, another non-album track, it spent eight weeks.

Music Video: The promotional video was compiled by Jim Yukich from backstage and soundcheck footage of the band on the road—a good deal of it shot by Phil Collins on his Sony Handycam. The 12-inch single release in the UK featured a live version (7:00) along with [143] INVISIBLE TOUCH, both recorded at the Forum, Inglewood, Los Angeles, between 13–17 October 1986.

Live Performances: 1986/7, 1992, 1998, 2007. The song was performed on each of the band's subsequent tours. Another crowd favorite spurred on by Collins' call and response vocal interplay with the audience at the song's top and tail. On the 1998 tour Ray Wilson gave his vocal interpretation, while Nir Zidkyahu was on drums and Anthony Drennan on bass.

Live Recordings: (1) The recording (7:00) from the Forum, Inglewood, Los Angeles, 13–17 October 1986 was the format of the 12-inch single release of the song. As on the other two live recordings released, the band was augmented by Daryl Stuermer (bass) and Chester Thompson (drums). This recording was engineered by Craig Schertz and George Massemburg.

(2) The band included a version (6:02) recorded at Knebworth, England, on 2 August 1992 on *The Way We Walk, Volume One: The Shorts*. The recording was engineered by Nick Davis and Geoff Callingham and produced by Davis, Robert Colby and the band. It would later be remixed (6:41) by Davis and included on the reissued *The Way We Walk* as part of the *Genesis Live 1973–2007* box set.

(3) A third live recording (6:01) taken from a performance at Parc des Princes, Paris, on 30 June 2007 was included on *Live Over Europe 2007*. The recording by Bernard Natier was produced by Nick Davis.

[150] THE BRAZILIAN

Music: Tony Banks/Phil Collins/Mike Rutherford
Length: 5:04
Tony Banks—Synthesizers; **Phil Collins**—Electronic Drums, Percussion; **Mike Rutherford**—Guitar, Bass
Recorded and Mixed at The Farm, Chiddingfold, Surrey, October 1985 to February 1986.
Producer: Genesis and Hugh Padgham. Engineer: Hugh Padgham. Assistant: Paul Gomersall.
2007 Remix/Remaster Release:
Mixed at The Farm, Surrey 2005/2006.
5.1 Surround sound and stereo mixes by Nick Davis. Assisted by Tom Mitchell.
UK Album Release: 9 June 1986 (CD/LP. *Invisible Touch*)
U.S. Album Release: 6 June 1986 (CD/LP. *Invisible Touch*)

The album closer, THE BRAZILIAN, was the only fully instrumental track included on *Invisible Touch* and was the result of studio experimentation. On occasions Banks would sample what he would call "noise in the room" with the Emulator as the trio were jamming. Sometimes from these samples good ideas would come from the new sounds and loops he created. Banks is often praised for his harmonic ear, but his skillful creation of new and interesting sounds through samples or by mixing different patches is often overlooked. On this occasion Banks recorded a twenty-second sample then honed it to four or five seconds and created a loop, which would form the intro and basis for the piece. Over this looped rhythm Banks improvised some simple and charming synth phrases giving the tune a very distinctive and quirky feel. The band ended up with three reels of improvisation, which Banks then edited down to the final structure using the best pieces. Collins added his electronic drums using his Simmons kit, further embellishing the tune's industrial feel. During the closing section Rutherford introduces a wailing lead guitar, which heightens the excitement and gives the piece a rousing conclusion.

The band had recorded two instrumentals during the sessions. The second, [151] DO THE NEUROTIC, was a more traditional piece. Banks, Collins and Rutherford had a choice to make as to which would close the album. Faced with a similar choice to that on *Abacab*, where they had to decide between the romantic [132] YOU MIGHT RECALL and the brash [125] WHO DUNNIT?, the trio here again opted for the quirky over the traditional. *Uncut*'s *The Ultimate Music Guide* series offered the following description: "...with its blaring, imperious synth motif and lurching rhythm, [it] sounds not unlike the maximalist sci-fi soundscapes recently conjured up by post-dubstep electronica artists such as Rustie and Ikonika."[23] THE BRAZILIAN is a dynamic and original sound that again blended old philosophies in a modern soundscape.

The piece was the second from the album to be used in a film, in this case the Raymond Briggs comic book animated adaptation *When the Wind Blows*, released on 26 October 1986. It also appeared on the associated soundtrack album, which included songs by David Bowie (who wrote the title song), Squeeze, Hugh Cornwell, Paul Hardcastle, Roger Waters and his Bleeding Heart Band.

The track also received a Grammy nomination for Best Pop Instrumental Performance (Orchestra, Group or Soloist) and went on to be used extensively by the BBC during their coverage of the 1987 World Athletics Championships.

Live Performances: 1986/7. The piece was impressively performed on the *Invisible Touch* tour, with Collins and Chester Thompson doubling up on drums.

Live Recordings: A recording (5:27) taken between 2–4 July 1987 at Wembley Stadium, London, was included on the [143] INVISIBLE TOUCH (Live) CD single release on 9 November 1992. The same recording (5:18) was later included on CD2 of the *Genesis Archive #2 1976–1992* box set. The lineup was augmented by Daryl Stuermer (bass) and Thompson. The recording was engineered by Geoff Callingham and Nick Davis.

[151] DO THE NEUROTIC

Music: Tony Banks/Phil Collins/Mike Rutherford
Length: 7:07
Tony Banks—Synthesizers; **Phil Collins**—Drums, Percussion; **Mike Rutherford**—Guitar, Bass
Recorded and Mixed at The Farm, Chiddingfold, Surrey, October 1985 to February 1986.
Producer: Genesis and Hugh Padgham. Engineer: Hugh Padgham. Assistant: Paul Gomersall.
2007 Remix/Remaster Release:
Mixed at The Farm, Surrey 2005/2006.
5.1 Surround sound and stereo mixes by Nick Davis. Assisted by Tom Mitchell.

UK Release: 25 August 1986 (B-side single b/w [146] In Too Deep. Virgin/Charisma. GENS 2) and 17 November 1986 ("B-side" CD single b/w [145] Land of Confusion, Land of Confusion [extended mix] and Feeding the Fire. Virgin/Charisma. SNEG 3-12)
U.S. Release: 5 August 1986 (B-side single b/w [149] Throwing It All Away. Atlantic. 7-89372)

Do the Neurotic is an uptempo instrumental, played in a jazzy style, which lost out to [150] The Brazilian as the closing track to *Invisible Touch*. This is a piece the band seemed to really enjoy playing as is evident in Collins' energetic drumming. Rutherford produces his best guitar work of the sessions here, and with Banks stabbing out synth chords the whole thing has an improvised feel about it reminiscent of some of their best instrumental work of the 1970s. While a tad overlong and lacking in a clear structure, it is still an enjoyable piece that has a more organic and traditional Genesis arrangement—no electronic drums here. The band's playing is extremely tight with each player's part complimenting the other to create a thrilling whole. The strength of Genesis had long been based around the core instrumental interaction between the Banks-Collins-Rutherford trio and this piece demonstrates their ability to bring out the best in each other. Banks later commented, "I think Do the Neurotic is probably the best we ever played together as a unit and it sounds really, really good."[24]

Some aspects of this instrumental—notably Collins' drum part—would be reworked into [155] Jesus He Knows Me (which was developed under the working title of "Do the New One") on the following Genesis album, *We Can't Dance*.

Single Release: The track would be used as a B-side for the various single versions of [146] In Too Deep (edited to 5:23 on the 7-inch single) and [145] Land of Confusion (CD single) in the UK and to [149] Throwing It All Away in the U.S. (again in edited form at 5:21). It would also be included on CD1 of the *Genesis Archive #2 1976–1992* box set and in remixed form on the *Extra Tracks* CD on the *Genesis 1983–1998* box set.

[152] Feeding the Fire

Music: Tony Banks/Phil Collins/Mike Rutherford
Lyrics: Tony Banks
Length: 5:53
Tony Banks—Synthesizers; **Phil Collins**—Lead & Backing Vocals, Drums, Percussion; **Mike Rutherford**—Guitar, Bass
Recorded and Mixed at The Farm, Chiddingfold, Surrey, October 1985 to February 1986.
Producer: Genesis and Hugh Padgham. Engineer: Hugh Padgham. Assistant: Paul Gomersall.
2007 Remix/Remaster Release:
Mixed at The Farm, Surrey 2005/2006.
5.1 Surround sound and stereo mixes by Nick Davis. Assisted by Tom Mitchell.
UK Release: 17 November 1986 (B-side single/CD single b/w Land of Confusion. CD version adds [151] Do the Neurotic. Virgin/Charisma. GENS 3/ SNEG 3-12)
U.S. Release: 18 November 1986 (B-side single b/w Land of Confusion. Atlantic. 7-89336)

Feeding the Fire is the heaviest and darkest song from the sessions. It features a blistering vocal performance from Collins over his own crisp backbeat which is directed by Banks' stuttering keyboard riff. Rutherford adds his own complimenting clipped rhythm guitar chords. The verse section is much softer, with Banks playing breathy synth pad chords behind a gentler guitar part and pulsing bass. The second verse dissolves into an instrumental bridge led by Banks over the same rhythmic tempo of the verse, before a searing vocal cry from Collins brings us back in with the main chorus hook. Banks' biting

15. Studio Album #13: *Invisible Touch*

lyrics look at the apathy of human nature, and Collins delivers his vocal performance with a sneering cynicism.

The result is a song that would not have been out of place on *Invisible Touch* and may well have balanced favorably with some of the more pop orientated songs. It was a song that Banks had championed but ultimately lost out on. Collins, despite also stating a liking for the song, sensed it did not feel complete and that was why it fell by the wayside. Another possible reason may be due to its extended and lighter bridge section, which has a similar feel to that used in [144] TONIGHT, TONIGHT, TONIGHT.

Single Release: The song was included as the B-side to the single release of [145] LAND OF CONFUSION in both the UK and the U.S. It would later be included (5:49) on CD1 of the box set *Genesis Archive #2 1976–1992* and then in remixed form on the *Extra Tracks* CD to the box set *Genesis 1983–1998*.

[153] I'D RATHER BE YOU

Music: Tony Banks/Phil Collins/Mike Rutherford
Lyrics: Phil Collins
Length: 4:03
Tony Banks—Synthesizers; **Phil Collins**—Lead & Backing Vocals, Electronic Drums, Percussion, Drum Machine; **Mike Rutherford**—Guitar, Bass
Recorded and Mixed at The Farm, Chiddingfold, Surrey, October 1985 to February 1986.
Producer: Genesis and Hugh Padgham. Engineer: Hugh Padgham. Assistant: Paul Gomersall.
2007 Remix/Remaster Release:
Mixed at The Farm, Surrey 2005/2006.
5.1 Surround sound and stereo mixes by Nick Davis. Assisted by Tom Mitchell.
UK Release: 15 June 1987 (B-side single b/w [149] THROWING IT ALL AWAY. Virgin/Charisma. GENS5)
U.S. Release: April (?) 1987 (B-side single b/w [146] IN TOO DEEP. Atlantic. 7-89316)

I'D RATHER BE YOU is the weakest track recorded during the *Invisible Touch* sessions and was wisely left off the album. It features the Motown shuffle that had been championed by Collins on much of his solo work. Here, however, the arrangement lacks the organic passion and guts of that work and is instead caught up in a synthetic sheen. As a result, the sound feels empty with uninspired keyboard work, with its weak simulated brass sound, from Banks and despite some funky, bass work from Rutherford. Collins' lyrics are told from the point of view of someone with a sense of envy over their partner's success. Collins had also commented how the songs that were not included on *Invisible Touch* felt unfinished or not as strong as the rest of the material. This is certainly the case here. There are the odd flourishes of melodic invention in Banks' lead synth phrasing on the outro, but it is not enough to rescue the song from being consigned to the band's B-list.

Single Release: The song would be the B-side to the June 1987 single releases [146] IN TOO DEEP in the U.S. and [149] THROWING IT ALL AWAY in the UK. It would later be included on CD1 of the *Genesis Archive #2 1976–1992* box set and in remixed form (4:04) on the *Extra Tracks* CD of the *Genesis 1983–1998* box set.

* * *

Following its early June release, *Invisible Touch* would become a multiplatinum mega-hit in both the UK and the U.S., producing a string of hit singles including their first U.S. #1 [143] INVISIBLE TOUCH. It was a #1 album in the UK for three weeks after release and peaked at #3 in the U.S. The album produced five top 5 singles in the U.S., while it remained in the UK charts for more than a year and overall would spend ninety-six weeks there, including seventy-seven weeks unbroken from its initial release (forty-two of which were in the Top 20). In summary, it was *Invisible Touch* that made Genesis one of the top-drawing rock acts in the world at the time.

It is no accident that the album became the band's best seller. The songs were of a consistently high standard, had great energy, were immaculately produced with a modern sound, that admittedly now sounds dated in places with its 1980s pop sheen and electronic drums. The performances were as dynamic and slick as the writing, showing the band had reached a confident new high.

The songs themselves were largely pop-rock in approach, ranging from the straight pop approach of [143] INVISIBLE TOUCH and [147] ANYTHING SHE DOES, via the smooth ballads [146] IN TOO DEEP and [149] THROWING IT ALL AWAY to more traditional Genesis fare such as the atmospheric [144] TONIGHT, TONIGHT, TONIGHT and the dynamic [148] DOMINO. [150] THE BRAZILIAN showcased the experimental side of the band and taken as a whole the album demonstrated that instead of resting on its laurels Genesis was continuing to evolve and set themselves new challenges.

The band were very pleased with their work. Banks commented, "I said the second side of *Genesis* wasn't so good, but I don't feel the same way about this one. It's very consistent and I'm so pleased it had a good reaction in America."[25] Rutherford agreed: "Other albums, some songs are great and some are OK, but pretty much all of the *Invisible Touch* album seemed to work. I think it was led by courage, but the fire was fueled by Phil's incredible solo success too."[26]

Some critics and older fans were swift to point to the seemingly more commercial approach and slicker production as evidence the band had lost its edge, but they were missing the point. J.D. Considine in *Rolling Stone* noted astutely, "every tune is carefully pruned so that each flourish delivers not an instrumental epiphany but a solid hook."[27] Stephen Thomas Erlewine in his retrospective review for *All Music Guide* offered a more typical view when he called it the band's "poppiest album, a sleek, streamlined affair built on electronic percussion and dressed in synths that somehow seem to be programmed, not played by Tony Banks."[28]

What many commentators missed was that with each successive album throughout their career Genesis had moved in a new direction from the last, something that undoubtedly kept them out of the firing line during the advent of punk. The band's change in writing style meant the songs were fully collaborative with each member having an influence. The approach started with *Abacab* then gained impetus with Genesis before achieving its natural fruition with *Invisible Touch*. The simpler song structures came as a result of the members' improving skills as writers aided by their use of drum machines and production tools to set up atmospheres. The approach meant the band felt less inclined to embellish and more inclined to develop individual ideas into whole songs. That the resultant album was so impressive both commercially and compositionally demonstrates how at home with each other the trio had become. *Invisible Touch* can certainly be viewed as the commercial peak of the band's career, demonstrating songwriters in total control of their craft. It ranks, alongside *Duke*, as their best and most consistent work as a trio.

The subsequent nine-month tour took in 112 shows and would confirm their status as one of the world's top live bands by attracting huge stadium audiences. The tour included three legs of the U.S. and Canada; a visit to Australia and New Zealand as well as japan; and two European legs culminating in four glorious nights at London's Wembley Stadium in July 1987.

16

Studio Album #14: *We Can't Dance*

UK Release: 11 November 1991. CD/2LP. Virgin. GEN CD3/ GEN LP3.
U.S. Release: 12 November 1991. CD. Atlantic. 7 82344–2.
Remix/Remaster Release:
UK Release: 1 October 2007. CD/SACD/DVD. Virgin. GENCDR3.
U.S. Release: 20 November 2007. CD/DVD. Atlantic/Rhino. R2 301820.

Album Tracks

[154] No Son of Mine
[155] Jesus He Knows Me
[156] Driving the Last Spike
[157] I Can't Dance
[158] Never a Time
[159] Dreaming While You Sleep
[160] Tell Me Why
[161] Living Forever
[162] Hold On My Heart
[163] Way of the World
[164] Since I Lost You
[165] Fading Lights

Other Songs Recorded

[166] On the Shoreline
[167] Hearts on Fire

The five-and-a-half-year gap between the release of *Invisible Touch* and *We Can't Dance* was the longest to date between Genesis albums. Phil Collins' solo career had gone from strength to strength, including him branching out into film acting by playing the starring role in 1988's *Buster* (to which he contributed songs for the soundtrack) and making a cameo appearance in 1991s *Hook*. He also had time to write and record his fourth solo album *…But Seriously*, which topped the UK Album chart for fifteen weeks and the U.S. chart for four weeks following its release on 20 November 1989. Collins followed this up with an extensive world tour and the live album *Serious Hits…. Live!* a year later.

Also, during the hiatus, Mike Rutherford and Tony Banks each recorded two albums. Rutherford's Mike + The Mechanics released *Living Years* in November 1988, which reached #2 in the UK Album chart and stayed on the chart for nineteen weeks. The album's success was buoyed by the popularity of its title track, which reached #2 in the UK Singles chart and #1 in the U.S., where the album peaked at #13. Rutherford followed up in April 1991 with another Mechanics album, *Word of Mouth*, which reached #11 on the UK Album chart but this time stalled at #107 in the U.S.

Tony Banks tried to emulate Rutherford's success by taking a band approach utilizing singers Alistair Gordon and Jayney Klimek for his August 1989 release *Bankstatement*. When that album failed to chart, Banks reverted to a solo identity for his April 1991 release *Still*. Here he utilized a variety of singers including Fish, Nik Kershaw, Andy Taylor and once again Jayney Klimek, but this album also failed to chart. Both albums had strong songs, but the lack of a focal point and Banks' natural aversion to the limelight will not have helped their commercial prospects.

Genesis had briefly reunited on 14 May 1988, performing a twenty-minute medley of their hits, including some solo material,[1] at the Atlantic 40th Anniversary show. On 30 June 1990, the band reconvened for a performance at the Silver Clef Award Winners Show at Knebworth. The bill also included Eric Clapton, Paul McCartney, Pink Floyd, Dire Straits, Status Quo, Tears for Fears, Cliff Richard, Elton John and Robert Plant. Collins also performed with his own band who also augmented Genesis during their short set.

Genesis finally regrouped at The Farm on 13 March 1991 to start writing and recording what was to be their fourteenth studio album and their last with Phil Collins.[2] Banks noted, "When you come back together again, you're not quite the same people as when you left and you keep introducing new elements into the group. Once you've been back a few days you slip into it very fast."[3] The band were a little rusty at the start of the sessions, but quickly got into the groove. With the advent of the compact disc, the band realized they could utilize up to 73 minutes of material rather than being limited to the circa 50 minutes that vinyl allowed. Over the next two and a half months the trio worked on fifteen new songs and recorded fourteen of them. The lyrics were, as usual, divided between the band members based on their energy for specific songs. This time Collins picked up a larger share due to Banks and Rutherford having to absent themselves for promotional activities on their albums *Still* and *Word of Mouth*. In all, Collins was responsible for the lyrics to seven of the twelve songs that made it onto the album.

For this project, Genesis employed a new producer/engineer in 28-year-old Nick Davis, who had worked previously with both Rutherford (engineer on *Living Years*) and Banks (co-producer/engineer on *Still*). Rutherford noted: "We were very happy with Hugh [Padgham], we all like his work, but it was time to do something different."[4] Davis was assisted in the studio by Mark Robinson, with Geoff Callingham and Mike Bowen offering further technical assistance. The change of engineer resulted in a return to a more organic sound and for the first time the whole album was digitally recorded.

Banks acknowledged Davis' challenge for him to move away from his tried and trusted keyboard sounds. He had acquired many new keyboards in the years between Genesis albums including the Korg 01/W Music Workstation, Korg Wavestation, Ensoniq VFX, Roland JD-800, Roland Rhodes VK-1000, and the sampling E-mu Emulator III. Rutherford avoided using the guitar synthesizer and instead stuck to his Fender Stratocaster along with two Steinbergers, one of which he adapted with a larger body. He used a Groove Tube amplifier, at the suggestion of technician Geoff Banks, to get an earthier sound. Collins chose to dispense with the controversial electronic Simmons kit, which by this time was already beginning to sound dated with its overly synthetic sound, and largely use his acoustic Premier and Gretsch kits. The recorded tracks were mixed on the studio's 56-channel SSL 4000E mixing console and the band were delighted with their new sound.

The recording sessions were also filmed for a 46-minute TV documentary—*No Admittance*. The presence of a film crew in the studio proved to be stifling for the band and the final footage would broadly concentrate on interviews along with shots of them putting the final touches to songs. Little of the actual creative process was captured. Banks reflected, "Every time they were around, we did no creative work at all. Because you just can't. It's just not the way we work. As soon as they were there, we shut off."[5]

The band took a six-week break in the summer, before returning to The Farm in late September to complete the mixing of the album. There were some debates over the sequencing of the album, with Banks wanting to include [166] ON THE SHORELINE. As usual a democratic vote decided the outcome and the track was omitted.

The title for the album, *We Can't Dance*, was adapted from the track [157] I CAN'T DANCE and was the band's response to the proliferation of dance music in the charts at the time.

[154] NO SON OF MINE

Music: Tony Banks/Phil Collins/Mike Rutherford
Lyrics: Phil Collins
Length: 6:40
Tony Banks—Synthesizers; **Phil Collins**—Lead & Backing Vocals, Drums, Percussion, Drum Machine; **Mike Rutherford**—Guitar, Bass
Recorded and Mixed at The Farm, Chiddingfold, Surrey, March to September 1991.
Producer: Genesis and Nick Davis. Engineer: Nick Davis. Assistant: Mark Robinson.
2007 Remix/Remaster Release:
Mixed at The Farm, Surrey 2005/2006.
5.1 Surround sound and stereo mixes by Nick Davis. Assisted by Tom Mitchell.
UK Release: 28 October 1991 (A-side single/CD single b/w [161] LIVING FOREVER. Virgin. GENS 6/ GENDG 6. 12-INCH and CD versions add [143] INVISIBLE TOUCH [live])
U.S. Release: 29 October 1991 (A-side single/CD single b/w [161] LIVING FOREVER. Atlantic. 7–87571/ 7 87571-2)
UK Album Release: 11 November 1991. (CD/2LP: *We Can't Dance*)
U.S. Album Release: 12 November 1991. (CD: *We Can't Dance*)

NO SON OF MINE is typically Genesis in composition and is a great choice as the album opener. The song opens with a tick-tock metronome and a thumping bass drum heartbeat sound over which Banks plays a growling sampled keyboard sound, immediately creating a sense of menace,[6] while Rutherford's bass pulses on each beat beneath. This leads into a heart-wrenching song about a young man forced to leave home, because of the domestic violence he suffers at the hands of his abusive father, and his subsequent attempt at reconciliation. The track's atmosphere is set during its hypnotic opening verse as Banks contributes some straight sustained chords in the key of E minor, which build into a rousing chorus, heightened by his change of keyboard texture as the father denounces his son. The song rotates between verse and chorus before playing out over a repeat of the title lyric with a sing-along *oh-oh* backing vocals reminiscent of The Police. Collins' vocal delivery is both powerful and moving. The singer demonstrates his ability to bring an emotional authenticity to the lyrics. Collins explained the origin of the title phrase: "I didn't know what I was singing at one point, but Mike said, 'It sounds like you're singing *No son of mine*. In fact, I hadn't been singing that, but that's what it sounded like. Straight away there was a thread, a handle to hang the song on."[7] From that spontaneous phrase, Collins would formulate ideas for the story he wanted to tell.

Advertisement to promote the October 1991 release of [154] No Son of Mine, the lead-off single from the album *We Can't Dance* (author's collection).

The song works as both social commentary and an encapsulation of the more natural sound Genesis were trying to achieve. There is a gritty earthiness to the sound and arrangement that provides a counterbalance to the sheen of *Invisible Touch*. The band had recaptured the distinctive live feel that had been a feature of many of their earlier albums. The result is one of the strongest cuts from the album and a song all the band members were very proud of.

Single Release: No Son of Mine was used as the lead-off single, being released three weeks in advance of the album. It was backed with [161] Living Forever for the 7-inch version. A live rendition of [143] Invisible Touch from the *Invisible Touch* tour was added for the CD single format. The single reached #6 in the UK, spending seven weeks on the chart in total. In the U.S., it peaked at #12 and spent twenty weeks on the chart. The radio edit (4:41) removed part of the second verse and faded the outro a minute earlier. A second edit (5:44) for the 1999 *Turn It On Again: The Hits* compilation album just faded the outro.

Music Video: A promotional video was shot by Jim Yukich with the band performing among actors playing out the story described in the lyrics. The sepia-toned monochrome photography became a generational metaphor for the polar viewpoints of the father and son.

Live Performances: 1992, 1998, 2007. No Son of Mine would be performed on each of the three subsequent tours—in 1992 and 2007 with Collins on vocals and in 1998 with Ray Wilson taking the microphone.

Live Recordings: (1) A recording (7:06) from Niedersachsenstadion, Hanover, Germany, on 13 July 1992 was included on *The Way We Walk, Volume One: The Shorts*. The band was augmented by Daryl Stuermer (bass) and Chester Thompson (drums) on both officially available live recordings. This recording was engineered by Nick Davis and Geoff Callingham and produced by Nick Davis, Robert Colby and the band. The track was later remixed (7:02) by Davis and reissued *The Way We Walk* as part of the *Genesis Live 1973-2007* box set.

(2) A recording (6:57) from the 2007 reunion tour at the Amsterdam Arena in the Netherlands on 1 July was later included on the reunion tour's *Live Over Europe 2007*. The recording by Bernard Natier was produced by Nick Davis.

[155] Jesus He Knows Me

Music: Tony Banks/Phil Collins/Mike Rutherford
Lyrics: Phil Collins
Length: 4:16
Tony Banks—Synthesizers; **Phil Collins**—Lead & Backing Vocals, Drums, Percussion; **Mike Rutherford**—Guitar, Bass
Recorded and Mixed at The Farm, Chiddingfold, Surrey, March to September 1991.
Producer: Genesis and Nick Davis. Engineer: Nick Davis. Assistant: Mark Robinson.
2007 Remix/Remaster Release:
Mixed at The Farm, Surrey 2005/2006.
5.1 Surround sound and stereo mixes by Nick Davis. Assisted by Tom Mitchell.
UK Release: 11 November 1991. (CD/2LP: *We Can't Dance*)
U.S. Release: 12 November 1991. (CD: *We Can't Dance*)
UK Single Release: 20 July 1992 (A-side single/CD single/"Invisible Series" CD single b/w [167] Hearts on Fire. Virgin. GENS 9/ GENDG 9/GENDX 9. CD single adds [157] I Can't Dance [The Other Mix]. "Invisible Series" CD single adds [145] Land of Confusion [live rehearsal version])
U.S. Single Release: 21 July 1992 ("A-side" CD single b/w [167] Hearts on Fire. Atlantic. 7-82344-2)

The album's second track, Jesus He Knows Me, is a direct contrast to the opening song, [154] No Son of Mine, with its cynical humor and uptempo approach. This satirical song, which became a radio favorite through its catchy chorus and humorous lyrics, pokes fun at the TV evangelists who dominate American households each Sunday, demanding money to keep their faith worship programs in business (and themselves in the lifestyle to which they are accustomed). A fast and energetic song, its working title "Do the New One" suggests its basis was in the instrumental [151] Do the Neurotic from the *Invisible Touch* album sessions—Collins' drum pattern from that tune was replicated to form the basis of this song.

The opening musical phrase is not Rutherford's guitar, as one might initially suspect on hearing it, but Banks' keyboard. Banks explained, "Phil was playing really fast on the drums and I started playing a chord sequence on top of it. It didn't start with the bit you hear at the front—that came later. I started playing this reggae rhythm on top of what he was doing because it was in the same sort of tempo and switched to playing reggae underneath it, so we got the middle eight part, then the intro developed out of the middle eight. I think it works pretty well."[8] The change of rhythm for the midsection was suggested by co-producer Nick Davis, who put forward the idea of a contrast to the fast-paced straight 4/4 rhythm of the rest of the piece. Harmonically, the song moves between four keys with the verse written in E flat minor before ascending to D flat for the pre-chorus run-in then finally settling on A flat minor for the chorus with the bridge in G minor. The result is a song that sounds deceptively simple with its natural rhythmic flow disguising the more complex harmonic transitions within.

Collins' lyrics were again developed from an ad lib of the chorus phrase during a jam session. He explored the TV evangelist theme after the band had been left flabbergasted by the impudence of the preachers requesting their audience donate huge sums of money to their respective practices. While they had been on tour in the southern states, the band had witnessed the evangelists' domination of the TV channels in the U.S. Bible Belt. Collins modeled the character in the song around one specific evangelist—Ernest Angley.[9] Collins explained, "Whenever, on a Sunday I'd surf the TV if ever I found him, I'd watch for as long as he was on. He had the worst wig I've ever seen, and his accent was *the* most outrageous thing you'll ever hear. A complete character and I loved him. It was he who I impersonated on the video. The figure of 18,000,000 dollars was drawn from another guy who went on TV saying that God had told him to get that much by the weekend!!! The strangest stories are usually founded on truth. No 666 thing."[10] Banks noted Collins' lyrics were of a much more cynical nature than his usual output, which tended to be more heartfelt.

The song was always a candidate for single release and it performed well on both sides of the Atlantic, despite being subject to censure. It demonstrated the band's ability to skillfully marry rhythm and melody to the cynicism of the lyrics in creating an appealing pop song.

Single Release: The single is a slightly remixed (4:17) version with enhanced chorus volume and was released in July 1992 in various formats. This was the fourth single from the album and the primary "B-side" was the non-album track [167] HEARTS ON FIRE. Other tracks on the various longer CD single releases included [157] I CAN'T DANCE (The Other Mix) and [145] LAND OF CONFUSION (Rehearsal Version). The single reached #20 in the UK and stayed on the chart for seven weeks. In the U.S. the single reached #21 on the *Billboard* Hot 100 and remained in the chart for a lengthy twenty weeks.

Music Video: A promotional video was shot by director Jim Yukich. Each member of the band played the part of a TV evangelist—with Collins delivering a wonderful impersonation of Ernest Angley. The video, which was popular on MTV, was nominated for a Brit Award in the British Video category in 1993. However, it was banned by the BBC, which felt the video may cause offense. Collins was staggered by the action of the broadcaster, saying, "I can't believe they got totally the wrong end of the stick, because there was nothing in there that was offensive other than to those people who *should* have been offended by it."[11]

Live Performances: 1992. The band had noted the hostile reaction they got in the Bible Belt of the southern U.S. states and had originally decided not to perform the song live on the 1992 tour. Fortunately, their cold feet quickly warmed up and the song was ultimately included, allowing Collins to act out his evangelist performance on stage. However, the song would not be performed on any later tours.

Live Recordings: A live recording (5:24) from Niedersachsenstadion, Hanover, Germany, on 11 July 1992 was included on the live album *The Way We Walk, Volume One: The Shorts*. The band was augmented by Daryl Stuermer (bass) and Chester Thompson (drums). The recording was engineered by Nick Davis and Geoff Callingham and produced by Davis, Robert Colby and the band. It was subsequently remixed by Davis and reissued on *The Way We Walk* as part of the *Genesis Live 1973–2007* box set.

[156] DRIVING THE LAST SPIKE

Music: Tony Banks/Phil Collins/Mike Rutherford
Lyrics: Phil Collins
Length: 10:08
Tony Banks—Synthesizers; **Phil Collins**—Lead & Backing Vocals, Drums, Percussion, Drum Machine; **Mike Rutherford**—Guitar, Bass
Recorded and Mixed at The Farm, Chiddingfold, Surrey, March to September 1991.
Producer: Genesis and Nick Davis. Engineer: Nick Davis. Assistant: Mark Robinson.
2007 Remix/Remaster Release:
Mixed at The Farm, Surrey 2005/2006.
5.1 Surround sound and stereo mixes by Nick Davis. Assisted by Tom Mitchell.
UK Release: 11 November 1991. (CD/2LP: *We Can't Dance*)
U.S. Release: 12 November 1991. (CD: *We Can't Dance*)

DRIVING THE LAST SPIKE was the first long track on the album and was developed under the working title "Irish"—an image conjured up by Banks' choice of keyboard sound patch and his lilting melancholic melody. The ambience created prompted Collins to write his lyrical story from the perspective of one of the 19th-century immigrant workers from Ireland who came to England to work on the railways. He had been inspired by the book *The Railway Navvies: A History of the Men Who Made the Railways* by Terry Coleman (Hutchinson, 1965), which had been given to him by the actor Dennis Waterman. It was the first time Collins had taken on such an extensive lyrical task for a song, although he had previously provided a less successful story-based lyric for [133] ME AND VIRGIL. The singer was very proud of his work and his lyrics are undeniably moving and keenly emphasized by the musical palette.

The song's melancholy ambience was created by a soothing pattern from Collins' E-mu 1200 drum machine[12] and Banks' pan pipe-like synth motif. These are accompanied by a lightly played lead guitar part from Rutherford. The music evocatively conveys the lyrical story which outlines the extremely hazardous conditions the engineers worked in, resulting in the loss of many lives. The song does feel a little too long as the themes are stretched out over ten minutes with little change in mood, rhythm or tempo away from its traditional verse-chorus structure. That said there are some strong instrumental moments, notably Rutherford's dramatic slashing guitar chords at the end of the chorus and some energetic drumming from Collins throughout. Rutherford noted, "That end section, that driving section is really basic. There's the keyboards, there's the drums, there's the trashy guitars. There isn't much in there and I like that. It sounds like a band, which I think is good."[13] Rutherford's Pete Townshend–like guitar licks during the finale mirrored his approach to the end section of [91] INSIDE AND OUT as Collins acknowledged, "We've done that stuff before. It's just that nobody's ever picked up on it. The feeling was Genesis are not in there, they're not hard rock."[14]

On the lyric sheet in the CD booklet the band provided an introductory note which read: "In the early 1800s, large groups of mainly unskilled laborers built England's Railways. The cost in human terms alone was very high." A life-size bronze statue of "The Unknown Navvy" at Gerrards Cross station in Buckinghamshire was part-funded by a £3,000 donation from Genesis.

Live Performances: 1992. The song was included in the set for the subsequent tour only.

Live Recordings: A recording (10:18) from Niedersachsenstadion, Hanover, Germany, on 13 July 1992 was included on the live album *The Way We Walk, Volume Two: The Longs*. The band was augmented by Daryl Stuermer (bass) and Chester Thompson (drums). The recording was engineered by Nick Davis and Geoff Callingham and produced by Nick Davis, Robert Colby and the band. It was remixed (10:19) by Davis for the reissue *The Way We Walk* on the box set *Genesis Live 1973–2007*.[15]

[157] I CAN'T DANCE

Music: Tony Banks/Phil Collins/Mike Rutherford
Lyrics: Phil Collins
Length: 4:01
Tony Banks—Synthesizers, Synth Drums; **Phil Collins**—Lead & Backing Vocals, Drums, Percussion; **Mike Rutherford**—Guitar, Bass
Recorded and Mixed at The Farm, Chiddingfold, Surrey, March to September 1991.
Producer: Genesis and Nick Davis. Engineer: Nick Davis. Assistant: Mark Robinson.
2007 Remix/Remaster Release:
Mixed at The Farm, Surrey 2005/2006.
5.1 Surround sound and stereo mixes by Nick Davis. Assisted by Tom Mitchell.
UK Release: 11 November 1991. (CD/2LP: *We Can't Dance*)
U.S. Release: 12 November 1991. (CD: *We Can't Dance*)
UK Single Release: 6 January 1992 (A-side single/CD single/"Invisible Series" CD single b/w [166] ON THE SHORELINE. Virgin. GENS 7/ GENSD 7/GENDG 7. 12-inch and CD single version adds I CAN'T DANCE [Sex Mix]. The "Invisible Series'" CD single adds [146] IN TOO DEEP [live] and [135] THAT'S ALL [live])
U.S. Single Release: 7 January 1992 (A-side single/CD single b/w [166] ON THE SHORELINE. Atlantic. 7–87532/85906–2. CD Maxi single version includes I CAN'T DANCE [Sex Mix], [146] IN TOO DEEP [live] and [135] THAT'S ALL [live])

On Boxing Day 1985, a famous TV commercial, advertising Levi's jeans, was broadcast for the first time and became an overnight sensation. Its story, which is played out to Marvin Gaye's "I Heard It Through the Grapevine," is of a young man in a launderette stripping down to his boxer shorts, under the adoring gaze of two girls, so that he can wash his denim jeans. The ad and its many follow-ups provided inspiration to Collins for his lyrics to this raunchy song based around Rutherford's dirty Keith Richards-esque guitar riff.[16] Collins recalled, "The lyrics were set around the scenario of the jeans commercials, just suggesting some of these hunks may not have too much else going for them apart from the fact that they look great."[17] This may suggest a certain degree of jealousy on the part of the singer, but the fact he performed the song with self-effacing humor against his own plain image in the music video shot to support the song's release as a single suggests otherwise.

Rutherford had originally been working on the 16-bar riff under a working reference title of "Heavy A Flat." As this initial title suggests the piece was originally much more aggressive than the slowed down and dirty final version used on the album, but the band had struggled to add anything to it other than big keyboard chords, mirroring Rutherford's riff, and Collins' heavy backbeat. All three felt it sounded too familiar, being similar in style to [73] SQUONK. Banks, meanwhile, had been experimenting with the Roland JD-800 keyboard and its drum kit presets. He used this patch to start playing along to Rutherford's riff. Immediately Banks' quirky synthetic drum loop lightened the tone, opening up new possibilities for the track.

The band further developed the song using Rutherford's repeated riff as its base while adding a Traffic inspired "Feelin' Alright"–styled groove by Banks as he played straight major-key chords on the Roland VK-1000 keyboard using an electric piano tone. Collins added real drums at 2:47 following the third verse, which served to lift the song toward its climax. Collins' vocal inflections on the chorus are said to have been inspired by Roland Gift of Fine Young Cannibals, who had chart hits at the time including "She Drives Me Crazy" and "Good Thing." Nick Davis used a close-miked technique to record Collins' vocal using an old valve microphone designed to create a more intimate sound.

The band decided to keep the song simple in order to retain its quirky feel. Collins wrote the lyrics very quickly, while Banks and Rutherford were recording their musical parts. The result was something each member acknowledged they would likely never have tried on previous albums. Banks said, "When we actually put the song down, we put some more chords in but left it really simple. We put it down in a few hours. It shows a certain direction we could go in for certain songs, which is totally opposite what Genesis used to do in the past, which was to overblow a thing—take one idea and make it massive. This was taking an idea and leaving it really small and making it work."[18] Rutherford was particularly pleased having aspired to write a song based on a simple guitar riff for some time.

The result is a song that leaves the listener smiling. Its relative simplicity is its virtue and it stands out on the album for that very reason. It is atypical of a band more famous for long suites and dramatic instrumental sequences. The self-restraint Genesis imposed on themselves was admirable and again reflected their willingness to constantly challenge their approach. In general, the older fan base disliked it, dismissing the song as disposable pop. The rest responded positively to the humor and the robotic walk featured in the music video, to make this a unique hit in the Genesis repertoire. Rutherford noted shortly after the album's release, "It's the most radical song. If it wasn't Phil that was singing, you'd have to be told that it was Genesis."[19]

The song received a Grammy nomination for Best Pop Performance by a Duo or Group with Vocals in 1993.

Single Release: An obvious single contender, on 30 December 1991 I CAN'T DANCE became the second song released as such from the album. Again, this was in various formats ranging from 7-inch vinyl to CD single. The prominent "B-side" was the non-album track [166] ON THE SHORELINE. The CD single (#2 in *The Invisible Series*) included live recordings of [146] IN TOO DEEP and [135] THAT'S ALL from the 1986/7 tour. The single was a Top 10 hit on both sides of the Atlantic peaking at #7 in each territory, spending nine weeks on the chart in the UK and twenty weeks in the U.S. A couple of remixes, a partly interesting as well as mildly annoying vogue at that time, were included as B-sides. These included the "Sex Mix" (6:59) compiled by Howard and Trevor Gray and the "Other Mix" (6:00) compiled by Ben Liebrand.

Music Video: The promotional video was shot by Jim Yukich and was a send-up of the Levi Strauss & Co. advertisements—notably the 1991 ad set in a pool hall backed with The Clash's "Should I Stay or Should I Go." Genesis would become indelibly linked with the awkward robotic walk they performed in time to the rhythm. Collins also spoofed Michael Jackson's dance routine from his "Black or White" video by retooling it as a tap dance at the end of the video before being dragged off the stage by his bandmates.

Live Performances: 1992, 1998, 2007. The song was performed live on each subsequent tour (with Ray Wilson on vocals in 1998).

Live Recordings: (1) A performance (6:54) from Niedersachsenstadion, Hanover, Germany, on 13 July 1992 was included on *The Way We Walk, Volume One: The Shorts.* The band was augmented by Daryl Stuermer (bass) and Chester Thompson (drums) on both officially available live recordings. This recording was engineered by Nick Davis and Geoff Callingham and produced by Nick Davis, Robert Colby and the band. It was remixed by Davis for the reissue of *The Way We Walk* as part of the *Genesis Live 1973–2007* box set.

(2) A performance (6:11) from the Olympiastadion, Munich, Bavaria, Germany, on 10 July 2007 was included on *Live Over Europe 2007*. The recording by Bernard Natier was produced by Nick Davis.

[158] NEVER A TIME

Music: Tony Banks/Phil Collins/Mike Rutherford
Lyrics: Mike Rutherford
Length: 3:50
Tony Banks—Electric Grand Piano, Synthesizers; **Phil Collins**—Lead & Backing Vocals, Drums, Percussion; **Mike Rutherford**—Guitar, Bass
Recorded and Mixed at The Farm, Chiddingfold, Surrey, March to September 1991.
Producer: Genesis and Nick Davis. Engineer: Nick Davis. Assistant: Mark Robinson.
2007 Remix/Remaster Release:
Mixed at The Farm, Surrey 2005/2006.
5.1 Surround sound and stereo mixes by Nick Davis. Assisted by Tom Mitchell.
UK Release: 11 November 1991. (CD/2LP: *We Can't Dance*)
U.S. Release: 12 November 1991. (CD: *We Can't Dance*)
U.S. Single Release: 19 October 1992 ("A-side" CD single b/w [144] TONIGHT, TONIGHT, TONIGHT [live] and [143] INVISIBLE TOUCH [live]. Atlantic. 87411-2)

NEVER A TIME is the first of three ballads on the album and follows the tradition set by [139] TAKING IT ALL TOO HARD and [146] IN TOO DEEP by being well-crafted, melodic and seemingly effortless in execution. The song's flow further demonstrates how adept Genesis had become at writing winning ballads, but to some it felt formulaic. The band's confidence in the material was evident in the working title for this song—"B.B. Hit" ("B.B." as in "Big Big"). Genesis had in mind a U.S. audience as Banks noted, "This is what we used to call a rock-a-ballad. It's the shortest track on the album. I think the Americans will like this, but I know nothing about singles—look at my track record on singles!"[20] Banks doesn't mean to suggest the band were pandering to their audience, that is something they have consistently said they avoid doing, it merely demonstrates the band by now had become very comfortable at writing winning pop songs. This included love songs and break-up songs that connected with a much wider audience than their progressive rock roots—a forte that had become most associated with the band's charismatic front man. While there can be little doubt that Collins' solo success ignited interest from new quarters, it would be wrong to suggest the singer/drummer was the sole catalyst. The lyrics here were written by Rutherford, who also provided the lyrics to Genesis' first hit love song [102] FOLLOW YOU, FOLLOW ME.

Musically the song is simply and traditionally structured around a standard verse-chorus-bridge layout. Rutherford's lyrics cover familiar territory about how in relationships you never find the right time to say the right thing. While the song is undoubtedly well crafted, it also feels a little *too* safe—the kind of song the modern Genesis could churn out in its sleep. As a result, NEVER A TIME never quite realizes the grand expectations of its working title. It was never performed live and was one of just two songs from the album ([164] SINCE I LOST YOU being the other) not rehearsed ahead of the subsequent tour.

Single Release: NEVER A TIME was released as a single on 19 October 1992 in the U.S., the best part of a year after the album. Included with the release were live versions of [144] TONIGHT, TONIGHT, TONIGHT and [143] INVISIBLE TOUCH. The release served a dual purpose in promoting the forthcoming live album *The Way We Walk, Volume One: The Shorts.* The single reached #21 on the *Billboard* Hot 100 and stayed on the chart for twenty weeks. The song was also released as a single in Holland with the same track listing and the addition of a live recording of [159] DREAMING WHILE YOU SLEEP.

[159] DREAMING WHILE YOU SLEEP

Music: Tony Banks/Phil Collins/Mike Rutherford
Lyrics: Mike Rutherford
Length: 7:16
Tony Banks—Synthesizers; **Phil Collins**—Lead & Backing Vocals, Drums, Percussion, Drum Machine; **Mike Rutherford**—Guitar, Bass, Bass Pedals
Recorded and Mixed at The Farm, Chiddingfold, Surrey, March to September 1991.
Producer: Genesis and Nick Davis. Engineer: Nick Davis. Assistant: Mark Robinson.
2007 Remix/Remaster Release:
Mixed at The Farm, Surrey 2005/2006.
5.1 Surround sound and stereo mixes by Nick Davis. Assisted by Tom Mitchell.
UK Release: 11 November 1991. (CD/2LP: *We Can't Dance*)
U.S. Release: 12 November 1991. (CD: *We Can't Dance*)

The darkest and most atmospheric track on the album has a rhythm and atmosphere reminiscent of Peter Gabriel's solo material, particularly recalling "San Jacinto." This is most notable in the way the song generates a mood from its sparse arrangement and the use bass note progressions to emphasize the drama, particularly the descending lines during the chorus. The song begins with Collins' programmed rolling drum machine pattern—earning the piece its working title of "Rolling Toms." This sequence plays throughout the song and is dramatically punctuated by Collins' loud ambient drum fill which punches holes into the space left open on the entrance to the chorus. A bass xylophone adds further rhythmic drive. All this rhythm and counter-rhythm means Banks can hang onto his chords for longer and create an aural image of the mind drifting with the protagonist being lost in his own reflections. Rutherford's distant weeping lead guitar adds to the dreamlike feel. His power guitar chords also help to heighten the impact of the chorus over which Collins' angst-ridden vocal completes the performance. The music is well-matched to Rutherford's lyrical description of a man racked with guilt, having been the cause of a young girl's injuries in a hit and run accident while he achingly hopes for her recovery. It is a powerful lyric, one of the best Rutherford provided for the band, and helps make this one of the most powerful songs on the album.

Live Performances: 1992 (U.S. leg and UK theater leg). The song was notably played at theater venues in the UK to take advantage of the acoustics to maximize the mood of the song.

Live Recordings: A live recording (7:55) from Earls Court Exhibition Centre, London, between 2–8 November 1992 was included as one of the B-sides to the [160] TELL MY WHY single in the UK and the Dutch release of [158] NEVER A TIME. The same recording (7:48) was also included on CD2 of the *Genesis Archive #2 1976–1992* box set. The band was augmented by Daryl Stuermer (bass) and Chester Thompson (drums). The recording was mixed by Nick Davis.

[160] TELL ME WHY

Music: Tony Banks/Phil Collins/Mike Rutherford
Lyrics: Phil Collins
Length: 4:59
Tony Banks—Electric Grand Piano, Synthesizers; **Phil Collins**—Lead & Backing Vocals, Drums, Percussion; **Mike Rutherford**—Guitar, Bass
Recorded and Mixed at The Farm, Chiddingfold, Surrey, March to September 1991.
Producer: Genesis and Nick Davis. Engineer: Nick Davis. Assistant: Mark Robinson.
2007 Remix/Remaster Release:
Mixed at The Farm, Surrey 2005/2006.
5.1 Surround sound and stereo mixes by Nick Davis. Assisted by Tom Mitchell.
UK Release: 11 November 1991. (CD/2LP: *We Can't Dance*)
U.S. Release: 12 November 1991. (CD: *We Can't Dance*)
UK Single Release: 8 February 1993 (A-side single/Two CD singles b/w [143] DREAMING WHILE YOU SLEEP [live]. Virgin. GENS 11/GENDG 11/GENDX 11. CD singles add [111] TURN IT ON AGAIN [live] and [144] TONIGHT, TONIGHT, TONIGHT [live] respectively)

Poster issued to UK record stores for the single release of [160] TELL ME WHY in February 1993 (courtesy Mark Kenyon/The Genesis Archive).

Two years before the release of *We Can't Dance*, Collins had a major solo hit with the song "Another Day in Paradise," aimed at raising awareness of the issues facing homeless people living on the streets of our cities. He was roundly criticized in the press for his rallying call—apparently millionaires are not allowed to be concerned about the welfare of people worse off than themselves. His social conscience surfaced again in his lyrics to this song about the refugee crisis created by the Gulf War. Here, however, the musical backdrop is at odds with the thematic sentiments of the protesting lyrics. So, we hear Collins singing about hunger, starvation and the problems of the world against a shuffling uptempo backbeat and a "happy" jangly guitar, created by Rutherford's use of a 12-string Rickenbacker guitar.[21] The effect is both contradictory and jarring and the execution felt somewhat forced and fell a little flat. The band's intentions, however, were honorable and indeed the royalties from the sales of the single release were donated to the Bosnian *Save the Children* and *Red Cross* charities. Banks later admitted, "I wasn't totally happy with the lyrics for TELL ME WHY where I felt that Phil had covered that ground before, and I would have preferred a slightly less burdensome lyric, and he took it into a field where it didn't need to go and when he was just playing the instrumental and he was 'nah-nah-ing' his way through the lyric it sounded great and we thought it could have been the big single off the album but with that lyric it was just impossible to release it."[22]

The song can therefore be considered a misstep and one of the lesser cuts on the album. There was certainly a stronger argument for the inclusion of [166] ON THE SHORELINE.

Single Release: TELL ME WHY was released as a single (more as a social statement than a commercial one) in the UK and Europe more than a year after the album, on 8 February 1993. The 7-inch single was backed with yet another live release of [143] INVISIBLE TOUCH, while the CD single included live renditions of [159] DREAMING WHILE YOU SLEEP and [144] TONIGHT, TONIGHT, TONIGHT. The single peaked at #40 in the UK but disappeared from the chart after only three weeks.

Music Video: A music video, shot in monochrome, was compiled blending performance footage of the band with newsreel shots of starving families in Africa and homeless people on the streets.

[161] LIVING FOREVER

Music: Tony Banks/Phil Collins/Mike Rutherford
Lyrics: Tony Banks
Length: 5:41
Tony Banks—Synthesizers; **Phil Collins**—Lead & Backing Vocals, Drums, Percussion, Drum Machine; **Mike Rutherford**—Guitar, Bass
Recorded and Mixed at The Farm, Chiddingfold, Surrey, March to September 1991.
Producer: Genesis and Nick Davis. Engineer: Nick Davis. Assistant: Mark Robinson.
2007 Remix/Remaster Release:
Mixed at The Farm, Surrey 2005/2006.
5.1 Surround sound and stereo mixes by Nick Davis. Assisted by Tom Mitchell.
UK Release: 28 October 1991 (B-side single/CD single b/w NO SON OF MINE. Virgin. GENS 6/ GENDG 6.)
U.S. Release: 29 October 1991 (B-side single/CD single b/w NO SON OF MINE. Atlantic. 7-87571/ 7 87571-2)
UK Album Release: 11 November 1991. (CD/2LP: *We Can't Dance*)
U.S. Album Release: 12 November 1991. (CD: *We Can't Dance*)

A number of tracks on *We Can't Dance* saw Genesis take a distinctly cynical view of life, whether it be over the hollow sentiments of the male model advertising jeans ([157] I

CAN'T DANCE) or the hard-faced corruption of the TV evangelists fleecing the American public for money ([155] JESUS HE KNOWS ME). LIVING FOREVER is another example of this approach. Here, Banks' lyrics take a poke at how health departments confusingly preach to us about what is best for our wellbeing; telling us something is good one minute and then bad the next, thereby giving out mixed messages and creating mass confusion.

The hip-hop rhythm laid down by wire brushes at the start of the song is not played for real, instead it is a drum machine pattern programmed by Collins using an E-mu SP1200 patch called "Jazz Kit Brushes." The pattern, written in about ten minutes during a lull in the sessions, earned the song its working title of "Hip Hop Brushes." The verse-chorus segments work around Rutherford's staccato guitar chords in B flat supported by his pulsing bass and backed by Banks' reggae-tinged keyboard rhythms. At 3:03 the song moves into a light and pleasant, if unspectacular, instrumental section allowing the band to stretch out and play. For the first part of his solo Banks plays diminished chords on the Ensoniq VFX, which add a hint of menace. Then, at 4:12, he lifts the piece into major chord territory and changes the tone using a lead patch on the Korg Wavestation, which gives the piece an instantly warmer and breezier feel more in tune with the song's theme. The song somehow feels incomplete with neither the vocal nor the instrumental section catching fire. In fact, the latter feels more like space filler. As a result, the track feels insubstantial and is memorable primarily for Banks' witty lyrics and their topical subject matter.

While the song was rehearsed for the subsequent tour it was not included in the final set and has never been performed in front of a live audience.

Single Release: LIVING FOREVER was the B-side to the lead single from the album, [154] NO SON OF MINE, and was therefore available three weeks before the album's official release in the UK.

[162] HOLD ON MY HEART

Music: Tony Banks/Phil Collins/Mike Rutherford
Lyrics: Phil Collins
Length: 4:38
Tony Banks—Synthesizers; **Phil Collins**—Lead & Backing Vocals, Drums, Percussion, Drum Machine; **Mike Rutherford**—Guitar, Bass
Recorded and Mixed at The Farm, Chiddingfold, Surrey, March to September 1991.
Producer: Genesis and Nick Davis. Engineer: Nick Davis. Assistant: Mark Robinson.
2007 Remix/Remaster Release:
Mixed at The Farm, Surrey 2005/2006.
5.1 Surround sound and stereo mixes by Nick Davis. Assisted by Tom Mitchell.
UK Release: 11 November 1991. (CD/2LP: *We Can't Dance*)
U.S. Release: 12 November 1991. (CD: *We Can't Dance*)
UK Single Release: 13 April 1992 (A-side single/ "Invisible Series" CD single b/w [163] WAY OF THE WORLD. Virgin. GENS 8/GENSD 8. "Invisible Series" CD single adds [136/137] HOME BY THE SEA [live] and [82] YOUR OWN SPECIAL WAY [live])
U.S. Single Release: 14 April 1992 (A-side single b/w [163] WAY OF THE WORLD. Atlantic. 7-87481/ GENSD 8)

HOLD ON MY HEART is a slow, restrained and moody ballad with a sleepy "one-in-the-morning" feel. Banks contributes some seductive harmonies, effectively alternating minor seventh and major chords using the soft pads on the Korg Wavestation synthesizer during the song's opening. He uses bass notes that differ from the root of the chord to create an expectation of resolution, which is only achieved as we enter the verse. Banks notes: "the opening chords are pretty exotic, actually, and I crept those in without them really noticing what was happening."[23] The high-pitched melodic tone that rides over the arrangement resembles the sound made by stroking the tops of wine glasses with a wet finger and as such it cuts through the thick chords like a piece of citrus fruit. The part was played on the Roland JD-800 synthesizer keyboard using one of the preset patches. Banks' chord structure proved reminiscent of Burt Bacharach in approach and the song was given the working title "Burt" as a reference to the songwriter. Rutherford provides an understated bass part as well as adding a light rhythmic guitar phrase, the latter reminiscent of his work on his Mike + The Mechanics hit "The Living Years." Collins' drumming is light and sensitive, offering percussive color to Banks' sustained chords. Collins' vocal is also beautifully delivered, notably during the bridge where he authentically conveys the sensitive nature of the song's lyrics about being hurt in love and tentatively embarking on a new relationship.

Originally, the song was to be titled "Hold On to My Heart" but was changed when there were worries that it may sound like a medical song! At one point the band felt the song would not make the album, but once they had added vocal harmonies and overdubs, its standing was elevated as Banks recalled, "Suddenly, having been something like number 13 in the rankings, it came up to number three or four. It's funny how these little things can affect the way you listen to the rest of the song."[24]

A lot of criticism about late-period Genesis from the music press and fans of the band's progressive period was that there was little to distinguish their songs from Phil Collins' solo material. This view is clearly simplistic and to some extent based on Collins' distinctive vocal delivery and penchant for heartfelt ballads. This criticism also does a great disservice to the contribution of Banks and Rutherford. Here the chord structure and ambience are created by Banks, although admittedly he styled his chord sequence to get the best out of Collins' voice. Collins confirmed, "A song like HOLD ON MY HEART might seem to be one of my romantic songs but all I did was sing along to some chords Tony was playing. The chemistry between us was kind of magical."[25] The result is very much a band package and a gently sublime one at that. It is one of the band's very best love songs.

Single Release: HOLD ON MY HEART was released as a single on 6 April 1992 in the UK and soon after in the U.S. reaching chart peaks of #16 and #12 respectively. It spent five weeks on the UK list and twenty weeks on the U.S. list. The B-side was [163] WAY OF THE WORLD with live renditions of [136/137] HOME BY THE SEA and [82] YOUR OWN SPECIAL WAY added for the CD single release.

Live Performances: 1992, 2007. The song was performed on the subsequent 1992 tour. In 1998, with Ray Wilson on vocals, it was rehearsed but ultimately not included in the set. Collins returned to vocal duties on the 2007 reunion tour where the song was again performed throughout.

Live Recordings: (1) A recording (5:41) from Niedersachsenstadion, Hanover, Germany, on 10 July 1992 was included on the live album *The Way We Walk, Volume One: The Shorts* and in remixed form (5:52) on the reissue as *The Way We Walk* as part of the *Genesis Live 1973–2007* box set. The band was augmented by Daryl Stuermer (bass) and Chester Thompson (drums) on both officially released live versions of the song. This recording was engineered by Nick Davis and Geoff Callingham produced by Davis, Robert Colby and the band.

(2) A further recording (5:58) from the AWD-Arena, Hanover, Germany, on 24 June 2007 was included on *Live Over Europe 2007*. The recording by Bernard Natier was produced by Nick Davis.

[163] Way of the World

Music: Tony Banks/Phil Collins/Mike Rutherford
Lyrics: Mike Rutherford
Length: 5:39
Tony Banks—Synthesizers; **Phil Collins**—Lead & Backing Vocals, Drums, Percussion; **Mike Rutherford**—Guitar, Bass
Recorded and Mixed at The Farm, Chiddingfold, Surrey, March to September 1991.
Producer: Genesis and Nick Davis. Engineer: Nick Davis. Assistant: Mark Robinson.
2007 Remix/Remaster Release:
Mixed at The Farm, Surrey 2005/2006.
5.1 Surround sound and stereo mixes by Nick Davis. Assisted by Tom Mitchell.
UK Release: 11 November 1991. (CD/2LP: *We Can't Dance*)
U.S. Release: 12 November 1991. (CD: *We Can't Dance*)
UK Single Release: 13 April 1992 (B-side single/"Invisible Series" CD single b/w [162] Hold On My Heart. Virgin. GENS 8/GENSD 8)
U.S. Single Release: 14 April 1992 (B-side single b/w [162] Hold On My Heart. Atlantic. 7-87481/GENSD 8)

Way of the World, which was developed under the working title "Spaghetti West," is an uptempo song with its lyrically philosophical approach acting as a balance to Collins' lyrics to [160] Tell Me Why. It has an infectious melody and it is surprising the song was not released as a single. Collins sets up the Motown shuffle rhythmic base and Rutherford adds some nice prodding bass lines along with a guiding snappy guitar riff, while Banks provides lush keyboard chords and countermelodies. The verses are sparsely arranged, but the chorus urges the rhythm forward with additional keyboard layers. At 4:12, Banks gets to add a brief and jaunty solo that acts as a bridge, mirroring the way the band structured their first major hit, [102] Follow You, Follow Me. The lyrical message about needing a balance in the world was perhaps a little twee and simplistic. Rutherford commented in a radio interview, "It's good to try to put things right, but you shouldn't forget there will always be a balance of highs and lows in the world."[26]

Ultimately, this is a neat pop song, which nods in the direction of Motown, while retaining that distinctive Genesis feel. While the song was rehearsed it was not included in the final set for the 1992 tour and has never been performed in front of a live audience.

Single Release: The song was included as a B-side to the [162] Hold On My Heart single released in April 1992.

[164] Since I Lost You

Music: Tony Banks/Phil Collins/Mike Rutherford
Lyrics: Phil Collins
Length: 4:09
Tony Banks—Electric Grand Piano, Synthesizers; **Phil Collins**—Lead & Backing Vocals, Drums, Percussion; **Mike Rutherford**—Guitar, Bass
Recorded and Mixed at The Farm, Chiddingfold, Surrey, March to September 1991.
Producer: Genesis and Nick Davis. Engineer: Nick Davis. Assistant: Mark Robinson.
2007 Remix/Remaster Release:
Mixed at The Farm, Surrey 2005/2006.
5.1 Surround sound and stereo mixes by Nick Davis. Assisted by Tom Mitchell.
UK Release: 11 November 1991. (CD/2LP: *We Can't Dance*)
U.S. Release: 12 November 1991. (CD: *We Can't Dance*)

This ballad, written in 6/8 time, is given the Phil Spector treatment, inspired by the sound he created for The Teddy Bears' "To Know Him Is to Love Him." For his drum part, Collins also added an echo effect designed to recall Spector's sound. Rutherford contributes a bluesy Eric Clapton–like lead guitar part over Banks' plodding piano chords. The song is in fact dedicated to Eric Clapton's son, Conor, who died in a tragic accident while Genesis were in the middle of recording *We Can't Dance*.[27] Banks and Collins had written the piece of piano-led music as they were alone in the studio on the day the news broke. Collins used some of the conversations he had with Clapton, a close friend, to bring across the raw emotion of the loss of a child into his lyrics and he did not tell his bandmates of the subject matter until they had been completed. Worried the song may feel intrusive on the grief of his friend, Collins contacted Clapton to gain his approval for the song to appear on the album. The lyrics moved Clapton so much on hearing the song that he gave the band his blessing. On the final recording Collins delivers a heartfelt vocal performance in a high register, which sounds a little awkward, but is not lacking in sincerity and is genuinely heart-breaking.

Live Performances: While the song has never been played live by the band, Collins performed it with Brad Cole on keyboards and Daryl Stuermer on guitar for his VH1 *Storytellers* TV special on 13 April 1997.

[165] FADING LIGHTS

Music: Tony Banks/Phil Collins/Mike Rutherford
Lyrics: Tony Banks
Length: 10:27
Tony Banks—Synthesizers; **Phil Collins**—Lead & Backing Vocals, Drums, Percussion, Drum Machine;
  Mike Rutherford—Guitar, Bass, Bass Pedals
Recorded and Mixed at The Farm, Chiddingfold, Surrey, March to September 1991.
Producer: Genesis and Nick Davis. Engineer: Nick Davis. Assistant: Mark Robinson.
2007 Remix/Remaster Release:
Mixed at The Farm, Surrey 2005/2006.
5.1 Surround sound and stereo mixes by Nick Davis. Assisted by Tom Mitchell.
UK Release: 11 November 1991. (CD/2LP: *We Can't Dance*)
U.S. Release: 12 November 1991. (CD: *We Can't Dance*)

If [164] SINCE I LOST YOU is poignant for very human reasons, FADING LIGHTS is poignant for its hidden prophecy about the band's future. Lyrically, the song reflects on events that have passed and Banks' words can now be seen as a metaphor for the band looking at itself and believing this will be the end of an era. Collins had intimated in the Electronic Press Kit issued with the album that he had wondered going into the album whether he would still find fulfillment in the band—concluding that he did. But the seeds of doubt had been sown and would come to fruition just over four years later, making this the last studio album the trio would record together. Banks later admitted he purposely wrote the lyrics to fit that scenario, specifically wanting to end the song and the album with one simple word— *remember*. If this is the case, he did not inform his band mates at the time as Collins later recalled, "There was no hint of prediction as far as I'm aware of. Tony wrote these lyrics, but I think the idea is more global than specific."[28]

Musically, the song has a mellow and sedate atmosphere created by Banks' gliding synth pad chords, complemented by a gentle undulating drum machine pattern.[29] The song opens with Banks playing an ascending two-note chord sequence suggesting a climb to a peak. The chorus melody, again sung in a high register by Collins that stretched his vocal range,[30] has echoes of [76] RIPPLES… from *A Trick of the Tail*, which also had a theme of the passing of time. The execution, however, is different and there is a lively midsong instrumental, assembled from material amassed through three or four hours of jamming, with the three members interplaying beautifully for one last progressive hurrah. This section is led by Banks' weaving synth lines and big punctuating chords, using three different tones from the Korg Wavestation, and is one of the band's most memorable instrumental pieces. Collins propels this section along with some tight, crisp drumming and adding some of his trademark fills. Rutherford contributes some of his signature power chords over the bedrock of his rumbling bass pedals. It is a wonderfully dynamic and exciting section that exits by slowing back down into the song's original gentle arrangement for its prophetic final verse and last line.

Collins saw elements of old and new Genesis in the song, "I think as though the middle part could be called traditional Genesis instrumentally, the actual song part is very untraditional. I mean, I think that it's very rare that we hang on a couple of chords … well four or maybe five chords on a very simple drum machine and a vocal—it's rare that we do that and in some respects it has both ends that Genesis do."[31] The sandwich structure of the song is certainly typical of the band (see [42], [76], [136]/[137] and [177]) and the song proves to be a fitting end to its most commercially successful era, wonderfully capturing the essence of one of rock music's most creative and original bands.

Live Performances: 1992. The song was performed on the subsequent tour by Genesis as a trio, with Daryl Stuermer and Chester Thompson taking a break during the set. Collins delivered a stronger vocal performance in the lowered key used for the song.

Live Recordings: A recording (10:55) from Niedersachsenstadion, Hanover, Germany, on 13 July 1992 was included on the live album *The Way We Walk, Volume Two: The Longs*. The recording was engineered by Nick Davis and Geoff Callingham and produced by Davis, Robert Colby and the band. It was later remixed (11:03) by Davis and included on the reissue *The Way We Walk* as part of the *Genesis Live 1973–2007* box set.

[166] ON THE SHORELINE

Music: Tony Banks/Phil Collins/Mike Rutherford
Lyrics: Tony Banks
Length: 4:49
Tony Banks—Synthesizers; **Phil Collins**—Lead & Backing Vocals, Drums, Percussion; **Mike Rutherford**—Guitar, Bass
Recorded and Mixed at The Farm, Chiddingfold, Surrey, March to September 1991.
Producer: Genesis and Nick Davis. Engineer: Nick Davis. Assistant: Mark Robinson.
2007 Remix/Remaster Release:
Mixed at The Farm, Surrey 2005/2006.
5.1 Surround sound and stereo mixes by Nick Davis. Assisted by Tom Mitchell.
UK Release: 6 January 1992 (B-side single/CD single/"Invisible Series" CD single b/w [157] I CAN'T DANCE. Virgin. GENS 7/ GENSD 7/GENDG 7)
U.S. Release: 7 January 1992 (B-side single/CD single b/w [157] I CAN'T DANCE. Atlantic. 7–87532/85906-2)

ON THE SHORELINE is a strong midtempo track, which must have narrowly missed out on inclusion on *We Can't Dance*. Banks was disappointed that the song failed to make the final cut, stating in an online chat in 2008 that he felt it was stronger than both [164] SINCE I LOST YOU and [158] NEVER A TIME. Even Collins later noted the song had a "very strong, very Zeppelin-like groove to it."[32] One reason for its exclusion may have been the need to attain a wider variety of songs on the album. There are moments here that are reminiscent of other songs included on *We Can't Dance*: the reuse of the sampled "elephant sound" from the intro to [154] NO SON OF MINE and the two-chord guitar phrasing and earthy sound is similar to that Rutherford used on [161] LIVING FOREVER. Lyrically, the song is about choices and contains some typical Banks phrases highlighting the contrasts and balance in life. The song has a traditional Genesis feel to it and is driven by a strong vocal performance from Collins, who manages to extract emotion from Banks' literate words.

ON THE SHORELINE was included as the lead-off track on *Genesis Archive #2 1976–1992*. It would later appear in remixed form (4:49) on the *Extra Tracks* CD from the *Genesis 1983–1998* box set. The song also featured on the Edel label's compilation album *Earthrise II*, which was aimed at raising funds and awareness for the protection of the rainforests.

Single Release: Initially released as the primary B-side for the [157] I CAN'T DANCE single in January 1992. A promo CD of ON THE SHORELINE was distributed to radio stations to promote the *Earthrise II* album. The song was also released alongside Shane McGowan's "Silent Scream" and Stereo MC's "Creation" as a three-track promo.

Music Video: A promotional video documentary utilizing footage highlighting the destruction of the rainforests was compiled for ON THE SHORELINE and would be played on TV music channels.

[167] HEARTS ON FIRE

Music: Tony Banks/Phil Collins/Mike Rutherford
Lyrics: Phil Collins
Length: 5:16
Tony Banks—Synthesizers, Synth Bass; **Phil Collins**—Lead & Backing Vocals, Drums, Percussion, Drum Machine; **Mike Rutherford**—Guitar, Bass
Recorded and Mixed at The Farm, Chiddingfold, Surrey, March to September 1991.
Producer: Genesis and Nick Davis. Engineer: Nick Davis. Assistant: Mark Robinson.
2007 Remix/Remaster Release:
Mixed at The Farm, Surrey 2005/2006.
5.1 Surround sound and stereo mixes by Nick Davis. Assisted by Tom Mitchell.
UK Release: 20 July 1992 (B-side single/CD single/"Invisible Series" CD single b/w [155] JESUS HE KNOWS ME. Virgin. GENS 9/ GENDG 9/GENDX 9)
U.S. Release: 21 July 1992 ("B-side" CD single b/w [155] JESUS HE KNOWS ME. Atlantic. 7–82344–2)

Developed under the working title "Bass Botty," which describes the Calypso rhythm to the music, HEARTS ON FIRE sees Collins deliver his vocal in a dubious seemingly cod-Caribbean accent—reminiscent of his misstep on [138] ILLEGAL ALIEN, although here it is less obvious. Banks' sequenced melodic bass synth line is the heart of the song and is mirrored by his lead synth part. There are other nice moments, including a short mid-song instrumental bridge that is reminiscent of that used in [119] ABACAB. While pleasantly melodic, the song is a lightweight confection that feels like a B-side. However, it is fondly remembered by Collins, something he noted in the Electronic Press Kit for *Genesis Archive #2 1976–1992* but is one of the least well-known pieces in the Genesis catalogue. Banks, too, felt the song should have been on the album, along with [166] ON THE SHORELINE. The song would briefly be known as "Give It Up" and would be named as such on an Austrian B-side single release.

Single Release: HEARTS ON FIRE was the primary B-side for the single release of [155]

Jesus He Knows Me in July 1992. It was later included on the *Genesis Archive #2 1976–1992* box set and in remixed form on the *Extra Tracks* CD for the *Genesis 1983–1998* box set.

* * *

We Can't Dance was released on 11 November in the UK (delayed to avoid simultaneous release with Michael Jackson's *Dangerous* and U2's *Achtung Baby,* which were released the week's before and after respectively), where it briefly topped the charts. In the U.S. the album reached #4 on the *Billboard* chart. *We Can't Dance* duplicated the commercial success of its predecessor and became the ninth biggest selling album in the UK in 1992, confirming Genesis' continued popularity with the music buying public. It is a thoroughly competent effort, which doesn't quite reach the heights of *Invisible Touch* but still delivers a high proportion of quality songs. The album is a small step away from the more pop orientated approach of its predecessor, although it still has its share of hits. The music here, though, is denser and contains a lot more instrumental work. The CD format afforded the band more space to try out different ideas and soundscapes, something the trio were keen to exploit.

Nick Davis produced a thicker and more organic finish to the sound, which contrasted with the spongy, sheen-like quality of Hugh Padgham's work on *Invisible Touch*. This is most noticeable when the guitar is dominant. Rutherford found a harder edge to his aural dynamic and his use of power chords found more resonance. As a result, the album feels less dated today than either of the previous two albums.

This time around the hits were quirkier and contained a large dose of cynical humor on songs such as [157] I Can't Dance and [155] Jesus He Knows Me. The more serious [154] No Son of Mine was released as the first single and had a traditional Genesis feel and performed well in the charts. In between these more direct tunes, there were longer pieces, which allowed the band to stretch out, both musically and lyrically. [165] Fading Lights and [159] Dreaming While You Sleep both demonstrated the band's strength in this area. [156] Driving the Last Spike was less successful, but still contained some interesting musical passages and fine lyrics.

Due to heavy solo project promotion workload for Banks (*Still*) and Rutherford (*Word of Mouth*), Collins wrote most of the lyrics for the album—his highest percentage contribution to any Genesis album by far. Like Peter Gabriel before him, Collins would leave Genesis following the album containing his largest overall lyrical contribution. There was no sense of dissatisfaction from Collins—in fact, the opposite was true as he confirmed in a radio interview: "We've had our longest break between albums, and yet we've come back with something we actually like an awful lot, and we had such a great time writing. It was a very easy album to write, it came quite quickly, and we really enjoyed the process."[33] Nevertheless, *We Can't Dance* would prove to be the band's last album with their charismatic front man.

As was becoming the norm for the band, the response of the music press was mixed. Max Bell writing for *Vox* was unimpressed, "Musically the album is soggy and dull."[34] David Browne in *Entertainment Weekly* noted, "At a time when everything is uncertain … you almost have to admire a record like *We Can't Dance*…. You know there will be a couple of fleeting moments when the band breaks out of its torpor—for instance, on the very polite primal stomp of I Can't Dance—and that such moments will just as quickly be subsumed by the rest of the musical quicksand."[35] Karav Manning in *Rolling Stone* was a little more positive: "Although *We Can't Dance* doesn't quite achieve the vulnerable grace of *Duke* or the exuberance of *Abacab*, Genesis has nevertheless delivered an elegantly spare—and even adventurous—album."[36] In his review for *All Music Guide*, Geoff Orens offered his opinion that "the record was the band's strongest musical statement in over a decade."[37] J.D. Considine writing for the *Baltimore Sun* noted, "Although there are quite a few rockers who have been recording as long as Collins, Banks and Rutherford, few ever produce albums that benefit from those years of experience as much as *We Can't Dance* does."[38]

Genesis released two live albums following their 1992 tour with the umbrella title of *The Way We Walk* split between *The Shorts* and *The Longs*. In retrospect, these albums are a neat finale to Phil Collins' tenure with the band, although this was not the intention at the time. Rutherford noted, "Live albums don't require the same amount of effort as studio albums, in terms of creating the actual material, and so Nick Davis, with Robert Colby co-producing mainly did most of the hard work. They would set up the mixes, then I'd come in with Tony Banks mainly, as Phil was away for quite a lot of that time, and we'd assess the tracks, comment on them and usually say 'yep' and leave again, because it was just where it should be."[39]

Genesis had recorded three studio albums since their last live release and the set had changed radically. These two live albums highlighted the songs in the current set. The decision to release separate CDs was reached by the band finding the balance for a double CD set awkward. They rationalized that their fans were split into two elements; those who liked the hits and those who liked the longer more demanding tunes. The decision was therefore made to split the tunes accordingly and release the discs two months apart, a decision that would certainly have pleased the accountants.

Once band activities returned to a state of hiatus, Collins became heavily ensconced in his highly personal album *Both Sides*. When he was asked by Rutherford to take part in a charity gig at Cowdray Ruins, on 18 September 1993, he agreed but felt very out of place at the gig and it was this feeling that convinced him it was time to leave the band. His personal

From left, Mike Rutherford, Tony Banks and Phil Collins rehearsing for Genesis' 1992 tour. Virgin/Charisma promotional photograph by David Scheimann (courtesy Mark Kenyon/The Genesis Archive).

life was also going through more traumas with his separation and then divorce from second wife Jill. He confided his decision to leave to manager Tony Smith, who encouraged him not to make any final decisions for a year or so as the band was inactive at this point anyway. Indeed, it would not be until three years later that Collins officially announced that he was leaving the band once Banks and Rutherford had been looking to set dates for the next Genesis project. He had recorded his most personal album to date and moved to Switzerland to be with his new love, Orianne Cevey. Collins met with the band over lunch during 1995 to advise them of his decision, telling them he wanted to concentrate more on his solo career and his new life in Switzerland with Orianne.

Collins explained his decision a year later, "I love Genesis, but life was getting very complicated. The more success I had, the more success Genesis had, the more pressures and the more demands there were on my time, and I just had no time for anything else, no personal life. Eventually Mike and Tony and I got together in my manager's house for lunch to discuss it, and the guys were fine, they realized that it was over for good."[40]

Collins' bandmates were both saddened, but not surprised, by his departure. Rutherford said, "For anyone in a band, there's always at least a slight compromise. Phil has so much in his life, his solo career, his acting, other stuff he wants to do, and Genesis is always two years at a stretch with an album and tour. He felt it was time to move on. It was very sad, actually, but very normal."[41] Banks added his thoughts, "I was sad when it finally happened because Phil's a good friend and we've had a good time together. I think there was a degree of loyalty and I think he got something from Genesis. But there came a point where he no longer wanted to make a compromise. He'd become almost bigger than the band, in a way, like Peter had, and it's a challenge for everyone."[42]

An announcement was made to the press on 29 March 1996, stating that Banks and Rutherford had decided to continue with the band and look for a new singer. The header was typically humorous: "Genesis end twenty-year experiment. Decide to replace Peter Gabriel as vocalist."

Part 5

Their Final Bow: June 1996–July 2000

Tony Banks (Keyboards)
Mike Rutherford (Guitars, Bass)
Ray Wilson (Vocals)

From left, Ray Wilson, Mike Rutherford and Tony Banks. The final studio line-up of Genesis for 1997's ...*Calling All Stations*.... Virgin promotional photograph by Kevin Westenberg (courtesy Mark Kenyon/The Genesis Archive).

17

Studio Album #15: *...Calling All Stations...*

UK Release: 1 September 1997. CD/2LP (3-sides). Virgin. GENCD 6/ GENLP 6
U.S. Release: 2 September 1997. CD. Atlantic. 83037-2p.
Remix/Remaster Release:
UK Release: 1 October 2007. CD/SACD/DVD. Virgin. GENCDR3.
U.S. Release: 20 November 2007. CD/DVD. Atlantic/Rhino. R2 300092.

Album Tracks

[168] CALLING ALL STATIONS
[169] CONGO
[170] SHIPWRECKED
[171] ALIEN AFTERNOON
[172] NOT ABOUT US
[173] IF THAT'S WHAT YOU NEED
[174] THE DIVIDING LINE
[175] UNCERTAIN WEATHER
[176] SMALL TALK
[177] THERE MUST BE SOME OTHER WAY
[178] ONE MAN'S FOOL

Other Songs Recorded

[179] PAPA HE SAID
[180] BANJO MAN
[181] PHRET
[182] 7/8
[183] ANYTHING NOW
[184] SIGN YOUR LIFE AWAY
[185] RUN OUT OF TIME
[U186] NOWHERE ELSE TO TURN

The first and only Genesis studio album to be released following the departure of Phil Collins ended a wait of nearly six years. Banks and Rutherford got together for some writing sessions in 1996, shortly after the announcement was made to the press of Phil Collins' departure. The pair decided to test whether the group was still viable from a writing point of view. They were very happy with the darker and harder material they were coming up with and so the search started for a singer and drummer to replace Collins.

After going through the usual round of auditions, Banks and Rutherford settled on Scot **RAYMOND "RAY" WILSON** (born in Dumfries, Scotland, on 8 September 1968) to take over as lead vocalist.[1] Wilson had enjoyed a #1 single, "Inside," with Stiltskin—a sub-Nirvana UK grunge-rock band. Stiltskin's album, *The Mind's Eye*, became a UK #12, but proved to be their only album.[2] Both Banks and Rutherford had listened to the album on the recommendation of Virgin executives and were impressed enough to make an approach to Wilson. When Wilson got the call from Genesis, he was in the middle of writing an album with his new band Cut.[3] Having passed the audition, he was forced to postpone the Cut project and go straight to work with Banks and Rutherford to finish off the new Genesis album. Wilson was announced as the band's new lead singer via a press release on 6 June 1997 in which Banks noted, "We listened to hundreds of tapes, but Ray's voice really stood out. It had a quality that really moved me. His voice is thicker and harks back more to the earlier Genesis."[4]

In the meantime, while most of the songs for the new Genesis album had already been written, there were areas where Banks and Rutherford were looking for Wilson to contribute. They encouraged Wilson to ad-lib vocal melodies in the way Phil Collins had done. This resulted in Wilson contributing melody lines and lyrics to three of the songs on the album and another two non-album tracks.

The other area that needed to be covered was that of the drummer. While Collins' vocals had been a major part of the band's identity on their last few albums, his distinctive drums had been the rhythmic heart of Genesis since 1970. In many ways this was the tougher vacancy to fill. In the end the stick duties were shared by two session drummers, Nir Zidkyahu (an Israeli living in New York) and Nick D'Virgilio (who was in a band called Spock's Beard).[5] This was after touring drummer Chester Thompson had touted for the job on a full-time basis, but was knocked back by Banks and Rutherford who were looking to forge a new direction.[6] Zidkyahu ended up with the lion's share of the album and the subsequent tour spot. The band had both drummers play on all the tracks during the auditions and then chose what they considered to be the strongest versions. One track, [171] ALIEN AFTERNOON, included contributions from both.

Nick Davis was again on board as co-producer and engineer and he was assisted by Ian Huffam. The album was recorded and mixed between January and June 1997. In all the band recorded nineteen tracks, of which eleven made the final album cut and all but one of the remaining were released as B-sides.

[168] CALLING ALL STATIONS

Music: Tony Banks/Mike Rutherford
Lyrics: Mike Rutherford
Length: 5:46
Tony Banks—Synthesizers; **Mike Rutherford**—Guitar, Bass; **Ray Wilson**—Lead & Backing Vocals; **Nir Zidkyahu**—Drums, Percussion
Recorded and Mixed at The Farm, Chiddingfold, Surrey, January to June 1997.
Producer: Nick Davis, Tony Banks and Mike Rutherford. Engineer: Nick Davis. Assistant: Ian Huffam.
2007 Remix/Remaster Release:
Mixed at The Farm, Surrey 2005/2006.
5.1 Surround sound and stereo mixes by Nick Davis. Assisted by Tom Mitchell.
UK Release: 1 September 1997 (CD: *...Calling All Stations...*)
U.S. Release: 2 September 1997 (CD: *...Calling All Stations...*)

The album opener and title track was also the first song worked on by Banks and Rutherford in their writing sessions. The pair wanted a rock-based opening to emphasize a change in approach, having already hinted at a darker, less commercial album during the writing and recording. The duo set up a drum machine pattern and Banks added a tense series of chord progressions and together they began to develop the song under the working title "Katmandu." The song is unusual in that, despite its relatively simple structure, there is no distinct chorus. It opens with a blistering guitar riff from Rutherford backed by Banks' dark and brooding chords. Like [154] NO SON OF MINE, which opened *We Can't Dance*, the song is written in E minor. The drum machine rhythm was replaced by Zidkyahu's real drums on the final recording, but the physically played pattern retained the machine's hypnotic quality through not straying from simply holding down the backbeat. This effect was further emphasized by Rutherford's regimented bass line. Wilson's vocal performance is very strong and increases in intensity as the song progresses giving it much needed drive. A brief instrumental bridge features some of Banks' trademark odd synth sounds. Rutherford even gets to contribute a brief guitar solo from 3:30 to 3:54.

There was nothing particularly new or exciting in Rutherford's lyrics dealing with themes of isolation and loneliness as he recalled: "The phrase 'calling all stations' was initially about someone who was stuck out in the Antarctic, along, with his radio fading, trying to get a message through, and realizing it was a lost cause. It's about isolation. It always fascinates me that, in this day of amazingly increased communication, we're getting more and more isolated."[7] Rutherford also tried out various vocal ideas himself before Wilson had come on board. Once he had joined the sessions, Wilson was encouraged to repeat the vocal melody lines Rutherford had written, but quickly the band realized Wilson was more than capable of developing his own ideas. Banks remembered, "We were very much experimenting with his voice to see what we could get out of it and some melodic lines were better than others, so we shaped the melody very much around his voice."[8]

While its rather monotonous approach may seem to work against the song, it was seemingly intentional aiming to conjure up the psychological torture of isolation suggested by the lyrics. The song oozes atmosphere in the same way that [134] MAMA had done, but it lacks that song's progression to its heightened climax and ultimately falls short of that classic.

Live Performances: 1998. Like all the songs from the album that made it into the live set, it would only be performed on the subsequent show with the band augmented by Anthony Drennan (guitar/bass) and Nir Zidkyahu (drums).

Live Recordings: While there has been no official live recording released, a performance recorded during the band's rehearsals at Bray Studios in January 1998 was included on a five-track promo disc which was used as a handout to an invited audience at a later rehearsal on 23 January. Surplus copies were then used as a competition prize.

[169] CONGO

Music: Tony Banks/Mike Rutherford
Lyrics: Tony Banks
Length: 4:52
Tony Banks—Synthesizers, Backing Vocals, Drum Machine (?); **Mike Rutherford**—Guitar, Bass, Backing Vocals, Drum Machine (?); **Ray Wilson**—Lead & Backing Vocals; **Nir Zidkyahu**—Drums, Percussion
Recorded and Mixed at The Farm, Chiddingfold, Surrey, January to June 1997.
Producer: Nick Davis, Tony Banks and Mike Rutherford. Engineer: Nick Davis. Assistant: Ian Huffam.
2007 Remix/Remaster Release:
Mixed at The Farm, Surrey 2005/2006.

17. Studio Album #15: …Calling All Stations… 277

Postcard issued by Virgin to promote the September 1997 single release of [169] Congo (author's collection).

    5.1 Surround sound and stereo mixes by Nick Davis. Assisted by Tom Mitchell.
    UK Release: 1 September 1997 (CD: …Calling All Stations…)
    U.S. Release: 2 September 1997 (CD: …Calling All Stations…)
    UK Single Release: 15 September 1997 ("A-side" CD single and enhanced CD single b/w [179] Papa He Said and [180] Banjo Man. Virgin. GENSD 12/ GENSDX12. Enhanced CD single omits the two studio B-sides and adds [137] Second Home by the Sea [edit] and a music video of Congo)

    Congo is the most commercial song on the album, but it is also the most awkwardly structured. The song originated from a loop Banks had developed in which he combined different musical fragments and slowed them down. The result was two contrasting moods as the dark rhythm is overlaid with a happier melodic phrase from Banks' keyboard. Banks knew Wilson's voice would suit the bluesy melody line he had written. While it may have been well matched to his range, Wilson had doubts about the song: "The single Congo has never been my favorite song, I make no bones about that. It is a bit too quirky for me and I think there are better alternatives, but the idea was that they wanted to establish the band in rock radio, you know."9

    The song opens with African chants that are abruptly broken by a treated synth/guitar phrase as the Caribbean rhythm continues beneath. Wilson sings the song's verse with a bluesy feel as he describes a controlling relationship. Banks' figurative use in his lyrics of the Congo as a place of exile for the controller, where he can lead in any way he wants, feels more than a little forced. However, the chorus is one of the band's infectious best with its catchy sing-along melody. Rutherford's bass is hooked on E, while Banks rotates between E major, D major and A major. The midsong break, switching from E major to G major, works in a similar way to that used on [145] Land of Confusion, being based around a softer synth sound before breaking back into the chorus. The track then strangely peters out, losing its impetus with a third section returning to the introductory keyboard riff leading to a rather abrupt fade. The song was restructured for its single release by replacing this third section with a repeat of the chorus, but this only served to make the song seem even more repetitive without a lifting key change.

It was notable that like Congo the arrangements on many of the songs on the album would suffer from Phil Collins' absence. One of Collins' great contributions to Genesis had been his ability to keep the songs musically interesting, with a keen ear for what did and did not work.

Single Release: The song was the first single released from the album, in its edited and remixed form (4:03), on 15 September 1997. It was released in CD format only in two versions. The single also included the non-album tracks [179] Papa He Said and [180] Banjo Man. Congo would reach #29 on the UK Singles chart. In the U.S. it was released as a promo CD single only to radio stations.

Music Video: A promotional video, directed by Howard Greenhalgh, was filmed in Malta seemingly depicting a scene of industrial slave labor with the band dressed in long black coats and wearing sunglasses to look suitably moody. The imagery was more interpretive of the theme than a literal translation of the lyrics.

Live Performances: 1998. The album version was performed on tour with an extended solo section at the song's conclusion for Rutherford's lead guitar.

Live Recordings: No official live recording has been released from the tour.

[170] Shipwrecked

Music: Tony Banks/Mike Rutherford
Lyrics: Mike Rutherford
Length: 4:24
Tony Banks—Synthesizers, Backing Vocals, Drum Machine (?); **Mike Rutherford**—Guitar, Bass, Drum Machine (?); **Ray Wilson**—Lead & Backing Vocals; **Nir Zidkyahu**—Drums, Percussion
Recorded and Mixed at The Farm, Chiddingfold, Surrey, January to June 1997.
Producer: Nick Davis, Tony Banks and Mike Rutherford. Engineer: Nick Davis. Assistant: Ian Huffam.
2007 Remix/Remaster Release:
Mixed at The Farm, Surrey 2005/2006.
5.1 Surround sound and stereo mixes by Nick Davis. Assisted by Tom Mitchell.
UK Release: 1 September 1997 (CD: ...*Calling All Stations*...)
U.S. Release: 2 September 1997 (CD: ...*Calling All Stations*...)
UK Single Release: 1 December 1997 ("A-side" two CD singles b/w [181] Phret and [182] 7/8. Virgin. GENSD14/GENDX14. The latter replaces the studio "B-sides" with No Son Of Mine [live], "Lover's Leap" from Supper's Ready and Turn It On Again [live] from the album launch)

The sound of tuning a radio dial finally settles onto a slow repeated guitar riff before a wash of keyboards comes in to mirror the riff and open the sonic landscape. Shipwrecked, written under the working title "1965," is another break-up song built around the theme of isolation and is again well sung by Wilson, with the lower register ideally suited to Wilson's husky voice. The song came from another of Banks' loops, this time sampled from the short guitar riff from Rutherford. Banks had taken the riff from a 25-minute improvisation for another song being recorded in the sessions—[183] Anything Now. Banks clipped the riff from the digital audio tape (DAT) and programmed it into his Emulator. He then played this back at a slower speed and created the loop. A simply structured song (verse-chorus-verse-chorus × 2-bridge-chorus) was built around the looped riff and as such the song doesn't really go anywhere. Banks admitted, "We were a bit stuck with some of the elements in it so what we did was overdub slowed down guitars on it to make the riff itself a bit more prominent, but we still couldn't get it as good as the original loop, so the original loop is quite loud."[10]

Rutherford wrote the lyrics and developed a vocal melody that didn't quite satisfy Banks, who then developed a second melody. Ultimately, they used a mix of the two. While Wilson delivered a strong vocal, he was never fully happy with the song. Indeed, while the band initially included the song in their live set it was quickly dropped. Wilson later stated the band had found it boring to play, being stuck in its slow tempo and again without a lifting key change.

Single Release: The song was released as the second CD single from the album (in two versions) on 1 December 1997. It peaked at #54 on the UK singles chart before disappearing after only two weeks in the Top 100.

Music Video: A promotional video was shot by Greg Masuak and produced by the Oil Factory. It is another arty shoot with the band interposed into the story of a girl seemingly isolated from everything around her.

Postcard issued by Virgin to promote the December 1997 single release of [170] SHIPWRECKED (author's collection).

Live Performances: 1998 (Europe early shows). The song initially formed part of the set of their subsequent tour but was dropped as the band refined the balance of the show.

Live Recordings: No official live recording was released from the tour.

[171] ALIEN AFTERNOON

Music: Tony Banks/Mike Rutherford
Lyrics: Tony Banks
Length: 7:52
Tony Banks—Synthesizers, Vocoder; **Mike Rutherford**—Guitar, Bass, Drum Machine; **Ray Wilson**—Lead & Backing Vocals; **Nick D'Virgilio**—Drums, Percussion (first half); **Nir Zidkyahu**—Drums, Percussion (second half)
Recorded and Mixed at The Farm, Chiddingfold, Surrey, January to June 1997.
Producer: Nick Davis, Tony Banks and Mike Rutherford. Engineer: Nick Davis. Assistant: Ian Huffam.

2007 Remix/Remaster Release:
Mixed at The Farm, Surrey 2005/2006.
5.1 Surround sound and stereo mixes by Nick Davis. Assisted by Tom Mitchell.
UK Release: 1 September 1997 (CD: ...*Calling All Stations*...)
U.S. Release: 2 September 1997 (CD: ...*Calling All Stations*...)

ALIEN AFTERNOON's theme is one of displacement with Banks and Rutherford developing the song under the working title of "Paris" using a drum pattern Rutherford had created. Banks improvised three or four different parts on top of this and then honed it down to the two sections, the first being Rutherford's preference and the second Banks.' These sections were linked together by a bridging repeat of the opening refrain. The resultant two-part song is one of the strongest from the sessions. The first half opens with some atmospheric and other-worldly soft synth chords in D minor from Banks, reminiscent of his opening to WATCHER OF THE SKIES if not as powerful, before oddly clicking into the reggae groove of its verse. Banks' humorous "A Day in the Life" inspired lyrics help this section through to the bridge, with Wilson's distant distorted vocals adding an extra dimension. From 4:58, The second half of the song switches key to D major and features the protagonist encountering alien life forms embodies in the repeated catchy choral vocoder work over Banks' rising keyboard chords, Rutherford's slashing guitar and the punctuating drum patterns from Zidkyahu. Wilson's vocals soar over this section to give the song an epic finale.

Live Performances: 1998 (occasionally). The song was regularly alternated with [177] THERE MUST BE SOME OTHER WAY during the subsequent tour. It included an elongated second section which allowed for an extended lead guitar solo from Rutherford.

Live Recordings: No official live recording was released from the tour.

[172] NOT ABOUT US

Music: Tony Banks/Mike Rutherford/Ray Wilson
Lyrics: Mike Rutherford/Ray Wilson
Length: 4:39
Tony Banks—Synthesizers; **Mike Rutherford**—Guitar, Acoustic Guitar, Bass, Backing Vocals; **Ray Wilson**—Lead & Backing Vocals; **Nir Zidkyahu**—Drums, Percussion
Recorded and Mixed at The Farm, Chiddingfold, Surrey, January to June 1997.
Producer: Nick Davis, Tony Banks and Mike Rutherford. Engineer: Nick Davis. Assistant: Ian Huffam.
2007 Remix/Remaster Release:
Mixed at The Farm, Surrey 2005/2006.
5.1 Surround sound and stereo mixes by Nick Davis. Assisted by Tom Mitchell.
UK Release: 1 September 1997 (CD: ...*Calling All Stations*...)
U.S. Release: 2 September 1997 (CD: ...*Calling All Stations*...)
UK Single Release: 23 February 1998 ("A-side" CD single b/w [183] ANYTHING NOW, [184] SIGN YOUR LIFE AWAY and [185] RUN OUT OF TIME. Virgin. GENSD15/ GENDX15. The latter CD single replaced the studio "B-sides" with acoustic versions of [40] DANCING WITH THE MOONLIT KNIGHT [opening; live], [102] FOLLOW YOU, FOLLOW ME [live] and NOT ABOUT US [live])
U.S. Single Release: 24 February 1998 (A-side single/CD single b/w [111] TURN IT ON AGAIN [live from Cape Canaveral]. Atlantic. 7–84043/2–84043)

NOT ABOUT US is a largely acoustic piece,[11] with some pleasant playing from Rutherford and an orchestral sound to the keyboard accompaniment from Banks. It is the strongest ballad on the album and has a Crowded House feel to it,[12] while some of the instrumental work harks back to *Duke* in its arrangement. Rutherford's tasteful opening acoustic guitar chords in G minor lead into a simple verse-chorus structure. Banks wrote the chord sequence for the chorus and Rutherford the melody line. Banks finds room for a very short simulated horn refrain in B flat minor from 3:25 to 3:37, which then leads into a playout back in G minor using the harmonies from the verse. Wilson improvised the vocal melody lines during his second audition for the band and his improvisations were used in the first verse. Wilson recalled, "The song developed from a jam session. I always wanted to get the idea across that people should remember that there is always some-one worse off than themselves."[13] Both Wilson and Rutherford contributed to the lyrics, for which Wilson also noted, "I've always seen it as being we (human beings) see ourselves as being a bit too important. There's more than just us small, insignificant people on this Earth."[14]

Single Release: On 23 February 1998, the song became the third CD single to be released from the album in edited (4:04) form with an earlier fade on the first of the two versions released. The single only reached #66 on the UK Singles chart.

Music Video: A promotional video was shot by Shaun Broughton and is another moody affair, which atmospherically captures the song's theme and again features the band in long black coats.

Live Performances: 1998. The song was performed as part of the midset acoustic section with Banks joining Rutherford and Anthony Drennan on acoustic guitar.

Live Recordings: A live acoustic recording (3:35) from a performance at RTL Studios, Paris, on 13 December 1997 was included on the second version of the CD single. The band was augmented by Drennan (guitar) and Nir Zidkyahu (percussion). The recording was engineered by Christopher Hedge and produced by Nick Davis.

[173] IF THAT'S WHAT YOU NEED

Music: Tony Banks/Mike Rutherford
Lyrics: Mike Rutherford
Length: 5:13
Tony Banks—Synthesizers; **Mike Rutherford**—Guitar, Bass; **Ray Wilson**—Lead & Backing Vocals; **Nick D'Virgilio**—Drums, Percussion
Recorded and Mixed at The Farm, Chiddingfold, Surrey, January to June 1997.
Producer: Nick Davis, Tony Banks and Mike Rutherford. Engineer: Nick Davis. Assistant: Ian Huffam.
2007 Remix/Remaster Release:
Mixed at The Farm, Surrey 2005/2006.
5.1 Surround sound and stereo mixes by Nick Davis. Assisted by Tom Mitchell.
UK Release: 1 September 1997 (CD: *...Calling All Stations...*)
U.S. Release: 2 September 1997 (CD: *...Calling All Stations...*)

Written under the working title of "Jelly," IF THAT'S WHAT YOU NEED was, like [170] SHIPWRECKED, developed from a recorded loop. It is a soggy ballad that seems to drag following the more spirited NOT ABOUT US. Maybe it is because there is so much that is familiar about it, suggesting a lack of inspiration from the writers. Banks' lush keyboard chords in E major are reminiscent in feel of those used on [162] HOLD ON MY HEART. Rutherford's rhythm guitar styling again mirrors parts he had played on most of his Mike + The Mechanic albums.

Lyrically, the song is about how we often have difficulty in communicating with the ones we love, never quite saying the right thing at the right time. Rutherford's lyrics were written from his awkward perspective. He later confirmed "It's written to my wife. It's about communicating, something I'm terribly bad at. At home, I mean. She has practically to drag information out of me, and feelings and facts."[15] The song follows a simple verse-chorus-bridge structure with Rutherford's lead guitar more prominent on the second chorus. There is a change of key to C major through its vocal bridge (2:50 to 3:14), before it returns to E major for a brief keyboard refrain by Banks. The final chorus is lifted by Rutherford's evocative lead guitar, but while Wilson manages to evoke some emotion from the lyrics, this is perhaps the least interesting track on the album, being musically bland and lyrically unremarkable.

[174] THE DIVIDING LINE

Music: Tony Banks/Mike Rutherford
Lyrics: Mike Rutherford
Length: 7:46
Tony Banks—Synthesizers, Synth Bass; **Mike Rutherford**—Guitar, Bass; **Ray Wilson**—Lead & Backing Vocals; **Nir Zidkyahu**—Drums, Percussion
Recorded and Mixed at The Farm, Chiddingfold, Surrey, January to June 1997.
Producer: Nick Davis, Tony Banks and Mike Rutherford. Engineer: Nick Davis. Assistant: Ian Huffam.
2007 Remix/Remaster Release:
Mixed at The Farm, Surrey 2005/2006.
5.1 Surround sound and stereo mixes by Nick Davis. Assisted by Tom Mitchell.
UK Release: 1 September 1997 (CD: ...*Calling All Stations*...)
U.S. Release: 2 September 1997 (CD: ...*Calling All Stations*...)

We return to classic Genesis with this driving, dynamic song written under the working title of "NYPD" due to the fast nature of the drum machine pattern Banks and Rutherford had set up to jam along to. At 119 beats-per-minute this is indeed the fastest track on the album, being urged along by a sequenced synth bass part from Banks over some clattering drums from Zidkyahu and raunchy guitar chords from Rutherford. Banks adds descending chords and a repeated spiraling synth phrase in A minor at 0:49 before Rutherford's guitar transitions to E major for the first vocal section.

Structurally, the song has two key vocal sections, but no distinct chorus. Instead, between 5:41 and 6:29, we are treated to a drum solo over the programmed synth bass pattern. Zidkyahu is obviously enjoying himself on this track and his confident, aggressive playing for once makes you forget Collins is not on board. Wilson also delivers one of his best vocal performances, creating a passionate interpretation of Rutherford's lyrics about the borders that separate us, using problems in our cities as his metaphoric canvas. The guitarist recalled, "I was inspired by a cartoon drawing of a street corner, in a sort of *Mad*-magazine style. One side was dangerous, the other was safe. It's about rich and poor and the dividing line between the two."[16]

The song is one of the few on the album that feels complete, with it having a natural ending rather than being faded out like all the others. It is one of the strongest cuts on the album and would become a live standout. Banks summarized the track saying, "It has a great rhythm track, but lyrically, it's a little bit simplistic. Melodically, it could have been better."[17]

Promo Single Release: A radio edit (5:39) of the song was released in late 1997 for U.S. radio play accompanied by the album version and a live performance of [111] TURN IT ON AGAIN from the band's album launch acoustic set at Cape Canaveral on 28 August 1997.

Live Performances: 1998. The song would thrive in the live environment, with Rutherford and Anthony Drennan performing a lead guitar duel during the song's intro and Zidkyahu obviously enjoying his drum solo.

Live Recordings: There is no official live recording of this dynamic song, which may have pointed the way forward for the band had they decided to continue beyond this album.

[175] UNCERTAIN WEATHER

Music: Tony Banks/Mike Rutherford
Lyrics: Tony Banks
Length: 5:30
Tony Banks—Synthesizers, Backing Vocals, Drum Machine (?); **Mike Rutherford**—Guitar, Bass, Backing Vocals; **Ray Wilson**—Lead & Backing Vocals; **Nick D'Virgilio**—Drums, Percussion
Recorded and Mixed at The Farm, Chiddingfold, Surrey, January to June 1997.
Producer: Nick Davis, Tony Banks and Mike Rutherford. Engineer: Nick Davis. Assistant: Ian Huffam.
2007 Remix/Remaster Release:
Mixed at The Farm, Surrey 2005/2006.
5.1 Surround sound and stereo mixes by Nick Davis. Assisted by Tom Mitchell.
UK Release: 1 September 1997 (CD: ...Calling All Stations...)
U.S. Release: 2 September 1997 (CD: ...Calling All Stations...)

UNCERTAIN WEATHER takes us back to midtempo territory and puts us back on familiar ground. It has a very traditional Genesis feel to it, almost to the point of predictability. Developed under the working title "Answering 12," the song opens with a gentle drum machine pattern likely programmed by Banks underpinning his string synth line. Banks wrote the vocal melody lines and insisted Wilson stick to them. Ultimately, the singer delivers a Gabriel-like timbre on the chorus that does the song no harm in conveying Banks' reflective lyrics recounting the story behind a photograph of a young soldier who never returned from whatever war he was fighting. The soaring, powerful and densely arranged chorus, heightened by the transition from D minor to F major, is typical of Banks and plays against the soft and brooding verse. It is therefore reminiscent of the keyboardist's work on *A Curious Feeling* as well as [93] UNDERTOW.

The song also includes one of Nick D'Virgilio's strongest drumming performances on the album as he deftly uses the tom-toms to add delicate rhythmic punctuation to Banks' melodies. Both drummers had played on all the tracks during the recording and the band ended up selecting what they felt was best for each. Here, D'Virgilio's lighter touch won out. UNCERTAIN WEATHER is an emotive, if familiar, addition to the album, but was never performed live by the band.

[176] SMALL TALK

Music: Tony Banks/Mike Rutherford/Ray Wilson
Lyrics: Ray Wilson
Length: 5:03
Tony Banks—Synthesizers, Backing Vocals; **Mike Rutherford**—Guitar, Bass, Backing Vocals; **Ray Wilson**—Lead & Backing Vocals; **Nick D'Virgilio**—Drums, Percussion
Recorded and Mixed at The Farm, Chiddingfold, Surrey, January to June 1997.
Producer: Nick Davis, Tony Banks and Mike Rutherford. Engineer: Nick Davis. Assistant: Ian Huffam.
2007 Remix/Remaster Release:
Mixed at The Farm, Surrey 2005/2006.
5.1 Surround sound and stereo mixes by Nick Davis. Assisted by Tom Mitchell.
UK Release: 1 September 1997 (CD: ...Calling All Stations...)
U.S. Release: 2 September 1997 (CD: ...Calling All Stations...)

SMALL TALK has a groove reminiscent of Peter Gabriel's "Sledgehammer," despite lacking that song's distinctive hook. Wilson wrote the lyrics and vocal melody, having more of an affinity with the music that Rutherford and Banks had written under the working title of "Morley." Banks' choice of synth sounds somewhat dates the song, giving it a distinctly 1980s feel and he also uses an unconvincing saxophone patch over the top. Rutherford provided the simple guitar riff which formed the basis of the song. The chorus has a three-part vocal harmony which allows Wilson to explore his range, but the singer was never fully satisfied with the end result noting, "I thought I really like this, I hope I can write something worthwhile and I felt with the song I almost got it but not quite. It misses a hook for me. If it had one it could have been a great single bit it is still a good song and I am happy with it."[18] There is an interlude in which Banks provides a pizzicato string overlay, switching from the A minor key of the main song to its relative C major, over sounds of people talking, maybe in a bar. The song then fades as Banks adds lush strings and Rutherford a weeping guitar.

Lyrically, SMALL TALK was inspired by Wilson's experiences with Stiltskin of the insincere way the music industry treats its artists. He referred to this in a promotional interview, "It's got sort of a double meaning. There's the small talk of the industry, the small talk you hear everywhere in the music industry. It's riddled with people not saying what they mean and telling you what you want to hear. Which is what happened in Stiltskin at the beginning. Then when it started to go wrong, it hanged quite dramatically. And that coupled with the relationship angle, as well."[19] The song would not have been out of place on a Tony Banks solo record, but it felt a little incongruous on this otherwise largely dark and brooding album. While the song was rehearsed ahead of the subsequent tour it was never performed in front of a live audience.

[177] THERE MUST BE SOME OTHER WAY

Music: Tony Banks/Mike Rutherford/Ray Wilson
Lyrics: Tony Banks/Ray Wilson
Length: 7:55
Tony Banks—Synthesizers, Drum Machine (?); **Mike Rutherford**—Guitar, Bass, Drum Machine (?); **Ray Wilson**—Lead & Backing Vocals; **Nir Zidkyahu**—Drums, Percussion
Recorded and Mixed at The Farm, Chiddingfold, Surrey, January to June 1997.
Producer: Nick Davis, Tony Banks and Mike Rutherford. Engineer: Nick Davis. Assistant: Ian Huffam.
2007 Remix/Remaster Release:
Mixed at The Farm, Surrey 2005/2006
5.1 Surround sound and stereo mixes by Nick Davis. Assisted by Tom Mitchell.
UK Release: 1 September 1997 (CD: ...Calling All Stations...)
U.S. Release: 2 September 1997 (CD: ...Calling All Stations...)

A cavernous sounding drum machine rhythm, which may have been the inspiration for the working title of "Thunder," is prompted by a three-note bass line from Rutherford to open THERE MUST BE SOME OTHER WAY. Banks adds descending string chords in E minor, which are reminiscent of Mike + The Mechanics' "Silent Running." This become the basis for the verse, which is a gently sung affair about a broken relationship. As the song transitions to its chorus via some slashing guitar from Rutherford, an intensive pick up in Wilson's vocals emphasizes the anguish and frustration of the song's subject. The pained exclamation of the song's title was improvised by Wilson during the audition process as Banks and Rutherford looked to test prospective singers on their ability to create vocal melodies and ad-lib lyrics. The phrase was used by Banks as the basis for his lyrics. The song then breaks into a midsong instrumental section (3:58 to 6:05) with Banks providing a neat, if familiar, synth solo that is reminiscent of the one he played on [165] FADING LIGHTS. It was his only extended solo on the album. The song then settles back into a reprise of the first section using the sandwich structure the band had employed several times throughout its catalogue. Not surprisingly, the song proved to be one of Banks' favorites from the album and while it plays to his strengths there is little here that feels new.

Live Performances: 1998. The song would be played regularly on the band's subsequent tour, occasionally being alternated with [171] ALIEN AFTERNOON.

Live Recordings: No official live recording of the song has been released.

[178] ONE MAN'S FOOL

Music: Tony Banks/Mike Rutherford
Lyrics: Tony Banks
Length: 8:46
Tony Banks—Synthesizers, Backing Vocals, Drum Machine (?); **Mike Rutherford**—Guitar, Bass, Backing Vocals, Drum Machine (?); **Ray Wilson**—Lead & Backing Vocals; **Nir Zidkyahu**—Drums, Percussion
Recorded and Mixed at The Farm, Chiddingfold, Surrey, January to June 1997.
Producer: Nick Davis, Tony Banks and Mike Rutherford. Engineer: Nick Davis. Assistant: Ian Huffam.
2007 Remix/Remaster Release:
Mixed at The Farm, Surrey 2005/2006.
5.1 Surround sound and stereo mixes by Nick Davis. Assisted by Tom Mitchell.
UK Release: 1 September 1997 (CD: *...Calling All Stations...*)
U.S. Release: 2 September 1997 (CD: *...Calling All Stations...*)

At close to nine minutes, ONE MAN'S FOOL is the longest track on the album and makes for a fine closer. Like the earlier [171] ALIEN AFTERNOON, it is a two-part song. Lyrically, it was inspired by the impacts of the Manchester bombing by the IRA in 1996. Banks' concept for the first section is that terrorists are too distanced from their victims to care about the results of their actions. For the second section Banks noted he "extends the idea a bit further really, dealing with certainty, people who are certain about things; how can you be so sure? I have always had a mistrust of certainty and the second half really deals with that, but it deals with it really in a more philosophical manner so it's less personal, it's less intense."[20] The themes have increased in significance in the post–9/11 world and the 2017 bomb at the Manchester Arena.

The song was developed under the working title of "Breathless." It opens with a pattering drum machine rhythm over which Banks adds some soft pad chords and Wilson provides evocative vocals. Zidkyahu's drums enter to signal the chorus with Banks switching to a brass sound as Rutherford's bass bubbles away underneath. After the verse and chorus rotating three times up to 3:48, the song changes dynamic. At 4:24 the key lifts from E flat minor to E flat major and the song enters its final, and musically joyous section. Rutherford's rhythm guitar adds to the urgency and Banks' rotating descending chords keep the section on course. Zidkyahu's drumming provides a heavy backbeat before doubling the beat from 7:03 as the play out increases in intensity and alternates between E flat major and F sharp major. The song has an anthemic close with Wilson lamenting his dreams over a repeated vocal phrase. Banks felt this was an area where Wilson lacked the emotion that Collins or Gabriel would have brought to the end section, noting, "If Phil had been there, I just know it would have taken off and gone somewhere else."[21] Nevertheless, the song, is one of the strongest on the album, despite never being performed live by the band.

* * *

Eight further tracks were recorded during the sessions, with seven of them released as "B-sides" across the three CD singles from the album. Other music worked on during the sessions but never surfacing went under the working titles of "Soft Delight," "Scotties," "Groan" (parts 1, 2 and 3—part 2 of which emerged as [168] CALLING ALL STATIONS and part 3 was later titled "Fast Echo").

[179] PAPA HE SAID

Music: Tony Banks/Mike Rutherford
Lyrics: Mike Rutherford
Length: 4:07
Tony Banks—Synthesizers; **Mike Rutherford**—Guitar, Bass; **Ray Wilson**—Lead & Backing Vocals; **Nir Zidkyahu** (?)—Drums, Percussion
Recorded and Mixed at The Farm, Chiddingfold, Surrey, January to June 1997.
Producer: Nick Davis, Tony Banks and Mike Rutherford. Engineer: Nick Davis. Assistant: Ian Huffam.
UK Release: 15 September 1997 ("B-side" CD single b/w [169] CONGO and c/w [180] BANJO MAN. Virgin. GENSD 12)

This throwaway song has its basis in Rutherford's Keith Richards–like guitar riff. The song alternates between the keys of B flat major and A minor, keys in which Wilson seems quite at home with his vocal delivery. However, the result is a song that is generally unsurprising and bland. Written under the working title "Tele," it carries a more organic sound than other songs recorded in the sessions with Rutherford's dirty sounding rhythm guitar and Banks' use of the organ patch giving the sound an organic feel. While not documented, it is likely Zidkyahu was the drummer used here and he introduces a cow bell to his percussion, adding to the Stones-like feel of the song. Lyrically, PAPA HE SAID potentially has dark undertones potentially relating to an abusive or domineering parent.

Single Release: The song was included on the CD single release of [169] CONGO, but not the *Genesis 1983–1998* box set.

[180] BANJO MAN

Music: Tony Banks/Mike Rutherford
Lyrics: Ray Wilson
Length: 4:21
Tony Banks—Synthesizers; **Mike Rutherford**—Guitar, Bass; **Ray Wilson**—Lead & Backing Vocals; **Nir Zidkyahu** (?)—Drums, Percussion
Recorded and Mixed at The Farm, Chiddingfold, Surrey, January to June 1997.
Producer: Nick Davis, Tony Banks and Mike Rutherford. Engineer: Nick Davis. Assistant: Ian Huffam.
UK Release: 15 September 1997 ("B-side" CD single b/w [169] CONGO and c/w [179] PAPA HE SAID. Virgin. GENSD 12)

BANJO MAN is a jaunty piece with Banks using a synth patch to simulate the banjo of the title as Wilson sings about an out-of-luck busker dreaming of the big time. The vocal is delivered in a high register in the key of B minor making Wilson sound uncannily like Sting in places. The song is not in character with the darker nature of the other material recorded during the sessions and is therefore an obvious leftover. Its quirky delivery is akin to that of [90] Pigeons, recorded during the *Wind & Wuthering* sessions, and while it makes the song distinctive there is little here that suggests it ever seriously challenged for a position on the album. Wilson was not a fan of the song despite having written the lyrics. Banks also commented later, "things like Banjo Man and a couple of others, we just felt were not really up there."22

Single Release: The song was included on the CD single release of [169] Congo but, like most of the leftovers from these sessions, not the *Genesis 1983–1998* box set.

[181] Phret

Music: Tony Banks/Mike Rutherford
Length: 4:06
Tony Banks—Synthesizers, Synth Bass; **Mike Rutherford**—Guitar, Bass; **Nick D'Virgilio**—Drums, Percussion
Recorded and Mixed at The Farm, Chiddingfold, Surrey, January to June 1997.
Producer: Nick Davis, Tony Banks and Mike Rutherford. Engineer: Nick Davis. Assistant: Ian Huffam.
UK Release: 1 December 1997 ("B-side" CD single b/w [170] Shipwrecked and c/w [182] 7/8. Virgin. GENSD14)

Another instrumental that retained its working title inspired by the melodic fretless bass line that provides the main hook of the track. The sound was played on the keyboard by Banks, who also adds some nice chiming synth sounds. Rutherford's accompanying rhythm guitar part helps give the tune a kind of Christmas seasonal feel. Alternating between G major and G minor keys the piece has two key parts, the first a quiet section with the second forming the main basis of the track adding D'Virgilio's drums into the mix. Ultimately, this insipid instrumental feels like a demo or backing track for a song that was never fully developed.

Single Release: The track was included on the CD single release of [170] Shipwrecked, but not the *Genesis 1983–1998* box set.

[182] 7/8

Music: Tony Banks/Mike Rutherford
Length: 5:08
Tony Banks—Electric Grand Piano, Synthesizers; **Mike Rutherford**—Guitar, Bass; **Nick D'Virgilio**—Drums, Percussion
Recorded and Mixed at The Farm, Chiddingfold, Surrey, January to June 1997.
Producer: Nick Davis, Tony Banks and Mike Rutherford. Engineer: Nick Davis. Assistant: Ian Huffam.
UK Release: 1 December 1997 ("B-side" CD single b/w [170] Shipwrecked and c/w [181] Phret. Virgin. GENSD14)

Following the time signature of its title, which was derived from Rutherford's guitar phrasing, this instrumental has some nice passages and surges, but lacks any distinctive hook. The piece is structured into three distinct parts in three different keys (E minor, G major and D minor), suggesting it was pasted together from separate jam sessions. Banks mirrors Rutherford's phrase with Rutherford then switching to rhythm guitar. Banks adds a piano to the second section from 1:18 to 1:57, while D'Virgilio contributes some effective drumming with good use of cymbals to emphasize Banks and Rutherford's musical interplay. Like [181] Phret, this is a track that feels as if it is incomplete and would potentially benefit from the addition of a vocal part or an overriding melody.

Single Release: The track was also included on the CD single release of [170] Shipwrecked, but not the *Genesis 1983–1998* box set.

[183] Anything Now

Music: Tony Banks/Mike Rutherford
Lyrics: Tony Banks
Length: 7:02
Tony Banks—Electric Grand Piano, Synthesizers; **Mike Rutherford**—Guitar, Bass, Bass Pedals; **Ray Wilson**—Lead & Backing Vocals; **Nir Zidkyahu**—Drums, Percussion
Recorded and Mixed at The Farm, Chiddingfold, Surrey, January to June 1997.
Producer: Nick Davis, Tony Banks and Mike Rutherford. Engineer: Nick Davis. Assistant: Ian Huffam.
2007 Remix/Remaster Release:
Mixed at The Farm, Surrey 2005/2006.
5.1 Surround sound and stereo mixes by Nick Davis. Assisted by Tom Mitchell.
UK Release: 23 February 1998 ("B-side" CD single b/w [172] Not About Us, c/w [184] Sign Your Life Away and [185] Run Out of Time. Virgin. GENSD15)
U.S. Release: 20 November 2007 (5-CD: *Genesis 1983–1998* Extra Tracks CD)

This is one of the strongest leftovers from the recording sessions, originally developed under the working title "Big Boy." It is an uptempo number with some nice guitar/keyboard phrases and interplay urged along by Rutherford's pulsing bass pedals before he switches to a more melodic fretless for the verse. The song's verse and chorus are reminiscent of the sound Rutherford would look for on a Mike + The Mechanics track. It is mainly written in B minor with sections switching to B major. The chorus is very catchy, although Wilson's vocal delivery is flat and lacking in emotional resonance. This was the major reason for the song's exclusion from the album as Banks noted, "we couldn't quite get Ray to sing it right. The piano solo in the middle is very unlike anything we've ever done. I would have loved to have it on there, but the vocal wasn't up to scratch."[23] At 3:48 to 5:45, the song breaks into an instrumental section with Banks contributing the aforementioned jazzy piano chords using the CP-70E electric grand before Zidkyahu picks up the tempo again to steer the band back into the main song. The optimistic tone of the lyrics endows Anything Now with a more positive outlook than much of the material eventually used on the album.

Single Release: The song was included as part of the CD single release of [172] Not About Us with two other non-album tracks ([184] and [185]). It would also be later included in remixed form [7:03] on the Extra Tracks CD of the *Genesis 1983–1998* box set.

[184] Sign Your Life Away

Music: Tony Banks/Mike Rutherford
Lyrics: Mike Rutherford
Length: 4:44
Tony Banks—Synthesizers; **Mike Rutherford**—Guitar, Guitar Synthesizer, Bass; **Ray Wilson**—Lead & Backing Vocals; **Nick D'Virgilio**—Drums, Percussion
Recorded and Mixed at The Farm, Chiddingfold, Surrey, January to June 1997.
Producer: Nick Davis, Tony Banks and Mike Rutherford. Engineer: Nick Davis. Assistant: Ian Huffam.
2007 Remix/Remaster Release:

Mixed at The Farm, Surrey 2005/2006.
5.1 Surround sound and stereo mixes by Nick Davis. Assisted by Tom Mitchell.
UK Release: 23 February 1998 ("B-side" CD single b/w [172] NOT ABOUT US, c/w [183] ANYTHING NOW and [185] RUN OUT OF TIME. Virgin. GENSD15)
U.S. Release: 20 November 2007 (5-CD: *Genesis 1983–1998* Extra Tracks CD)

This fast-paced straight-ahead Rutherford led guitar rocker is uncharacteristic of the band. It is a lyrically cynical song that explores how people in positions of power mislead those who depend on them. The song opens with a siren-like sound from Rutherford's guitar and a strong backbeat from D'Virgilio.[24] Banks' arpeggios on the verse give the song a musical contrast. SIGN YOUR LIFE AWAY is aggressive in contrast to the general midtempo feel of the rest of the songs recorded during the sessions. Wilson seems much more at home as he delivers a stronger vocal here compared to his less than assured performance on tracks like [183] ANYTHING NOW. A two-part bridge from 3:05 to 3:44, sees the second part allow space for Rutherford to provide a distorted guitar riff. The song did at least offer something different and added contrast to the generally midtempo approach to many of the songs written for the album.

Single Release: The song was one of three non-album tracks included as part of the CD single release of [172] NOT ABOUT US. It would also be later included in remixed form [4:45] on the *Extra Tracks* CD of the *Genesis 1983–1998* box set.

[185] RUN OUT OF TIME

Music: Tony Banks/Mike Rutherford
Lyrics: Tony Banks (?)
Length: 6:35
Tony Banks—Synthesizers; **Mike Rutherford**—Guitar, Bass; **Ray Wilson**—Lead & Backing Vocals; **Nir Zidkyahu**—Drums, Percussion
Recorded and Mixed at The Farm, Chiddingfold, Surrey, January to June 1997.
Producer: Nick Davis, Tony Banks and Mike Rutherford. Engineer: Nick Davis. Assistant: Ian Huffam.
2007 Remix/Remaster Release:
Mixed at The Farm, Surrey 2005/2006
5.1 Surround sound and stereo mixes by Nick Davis. Assisted by Tom Mitchell.
UK Release: 23 February 1998 ("B-side" CD single b/w [172] NOT ABOUT US, c/w [183] ANYTHING NOW and [184] SIGN YOUR LIFE AWAY. Virgin. GENSD15)
U.S. Release: 20 November 2007 (5-CD: *Genesis 1983–1998* Extra Tracks CD)

The dark and brooding sound Banks and Rutherford had been looking for during the sessions is no more evident than on this long ballad, which surprisingly failed to make the album. Banks' haunting opening sax patch[25] in G minor gives the track a late evening-feel emphasized by the accompanying world-weary lyric, effectively delivered by Wilson. Banks is at his experimental best in his use of harmonies, notably during the transition from verse to chorus transitioning from B flat major to G minor. The song builds into a wonderfully evocative bridge, which is full of Banks' trademark chord progressions. While moody and evocative, the song is perhaps a tad overlong.[26] Judging by its lyrical style, the words to this song were most likely written by Banks.

Single Release: The song was one of three non-album tracks included as part of the CD single release of [172] NOT ABOUT US. It would also be later included in remixed form with a more sensitive fade-out [6:31] on the *Extra Tracks* CD of the *Genesis 1983–1998* box set. Another edit of the song (4:40) was included on a four-track disc circulated to Virgin executives as a selection of B-sides.

[U186] Nowhere Else to Turn

Music: Tony Banks/Mike Rutherford
Lyrics: Ray Wilson
Length: 4:31
Tony Banks—Synthesizers; **Mike Rutherford**—Guitar, Bass; **Ray Wilson**—Lead & Backing Vocals; **Nir Zidkyahu**—Drums, Percussion
Recorded and Mixed at The Farm, Chiddingfold, Surrey, January to June 1997.
Producer: Nick Davis, Tony Banks and Mike Rutherford. Engineer: Nick Davis. Assistant: Ian Huffam
UK/U.S. Release: Unreleased.

This is another track that is reminiscent of Mike + The Mechanics, with its guitar riff driven catchy chorus and Rutherford's trademark rhythm guitar. Banks adds synth chords underneath but there is little here to get excited about. During the writing process the song was progressed under the working titles "Rosin" and "Cold Winter's Night." Wilson contributed the lyrics about yet another broken relationship where the protagonist is desperate to patch things up, if only for one night. Musically the song is unremarkable and was understandably omitted from the album. When later asked about this Wilson replied, "I don't know why it wasn't used. A money thing, maybe? Or it might be that it was crap."[27]

The song was later included as part of a four-track sampler CD-R used to showcase the non-album tracks with executives for them to decide which should be included on the [172] Not About Us CD single. Nowhere Else to Turn was the song omitted and has never been officially released but is widely available on the internet as an MP3 download.

* * *

The big question confronting Genesis as they released ...*Calling All Stations*... on 1 September 1997 was would they still be viable without the charismatic presence of Phil Collins. The answer became quickly apparent as sales failed to match the stratospheric numbers of the previous three albums. From a purely artistic point of view ...*Calling All Stations*... can be viewed as a continuation of the pop-rock approach they had adopted since 1980, albeit with a much darker tone here.[28] Rutherford and Banks' writing is more self-indulgent here and lacks Collins' direct approach along with his editing and arrangement skills. As a result, many of the songs feel cluttered and have a similarity of tempo with most faded out rather than reaching their natural conclusion.

After a tremendous opening the album suffers from a soggy center, with consecutive ballads, and an almost overindulgent end, with two long pieces placed in the home stretch to close out the set. Some better sequencing of the running order may have given the album a more fluid feel. A couple of the more uptempo songs omitted may also have provided a better contrast.

The job of filling Collins' shoes fell to three people in the end. Ray Wilson is an adequate and sometimes expressive, if undistinguished, singer. He has a rock singer's huskiness to his voice and is more at home with the heavy or moody songs. As he joined the sessions when most of the music had already been written, he could only contribute compositionally to a handful of tracks. Banks and Rutherford had also generally given him B-list tracks to work on.

While Collins' distinctive vocals was a key ingredient of their music from 1976, his absence is also heavily felt in the drumming department. His melodic and inventive drumming is replaced here by largely regimented performances. As the drummers were not involved in the creative process, they had to work from pre-programmed drum machine

17. Studio Album #15: ...Calling All Stations... 291

patterns and their resultant efforts generally lacked the fluency Collins would have brought to the sessions. Nir Zidkyahu does show signs of there being a more expressive drummer lurking under the surface, notably on [174] THE DIVIDING LINE and [178] ONE MAN'S FOOL, where his style comes closest to emulating his predecessor. His live performances would better demonstrate his talents. D'Virgilio also offers some cultured playing on [175] UNCERTAIN WEATHER, but otherwise the playing of both, while competent, lacks the inventiveness Collins would have brought to the project.

On a commercial level, the album spelled the death of the band in the U.S., where it peaked at #54 and remained on the chart for only five weeks. The album also saw a significant dip in sales in the UK staying on the chart for just eight weeks, despite entering the at

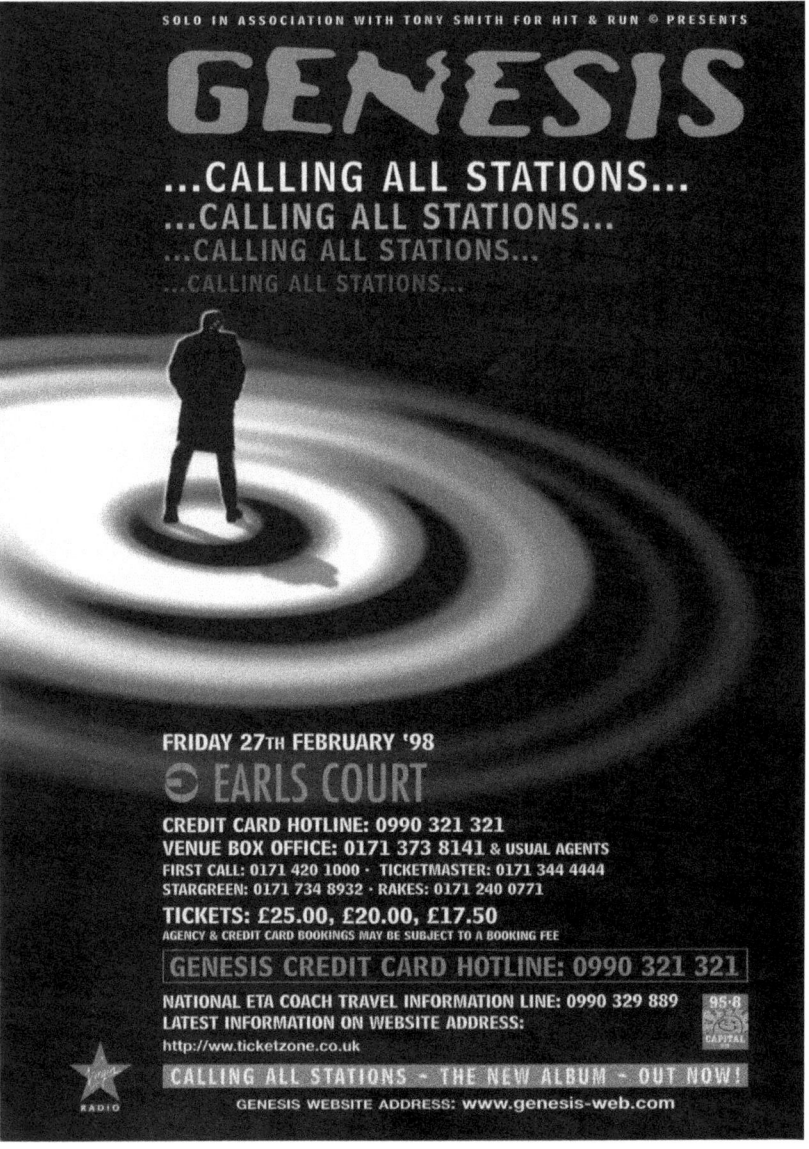

Poster advertising Genesis' Earl's Court concert in London on 27 February 1998 (author's collection).

#2. The fact that there was a six-year gap between albums did not help matters. The music scene had changed dramatically with the advent of grunge and indie rock/pop and Genesis had been away for too long. This is something Rutherford readily acknowledged, "Unfortunately, we hit the time when many of the older bands got less radio play just by definition of categories. It was quite hard, as we had something new to say but we weren't afforded as good a platform to show it."[29]

The critics were largely negative about the album with the occasional exception. *Mojo* were one of the more positive commentators noting, "the 10 million who bought *We Can't Dance* will feel at home here."[30] *All Music Guide*'s Stephen Thomas Erlewine review was more typical in his assessment: "It wants to be an art rock album, but not at the expense of losing the pop audience—which makes it all the stranger that the group doesn't really write pop songs on …*Calling All Stations*…. That may be because Wilson's voice isn't suited for pop, but works well with languid, synthesized prog settings. But even ponderous prog rock has to have musical themes worth exploring, and on that level, Genesis come up dry on …*Calling All Stations*…"[31] In its review *Rolling Stone* commented, "the ultimate problem here is the usual one: the dearth of decent material beyond a few pleasant if generic FM-rock tunes."[32] Peter Kane observed pretty accurately in *Q* that the album was, "One-paced and one-dimensional, their time might just be up."[33]

…*Calling All Stations*… would prove to be Wilson's only recording with Genesis following the album's poor sales and the cancellation of a tour in the U.S. The band did, however, complete a 47-date tour of Europe commencing on 23 January 1998. For this tour, guitarist Anthony Drennan[34] and drummer Nir Zidkyahu made up the rest of the lineup. The last two dates played by the band were on 30 and 31 May 1998 at the Rock am/im Ring Festival at Nürburgring in Germany.

Once the tour was completed the band considered its options. Banks and Wilson were keen to continue and return to the studio to record a follow-up.[35] However, Rutherford was not of the same mind set saying later, "Ray did a fantastic job and he often doesn't get enough credit. He was great live and it was a very hard gig. However, I just didn't want to have to keep making albums and touring solidly for the next three or four years."[36] Rutherford also cited that he and Banks were further apart from a writing perspective than he had perceived and added he missed Collins' input and ability to be the glue in the middle. Banks understood Rutherford's reasons, "Genesis had been just a fantastic thing, we decided let's just leave it on a high rather than try to take it right down to just doing the low sales again. So, we decided to knock it on the head."[37]

The decision to put the band on ice, made toward the end of 1999, was frustrating to Wilson who had put his own career on hold to join the band for what he believed would be more than just one album. He said, "From my point of view, I look at it and say, 'Well, that's not what your intention was in the beginning, guys. You can't just say that because it didn't take off in America, all right that's it. We give in. We go home. If you told me that in the first place, I would never have joined the band.' So, there is a little bit of resentment there, because I feel that they didn't have the courage to continue when I think they should have."[38]

Ray Wilson's contract with Genesis expired in July 2000 and was not renewed, effectively ending the band's recording career. The songs recorded during the …*Calling All Stations*… sessions would be the last batch of original material released by the band.

It would not, however, be the last we would hear from Genesis.

Part 6

Looking Back and Reunions

18

SINCE 1998

While Genesis had effectively ceased as a recording unit in 1997, the individual members have continued with their solo careers. Tony Banks has recorded three classical albums and Mike Rutherford has reignited his Mike + The Mechanics project, with new singers Andrew Roachford and Tim Howar. Ray Wilson has released a series of albums and continues to regularly tour Europe, performing his own material and many Genesis songs from all eras. Steve Hackett too produces albums and tours on a regular basis—including two albums of new recordings of Genesis songs and his most recent tours have focused heavily on Genesis material. Phil Collins retired from recording and performing after his 2004/5 solo tour, only to return in 2010 with a Motown covers album and then from 2017 with a live show that crossed the world in clusters of shows to break up the schedule. Peter Gabriel remains the least productive in terms of new studio recordings with no full album of original material since 2002's *Up*, but he has revisited early material and released a covers album. He also toured extensively between 2012 and 2014 and again with Sting in 2016.

Genesis have reunited on a wide range of activities since their last album release. On 22 June 1998, shortly after the completion of the …*Calling All Stations*…. European tour, the band released the 52-track 4-CD box set *Genesis Archive 1967–75*. The set included early demos, singles, BBC session recordings and B-sides. Also included were five live tracks from their show at the Rainbow Theatre in London, England, on 20 October 1973 and a live recording of their album *The Lamb Lies Down on Broadway* at the Shrine Auditorium, Los Angeles, on 24 January 1975.[1] To promote the box set a photo session and dinner was organized to include Tony Banks, Mike Rutherford, Phil Collins, Peter Gabriel, Steve Hackett, Anthony Phillips, John Silver and Chris Stewart (who attended the dinner only). Interviews were also recorded for a 45-minute documentary for VH-1, which was narrated by Ray Wilson.

The initial plan to release the box set ahead of Christmas in 1995 was postponed for unstated legal reasons. There would be further delays from other provisionally set dates—not least of which was caused by the band releasing …*Calling All Stations*…. The original plan was for three box sets with the second covering the period 1976–81 and the last from 1982 to date. Ultimately this was scaled down to two sets, the second covering 1976–1992.

The *Genesis Archive 1967–75* box set was well received by fans and critics alike and sold strongly enough to enter the UK Albums chart at #35.

* * *

In 1998, past members of Genesis met to promote the release of the *Genesis Archive 1967–1975* box set. From left, Tony Banks, Steve Hackett, Peter Gabriel, Anthony Phillips, Mike Rutherford, John Silver and Phil Collins. Virgin promotional photograph by Lauren Haynes (courtesy Mark Kenyon/The Genesis Archive).

[186] THE CARPET CRAWLERS 1999

Band Credit: Tony Banks/Phil Collins/Peter Gabriel/Steve Hackett/Mike Rutherford
Music: Tony Banks/Mike Rutherford
Lyrics: Peter Gabriel
Length: 5:40
Tony Banks—Synthesizers and Additional Programming; **Phil Collins**—Lead Vocals (third verse), Backing Vocals, Drums; **Peter Gabriel**—Lead Vocals (intro, first and second verse), Backing Vocals, Additional Programming; **Steve Hackett**—Guitar; **Mike Rutherford**—Bass; **Richard Evans**—Additional Guitar; **Garry Hughes**—Additional Programming; **Jamie Muhoberac**—Additional Programming; **Andy Richards**—Additional Programming
Recorded and Mixed at Sarm Hookend; Sarm Workshops; Aquarius Studios; Fisher Lane Farm, Surrey; Real World Studios & Crown Studios, Twickenham, 1995–1999.
Producer: Trevor Horn. Engineer: Steve Fitzmaurice, Tim Weidner and Tim Willis. Assistant Engineers: Alex Black, Andre Coulam, Justin Fraser & Dan Vickers.
Mixed by Richard Lowe.
Mastered by Nick Davis and Tim Young.
Production Coordinator: Augusta Quiney.
UK Release: 25 October 1999. (CD: *Turn It On Again—The Hits*)
U.S. Release: 26 October 1999. (CD: *Turn It On Again—The Hits*)

A little more than a year later, on 25 October 1999, Genesis released *Turn It On Again: The Hits*—a compilation of their major singles. Included in the collection was a new recording of [57] CARPET CRAWLERS. The track, which was renamed THE CARPET CRAWLERS 1999, was also released as a CD single across Europe on 2 November 1999 (but not in the UK or U.S.). Each band member recorded their part separately in their home studios, mostly during 1995, digitally sending their contributions to producer Trevor Horn who compiled the song. It was Gabriel's idea to use Horn as producer, to ensure some independent input and reduce the potential for disagreements between the band. Horn employed a contemporary production approach to the song, including additional studio drum and keyboard programming. This had the effect of sucking some of the heart from the song. Banks commented, "It was nice working with Trevor; I'm an admirer of his. He's a talented chap, so it was fun to have done that. We had a good time just getting together at Peter's studio at Real World. Good food. We ate a lot, as I remember—and played a lot of tennis."[2] Hackett also referenced some heavy rhythm guitar work he had produced that was not included in the final version, "we all worked separately on this project and didn't actually record it together in a studio as a band. Our tracks were then given to Trevor Horn to mix. Although it came off quite well, I felt the floating quality you get as a band was absent. I recorded a lot of rhythm heavy guitar work but most of it was sadly left off of the final recording."[3] It was also originally intended to have Ray Wilson sing the fourth verse, but the idea was scrapped at the eleventh hour and the verse was omitted from the song, resulting in Gabriel and Collins sharing lead vocal duties. Originally it was intended that only Gabriel provide the lead vocals—Collins getting a call late in the recording process with a request to add his lead to the third verse.

It was initially intended to include the song on the *Genesis Archive 1967–75* box set, but it was held back for the release of *Turn It On Again—The Hits*, which reached #4 in the UK and would stay on the chart for thirteen weeks. The compilation album would be repackaged as a double-CD release eight years later to promote the band's reunion tour.

Single Release: A radio edit was released as a promo CD in both the UK (4:00) and the U.S. (4:13). The full version of the European single release on 2 November 1999 was backed with [102] FOLLOW YOU, FOLLOW ME and [111] TURN IT ON AGAIN.

Music Video: An artistic promotional video, which did not feature the band, was shot by Tom Baxandall.

* * *

Genesis' manager, Tony Smith, was celebrated at the Music Managers Forum on 21 September 2000 where Smith was presented with the Peter Grant Award for Music management. The event was attended by Tony Banks, Phil Collins and Mike Rutherford as well as Peter Gabriel. Banks, Collins and Rutherford prepared a short acoustic set for the evening, which they rehearsed at their Fisher Lane Farm studio. The rehearsals were filmed by a crew preparing the DVD *The Genesis Songbook*, which was released in 2001. The crew captured the trio rehearsing acoustic performances of [102] FOLLOW YOU, FOLLOW ME and [88] AFTERGLOW. Daryl Stuermer joined his friends for the set, which was performed at the Park Lane Hilton in London. The set was restricted to three songs: [143] INVISIBLE TOUCH, FOLLOW YOU, FOLLOW ME and [157] I CAN'T DANCE.

The 3-CD box set, *Genesis Archive #2 1976–1992* was released on 6 November 2000 and captured the full period of Collins' tenure as singer. The collection mixed previously unreleased live material with B-sides and 12-inch single remixes. One of the main points of interest was a work-in-progress version of [134] MAMA (10:43), which demonstrated how the band extracted the best material from extended jams. The track list was compiled with the help of fans and Tony Banks played a key part in its compilation. Fans were upset that the set excluded two of the non-album tracks from the period in [89] MATCH OF THE DAY and [133] ME & VIRGIL. Banks, Collins and Rutherford promoted the release with press interviews and a second, shorter (22 minutes) VH1 documentary.

A 3-CD "Best of" set was released on 29 November 2004 as *Platinum Collection*. A U.S. release followed ten months later, on 13 September 2005. The set was a broader representation of the band's output than *Turn It On Again: The Hits* and included several remixed versions of key tracks from all periods of the band and served as a taster for the full rerelease of the band's back-catalogue in remixed and remastered form. Nick Davis had been working on the remixes under the supervision of Tony Banks. The *Platinum Collection* would reach #21 in the UK Album chart and spent fourteen weeks in the Top 100.

Banks, Collins, Rutherford, Gabriel and Hackett met in Glasgow on 20 November 2005, where Collins was performing on his "First Final Farewell Tour," to discuss a potential reunion tour. The aim was to present a complete performance of *The Lamb Lies Down on Broadway*, which had just celebrated its thirtieth anniversary. At the meeting the band failed to reach an agreement with Gabriel unable and/or unwilling to commit to the venture. Hackett and Gabriel left the meeting at that point leaving the trio of Banks, Collins and Rutherford to discuss a reunion of their 1978–1993 live lineup. The three quickly agreed to commit to a tour once their diaries had become open. A short European tour was finally announced at a press conference on 7 November 2006 and a similar American tour was announced in New York on 7 March 2007. The "Turn It On Again Tour" would see the band again augmented by Daryl Stuermer and Chester Thompson.

Initial rehearsals took place in New York in October 2006 and final rehearsals in Cossonay in Switzerland and Brussels in Belgium, during April and May 2007. The European

Genesis re-united in 2007 for their *Turn It On Again* tour. From left, Chester Thompson, Mike Rutherford, Phil Collins, Tony Banks and Daryl Stuermer. Virgin promotional photograph by Stephanie Pistel (author's collection).

leg took in twenty-three dates starting on 11 June 2007 in Helsinki and included an appearance at the Live Earth concert at Wembley Stadium, London on 7 July. The European leg climaxed with a free concert to approximately half-a-million people at Circus Maximus in Rome on 14 July. The U.S. leg of the tour took in a further twenty-five dates between 7 September and 13 October 2007, with the last performance of the band being witnessed at the Hollywood Bowl in Los Angeles. Banks, Collins and Rutherford had seen the tour as a farewell and thank-you to the fans, a chance to say "good-bye" properly.

Soundboard recordings of all the shows were made available to fans by the Encore Series team at TheMusic.com. An official live album, *Live Over Europe 2007*, was released on 20 November 2007 in the U.S. and six days later in the UK, where it peaked at #51 in the Album chart. The Rome performance was filmed for the DVD *When in Rome 2007*, released on 26 May 2008 in the UK and 10 June in the U.S. The DVD included the tour documentary *Come Rain or Shine*, which was also premiered in cinemas in the UK on 20 May 2008, with all the three band members in attendance.

Also under way was a project to remix and remaster all the band's studio albums, excepting *From Genesis to Revelation*, for which the rights were still owned by Jonatan King. The albums were split into three box sets released over an 18-month period: *Genesis 1970–1975* (released 10 November 2008), *Genesis 1976–1982* (released 2 April 2007) and *Genesis 1983–1998* (released 1 October 2007). Each box set featured a stereo and 5.1 surround remix of the original albums as well as adding all non-album tracks. Video material including performances, music videos and interviews, was also included as a second disc on DVD for each album. The project was extended to a box set of the band's live albums, which was released on 14 September 2009 as *Genesis Live 1973–2007*. Finally, the band's live DVDs were released as *Genesis: The Movie Box 1981–2007* on 16 November 2009 and a week later in the U.S. All the remixes and remasters were undertaken by Nick Davis and supervised by the band.

The 2007 reunion tour was a huge success. Here, the band perform [162] Hold On My Heart at Old Trafford, Manchester, on 7 July 2007, the last time the author saw Genesis live. From left, Daryl Stuermer, Mike Rutherford, Phil Collins and Tony Banks with drummer Chester Thompson hidden behind Rutherford. (photograph by Andrew St. Denis, Lincolnimp68/Wikimedia Commons).

Genesis were inducted into the Rock and Roll Hall of Fame in March 2010. Due to commitments elsewhere, Peter Gabriel was unable to join his former bandmates for the event. While Banks, Collins, Hackett and Rutherford all attended, they declined to perform. The band Phish offered renditions [33] WATCHER OF THE SKIES and [120] NO REPLY AT ALL on their behalf.

In 2014 the BBC commissioned a documentary about Genesis, which was to highlight the success of the band as well as the members individually. The focus was on Banks, Collins, Gabriel, Hackett and Rutherford. To accompany the documentary, a new 3-CD compilation, *R-Kive*, was released on 22 September 2014 in the UK and a week later in other territories. The 37-track collection included selections from all eras of the band along with three selected solo tracks from each of the five members. The accompanying TV documentary, *Genesis: Together and Apart*, had a troubled production, in that it was poorly edited and initially only featured the solo careers of Gabriel and Collins. Changes were made to incorporate Banks and Rutherford, but no mention of Hackett's career was included and Ray Wilson's stint with the band was ignored. All five former band members were interviewed individually and as a group for the film. While the five also attended a premiere screening, each of them later expressed their disappointment in the final cut. A DVD/Blu-ray package of the documentary, retitled *Genesis: Sum of the Parts* was released

The author's tickets for the Old Trafford, Manchester, gig on 7 July 2007 (author's collection).

The "classic" five-man line-up together again at a photo shoot in 2014 to promote the BBC documentary *Genesis: Together and Apart* (released on Blu-ray as *Genesis: Sum of the Parts*). From left, Peter Gabriel, Steve Hackett, Mike Rutherford, Phil Collins and Tony Banks (Gelring/BBC promotional photograph by Patrick Balls).

in late October 2014. To date this is the last active piece of work the band has undertaken collectively.

It was during the 2007 reunion tour that Phil Collins developed problems with vertebrae in his neck and hands—wear and tear from a lifetime of drumming and bad posture. The injury initially restricted his ability to play drums—he had to tape the sticks to his hands for his studio album recording of Motown covers, *Going Back*, during 2009/10. Other health issues blighted the singer, notably back problems which resulted in a series of operations and a dependency on painkillers, which when mixed with alcohol caused further issues. The surgery left Collins suffering from a condition known as "drop foot" with the singer unable to stand for long periods and having to walk with the aid of a stick. He was now also no longer able to play drums. While Collins eventually came out of retirement to perform his successful "Not Dead Yet" tour in various legs from 2017, he was immobile and had to deliver his songs almost exclusively from a chair at the front of the stage. His 16-year-old son, Nicholas, took on drum duties with a skill that will undoubtedly have made his father proud.

Collins' condition led many to believe that any further Genesis reunion was extremely unlikely. However, on 4 March 2020, Banks, Collins and Rutherford surprised everyone by announcing they would be reuniting for a tour of the UK in November and December of 2020 with Nic Collins taking the drum stool and Daryl Stuermer again filling guitar and bass duties. US and European dates would likely follow if the band adopted Collins' lead in splitting touring activity into bite-sized chunks.

While the band is again active as a live proposition, the back catalogue of studio recordings has been exhausted and we are assured all available material has been released. What we are left with is an extraordinarily diverse catalogue of musical invention spanning fifteen studio albums of consistently high quality. Genesis' legacy will live on through these recordings long after the band finally call it a day and their music will remain with us until our supper is ready.

Discography

What follows is a summary of all the officially released recordings of Genesis in the UK and U.S. The studio albums, which are covered in detail in the main text with their associated track lists and catalogue details, are merely shown here for completeness. The band's live and compilation albums, as well as box set releases, list the tracks included along with any key notes (e.g., "Excerpt," where the song is included as part of a medley or is played in abbreviated format). Also listed are the official solo album releases for each of the band members. For the sake of space, as each band member undoubtedly deserves a book of his own to do any justice to his solo output, the album tracks have not been listed.

Genesis Studio Albums

(See individual album sections for details and tracks included)

From Genesis to Revelation (UK: 1969, U.S: 1974)
Trespass (UK: 1970, U.S.: 1971)
Nursery Cryme (UK: 1971, U.S.: 1972)
Foxtrot (1972)
Selling England by the Pound (1973)
The Lamb Lies Down on Broadway (1974)
A Trick of the Tail (1976)
Wind & Wuthering (1976)

…And Then There Were Three… (1978)
Duke (1980)
Abacab (1981)
Genesis (1983)
Invisible Touch (1986)
We Can't Dance (1991)
…Calling All Stations… (1997)

Genesis Live Albums

Genesis Live (1973)

Original (UK: LP. Charisma. CLASS 1; U.S.: LP. Charisma CAS 1666):
 [33] WATCHER OF THE SKIES / [35] GET 'EM OUT BY FRIDAY / [27] THE RETURN OF THE GIANT HOGWEED / [25] THE MUSICAL BOX / [24] THE KNIFE.
2009 Reissue (UK: CD. Virgin. 5099968650520; U.S.: CD. Atlantic/Rhino. R2 521143):
 [33] WATCHER OF THE SKIES / [35] GET 'EM OUT BY FRIDAY / [27] THE RETURN OF THE GIANT HOGWEED / [25] THE MUSICAL BOX / [24] THE KNIFE / [54] BACK IN N.Y.C. / [49] FLY ON A WINDSHIELD / [50] BROADWAY MELODY OF 1974 / [61] ANYWAY / [58] THE CHAMBER OF 32 DOORS.

Seconds Out (1977)

Original (UK: 2LP. Charisma. GE 2001; U.S.: 2LP. Atlantic. SD 2–9002)
2009 Reissue (UK: 2-CD. Virgin 724383988723; U.S.: 2-CD. Atlantic/Rhino. R2 521143):
 [73] SQUONK / [57] THE CARPET CRAWL / [75] ROBBERY, ASSAULT AND BATTERY / [88] AFTERGLOW / [42] FIRTH OF FIFTH / [41] I KNOW WHAT I LIKE (IN YOUR WARDROBE) / [48] THE LAMB LIES DOWN ON BROADWAY / [25] THE MUSICAL BOX (CLOSING SECTION) / [38] SUPPER'S READY / [46] THE CINEMA SHOW / [71] DANCE ON A VOLCANO / [78] LOS ENDOS.

Three Sides Live (1982)

Original (UK: 2LP. Charisma. GE 2001; U.S.: 2LP. Atlantic. SD 2–2000)
2009 Reissue (UK: 2-CD. Virgin 724383988723; U.S. 2-CD. Atlantic/Rhino. R2 521143): UK and UK/U.S. Reissue:

[111] Turn It On Again / [123/124] Dodo / [119] Abacab / [105] Behind the Lines / [106] Duchess / [121] Me & Sarah Jane / [102] Follow You, Follow Me / [109] Misunderstanding / [52] In the Cage (Medley—[45] Cinema Show [Excerpt]—[65] Slippermen [Excerpt]) / [88] Afterglow / [81] One for the Vine / [31] Fountain of Salmacis / [70/33] It. / Watcher of the Skies.
U.S. Original: [111] Turn It On Again / [123/124] Dodo / [119] Abacab / [105] Behind the Lines / [106] Duchess / [121] Me & Sarah Jane / [102] Follow You, Follow Me / [109] Misunderstanding / [52] In the Cage (Medley—[45] Cinema Show [Excerpt]—[65] Slippermen [Excerpt]) / [88] Afterglow / [131] Paperlate / [132] You Might Recall / [133] Me and Virgil / [118] Evidence of Autumn / [117] Open Door.

Live–The Way We Walk, Vol I: The Shorts (1992)

Live–The Way We Walk, Vol II: The Longs (1993)

I: *The Shorts* (UK: CD. Virgin. GEN CD 4; U.S.: CD. Atlantic. 82452-2):
I: [145] Land of Confusion / [154] No Son of Mine / [155] Jesus He Knows Me / [149] Throwing It All Away / [157] I Can't Dance / [134] Mama / [162] Hold On My Heart / [135] That's All / [146] In Too Deep / [144] Tonight, Tonight, Tonight (Excerpt) / [143] Invisible Touch.
II: *The Longs* (UK: CD. Virgin. GEN CD 5; U.S.: CD. Atlantic. 82461-2):
II: Old Medley ([71] Dance on a Volcano [Excerpt] / [48] Lamb Lies Down on Broadway [Excerpt] / [25] The Musical Box [Excerpt] / [42] Firth of Fifth [Excerpt] / [41] I Know What I Like... [Excerpt]) / [156] Driving the Last Spike / [148] Domino / [165] Fading Lights / [136/137] Home by the Sea / Second Home by The Sea / [n/a] Drum Duet.
The Way We Walk 2009 Reissue (UK: 2-CD. Virgin. 5099968650827; U.S.: 2-CD. Atlantic/Rhino. [?]):
[145] Land of Confusion / [154] No Son of Mine / [156] Driving the Last Spike / Old Medley ([71] Dance on a Volcano / [48] Lamb Lies Down on Broadway / [25] The Musical Box / [42] Firth of Fifth / [41] I Know What I Like...) / [149] Throwing It All Away / [165] Fading Lights / [155] Jesus He Knows Me / [136/137] Home by the Sea/Second Home by the Sea / [162] Hold On My Heart / [148] Domino / [n/a] The Drum Thing (Drum Duet) / [157] I Can't Dance / [144] Tonight, Tonight, Tonight / [143] Invisible Touch / [111] Turn It On Again / [134] Mama / [135] That's All / [146] In Too Deep.

Live Over Europe 2007 (2007)

Original: (UK: 2-CD. Virgin. 5099951132927; U.S.: 2-CD. Atlantic/Rhino 375100-2):
[105/116] Duke's Intro / [111] Turn It On Again / [154] No Son of Mine / [145] Land of Confusion / [52] In The Cage (medley—[45] Cinema Show [Excerpt]—[115] Duke's Travels [Excerpt]) / [88] Afterglow / [162] Hold On My Heart / [136/137] Home by the Sea / [102] Follow You, Follow Me / [42] Firth of Fifth (Excerpt) / [41] I Know What I Like (In Your Wardrobe) / [134] Mama / [76] Ripples... / [149] Throwing It All Away / [148] Domino / [n/a] Conversations with 2 Stools / [78] Los Endos / [144] Tonight, Tonight, Tonight (Excerpt) / [143] Invisible Touch / [157] I Can't Dance / [57] Carpet Crawlers.

Genesis Compilation Albums and Box Sets

Genesis Archive 1967–75 (1998)

Original (UK: 4-CD. Virgin. CD BOX 6; U.S.: 4-CD. Atlantic. 82858-2):
CD 1 and 2: *Live at the Shrine Auditorium, Los Angeles, 24 January 1975:* [48] The Lamb Lies Down on Broadway / [49] Fly on a Windshield /[50] Broadway Melody of 1974 / [51] Cuckoo Cocoon / [52] In the Cage / [53] The Grand Parade of Lifeless Packaging / [54] Back in N.Y.C. / [55] Hairless Heart / [56] Counting Out Time / [57] Carpet Crawlers / [58] The Chamber of 32 Doors / [59] Lilywhite Lilith / [60] The Waiting Room / [61] Anyway / [62] Here Comes the Supernatural Anaesthetist / [63] The Lamia / [64] Silent Sorrow in Empty Boats / [65] The Colony of Slippermen / [66] Ravine / [67] The Light Dies Down on Broadway / [68] Riding the Scree / [69] In the Rapids / [70] It.
CD 3: *Live at the Rainbow Theatre, London, 20 October 1973:* [40] Dancing with the Moonlit Knight; [42] Firth of Fifth; [43] More Fool Me; [38] Supper's Ready; [41] I Know What I Like (In Your Wardrobe); *plus* [22] Stagnation (BBC Session); [39] Twilight Alehouse; [32] Happy the Man; [33] Watcher of the Skies (Single Edit).
CD4: [10] In the Wilderness (Rough Mix) / [D18g] Shepherd (BBC Session) / [D18f] Pacidy (BBC Session) / [D18h] Let Us Now Make Love (BBC Session) / [D18a] Going Out to Get You (Demo) /

[23] Dusk (Demo) / [17] Build Me a Mountain (Rough Mix) / [18] Image Blown Out (Rough Mix) / [13] One Day (Rough Mix) / [5] Where the Sour Turns to Sweet (Demo) / [6] In the Beginning (Demo) / [D4a] The Magic of Time (Demo) / [D4b] Hey! (Demo) / {D0d} Hidden in the World of Dawn (Demo) / [D0e] Sea Bee (Demo) / [D0f] The Mystery of the Flannan Isle Lighthouse (Demo) / [D0g] Hair on the Arms and Legs (Demo) / [D0b] She Is Beautiful (Demo) / [D0c] Try a Little Sadness (Demo) / [D0a] Patricia (Demo).

Turn It On Again: The Hits (1999)

Original (UK: CD. Virgin. GENCD 8; U.S.: CD. Atlantic. 83244–2):
 [111] Turn It On Again / [143] Invisible Touch / [134] Mama (Radio edit) / [145] Land of Confusion / [157] I Can't Dance / [102] Follow You Follow Me / [162] Hold On My Heart / [119] Abacab (UK single edit) / [41] I Know What I Like (In Your Wardrobe) / [154] No Son of Mine (Edited version) / [144] Tonight, Tonight, Tonight (New edit of single version) / [146] In Too Deep / [169] Congo (Single version) / [155] Jesus He Knows Me (Single mix) / [135] That's All / [109] Misunderstanding / [149] Throwing It All Away / [186] The Carpet Crawlers 1999.

2007 Tour Edition (UK: 2-CD. Virgin. GENCDZ 8; U.S.: 2-CD. Atlantic/Rhino. R2 281852):
 [111] Turn It On Again / [154] No Son of Mine (Edited version) / [157] I Can't Dance / [162] Hold On My Heart / [155] Jesus He Knows Me (Single mix) / [160] Tell Me Why / [143] Invisible Touch / [145] Land of Confusion / [144] Tonight, Tonight, Tonight (New edit of single version) / [146] In Too Deep / [149] Throwing It All Away / [134] Mama (Radio edit) / [135] That's All / [138] Illegal Alien / [119] Abacab (UK single edit) / [120] No Reply at All / [186] The Carpet Crawlers 1999 / [131] Paperlate / [122] Keep It Dark / [126] Man on the Corner / [106] Duchess (Single version) / [109] Misunderstanding / [102] Follow You, Follow Me / [98] Many Too Many / [82] Your Own Special Way / [88] Afterglow / [90] Pigeons / [91] Inside and Out / [77] A Trick of the Tail / [56] Counting Out Time / [41] I Know What I Like (In Your Wardrobe) / [32] Happy the Man / [24] The Knife (Part 1) (Single version) / [169] Congo (Single version).

Genesis Archive #2: 1976–1992 (2000)

Original (UK: 3-CD. Virgin. CDBOX7; U.S.: 3-CD. Atlantic. 83410–2):
 [166] On the Shoreline / [167] Hearts on Fire / [132] You Might Recall / [131] Paperlate / [118] Evidence of Autumn / [151] Do the Neurotic / [153] I'd Rather Be You / [129] Naminanu / [91] Inside and Out / [152] Feeding the Fire / [157] I Can't Dance (12-inch remix) / [130] Submarine (alternative version) / [138] Illegal Alien (live at the Forum, Los Angeles, on 14 January 1984) / [159] Dreaming While You Sleep (live at Earls Court Exhibition Centre, London, in November 1992) / [142] It's Gonna Get Better (live at the Forum, Los Angeles, on 14 January 1984) / [97] Deep in the Motherlode (live at Theatre Royal, Drury Lane, London, on 5 May 1980) / [76] Ripples… (live at the Lyceum Theatre, London, on 6 May 1980) / [150] The Brazilian (live at Wembley Stadium, London, on 4 July 1987) / [82] Your Own Special Way (live at the Sydney Entertainment Centre in December 1986) / [96] Burning Rope (live at the Hofheinz Pavilion, Houston, on 22 October 1978) / [72] Entangled (live at Bingley Hall, Staffordshire, on 10 July 1976) / [115/116] Duke's Travels/Duke's End (live at the Lyceum Theatre, London, on 7 May 1980) / [143] Invisible Touch (12-inch remix) / [145] Land of Confusion (12-inch remix) / [144] Tonight, Tonight, Tonight (12-inch remix) / [120] No Reply at All (live at the Savoy Theatre, New York City, on 28 November 1981) / [126] Man on the Corner (live at the Savoy Theatre, New York City, on 28 November 1981) / [101] The Lady Lies (live at the Lyceum Theatre, London, on 6 May 1980) / [117] Open Door / [103] The Day the Light Went Out / [104] Vancouver / [90] Pigeons / [79] It's Yourself (early fade) / [134] Mama (work in progress).

Platinum Collection (UK: 2004; U.S.: 2005)

Original: (UK: 3-CD. Virgin. 724386373427; U.S.: 3-CD. Atlantic/Rhino. 78446):
 [154] No Son of Mine / [157] I Can't Dance / [155] Jesus He Knows Me / [162] Hold On My Heart / [143] Invisible Touch / [149] Throwing It All Away / [144] Tonight, Tonight, Tonight (Edited version) / [145] Land of Confusion / [146] In Too Deep / [134] Mama / [135] That's All / [136/137] Home by the Sea/Second Home by the Sea / [138] Illegal Alien / [131] Paperlate / [168] Calling All Stations / [119] Abacab / [122] Keep it Dark / [111] Turn It On Again / [105] Behind the Lines / [106] Duchess / [109] Misunderstanding / [98] Many Too Many / [102] Follow You Follow Me / [93] Undertow / [87] …In That Quiet Earth / [88] Afterglow / [82] Your Own Special Way / [77] A Trick of the Tail / [76] Ripples… / [78] Los Endos / [48] The Lamb Lies Down on Broadway / [56] Counting Out Time / [57] Carpet Crawlers / [42] Firth of Fifth / [46] The

Cinema Show / [41] I Know What I Like (In Your Wardrobe) / [38] Supper's Ready / [25] The Musical Box / [24] The Knife.

Genesis 1976–1982 (2007)

Original: (UK: 6-CD/6DVD. Virgin. CDBOX 12; U.S.: 6-CD/6DVD, Atlantic/Rhino. R2 125436):
  Includes the albums: *A Trick of the Tail* (1976); *Wind & Wuthering* (1976); *...And Then There Were Three...* (1978); *Duke* (1980); *Abacab* (1981).
Extra Tracks CD:
  [131] Paperlate / [118] Evidence of Autumn / [90] Pigeons / [132] You Might Recall / [129] Naminanu / [91] Inside and Out / [104] Vancouver / [133] Me and Virgil / [79] It's Yourself / [89] Match of the Day / [117] Open Door / [103] The Day the Light Went Out / [130] Submarine.

Genesis 1983–1998 (2007)

Original: (UK: 5CD/5DVD. Virgin. CDBOX 13; U.S.: 5CD/5DVD. Atlantic/Rhino. 081227996413):
  Includes the albums: *Genesis* (1983); *Invisible Touch* (1986); *We Can't Dance* (1991); *...Calling All Stations...* (1997).
Extra Tracks CD:
  [166] On the Shoreline / [167] Hearts on Fire / [151] Do the Neurotic / [152] Feeding the Fire / [153] I'd Rather Be You / [183] Anything Now / [184] Sign Your Life Away / [185] Run Out of Time.

Genesis 1970–1975 (2008)

Original: (UK: 7CD/6DVD. Virgin. CDBOX 13; U.S.: 7CD/6DVD. Atlantic/Rhino. R2 513942):
  Includes the albums: *Trespass* (1970); *Nursery Cryme* (1971); *Foxtrot* (1972); *Selling England by the Pound* (1973); *The Lamb Lies Down on Broadway* (1974).
Extra Tracks CD:
  [32] Happy the Man / [39] Twilight Alehouse / [D18a] Going Out to Get You (Demo) / [D18g] Shepherd (BBC Session) / [D18f] Pacidy (BBC Session) / [D18h] Let Us Now Make Love (BBC Session) / [D18b] Provocation (BBC Recording) / [D18c] Frustration (BBC Recording) / [D18d] Manipulation (BBC Recording) / [D18e] Resignation (BBC Recording).

Genesis Live 1973–2007 (2009)

Original: (UK: 8CD/3DVD. Virgin. CDBOX 17; U.S.: 8CD/3DVD. Atlantic/Rhino. R2 521143):
  Includes the albums: *Genesis Live* (2009 reissue); *Seconds Out* (1977); *Three Sides Live* (1982); *The Way We Walk* (2009 reissue) plus a slot for *Live Over Europe 2007* (2007).
Live at the Rainbow (1973) CD/DVD-A:
  Watcher of the Skies (DVD-A only) / [40] Dancing with the Moonlit Knight / [46] The Cinema Show / [41] I Know What I Like (In Your Wardrobe) / [42] Firth of Fifth / [25] The Musical Box (DVD-A only) / [43] More Fool Me / [44] The Battle of Epping Forest / [38] Supper's Ready.

R–Kive (2014)

Original: (UK: 3-CD. Virgin EMI/UMC. RKIVE 1; U.S.: 3-CD. Rhino. R2 545742):
  [24] The Knife / [25] The Musical Box / [38] Supper's Ready / [46] The Cinema Show / [41] I Know What I Like (In Your Wardrobe) / [48] The Lamb Lies Down on Broadway / [54] Back in N.Y.C. / [57] Carpet Crawlers / "Ace of Wands" (Steve Hackett) / [76] Ripples... / [88] Afterglow / "Solsbury Hill" (Peter Gabriel) / [102] Follow You Follow Me / "For a While" (Tony Banks) / "Every Day" (Steve Hackett) / "Biko" (Peter Gabriel) / [111] Turn It On Again / "In the Air Tonight" (Phil Collins) / [119] Abacab / [134] Mama / [135] That's All / "Easy Lover" (Phil Collins & Philip Bailey) / "Silent Running (On Dangerous Ground)" (Mike + The Mechanics) / [143] Invisible Touch / [145] Land of Confusion / [144] Tonight, Tonight, Tonight / "The Living Years" (Mike + The Mechanics) / "Red Day on Blue Street" (Tony Banks) / [157] I Can't Dance / [154] No Son of Mine / [162] Hold On My Heart / "Over My Shoulder" (Mike + The Mechanics) / [168] Calling All Stations / "Signal to Noise" (Peter Gabriel) / "Wake Up Call" (Phil Collins) / "Nomads" (Steve Hackett) / "Siren" (Tony Banks).

50 Years Ago (2017)

Original: (MP3 Download: Jonjo Music Ltd.):
  [12] In Hiding (Vocals) / [13] One Day (New Stereo Mix) / [3] A Winter's Tale / [16] A Place to Call My Own (Vocals) / [1] The Silent Sun / [12] In Hiding (New Stereo Mix) / [4] On the Trail of the One Eyed Hound (New Stereo Mix) / [5] Where the Sour Turns to Sweet / [16]

A Place to Call My Own (New Mix) / [13] One Day / [15] In Limbo / [9] Am I Very Wrong? / [8] The Serpent / [8] The Serpent (Vocals) / [1] The Silent Sun (Alternate New Mix) / [11] The Conqueror / [18] Image Blown Out / [2] That's Me / [10] In the Wilderness / [14] The Window / [6] In the Beginning (New Mix) / [7] Fireside Song (New Mix) / [5] Where the Sour Turns to Sweet (New Mix).

Anthony Phillips Albums

Studio Albums

The Geese & the Ghost (1977)
Wise After the Event (1978)
Private Parts & Pieces (1978)
Sides (1979)
Private Parts & Pieces II: Back to the Pavilion (1980)
1984 (1981)
Private Parts & Pieces III: Antiques (1982, with Enrique Berro Garcia)
Invisible Men (1983, with Richard Scott)
Private Parts & Pieces IV: A Catch at the Tables (1984)
Private Parts & Pieces V: Twelve (1985)
Private Parts & Pieces VI: Ivory Moon (1986)
Private Parts & Pieces VII: Slow Waves, Soft Stars (1987)
Tarka (1988, with Harry Williamson)
Missing Links Volume One: Finger Painting (1989)
Slow Dance (1990)
Private Parts & Pieces VIII: New England (1992)
Sail the World (1994)
Missing Links Volume Two: The Sky Road (1994)
Gypsy Suite (1995, with Harry Williamson)
The Living Room Concert (1995)
The Meadows of Englewood (1996, with Guillermo Cazenave)
Private Parts & Pieces IX: Dragonfly Dreams (1996, with Enrique Berro Garcia)
Missing Links Volume 3: Time and Tide (1997, with Joji Hirota)
Live Radio Sessions (1998, with Guillermo Cazenave)
Private Parts & Pieces X: Soirée (1999)
Radio Clyde (2003, recorded in 1978)
Field Day (2005)
Wildlife (2007, with Joji Hirota)
Missing Links Volume IV: Pathways & Promenades (2009)
Ahead of the Field: Music for TV and Film (2010)
Seventh Heaven (2012, with Andrew Skeet)
Private Parts & Pieces XI: City of Dreams (2012)
Strings of Light (2019)

Compilations

Harvest of the Heart (1985)
Anthology (1995)
Legend (1997, released in Argentina only)
Archive Collection Volume I (1998)
Legend (1999, different release from above)
Soft Vivace (2002)
Soundscapes (2003)
Archive Collection Volume II (2004)
Harvest of the Heart: An Anthology (2014)
Private Parts & Pieces I—IV (2015)
Private Parts & Pieces V—VIII (2016)
Private Parts & Pieces IX—XI (2018)

Peter Gabriel Albums

Studio Albums

Peter Gabriel (1977)
Peter Gabriel (1978)
Peter Gabriel (1980)
Peter Gabriel (1982)
So (1986)
Us (1992)
Up (2002)
Big Blue Ball (2008, with multiple artists)
Scratch My Back (2010, orchestral covers)
New Blood (2011, orchestral rerecordings)
And I'll Scratch Yours (2013, multiple artists covering Gabriel's songs)

Soundtrack Albums

Birdy (1985)
Passion (1989)
OVO (2000)
Long Walk Home: Music from the Rabbit-Proof Fence (2002)

Live Albums

Plays Live (1983)
Plays Live Highlights (1985)
Secret World Live (1994)
Live Blood (2012)
Back to Front: Live in London (2014, with Blu-ray/DVD)
Growing Up Live (2019, with Blu-ray/DVD)

Discography

Compilations

Shaking the Tree: Sixteen Golden Greats (1990)
Hit (2003)
Rated PG (2019, songs from the movies)
Flotsam and Jetsam (2019, rarities collection—download only)

Steve Hackett Albums

Studio Albums

Voyage of the Acolyte (1975)
Please Don't Touch (1978)
Spectral Mornings (1979)
Defector (1980)
Cured (1981)
Highly Strung (1983)
Bay of Kings (1983)
Till We Have Faces (1984)
Momentum (1988)
Guitar Noir (1993)
Blues with a Feeling (1995)
Genesis Revisited (1996)
A Midsummer Night's Dream (1997, with Royal Philharmonic Orchestra)
Darktown (1999)
Feedback 86 (2000, previously unreleased album from 1986)
To Watch the Storms (2003)
Metamorpheus (2005, with The Underworld Orchestra)
Wild Orchids (2006)
Tribute (2008)
Out of the Tunnel's Mouth (2009)
Beyond the Shrouded Horizon (2011)
Genesis Revisited II (2012)
Wolflight (2015)
The Night Siren (2017)
At the Edge of Light (2019)
With Quiet World:
The Road (1970)
With GTR:
GTR (1986)
With Squackett:
A Life Within a Day (2012, with Chris Squire)
With John Hackett:
Sketches of Satie (2000)

Live Albums

Time Lapse (1992)
There Are Many Sides to the Night (1995)
The Tokyo Tapes (1998)
Live Archive 70's 80's 90's (2001)
Live Archive Newcastle 70's (2001)
Somewhere in South America... (2002)
Hungarian Horizons (2003)
Live Archive NEARfest (2003)
Live Archive 03 (2004)
Live Archive 04 (2004)
Live Archive 05 (2005)
Live Archive 83 (2006, acoustic duo recording with John Hackett)
Live Rails (2010)
Genesis Revisited: Live at Hammersmith (2013)
Genesis Revisited: Live at the Royal Albert Hall (2014)
The Total Experience Live in Liverpool (2016)
Wuthering Nights: Live in Birmingham (2018)
With GTR:
King Biscuit Flower Hour Presents GTR (1997)

Compilations

The Unauthorised Biography (1992)
Genesis Files (2002)
Premonitions: The Charisma Recordings 1975–1983 (2015)
Broken Skies Outspread Wings (2018)

Tony Banks Albums

Studio Albums

A Curious Feeling (1979)
The Fugitive (1983)
Still (1991)
Seven: A Suite for Orchestra (2004, orchestral)
Six Pieces for Orchestra (2012, orchestral)
Five (2018, orchestral)
As Bankstatement:
Bankstatement (1989)
As Strictly Inc.:
Strictly Inc (1995)

Soundtrack Albums

The Wicked Lady (1983)
Soundtracks (1986, music from the films *Quicksilver* and *Lorca and the Outlaws*)

Compilation Albums

A Chord Too Far (2015)

Mike Rutherford Albums

Studio Albums

Smallcreep's Day (1980)
Acting Very Strange (1982)
As Mike + The Mechanics:
Mike + The Mechanics (1985)
Living Years (1988)
Word of Mouth (1991)
Beggar on a Beach of Gold (1995)
Mike & The Mechanics (M6) (1999)
Rewired (2004)
The Road (2011)
Let Me Fly (2017)
Out of the Blue (2019, includes rerecordings of old songs plus three new songs)

Compilation Albums

As Mike + The Mechanics:
Hits (1996)
The Singles 1985–2014 (2014, 2-CD version includes B-sides)
Silent Running: The Masters Collection (2018)

Phil Collins Albums

Studio Albums

Face Value (1981)
Hello, I Must Be Going! (1982)
No Jacket Required (1985)
…But Seriously (1989)
Both Sides (1993)
Dance into the Light (1996)
Testify (2002)
Going Back (2010, covers—mainly Motown)

Soundtrack Albums

Tarzan (1999)
Brother Bear (2003)

Live Albums

Serious Hits…. Live! (1990)
A Hot Night in Paris (1999, as the Phil Collins Big Band)

Compilation Albums

…Hits (1998)
Love Songs: A Compilation…. Old and New (2004)
The Singles (2016, 3-CD version is expanded)
Plays Well with Others (2018, sessions, collaborations, etc.)

Ray Wilson Albums

Studio Albums

Change (2003)
The Next Best Thing (2004)
Propaganda Man (2008)
Chasing Rainbows (2013)
Song for a Friend (2016)
Makes Me Think of Home (2016)
With Guaranteed Pure:
Swing Your Bag (1993)
With Stiltskin:
The Mind's Eye (1994)
She (2006)
Unfulfillment (2011)
With Cut:
Millionairhead (1999)

Live Albums

Live and Acoustic (2002) (previously titled "Unplugged")
Ray Wilson Live (2005)
An Audience and Ray Wilson (2006)
Ray Wilson and the Berlin Symphony Ensemble, *Genesis Klassik Live in Berlin* (2009)
Ray Wilson and the Berlin Symphony Ensemble, *Genesis Classic Live in Poznan* (2011)
Up Close and Personal—Live at SWR1 (2014)
Genesis vs. Stiltskin—20 Years and More (2014)
Time and Distance (2017)
ZDF@Bauhaus—May 20, 2018 (2018)
With Stiltskin:
Stiltskin Live (2007)

Compilation Albums

Upon My Life (2019)

Chapter Notes

Epigraphs

1. *1973–2007 Live*. CD Booklet, 2009.
2. *Platinum Collection*. CD Booklet, 2004.
3. *Platinum Collection*. CD Booklet, 2004.
4. *Genesis Revisited*. CD Booklet, 1996.
5. *R-Kive*. CD Booklet, 2014.

Chapter 1

1. Charterhouse School was founded in 1611 on the site of an old Carthusian monastery in Charterhouse Square, Smithfield, London, and moved to its present location in 1872. The school has a joint claim to have founded Association Football. Up until the 1970s the school was all male. Girls were admitted to the sixth form from then on. Old boys are known as Old Carthusians. As a private boarding school, Charterhouse was increasingly seen as an anachronism for its formal and conventionalist approach to schooling. The school was divided into houses, with Banks, Gabriel and later Phillips placed in Duckites house (actually Girdlestonites, but generally known as "Duckites" because Mr. Girdleston, whom the house was named after, walked like a duck), while Rutherford was in Lockites. Former pupils are known as Old Carthusians in reference to the monastery.
2. Fielder, Hugh. *The Book of Genesis*. London: Sidgwick & Jackson, 1984.
3. Rutherford's father had prepared his own memoirs covering his naval career but failed to find publishing interest. On discovering the manuscript in his father's possessions, Rutherford came up with the idea of blending his father's story with his own. This he does by interweaving events of their contrasting careers in his autobiography *The Living Years: The First Genesis Memoir*. London: Constable & Robin, 2014. The book vividly captures the differences between the war generation and the one that followed and the strains that placed on family relationships.
4. Rivers Maitland Alexander Job was born in 1950 and was a talented but eccentric musician who played guitar and bass. He became a member of Anon, one of the bands that would ultimately fuse into Genesis. His parents later withdrew him from Charterhouse due to disciplinary issues and Job would later go on to join the band Savoy Brown, featuring on their 1968 album *Getting to the Point* and its follow-up *Blue Matter*. He then drifted away from music and into obscurity before dying prematurely in 1979.
5. Ling, Dave. "School: Mike Rutherford and Tony Banks." *Classic Rock*, 16 July 2014.
6. Richard Macphail noted the band was often referred to as The Anon, using the definite article. This was compounded by Rob Tyrell's sister, Marcia, painting the band name as such on his drums. (Macphail, Richard, with Chris Charlesworth. *My Book of Genesis*. London: Argyll & Bute, 2017).
7. Richard Paul Macphail was born on 17 September 1950. He played in essential role on the band's road to success, being involved in the early school bands, before becoming their road manager, technician, driver, and all-round supporter. His association with the band finished in 1973, but was briefly re-ignited in 1976, when he acted as road manager. He later worked in the same capacity for Peter Gabriel for a short period. His memoir, *My Book of Genesis* (Argyll & Bute, 2017), tells of his time with the band and is a must-read for followers.
8. One of the actions that reportedly contributed to River Job's exclusion from Charterhouse was that he had thrown a lead at the music master when he pulled the plug on Anon's concert before they had finished the set.
9. A CD single of the recording (2:59), made at Tony Pike Sound Studios, 31 Dryburgh Road, London, was released in November 2011 by Genesis' German fan website *It* (https://www.genesis-news.com/c--FanclubCD-2011-Anon-Pennsylvania-Flickhouse-s461.html). The recording features a mono and enhanced (pseudo stereo) version of the song. The band was: Rivers Job (bass), Richard Macphail (lead vocals), Rob Tyrell (drums), Mike Rutherford (rhythm guitar), Anthony Phillips (lead guitar). The recording was produced by Brian Roberts and remastered by Jonathan Dann and Tom Morgenstern. Macphail also sang with other bands, such as The Austin Hippy Blues, before taking on the role of Genesis' road manager between 1969 and 1973 and becoming a key figure in the band's development.
10. Brian Roberts lived in Chiswick. He had converted a room over the garage to his parents' house

into a music studio and the band recorded many of their early demos there. After Roberts had moved home, he remembered he had left many of his tape recordings in his attic, but by the time he returned he discovered they had been discarded.

11. Jonathan King was born Kenneth George King on 6 December 1944. A former Charterhouse pupil he had made his name in the music business as both a performer and producer. His 1965 hit, "Everyone's Gone to the Moon," put him on the musical map and his output was prolific during the late 1960s and into the 1970s. He became a record exec at Decca and set up his own label, UK Records. He later gave the Bay City Rollers and 10cc similar starts to their careers. In the late 1970s, he became a TV presenter and personality, working regularly on *Top of the Pops*. He moved to New York in the 1980s and presented the TV show *Entertainment USA*. In 2001, he was convicted of child sexual abuse and received a seven-year prison sentence, effectively ending his show business career. Since then he has written a number of frank books about his life including in 2009, *65: My Life So Far*. While the band have remained grateful to King for giving them the opportunity to record their songs, they feel the producer has often overplayed his contribution to the band's success, disagreeing that he managed their early career.

12. The song is also referred to as "She's So Beautiful."

13. Initially King persuaded the band to sign a five-year contract with a five-year option, until the parents of the boys wisely intervened and reduced the contract to one year with a one-year option.

14. Gallo, Armando. *Genesis: I Know What I Like*. Los Angeles: DIY, 1979.

15. "Genesis—The Greatest Story Ever Told." Repertoire Records. 29 July 2011. Retrieved 24 September 2018. https://www.repertoirerecords.com/spotlight/genesis-the-greatest-story-ever-told.

16. Flannan Isles Lighthouse is situated near the highest point on Eilean Mòr, one of the Flannan Isles in the Outer Hebrides off the west coast of Scotland. The mystery was based on an incident in 1900 whereupon noticing no light emanating from the lighthouse, a search team arrived to find no sign of the three keepers.

17. Some sources state THE SILENT SUN single was released on 22 or 23 February 1968, while others state 2 February, which is also the date noted on the label of the demo version of the single and quoted in Decca's promo material including advance ordering information for dealers. It is likely the 2 February date was the release date for advance copies of the single. In his book, *My Book of Genesis*, Richard Macphail distinctly remembers the single being officially released on a Thursday and the same day as Chris Welch's review appeared in *Melody Maker*, which only fits with 22 February, so this is the date I have gone with.

18. Another name suggested for the band by King was Gabriel's Angels, which perhaps understandably only Gabriel liked. Phillips had suggested Champagne Meadow, which was also quickly discarded by the others.

19. "Genesis—The Greatest Story Ever Told." Repertoire Records, 29 July 2011. Retrieved 24 September 2018. September 2018. https://www.repertoirerecords.com/spotlight/genesis-the-greatest-story-ever-told.

20. The outfits, bought in London's Carnaby Street, were a mix of black jackets and white shirts and trousers or vice versa. A promo photograph shows Gabriel and Rutherford in white jackets, while Banks, Phillips and Stewart opted for black.

21. Platts, Robin. *Genesis: Inside & Out*. London: Collector's Guide, 2001.

22. Johnson, Derek. SILENT SUN single review. *New Musical Express*, 8 March 1968.

23. "Genesis Revelations: Interview with Anthony Phillips." *The Waiting Room Online #15*. 28 April 1989. Retrieved 23 August 2019. www.twronline.net

24. This is the release date quoted on Decca's demo pressing of the single.

25. Johnson, Derek. A WINTER'S TALE single review. *New Musical Express*, 11 May 1968.

26. In an interview with Dave Negrin for his *World of Genesis* (www.worldofgenesis.com/ChrisStewart-interview-0805.htm) website on 5 August 2005 (retrieved 26 September 2018), Stewart conceded the band had made the right decision: "I was still at school, and they were allowed to leave. Their parents said that they figured that it was quite a promising career, and it was rightly worth leaving. My parents said, 'No! You sit your exams out! That doesn't look like a very promising career at all!' That, apart from the fact that I was also a rotten drummer, were two of the reasons that I was given the boot from Genesis... and very justifiably, too." On leaving school Stewart went to work on a building site. Stewart would later go on to become a best-selling author of several books describing his experiences as a remote farmer in Spain. His 1999 book *Driving Over Lemons* became an international best-seller.

27. Silver was the founder member of the first pop group at St. Edward's School. He was a major jazz fan, with Stan Kenton's big band being a favorite of his.

28. Thomas had worked with Peter Gabriel in the band The Spoken Word. Members of the band stayed at his flat in Branham Gardens, Earl's Court, London, for a period.

29. The session also included the songs "I'm Here," "2:30 Parktime (a.m. p.m.)" and "There Was a Movement."

Chapter 2

1. The album title is a reference to a challenge from an American band called Genesis over the band name. Genesis were intending to rename their band Revelation, but ultimately decided against it. There is no band name reference on the album cover.

2. Banks and Gabriel would write their songs at a flat they shared Earl's Court with mutual friend David Thomas.

3. Arthur Greenslade (4 May 1923–27 November 2003) had worked with a range of performers and some of the biggest artists of the day including

Tom Jones, Dusty Springfield, Engelbert Humperdinck, Johnny Mathis, Billy Fury and Val Doonican. He employed Lou Warburton, another musical arranger, to act as conductor. Lewis "Lou" Warburton started out as a saxophone player in several orchestras, before starting his own. He worked as a musical director and arranger for The Hollies and Cilla Black among others.

4. Negrin, Dave. "The Man Who Would Be King—An Interview with Jonathan King." *WorldofGenesis.com*, 29 April 2005. Retrieved 24 March 2019. www.worldofgenesis.com/JonathanKing-Interview.htm.

5. This is the release date quoted on Decca's demo pressing of the single.

6. Banks, Tony, Phil Collins, Peter Gabriel, Steve Hackett and Mike Rutherford. Ed. Philip Dodd. *Genesis; Chapter & Verse*. London: Weidenfeld & Nicolson, 2007.

7. Fielder, Hugh. *The Book of Genesis*. London: Sidgwick & Jackson, 1984.

8. Gallo, Armando. *Genesis: I Know What I Like*. Los Angeles: DIY, 1979.

9. The initial sessions in August 1968 were recorded on 4-track equipment. When King decided to add orchestration in November, the original 4-track was mixed down to a band track and vocal track on a new 4-track tape, with the orchestration or backing vocals taking one or both of the third and fourth tracks of the new tape.

10. Young, Jon. "Genesis Look at Themselves—An Autodiscography." *Trouser Press*, March 1982.

11. *Trespass* reissue DVD interview, 2008.

12. Williams, Mark. Review of *From Genesis to Revelation*. *International Times* (#57), 23 May-5 June 1969.

13. Press release. Jonjo Music Ltd., 1 May 2017.

Chapter 3

1. Gallo, Armando. *Genesis—I Know What I Like*. Los Angeles: DIY, 1979.

2. The Mellotron was the first keyboard to give musicians access to an orchestral canvas. These sounds were stored on tape, making the instrument heavy and unwieldly. The Beatles had used the instrument for their single "Strawberry Fields Forever" demonstrating the impact it would have on popular music.

3. Silver attended Cornell University in New York state, where he studied in the School of Hotel Administration. He continued to play drums in bands there for a period, too. Eventually he changed career tac altogether to work in TV production on news and current affairs back in the UK, working at Granada and Thames Television among others. He later moved into IT working on video editing systems.

4. Mayhew had learned to play drums at 16 and joined the school band. He played in a variety of bands in Suffolk, playing air force bases, pubs and clubs. He had been in a band called Milton's Fingers, but had left them, and moved back to London.

5. "Genesis Revelations: Interview with Anthony Phillips." *The Waiting Room Online #15*. 28 April 1989. Retrieved 4 August 2019. www.twronline.net

6. Tony Hill-Smith was a friend of Peter Gabriel's, who was a guitarist with a group called Design. He was a keen supporter and provider of encouragement to the band. He would regularly drop in on the band's rehearsals and was photographed with the band with Brian Roberts at Roberts' grandmothers' house for a feature in the *East Grinstead Courier* on 31 July 1969.

7. In "Beyond the Shrouded Riffs," an interview for *Genesis-News.com* (www.genesis-news.com/c-Steve-Hackett-Interview-in-Aschaffenburg-ColosSaal-23112011-s470.html) on 23 November 2011 (retrieved 4 August 2019), Hackett recalled that the songs were only really sketches recorded to demo standard at the time of recording. Rutherford later contradicted this view in "Genesis of a Mechanic—An Interview with Mike Rutherford," an interview he gave to *The World of Genesis* website three years later (retrieved 4 August 2019), where he stated the songs were complete recordings. (www.worldofgenesis.com/MikeRutherford-interview2004-page2.htm). Tony Banks recalled in *Chapter & Verse* that GOING OUT TO GET YOU was a key part of their live set and the reason that they never put it on an album was that Anthony Phillips had been the main writer and by the time it was considered as a potential single he had left the band.

8. A live version of GOING OUT TO GET YOU unofficially recorded in Italy in 1972 can be heard on a *YouTube* post, where the changes in the song are evident. https://www.youtube.com/watch?v=-hlq7J-NJe2Q

9. Mick Jackson was an obscure painter, who was seemingly fascinating enough for the BBC to invest in making a documentary about his work. Jackson's subject matter was often controversial, including sexually charged and provocative depictions of bondage and domination.

10. Peter Gabriel added flute to Stevens' song "Katmandu" on the 1970 album *Mona Bone Jakon*.

11. The band were impressed by Samwell-Smith's work and asked him to become their full-time producer. He declined, citing his commitments to Cat Stevens.

12. The 7½-inch reel to reel tapes along with handwritten notes about the film apparently lay in a barn in Europe for 15 years before being discovered.

13. Gabriel recalled in his liner notes to the *Genesis 1970–1975* box set that a lack of studio time, due to the need to lay down the instrumental tracks, meant he was only able to lay down a guide vocal track.

14. The piece had been developed under the working title "F Sharp" in reference to the guitar tuning chosen by Phillips.

15. It is widely accepted that Phillips was the principal writer, but the group policy of band accreditation meant that by the time the song was further developed into [25] THE MUSICAL BOX, Phillips was no longer a part of the band and therefore received no credit when it was included on *Nursery Cryme*.

16. Rutherford remembered in his memoir that

this session was the only early recording of the band to have a professional sound.

17. "Genesis Revelations: Interview with Anthony Phillips." *The Waiting Room Online #15*. 28 April 1989. www.twronline.net

Chapter 4

1. Rare Bird had two keyboard players, one of whom was Dave Kaffinetti, who had created a new sound by playing his electric piano through a fuzz box, giving it a similar sound to a guitar. Tony Banks remembered this technique later, when he had to cover the guitar parts once Anthony Phillips had left the band.

2. Tony Stratton-Smith (born 29 October 1933, died 19 March 1987) had started his career as a sports journalist and found himself becoming fascinated with music management, having seen the part Brian Epstein played in the success of the Beatles. In 1968, he took over management of The Nice, one of Genesis' favorite bands at the time, and shortly after formed his own record label, The Famous Charisma Label, in 1969. Along with The Nice, the label supported acts such as Lindisfarne, Van Der Graaf Generator, String Driven Thing and Hawkwind and later Peter Hammill, Vivian Stanshall and the Monty Python group of comedians. The label was managed day to day by Gail Colson. Other office staff at Charisma included Fred Munt (later to become Gail Colson's husband), Eve Slater, Chris Briggs and Glen Colson (Gail's brother) as press officer.

3. Genesis had also been considered by Island Records (on the recommendation of Mott the Hoople, who Genesis had supported) and Chrysalis. Additionally, Mike Pinder of the Moody Blues was keen on the band and looked to sign them for the Blues' Threshold Label. They even got as far as recording a version of [19] Looking for Someone. Banks was put off signing for the label when the producer refused to re-record to remove a mistake he had made.

4. Gallo, Armando. *Genesis: I Know What I Like*. Los Angeles: DIY, 1979.

5. There were also many other songs the band had written or covered during the period between *From Genesis to Revelation* and *Trespass* which were not recorded, including: "Movement" (an extended piece, for which some sections would later be developed into separate songs), "Everywhere Is Here," "Stranger," "Babies," "Chobham Chords," "Classic," "Digby of the Rambling Lake," "Eastern Magic Boogie," "Epic," "Grandma," "Key to Love," "Little Leaf," "Masochistic Man," "Moss," "Silver Song" (later recorded by Anthony Phillips with Phil Collins on vocals), "Think Again," "Wandering Waterlily" and "Wooden Mask" (believed to have been recorded at the *Nursery Cryme* sessions as a potential B-side to a proposed single release for [D18a] Going Out to Get You. Live covers included: "Black Sheep," "Crossroads," "Do I Still Figure in Your Life?" and "Stumble."

6. Welch, Chris. *Genesis: The Complete Guide to their Music*. London: Omnibus, 2011.

7. The new equipment the band used for the recording included a secondhand Ludwig drum kit and separate snare drum they bought for John Mayhew.

8. Watts, Michael. "Reading from the Book of Genesis." *Melody Maker*, 23 January 1971.

9. Phillips had contracted a bout of glandular fever a few months before the album was recorded, and he had never properly recovered. It had drained him of energy and added anxiety to his stage performances. His condition would come to have more serious consequences for the band.

10. Gerhardts, Christian. "Evolution of Genesis Event 2006." "Question Time with John Mayhew." *It (Genesis-News.com)*, 2006. Retrieved 4 August 2019. https://www.genesis-news.com/c-Genesis-Interview-with-John-Mayhew-2006-s159.html).

11. Reed, Ryan. "20 Insanely Great Genesis Songs Only Hardcore Fans Know," *Rolling Stone*, 10 October 2014. Retrieved 1 March 2019. https://www.rollingstone.com/music/music-lists/20-insanely-great-genesis-songs-only-hardcore-fans-know-157999/the-carpet-crawlers-1999-148785.

12. *White Fang*, by Jack London, was published in the United States by Macmillan in 1906. The story is written from the perspective of White Fang, a wolf-dog living in the north west territories of Canada. It is a morality tale that contrasts the violent animal world with the equally violent human world. The novel is a companion piece to London's more famous 1903 work, *The Call of the Wild*. The story has also been filmed many times over the years, most recently as a French animation in 2018.

13. Phillips later admitted this in an interview in March 2001 with *Mojo* Magazine: "the irony was that he was singing it on stage, but he didn't realize that I had written about his girlfriend." (Collis, Clark. "Bloody Students." *Mojo*, March 2001).

14. Banks hired the Mellotron for the *Trespass* recordings and had only a day to use it on the two tracks he'd earmarked—this one and [22] Stagnation.

15. The band recall the length of "The Movement" being from between thirteen and twenty minutes.

16. Young, Jon. "Genesis Look at Themselves—An Autodiscography." *Trouser Press*, March 1982.

17. Roberts, Chris. "The Prog Interview: Tony Banks." *Prog*, 1 March 2018.

18. Gabriel played the flute to give him something to do during the instrumental sections as Banks had declared the keyboards as his territory and off-limits to the singer.

19. Interview with Tony Banks. *The Waiting Room Online*. 9 April 1994. Retrieved 4 August 2019. www.twronline.net

20. Watts, Michael. Review of *Trespass*. *Melody Maker*, 12 December 1970.

21. Gilbert, Jerry. Review of *Trespass*. *Sounds*, October 1970.

Chapter 5

1. After leaving the band, Anthony Phillips went about studying music at the Guildhall School of

Music and Drama. He carved out a solo career for himself. In the early days he was helped by Mike Rutherford and Phil Collins—notably on his 1977 release *The Geese and the Ghost*. He went on to play keyboards on Mike Rutherford's debut solo album, *Smallcreep's Day*, in 1979. He has produced a series of largely instrumental albums, many under the title of *Private Parts & Pieces*, and writes music for advertising and soundtracks.

2. Interviewed for German fan website *It*, Mayhew recalled, "I was asked to leave. I just technically wasn't good enough, that's the truth of the matter." After Mayhew left the band, he briefly went back to becoming a jobbing musician. He played in bands that toured Europe, mainly American air bases in Germany and Poland. During this period, he met his second wife in Norway and in 1977 the couple eventually emigrated to New Zealand and then Australia where he gave up drumming and became a decorative artist. He was out of contact with the band for more than 30 years. Mayhew moved to Scotland in the early 2000s, where he discussed with student Dave Burgess that he used to play drums and Burgess, being a big Genesis fan, put two and two together, eventually contacting Genesis' management, instigating a link-up with Mayhew. He was able to contribute his recollections for the band's official autobiography, *Genesis: Chapter & Verse*. Mayhew died of a heart condition in Glasgow, Scotland, on 26 March 2009, the day before his 62nd birthday. (Gerhardts, Christian. "Evolution of Genesis Event 2006." "Question Time with John Mayhew." *It (Genesis-News.com)*, 2006. Retrieved 4 August 2019. https://www.genesis-news.com/c-Genesis-Interview-with-John-Mayhew-2006-s159.html).

3. Phil Collins recalled in his book, *Not Dead Yet: The Autobiography* (London: Penguin Random House, 2016), "I'm thinking that if we present ourselves at this audition as a package, we'll stand a better chance of getting the gig."

4. Tony Stratton-Smith had the idea of taking his three top bands—Lindisfarne, Van Der Graaf Generator and Genesis—around the country as a package. Customers would buy tickets for thirty pence or six shillings in old money (hence the christening of the "Six-Bob" tour). The venture was a success, giving exposure to all the bands to a broader audience.

5. [25] THE MUSICAL BOX and [27] THE RETURN OF THE GIANT HOGWEED had been written before the band started writing at the rehearsals.

6. Gallo, Armando. *Genesis: I Know What I Like*. Los Angeles: DIY, 1979.

7. *Genesis Archive 1967–75* Interview Disc, 1998.

8. Interview with Steve Hackett. *BBC Radio Hallam*, 5 May 1978.

9. The reference "F#" refers to Phillips and Rutherford tuning each of the top three strings on their 12-string guitars to F sharp.

10. Young, Jon. "Genesis Look at Themselves—An Autodiscography." *Trouser Press*, March 1982.

11. The house contained a formal garden and croquet lawn.

12. Snow, Matt. "The Man Who Fell to Earth," *Mojo*, April 2010.

13. Rutherford had been encouraged by Gabriel to create a sound matching that of The Who's Pete Townshend with his slashing guitar riffs.

14. Finger-tapping is the technique of hammering the index finger onto the string against the guitar's fretboard.

15. The band had also been influenced by a song called "The Weaver's Answer" by Family, with Collins replicating the rolling drum sound in the midsong instrumental section.

16. Clarke, Steve. "The Genesis Guide to Genesis." *New Musical Express*, 1 January 1977.

17. Collins, Phil. *Not Dead Yet: The Autobiography*. London: Penguin Random House, 2016.

18. The hogweed is technically known as Heracleum mantegazzianum and is a toxic plant, which can cause severe skin inflammation and is native to the Caucasus region and Central Asia. It became an invasive species to Europe and the UK. The band imagined a story of the plant being taken from Russia by a Victorian explorer and introduced into England.

19. Gabriel and Collins' combined vocals was recorded onto one track, so the voices could not be separated when it came to remix the album.

20. Rutherford, Mike. *The Living Years: The First Genesis Memoir*. London: Constable & Robinson, 2014.

21. Young, Jon. "Genesis Look at Themselves—An Autodiscography." *Trouser Press*, March 1982.

22. Steve Hackett interviewed by Aymeric Leroy. June 1998.

23. The album liner notes describe a Hermaphrodite as a flower containing both male and female organs and the legend surrounding it. It then goes on the explain that Hermaphroditus was the son of Hermes and Aphrodite, born out of a secret love affair. The boy was left at Mount Ida with the nymphs who lived there and grew up in the wild woods where he encountered a water nymph (Salmacis). He placed a curse on the waters which meant anyone who bathed in them would become a hermaphrodite. Salmacis Fountain is near the ancient Mausoleum of Halicarnassus in Bodrum, Turkey, and today is a tourist attraction.

24. Fielder, Hugh. *The Book of Genesis*. London: Sidgwick & Jackson, 1984.

25. Couture, Francios. THE FOUNTAIN OF SALMACIS song review. *All Music Guide*. Retrieved 15 September 2019. www.allmusic.com/song/the-fountain-of-salmacis-mt0050899757.

26. The album would not appear on the UK Albums chart until its rerelease in May 1974, when it peaked at #39.

27. Gallo, Armando. *Genesis: I Know What I Like*. Los Angeles: DIY, 1979.

28. Gilbert, Jerry. *Nursery Cryme* review. *Sounds*, 4 December 1971.

29. Cromelin, Richard. *Nursery Cryme* review. *Rolling Stone*, 26 October 1971.

30. Gallo, Armando. *Genesis: I Know What I Like*. Los Angeles: DIY, 1979.

31. A promo version of the single was released to radio DJs on 12 May 1972 but failed to generate enough interest to force the band into the UK Singles chart. The single would be rereleased in October

1972, with a picture sleeve cover, but again without success.
   32. Interview with Tony Banks. *The Waiting Room Online*, 1994
   33. Welch, Chris. "The Book of Genesis." *Melody Maker*, 20 July 1972.
   34. *The Waiting Room Online*. March 1996.
   35. Welch, Chris. Review of Happy the Man *Melody Maker*, 3 July 1972.

Chapter 6

   1. Phil Collins' mother, June, managed the Barbara Speake Stage School in Acton and had access to various venues, one of which was the Una Billings School of Dancing.
   2. Roberts, Chris. "Genesis: Foxtrot Was Where We First Started to Become Significant." *Prog*, 6 October 2016. Retrieved 24 September 2018. https://www.loudersound.com/features/genesis-fox-on-the-run.
   3. Potter did not like Banks' atmospheric introduction to Watcher of the Skies and felt the song would be better off without it, likening Banks' work to the soundtrack to *2001: A Space Odyssey*. Ironically Banks was approached to work on the sequel to that film in 1984, a project he ultimately left when director Peter Hyams proved to be less than enthusiastic about his work.
   4. *Metal Hammer Genesis Special*. July 1987
   5. During the sessions Genesis also rehearsed a piece largely written by Rutherford in 3/4 time that was not used on the album but would become the end section of "Shadow of Hierophant" on Steve Hackett's 1975 debut solo album *Voyage of the Acolyte*. The band was also working on an embryonic version of [42] Firth of Fifth, which would be recorded on their next studio album, *Selling England by the Pound*.
   6. Hackett, Steve. *Watcher of the Skies: Genesis Revisited*. Liner notes. 1996.
   7. Collins was inspired by watching the band Yes perform into trying out more complex drum patterns and time signatures.
   8. Roberts, Chris. "Genesis: Foxtrot Was Where We First Started to Become Significant." *Prog*. 6 October 2016. Retrieved 24 September 2018. https://www.loudersound.com/features/genesis-fox-on-the-run.
   9. The song was premiered at the Lincoln Festival on Sunday 28 May 1972.
   10. The line in question is: "Then felt I like some watcher of the skies / When a new planet swims into his ken."
   11. Hewitt, Alan. "Between the Tape Deck and the Teacup." *The Waiting Room Online*. 21 August 1997. Retrieved 5 August 2019. www.twronline.net.
   12. Gallo, Armando. *Genesis: I Know What I Like*. Los Angeles: DIY, 1979.
   13. *HackettSongs*. 12 October 2012. Retrieved 24 September 2018. www.hackettsongs.com/blog/steve97.html.
   14. *Foxtrot* 2008 reissue DVD Interview.
   15. Fielder, Hugh. *The Book of Genesis*. London: Sidgwick & Jackson, 1984.
   16. Romano, Will. "A Different View: Steve Hackett." *Modern Drummer*, April 2013.
   17. The lyrics for each section of the song were interpreted by the band in their program notes for the *Foxtrot* tour as follows:

i.) Lover's Leap
In which two lovers are lost in each other's eyes and found again transformed in the bodies of another male and female.

ii.) The Guaranteed Eternal Sanctuary Man
The lovers come across a town dominated by two characters: one a benevolent farmer, and the other the head of a highly disciplined scientific religion. The latter likes to be known as "The Guaranteed Eternal Sanctuary Man" and claims to contain a secret new ingredient capable of fighting fire. This is a falsehood, an untruth, a whopper and a taradiddle, or to put it in clearer terms; a lie.

iii.) Ikhnaton and Itsacon and Their Band of Merry Men
Who the lovers see clad in grays and purples, awaiting to be summoned out of the ground. At the G.E.S.M.'s command they pour forth, from the bowels of the earth, to attack all those without an up-to-date "Eternal Life Licence" which were obtainable at the head office of the G.E.S.M.'s religion.

iv.) How Dare I Be So Beautiful?
In which our intrepid heroes investigate the aftermath of the battle and discover a solitary figure, obsessed by his own image. They witness an unusual transmutation, and are pulled into their own reflections in the water.

v.) Willow Farm
Climbing out of the pool, they are once again in a different existence. They're right in the middle of a myriad of bright colors, filled with all manner of objects, plants, animals and humans. Life flows freely and everything is mindlessly busy. At random, a whistle blows and every single thing is instantly changed into another.

vi.) Apocalypse in 9/8 (Co-Starring the Delicious Talents of Gabble Ratchet)
At one whistle the lovers become seeds in the soil, where they recognize other seeds to be people from the world in which they had originated. While they wait for Spring, they are returned to their old world to see the Apocalypse of St. John in full progress. The seven trumpeters cause a sensation, the fox keeps throwing sixes, and Pythagoras (a Greek extra) is deliriously happy as he manages to put exactly the right amount of milk and honey on his corn flakes.

vii) As Sure as Eggs is Eggs (Aching Mens' Feet)
Above all else an egg is an egg. "And did those feet……" making ends meet.

As for Gabble Ratchet—apparently it is the sound of wild geese that heralds the arrival of archangels (or something similar).

18. For live performances of the song, Banks would use the Hammond organ as he was unable to recreate the piano effect on stage.

19. Gallo, Armando. *Genesis: I Know What I Like*. Los Angeles: DIY, 1980.

20. The reference to Gabble Ratchet is apparently a link to the Hounds of Hell, usually portrayed as geese—hence the sound effect during this piece. They are also referred to as Gabriel's Hounds with the obvious link to the singer.

21. Tyler, Tony. "Genesis: Poised on the Brink." *New Musical Express*, 18 November 1972.

22. Collins, Phil. *Not Dead Yet: The Autobiography*. London: Penguin Random House, 2016.

23. Roberts, Chris. "The Prog Interview: Tony Banks." *Prog*, 1 March 2018.

24. Wiser, Carl. Interview with Tony Banks. *Songfacts*, 20 February 2018. Retrieved 24 September 2018. www.songfacts.com/blog/interviews/tony_banks.

25. The title is a play on x=x (eggs is eggs), and denotes certainty and faith as good defeats evil, while "Aching Men's Feet" is a play on the phrase "Making ends meet."

26. Banks, Tony, Phil Collins, Peter Gabriel, Steve Hackett and Mike Rutherford. Ed. Philip Dodd. *Genesis; Chapter & Verse*. London: Weidenfeld & Nicolson, 2007.

27. Clarke, Steve. "The Genesis Guide to Genesis." *New Musical Express*, 1 January 1977.

28. "Interview with Tony Banks." *Songfacts.com*, 20 February 2018. Retrieved 24 September 2018. www.songfacts.com/blog/interviews/tony_banks.

29. Collins, Phil. *Not Dead Yet: The Autobiography*. London: Penguin Random House, 2016.

30. *Foxtrot* 2008 reissue DVD Interview.

31. The album title, *Foxtrot*, was inspired by Whitehead's painting and not the other way around.

32. Whitehad, Paul. "Cover Story—*Foxtrot*." *RockPop Gallery*, 8 June 2007. Retrieved 24 September 2018. rockpopgallery.typepad.com/rockpop_gallery_news/2007/06/cover_story_fox.html.

33. Gallo, Armando. *Genesis: I Know What I Like*. Los Angeles: DIY, 1979.

34. Gilbert, Jerry, Review of *Foxtrot*. *Sounds*, 30 September 1972.

35. *Billboard*, 9 December 1972.

36. Described by Gabriel, in his interview for the *Foxtrot* 2008 reissue DVD, as a "visceral sense of shock."

37. The show was cancelled as the promoter, Rikki Farr, said the tickets could not be printed in time. The band had planned to do two sets, the first featuring older material such as [22] STAGNATION and the second featuring their current set.

38. The 2009 remix/remaster added five tracks recorded from the show at the Shrine Auditorium in LA in 1975 on the tour of *The Lamb Lies Down on Broadway*. These tracks work as a sampler of the full *Lamb* show, but also highlight some of the limitations the band had in bringing that material to life.

39. Hewitt, Alan. "Genesis Revelations—Steve Hackett in Conversation about his Career with Genesis." *The Waiting Room Online*, March 1996. Retrieved 6 August 2019. www.twronline.net.

Chapter 7

1. *BBC Radio Hallam*, 5 May 1978.

2. Young, Jon. "Genesis Look at Themselves—An Autodiscography." *Trouser Press*, March 1982.

3. Fielder, Hugh. *The Book of Genesis*. London: Sidgwick & Jackson, 1984.

4. Fielder, Hugh. *The Book of Genesis*. London: Sidgwick & Jackson, 1984.

5. Harvey, Peter. "Our Act Was Slowly Taking Us Over." *Record Mirror*, 19 January 1974.

6. Greene, Andy. "Genesis Guitarist Steve Hackett Talks 'Selling England by the Pound' Tour." *Rolling Stone*, 5 September 2019. Retrieved 6 September 2019. www.rollingstone.com/music/music-features/genesis-steve-hackett-interview-selling-england-by-the-pound-tour-879695/?fbclid=IwAR3RiM7YqK5djtbQ47OpRR5T4HYJM-AZUvuSpTp17VY8tjlO64UZk7fmLf0.

7. Buckley, David. "In an English Country Garden." *Q Classic: Pink Floyd and the Story of Prog Rock*, July 2005.

8. Genesis referred to this section of music as "Disney."

9. This release date is the most likely based on music press coverage and band interviews at the time. The release of the single had been delayed due to a vinyl shortage in the industry.

10. Negrin, Dave. "Tales of the Tape." *World of Genesis*, 2 July 2006. Retrieved 24 September 2018. www.worldofgenesis.com/JohnBurns-interview2006.htm.

11. Gilbert, Jerry. "Genesis Know What They Like…" *Sounds*, 27 April 1974.

12. The song's title is an obvious pun on the Firth of Forth river mouth in Scotland.

13. Clarke, Steve. "The Genesis Guide to Genesis." *New Musical Express*, 1 January 1977.

14. Greene, Andy. "Genesis Guitarist Steve Hackett Talks 'Selling England by the Pound' Tour." *Rolling Stone*, 5 September 2019. Retrieved 6 September 2019. www.rollingstone.com/music/music-features/genesis-steve-hackett-interview-selling-england-by-the-pound-tour-879695/?fbclid=IwAR3RiM7YqK5djtbQ47OpRR5T4HYJM-AZUvuSpTp17VY8tjlO64UZk7fmLf0.

15. Mackintosh, Hamish. "Tony Banks: The 10 Records That Changed My Life." *MusicRadar*, 14 August 2015. Retrieved 24 September 2018. https://www.musicradar.com/news/tech/tony-banks-the-10-records-that-changed-my-life-626411.

16. Negrin, Dave. "Tales of the Tape." *World of Genesis*. 2 July 2006. Retrieved 24 September 2018. www.worldofgenesis.com/JohnBurns-interview2006.htm.

17. The *Times* article, dated 5 April 1972, stated: "One gang even challenged another to a private battle in Epping Forest. About 50 men, armed with knuckledusters, heavy boots and razors, arrived. Combatants left the area suffering serious injuries. The

winning gang, made up mainly of young men, won the concession to a protection racket in a small area of east London."

18. Schacht, Janis. *Genesis*. New York: Proteus Books, 1985.

19. *Virgin Online* Web Chat. 27 November 1998.

20. *Selling England by the Pound* reissue DVD interview, 2008.

21. *Selling England by the Pound* reissue DVD interview, 2008.

22. Banks, Tony, Phil Collins, Peter Gabriel, Steve Hackett and Mike Rutherford. Ed. Phillip Dodd. *Genesis: Chapter & Verse*. London: Weidenfeld and Nicolson, 2007.

23. Gallo, Armando. *Genesis: I Know What I Like*. Los Angeles: DIY, 1979.

24. Tony Banks Interview. *Songfacts.com*. Retrieved 14 February 2019. www.songfacts.com/detail.php?id=32937.

25. Rutherford, Mike. *The Living Years: The First Genesis Memoir*. London: Constable & Robinson, 2014.

26. Gallo, Armando. *Genesis: I Know What I Like*. Los Angeles: DIY, 1979.

27. Review of *Selling England by the Pound*. *Sounds*, 29 September 1973.

28. Charone, Barbara. "The Pound Recovers." *New Musical Express*, 29 September 1973.

29. Gambaccini, Paul. *Selling England by the Pound* review. *Rolling Stone*, 14 March 1974.

30. Blake, Mark. "Anyone for Croquet with a Severed Head? Ghosts in the Front Garden? And Who's Best: Gabriel or Collins?' *Planet Rock*, Issue #13, April 2019.

31. Erlewine, Stephen Thomas. *Selling England by the Pound* review. *All Music Guide*. Retrieved 13 April 2019. https://www.allmusic.com/album/selling-england-by-the-pound-mw0000189986.

32. The set included: [33] WATCHER OF THE SKIES, [40] DANCING WITH THE MOONLIT KNIGHT, [41] I KNOW WHAT I LIKE, THE [25] MUSICAL BOX and [38] SUPPER'S READY. The 61-minute film, shot in 16mm, was made available on the DVD Extras Disc of the remixed *Selling England by the Pound* album released as part of the *Genesis 1970–1975* box set.

33. Welch, Chris. "Genesis: England Rules the Waves!" *Melody Maker*, 25 May 1974.

34. According to Collins the debt amounted to £150,000. Rutherford remember it at £400,000.

35. Harvey, Peter. "Our Act Was Slowly Taking Us Over." *Record Mirror*, 19 January 1974.

Chapter 8

1. Gabriel had come up with the name Rael, through experimentation with the sounds of words, and thought the name would avoid any ethnic stereotyping. He hadn't at that point realized that fellow English band The Who had also used the name for a "mini-opera" on their 1967 album *The Who Sell Out*.

2. Rutherford essentially saw *The Little Prince* as a children's story aimed at grown-ups.

3. *Cheap Thrills*. March 1977.

4. Rutherford acknowledged in his memoir that he could see that the music could bring alive the imagery the story created. (Rutherford, Mike. *The Living Years: The First Genesis Memoir*. London: Constable & Robinson, 2014).

5. Charone, Barbara. *Rolling Stone*. "Genesis: To Them It's Only Rock & Role." 2 January 1975.

6. Fielder, Hugh. *The Book of Genesis*. London: Sidgwick & Jackson, 1984.

7. Friedkin had also approached Tangerine Dream for musical ideas and Philippe Drier, one of the founders of *Heavy Metal* comic books in France, for design ideas. The sci-fi film would not materialize, but Friedkin went on to use Tangerine Dream on the soundtrack to his next movie, *Sorcerer*, released in 1977.

8. Collins was chief archivist of the band's writing and rehearsal sessions, using his Nakamichi cassette recorder to capture the sessions and help identify the strongest moments.

9. According to Holm-Hudson (p. 52) the recording equipment used included: Two 3M 24-track recorders, a Helios Electronics 30-input mixing console, Altec monitors and two A62 Studers for mastering

10. Easlea, Daryl. "Genesis: 'I Was Aware There Was Something Going on With Peter.'" *Prog*, 18 November 2016. Retrieved 24 September 2018. https://www.loudersound.com/features/genesis-i-was-aware-there-was-something-going-on-with-peter.

11. Island Studios was based in a converted church in Notting Hill. There were two studios in the building, with the upstairs one being the best equipped. Genesis were using the studio downstairs.

12. Tony Banks: "We never finished it properly, it was a rush job. It finalized the split between us and Pete, that's certain." (Jones, Cliff. "Genesis: Chapter & Verse." *RCD*, June 1994 [?]).

13. Hewitt, Alan. "The Genesis of a Guitarist—Steve Hackett Reminisces to Alan about his Career with Genesis." *The Waiting Room Online*. 22 August 1997. Retrieved 9 August 2019. www.twronline.net.

14. The icons referenced included comedian Lenny Bruce; philosopher Marshall McLuhan; Groucho Marx; criminal Caryl Chessman, who was executed in the gas chamber; and movie producer Howard Hughes. References are also made to the Ku Klux Klan serving hot soul food; Glenn Miller's "In the Mood"; Elvis' blue suede shoes; Winston cigarettes and the pop standard "Needles and Pins."

15. This version can be seen on the *Genesis: In Concert* film captured at the Apollo Theatre in Glasgow, Scotland, on 9 July 1976, and Bingley Hall in Staffordshire, England, on 10 July 1976. The film was released as a DVD extra on the *A Trick of the Tail* disc in the box set *Genesis 1976–1982*.

16. The song was referenced as "Claustrophobia" during its recording.

17. *Genesis Official Website*, 23 November 2001. No longer available.

18. Easlea, Daryl. *Prog*. "Genesis, Peter Gabriel, and the Story of The Lamb Lies Down on Broadway." 18 November 2016. Retrieved 9 August 2019. https://

www.loudersound.com/features/genesis-i-was-aware-there-was-something-going-on-with-peter.

19. The release date used here is based on information published at the time by fan newsletter *The Hogweed Youth Movement*. Other sources have referenced 1 and 8 November as potential release dates.

20. Irwin, Colin. "Genesis: What a Dreary Time." *Melody Maker*, 16 November 1974.

21. The other being [53] THE GRAND PARADE OF LIFELESS PACKAGING.

22. Rutherford, Mike. *The Living Years: The First Genesis Memoir*. London: Constable & Robinson, 2014.

23. The single removes the first linking vocal section, something the band would emulate in live performances from 1976.

24. Irwin, Colin. THE CARPET CRAWLERS single review. *Melody Maker*, 26 April 1975.

25. Childs, Andy. THE CARPET CRAWLERS single review. *Zig Zag*, April 1975.

26. The song was developed under the working title of "Countryman."

27. Fielder, Hugh. *The Book of Genesis*. London: Sidgwick & Jackson, 1984.

28. Banks, Tony, Phil Collins, Peter Gabriel, Steve Hackett and Mike Rutherford. Ed. Phillip Dodd. *Genesis: Chapter & Verse*. London: Weidenfeld and Nicolson, 2007.

29. Dallas, Karl. "Banks' Holiday." *Melody Maker*, 7 June 1975.

30. Hackett, Steve. "Genesis Revisited and Remembered." *HackettSongs*. 12 October 2012. Retrieved 7 June 2017. www.hackettsongs.com/blog/steve97.html.

31. Negrin, Dave. "Tales of the Tape." *World of Genesis*, 2 July 2006. Retrieved 24 September 2018. www.worldofgenesis.com/JohnBurns-interview2006.htm.

32. Bonner, Michael. "Genesis Interviewed: 'We Ended Up as a Three-Piece Because We Had Too Many Ideas for a Five-Piece…'" *Uncut*, 10 September 2015. Retrieved 19 January 2019. https://www.uncut.co.uk/blog/the-view-from-here/genesis-interviewed-we-ended-up-as-a-three-piece-because-we-had-too-many-ideas-for-a-five-piece-70663/5#xvGVCl00Ep8QkGbS.99.

33. Charone, Barbara. *The Lamb Lies Down on Broadway* review. *Sounds*, 23 November 1974.

34. Welch, Chris. *The Lamb Lies Down on Broadway* review. *Melody Maker*, 23 November 1974.

35. Erskins, Pete. *The Lamb Lies Down on Broadway* review. *New Musical Express*, 30 November 1974.

36. Erlewine, Stephen Thomas. *The Lamb Lies Down on Broadway* review. *All Music Guide*. Retrieved 20 February 2019. https://www.allmusic.com/album/the-lamb-lies-down-on-broadway-mw0000650187.

37. Michaud, Jon. The "Ulysses of Concept Albums." *The New Yorker*. 28 February 2014. Retrieved 20 February 2019. https://www.newyorker.com/culture/culture-desk/the-ulysses-of-concept-albums.

38. "*The Lamb Lies Down on Broadway* by Genesis." *Classic Rock Review*. 31 August 2014. Retrieved 20 February 2019. www.classicrockreview.com/2014/08/1974-genesis-lamb-lies-down.

39. *ZigZag*. #53, June 1975.

40. Rutherford, Mike. *The Living Years: The First Genesis Memoir*. London: Constable & Robinson, 2014.

41. Collins, Phil. *Not Dead Yet: The Autobiography*. London: Penguin Random House, 20 October 2016.

42. Bungey, John. "Mallets in Wonderland." *Mojo*, July 1998.

43. Jones, Cliff. "Genesis: Chapter & Verse." *RCD*, June 1994 [?].

44. Hackett severed his tendon in the fleshy part of his thumb as he squeezed too hard on a wine glass. He spent five days in hospital where he had a tendon graft followed by a few weeks of physiotherapy.

45. *Genesis Archive 1967–75*. Interview disc.

46. Gabriel's press release read as follows:

"I had a dream, eye's dream. Then I had another dream with the body and soul of a rock star. When it didn't feel good I packed it in. Looking back for the musical and non-musical reasons, this is what I came up with:

OUT, ANGELS OUT—an investigation.

The vehicle we had built as a co-op to serve our songwriting became our master and had cooped us up inside the success we had wanted. It affected the attitudes and the spirit of the whole band. the music had not dried up and I still respect the other musicians, but our roles had set in hard. To get an idea through "Genesis the Big" meant shifting a lot more concrete than before. For any band, transferring the heart from idealistic enthusiasm to professionalism is a difficult operation. I believe the use of sound and visual images can be developed to do much more than we have done. But on a large scale it needs one clear and coherent direction, which our pseudo-democratic committee system could not provide. As an artist, I need to absorb a wide variety of experiences. It is difficult to respond to intuition and impulse within the long-term planning that the band needed. I felt I should look at/learn about/develop myself, my creative bits and pieces and pick up on a lot of work going on outside music. Even the hidden delights of vegetable growing and community living are beginning to reveal their secrets. I could not expect the band to tie in their schedules with my bondage to cabbages. The increase in money and power, if I had stayed, would have anchored me to the spotlights. It was important to me to give space to my family, which I wanted to hold together, and to liberate the daddy in me. Although I have seen and learnt a great deal in the last seven years, I found I had begun to look at things as the famous Gabriel, despite hiding my occupation whenever possible, hitching lifts, etc. I had begun to think in business terms; very useful for an often bitten once shy musician, but treating records and audiences as money was taking me away from them. When performing, there were less shivers up and down the spine. I believe the world has soon to go through a difficult period of changes. I'm excited by some of the areas coming through to the surface which seem to have been hidden away in people's minds. I want to explore and be prepared to be open and flexible enough to respond, not tied in to the old hierarchy. Much of my psyche's ambitions as 'Gabriel archetypal rock star' have been fulfilled—a lot of the ego-gratification and the need to attract young ladies, perhaps the result of frequent rejection as "Gabriel acne-struck public school boy." However, I can still get off playing the star game once in a while. My future within music, if it exists, will be in as many situations as possible. It's good to see a growing number of artists breaking down the pigeonholes. This is the difference between the profitable, compartmentalized, battery chicken and the free-range. Why did the chicken cross the road anyway? There is no animosity between myself and the band or management. The decision had been made some time ago and we have talked about our new direction. The reason why my leaving was not announced earlier was because I had been asked to delay until they had found a replacement to plug up the hole. It is not impossible that some of them might work with me on other projects. The following guesswork has little in common with truth: Gabriel left Genesis. 1) To work in theatre. 2) To make more money as a solo artist. 3) To do a "Bowie." 4) To do a "Ferry." 5) To do a "Furry Boa round my neck and hang myself with it." 6) To go see an institution. 7) To go senile in the sticks. I do not express myself adequately in interviews and I felt I owed it to the people who have put a lot of love and energy supporting the band to give an accurate picture of my reasons."

47. Tyler, Tony. "Thinks... Where in Hell's Name We Gonna Rake Up Another Guy with a Mush Like That." *New Musical Express*, 13 September 1975.

48. Welch, Chris. "Gabriel Tells All!" *Melody Maker*, 6 December 1975.

49. Bell, Max. "Bathtub Confidential: Former Genesis Star Braves Humiliation of Nude Stunt." *New Musical Express*, 27 December 1975.

Chapter 9

1. Collins linked up with the other five musicians, three (bass player Percy Jones, keyboard player Robin Lumley and guitarist John Goodsall) of whom would eventually form the nucleus of Brand X with Collins, in late 1974. He was contacted by Richard Williams, a former *Melody Maker* journalist who was now head of A&R at Island Records. Brand X would fuse rock and jazz into an inventive, if self-indulgent, sound. The outlet gave Collins release from his day job with Genesis and allowed him to further develop his drumming skills.

2. *A Trick of the Tail* reissue interview, 2007.

3. Phil Collins had drum lessons here in his teens. Genesis rented the rehearsal room, situated beside a hairdresser's shop, for £175 a week.

4. Interview for Genesis Official Website, 23 November 2001. No longer available.

5. Collins worked with David Hentschel as drummer on his album *Startling Music*, a collection of instrumental version s of the songs from Ringo Starr's solo album *Ringo*, recorded at Ringo's house, as well as his scores for the films *Operation Daybreak* and later *The Squeeze*.

6. Among those who sent in tapes to the band were Nick Lowe, Mick Rogers of Manfred Mann's Earth Band, Brinsley Schwarz and Noel McCalla (who eventually worked with Rutherford on *Smallcreep's Day*).

7. Keddie, Gibson. "The Long and the Short of It." *Guitarist*, February 1993.

8. Prasad, Anil. "Genesis: Turning It on Again." *Innerviews*, 2007. Retrieved 24 September 2018. www.innerviews.org/inner/genesis.html.

9. Guarisco, Donald. Dance on a Volcano review. *All Music Guide*. Retrieved 20 February 2019. https://www.allmusic.com/song/dance-on-a-volcano-mt0045363089.

10. *A Trick of the Tail* reissue interview, 2007.

11. Karyn. "*A Trick of the Tail* and *Wind & Wuthering* by Genesis." Classic Rock Review, 9 November 2011. Retrieved 20 February 2019. www.classicrockreview.com/2011/11/1976-genesis-double-review.

12. Shasho, Ray. Steve Hackett interview. *Examiner,com.* 11 December 2013.

13. Banks, Tony, Phil Collins, Peter Gabriel, Steve Hackett and Mike Rutherford. Ed. Phillip Dodd. *Genesis: Chapter & Verse*. London: Weidenfeld and Nicolson, 2007.

14. Steve Hackett, Virgin Online Chat, 27 November 1998.

15. Clarke, Steve. "The Genesis Guide to Genesis." *New Musical Express*, 1 January 1977.

16. Rutherford took a description from Argentinian writer Jorge Luis Borges' *Book of Imaginary Beings*, originally published in Spanish in 1957 and in English in 1969. The "squonk" was reputed to live in the Hemlock forests in northern Pennsylvania. This description originated from a book written by William T. Cox in 1910 and titled *Fearsome Creatures of the Lumberwoods, with a Few Desert and Mountain Beasts*. Rutherford basically recounted the myth in lyric form right down to the finale where the creature, captured and bagged by a hunter, dissolves in its own tears.

17. Mann, Richard. "Beggar's Banquet." *Guitarist*, 1995.

18. Roberts, Chris. "The Prog Interview: Tony Banks." *Prog*, 1 March 2018.

19. Collins, Phil. *Not Dead Yet: The Autobiography*. London: Penguin Random House, 20 October 2016.

20. "Tony Banks & the Evolution of Genesis." *Keyboard* Magazine, November 1984.

21. Welch, Chris. "Genesis Re-Born." *Melody Maker*, 7 February 1976.
22. Shacht, Janis. *Genesis*. New York: Proteus, 1985.
23. Charone, Barbara. "A Trick and a Triumph." *Sounds*. 7 February 1976.
24. Negrin, Dave. "Hackett to Bits." *The World of Genesis*, 14 August 2001. Retrieved 24 September 2018. www.worldofgenesis.com/SteveHackett-interview-2001.htm.
25. *The Inheritors* by William Golding was published in 1955 and its hardcover featured a painting of a beast with horns called The Sorcerer. The book follows a tribe of prehistoric Neanderthals to their extinction at the hands of homo sapiens. It is the last chapter of the book—written from the human point of view—that provided the inspiration for Banks' lyrics.
26. Collins came up with the title for the track, which obviously signifies "The End."
27. Clarke, Steve. "The Genesis Guide to Genesis." *New Musical Express*, 1 January 1977.
28. Romano, Will. "A Different View: Steve Hackett." *Modern Drummer*, April 2013.
29. Clarke, Steve. "The Genesis Guide to Genesis." *New Musical Express*, 1 January 1977.
30. Platts, Robin. *Genesis: Inside and Out*. Burlington: Collector's Guide, 2001.
31. Charone, Barbara. "Genesis: Chapter II.'" *Sounds*, 14 February 1976.
32. Welch, Chris. "Genesis Re-Born." *Melody Maker*, 7 February 1976.
33. Charone, Barbara. "Genesis: Supper Is Definitely Ready." *Sounds*, 15 May 1976.

Chapter 10

1. *Genesis: A History*. DVD. BBC Scotland, 1990.
2. Young, Jon. "Genesis Look at Themselves—An Autodiscography." *Trouser Press*, March 1982.
3. Hewitt, Alan. "Between the Tape Deck and the Teacup." *The Waiting Room*, 21 August 1997.
4. Young, Jon. "Genesis Look at Themselves—An Autodiscography." *Trouser Press*, March 1982.
5. Easlea, Daryl. "Lost in the Afterglow." *Prog*, 25 April 2017.
6. Banks, Tony, Phil Collins, Peter Gabriel, Steve Hackett and Mike Rutherford. Ed. Phillip Dodd. *Genesis: Chapter & Verse*. London: Weidenfeld and Nicolson, 2007.
7. *The Flight of the Heron* was the first book in Dorothy Kathleen Broster's Jacobite trilogy and was first published in 1925. The other books in the series were *The Gleam in the North* (1927) and *The Dark Mile* (1929).
8. Easlea, Daryl. "*Wind & Wuthering*: Genesis Look Back on Their Boldest Prog Statement." Prog. 22 April 2017. Retrieved 23 February 2019. https://www.loudersound.com/features/wind-wuthering-genesis-look-back-on-their-boldest-prog-statement.
9. Sutcliffe, Phil. "Help!." *Mojo*, April 2007.
10. Clarke, Steve. "The Genesis Guide to Genesis." *New Musical Express*, 1 January 1977.
11. Moorcock's novel is the second in a series involving adventurer Eternal Champion. The others are *The Eternal Champion* (1970) and *The Dragon in the Sword* (1987). In addition, a comic book, *The Swords of Heaven, the Flowers of Hell*, was published in 1979.
12. Rutherford himself cannot recall the tuning and when the band performed it live, he approximated the harmonics as best he could using straight chords.
13. Young, Jon. "Genesis Look at Themselves—An Autodiscography." *Trouser Press*, March 1982.
14. Young, Jon. "Genesis Look at Themselves—An Autodiscography." *Trouser Press*, March 1982.
15. *Genesis: Wind & Wuthering*. Reissues Interview, 2007.
16. Fielder, Hugh. *The Book of Genesis*. London: Sidgwick & Jackson, 1984.
17. Phil Collins Official Website Forum, 26 November 2004. No longer available.
18. Easlea, Daryl. "*Wind & Wuthering*: Genesis Look Back on Their Boldest Prog Statement." Prog. 22 April 2017. Retrieved 23 February 2019. https://www.loudersound.com/features/wind-wuthering-genesis-look-back-on-their-boldest-prog-statement.
19. Jimmy Webb (born 1946) is a renowned American songwriter who wrote a string of pop standards including "Up, Up and Away," "By the Time I Get to Phoenix," "Wichita Lineman," "Galveston" and one of Banks' favorite songs at the time, "MacArthur Park."
20. Banks, Tony, Phil Collins, Peter Gabriel, Steve Hackett and Mike Rutherford. Ed. Phillip Dodd. *Genesis: Chapter & Verse*. London: Weidenfeld and Nicolson, 2007.
21. Easlea, Daryl. "*Wind & Wuthering*: Genesis Look Back on Their Boldest Prog Statement." Prog. 22 April 2017. Retrieved 23 February 2019. https://www.loudersound.com/features/wind-wuthering-genesis-look-back-on-their-boldest-prog-statement.
22. Milano, Dominic. "Tony Banks & The Evolution of Genesis." *Keyboard* Magazine, November 1984.
23. Phil Collins Q&A, Official Website, 2 November 2004.
24. Easlea, Daryl. "*Wind & Wuthering*: Genesis Look Back on Their Boldest Prog Statement." Prog. 22 April 2017. Retrieved 23 February 2019. https://www.loudersound.com/features/wind-wuthering-genesis-look-back-on-their-boldest-prog-statement.
25. Hewitt, Alan. Interview with Tony Banks. *The Waiting Room*. 13 March 2004. Retrieved 11 August 2019. www.twronline.net
26. Easlea, Daryl. "*Wind & Wuthering*: Genesis Look Back on Their Boldest Prog Statement." Prog. 22 April 2017. Retrieved 23 February 2019. https://www.loudersound.com/features/wind-wuthering-genesis-look-back-on-their-boldest-prog-statement.
27. Hewitt, Alan. "Distant Memories—Genesis Archive 1967-75 The Interviews." *The Waiting Room*. 12 September 2000. Retrieved 25 September 2018. www.twronline.net.
28. *Circus*. 31 March 1977.
29. *Genesis: Wind & Wuthering*. Reissues Interview. 2006.

30. Brown, David. *Wind & Wuthering* review. *Record Mirror.* 18 December 1976.
31. Charone, Barbara. "Wuthering Heights." *Sounds.* 18 December 1976.
32. Fielder, Hugh. *The Book of Genesis.* London: Sidgwick & Jackson, 1984.
33. Orme, John. "Genesis Down to Trio as Hackett Goes Solo." *Melody Maker,* 8 October 1976.

Chapter 11

1. Young, Jon. "Genesis Look at Themselves—An Autodiscography." *Trouser Press*, March 1982.
2. Elliott, Paul. "The Last Hurrah." *Mojo,* August 2007.
3. Lester, Paul. "The Story Behind the Song: Follow You, Follow Me by Genesis." *Loudersound.com*,18 July 2017. Retrieved 25 September 2018 https://www.loudersound.com/features/the-story-behind-the-song-follow-you-follow-me-by-genesis.
4. Prasad, Anil. "Genesis: Turning It on Again." *Innerviews*, 2007. Retrieved 25 September 2018. www.innerviews.org/inner/genesis.html.
5. *Genesis: A History.* DVD. BBC Scotland, 1990.
6. Milano, Dominic. "Tony Banks." *Contemporary Keyboard,* July 1978.
7. Fielder, Hugh. "Genesis Track by Track." *Sounds,* 1 April 1978.
8. Interview with Genesis by Nicky Horne. *BBC Radio One*, March 1978.
9. Interview with Genesis by Nicky Horne. *BBC Radio One*, March 1978.
10. Platts, Robin. *Genesis: Inside & Out.* London: Collector's Guide, 2001.
11. *Genesis …And Then There Were Three….* Reissues DVD interview, 2007.
12. Interview with Genesis by Nicky Horne. *BBC Radio One*, March 1978.
13. Interview with Genesis by Nicky Horne. *BBC Radio One*, March 1978.
14. Fielder, Hugh. "Genesis Track by Track." *Sounds,* 1 April 1978.
15. Miller, William F. "Phil Collins: Drummer to the Core!" *Modern Drummer,* March 1997.
16. Roberts, Chris. "The Prog Interview: Tony Banks." *Prog,* 1 March 2018.
17. This would be the last time Banks used the Mellotron on a Genesis album.
18. *Genesis …And Then There Were Three….* Reissues DVD interview, 2007.
19. Fielder, Hugh. "Genesis Track by Track." *Sounds,* 1 April 1978.
20. Little Nemo, who dreamed himself into various adventures, was created by American cartoonist Winsor McCay and ran as a comic strip in *New York Herald* and later *New York American* from 1905 to 1926.
21. Jones, Tim. *Record Collector* #256, "Genesis—Turning It on Again." December 2000.
22. Fielder, Hugh. "Genesis Track by Track." *Sounds,* 1 April 1978.
23. *Genesis …And Then There Were Three….* Reissues DVD interview, 2007.

24. Erlewine, Stephen Thomas. *…And Then There Were Three…* album review. *All Music Guide.* Retrieved 24 February 2019. https://www.allmusic.com/album/and-then-there-were-three-mw0000190103.
25. "Genesis: A Revelation." *International Musician and Recording World*, March 1982.
26. Hewitt, Alan. Interview with Tony Banks. *The Waiting Room*, 3 December 2004. Retrieved 25 September 2018. www.twronline.net.
27. Banks, Tony, Phil Collins, Peter Gabriel, Steve Hackett and Mike Rutherford. Ed. Phillip Dodd. *Genesis: Chapter & Verse.* London: Weidenfeld and Nicolson, 2007.
28. *Metal Hammer Genesis Special,* July 1987.
29. Welch, Chris. "Genesis Hit Back." *Melody Maker,* 19 August 1978.
30. Clarke, Steve. "Three Too Many." *New Musical Express,* 1 April 1978.
31. Bloom, Michael. *…And Then There Were Three…* review. *Rolling Stone,* 10 August 1978.
32. Welch, Chris. "Genesis: Tricks and Treats." *Melody Maker,* 1 April 1978
33. Fielder, Hugh. "The Triumphant Triumvirate." *Sounds.* 1 April 1978.
34. Elliott Randall of Steely Dan had also been auditioned by Rutherford. Rutherford stated in his memoir that Randall lost out to Daryl Stuermer because of his session approach to the songs, whereas Stuermer would see straight away the songs had to be interpreted as written.

Chapter 12

1. Young, Jon. "Genesis Look at Themselves—An Autodiscography." *Trouser Press*, March 1982.
2. *Duke* Reissues DVD interview, 2006.
3. All three members of Genesis had been presented with a CR-78 drum machine by Roland during the Japanese leg of their 1978 tour.
4. Young, Jon. "Genesis Look at Themselves—An Autodiscography." *Trouser Press*, March 1982.
5. *Duke* Reissues DVD interview, 2006.
6. Interview with Kid Jensen. *BBC Radio One*, March 1980.
7. Phil Collins Official website (no longer available). Phil Collins' personal post on 24 October 2004.
8. Sutcliffe, Phil. "Help!" *Mojo,* April 2007.
9. *Duke* Reissues DVD interview, 2006.
10. *Duke* Reissues DVD interview, 2006.
11. The grand opening fanfare led to the working title for the group material of "The Duke."
12. Interview with Genesis. *Rockline,* 29 July 1982.
13. *Genesis: A History.* DVD. BBC Scotland, 1990.
14. *Duke* Reissues DVD interview, 2006.
15. *Duke* Reissues DVD interview, 2006.
16. Chick, Stevie. "Genesis: 10 of the Best." *The Guardian*, 3 September 2014. Retrieved 20 February 2019. https://www.theguardian.com/music/musicblog/2014/sep/03/genesis-10-of-the-best.
17. McMahon, Scott. *The Genesis Discography 1967–1996,* January 1998 Edition. Document download no longer available.

18. Fielder, Hugh. *The Book of Genesis*. London: Sidgwick & Jackson, 1984.
19. Banks is quite self-effacing in his assessment of his lack of commercial success and this was the title he gave to the four-CD retrospective box set of his solo material released in 2015.
20. Couture, Francis. Heathaze song review. *All Music Guide*. Retrieved 24 February 2019. www.allmusic.com/song/heathaze-mt0009325040.
21. See [105].
22. Rutherford had experimented with a different tuning on his guitar, retuning the high E string to D. It was a tuning he would use more going forward.
23. *The Genesis Songbook*. DVD. Eagle Vision, 2001.
24. Janisch, Helmut, "Flowers for Algernon?" *Genesis-News.com (it)*, 30 September 2009. Retrieved 25 September 2018. https://www.genesis-news.com/c-Tony-Banks-A-Curious-Interview-30th-September-2009-s351.html.
25. Interview with Kid Jensen. *BBC Radio One*, March 1980.
26. Couture, Francis. Alone Tonight song review. *All Music Guide*. Retrieved 24 February 2019. https://www.allmusic.com/song/alone-tonight-mt0002259138.
27. "Genesis: A Revelation." *International Musician and Recording World*, March 1982.
28. Barber, Lynden. "Facing Up to New Values." *Melody Maker*, 7 February 1981.
29. *Classic Albums: Face Value*. DVD. Eagle Rock, 1999.
30. Fielder, Hugh. "Duke of Hazard." *Sounds*, 10 May 1980.
31. Interview with Mike Rutherford and Phil Collins by Nicky Horne. *Capitol Radio*. 5 February 1980.
32. Interview with Tony Banks, Phil Collins and Mike Rutherford at Shepperton Studios. *BBC Radio Hallam*, 29 September 1981.
33. "The A to Z of Genesis": Interview with Tony Banks. *The Waiting Room Online #31*, November 1995. Retrieved 23 August 2019. www.twronline.net
34. Fielder, Hugh. "Duke of Hazard." *Sounds*, 10 May 1980.
35. Hanna, Lynn. *Duke* album review. *New Musical Express*, 5 April 1980.
36. Fielder, Hugh. "Power Pomp Supremos." *Sounds*, 5 April 1980.
37. Erlewine, Stephen Thomas. *Duke* album review. *All Music Guide*. Retrieved 24 February 2019. https://www.allmusic.com/album/duke-mw0000189985.
38. Interview with Genesis. *Rockline*, 29 July 1982.

Chapter 13

1. Two UK release dates are regularly quoted. Monday, 14 September, and Friday, 18 September. I have gone with the latter, purely from the memory of a friend having bought the album just before the weekend and it not yet being stocked in my local record store. The British Phonographic Institute (BPI) also holds this date in its certification database. It wouldn't be until 1989 when release dates were standardized as a Monday in the UK and Tuesday in the U.S. From 2015 this reverted to Friday internationally.
2. Platts, Robin. *Genesis: Inside & Out*. London: Collector's Guide, 2001.
3. Hilton, Kevin. "'Out came this ginormous sound': Hugh Padgham on 'accidentally discovering' the Gated Reverb Drum Sound." *PSN Europe*. 21 February 2018. Retrieved 25 February 2019. https://www.psneurope.com/studio/reverb-sound-discovery-hugh-padgham.
4. Townsend, Martin. "We Can't Dance." *Vox*, December 1991.
5. *Melody Maker*. Issue unknown, 1981.
6. Fricke, David. "Genesis: Art Rockers Go Pop." *Rolling Stone*, 18 March 1982.
7. Fielder, Hugh. "The Great Escape." *Sounds*, 26 September 1981.
8. Fielder, Hugh. "The Great Escape." *Sounds*, 26 September 1981.
9. Interview with Genesis. *Hallam FM* Radio, 28 September 1981.
10. Barnes, Stuart and Frank Rogers. "So, that's what it does!" *The Waiting Room*, 27 June 2015. Retrieved 25 September 2018. www.twronline.net/issues/twr94/twr94_tb_interview_part2.htm.
11. "Has the Hard-Rocking Trio Taken Its Biggest Gamble Yet with *Abacab*?" *Circus*, 31 January 1982.
12. Interview with Mike Rutherford. *Guitar for the Practising Musician*, August 1984.
13. *Abacab* Reissues DVD interview, 2006.
14. Interview with Genesis. *Hallam FM* Radio, 28 September 1981.
15. Schacht, Janis. *Genesis*. New York: Proteus Books, 1985.
16. Interview with Genesis. *Hallam FM* Radio, 28 September 1981.
17. Parker, Joe. "Genesis," *Record Collector*, October 1997.
18. Interview with Genesis. *Hallam FM* Radio, 28 September 1981.
19. Interview with Richard Skinner. *BBC Radio One*, 12 September 1981).
20. Parker, Joe. "Genesis," *Record Collector*, October 1997.
21. *Abacab* Reissues DVD Interview. 2006.
22. The working title was "Vocal 3/4."
23. *Phil Collins Official Website* Forum, 14 February 2005.
24. Reed, Ryan. "20 Insanely Great Genesis Songs Only Hardcore Fans Know." *Rolling Stone*, 10 October 2014. Retrieved 23 September 2019. www.rollingstone.com/music/music-lists/20-insanely-great-genesis-songs-only-hardcore-fans-know-157999/naminanu-152569/.
25. The final section of the piece was repeated to lengthen the track.
26. The *3x3* EP included several nods to the band's heroes. The cover photo included their recreation of The Beatles' "Twist and Shout" single cover; the title mimicked the Rolling Stones' own EP *5x5* and LP *12x5*; and sleeve notes were written by The Beatles' former press officer, Tony Barrow.
27. Sleeve Notes. *3x3* EP, May 1982.

28. Thompson, Dave. *3x3* EP review. *All Music Guide.* Retrieved 22 September 2019. www.allmusic.com/album/3-x-3-mw0000839393.
29. The song had been subject to a friendly wager within the band about whether it would become a big hit, with Collins and Rutherford on the one side believing it would and Banks on the other.
30. *3x3* EP. Sleeve notes, May 1982.
31. *Phil Collins Official Website* Forum, 17 January 2005. No longer available.
32. Fielder, Hugh. *The Book of Genesis.* London: Sidgwick & Jackson, 1984.
33. *The Waiting Room*, 13 March 2004.
34. "Has the Hard-Rocking Trio Taken Its Biggest Gamble Yet with *Abacab*?" *Circus*, 31 January 1982.
35. Fielder, Hugh. *The Book of Genesis.* London: Sidgwick & Jackson, 1984.
36. Colbert, Paul. "New Values." *Melody Maker*, 26 September 1981.
37. Fricke, David. *Rolling Stone.* "Genesis: Art Rockers Go Pop." 18 March 1982.
38. Wheatley, Cathi, "Three Wise Men." *Sounds*, 26 September 1981.
39. Erlewine, Stephen Thomas. *Abacab* album review. *All Music Guide.* Retrieved 1 March 2019. https://www.allmusic.com/album/abacab-mw0000650185.
40. Interview with Matt Lathrum, 20 January 2000.
41. Kamin, Philip and Peter Goddard. *Genesis: Peter Gabriel, Phil Collins & Beyond.* Stoddard, 1984.
42. Gabriel had organized the previous year's WOMAD World Music Festival, which was a financial disaster, leaving the venture heavily in debt.

Chapter 14

1. *Genesis: A History.* DVD. BBC Scotland, 1990.
2. "Three into One." Wavelength 3-LP vinyl radio show interview.
3. Hugh Padgham had introduced the track to the band, having brought it into the studio one day. The band loved the song and Collins picked up on the laugh employed by the rapper, honing it into something more sinister.
4. *Metal Hammer Genesis Special*, July 1987.
5. Genesis radio interview. *In the Studio* with Redbeard, 1987.
6. Hewitt, Alan. "The A to Z of Genesis." *The Waiting Room*, August 1997. Retrieved 25 September 2018. www.twronline.net.
7. There is no definitive source quoted on the CD single release and while the remainder of the *Invisible Series* of CD singles released for songs from *We Can't Dance* included recordings from their 1986/7 tour, it is believed this version of HOME BY THE SEA was from the previous tour.
8. *Kerrang* issue # 62, 27 February to 3 March 1984.
9. *Hitmen*, 1986.
10. Jones, Cliff. "Genesis: Chapter & Verse." *RCD*, June 1994 (?)
11. *Genesis Official Website*, 23 November 2001.
12. *Genesis Official Website*, 23 November 2001.
13. The album version blends the first half of the first verse with the second half of the second verse from the longer version released on the 12-inch [134] MAMA single and removes an interlinking chorus.
14. *Metal Hammer Genesis Special*, 1987.
15. Radio interview with Genesis. *In the Studio* with Redbeard, 1987.
16. Fielder, Hugh. "Mama from Heaven." *Sounds*, 8(?) October 1983.
17. Considine, J.D. *Genesis* album review. *Rolling Stone*, Issue #419, 1983.
18. Erlewine, Stephen Thomas. *Genesis* album review. *All Music Guide.* Retrieved 1 March 2019. https://www.allmusic.com/album/genesis-mw0000650186,

Chapter 15

1. *Invisible Touch* Press Kit. Virgin, 2 June 1986.
2. "Classic Albums." *BBC Radio One*, 3 June 1989.
3. *Invisible Touch* Press Kit. Virgin, 2 June 1986.
4. Barnett, Laura. "Phil Collins and Mike Rutherford: How We Made *Invisible Touch*." *The Guardian*, 14 October 2014.
5. Greenwald, Ted. "Tony Banks." *Keyboard*, February 1987.
6. *Phil Collins Official website*, 17 October 2005.
7. Unknown U.S. Radio Interview, 1986.
8. Goodyear, Tim. "And Then There Was One." *E&MM*, July 1986.
9. "Classic Albums." *BBC Radio One*, 3 June 1989.
10. The song would also be used in the 2000 movie *American Psycho*, when Patrick Bateman (played by Christian Bale) describes it as "the most moving pop song of the 1980s, about monogamy and commitment" as he plays the song to two prostitutes about the meet their maker.
11. This account comes from the book *Very Naughty Boys* by Robert Sellers (London: Titan, 2013), which is a history of HandMade Films.
12. *Billboard* Magazine. Vol. 99 No. 10, 7 March 1987.
13. The song was developed under the working title "Snake."
14. Unknown U.S. radio interview, 1986.
15. The band were all fans of Benny Hill, who, according to video director Jim Yukich in his liner notes for the *Genesis 1983–1998* box set, asked for £50,000 to appear. When the band realized Hill wasn't joking, he was hired anyway and adopted his Fred Scuttle character for the part.
16. Radio Interview. *CBAK 4028*, 16 June 1986.
17. *The Way We Walk.* DVD. Interview with Tony Banks, 3 December 2001.
18. "Classic Albums." *BBC Radio One*, 3 June 1989.
19. Blake, Mark. "…But Seriously…" *Prog*, 2 March 2016.
20. Genesis often applied names as a memory jogger for a musical segment that may have been

inspired by or been reminiscent of another band. The likelihood here is the original riff Rutherford developed had a Led Zeppelin feel that prompted the working title. The other link is Collins' love of the Marx Brothers—Groucho, Chico, Harpo and Zeppo. Collins used one of Groucho's saying as the title of his second album, *Hello, I Must Be Going!*

21. Unknown U.S. radio interview, 1986.
22. Couture, Francis. THROWING IT ALL AWAY song review. *All Music Guide.* Retrieved 4 March 2019. https://www.allmusic.com/song/throwing-it-all-away-mt0010318779.
23. Richards, Sam. *Invisible Touch* review. *The Ultimate Music Guide: Genesis (Uncut).* March 2017.
24. Pradad, Anil. "Tony Banks: Beyond the Physical." *Innerviews.* 29 September 2019. Retrieved 29 September 2019. www.innerviews.org/inner/tony-banks.
25. "The Invisible Report." *Metal Hammer/Hurricane,* 1987.
26. Wingate, Jonathan. "We've Been Uncool for Most of Our Career." *Record Collector,* April 2005.
27. Considine, J.D. *Invisible Touch* album review. *Rolling Stone,* Issue #480, 14 August 1986
28. Erlewine, Stephen Thomas. *Invisible Touch* album review. *All Music Guide.* Retrieved 4 March 2019. https://www.allmusic.com/album/invisible-touch-mw0000190104.

Chapter 16

1. This was the only occasion in which the band covered solo material with segments of Rutherford's Mike + the Mechanics song "All I Need Is a Miracle," Banks' "Shortcut to Somewhere" and Collins' own cover of the Supremes' "You Can't Hurry Love" incorporated into the medley.
2. The band had initially been intending to regroup in 1990, but plans were put back a year following the success of Collins' *…But Seriously* album and his subsequent extended *Seriously Live* tour.
3. *We Can't Dance* Press Kit, November 1991.
4. Townsend, Martin. "We Can't Dance." *Vox,* December 1991.
5. Considine, J.D. "Genesis: Three for the Road." *Musician,* June 1992.
6. Tony Banks had sampled Rutherford's guitar on the Emulator III and then played it back over three notes lower down in the register, deepening its overall tone and creating a noise like an elephant—hence the working title for the song, "Elephantus.' The sound would also be used in the opening of the non-album track [166] ON THE SHORELINE.
7. Welch, Chris. "Genesis—Regenerators." *Rock Attack,* Vol 5. 1991.
8. *The Way We Walk—Live in Concert.* DVD, 2002.
9. Ernest Angley was born on 9 August 1921 in Gaston County, North Carolina. Raised as a Baptist by the age of 18 he saw Jesus Christ as his savior. He worked as a travelling evangelist in the 1950s. His one-hour TV show, *The Ernest Angley Hour,* brought him to the attention of the nation. Among his more controversial claims was that faith in Jesus could cure HIV/AIDS.
10. *Phil Collins Official Website* Forum, 17 December 2004. No longer available.
11. Colbert, Paul. "Cut Loose." *Vox,* December 1992.
12. Collins' programmed drum machine part was based on an earlier pattern written by Rutherford. Collins smoothed off the rough edges and captures the essence.
13. Townsend, Martin. "We Can't Dance." *Vox,* December 1991.
14. Townsend, Martin. "We Can't Dance." *Vox,* December 1991.
15. An edited performance (4:14), the last part of the song, from an early live show was included as part of a promo CD with the full album version and a shorter album version edit (4:16).
16. The song's working title of "Blue Jeans" telegraphed the band's intent at an early stage.
17. Gary Davies Show. *BBC Radio One,* November 1991.
18. *The Way We Walk—Live in Concert.* DVD, 2002.
19. Gary Davies Show. *BBC Radio One,* November 1991.
20. Welch, Chris. "Genesis—Regenerators." *Rock Attack,* Vol 5. 1991.
21. The song was developed under the working title of "Rickenbacker." Phil Collins' comments on the song demonstrate how confused the band's thinking was: "It has overtones of The Beatles and The Byrds. In fact, it is a nineties protest song about bad news on TV." (Welch, Chris. "Genesis—Regenerators." *Rock Attack,* Vol 5. 1991.)
22. *The Waiting Room,* Approx. 1997. www.twronline.net.
23. Wiser, Carl. Interview with Tony Banks. *Songfacts,* 20 February 2018. Retrieved 25 September 2018. www.songfacts.com/blog/interviews/tony_banks.
24. Doershuk, Robert L. "Genesis: We Can't Dance." *Keyboard,* February 1992.
25. *Platinum Collection.* CD booklet. 2004.
26. Gary Davies Show. *BBC Radio One,* November 1991.
27. While recording the album Genesis learned of the death of Eric Clapton's 4-year old son, Conor, on 20 March 1991, who fell from the 53rd floor window of his mother's friend's New York City apartment at 117 East 57th Street. Clapton himself expressed his personal grief in the multi-Grammy winning song he wrote with Will Jennings, "Tears in Heaven."
28. *Phil Collins Official Website.* Forum, 2 November 2004. No longer available.
29. The working title for the song was "Nile" as the music reminded the band of a boat slowly floating down that vast river. The drum machine pattern was later sampled by Enigma for the song "I Love You…I'll Kill You" on their second album, *The Cross of Changes.*
30. The song would be transposed to a lower key when played on tour to protect Collins' voice. As a

result, his vocal performance is stronger on the live version than the studio recording.

31. Genesis Interview. *Radio Forth*, November 1991.

32. *Genesis Archive #2 1976–1992* Electronic Press Kit, November 2000.

33. Interview with Genesis. *Rockline* Radio Show, 25 November 1991.

34. Bell, Max. "Dancing in the Dark." *Vox*, December 1991.

35. Browne, David. *We Can't Dance* review. *Entertainment Weekly*, 15 November 1991.

36. Manning, Karav. *We Can't Dance* review. Rolling Stone, 9 January 1992.

37. Orens, Geoff. *We Can't Dance* album review. *All Music Guide*. Retrieved 6 March 2019. https://www.allmusic.com/album/we-cant-dance-mw0000269602.

38. Considine, J.D. "Genesis Pulls Away from Pop Frivolity but Stays Tuneful." *Star Tribune/Baltimore Sun*. 15 December 1991.

39. Keddie, Gibson. "The Long and the Short of It." *Guitarist*, February 1993).

40. "Phil Collins Speaks of New Life with Girlfriend Orianne Cevey and without Genesis." *Hello*, 15 February 1997.

41. *E Online*, 1997. No longer available.

42. Maconie, Stuart. "Okay son, you're in!" *Q*. September 1997.

Chapter 17

1. Other singers auditioned included Francis Dunnery, Nick Van Eede and David Longdon. Dunnery had been the singer with It Bites between 1982 and 1990, while Van Eede was best known as lead vocalist with Cutting Crew from 1985 to 1993. Van Eede got as far as being in the last two, alongside Wilson. Cutting Crew reformed in 2005. Longdon joined progressive rock band Big Big Train in 2009. Longdon and Wilson were tested over a period of six months, between May and November 1996, before Banks and Rutherford finally decided on Wilson.

2. Wilson was to reuse the band name in 2006 with new members and record two further albums—*She* (2006) and *Unfulfillment* (2011) along with the live recording *Ray Wilson and Stiltskin Live* (2007).

3. The Cut album *Millionairhead* would be released in 1999.

4. Virgin Press Release, 6 June 1997.

5. Nick D'Virgilio: "I found out where the Hit-n-Run offices were located in London and went there with a Spock's Beard CD…I did end up getting a phone call from Nick Davis about 6 months later on a Sunday morning asking for some other things that I had recorded on. I sent them whatever I could find and they called back to say they wanted me to come an audition. They flew me to the UK and I went to The Farm and jammed with Tony and Mike. I was on cloud 9!" (Giammetti, Mario. "Nick D'Virgilio exclusive interview." *Dusk* #68, September 2011. Retrieved 6 October 2018. www.dusk.it/bigbigtrain/interview.htm).

6. Chester Thompson: "I proposed to jam with the guys to see if there was a real chemistry there. Because, at that point, if it was going to continue, I was not going to be content to continue as a side man. If they were willing to open it up to be a real group, then I certainly would have leaped at the chance. But again, like I said, it's their band; and Mike made it very clear that it was their band, and that they were not at all interested in sharing anything. So, that was that." (Negrin, Dave. "A Joyful Noise." *World of Genesis*, 10 February 2002. Retrieved 25 September 2018. www.worldofgenesis.com/ChesterThompson-interview-2002.htm).

7. *Jam!* Website, 10 September 1997. No longer available.

8. Hewitt, Alan, and Simon Pound. "An Alien Afternoon with Tony Banks." *The Waiting Room*, 22 August 1997. Retrieved 25 September 2018. www.twronline.net.

9. Hewitt, Alan, Simon Pound and Ian Jones. "Another Chiddingfold Afternoon." *The Waiting Room*, 25 September 1997. Retrieved 25 September 2018. www.twronline.net.

10. Hewitt, Alan, and Simon Pound. "An Alien Afternoon with Tony Banks." *The Waiting Room*, 22 August 1997. Retrieved 25 September 2018. www.twronline.net.

11. The working title for the song was "Acoustic EMI."

12. The Australian band was one of Rutherford's favorites at the time.

13. Progsheet.net, 2006. No longer available.

14. *Jam!* 10 September 1997.

15. Walsh, John. "Charterhouse Blues." *The Independent*, 2 August 1997.

16. *Jam!* 10 September 1997. No longer available.

17. Pradad, Anil. "Tony Banks: Beyond the Physical." *Innerviews*. 29 September 2019. Retrieved 29 September 2019. www.innerviews.org/inner/tony-banks.

18. Hewitt, Alan, Simon Pound and Ian Jones. "Another Chiddingfold Afternoon." *The Waiting Room*, 25 September 1997. Retrieved 25 September 2018. www.twronline.net.

19. *Jam!* 10 September 1997. No longer available.

20. Hewitt, Alan, and Simon Pound. "An Alien Afternoon with Tony Banks." *The Waiting Room*, 22 August 1997. Retrieved 25 September 2018. www.twronline.net.

21. Banks, Tony, Phil Collins, Peter Gabriel, Steve Hackett and Mike Rutherford. Ed. Phillip Dodd. *Genesis: Chapter & Verse*. London: Weidenfeld and Nicolson, 2007.

22. Interview with Tony Banks. *Genesis-news.com*, 7 July 2007. No longer available.

23. *Genesis Official Site*. Web Chat, 20 May 2008. No longer available.

24. The working title for the song was "Fuzz Intro" recalling the treated fuzz box sound applied to Rutherford's guitar.

25. The working title for the song was "Chicago Sax."

26. An earlier cut ran to 4:40. The song was to be included on the album but was pulled very late in the day as the album was re-sequenced.

27. Hewitt, Alan. "There must be some other way to do an interview!" *The Waiting Room* online. November 2000. Retrieved 10 March 2019. www.twronline.net.

28. Tony Banks: "We wanted to get back to perhaps slightly more drama than we'd had in recent years, a bit more weight." (*Toronto Sun*, 15 July 1997).

29. *Total Guitar*, April 2000.

30. Bungey, John. "In the Beginning, Again." *Mojo*, September 1997.

31. Erlewine, Stephen Thomas. ...*Calling All Stations*... album review. *All Music Guide*. Retrieved 10 March 2019. https://www.allmusic.com/album/calling-all-stations-mw0000026641.

32. ...*Calling All Stations*... album review. *Rolling Stone*, Issue #772, 1997.

33. Kane, Peter. ...*Calling All Stations*... album review. *Q*, September 1997.

34. Daryl Stuermer was unavailable as he had been touring with Phil Collins.

35. Ahead of the album's release Ray Wilson was looking forward to a follow-up when in an interview on *Capitol Radio* on 6 June 1997 he said, "I'd like to see the next album go back more, in fact I'd like us to step completely back and stop being a pop band in any way and just be a Genesis."

36. Prasad, Anil. "Genesis: Turning It on Again." *Innerviews*, 2007. Retrieved 25 September 2018. www.innerviews.org/inner/genesis.html.

37. Negrin, Dave. "Suite Success." *World of Genesis*, 17 April 2004. Retrieved 25 September 2018. www.worldofgenesis.com/TonyBanksInterview2004.htm.

38. Negrin, Dave. "Inside the Mind's Eye of Ray Wilson." *World of Genesis*, 29 May 2001. Retrieved 25 September 2018. www.worldofgenesis.com/RayWilson-Interview2001.htm.

Chapter 18

1. Both Peter Gabriel and Steve Hackett provided live overdubs for the live releases to cover up mistakes and inadequate performances. Gabriel had had difficulty with conveying his vocals through some heavy costumes and some of his delivery suffered as a result. Ever the perfectionist, Gabriel would make a significant number of changes.

2. Reed, Ryan. "Tony Banks Says Genesis Are Probably Done for Good: Exclusive Interview." *Ultimate Classic Rock*, March 2018. Retrieved 25 September 2018. ultimateclassicrock.com/genesis-no-reunion-tony-banks.

3. DellaSala, Gene. "Interview with Former Genesis Guitarist Steve Hackett." *Audioholics Magazine*, 24 January 2007. Retrieved 25 September 2018. https://www.audioholics.com/music-reviews/interview-with-former-genesis-guitarist-steve-hackett-1.

Bibliography

On Genesis and Members

Banks, Tony, Phil Collins, Peter Gabriel, Steve Hackett and Mike Rutherford. Philip Dodd (ed.) *Genesis: Chapter and Verse*. Weidenfeld and Nicolson, 2007.
Bowler, Dave, and Bryan Dray. *Genesis: A Biography*. Sidgwick & Jackson, 1993.
Bowman, Durrel. *Experiencing Peter Gabriel: A Listener's Companion*. R&L, 2016.
Bright, Spencer. *Peter Gabriel: An Authorised Biography*. Headline, 1989. Rev. ed., Sidgwick & Jackson, 1999.
Bruford, Bill. *Bill Bruford: The Autobiography*. London: Jawbone, 2009.
Carruthers, Rob. *Genesis: The Gabriel Era (Rock Retrospectives)*. Angry Penguin, 2007.
Coleman, Ray. *Phil Collins: The Definitive Biography*. Simon & Schuster, 1997.
Collins, Phil. *Not Dead Yet: The Autobiography*. Penguin/Random House, 2016.
Demont, Max. *Genesis: Counting Out Time: Worldwide Singles Discography Vol. 1*. Self-published, 1993.
Drewett, Michael, Sarah Hill and Kimi Kärki (eds). *Peter Gabriel, from Genesis to Growing Up*. Farnham, Surrey, UK: Ashgate, 2012.
Easlea, Daryl. *Without Frontiers: The Life and Music of Peter Gabriel*. London: Omnibus, 2013.
Ellis, Robert. *Genesis—The Lamb Lies Down on Broadway: The Ultimate Record*. London: Rock Library, 2014.
Fielder, Hugh. *The Book of Genesis*. London: Sidgwick & Jackson, 1984.
Gallo, Armando. *From One Fan to Another*. London: Omnibus, 1984.
_____. *Genesis: I Know What I Like*. DIY, 1979. [Update of *Genesis: The Evolution of a Rock Band*].
_____. *Genesis: The Evolution of a Rock Band*. Sidgwick & Jackson, 1978.
_____. *Peter Gabriel*. London: Omnibus, 1986.
Hewitt, Alan. *Genesis Revisited*. Godalming: Willow Farm, 2006. [Update of *Opening the Musical Box: A Genesis Chronicle*).
_____. *Opening the Musical Box: A Genesis Chronicle*. London: Firefly, 2001.
_____. *A Selection of Shows: Genesis & Solo Live Guide 1976-2014*. Bedford: Wymer, 2015.
_____. *Sketches of Hackett: The Authorised Biography*. Bedford: Wymer, 2009.
Holm-Hudson, Kevin. *Genesis and the Lamb Lies Down on Broadway*. Farnham, Surrey, UK: Ashgate, 2008.
MacFarlane, Stuart. *On Track... Genesis: Every Album, Every Song*. Tewkesbury: Sonicbond, 2019.
Macphail, Richard. *My Book of Genesis*. Bedford: Wymer, 2018.
Mulvey, John (ed.). *Genesis: The Ultimate Music Guide*. 2019.
Parkyn, Geoff. *Genesis: The Illustrated Discography*. London: Omnibus, 1983.
Platts, Robin. *Genesis Inside & Out*. Collector's Guide Publishing, 2001. [Updated and republished as *Genesis: Behind the Lines, 1967-2007*, 2007.]
Russell, Paul. *Genesis: Play Me My Song—A Live Guide 1969 to 1975*. Wembley: SAF, 2004.
Rutherford, Mike. *The Living Years: The First Genesis Memoir*. London: Constable & Robinson, 2014.
St. Michael, Mick. *Peter Gabriel: In His Own Words*. London: Omnibus, 1994.
Schacht, Janis. *Genesis*. London: Proteus, 1985.
Thompson, Dave. *Turn It On Again: Peter Gabriel, Phil Collins and Genesis*. San Francisco: Backbeat, 2005.
Waller, Johnny. *The Phil Collins Story*. London: Zomba, 1985.
Welch, Chris. *The Complete Guide to the Music of Genesis*. London: Omnibus, 1995.
_____. *The Secret Life of Peter Gabriel*. London: Omnibus, 1998.

On Music

Brackett, Nathan, Christian David Hoard. *The New Rolling Stone Album Guide*. New York: Simon & Schuster, 2004, pp. 327-328.
Buckley, Peter. *The Rough Guide to Rock*, 3rd ed. London: Rough Guides, 2003.

Frame, Pete. *The Complete Rock Family Trees*. London: Omnibus, 1983.
Graff, Gary, and Daniel Durchholz (eds). *MusicHound Rock: The Essential Album Guide*. Farmington Hills, MI: Visible Ink, 1999.
Hegarty, Paul, and Martin Halliwell. *Beyond and Before: Progressive Rock Since the 1960s*. New York: Continuum, 2011.
Macan, Edward. *Rocking the Classics: English Progressive Rock and the Counterculture*. London: Oxford University Press, 1997.
Romano, Will. *Mountains Come Out of the Sky: The Complete Illustrated History of Prog Rock*. San Francisco: Backbeat, 2010.

Official Internet Resources

Genesis: www.genesis-music.com, facebook.com/genesis, twitter.co/genesis_band.
Tony Banks: www.tonybanksmusic.com, facebook.com/tonybanksofficial.
Phil Collins: www.philcollins.com, facebook.com/philcollins, twitter.com/PhilCollinsFeed.
Peter Gabriel: petergabriel.com, facebook.com/PeterGabriel, twitter.com/itspetergabriel.
Steve Hackett: www.hackettsongs.com, facebook.com/stevehackettofficial, twitter.com/HackettOfficial.
Anthony Phillips: www.anthonyphillips.co.uk, facebook.com/AnthonyPhillipsOfficial.
Mike Rutherford: http://mikeandthemechanics.com, facebook.com/mikeandthemechanicsofficial, twitter.com/officialmatm.
Ray Wilson: www.raywilson.ne, www.facebook.com/raywilsonofficial.

Other Recommended Internet Resources

The Genesis Archive: http://thegenesisarchive.co.uk/, www.facebook.com/TheGenesisArchive/, twitter.com/genesisarchive, youtube.com/thegenesisarchive.
A Genesis Discography: www.genesis-discography.org.
The Genesis Museum: www.genesismuseum.com.
Genesis News.com: www.genesis-news.com, facebook.com/Genesis.News, twitter.com/genesis_news The Waiting Room Online: www.twronline.net.
Genesis—The Movement: www.genesis-movement.org.
World of Genesis: www.worldofgenesis.com, twitter.com/WorldofGenesis.

Song Title Index

Figures in **bold** refer to main song entry

Song Title (Cat No.)

Abacab (119) 7, 200, **202–4**, 206, 208, 209, 210, 212, 213, 218, 236, 269
After the Ordeal (45) 87, **96–7**, 100
Afterglow (88) 146, 148, **156–7**, 160, 161, 167, 196, 296
Aisle of Plenty (47) 87, 90, **98–9**
Alien Afternoon (171) 274, 275, **279–80**, 285
All in a Mouse's Night (84) 146, **153–4**
Alone Tonight (112) 181, **193**, 195
Am I Very Wrong? (9) 27, **31–2**
Another Record (128) 7, 200, 203, **212–3**
Anything Now (183) 274, 278, 280, **288**, 289
Anything She Does (147) 233, **242–3**, 250
Anyway (61) 43, 101, **119–20**, 121,

Back in N.Y.C. (54) 6, 101, 105, **110–11**, 112, 129, 187
Ballad of Big (94) 164, **167–8**, 174
Banjo Man (180) 274, 277, 278, **286–7**
The Battle of Epping Forest (44) 2, 66, 87, **95–6**, 100
Behind the Lines (105) 181, **183–5**, 186, 187, 188, 189, 190, 191, 195, 196
Blood on the Rooftops (85) 146, 148, **154**, 161, 171
The Brazilian (150) 8, 233, 236, **246–7**, 248, 250
Broadway Melody of 1974 (50) 101, **107**
Build Me a Mountain (17) 27, **36–7**
Burning Rope (96) 164, **168–9**, 171, 179

Calling All Stations (168) 274, 275–6, 286,

Can-Utility and the Coastliners (36) 72, **77–8**, 84
Carpet Crawlers (57) 6, 10, 90, 101, 105, **114–6**, 117, 119, 129, 133, 158, 296
The Carpet Crawlers 1999 (186) 11, 12, **295–6**
The Chamber of 32 Doors (58) 101, 115, **116–7**
The Cinema Show (46) 2, 6, 87, 89, 90, **97–8**, 99, 100, 133, 161, 196, 230
The Colony of Slippermen (65) 6, 101, **122–4**
Congo (169) 226, 274, **276–8**, 286, 287
The Conqueror (11) 27, **33**
Counting Out Time (56) 6, 101, 105, **112–4**, 115, 125, 126, 129
Cuckoo Cocoon (51) 101, **107–8**
Cul-De-Sac (113) 181, **194**, 197, 198

Dance on a Volcano (71) 132, 133, **134–5**, 138, 141, 142, 144
Dancing with the Moonlit Knight (40) 6, 87, **89–90**, 99, 214, 280, 317n32
The Day the Light Went Out (103) 164, 171, **177**, 178
Deep in the Motherlode (97) 164, 167, **169–70**, 172
The Dividing Line (174) 9, 274, **282–3**, 291
Do the Neurotic (151) 233, 239, 241, 242, 245, 246, **247–8**, 255
Dodo (123) 200, 204, **208–9**, 213, 214, 218, 244; *see also Lurker*
Domino (I: In the Glow of the Night; II: The Last Domino) (148) 2, 8, 233, 236, 238, **243–5**, 250
Down and Out (92) 164, **165–6**, 179
Dreaming While You Sleep (159) 251, **261**, 262, 263, 270

Driving the Last Spike (156) 251, **257–8**, 270
Duchess (106) 1, 7, 181, 183, **185–6**, 187, 196, 197, 198, 199, 213
Duke's End (116) 181, 183, 185, **195–6**; *see also Duke's Travels*
Duke's Travels (115) 181, 183, 187, 191, **195–6**; *see also Duke's End*
Dusk (23) 40, 41, 45, 47, 48, **53–4**

Eleventh Earl of Mar (80) 146, **148–9**
Entangled (72) 132, 133, **135–6**, 138, 139, 141, 144
Evidence of Autumn (118) 181, 188, 189, 190, **197–8**

Fading Lights (165) 8, 251, **267–8**, 270, 285
Feeding the Fire (152) 233, 239, 241, **248–9**
Fireside Song (7) 27, **30–1**, 38
Firth of Fifth (42) 2, 6, 87, **92–4**, 95, 97, 100, 133, 224, 226, 268, 315n5
Fly on a Windshield (49) 101, **106–7**
Follow You, Follow Me (102) 1, 7, 159, 164, 167, 168, 171, **174–7**, 178, 179, 229, 260, 266, 280, 296
For Absent Friends (26) 58, **63–4**, 68, 69, 94, 133
The Fountain of Salmacis (31) 6, 42, 44, 58, 63, 64, **67–8**, 69, 148
Frustration (D18c) 21, **43**, 119

Get 'Em Out by Friday (35) 66, 72, **76–7**, 83
Going Out to Get You (D18a) **41–2**, 312ch3n7, 313n5
The Grand Parade of Lifeless Packaging (53) 101, 105, **109–10**, 318n21

Guide Vocal (107) 181, 183, 184, **186–7**, 191, 196

Hair on the Arms and Legs (D0g) 19, **20–1**
Hairless Heart (55) 101, **112**
Happy the Man (32) 12, 58, 65, **70–1**
Harlequin (30) 58, **66–7**, 69
Harold the Barrel (29) 58, **66**, 69, 133, 140
Hearts on Fire (167) 251, 255, 256, **269–70**
Heathaze (110) 181, **189–90**
Here Comes the Supernatural Anaesthetist (62) 101, 103, **120**
Hey! (D4b) 19, **25–6**
Hidden in the World of Dawn (D0d) **19**
Hold On My Heart (162) 152, 227, 251, **264–5**, 266, 281, 298
Home by the Sea (136) 8, 220, 224, 225, **226–7**, 228, 232, 264, 265, 268, 277, 323ch14n7; *see also Second Home by the Sea*
Horizons (37) 72, 73, **78–9**, 84

I Can't Dance (157) 242, 251, 253, 255, 256, **258–60**, 268, 269, 270, 296
I Know What I Like (in Your Wardrobe) (41) 6, 53, 86, 87, **90–2**, 95, 97, 99, 100, 317n32
I'd Rather Be You (153) 233, 241, 242, 245, 246, **249**
If That's What You Need (173) 274, **281–2**
Illegal Alien (138) 8, 191, 220, **227–8**, 230, 232, 269
Image Blown Out (18) 17, 27, **37**
In Hiding (12) 17, 27, 29, **33–4**
In Limbo (15) 27, **35–6**, 38
...In That Quiet Earth (87) 83, 146, 150, **155–6**, 160, 178
In the Beginning (6) 19, 27, **29–30**, 31, 38
In the Cage (52) 6, 83, 98, 101, **108–9**, 111, 124, 126, 129, 156, 157, 196
In the Rapids (69) 101, **126–7**
In the Wilderness (10) 27, **32–33**
In Too Deep (146) 233, **241–2**, 248, 249, 250, 258, 259, 260
Inside and Out (91) 146, 157, **158–9**, 161, 174, 244, 257
Invisible Touch (143) 204, 233, **235–7**, 238, 239, 243, 244, 245, 246, 247, 249, 250, 253, 254, 260, 261, 263, 296
It. (70) 75, 101, 126, **127–8**, 129
It's Gonna Get Better (142) 220, 222, 223, **231**, 232
It's Yourself (79) 132, 139, **142–3**, 150, 151

Jesus He Knows Me (155) 228, 241, 248, 251, **255–7**, 264, 269, 270,
Just a Job to Do (140) 220, **229–30**, 232

Keep It Dark (122) 7, 200, 203, **206–8**, 213, 218, 219
The Knife (24) 41, 42, 47, 48, **54–5**, 59, 64, 65, 69, 85, 129, 133, 213

The Lady Lies (101) 164, **173–4**
The Lamb Lies Down on Broadway (48) 6, 63, 101, **104–6**, 112, 114, 115, 129, 204,
The Lamia (63) 101, 103, **121**, 122, 125
Land of Confusion (145) 233, **239–41**, 248, 249, 255, 256, 277
Let Us Now Make Love (D18h) 45, **46**
The Light Dies Down on Broadway (67) 101, 103, **124–5**
Like It or Not (127) 200, **211–2**
Lilywhite Lilith (59) 101, **117–8**, 119, 153
Living Forever (161) 251, 253, 254, **263–4**, 269
Looking for Someone (19) 42, 45, 47, 48, **49–50**, 52, 55, 313n3
Los Endos (78) 6, 132, 135, **141–2**, 143, 144, 153, 178
Lurker (124) 200, **208–9**, 213, 214, 218, 244; *see also Dodo*

Mad Man Moon (74) 76, 132, **137–8**, 144, 149
The Magic of Time (D4a) 19, **25**, 32
Mama (134) 8, 171, 220, **222–4**, 228, 231, 232, 238, 276, 296, 323ch14n13
Man of Our Times (108) 181, **187**, 198
Man on the Corner (126) 200, **210–1**, 214
Manipulation (D18d) **43**, 44, 62
Many Too Many (98) 164, 167, **170–1**, 172, 175, 177, 178, 179, 229
Match of the Day (89) 146, **157–8**, 161, 164, 177, 297
Me and Sarah Jane (121) 200, **205–6**
Me and Virgil (133) 200, 216, **217–8**, 257
Misunderstanding (109) 181, 182, 184, 185, 186, **187–9**, 191, 197, 198, 199
More Fool Me (43) 87, **94–5**, 100, 133
The Musical Box (25) 6, 9, 19, 43, 44, 58, 59, **61–3**, 64, 68, 69, 80, 85, 90, 129, 312n15, 314n5

The Mystery of the Flannan Isle Lighthouse (D0f) 19, **20**

Naminanu (129) 200, 203, 206, 207, 209, **213**, 214
Never a Time (158) 251, **260–1**, 268
No Reply at All (120) 200, 203, **204–5**, 208, 209, 214, 299
No Son of Mine (154) 237, 251, **253–5**, 263, 264, 269, 270, 276, 278
Not About Us (172) 90, 176, 274, **280–1**, 288, 289, 290
Nowhere Else to Turn (U186) 11, 274, **290**

On the Shoreline (166) 251, 253, 258, 259, 263, **268–9**, 324n6
One Day (13) 27, **34**
One-Eyed Hound (4) 22, 23, **24**
One for the Vine (81) 146, **149–50**, 152, 169, 197
One Man's Fool (178) 274, **285–6**, 291
Open Door (117) 181, 185, 186, **196–7**

Pacidy (D18f) 41, **44–5**
Papa He Said (179) 274, 277, 278, **286**
Paperlate (131) 90, 200, 204, **214–6**, 217, 238, 243
Patricia (D0a) 11, **16–7**, 34
Phret (181) 274, 278, **287**, 288
Pigeons (90) 146, 157, **158**, 161, 164, 287
A Place to Call My Own (16) 27, **36**
Please Don't Ask (114) 181, 182, **194–5**
Provocation (D18b) **42**, 49, 67

Ravine (66) 101, **124**, 155
Resignation (D18e) **44**
The Return of the Giant Hogweed (27) 58, **64–5**, 69, 314n5
Riding the Scree (68) 101, 112, **125–6**
Ripples... (76) 6, 132, 133, 135, 136, 138, **139–40**, 141, 143, 144, 159, 190, 268
Robbery, Assault and Battery (75) 132, **138–9**
Run Out of Time (185) 274, 280, 288, **289**

Say It's Alright Joe (100) 164, **172–3**, 178, 179
Scenes from a Night's Dream (99) 164, 167, 170, **172**, 179
Sea Bee (D0e) **19–20**
Second Home by the Sea (137) 8, 220, 224, 225, **226–7**, 232, 268, 277; *see also Home by the Sea*

Song Title Index

The Serpent (8) 18, 27, 30, 31, 38
7/8 (182) 274, 278, 287–8
Seven Stones (28) 58, 65, 69, 70
She is Beautiful (D0b) 11, 16, 17–8, 31
Shepherd (D18g) 45–6
Shipwrecked (170) 83, 193, 274, 278–9, 281, 287, 288
Sign Your Life Away (184) 274, 280, **288–9**
Silent Sorrow in Empty Boats (64) 101, **121–2**, 124
The Silent Sun (1) 11, **21–2**, 23, 27, 29, 36, 311n17
Silver Rainbow (141) 220, 228, 229, **230–1**, 232
Since I Lost You (164) 251, 260, **266–7**, 268
Small Talk (176) 274, **283–4**
Snowbound (95) 164, **168**
Squonk (73) 6, 132, 133, 134, **136–7**, 141, 142, 144, 258
Stagnation (22) 6, 40, 45, 47, 48, **52–3**, 54, 55, 59, 62, 92, 313n14, 316n37
Submarine (130) 200, 209, 211, **213–4**
Supper's Ready (38) 2, 3, 6, 9, 10, 40, 66, 72, 73, 75, **79–83**, 84, 85, 101, 111, 133, 142, 156, 161, 183, 185, 194, 278, 315n17, 317n32

Taking It All Too Hard (139) 220, 224, 225, **228–9**, 230, 231, 232, 260
Tell Me Why (160) 193, 239, 251, **262–3**, 266
That's All (135) 8, 94, 220, **224–5**, 226, 228, 229, 232, 258, 259
That's Me (2) 16, 21, **22–3**
There Must Be Some Other Way (177) 268, 274, 280, **284–5**
Throwing It All Away (149) 233, 237, **245–6**, 248, 249, 250
Time Table (34) 72, **76**, 84
Tonight, Tonight, Tonight (144) 187, 216, 233, **237–9**, 243, 244, 249, 250, 260, 261, 262, 263
A Trick of the Tail (77) 37, 132, 136, 138, 139, **140–1**, 144
Try a Little Sadness (D0c) 16, 17, **18**
Turn It On Again (111) 181, 183, 184, 185, **190–3**, 196, 197, 198, 199, 227, 228, 262, 278, 280, 282, 296
Twilight Alehouse (39) 59, 72, **86**, 90

Uncertain Weather (175) 274, **283**, 291
Undertow (93) 164, **166–7**, 171, 172, 178, 283

Unquiet Slumbers for the Sleepers… (86) 124, 146, **155**, 161

Vancouver (104) 143, 164, 171, **177–8**
Visions of Angels (21) 47, 50, **51–2**, 54

The Waiting Room (60) 101, 103, 114, 115, **118–9**, 153
Watcher of the Skies (33) 72, **73–6**, 82, 83, 127, 129, 280, 299, 315n3, 317n32
Way of the World (163) 251, 264, 265, **266**
Where the Sour Turns to Sweet (5) 17, 22, 27, **29**, 34, 38
White Mountain (20) 40, 41, 47, **50–1**
Who Dunnit? (125) 7, 203, **209–10**, 216, 219, 247
Window (14) 27, **35**, 38
A Winter's Tale (3) 21, **23–4**
Wot Gorilla? (83) 119, 146, 148, **152–3**, 159, 161, 213

You Might Recall (132) 200, 210, 214, **216–7**, 247
Your Own Special Way (82) 143, 146, 148, **150–2**, 154, 155, 156, 159, 160, 161, 264, 265

General Index

Abacab 7, 8, 9, 90, 200–219, 220, 221, 225, 232, 247, 250, 270
Abba 183, 198, 221
Achtung Baby 270
Acting Very Strange 220
Alexander, John 17
Alice in Wonderland 230
"All Day and All of the Night" 191
"All I Need Is a Miracle" 233, 324*n*1
Allom, Tom 28
American Psycho 323*ch*15*n*10
And Then There Were None 164
…And Then There Were Three… 5, 6, 7, 164–180, 181, 182, 184, 198, 229
Anderson, Jon 134
Angley, Ernest 256, 324*n*9
The Animals 14
Anon 15–6, 310*n*6, 310*n*8
"Another Day in Paradise" 263
Another Green World 104
Anthony, John 47–9, 54, 56, 60, 61, 80
Ark 2 59

"Babies" 313*n*5
Bach, Johann Sebastian 79
Bacharach, Burt 109, 265
Bailey, Philip 233
Baker, Ginger 91
Bale, Christian 323*ch*15*n*10
Banks, Geoff 252
Banks, Tony: birth 14; childhood 4, 14–5; first use of synthesizers 89; influences 4, 15–6; orchestral work 132; purchase of Mellotron 74, 88; reunion (2007) 297–8; reunion (2020) 300; reunion discussions (2005) 297; solo work 167, 181, 205, 220, 233–4, 251–2; *passim*
Bankstatement 252
"Barnaby's Adventure" 19
Barnard, Mick 59, 62
Barrow, Tony 322*ch*13*n*26
Baxandall, Tom 296

The Beach Boys 4, 25, 182, 188
The Beatles 1–2, 4, 9, 14, 15, 16, 24, 34, 37, 65, 76, 91, 143, 178, 206, 224, 225, 232, 312*n*2, 313*n*2, 322*ch*13*n*26, 324*ch*16*n*21
The Bee Gees 21
Big Big Train 325*n*1
"Black or White" 259
"Black Sheep" 313*n*5
Blackburn, Tony 23
Blade Runner 239
"The Block" 95
"Bohemian Rhapsody" 138
"Bolero" 107
Book of Imaginary Beings 319*n*16
Booker T and the MGs 203
Borboletta 142
Borges, Jorge Luis 319*n*16
Both Sides 271
Bowen, Mike 252
Bowie, David 247
Brand X 88, 132, 133, 142, 145, 182, 319*n*1
Brave New World 110
Bream, Julian 79
Briggs, Chris 313*n*2
Brontë, Emily 148
Broster, Dorothy Kathleen 149, 320*n*7
Broughton, Shaun 281
Brown, James 15, 93
Brubeck, Dave 25
Bruce, Lenny 317*n*14
Bruford, Bill 144–5, 160, 161
Bryant, Bridgette 192
Buchan, John 148
Burns, John 10, 73, 79, 89, 90, 94, 99, 103, 123
Buster 251
…But Seriously 251
Butch Cassidy and the Sundance Kid 109
Byrd, William 79
The Byrds 324*n*21

Cable, Robin 48–9
Calamity the Cow 59
The Call of the Wild 313*n*12

…Calling All Stations… 8, 10, 83, 193, 274–92, 294
Callingham, Geoff 221, 252
Carrack, Paul 89
"Cars" 187
Caryl, Ronnie 59
Charterhouse School 4, 14–7, 310*n*1, 310*n*8
Chessman, Caryl 317*n*14
"Chi Ti Ha Dato La Sua Vita" 24
Childhood's End 74
Chinese Wall 233
"Chobham Chords" 313*n*5
Christie, Agatha 164
Clapton, Eric 233, 252, 267, 324*ch*16*n*27
Clarke, Arthur C. 74
The Clash 259
"Classic" 313*n*5
Colby, Robert 271
Cole, Brad 192, 267
Coleman, Terry 257
Collins, Nicholas ("Nic") 300
Collins, Phil: becomes lead singer 6, 133–4; birth 58; childhood 59; collaboration with Hackett 132; collaboration with Phillips 88, 132; family 148, 315*n*1; film work 251; gated drum sound 7, 201; health issues 300; influences 4, 88, 136, 141–2, 213, 315*n*7; joins Genesis 58–9; leaves Genesis 8, 270–2, 274; marital problems 178, 181–2, 195, 272; "Not Dead Yet" tour 300; retirement 294; reunion (2007) 297–8; reunion (2020) 300; reunion discussions (2005) 297; session work 88, 104, 132, 221, 233, 319*n*5; solo work 182, 220–1, 233, 251, 294, 297, 300; *passim*; *see also* Brand X; Flaming Youth; Hickory; Zox and the Radar Boys
Colman, Mick 16, 17
Colson, Gail 313*n*2
Colson, Glen 313*n*2

333

Come Rain or Shine 298
"Compression" 89
Conroy, Paul 85
Cornwell, Hugh 247
Cox, William T. 319*n*16
"Creation" 269
The Cross of Changes 324*ch*16*n*29
"Crossroads" 313*n*5
Crowded House 280
A Curious Feeling 167, 181, 191, 194, 283
Cut 275, 325*n*3
Cutting Crew 325*n*1

Dangerous 270
Dauncey, Pete 53
Davis, Nick 55, 68, 83, 98, 252
Davis, Rahmlee Michael 192
"A Day in the Life" 34, 280
Day of the Triffids 64
"Déjà vu" 89
de Saint-Exupéry, Antoine 102
Dickens, Charles 62
"Digby of the Rambling Lake" 313*n*5
Dire Straits 252
Disturbed 240
"Do I Still Figure in Your Life" 313*n*5
"Don't Want You Back" 16
The Doors 4
Drake, Nick 46
The Dream 91
Drennan, Anthony 292
Drier, Philippe 317*n*7
The Drifters 105
Driving Over Lemons 311*n*26
Duke 1, 7, 90, 171, 174, 181–199, 200, 212, 214, 216, 217, 218, 219, 220, 250, 270, 280
Dunnery, Francis 325*n*1
D'Virgilio, Nick 275, 283, 287, 289, 291, 325*n*5

Earth, Wind & Fire 1, 7, 184, 190, 200, 203, 204, 214, 218, 233, 243
Earthrise II 269
"Eastern Magic Boogie" 313*n*5
Easybeats 203
El Topo 102
Elgie, Colin 143
Eliot, T.S. 97
ELO (Electric Light Orchestra) 182
ELP (Emerson, Lake and Palmer) 3–4, 9, 98, 201
Emerson, Keith 4, 61, 69, 81
Enigma 324*ch*16*n*29
Eno, Brian 104, 109, 110, 122, 123, 132
"Epic" 313*n*5
Erskine, John 149
Everett, Kenny 22

"Everybody Needs Somebody to Love" 191, 192
"Everyone's Gone to the Moon" 17
"Everywhere Is Here" 19, 313*n*5
The Exorcist 103

"F#" 19, 43, 62, 312*ch*3*n*14, 314*n*9
Face Value 7, 184, 186, 189, 194, 195, 200, 201, 211, 214, 217, 218
Fairport Convention 4, 40
Family 4, 40, 314*n*15
"Family" 53
Fearsome Creatures of the Lumberwoods, with a Few Desert and Mountain Beasts 319*n*16
"Feelin' Alright" 259
"Field of Eternity" 45
Fine Young Cannibals 259
Fish 252
Fisher Lane Farm Studio ("The Farm") 201, 220, 234, 235, 252, 253, 296
5x5 322*ch*13*n*26
Flaming Youth 59
The Flight of the Heron 149, 320*n*7
Fluide Glacial 77
"Fourteen Years Too Long" 19
Foxtrot 6, 9, 10, 66, 72–86, 89, 91, 92, 99, 129, 140, 143
Friars Club 59, 60, 69
Frida 221
"Friday on My Mind" 203
Friedkin, William 103, 317*n*7
Fripp, Robert 74
From Genesis to Revelation 17, 18, 22, 23, 24, 27–39, 40, 49, 51, 53
"From the Bottom of a Well" 19, 29
"From the Undertow" 167
The Fugitive 205, 220

Gabriel, Jill 51, 80, 104, 272
Gabriel, Peter: birth 14; childhood 4, 14–5; collaboration with William Friedkin 103; costumes 74, 75, 85, 100, 121, 123, 129; early career options 40–1; influences 4, 15–6, 25, 102; leaves Genesis 6, 129–30, 132–3, 318*n*46; overdubs on *Archive* releases 90, 105, 326*n*1; pioneering use of sound 7; press release 318*n*46; reunion discussions (2005) 297; solo work 7, 294; stage antics 60, 70, 85; WOMAD 83, 219, 323*n*42; *passim*
Gallagher, Noel 33
Gallo, Armando 2, 99
The Garden Wall 16
Gaye, Marvin 258

The Geese and the Ghost 88, 132
Genesis 8, 220–232, 250
Genesis Archive 1967-75 294
Genesis Archive #2 1976–1992 296
Genesis: In Concert 145
Genesis Live 74, 85, 103
Genesis 1970–1975 298
Genesis 1976–1982 298
Genesis 1983–1998 298
"Genesis Plays Jackson" / *The Jackson Tapes* 21, 42–4, 49, 62
Genesis Revisited 89
The Genesis Songbook 296
Genesis: Sum of the Parts 299
Genesis: The Movie Box 1981-2007 298
Genesis: Together and Apart 299
George & Mildred 225
"Get Off My Cloud" 33
"Getting Better" 140
Gibb, Robin 21
Gift, Roland 259
"The Glamourous Life" 236
Glorious Fool 221
"God If I Saw Her Now" 132
Going Back 300
Golding, William 320*ch*9*n*25
Gomersall, Mark 235
Goodsall, John 319*n*1
Gordon, Alistair 252
Gotlib 77
Gowers, Bruce 138, 140, 141
"Grandma" 313*n*5
Grandmaster Flash and the Furious Five 223
Gray, Howard 259
Gray, Trevor 259
Great Expectations 62
Greeley, Horace 170
Green, Frank J. 164
Greenhalgh, Howard 278
Greenslade, Arthur 23, 28, 29, 311–2*ch*2*n*3

Hackett, Steve: birth 59; childhood 59; collaboration with Collins and Rutherford 132; finger-tapping technique 62, 64, 80, 89, 314*n*14; hand injury 29; influences 59; joins Genesis 59–60; leaves Genesis 6, 161–2; overdubs on *Archive* releases 93–4, 326*n*1; reunion discussions (2005) 297; revisiting Genesis 89, 294; solo work 132, 133, 147, 294, 315*n*5; *passim*
Hammill, Peter 313*n*2
Hardcastle, Paul 247
Harrison, George 9
"Have Yourself a Merry Little Christmas" 156
Hawkwind 244, 313*n*2

General Index

Headley Grange 103
Heavy Metal 317*n*7
Hello, I Must Be Going! 221, 324*ch*15*n*20
Hendrix, Jimi 4
Hentschel, David 7, 49, 60, 133, 147, 148, 156, 165, 175, 183, 187, 201, 319*n*5
Hickory 59
Hill, Benny 243, 323*ch*15*n*15
Hill-Smith, Tony 41, 53, 312*ch*3*n*6
Hipgnosis 128, 143
Hitchcock, David 73, 79
"Hold the Line" 188
Holding, William 140
Holland 182
Hook 251
"Hoping Love Will Last" 147
Horn, Trevor 115, 296
Hoskins, Bob 241–2
The House of the Four Winds 148–9
Howar, Tim 294
Huffam, Ian 275
Hughes, Howard 317*n*14
"Humanity" 19
Huxley, Aldous 110
Hyams, Peter 315*n*3

"(I Can't Get No) Satisfaction" 191
"I Heard It Through the Grapevine" 258
"I Love You…I'll Kill You" 324*ch*16*n*29
"If Leaving Me Is Easy" 182
"If Love Is the Law" 33
"I'm Here" 19, 22, 311*n*29
"I'm Not in Love" 156
In Concert (BBC) 63, 65, 68
"In the Air Tonight" 7, 182, 186, 201, 223
In the Court of the Crimson King 4, 41, 196
"In the Midnight Hour" 191, 192
"In the Mood" 317*n*14
The Inheritors 140, 320*ch*9*n*25
"Inside" 8, 275
"Intruder" 7, 201
Invisible Touch 3, 8, 10, 232, 233–50, 251, 254, 255, 270
Island Studios 72, 89, 104, 105, 317*n*11
"It's a Man's Man's Man's World" 93
"It's Only Rock and Roll" 127

Jackson, Michael 1, 8, 259, 270
Jackson, Mick 42–4, 73, 119, 312*ch*3*n*9
James, Henry 62
Jennings, Will 324*ch*16*n*27
Jesus Christ Superstar 32
Jethro Tull 4

Job, Rivers 15–6, 310*n*4, 310*n*8, 310*n*9
John, Elton 252
Johnson, Alphonso 161
Johnston, Barry 41, 53
Jones, Ken 17
Jones, Percy 319*n*1

"Kashmir" 136
"Katmandu" 312*ch*3*n*10
Keats, John 74
Kershaw, Nik 252
"Ketch" 67
"Key to Love" 313*n*5
Kim, Harry 192
King, Ben E. 93
King, Jonathan 3, 4, 17, 18, 19, 22, 24, 31, 37, 38–9, 41, 55, 80, 311*n*11, 312*ch*2*n*4
King Biscuit 85
King Canute 78
King Crimson 4, 41, 59, 74, 144, 196
Klimek, Jayney 252
Knievel, Evel 126
Koechlin, Lionel 199
Ku Klux Klan 317*n*14

The Lamb Lies Down on Broadway 5, 6, 9, 10, 43, 82, 99, 101–130, 134, 137, 143, 153, 196, 202, 204, 294, 297, 316*n*38
"The Last Time" 191
Led Zeppelin 103, 136–7, 269, 324*ch*15*n*20
Lennon, John 9, 223, 224
Levine, Steve 39
Liebrand, Ben 259
Lindisfarne 48, 73, 313*n*2, 314*n*4
"Listen on Five" 16
"Little Leaf" 313*n*5
The Little Prince 102, 317*n*2
Live Over Europe 2007 298
Living Years 251
"The Living Years" 265
The Living Years: The First Genesis Memoir 310*n*3
Lloyd-Webber, Andrew 32
London, Jack 50, 313*n*12
Longdon, David 325*n*1
Lorca and the Outlaws 234
"Lost in a Drawer" 19
Lowe, Nick 319*n*6
Ludwig, Bob 235
Lumley, Robin 319*n*1

Macpahil, Richard 15, 16, 40, 42, 47, 79, 310*n*6, 310*n*7, 310*n*9, 311*n*7
"Magical Mystery Tour" 206
Mahavishnu Orchestra 88
Mancini, Henry 76
Manfred Mann's Earth Band 319*n*6

The Marquee Club 47, 69
"Martha My Dear" 225
Martyn, John 221
Marvin, Hank 15
The Marx Brothers/Marx, Groucho 317*n*14, 324*ch*15*n*20
Mary Poppins 135
"Masochistic Man" 313*n*5
Masuak, Greg 279
Mayhew, John 41, 43, 44, 45, 46, 49, 50, 51, 52, 53, 54, 55, 58, 312*ch*3*n*4, 313*n*7, 314*n*2
Maylam, Tony 145
McAuliffe, Vivienne 132
McCalla, Noel 319*n*6
McCartney, Paul 9, 224, 225, 252
McCay, Winsor 321*n*20
McCullar, Arnold 192
McGowan, Shane 269
McLuhan, Marshall 317*n*14
Mercer, Johnny 173
Mike + the Mechanics 8, 151, 233, 251–2, 265, 284, 288, 290, 294, 324*n*1
Mike Douglas Show 161
Millionairhead 325*n*3
The Mind's Eye 275
Mona Lisa 241–2
Monty Python 66, 81, 313*n*2
The Moody Blues 4, 28, 313*n*3
The Moon's a Balloon 223
Moorcock, Michael 150, 320*n*11
"More Trouble Every Day" 161
"Moss" 313*n*5
Mott the Hoople 313*n*3
"The Movement" 52, 313*n*5, 313*n*15
Munt, Fred 313*n*2
Music for Films 104
My Book of Genesis 310*n*7

"Needles and Pins" 317*n*14
New York City blackout 177
Newman, Randy 25
The Nice 4, 54, 313*n*2
Nightride 45–6, 53, 54
Niven, David 223
No Admittance 253
No Jacket Required 233
Numan, Gary 7, 111, 187
Nursery Cryme 5, 6, 9, 42, 44, 58–71, 84, 94, 133, 178, 312*n*15, 313*n*5

"Old Medley" 63
Oliver! 59
Omar 128
"On Broadway" 105
"On First Looking into Chapman's Homer" 74
"One for My Baby" 173
"Only Your Love" 88
Operation Daybreak 319*n*5

Orme, Stuart 186, 189, 191, 205, 208, 211, 223, 228
Out of Our Heads 16

Padgham, Hugh 7, 201, 202, 204, 217, 218, 221, 223, 235, 252, 322*n*3, 323*ch*14*n*3
Peel, John 75, 77, 86
"Pennsylvania Flickhouse" 16
Pet Sounds 4
Phillips, Anthony: birth 15; childhood 4, 15; illness 58, 313*n*9; influences 4, 16; leaves Genesis 58; solo and collaborative work 88, 132, 313–4*ch*5*n*1; *passim*
Phish 10, 74, 299
Phoenix in Obsidian 150
Physical Graffiti 103
Pictures at Eleven 221
Pilgrim's Progress 102
"Pinball Wizard" 192
Pinder, Mike 313*n*3
Pink Floyd 4, 9, 161, 252
Plant, Robert 221, 252
Platinum Collection 297
Platt, Tony 73
"Please Don't Touch" 147, 153
Please Don't Touch 147
Polar Studios 183, 195, 198
The Police 7, 253
Poor, Kim 135
Potoker, John "Tokes" 236, 238, 241
Potter, Bob 73, 78, 79, 315*n*3
"Prelude of Suite No. 1 in G major" 79
Prince 236
Private Parts and Pieces 45
Private Parts and Pieces VI: Ivory Moon 46
Procol Harum 4
Product 182
"Promise of a Fisherman" 142

Queen 138
Quicksilver 234
Quiet World 60

R-Kive 299
The Railway Navvies: A History of the Men Who Made the Railways 257
"Raindrops Keep Falling on My Head" 109
Randall, Elliott 321*n*24
Rare Bird 47, 48, 313*ch*4*n*1
Ravel, Maurice 107
Ray Wilson and Stiltskin Live 325*n*2
"Reach Out (I'll Be There)" 192
Redding, Otis 4, 15, 16, 18, 93
Regent Sound Studios 17, 18, 19, 20, 25, 27, 39, 41, 53

Reinhardt, Django 216
Richard, Cliff 15, 252
Richards, Keith 239, 258, 286
Roachford, Andrew 294
Roberts, Brian 16–7, 28, 40, 41, 54, 310–1*n*10, 312*ch*3*n*6
Robinson, Mark 252
Rock and Roll Hall of Fame 10, 74, 299
"Rocky Mountain Way" 188
Rogers, Mick 319*n*6
The Rolling Stones 4, 15–6, 33, 41, 127, 203, 322*ch*13*n*26
"Rondo" 54
Ronocoroni, Joe 17, 21
Rossetti, Christina Georgina 150
Roxy and Elsewhere (Live) 161
Rutherford, Mike: birth 15; childhood 4, 15; collaboration with Hackett 132; collaboration with Phillips 88, 132; influences 4, 15–6; memoir 310*n*3; relationship with father 310*n*3; reunion (2007) 297–8; reunion (2020) 300; reunion discussions (2005) 297; solo work 89, 181, 220, 233, 251–2; *passim*; *see also* Mike + the Mechanics

"Sail on Sailor" 182, 188
Samwell-Smith, Paul 42, 73, 313*ch*3*n*11
"San Jacinto" 261
Santana 142
Schwarz, Brinsley 319*n*6
Seconds Out 6, 161–2, 219
Selling England by the Pound 6, 9–10, 66, 79, 85, 87–100, 101, 133, 196, 198, 315*n*5, 317*n*32
Sergeant Pepper's Lonely Hearts Club Band 4
Serious Hits…Live! 251
"Shadow of Hierophant" 132, 315*n*5
The Shadows 15
Shakespeare, William 97
She 325*n*2
"She Drives Me Crazy" 259
Sheila E 236
"She's Leaving Home" 178
"Shortcut to Somewhere" 324*n*1
"Should I Stay or Should I Go" 259
The Shout 167
"Silent Running" 233, 284
"Silent Scream" 269
Silver, John 25, 26, 31, 32, 33, 35, 37, 38, 41, 48, 88, 294, 295, 311*n*27, 312*ch*3*n*3
"Silver Machine" 244
"Silver Song" 88, 313*n*5
Simone, Nina 4
Sinatra, Frank 173

"Sitting on Top of the World" 19
"Six-Bob" Tour 60, 314*n*4
"Six of the Best" reunion concert (1982) 219
Sklar, Leland 192
Slater, Eve 313*n*2
Sledge, Percy 16
"Sledgehammer" 236, 284
Smallcreep's Day 89, 181, 191, 314*n*1, 319*n*6
Smith, Tony 100, 130, 182, 272, 296
Solé, Jean 77
Something's Going On 221
Sorcerer 317*n*7
Sounds of the Seventies 53, 63, 64–5, 66, 68
Soundtracks 234
Spector, Phil 267
Spitting Image 240, 241
Spock's Beard 325*n*5
Spot the Pigeon 157–9
Squeeze 247
The Squeeze 319*n*5
Stanshall, Vivian 313*n*2
"Star of Sirius" 132
Startling Music 319*n*5
Status Quo 252
Stereo MC 269
Stevens, Cat 42, 312*ch*3*n*10
Stewart, Chris 16, 23, 24, 25, 294, 311*n*20, 311*n*26
Still 252, 270
Stiltskin 8, 275, 284
Sting 286, 294
Stopps, David 59, 69
"Stranger" 313*n*5
Stratton-Smith, Tony 5, 47, 48, 59, 60, 67, 69, 83, 91, 98, 100, 103, 130, 132, 313*n*2, 314*n*4
"Strawberry Fields Forever" 65
Strickland, Mick 133
String Driven Thing 313*n*2
Stuermer, Daryl: joins Genesis touring band 179–80, 321*n*24; Music Managers Forum reunion 296; reunion (2007) 297–8; reunion (2020) 300; *passim*
"Stumble" 313*n*5
"Sussudio" 233
Swanwick, Betty 91, 99

"Take Five" 25
"Take Me Home" 233
"Take this Heart" 88
Taking Tiger Mountain (By Strategy) 104
Tales from Topographic Oceans 105, 128
"Talkin' About You" 16
Tangerine Dream 317*n*7
Tauber, Doris 173
Taylor, Andy 252
Tears for Fears 252

General Index

"Tears in Heaven" 324*ch*16*n*27
The Teddy Bears 267
10cc 156
"Ten Little Indians" 164
Ten Thousand Fists 240
"That's How Strong My Love Is" 16
"There Was a Movement" 19, 311*n*29
"Think Again" 313*n*5
Thomas, David 25, 27, 32, 35, 311*n*28, 311*ch*2*n*2
Thompson, Chester: joins Genesis touring band 161; overlooked for …*Calling All Stations*… Tour 275, 325*n*6; reunion (2007) 297–8; *passim*
3x3 214–8, 322*ch*13*n*26
Three Dates with Genesis 171
Three Sides Live 216, 217, 219
"To Love Somebody" 21
Tommy 105
Top Gear 75, 77, 86
Top of the Pops 22, 91, 179, 199, 216, 311*n*11
Toto 189
Townshend, Pete 23, 30, 159, 257, 314*n*13
Traffic 259
Trespass 5, 6, 24, 42, 45, 46, 47–56, 58, 60, 65, 68, 70
A Trick of the Tail 5, 6, 7, 9, 10, 51, 60, 132–145, 146, 148, 149, 159, 268, 317*n*15
Turn It On Again: The Hits 295, 296, 297
The Turn of the Screw 62
"Twist and Shout" 322*ch*13*n*26
"2:30 Parktime (a.m. p.m.)" 19, 311*n*29
Tyrell, Rob 15, 310*n*6, 310*n*9

Unfulfillment 325*n*2
Unorthodox Behaviour 145
Up 294
U2 8, 270

Van Der Graaf Generator 4, 48, 313*n*2, 314*n*4
Van Eede, Nick 325*n*1
"Victory at Sea" 122
Voyage of the Acolyte 6, 132, 133, 161, 315*n*5

Wakeman, Rick 145
Walsh, Joe 188
"Wandering Waterlily" 313*n*5
Warburton, Lewis ("Lou") 312*ch*2*n*3
Washington, Thomas 204
The Wasteland 97
Waterman, Dennis 257
Waters, Roger 247
Watts, Charlie 33
The Way We Walk (*Shorts* and *Longs*) 271
We Can't Dance 5, 8, 10, 228, 248, 251–72, 276, 292, 323*ch*14*n*7
Weather Report 142, 153, 161, 176, 180
"The Weaver's Answer" 314*n*15
Webb, Jimmy 154, 320*n*19
West Side Story 102
"We've Got a Good Thing Going" 16
When in Rome 2007 298
When the Wind Blows 247
"Which Way the Wind Blows" 132
White, Fred 192
White Fang 50, 313*n*12
White Rock 145

Whitehead, Paul 55, 69, 84, 85, 99, 316*n*31
The Who 4, 15, 23, 105, 314*n*13, 317*n*1
Who Built the Moon 33
"Who Has Seen the Wind?" 150
The Who Sell Out 317*n*1
The Wicked Lady 220
Wilson, Ray: birth 275; contract termination 292; early career 275; joins Genesis 8, 275; overlooked for *The Carpet Crawlers 1999* 296; solo work 275, 294; *passim*
Wind & Wuthering 3, 6, 10, 124, 146–62, 164, 197, 287
The Wiz 161
Wonder, Stevie 171
"Wooden Mask" 42, 313*n*5
Word of Mouth 252, 270
Wuthering Heights 148

Yes 3, 4, 9, 105, 134, 142, 144, 145, 161, 315*n*7
"You Can't Hurry Love" 324*n*1
"You Got to Be Perfect" 19
"Your Mother Should Know" 140
Yukich, Jim 225, 227, 236, 238, 241, 242, 243, 246, 255, 256, 259, 323*ch*15*n*15

Zappa, Frank 161
Zawinul, Joe 213
Zidkyahu, Nir 275, 276, 280, 282, 285, 286, 288, 291, 292
The Zombies 4, 17
Zox and the Radar Boys 88

www.ingramcontent.com/pod-product-compliance
Ingram Content Group UK Ltd.
Pitfield, Milton Keynes, MK11 3LW, UK
UKHW051850210426
5322IPUK00025B/654